STUDIES ON THE CIVILIZATION AND CULTURE OF NUZI AND THE HURRIANS

Volume 3

Studies on the Civilization and Culture of Nuzi and the Hurrians

Edited by

David I. Owen
and
Martha A. Morrison

1. *In Honor of Ernest R. Lacheman on His Seventy-fifth Birthday, April 29, 1981*. Edited by M. A. Morrison and D. I. Owen. 1981.
2. *General Studies and Excavations at Nuzi 9/1*. Edited by D. I. Owen and M. A. Morrison. 1987.
3. *Joint Expedition with the Iraq Museum at Nuzi VII: Miscellaneous Texts.* By Ernest R. Lacheman† and Maynard P. Maidman. 1989.

JOINT EXPEDITION WITH THE IRAQ MUSEUM AT NUZI

VII

Miscellaneous Texts

By

ERNEST R. LACHEMAN†
and
MAYNARD P. MAIDMAN

EISENBRAUNS
WINONA LAKE
1989

Library of Congress Cataloging-in-Publication Data

Lacheman, Ernest René, 1906–
Joint expedition with the Iraq Museum at Nuzi VII / by Ernest Lacheman and Maynard P. Maidman.
p. cm.—(Studies on the civilization and culture of Nuzi and the Hurrians; v. 3–)
"Between 1927 and 1939, six volumes of Nuzi texts were published as Joint expeditions with the Iraq Museum at Nuzi, under the imprint of the American Schools of Oriental Research, Publications of the Baghdad School, Texts"—CIP pref.
Includes bibliographical references and index.
Contents: pt. 1. Miscellaneous texts.
ISBN 0-931464-45-5 (pt. 1)
1. Akkadian language—Texts. 2. Nuzi (Ancient city) I. Maidman, M. P. II. Title. III. Series: Studies on the civilization and culture of Nuzi and the Hurrians; v. 3, etc.
PJ3721.N8L3 1989 89-1382
492'.1—dc20 CIP

to Morton Smith

1. Tablet baking kiln being filled. From left to right: Emmanuel Wilensky, Bill Chiera, Edward Chiera, Nina Chiera, Ephraim Speiser. Season of 1927–28.

2. Loading crates of objects for shipment home. Season of 1927–28.

CONTENTS

Abbreviations

A — siglum for tablets in the collection of the Oriental Institute, University of Chicago

AAN — *Anthroponymie et Anthropologie de Nuzi*, vol. 1: *Les anthroponymes*, by E. Cassin and J.-J. Glassner (Malibu, CA: Undena, 1977).

AASOR — Annual of the American Schools of Oriental Research

AfO — *Archiv für Orientforschung*

AJSL — *American Journal of Semitic Languages and Literatures*

AOAT(S) — Alter Orient und Altes Testament (Sonderreihe)

BASOR — *Bulletin of the American Schools of Oriental Research*

CAD — *The Assyrian Dictionary of the Oriental Institute of the University of Chicago* (Chicago: Oriental Institute, 1956–)

HSS — Harvard Semitic Series

JAOS — *Journal of the American Oriental Society*

JEN — *Joint Expedition with the Iraq Museum at Nuzi*, by E. Chiera et al. (6 vols., Paris: Geuthner, 1927–39)

*JEN*u — siglum for unpublished texts from the Joint Expedition with the Iraq Museum at Nuzi

NPN — *Nuzi Personal Names*, by I. J. Gelb, P. M. Purves, and A. A. MacRae (Chicago: University of Chicago, 1943)

SCCNH 1 — *Studies on the Civilization and Culture of Nuzi and the Hurrians*, vol. 1: *In Honor of Ernest R. Lacheman on His Seventy-Fifth Birthday*, ed. M. A. Morrison and D. I. Owen (Winona Lake, Indiana: Eisenbrauns, 1981)

SCCNH 2 — *Studies on the Civilization and Culture of Nuzi and the Hurrians*, vol. 2: *General Studies and Excavations at Nuzi 9/1*, ed. D. I. Owen and M. A. Morrison (Winona Lake, Indiana: Eisenbrauns, 1987)

SMN — siglum for tablets excavated at Nuzi in the Semitic Museum, Harvard University

THNT — *Two Hundred Nuzi Texts from the Oriental Institute of the University of Chicago*, by M. P. Maidman (forthcoming)

ZA — *Zeitschrift für Assyriologie*

Foreword

The current volume fulfills one of the major goals that we had set out at the outset of the Nuzi Publication Project, that is, to make available, as quickly as possible, all of the copies of Nuzi tablets that Ernest R. Lacheman had left in various states of completion. It did not take long for the editors to recognize the enormity of the task of editing the Lacheman legacy. In their desire to promptly publish so many texts, Maynard P. Maidman was invited to undertake the preparation for publication of the copies that Lacheman had planned to include in *JEN* VII. His familiarity with the *JEN* corpus enabled him to tackle quickly the many difficulties that the project entailed. With amazingly quick and thorough preparation he brought the first of three stages of his work to completion. The publication below is more than simply the reproduction of Lacheman's copies. It represents meticulous collations of all tablets (mostly on originals or on a few casts), annotations of and corrections to the copies, a detailed catalogue, and an introduction. The second part of his project, to appear in a later volume, will contain a full edition of these texts, while a third and final part will bring Lacheman's ultimate goal, the full publication of the remaining *JEN*u holdings in Chicago's Oriental Institute to completion.

Mrs. Eunice Lacheman turned over her husband's papers to Professor Owen. Many of these contained notes and collations to the *JEN*u tablets. Furthermore, plaster casts, latex molds, and occasional photographs of the tablets, all made by Lacheman, were often helpful in the preparation of the texts for final publication. All relevant material was made available to Maidman by the editors. Mrs. Lacheman continued to take an active interest in the progress of our work. Without her cooperation its publication may never have taken place.

We would like to thank Professor Maidman for undertaking such a demanding task and Professor J. A. Brinkman and the authorities at the Oriental Institute for facilitating Maidman's visits to Chicago and his work on the tablets. Assyriology in general and Nuzi Studies in particular owe them all a great debt.

David I. Owen
Martha A. Morrison
1 June 1987

Preface

Between 1927 and 1939, six volumes of Nuzi texts were published as *Joint Expedition with the Iraq Museum at Nuzi*, under the imprint of the American Schools of Oriental Research, Publications of the Baghdad School, Texts. The present volume continues that series after a hiatus of some fifty years.

The resumption of the series came about under the following circumstances. When Ernest R. Lacheman died on 18 October 1982, he left behind a mass of unpublished copies and studies of the Nuzi texts. He had appointed David I. Owen as his literary executor. Owen, assisted by Martha A. Morrison, began to organize Lacheman's papers and to oversee their publication, an enormous task that continues to this day. Part of Lacheman's legacy consisted of copies of 200 unpublished Chicago tablets from the first season of excavations at Nuzi. Owen invited me to prepare those copies for publication, a project I embraced with enthusiasm.

Complications quickly arose, however. The Iraq Museum requested immediate return of their Nuzi texts from both Harvard University and the University of Chicago. In response, the Oriental Institute of the University of Chicago dispatched an initial shipment of 145 tablets to Baghdad, but not all of those tablets had been published.

I hastened to Chicago to evaluate the state of the collection, the plans for returning the tablets, and, through my own collation, the quality of Lacheman's copies. J. A. Brinkman, the curator of the tablet collection, offered his complete cooperation and arranged for the orderly return of the Nuzi texts—the published ones first. During this first trip to Chicago, I began the work of classifying and cataloguing the tablets and achieved, in large part, the identification of the Lacheman copies with the original tablets.

Next, during two brief stays in Chicago in February and August of 1983, I collated Lacheman's copies with 199 original tablets or casts. (The 200th text was identified and collated on a later occasion.) Work on the manuscript of the copies and editing these texts commenced in late April 1984. *JEN* VII is the first fruit of that work. The great amount of material that had to be processed in brief periods of time spent in Chicago necessitated certain limitations: measurements of the tablets were not taken and, more important, identification of seal impressions based on Edith Porada's *Seal Impressions of Nuzi* could not be undertaken with thoroughness.

The demands of this project meant that a variety of individuals and institutions were called upon and acted on my behalf in an extraordinarily generous and innovative manner. They deserve special thanks. My chairman and colleague in the Department of History at York University in Toronto, Professor Susan Houston, responded quickly and effectively to the need of the moment and obtained for me the necessary funds for two trips to Chicago in three months. Her successor as chairman, Professor Paul Lovejoy, proved no less supportive of my efforts. His encouragement and moral support have been unfailing and have provided a happy additional stimulus to my work.

York University has regularly extended to me financial support during the course of this project. Its encouragement of this scholarly enterprise during a period of severe budgetary constraints demonstrates its commitment to research. Barbara Crutchley of the Office of Research Administration was especially helpful in expediting my requests for funding. Major financial aid has been granted me by the Social Sciences and Humanities Research Council of Canada. In addition to minor grants, the Council has awarded me a leave fellowship and research grant. These have helped enable me to spend the 1985–86 academic year in Chicago and I am happy to acknowledge here the Council's generous support.

In Chicago, the roster of those who have helped me is also long. The aid and cooperation of J. A. Brinkman have made this project feasible. At various stages, the suggestions and logistical help of Joachim Oelsner, Erica Reiner, and Martha Roth have been helpful. To Roth and her husband, Bryon Rosner, go my thanks for their hospitality during my visits to Chicago.

David I. Owen and Martha A. Morrison have provided me with the opportunity to publish and edit these texts. Their help in matters scholarly and editorial has been extensive and valuable. For all this, I am very grateful.

Of those to whom I owe thanks, none deserve more than my wife, Ellen, and my children, Daniel and Aviva. They have sacrificed much: they suffered my absences when I was in Chicago; they often suffered from my presence when I was not.

I dedicate this book to Morton Smith of Columbia University. My first professor of ancient history, Smith imparted material, taught discipline, practiced honesty, and demonstrated wit. He does these things still. May he continue to do so for many years to come.

M. P. Maidman
January 1989

Introduction

The Project: History and Present Circumstances

Ernest R. Lacheman's bibliography bears eloquent witness to a lifetime of scholarly productivity.[1] Most of this effort was devoted to the publication and elucidation of the texts from Nuzi. Few areas of Assyriology have enjoyed and benefited from the unremitting dedication of one of its students as has Nuzi from the work of Lacheman. Lacheman's constancy ensured that new contributions to the field bearing his mark would continue to appear even after his death. Surely, the most significant of these posthumous contributions are the many hundreds of his hand copies, photographs, casts, and molds of unpublished Nuzi texts. In the sense that Nuzi texts will continue to appear as the result of his labors, Lacheman's legacy continues his life.

The majority of the unpublished material stems from the SMN collection—the Harvard texts excavated at Nuzi over the course of four seasons from 1927 to 1931. Publication of these tablets copied by Lacheman is now well under way with the appearance of "Excavations at Nuzi 9/1."[2] A smaller but still substantial body of work is based on the *JEN*u texts, all housed until recently in the Oriental Institute of the University of Chicago. These tablets were recovered during the first season of excavations at Yorghan Tepe in 1925–26. Lacheman left behind copies of 200 of these texts.[3] On the basis of these copies, a two-part project has been designed: (1) the present volume, *JEN* VII, containing facsimiles of these 200 tablets with Lacheman's copies as the very substantial foundation; and (2) a second volume, *Two Hundred Nuzi Texts from the Oriental Institute of the University of Chicago* (hereafter *THNT*), consisting of editions of these 200 tablets with transliterations, translations, notes, and indexes.[4]

[1] "Bibliography of Ernest R. Lacheman," compiled by M. A. Morrison and D. I. Owen, *SCCNH* 1:xix–xxi [*Lacheman Anniversary Volume*].

[2] In *SCCNH* 2:355–702.

[3] Professor Owen informs me that he has identified casts and molds of nearly all of the tablets that Lacheman copied for *JEN* VII. This means that we can collate texts even after they have been returned to Baghdad. However, close to 600 additional texts and major fragments (and about 1300 other fragments) from the Chicago collection remain unpublished and uncopied. I am currently preparing many of these items for publication. Katarzyna Grosz is also preparing some of this material for publication.

[4] The notes justify the transliterations and, in the process, also correct errors in the copies, as discussed below. Because of the discrepancy between copies and transliterations, and for

The project of publishing the Chicago texts differs from that of publishing the Harvard materials. This is due to two factors, each of which seriously complicates the publication of the Chicago texts. The first factor involves the context, both scholarly and personal, in which Lacheman studied both the Chicago and Harvard tablets.[5] His initial exposure to Nuzi was in 1931 as a graduate student at Harvard University. Robert H. Pfeiffer encouraged Lacheman to use the several thousand Nuzi texts in the Harvard collection as the basis of his doctorate. After accepting this suggestion, Lacheman went to the Oriental Institute where Edward Chiera was engaged in publishing the tablets excavated during the first season.[6] But, except for his relatively brief Chicago interlude (1932–35), Lacheman lived virtually his entire adult life in the Boston area, where he had quick and easy access to the Harvard texts. Therefore, the focus of his Nuzi studies was naturally the tablets in Harvard's Semitic Museum. Presentation of many of these tablets formed the basis of his (unpublished) Harvard University dissertation. The study, photography, copying, making molds and casts, and collating and recollating of these and most of the rest of the Semitic Museum Nuzi texts occupied him for the remainder of his life. He published over 1800 of the Harvard texts. Predictably, Lacheman's posthumous legacy includes copies of over 500 Harvard texts, practically all of them extremely accurate.

By contrast, Lacheman's ongoing interest in the Chicago Nuzi texts was far less intense. In addition to publishing 118 copies of these texts, Lacheman copied an additional 200 Chicago tablets, the basis of the present volume, and made tentative transliterations of these and still others of the Chicago Nuzi texts.[7] Collation of his copies with the originals was obviously a logistical problem of considerable dimensions although he did borrow tablets from the Oriental Institute on extended loan. While some collation and recopying was accomplished, no thoroughgoing "cleaning up" of these copies was ever

---

other reasons as well (also noted below), the first volume (*JEN* VII) should be used in close conjunction with the second (*THNT*).

[5] For sketches of Lacheman's life and career, see Owen, Morrison, and C. H. Gordon, "Ernest René Lacheman, A Tribute," *SCCNH* 1:xv–xvii; and Owen, "Ernest René Lacheman (1906–1982)," *AfO* 29–30 (1983–84) 330–32.

[6] These were published as *JEN* I–V. *JEN* VI was prepared by Lacheman himself.

[7] The 118 texts were published in "New Nuzi Texts and a New Method of Copying Cuneiform Tablets," *JAOS* 55 (1935) 429–31, plates 1–6 (4 copies); *JEN* VI (114 copies). Copies of the 200 additional tablets from Chicago have been recovered from Lacheman's papers. Circumstantial evidence suggests that few, if any, copies have gone undetected. I am very much indebted to David I. Owen for making available to me Lacheman's papers, manuscripts, and other materials relating to Nuzi. They have been very valuable in resolving many problems encountered in preparing the Chicago texts for publication. Indeed, in several cases, they virtually constitute a primary source for these texts. (For details, see *THNT*.)

achieved. The result was a series of copies whose finished character cannot begin to match that of his Harvard copies.[8]

The second factor complicating the publication of Lacheman's copies of the Chicago texts arises from more recent events. These events turned the process of preparing his copies for publication into a salvage project of sorts. Almost immediately following Lacheman's death, the Iraqi authorities urgently requested the return of their Nuzi tablets housed at Harvard and Chicago. Both universities immediately began preparing the tablets for return to Baghdad. Although neither the Harvard nor the Chicago material is in any danger, nevertheless the description "salvage operation" appropriately describes the effect of the return of the tablets on the publication of the Nuzi texts. Speed and initial perceptions held priority over deliberation and judgments considered at length. Obtaining essential information from all relevant tablets was a greater desideratum than culling all possible data from each individual document.

The Character of the Publication

As already noted, the copies of the Chicago texts were much less complete than their Harvard counterparts. Nonetheless, Lacheman's copies are retained as the foundation of the present publication. These copies have been collated with the original tablets, modified where necessary, and—ignoring aesthetic

[8] Lacheman's "Chicago" copies have several sorts of problems, mostly errors of omission. The problems are detailed in the following section of the introduction. In general terms, flaws in Lacheman's copies seem to pattern out in a significant manner. The earlier texts, that is, those closer to *JEN* 674 than to *JEN* 881, are generally freer of error than the later texts. There is at least one reason for this, probably two. First, the earlier tablets tend to be better preserved than the later ones. Lacheman clearly intended to publish as much as possible as quickly as possible—and complete, well-preserved texts were easier to deal with than those that were damaged or broken. The latter were put off until the former were treated, that is, the latter were assigned higher publication numbers. Second, and related to the first, Lacheman clearly devoted less time and attention to those texts that came later in his series. Indeed, his unpublished notes indicate the intention to copy tablets well into the 1,000s. Yet he only got as far as the 880s.

It is noted below that Lacheman himself understood that, to a large degree, his copies were not yet publishable. Yet, the reader may still get the impression that Lacheman's skills as a copyist were not of a high order. This impression would be false. Where he had the time and the tablet at his disposal, his copies are exemplary. Among these 200 copies, there are many instances of superb craftsmanship. Many of the tablets are in wretched condition and Lacheman's copies of these are often dazzling demonstrations of how sensitive an eye can be to the vague shapes of signs. To the student who may have the opportunity to judge for himself, compare, for example, the copy of *JEN* 835 with the original tablet.

Finally, according to Owen, Lacheman had apparently made casts of nearly all of the *JEN*u tablets he had copied. These casts may ultimately provide additional data on the texts in *JEN* VII since, according to Owen, some casts are in better condition that the original tablets.

considerations—are presented as hybrid copies with appropriate catalogues and comments.

Collation

Of the 200 Lacheman copies, I have collated 190 with the original tablets. In ten other cases (*JEN* 676, 726, 764, 768, 784, 787, 804, 818 [=875], 840, and 860), only casts were available for collations.

Collations from casts were not as successful as collations from the originals. Yet, collation from the originals was not without its own problems. Some of the original tablets were in much poorer condition at the time of collation than when Lacheman made his copies. Still others had deteriorated moderately or slightly. Details regarding the latest condition of the tablets will be given in *THNT*.

On the other hand, it was sometimes the case that tablets were actually in better condition at the time of collation than when originally copied. Frequently, during the course of collation, tablets were cleaned. Also, many joins were made.[9] Due to these and other circumstances, copies were often collated two, three, or even more times. As with the tablets that suffered over the years, details regarding the "improvement" of individual tablets are set forth in *THNT*.

Finally, indirect help in collation came from other sources. Readings from *NPN*, the *CAD* Nuzi file (upon which the *NPN* readings are mostly based), and Lacheman's unpublished papers were all compared with the tablets at appropriate junctures. Details will be presented in *THNT*.

Alteration of the Copies: General Remarks

The retention of the Lacheman copies as the basis of publication was the most important, but not the only, decision involved in this project. The state of the copies and the conditions under which collations were made forced compromise in several other areas. While additions to the copies were made freely to correct Lacheman's omissions, his erroneous inclusions were not deleted. This decision, an uncomfortable one indeed, requires explanation. Due partially to the decades-long delay in publishing the Chicago Nuzi texts, copies of Lacheman's "Chicago" texts have been circulating privately for years. These copies have formed the basis of study and even of historical reconstruction that have appeared in print. I believe, therefore, that *undimin-*

[9] Some joins were made in the years between copying and the most recent collation. See Lacheman, "A Propos of Criticism in Assyriology," *BASOR* 81 (1941) 22. I made others. Several were made in 1985 by Zhi Yang, then a graduate student at the University of Chicago, in the course of cataloguing work. I should like to thank her for her efforts on this phase of the project.

ished copies are legitimately needed as a basis for bringing those studies and reconstructions into line with the more fully presented evidence made available through this project. Fully corrected versions, including deletions, are reflected in the transliterations in *THNT* and explicit notation of errors in Lacheman's copies are made there in the notes to the transliterations.[10]

Additions and Other Changes to the Copies

More significant than the relatively few errors present in Lacheman's copies are the many additions his copies required. In general terms, my overarching goal has been the publication of texts with as much accurate information as possible, presented as unambiguously as possible. These considerations result in the addition of substantive matter to the copies and to darkening, retracing, and otherwise clarifying Lacheman's manuscript to make it more legible.

There are several types of additions. First, shapes of signs occasionally have been modified by addition of lines or wedges in order to reflect more closely the actual script of the tablet, that is, to correct a flaw in the copy. (I ignored some minor errors regarding shapes of signs where no change of interpretation or addition of data results.) This has been hazarded only where disruption of the copy does not result and where Lacheman clearly meant the same sign to be represented. If either of these two criteria is not fulfilled, the sign has been left undisturbed and, in cases of significantly inaccurately rendered sign forms, a more accurate form is presented at the appropriate place in *THNT*.

Second, signs and series of signs have been added, especially at the start and end of lines and along the edges. On rare occasion, a whole surface has been restored. Lacheman sometimes ignored signs and even whole lines of text. The signs and seal impressions on or near the edges of tablets are especially prone to be missing from Lacheman's copies. Several causes for these errors may be detected. Most obvious, many of Lacheman's copies were based on photographs of the tablets rather than on the tablets themselves. His technique for copying text on photographic prints, for all its benefits, does have weaknesses.[11] Signs and lines at the edges of a tablet, that is, at the periphery of the camera's depth of field, become obscure and are liable to be missed in the process of copying.[12] Furthermore, faint signs, indistinct lines, even badly

[10] It is, of course, possible that, in some cases, Lacheman's reading is to be preferred to mine. Therefore, retention of his readings is of further benefit inasmuch as Lacheman's signs and my alterations of those signs in the text editions can be compared. The reader, then, can judge each issue for himself.

[11] For details of his technique, see "New Nuzi Texts," 429–30.

[12] On this point see Julius Lewy, "A New Volume of Nuzi Texts [review of *JEN* VI]," *BASOR* 79 (1940) 31.

damaged but still visible surfaces could be, and often were, overlooked in his perusal of photographs. For example, a tablet with an eroded obverse containing only a half dozen partially preserved lines would be ignored; the reverse of the same tablet looking as if its fifteen or twenty complete lines had been written only an hour ago would be copied accurately. Even where Lacheman recollated his copies, that task was very frequently undertaken by comparison of the copy with the photograph, not the original. This tended to ensure the copy's fidelity to the photo, not to the tablet, and to perpetuate flaws in the copy. One further peculiarity should be noted. Sometimes a photograph would be marred by a (usually circular) lacuna in the print. Lacheman would interpret this as a gap in the tablet and reproduce that gap where none, in fact, existed.

Many additions have come about, as noted above, because of the improved condition of some tablets due to cleaning and joins subsequent to the time of the original copy.

As in the case of the forms of individual signs, I have added whole signs where they do not disrupt the copy as a whole or do not otherwise strain too badly the eye of the reader. Thus, not all possible additions have been made to the copies, but these signs do appear as part of *THNT*. In the transliterations, these signs are marked by a special siglum indicating their presence on the tablet but not in the copy. Where whole lines have not been added to the copy, this is indicated in the present volume by an asterisk and by the remark: "Additional text; see *THNT*." This accounts for apparent discrepancies in the line numbering of the copies. Thus, for example, *JEN* 674:37 is followed by an asterisk, then by line 40 (left edge). The asterisk alerts the reader to an omission, in this case an omission of two lines of text and a seal impression. In the transliteration, the lines present on the tablet but not added to the copy are indicated by a special siglum. Because of this category of "invisible" addition especially, the text copies should be used together with *THNT*.

A third type of addition to these copies deals with seal impressions. Lacheman frequently indicates the presence of seal impressions on the tablets by means of "seal impression" or "S.I." Where an impression is visible and Lacheman has omitted any indication of this, it is probably an indication that the copy was not completed. Compare, for example, the "finished" *JEN* 677 with *JEN* 839, where Lacheman failed to indicate the presence of impressions (a similar phenomenon appears among Lacheman's published texts). In any case, where the presence of a seal impression was not noted in the copy, I have added "seal impression" or "S.I." at the appropriate place.

Three further types of alterations involve changes rather than additions to the copies. I have changed Lacheman's line numbering where new lines have been added or where Lacheman simply miscounted. In one type of case, line numbering is a matter of judgment, namely at the end of many texts where lines of text are interspersed with seal impressions and where some lines of text are written perpendicular to others (see, for example, *JEN* 758). I have numbered these lines in the order that I believe the scribe intended them to be read.[13] I have numbered only those lines at least one trace of which is actually preserved. Descriptions of lacunae, that is, the number of missing lines in a gap, are detailed in *THNT*. Note that continuations of lines—those marked by scribes with the *Glossenkeil*, 𒑱—are not numbered separately.

A second type of change pertains to assigning lines of text to the different surfaces of the tablet. Lacheman would occasionally misassign to the wrong surface lines at the bottom of the obverse, on the lower edge, or at the start of the reverse. I have corrected these errors by means of marginal notes in the copies. Sometimes I have altered the outline of the tablet as originally depicted by Lacheman.

Finally, a last type of change is to be noted. *JEN* 837/838 consists of three clusters of context, two representing the obverse and one the reverse. Lacheman copied the smaller of the obverse clusters and the reverse as a single text, *JEN* 837, and the other cluster as another text, *JEN* 838, because he misinterpreted a series of three photographic prints. In addition to "renaming" the text 837/838 (to maintain the integrity of the text numbering scheme), I have rearranged the layout of the copies to reflect the state of the actual tablet.

One result of the changes to the copies described above is that many hundreds of corrective additions have been made without explicit statement to that effect. This failure to note each addition saves an enormous amount of space in *THNT* and spares the reader's patience as well. A great many of these additions will escape general notice. It should, therefore, be emphasized that what is presented in the present volume can no longer be considered a series of copies by Lacheman. It is now a composite manuscript. Responsibility for its strengths and weaknesses alike is shared by Lacheman and me. I assert this, not to deflect criticism from myself or to claim undeserved credit, but to protect Lacheman's interests. He can no longer do this for himself.

Other Idiosyncrasies of the Copies

Five peculiarities of Lacheman's copies require attention. First, blank areas, especially at the end of lines, may signify one of several underlying features of the tablet. To begin with, the blank may represent a preserved surface with nothing written upon it. This is obvious and needs no further comment. A blank area on the reverse may, on the other hand, represent the space taken up by a line of text wrapping around from the obverse. Where this is the case and where the interpretation of the document is thereby affected, I

[13] The order in which the lines are to be read is not, of course, necessarily the order in which the lines were written. Scribal omission of clauses or thought units is sometimes corrected by the scribe by his later insertion of lines of text, in a smaller hand, between previously written lines.

note this feature in *THNT*. Finally, a blank space may indicate effaced signs or a broken surface. This is a sign that Lacheman's copy is not a finished one and that he failed to indicate abraded or destroyed surfaces by means of his usual device, a series of diagonal, parallel lines. Compare, for example, *JEN* 842 obverse (marred surface indicated by Lacheman) with *JEN* 842 reverse (marred surface left unindicated by Lacheman and supplied by me). Copies similarly "incomplete" are published, for example, as *HSS* XV:224 and 251. Failure to indicate a damaged surface may lead, potentially, to misinterpretation of lines, for example, by underestimating the length of the line of text. Where I have detected this possibility (and wherever else practicable), I have made good those omissions, either in the particular copy or by means of the notes to the texts in *THNT*.

It should be noted and emphasized that Lacheman himself was perfectly aware that his copies were not ready for publication. His unpublished papers in several places imply this realization. Indeed, he left some of his copies partially corrected; others survive in two or more versions, each in a different state of completion. Compare for example, *JEN* 821 and 822, two representations of the same tablet.

A second peculiarity, especially frequent in incomplete copies, is Lacheman's failure to render the outline of the tablet. Compare, for example, the deficient *JEN* 674 with the complete *JEN* 676. To indicate the extent of breaks in the tablet, where breaks may affect interpretation of the text, I have either supplied the outline or described in the text edition the extent of any break. Occasionally, I use a heavy line to indicate, not a tablet's edge, but the start or end of a break. Thus, for example, the vertical line at the left of *JEN* 803 obverse does not represent the left edge of the tablet, but a break along the left side.

A third peculiarity of these texts is that, to save space in the copy, Lacheman frequently "shortened" the length of the reverse where seal impressions run the width of the tablet's surface. He accomplished this by indicating the presence (and full width) of a seal impression without giving the true extent of the length of the impression. The result is that the obverse of a tablet can appear far longer than its reverse. Where Lacheman indicates the shape of a tablet by means of an outline, this shortening of the reverse is indicated by means of breaks in the otherwise continuous outline. For an example of these several features, see *JEN* 769.

A fourth distinctive feature pertains to seal impressions. As mentioned above, Lacheman often indicated the presence of seal impressions by means of "seal impression" or "S.I."[14] Frequently, he further identified seal impressions by means of a number, usually preceded by "Po".[15] These numbers correspond

[14] As noted above, where he failed to indicate the presence of seal impressions, I have supplemented his notations exhaustively.

[15] Where Lacheman included the number without the "Po" prefix, I have supplied it.

to the Nuzi seal impressions enumerated and photographed in Edith Porada, *Seal Impressions of Nuzi.*[16] For reasons of time, no attempt has been made to supplement Lacheman's "Po" identifications nor has each number been checked against Porada's monograph. Occasionally, minor additions and corrections have been made (see especially *THNT*, note to *JEN* 753:18–21). Essentially, with respect to the detailed identification of seal impressions, Lacheman's manuscript has been left unaltered. It should be noted that where, in the same text, Lacheman identifies more than one seal impression by the same "Po" number, no error on his part need necessarily be assumed. Note, for example, the triple appearance of the seal impression, Po 580, accurately recorded in *JEN* 675. Multiple use of the same seal in individual Nuzi texts is occasionally observed (for further on this issue, see *THNT*, note to *JEN* 675:45). Finally, where "seal impression" or "S.I." appears other than right side up, this indicates the orientation of the impression. Where these indicators are right side up, this indicates either the orientation of the impression or uncertainty regarding the orientation.

The numbering of text copies in *JEN* VII is a fifth item deserving note. Lacheman adopted the system initiated by Chiera (*JEN* I–IV) and continued by Gelb (*JEN* V) and Lacheman himself (*JEN* VI) of numbering the Nuzi texts consecutively between volumes and not starting each volume with text #1. Thus, this volume of texts begins with #674. This method of numbering has been preserved as far as possible in order to maintain the consistency of the *JEN* series. Furthermore, the numbers assigned to the individual texts by Lacheman have been maintained wherever possible. This was done in order to avoid confusion since, as noted above, copies of these texts have circulated privately for some time. These copies were already numbered by Lacheman; to change those numbers now would necessitate a concordance or other device to identify "old" with "new" numbers, adding yet another layer of information on these tablets to the several already in existence.

This apparently straightforward and simple decision, however, involves certain drawbacks. Lacheman was not entirely systematic in his copying and numbering of the 200 texts. Several times, he copied the same text more than once and then assigned each of the copies a discrete number. Once, he mistook the copy of one text for copies of two, as already noted above. He also, apparently, skipped numbers.[17] The fact that the contents of this volume, *JEN* 674–881, consist of only 200 texts represents a consequence of these three types of anomalies.[18]

[16] AASOR 24. New Haven, Conn.: American Schools of Oriental Research, 1947, pp. 126–38, pls. I–LIV.

[17] The internal evidence of Lacheman's unpublished papers suggests that these gaps represent genuine omissions and not failure to find missing copies among Lacheman's manuscripts.

[18] In this area, as in others, Lacheman himself recognized contradictions, omissions, and inconsistencies. He certainly intended to correct these faults himself.

With regard to multiple copies of the same text, I have retained all copies, each with its own number. My modifications to these texts are made only in one copy each. That copy has been chosen as the best of the alternatives. The others have been retained, (*a*) to maintain the integrity of the numbering system as a whole (as mentioned above), (*b*) because, on occasion, they contribute better readings than are found in the main copies, and (*c*) to allow the reader to note the different types of copies found frequently in the Lacheman papers. In the following list, the main copy appears in the left hand column:

706 = 793
753 = 712, 877
813 = 879
818 = 875
822 = 821
869 = 801

With regard to Lacheman's misinterpretation of one text as two, his *JEN* 837 and 838 are one text. It is now numbered: *JEN* 837/838.

Finally with respect to the filling in of gaps in the numbering, it appears very likely that *JEN* 821 and 881 never existed as copies. On the other hand, copies of *JEN* 882 and 887 are attested (there is no evidence that *JEN* 883–86 were ever copied). The following changes, therefore, were made to Lacheman's numbering system:

present number	*"old" number*
821	828
828	887
881	882

JEN 828 was shifted to *JEN* 821 to juxtapose it directly with *JEN* 822, another copy of the same text. Also, Lacheman himself once renumbered *JEN* 887 as *JEN* 828 as well. Thus, the missing *JEN* 828 and 881 are supplied by the "old" *JEN* 887 and 882, respectively.

The Content and Significance of These Texts

The content of these tablets is typical of the tablets published in *JEN* I–VI and, indeed, of the Chicago tablets as a whole, published and unpublished. Table 1 (pages 12–13) demonstrates this at a glance.

The present collection is significant in several respects. First, these texts are significant in cumulative terms. About 675 tablets from the western suburbs of Nuzi have already been published. The present publication raises that total by 200. Already, we are beginning to perceive with greater definition the original contours of these private family archives. Some circumstantial evidence suggests that, in at least one case, the recovered archival material approximates that which was stored in antiquity.

The Harvard texts now being published (*SCCNH* 2, 4, and 5) are also expanding our appreciation of different types of archive-keeping organizations. As in the case of the Chicago collection, private archives are well represented. These stem from both the suburbs and—unexpectedly—the main mound. In addition, there are the records of the different "public" or institutional organizations. As more of these tablets from Chicago and Harvard are published, we shall better be able to assess the extent and significance of the several archive-keeping organizations in the context of Nuzi's social and economic life. And ultimately, we should better be able to reconstruct both the daily life of Nuzi and the socioeconomic patterns of this late Bronze Age community.

This group is also significant at the level of the individual text. Among the two hundred documents, there are several for which the published Nuzi material provides few if any analogues. *JEN* 812 and 869 provide two examples of the ill-attested personal exchange text. Thus the *šupe*ᵓᵓ*ultu* text genre, like the *mārūtu* and *tidennūtu* genres, is a transaction type where persons, as well as real estate, can be the objects of transfer. *JEN* 828, to cite another instance, is a unique and important text, recording the responsibility of individuals in bearing the *ilku* impost. The impost itself is attached to land. The very existence of such a text may undermine the popular notion that the *ilku* is the permanent responsibility of individuals within specific families, whether or not they currently hold title to real estate.

Other texts are not themselves unique or even unusual but nevertheless shed light on individual points of historical and linguistic interest. *JEN* 699, a declaration text (*lišānšu*), is one such document. In its relationship to *JEN* 467, this text too reveals that the *ilku* is indeed transferable along with the land to which it attaches.[19] I had noted this text (as "Nu 65") and its significance in preliminary fashion in my doctoral dissertation.[20] Another text, *JEN* 764, likely clears up a long standing crux on the relative values of the surface measures, *kumānu* and *ḫararnu*. The former is probably equal to ½ *awiḫaru*, while the latter probably equals ¼ *awiḫaru*. (See *THNT*, note to *JEN* 764:5: *ḫ*[*a*]-*ra-ar-n*[*i*], for the evidence for these values.)

Finally, the texts of *JEN* VII are significant because they promise correction of an unfortunate trend in Nuzi studies. A large number of the Chicago texts were among the first to be published in the late 1920s and 1930s. These represented documentation of private family activity. The first volumes of the Harvard texts similarly dealt with the private activities of families dwelling in

[19] See also *JEN* 789, especially lines 20–22 in this context.

[20] "A Socio-economic Analysis of a Nuzi Family Archive" (Ph.D. diss., University of Pennsylvania, 1976; University Microfilms 77-861) 321 n. 84. I plan to continue the discussion of the *ilku* at Nuzi, based in part on this new material, in a forthcoming study.

TABLE 1. *JEN VII: A Synopsis*

Text Genre \ Chief Principal Party	Teḫip-Tilla son of Puḫi-šenni	Enna-mati son of Teḫip-Tilla	Sons of Enna-mati	Teḫip-Tilla household	Tarmi-Tilla son of Šurki-Tilla	Ḫui-te son of Mušeya
ṭuppi mārūti (real estate)	83 See note *a*	3 750, 776, 780 (plus *lišānšu*)	1 779 (Pakla-piti son of Enna-mati)	3 734, 737, 774 See also note *b*	1 783	3 784, 789, 842
lišānšu relating to *mārūtu* (real estate)	5 682, 699 (in-directly), 740, 775, 777					
*ṭuppi šupe*ᵓᵓ*ulti* (real estate)	18 See note *c*	5 810, 811, 814, 815, 858			2 816, 837/838	
lišānšu relating to *šupe*ᵓᵓ*ultu* (real estate)	3 706, 711, 753?					
ṭuppi tidennūti (real estate)	1 836?				2 781?, 826?	5 822, 824, 830, 832, 833
lišānšu relating to *tidennūtu* (real estate)						
record of litigation	4 713, 846, 847, 850	3 848, 851 (see also note *e*), 873			1 849 (jointly with his brother Zike)	1 860?
other	7 See note *g*	1 812 (per-sonal *ṭuppi šupe*ᵓᵓ*ulti*)	1 819 (see also note *h*)		2 820 (see also note *i*), 864 (barley loan?)	
obscure	1 696 (Teḫip-Tilla, prob-ably)		1 853 (Takku son of Enna-mati)			
Total	122	12	3	3	8	9

a 674, 675, 676, 677, 678, 679, 680, 681, 683, 684, 685, 686, 687, 689 (real estate and *mobilia* are ceded), 690, 691, 692, 693, 694, 695, 698, 700, 701, 702, 703, 704, 705, 709, 710, 714, 715, 716, 717, 718, 719, 720, 721, 722, 723, 724, 725, 726, 727, 728, 729, 730, 731, 732, 733, 735, 736, 738, 739, 741 (plus *lišānšu*), 742 (plus *lišānšu*), 743, 744 (plus *lišānšu*?), 745, 746, 747, 749 (plus *lišānšu*), 751, 752, 755, 756, 757?, 758, 759, 760, 761 (plus *lišānšu*), 763, 764, 765, 766, 767, 768, 770, 772 (plus *lišānšu*), 773, 778, 841, 843?, 855.

b 734 and 774 were undertaken by the same agent; 737 was undertaken by a slave of Teḫip-Tilla.

c 697, 748, 762, 791, 792, 795, 796, 797 (perhaps not involving Teḫip-Tilla), 798, 799, 802, 803, 804, 805, 806 (plus elements approximating a *lišānšu*), 808, 809, 813.

d 823 (Rm. 4), 825 (Rm. 1), 827 (Rm. 14), 831 (Rm. 1), 834 (Rm. 15), 840 (Rm. 13).

e The format and (probably) the function of 851 are atypical.

f 861 (Rm. 16; a type of deposition), 862 (Rm. 4; a type of deposition), 874 (Rm. 11).

Itḫ-apu son of Ḫašiya	Kel-Tešup son of Ḫutiya	Ḫilpiš-šuḫ son of Šuḫun-zirira	Mat-Tešup son of Ḫilpiš-šuḫ	Others	Obscure	Total
3 785, 786, 787	1 790?	1 788		2 707 (Rm. 16), 782 (Rm. 13)		101
						5
	3 817, 818, 881			1 807 (Rm. 4)		29
						3
		1 835 (N.B.: Ḫilpiš-šuḫ is the borrower)		6 See note *d*		15
				1 839 (Rm. 13)		1
			1 852	1 865 (Rm. 15)	3 See note *f*	14
	2 See note *j*	1 794 (*ṭuppi tamgurti*)	1 880 (a will)	10 See note *k*	2 See note *l*	27
					3 See note *m*	5
3	6	3	2	21	8	200

g 688 (*qīštu* contract), 708 (*kallūtu* contract), 769 (servitude contract), 771 (real estate catalogue), 844 (personal *tidennūtu*?), 867 (possible servitude contract preceding a clear *lišānšu* regarding entry into servitude), 869 (personal *ṭuppi šupeʾʾulti*; plus *lišānšu*).

h 819 is possibly a receipt, possibly of Pakla-piti son of Enna-mati.

i 820 is probably a personal *ṭuppi tidennūti*.

j 859 (possibly a servitude contract), 871 (purchase [?] of a door).

k 829 (Rm. 13; *lišānšu* of a personal *tidennūtu*), 845 (Rm. 13; statement regarding a slave sale), 856 (Rm. 4 or 12; loan document), 857 (Rm. 4; real estate transaction), 863 (Rm. 13; *lišānšu* regarding real estate), 866 (Rm. 16; statement regarding real estate), 868 (Rm. 16; genuine adoption), 870 (Rm. 4; genuine adoption), 872 (Rm. 12; list of field measurers), 876 (Rm. 11; list of grain disbursements).

l 800 (Rm. 15; field list), 828 (Rm. 11; cadastre for *ilku*).

m 754 (Rm. 11), 854 (Rm. 16), 878 (Rm. 16).

the suburbs of Nuzi. In consequence, studies of family law, the economic functioning of the family, and related issues were among the first to appear in the Nuzi literature.

Subsequent to the first volumes of texts came Lacheman's publication of significant parts of the archives of the great government and temple organizations. This material, coupled with an increasing interest among Assyriologists and historians in the economic history of organizations, led to an appropriate corrective: the once neglected bureaucratic material became more and more the focus of scholarly interest and scrutiny. The importance of bureaucratic complexes is no longer denied or sloughed off as unworthy of careful examination.

In the course of this shift of focus, however, the private archives have themselves become neglected. Worse, they and the significance of the activity they reflect have been largely ignored. Only the great urban organizations and extended family communes have been judged as vital to the economic dynamic of Nuzi.[21] The notion of the private *oikos*—economically viable, based on the nuclear family, and largely independent of the great organizations—has been all but lost in the recent scholarly literature. Where present at all, discussion of private archives and the institutions they represent has often been punctuated by fanciful interpretations. These interpretations, more often than not, are based on groundless restorations of partially destroyed, unpublished texts, including texts now to be found in this volume. *JEN* VII and the published (*SCCNH* 2:167–201, 355–702) and forthcoming (*SCCNH* 4) studies by Martha A. Morrison of important private archives from the main mound should stimulate a needed shift in Nuzi studies. First, these new texts should end the neglect suffered by the private *oikos* in current scholarship. Second, it should temper the overly imaginative, arbitrary restorations of damaged tablets that have too often marked—and marred—Nuzi scholarship.[22]

[21] This assumes that extended family communes actually are attested in the Nuzi texts. The evidence for this is slight, at best.

[22] Accurate publication and competent editions should result in a generally higher level of reasonable speculation about Nuzi. With the encouragement of the Oriental Institute, I have been engaged in a project to catalogue the Nuzi holdings entrusted to the Institute in the late 1920s. For this initiative, hearty thanks are to be rendered to the curator of the Institute's tablet collection, Professor J. A. Brinkman. As this volume goes to press, I am pleased to note that the research for the catalogue has now been completed. This work will join two others, the catalogue of the British Museum Nuzi tablets (now complete, see M. P. Maidman, "The Nuzi Texts of the British Museum," *ZA* 76 [1986] 254–88) and the catalogue of the Harvard Semitic Museum material (being prepared by Professors D. I. Owen and M. A. Morrison), to provide scholars with a long needed guide as to what is and what is not to be found in the Nuzi texts.

Register of Tablets

*JEN*u[1]	*JEN*	*JEN*u	*JEN*
1	849	285	702
7	839	289	710
10	845	295	827
28	782	297	756
41	810	298	858
63	855	299	711
65	699	300+1142[6]	714
70a	791	305[7]	759
81	698	309	867
84	873	311	745
89	770	312[7]	—
92	776	313	716
96	700	319	767
101[2]	676	320	790
104	694	321	800
118	820	329a[8]	—
119	826	339[8]	866
128	781	346[9]	704
143	874	348a(+)348b	794
155	792	348b(+)348a	794
164	856	350	811
173	686	351	732
183	738	353[10]	861
189	878	354	779
190	854	356	683
212	783	357	778
215	816	359+538	798
220 [= A11906][3]	872	362	687
221 [= A11907]	763	363a+363b	690
223	706 [= *JEN* 793][4]	363b+363a	690
225	739	367	719
229	869 [= *JEN* 801]	381[11]	813 [= *JEN* 879]
233	843	383	769
235	692	387	795
239 [= A11911]	819	396	735
240	750	397	697
244[5]	703	398	774
258	753 [= *JEN* 712, 877]	399	717
		412	734

*JEN*u	*JEN*	*JEN*u	*JEN*
414	747	637	864
421	749	648	846
423	852	652	862
435	708	654	755
439	841	663	847
442	850	668	844
448	760	678	754
459(+)459B	796	679	871
459B(+)459	796	686	728
485	701	690+634	736
512	799	698	705
514	727	710	859
517+519	742	727	674
519+517	742	731 frag. 3 + 611	762
523	715	734	740
529a	802	736	814
532	853	737	733
533	812	743	803
538+359	798	752	721
539	730	760	722
546	837/838	762	805
555	720	768	851
564	678	772	784
568	766	775	832
569	685	782	744
578	696	783	768
580	865	785	780
583	731	790	723
590	675	791	824
596	797	792	833
597	758	793	785
604	718	797	789
605	684	799	831
610	677	800	786
611+731 frag. 3	762	802	818 [= *JEN* 875]
613	765	804	691
615	729	806	726
617	775	807	752
620	881	811	870
621	748	813	860
623	848	818	823
624	751	820	772
625[12]	741	822	777
627	829	824	815
628	693	826	773
629	817	827	724
631	868	829	834
632	822 [= *JEN* 821]	847	680
634+690	736	851	835

*JEN*u	*JEN*	*JEN*u	*JEN*
853	787	972	830
"854" [= A11951][13]	788	976	804
855	857	977	681
856	807	979	825
858	828	981	688
859	880	985	682
862	771	986	709
880	689	998	808
883	746	1004	809
885	757	1007	679
893	876	1028	842
900 [= A11958]	806	1029	764
916	743	1030	737
917 [= A11963]	725	1044a	713
924	840	1136	863
941	707	1142+300[14]	714
958	836	1144	695
963	761		

[1] The *JEN*u numbers employed in this register are provisional. As stated above (p. 14 n. 22), an exhaustive catalogue of the Nuzi texts in the Oriental Institute is now in preparation. When complete, some slight modification will be necessary both to the numbers given here and to some of the footnotes to this register (e.g., n. 7).

[2] *JEN* 676 is identified in the *CAD* Nuzi file and in Lacheman's papers as *JEN*u 591 (not as *JEN*u 101). However, the tablet actually bearing that number is a different text. It has been published as *JEN* 652. In *JEN* VI, "Description of the Tablets," the catalogue number of *JEN* 652 is erroneously given as *JEN*u 101. This last number, in turn, represents the present text, *JEN* 676. (Part of the confusion may have to do with the fact that *JEN* 652 is published on plate 591 in the volume in which it appears.) In short, *JEN* 676 and 652 are to be identified with *JEN*u 101 and 591 respectively, not (as has been assumed) with *JEN*u 591 and 101 respectively. I would like to thank Martha Roth for puzzling out this problem with me.

[3] The designation in brackets represents the Oriental Institute accession number of this tablet. The Institute has accessioned 100 Nuzi tablets from among the *JEN*u texts. In the text and notes that follow, tablets identified as A119xx are accessions of the Oriental Institute.

[4] On the reasons for the same tablet being represented in the present volume by more than one copy, see above, p. 10.

[5] The *CAD* Nuzi file indicates a join, *JEN*u 244+282b. Although there exists evidence of at least one join, there is no apparent separate item, *JEN*u 282b.

[6] This joined tablet bears only the number 300. However, the join, 300+1142, is indicated on the card in the box with this tablet. It is also asserted in the *CAD* Nuzi file for *JEN*u 300 and *JEN*u 1142. Finally, the data in the file for these two entries conform to what is now a single tablet.

[7] The Oriental Institute catalogues *JEN* 759 as *JEN*u 305. The same text is represented in *NPN* (in order of decreasing frequency) as *JEN*u 312B, 312a, and 312.

[8] Lacheman identified *JEN* 866 as *JEN*u 329a. However, this tablet is now clearly labeled (*JEN*u) 339. The numbering may have undergone change.

[9] Various sources identify this tablet as *JEN*u 911. However, it is clear that *JEN*u 346 = *JEN* 704 and that *JEN*u 911 is a different tablet.

[10] *Nuzi-Bibliographie* (AOATS 11) 199, incorrectly equates *JEN*u 353 with *JEN* 286.

[11] *JEN* II, p. 8 and *Nuzi-Bibliographie* (AOATS 11) 199 (following *JEN* II) incorrectly equate *JEN*u 381 with *JEN* 205.

[12] The Oriental Institute records and the tablet itself indicate a join, *JEN*u 625+878. A join, in fact, is visible. Yet, on the tablet, the number 878 is crossed out. Furthermore, *JEN*u 878 has been published as *JEN* 330. Collation of *JEN* 330 against a cast of *JEN*u 878 confirms this identification. (The original of *JEN*u 878 was returned to Baghdad before I could collate it.) It appears that a part of what is now *JEN* 741 was once stored in the same box as *JEN*u 878 (= *JEN* 330) and given the same number. A join with *JEN*u 625 was subsequently made.

[13] This tablet is cited in *NPN* and in the *CAD* Nuzi file as *JEN*u 854. However, this is not correct: (*a*) the tablet, which does have "A11951" written on it, bears no "854" on its surface (it seems to have "584" indistinctly written [*JEN*u 584 is, however, stored elsewhere]), and (*b*) *JEN*u 854 is another item in its own box.

[14] See n. 6 above.

Catalogue of Texts

This catalogue is, for the most part, straightforward. For each text, the following information, where known, is provided: publication number, museum number, archaeological provenience within the western suburban complex of Nuzi, and partial description of the contents of the text. The last two items require further comment.

Archaeological provenience

There is no single, authoritative catalogue defining the findspot of each Oriental Institute Nuzi text. Four main sources of pertinent information have been used in the compilation of this part of the catalogue. It appears likely that, in most cases, all four sources derive from the same original data. However, these sources occasionally disagree with each other and display other signs (e.g., lack of any datum) of deriving, at least in part, from different informational "traditions." Conflicting data are, of course, noted *ad loc.* Otherwise, no attempt has been made in the catalogue to note from which source(s) the data have been gleaned. Where no source indicates a find spot, "Rm. ?" in the catalogue reflects this fact. The four sources are:

1. The boxes in which the tablets are stored. For the most part, each tablet is kept in its own box. These boxes also contain cards upon which is listed (usually) the *JEN*u number, the room number, a month and day notation, and a siglum indicating whether or not the tablet was transliterated for the *CAD* Nuzi file. These cards were most likely first written in the late 1920s.
2. A list based on a catalogue created by Edward Chiera. In December 1973, during a visit to the Oriental Institute, I examined a box containing hundreds of pieces of paper, each containing a *JEN*u number and most containing a room number. Chiera had made this file and included in it slips of paper for all tablets supposedly copied up to October 1928. The file included information on *JEN*u 1–1024. This means that Chiera never finished the file since, in formal terms, there are 1171 *JEN*u numbers. (Actually there are far more than 1171 tablets and fragments distributed among these numbers.) For *JEN*u 1–312 inclusive, I noted the room numbers from this catalogue. After that number, however, I noted only those *JEN*u numbers found in rooms 13, 15, and 16, (i.e., from a Teḫip-Tilla Family archaeological provenience), as well as those numbers with

no indication of a room number at all. The absence of a *JEN*u number from my list indicates, by extension, that the tablet *is* linked with a particular room in the western suburbs, but a room other than 13, 15, or 16. These details of my derivative list based on Chiera's catalogue assume importance because, between 1973 and December 1982 (when I was next at the Oriental Institute), the box and its contents disappeared. My partial list, therefore, is, for the moment, the only reflex of that Chiera catalogue.

3. Lacheman's unpublished papers. Among Lacheman's manuscripts and notes, there are frequent references to the archaeological provenience of many of the Chicago Nuzi texts.
4. Research notes of Edith Porada. As part of her doctoral research, Porada drew hundreds of seal impressions from the Oriental Institute Nuzi collection. She identified these impressions by their *JEN*u numbers and, in addition, included in her notes the room numbers of the tablets containing the impressions whenever she had this information at her disposal. I should like to thank Professor Porada for making these notes available and for generously allowing me to cite them in this catalogue.

As intimated above, it appears that, for the most part, all four sources derive ultimately from Chiera's field notes of the 1925–1926 season at Yorghan Tepe.

Partial Description of the Contents of the Text

In general, these descriptions are confined to noting the text genre, identities of principal parties, type of real estate, location of real estate (if real estate is involved), and identity of the scribe, unless of course these data are lacking in the text. Failing such specificity (e.g., in badly broken texts such as *JEN* 857) a gist of the contents of the text is hazarded.

Inasmuch as the catalogue aims to present a general description only, *mobilia* involved in contracts, especially in real estate contracts, are most usually not itemized. In similar fashion, the amount of land mentioned in real estate texts is also not noted. Toponyms indicating major landmarks are given. Thus, GNs appearing without further specification represent town (i.e., URU) names. Other toponyms (e.g., canal and *dimtu* names) are also included. Designations such as "by the field of PN" are not included.

Frequently, data are enclosed within parentheses. This indicates either that the datum is lost in a lacuna or that it does not appear in the text at all. In either case, restoration is based on a parallel or otherwise related text. Where not self-evident, justifications for these restorations are detailed at the appropriate points in *THNT*. Only where parenthetical data are followed by a question mark or by words such as "possibly" and "probably" are those data to be deemed questionable.

Notation of text genres and other data (e.g., PNs) based on partially preserved words or signs are *not* set off by parentheses in the catalogue. Damaged material is symbolized as follows:

. . . indicates totally effaced data
x indicates an unintelligible or broken sign

Where possible, the description of the text starts with the name of the text genre. The genre is usually named after the initial, formulaic words of the text. The following is a list (together with brief explanations) of the Akkadian genre names used in this catalogue and, where an Akkadian name is lacking, the English substitutes that I have used.

catalogue: a detailed "list," *q.v.*

contract of "daughter-in-lawship": *JEN* 708; *kallūtu* is accomplished; cf. *JEN* 437 for format

contract of servitude: *JEN* 769; *ardūtu* is accomplished; cf. *JEN* 611 for format

lišānšu: a 'declaration'; this may relate to a *mārūtu*, *šupeʾʾultu*, or other transaction; it may appear alone or appended to the formulation of another genre

list: items are listed *seriatim*

loan document: *JEN* 856; no distinguishing superscription

qīštu contract: *JEN* 688; no distinguishing superscription

receipt: *JEN* 819, perhaps; no distinguishing superscription

record of litigation = PN_1 *itti* PN_2 *ina dini* (. . .) *ana pani dayyāni* (. . .) *ītelūma*

ṭuppi mārtūti: a 'tablet of adoption of a female'

ṭuppi mārūti: a 'tablet of adoption'; unless otherwise indicated, real estate (not genuine) adoption is meant

ṭuppi šimuti (*sic*): a will

ṭuppi šupeʾʾulti: a 'tablet of exchange'; unless otherwise indicated, the exchange involves real estate only

ṭuppi tidennūti: a 'tablet of antichretic loan'; the type of loan, whether based on real estate or a person, is indicated in each description

ṭuppišu (*sic*; see *JEN* 794:1) *tamgurti*: a 'tablet of agreement'

umma: a 'statement' of an individual

The following tablets lack superscription and their precise genre is at least somewhat unclear: *JEN* 688, 754, 853, 854, 857, 864, and 878.

Personal names are rendered, where possible, according to the spellings established in *NPN*, except that "y" is substituted for "i̯".

Catalogue of Texts

JEN 674 (*JEN*u 727; Rm. 15[1]) *ṭuppi mārūti*. Teḫip-Tilla (son of Puḫi-šenni) obtains from Kuššiya, Arip-apu, and Teḫip-apu sons of . . . -uzzi land in or by the *dimtu* of Kunatu (in Apena). Scribe: Taya son of Apil-Sin.

JEN 675 (*JEN*u 590; Rm. 15) (*ṭuppi*) *mārūti*. Teḫip-Tilla son of Puḫi-šenni obtains from Abeya son of Kip-apu, . . . -ya son of Ḫanaya, Šummi-(ya?) son of Ḫanaya, Eteš-šenni son of Zi-/Ke- . . . -a-a, and Ur?- . . . son of Wanti- . . . land in the *dimtu* of (Šulmiy)a? in Apena. Scribe: Taya (son of Apil-Sin).

JEN 676 (*JEN*u 101; Rm. 15?[2]) *ṭuppi mārūti*. Teḫip-Tilla son of Puḫi-šenni obtains from Šenneya son of Turari land in the *dimtu* of Šulmiya in Apena. Scribe: Taya (son of Apil-Sin).

JEN 677 (*JEN*u 610; Rm. 15) *ṭuppi mārūti*. Teḫip-Tilla son of Puḫi-šenni obtains from Tupk-apu son of Ar?- . . . land in the *dimtu* of Sulae in Apena. Scribe: Taya (son of Apil-Sin).

JEN 678 (*JEN*u 564; Rm. 15) *ṭuppi mārūti*. Teḫip-Tilla son of Puḫi-šenni obtains from Taya son of Akkul-enni land in the *dimtu* of Sulae in Apena. Scribe: Taya (son of Apil-Sin).

JEN 679 (*JEN*u 1007; Rm. 15) (*ṭuppi mārūti*). Teḫip-Tilla son of Puḫi-šenni obtains from Meleya son of (Ḫutiya) and Ma?- . . . son of Ḫutiya land by the *dimtu* of Kunatu in Apena. Scribe: Taya (son of Apil-Sin).

JEN 680 (*JEN*u 847; Rm. 15) (*ṭuppi*) *mārūti*. Teḫip-Tilla son of Puḫi-šenni obtains from Epuzi son of Ḫanakka and Šešwaya son of . . . land in the *dimtu* of Šulmiya in Apena. Scribe: Taya son of Apil-Sin.

JEN 681 (*JEN*u 977; Rm. 16?[3]) (*ṭuppi mārūti*). Teḫip-Tilla son of Puḫi-šenni obtains from Inniki son of (Ḫašiya) land by the *dimtu* of Tanna-tašši (in Turša?). Scribe: Taya (son of Apil-Sin).

[1] Room 15 as the locus appears both on the card in the box with this tablet and in Lacheman's unpublished notes. The Chiera catalogue gives the locus as room 11. This latter is most unlikely. All other Teḫip-Tilla Apena real estate *ṭuppi mārūti* texts (with the possible exception of *JEN* 676) come from room 15.

[2] On the catalogue number of this tablet, see above, Register of Tablets, n. 2. Lacheman's unpublished papers and Porada's notes both indicate room 15 as the findspot for this tablet. This is quite plausible (see above, n. 1). However the card in the box with this tablet and the Chiera catalogue give room 16 as the findspot.

[3] None of the sources used for this catalogue lists a room number for this tablet. However, the tablet has close links to *JEN* 683 from room 16. It is, therefore, plausible that *JEN* 681 comes from that room as well. On the connections of *JEN* 681 and 683, see *THNT*, comments to *JEN* 681.

JEN 682 (*JEN*u 985; Rm. 16) *lišānšu* relating to a *mārūtu*. Teḫip-Tilla (son of Puḫi-šenni) obtains from Ziliya son of Tenteya land in Nuzi?. Scribe: Balṭu-kašid son of Apil-Sin.

JEN 683 (*JEN*u 356; Rm. 16) *ṭuppi mārūti*. Teḫip-Tilla son of Puḫi-šenni obtains from Inniki son of Ḫašiya land by the *dimtu* of Naniya and by land of (the *dimtu* of?) Tanna-taššі (in Turša?). Scribe: Taya son of Apil-Sin.

JEN 684 (*JEN*u 605; Rm. 15) *ṭuppi mārūti*. Teḫip-Tilla son of Puḫi-šenni obtains from Tai-šenni son of A-x-. . . -šu land by the x-elḫue Canal in Šinina. Scribe: Taya son of Apil-Sin.

JEN 685 (*JEN*u 569; Rm. 15) (*ṭuppi mārūti*). Teḫip-Tilla son of Puḫi-šenni obtains from Ṭâb-Tilla son of Šukriya land in Šinina. Scribe: Taya (son of Apil-Sin).

JEN 686 (*JEN*u 173; Rm. 16) *ṭuppi mārūti*. Teḫip-Tilla son of Puḫi-šenni obtains from Šumuli son of Arip-enni land by the "Yarru" (near Artiḫi). Scribe: Itḫ-apiḫe son of Taya.

JEN 687 (*JEN*u 362; Rm. 16) *ṭuppi mārūti*. Teḫip-Tilla son of Puḫi-šenni obtains from Pui-tae son of Eteš-šenni land in Artiḫi. Scribe: Itḫ-apiḫe (son of Taya).

JEN 688 (*JEN*u 981; Rm. 16) *Qīštu* contract.[4] Teḫip-Tilla son of Puḫi-šenni obtains from Wantiya son of Tur-marti land in Nuzi. Scribe: Taya son of Apil-Sin.

JEN 689 (*JEN*u 880; Rm. 16) (*ṭuppi*) *mārūti* involving cession of *mobilia* together with real estate. Teḫip-Tilla son of Puḫi-šenni obtains from Tai-šenni son of Aḫušina land and a female slave. Scribe: Taya son of Apil-Sin.

JEN 690 (*JEN*u 363a+363b; Rm. 16) (*ṭuppi*) *mārūti*. Teḫip-Tilla son of Puḫi-šenni obtains from Paliya son of . . . -x-x- . . . *kuppātu*-structures and *paiḫu*-land (in Unap-še). Scribe: Taya (son of Apil-Sin).

JEN 691 (*JEN*u 804; Rm. 15) *ṭuppi mārūti*. Teḫip-Tilla son of Puḫi-šenni obtains from Šalim-pûti (son of? / and?) . . . -unnanni land by the road to Apena.[5] Scribe: Ila-nîšū son of Sin-napšir.

JEN 692 (*JEN*u 235; Rm. 16) *ṭuppi mārūti*. Teḫip-Tilla son of Puḫi-šenni obtains from Tai-Tilla son of Wantiya land in the *dimti piršanni*, by the Akip-tašenni Canal (in Zizza). Scribe: Taya son of Apil-Sin.

[4] See *THNT*, comment to *JEN* 688.
[5] For possible locations of this land, see *THNT*, comment to *JEN* 691:8–9.

JEN 693 (*JEN*u 628; Rm. 15) *ṭuppi mārūti.* Teḫip-Tilla son of Puḫi-šenni obtains from Waratteya son of (Puḫi?)ya[6] kuppātu-structures and land by the road to Ulamme, in Nuzi. Scribe: Taya son of Apil-Sin.

JEN 694 (*JEN*u 104; Rm. 16) *ṭuppi mārūti.* Teḫip-Tilla son of Puḫi-šenni obtains from Ḫutiya son of . . . land by the *dimtu* of . . . by the road to the *dimtu* of U(lūliya, probably) in Unap-še. Scribes: Šumu-libšī son of Taya and Itḫ-apiḫe son of Taya.[7]

JEN 695 (*JEN*u 1144; Rm. ?) *ṭuppi mārūti.* Teḫip-Tilla son of Puḫi-šenni obtains from Aḫu-waqar son of (Apil- . . . ?) and X- . . . -AḪ?- . . . (real estate). Scribe: Taya son of Apil-Sin.

JEN 696 (*JEN*u 578; Rm. 15) *lišānšu*; content obscure. Itḫišta son of Ar-tae makes a declaration, probably regarding *mobilia* (possibly obtained from Teḫip-Tilla son of Puḫi-šenni). Scribe: Taya (son of Apil-Sin).

JEN 697 (*JEN*u 397; Rm. 16) (*ṭuppi šupeʾʾulti*). Teḫip-Tilla (son of Puḫi-šenni) obtains from Itḫ-apu and Ḫalu-šenni (real estate) near the *dimtu* of . . . in exchange for (real estate) in the *dimtu* of Anita (in Zizza) and an additional payment of *mobilia.* Scribe: Taya son of Apil-Sin.

JEN 698 (*JEN*u 81; Rm. 16[8]) *ṭuppi mārūti.* Teḫip-Tilla (son of Puḫi-šenni) obtains from Punniya son of . . . land in or by the *dimtu* of Ukin-zaḫ by the . . . -AN- . . . ? Canal (in Unap-še). Scribe: Sin-iqîša.

JEN 699 (*JEN*u 65; Rm. 15) *lišānšu*s (relating to a *mārūtu*). Šeḫliya son of Akaya; Ḫutiya, (Ar-teya,) Zike, (Ataya,) and Kipiya sons of Tamar-tae; Šukriya and Ḫaip-šarri sons of Maliya; and Eḫliya son of Akkul-enni aver that their fathers had ceded to Teḫip-Tilla son of Puḫi-šenni land once belonging to Minaš-šuk son of Zaziya. That land was by the Nirašši Canal, by the road to Tarkulli (in Nuzi). The "brothers" reconfirm that cession. Keliya son of Un-Tešup, in his own statement (i.e., *umma*), concurs. Scribe: Iniya son of Kiannipu.

JEN 700 (*JEN*u 96; Rm. 16) *ṭuppi mārūti.* Teḫip-Tilla son of Puḫi-šenni obtains from Tae son of Tain-šuḫ land in the vicinity of (the *dimtu* of?) Šurkum-atal in Artiḫi. Scribe: Itḫ-apiḫe (son of Taya).

JEN 701 (*JEN*u 485; Rm. ?) *ṭuppi mārūti.* Teḫip-Tilla son of Puḫi-šenni obtains from Kapatta son of X- . . . land. Scribe: Ḫutiya (son of) Uta-mansi.

[6] On the evidence for this patronymic, see *THNT,* comment to *JEN* 693:2.

[7] Regarding the actual writer of this text, see *THNT,* comment to *JEN* 694:29.

[8] The card in the box with this tablet and Chiera's catalogue both assign this tablet to room 16. Lacheman once noted the same datum but crossed it out, replacing 16 with 15.

JEN 702 (*JEN*u 285; Rm. 16) *ṭuppi mārūti*. Teḫip-Tilla son of Puḫi-šenni obtains from Šelwin-atal son of Ar-šalipe land in Artiḫi. Scribe: Iškur-andul son of Ziniya.

JEN 703 (*JEN*u 244;[9] Rm. 16) *ṭuppi* (*mārūti*). Teḫip-Tilla son of Puḫi-šenni obtains from Šukr-apu (son of Eteya), Niḫriya (son of Ennaya), Tur-šenni son of Zilip-kanari, and Naniya son of Šurukkaya[10] land by the *dimtu* of Akawatil and by the *dimtu* of Umpin-api (in Unap-še). Scribe: Taya son of Apil-Sin.

JEN 704 (*JEN*u 346; Rm. ?)[11] *ṭuppi mārūti*. Teḫip-Tilla son of Puḫi-šenni obtains from Inb-ilišu son of ŠU-MA-^{d}IM land in or by Ḫulumeni. Scribe: Taya son of Apil-Sin.

JEN 705 (*JEN*u 698; Rm. 16) *ṭuppi mārūti*. Teḫip-Tilla son of Puḫi-šenni obtains from Šeḫala son of Ar-Tešup land by the road to Dūr-ubla (in Artiḫi?). Scribe: Itḫ-apiḫe (son of Taya).

JEN 706 (*JEN*u 223; Rm. 15) *lišānšu* relating to a *šupe*ʾʾ*ultu*. Teḫip-Tilla (son of Puḫi-šenni) obtains from Teḫip?-x- . . . land in the *dimtu* of Kip-Tešup (in Nuzi) in exchange for land. . . . This tablet also appears as *JEN* 793.

JEN 707 (*JEN*u 941; Rm. 16) *ṭuppi mārūti*. Alkiya son of (Milki-Tešup, probably) obtains from Teššuya[12] son of . . . structures, orchard land, and *ḫalaḫwu*-land by the (Killi) Canal (in Artiḫi).

JEN 708 (*JEN*u 435; Rm. 16) (Contract of "daughter-in-lawship.") Teḫip-Tilla (son of Puḫi-šenni) obtains from Šaš-kuli daughter of Pi-si?- . . . , a female slave. Scribe: Taya (son of Apil-Sin).

JEN 709 (*JEN*u 986; Rm. 16) *ṭuppi mārūti*. Teḫip-Tilla son of Puḫi-šenni obtains from Taya son of Ipša-ḫalu land by the *dimtu* of Apliya and by the *dimtu* of Akawatil in Unap-še. Scribe: Taya (son of Apil-Sin).

JEN 710 (*JEN*u 289; Rm. 16) *ṭuppi mārūti*. Teḫip-Tilla son of Puḫi-šenni obtains from Kittaya son of Ṣill-abi land in Artiḫi. Scribe: Itḫ-apiḫe (son of Taya).

[9] Regarding a supposed join, *JEN*u 244+282b, see above, Register of Tablets, n. 5.

[10] The name of a fifth adopter, probably "Zilip-apu son of Ipša-(ḫalu)," has been erased from the text (probably three times). See *THNT*, comment to *JEN* 703:6.

[11] On the identification of *JEN* 704 with *JEN*u 346, see above, Register of Tablets, n. 9. Although room 11 is listed as the findspot on the card in the box with this tablet (possibly also in Chiera's catalogue as well), *JEN* 704 should have been found in a Teḫip-Tilla archaeological context, room 15 or 16, rather than in room 11.

[12] The normalization "Teššuya" for *Te-eš-šu-a-a* follows an unpublished suggestion by Lacheman in a parallel situation. This spelling does not appear in *NPN* or *AAN*.

JEN 711 (*JEN*u 299; Rm. 15) (*lišānšu* relating to a *šupe*ʾʾ*ultu*). Teḫip-Tilla (son of Puḫi-šenni) and . . . exchange land in (the *dimtu* of) Šumaš-šawalli (in Nuzi). Scribe: Itḫ-apiḫe (son of Taya).

JEN 712 See *JEN* 753.

JEN 713 (*JEN*u 1044a; Rm. ?) Record of litigation. Teḫip-Tilla (son of Puḫi-šenni) defeats Ḫuišša son of Ḫurpi-šenni and, in consequence, obtains from him *mobilia*.

JEN 714 (*JEN*u 300+1142; Rm. 15[13]) *ṭuppi mārūti*. Teḫip-Tilla son of Puḫi-šenni obtains from Šumma-ilu son of Ikkin orchard land in Ulamme. Scribe: Itḫ-apiḫe (son of Taya).

JEN 715 (*JEN*u 523; Rm. 15) *ṭuppi mārūti*. Teḫip-Tilla (son of Puḫi-šenni) obtains from Šukri- . . . land (in Nuzi). Scribe: Nanna-mansi son of Taya.

JEN 716 (*JEN*u 313; Rm. 15) *ṭuppi mārūti*. Teḫip-Tilla son of Puḫi-šenni[14] obtains from Tulpi-šenni son of Turari land in or near Lupti (probably near Artiḫi). Scribe: Itḫ-apiḫe son of Taya.

JEN 717 (*JEN*u 399; Rm. 16) (*ṭuppi mārūti*). Teḫip-Tilla son of Puḫi-šenni obtains from Elḫip- . . . land in or near the *dimtu* of Teḫip-Tilla (in Zizza). Scribe: Itḫ-apiḫe (son of Taya).

JEN 718 (*JEN*u 604; Rm. 15) *ṭuppi mārūti*. Teḫip-Tilla son of Puḫi-šenni obtains from Tai-šenni son of Akap-tukke land on the road to Našmur. Scribe: Šamaš-ilu-ina-mâti? and, possibly, Zil-teya (son of Tauka).

JEN 719 (*JEN*u 367; Rm. 16) *ṭuppi mārūti*. Teḫip-Tilla son of Puḫi-šenni obtains from Na-x- . . . -ya? son of Kintar, Šun-tari son of Ḫani-kuzzi, Nai-šeri son of Apuzi, Aminipe son of Wantiya, Milkiya son of Apuzi, and Ninu-atal son of Apuzi land in Erišpa. Scribe: Itḫ-apiḫe (son of Taya).

JEN 720 (*JEN*u 555; Rm. 15) *ṭuppi mārūti*. Teḫip-Tilla son of Puḫi-šenni obtains from Ḫui-Tešup son of Naniya land by the "Yarru" (near Artiḫi). Scribe: Itḫ-apiḫe (son of Taya).

JEN 721 (*JEN*u 752; Rm. 16) *ṭuppi mārūti*. Teḫip-Tilla son of Puḫi-šenni obtains from Ar-šali son of Šukriya land (in the town of Arrapḫa?). Scribe: Itḫ-apiḫe son of Taya.

JEN 722 (*JEN*u 760; Rm. 16) *ṭuppi mārūti*. Teḫip-Tilla son of Puḫi-šenni obtains from Puḫu-menni daughter of Ḫana- . . . and from Šeš-

[13] For further on the join, see above, Register of Tablets, n. 6. The room 15 findspot is attested for *JEN*u 300 only. No findspot is noted for *JEN*u 1142.

[14] *JEN* 716:2–3 identifies the adoptee as "Teḫip-Tilla son of Teḫip-Tilla," an obvious scribal lapse.

wikka and Wantip-ukur sons of Turari land by the road to Anzugalli (in Nuzi). Scribe: Itḫ-apiḫe son of (Taya).

JEN 723 (*JEN*u 790; Rm. 16) *ṭuppi* (*mārūti*). Teḫip-Tilla (son of Puḫi-šenni) obtains from Ar-Tešup (son of Ipša-ḫalu?) land by the *dimtu* of . . . (in Unap-še?). Scribe: Itḫ-apiḫe son of Taya.

JEN 724 (*JEN*u 827; Rm. 15) *ṭuppi mārūti*. Teḫip-Tilla son of Puḫi-šenni obtains from Šemi son of Eḫlip-apu land (by the road to?) Nuḫ- . . . ?. Scribe: Itḫ-apiḫe (son of Taya).

JEN 725 (*JEN*u 917 = A11963; Rm. 15) *ṭuppi mārūti*. Teḫip-Tilla son of Puḫi-šenni obtains from Enna-mati son of Kamputtu land by the road to x-. . . . Scribe: Itḫ-apiḫe son of Taya.

JEN 726 (*JEN*u 806;[15] Rm. 16) *ṭuppi mārūti*. Teḫip-Tilla son of Puḫi-šenni obtains from Zaziya (son of Ḫašip-apu?) land by the road to or in the town of Arrapḫa. Scribe: Itḫ-apiḫe son of Taya.

JEN 727 (*JEN*u 514; Rm. 16) *ṭuppi mārūti*. Teḫip-Tilla son of Puḫi-šenni obtains from Šilwa-Tešup son of A(ta?)ya land in the *dimtu* of Kipantil (in Nuzi). Scribe: (Itḫ-apiḫe?) son of Taya?.

JEN 728 (*JEN*u 686; Rm. 16) *ṭuppi mārūti*. Teḫip-Tilla son of Puḫi-šenni obtains from Ipšaya son of Keliya land (in Artiḫi, probably). (Scribe: Itḫ-apiḫe son of Taya.)

JEN 729 (*JEN*u 615; Rm. 15) (*ṭuppi*) *mārūti*. Teḫip-Tilla son of Puḫi-šenni obtains from Ipša-ḫalu son of Šurkum-atal land. Scribe: Artašenni son of Apil-Sin.

JEN 730 (*JEN*u 539; Rm. 15) (*ṭuppi mārūti*). Teḫip-Tilla son of Puḫi-šenni obtains from Tupki-Tilla (son of? . . .) orchard land in Nuzi. Scribe: Artašenni (son of Apil-Sin).

JEN 731 (*JEN*u 583; Rm. 15) *ṭuppi mārūti*. Teḫip-Tilla son of Puḫi-šenni obtains from Muš-teya son of En-šaku land (by the road to Našm)ur? Scribes: Zil-teya (son of Tauka), possibly, and Erwi-šarri (son of Teššuya), possibly.

JEN 732 (*JEN*u 351; Rm. 16) (*ṭuppi mārūti*). Teḫip-Tilla son of Puḫi-šenni obtains from Šukr-apu son of x- . . . land (in Unap-še, probably). Scribe: (Taya son Apil-Sin?).

JEN 733 (*JEN*u 737; Rm. 15) *ṭuppi mārūti*. Teḫip-Tilla son of Puḫi-šenni obtains from Riš-keya son of Purna-ni?-x- . . . land in Karanna-of-Puḫi-šenni. Scribe: Naniya son of Lu-Nanna.

[15] *JEN*u 806 is the correct catalogue number, not 866, as in Noel Kenneth Weeks, "The Real Estate Interests of a Nuzi Family" (Ph.D. diss., Brandeis University, 1971) 337.

JEN 734 (*JEN*u 412; Rm. 16) *ṭuppi mārūti*. Minaya (son of Ipša-ḫalu) obtains from Teššuya son of Wantiya land, structures, and a threshing floor.

JEN 735 (*JEN*u 396; Rm. 16) *ṭuppi mārūti*. Teḫip-Tilla son of Puḫi-šenni obtains from Mušeya son of Sin-êriš land in Ḫurāṣina-ṣeḫru. Scribe: Balṭu-kašid (son of Apil-Sin).

JEN 736 (*JEN*u 634+690; Rm. 16[16]) *ṭuppi mārūti*. Teḫip-Tilla son of Puḫi-šenni obtains from Šennape son of Ḫairalla land by the *dimtu* of Akawatil and by the *dimtu* of Ulūliya in Unap-še. Scribe: (Waqar-bêli son of Taya).

JEN 737 (*JEN*u 1030; Rm. 15) *ṭuppi mārūti*. Antaya slave of Teḫip-Tilla obtains from Zike and Naḫiš-šalmu sons of Akkuya structures in the heart of (Nuz)i?.

JEN 738 (*JEN*u 183; Rm. 16) (*ṭuppi mārūti*). Teḫip-Tilla (son of Puḫi-šenni) obtains from Arik-keya (land, probably orchard land, in?) Atakkal. Scribe: (Balṭu-kašid son of Apil-Sin?).[17]

JEN 739 (*JEN*u 225; Rm. 15) *ṭuppi mārūti*. Teḫip-Tilla son of Puḫi-šenni obtains from Iriri-Tilla son of Šekaru land in the *dimtu* of Šak-ruššе? (if so, in Unap-še?). Scribe: Zil-teya son of Tauka, possibly.

JEN 740 (*JEN*u 734; Rm. 15) *lišānšu* relating to a *mārūtu*. Teḫip-Tilla son of Puḫi-šenni obtains from Kešḫaya son of Kinniya a threshing floor in Nuzi, by the road to Anzugalli. Scribe: ^{d}AK.DINGIR.RA (son of Sin-napšir), likely.

JEN 741 (*JEN*u 625; Rm. 15?[18]) *ṭuppi mārūti* and *lišānšu*. Teḫip-Tilla son of Puḫi-šenni obtains from Taya son of Ḫapi-ašu land in Unap-še, by the road to Turša. Taya declares he has received payment from Teḫip-Tilla. Scribe: Iluya (son of Sin-napšir?).

JEN 742 (*JEN*u 517+519; Rm. 16[19]) *ṭuppi mārūti* and *lišānšu*. Teḫip-Tilla son of Puḫi-šenni obtains from Ar-Tešup son of Ipša-ḫalu and

[16] This datum derives from a single source, Chiera's catalogue note for *JEN*u 690, and is consistent with the text's contents. For *JEN*u 634, Chiera's catalogue indicates a room other than rooms 13, 15, or 16. This is most unlikely.

[17] The writer of this text may be the scribe who wrote *JEN* 76 since these two texts otherwise show striking correspondences. For details, see *THNT*, comments to *JEN* 738. The identity of the scribe of *JEN* 76 is discussed by Pierre M. Purves, "The Early Scribes of Nuzi," *AJSL* 57 (1940) 173 n. 51. Contrast the conclusion of Gernot Wilhelm, *Untersuchungen zum Hurro-Akkadischen von Nuzi* (AOAT 9; Kevelaer: Butzon & Bercker, 1970) 10, 11 n. 7 (the first n. 7).

[18] On an alleged join, *JEN*u 625+878, see above, Register of Tablets, n. 12. The card in the box for *JEN*u 625 records the findspot as room 15. Chiera's catalogue gives the findspot as room 16. In light of n. 12 of the Register of Tablets, the datum that *JEN*u 878 comes from room 16 has no relevance to *JEN* 741.

[19] This findspot is recorded for both *JEN*u 517 and 519.

from Ḫanaya son of Ar-Tešup land by the *dimtu* of Eniya and by the road to the *dimtu* of Ulūliya (in Unap-še). Ḫanaya (probably alone) declares he has received payment from (Teḫip-Tilla). Scribe: Uta-andul (son of Taya).

JEN 743 (*JEN*u 916; Rm. 16) *ṭuppi mārūti.* Teḫip-Tilla son of Puḫi-šenni obtains from Apakke son of Paliya land by the *dimtu* of Akawatil, by the *dimtu* of Inb-ilišu, and by the road to the *dimtu* of UD-ḫušše (in Unap-še). Scribe: Iškur-andul son of Ziniya.

JEN 744 (*JEN*u 782; Rm. 16) (*ṭuppi*) *mārūti* (and *lišānšu*?). Teḫip-Tilla son of Puḫi-šenni obtains from Niḫriya son of Ennaya land by the *dimtu* of (Akawatil?) and (by?) the *dimtu* of Ulūliya (in Unap-še). Scribe: Iluya (son of Sin-napšir?).

JEN 745 (*JEN*u 311; Rm. 16) *ṭuppi mārūti.* Teḫip-Tilla son of Puḫi-šenni obtains from Elḫip-šarri son of Turru land by the *dimtu* of Teḫip-Tilla (in Zizza). Scribe: Ar-Tešup son of Taya.

JEN 746 (*JEN*u 883; Rm. 16) (*ṭuppi mārūti*). Teḫip-Tilla son of Puḫi-šenni obtains from Wantiš-še son of Turari, Eḫ- . . . -x-šeli son of Ari-kurri, Ḫašum-atal son of Ari-kurri, and Tae? son of x- . . . land in Nuzi in the *dimtu* of Šumaššawalli, (by?) the *dimtu* of Zi(ke)?/Awi(lu)?. Scribe: Taya (son of Apil-Sin).

JEN 747 (*JEN*u 414; Rm. 16) *ṭuppi mārūti.* Teḫip-Tilla son of Puḫi-šenni obtains from Iluya son of Ḫamattar *paiḫu*-land in Unap-še. Scribe: Urḫiya son of Keliya.

JEN 748 (*JEN*u 621; Rm. 15) (*ṭuppi*) *šupeʾʾulti.* Teḫip-Tilla son of Puḫi-šenni obtains from Unap-tae (son of Naya) structures in Nuzi in exchange for structures in Nuzi and an additional payment of *mobilia.* Scribe: Artašenni son of Apil-Sin.

JEN 749 (*JEN*u 421; Rm. 16[20]) (*ṭuppi mārūti* and *lišānšu*). Teḫip-Tilla (son of Puḫi-šenni) obtains from Taya (son of . . .) land in Unap-še. Taya declares he has received payment (from Teḫip-Tilla). Scribe: (E-/Še-ḫli?)-Tešup son of Sin-ibnī.

JEN 750 (*JEN*u 240; Rm. 16) *ṭuppi mārūti.* Enna-mati son of Teḫip-Tilla obtains from Kipaya son of Ilapri structures in Nuzi and, it seems, a cistern. Scribe: Iškur-andul son of Ziniya.

JEN 751 (*JEN*u 624; Rm. 16) *ṭuppi mārūti.* Teḫip-Tilla son of Puḫi-šenni obtains from Paya son of Ibašši-ilu land by the *dimtu* of (. . . ?-)x-taya and the *dimtu* of Akawatil (in Unap-še). Scribe: Šumu-libšī son of Taya.

[20] The sources for this datum are the card in the box with this tablet and Lacheman's notes. The tablet's contents are consistent with this findspot. Chiera's catalogue lists the findspot as room 11. This is most unlikely.

JEN 752 (*JEN*u 807; Rm. 16) *ṭuppi mārūti.* Teḫip-Tilla son of Puḫi-šenni obtains from Itḫ-apu son of Ipša-ḫalu land in the *dimti piršanni* of Teḫip-Tilla (in Zizza). Scribe: Uta-andul son of Taya.

JEN 753 (*JEN*u 258; Rm. 15[21]) (*lišānšu*, probably relating to a *šupeʾultu*). Teḫip-Tilla (son of Puḫi-šenni) obtains from Ḫupita son of Keliya land (by) the Nirašši (Canal) (in? Nu)zi? in exchange for land (in) . . . (and an additional payment of *mobilia*?). Scribe:. . . . This tablet also appears as *JEN* 712, 877.

JEN 754 (*JEN*u 678; Rm. 11) Contents obscure. Transfer of real estate and other property appears likely. Personal names include "Kuššiya" and "Šeḫel-Tešup."

JEN 755 (*JEN*u 654; Rm. ?) *ṭuppi mārūti.* Teḫip-Tilla (son of Puḫi-šenni) obtains from Šekaru son of Ḫutiya (structures? in Nuzi?). Scribe: Balṭu-kašid (son of Apil-Sin).

JEN 756 (*JEN*u 297; Rm. 16) (*ṭuppi mārūti.* Teḫip-Tilla son of Puḫi-šenni obtains from . . . land in Unap-še. Scribe:) Taya son of Apil-Sin.

JEN 757 (*JEN*u 885; Rm. 16) (*ṭuppi mārūti*, most likely). Teḫip-Tilla (son of Puḫi-šenni) obtains from Niḫriya son of . . . -riya (probably) land near Akip-apu, a tower, and a fold, (all in) Unap-še. Scribe: (E-/Še-ḫ)li-Tešup son of Sin-ibnī.

JEN 758 (*JEN*u 597; Rm. 15) *ṭuppi* (*mārūti*). Teḫip-Tilla son of Puḫi-šenni obtains from Nan-Tešup son of Kipi-Tilla land by the *dimtu* of Šakrušše (in Unap-še?). Scribe: Enna-mati (son of Šamaš-ilu-ina-mâti).

JEN 759 (*JEN*u 305;[22] Rm. 15) *ṭuppi mārūti.* Teḫip-Tilla (son of Puḫi-šenni) obtains from Minaš-šuk (son of . . .) land in. . . . Scribe: Erwi-šarri (son of Teššuya?) and, possibly, Zil-teya son of Tauka.

JEN 760 (*JEN*u 448; Rm. 16) *ṭuppi mārūti.* Teḫip-Tilla son of Puḫi-šenni obtains from Šamaḫul son of Paḫur orchard land in Purulli. Scribe: Ḫamanna.

JEN 761 (*JEN*u 963; Rm. 16) *ṭuppi mārūti* and *lišānšu.* Teḫip-Tilla son of Puḫi-šenni obtains from Tayuki son of A-x- . . . -x land in Unap-še by the *dimtu* of Akawatil and near the town of Akip-apu. Tayuki declares he has received payment (from Teḫip-Tilla). (Scribe?: E-/Še-ḫ)li-Te(šup son of Sin-ibnī?).

[21] The findspot for this tablet is noted in Chiera's catalogue. On the card in the same box with the text, 16 has been overwritten with 15.

[22] On the catalogue number(s) of this tablet, see above, Register of Tablets, n. 7.

JEN 762 (*JEN*u 611+731 fragment 3; Rm. 15[23]) *ṭuppi šupeʾʾulti.* Teḫip-Tilla son of Puḫi-šenni and Na?-. . . (son of) . . . -te exchange orchard land in Nuzi. Na?-. . . may receive an additional payment of *mobilia.* Scribe: Artašenni (son of Apil-Sin).

JEN 763 (*JEN*u 221 = A11907; Rm. 15) *ṭuppi mārūti.* Teḫip-Tilla (son of Puḫi-šenni) obtains from . . . -x-x? (and?) Šur-Tešup son(s?) of (Teḫip?)-Tilla (land) by the *dimtu* of Šakrušše (in Unap-še?). (Scribe): Enna-mati (son of Šamaš-ilu-ina-mâti).

JEN 764 (*JEN*u 1029; Rm. 15[24]) *ṭuppi mārūti.* Teḫip-Tilla son of Puḫi-šenni obtains from Puḫiya son of BE-x-. . . land by the *dimtu* of Šakrušše (in Unap-še?). (Scribe): Enna-mati (son of Šamaš-ilu-ina-mâti).

JEN 765 (*JEN*u 613; Rm. 15) *ṭuppi mārūti.* Teḫip-Tilla son of Puḫi-šenni obtains from Wantiya son of Purniya and Ḫašuar son of Purniya two (probably adjacent) plots of land owned individually by each in the *dimtu* of Šakrušše (in Unap-še?). (Scribe): Enna-mati (son of Šamaš-ilu-ina-mâti).

JEN 766 (*JEN*u 568;[25] Rm. 15) (*ṭuppi mārūti*). Teḫip-Tilla (son of Puḫi-šenni) obtains from . . . -x (son of . . . real estate in) Šinina. Scribe: (Taya son of) Apil-Sin.

JEN 767 (*JEN*u 319; Rm. 15) (*ṭuppi mārūti*). Teḫip-Tilla son of Puḫi-šenni obtains from Ikkiya son of Kakiya land by the . . . Canal, (in?) Purulli. (Scribe: Itḫ-apiḫe son of Taya?).

JEN 768 (*JEN*u 783; Rm. 16) (*ṭuppi mārūti*). Teḫip-Tilla son of Puḫi-šenni obtains from Turari son of Pu-x-. . . land in the (*dimti*) *piršanni* (of) Teḫip-Tilla (in Zizza). Scribe: Waqar-bêli son of Taya.

JEN 769 (*JEN*u 383; Rm. 16) Contract of servitude. Abutteya (son of . . .) enters the household of Teḫip-Tilla son of Puḫi-šenni. Scribe: Itḫ-apiḫe (son of Taya).

JEN 770 (*JEN*u 89; Rm. 16) (*ṭuppi mārūti*). Teḫip-Tilla son of Puḫi-šenni obtains from Šukr-apu son of Eteya land by the *dimtu* of Akawatil, by the road linking Unap-še to the *dimtu* of Ulūliya (in Unap-še).

[23] The cards in the boxes for *JEN*u 611 and 731 associate these tablets with room 15. Lacheman's papers also note that *JEN*u 611+731 comes from room 15. Chiera's catalogue assigns no room number to *JEN*u 611 and room 16 to *JEN*u 731.

[24] This datum comes from Lacheman's papers only. A secondary Oriental Institute record of what appeared on the card in the box with this tablet has room 18 (*sic*). The card itself is no longer present.

[25] Two sizeable tablet fragments bear this number. *JEN* 766 represents the larger of the two fragments. The fragments come from different tablets.

(Scribe: Very likely possibilities are Taya son of Apil-Sin and Itḫ-apiḫe son of Taya.[26])

JEN 771 (*JEN*u 862; Rm. 16) Catalogue of real estate. At least four land holdings (of Teḫip-Tilla son of Puḫi-šenni) are described in the surviving part of the text. Two are located in the *dimti maḫa*ZI, one of those by a canal. (All are most probably located in Artiḫi.)

JEN 772 (*JEN*u 820; Rm. 16) (*ṭuppi mārūti*) and *lišānšu*. Teḫip-Tilla son of Puḫi-šenni obtains from Pal-Tešup (son of . . .) land by the *dimtu* of (T)ur-šenni? (in Unap-še). Pal-Tešup declares he has received payment. Scribe: Iškur-andul son of Ziniya.

JEN 773 (*JEN*u 826; Rm. 15) *ṭuppi* (*mārūti*). Teḫip-Tilla son of Puḫi-šenni obtains from GA- . . . and . . . sons? of x- . . . -x- . . . land by the *dimtu* (of?) KI-x- . . . -x- . . . -x-ma?.

JEN 774 (*JEN*u 398; Rm. 16) *ṭuppi mārūti*. Minaya son of Ipša-ḫalu obtains from Šurukka son of Tauḫḫe all the latter's real estate, including land, structures, and a threshing floor (probably in the *dimtu* of Eniya in Unap-še). Scribe: Balṭu-kašid (son of Apil-Sin).

JEN 775 (*JEN*u 617; Rm. 15) (*lišānšu* relating to a *mārūtu*). Teḫip-Tilla (son of Puḫi-šenni) obtains from (. . .) land by the . . . ? Canal, probably.

JEN 776 (*JEN*u 92; Rm. 15[27]) *ṭuppi mārūti*. Enna-mati son of Teḫip-Tilla obtains from Ḫišmeya son of Ithišta land (in Tente, most likely). Scribe: Zunzu (son of Intiya).

JEN 777 (*JEN*u 822; Rm. 15) (*lišānšu*) relating to a *mārūtu*. Teḫip-Tilla son of Puḫi-šenni obtains from Taya son of A-x- . . . land. Scribe: Itḫ-apiḫe (son of Taya).

JEN 778 (*JEN*u 357; Rm. 16) (*ṭuppi mārūti*. Teḫip-Tilla son of Puḫi-šenni obtains from) Elḫip-šarri (son of . . . real estate [in Nuzi?]). Scribe: Waqar-bêli (son of Taya).

JEN 779 (*JEN*u 354; Rm. 16) *ṭuppi* (*mārūti*). Pakla-piti son of Enna-mati obtains from Ḫanakka son of Še-x- . . . land in Nuzi (near?) Til Zara-mu?-ḫi. Scribe: ^{d}AK.DINGIR.RA son of Sin-napšir.[28]

JEN 780 (*JEN*u 785; Rm. 16) *ṭuppi mārūti* and *lišānšu*. Enna-mati (son of Teḫip-Tilla) obtains from Šur-Tešup and Eḫli-Tešup sons of T(eḫip-

[26] Taya wrote *JEN* 703 and Itḫ-apiḫe wrote *JEN* 586. On the relevance of those texts to the present document, see *THNT*, comment to *JEN* 770:19.

[27] *JEN*u 92 is identified by all relevant sources but Lacheman (who does not comment on this point) as coming from room 15. *JEN*u 1127, consisting of four pieces, is defined by the card in the box with these pieces as coming from room 12. It is most unlikely that the fragment joining *JEN*u 92 comes from room 12.

[28] For further on the identity of the scribe of this tablet, see *THNT*, comment to *JEN* 779:40b–41a.

Tilla, probably) orchard land near the road to the *dimtu* of Ḫuišše. Šur-Tešup and Eḫli-Tešup declare (they have received payment from) Enna-mati. Scribe: Nanna-adaḫ.

JEN 781 (*JEN*u 128; Rm. 13) *ṭuppi t*(*idennūti*?) based on real estate. Tarmi-Tilla son of Šurki-Tilla receives from Ḫušḫuša wife? of? Ḫanaya land in Nuzi (by the road to) Atakkal (for a loan of?) *mobilia*. Scribe: Turar-Tešup son of Itḫ-apiḫe.

JEN 782 (*JEN*u 28; Rm. 13) (*ṭuppi mārūti*). Utḫap-tae son of Muš-teya obtains from Turariya and Kanaya son(s)? of x- . . . ? land near the town of . . . -x-GAL.

JEN 783 (*JEN*u 212; Rm. 13) (*ṭuppi mārūti*). Tarmi-Tilla (son of Šurki-Tilla) obtains from Šilaḫi land.

JEN 784 (*JEN*u 772; Rm. 1) *ṭuppi mārūti*. Ḫui-te (son of Mušeya) obtains from Šešerpa son of Itḫ-apu a structure in Ḫurāṣina-ṣeḫru. Scribe: I(ri)ri (probably), son of. . . .

JEN 785 (*JEN*u 793; Rm. 1) *ṭuppi mārūti*. Itḫ-apu son of Ḫašiya obtains from Turari son of Ila-nîšū land in? Ḫurāṣina-ṣeḫru by the road to? (lit., in) the town of Takku (that is, *Ta-ku-wa* [line 8]).

JEN 786 (*JEN*u 800; Rm. 1) *ṭuppi mārūti*. Itḫ-apu son of Ḫašiya obtains from Arik-kamari son of Puramizi land in Ḫurāṣina-ṣeḫru?. Scribe: Arip-urašše.

JEN 787 (*JEN*u 853; Rm. 1) *ṭuppi mārūti*. Itḫ-apu son of Ḫašiya obtains from Zume son of Mutta land in Ḫurāṣina-ṣeḫru by the road to Zipu-ša?. Scribe: Šamaš-bārī.

JEN 788 (*JEN*u "854" = A11951;[29] Rm. ?) *ṭuppi mārūti*. Hilpiš-šuḫ son of Šuḫun-zirira obtains from Akkul-enni son of Itḫ-apu structures in Temtena. Scribe: Ad(ašše?)ya.

JEN 789 (*JEN*u 797; Rm. 1) (*ṭuppi*) *mārūti* (atypically formulated). Ḫui-te son of Mušeya obtains from Šešerpa son of Itḫ-apu land, structures (and?) threshing floor(s), orchard land, (and?) Šešerpa's inheritance share, and other property in Ḫurāṣina-ṣeḫru and in the town of x-. . . . (This share may be equal to or in addition to the) tablets and the land described in them (all in Ḫurāṣina-ṣeḫru, probably) tendered to Ḫui-te.[30] In addition to the "gift" of *mobilia*, Ḫui-te gives to Šešerpa two houses in the outskirts (of Ḫurāṣina-ṣeḫru, probably). Scribe: (I)riri, probably.

[29] On the *JEN*u number of this tablet, see above, register of tablets, n. 13.

[30] I believe it likely that the real estate *is* the inheritance share and that the tablets document the same property.

JEN 790 (*JEN*u 320; Rm. 11) *ṭuppi mārūti* and (*lišānšu*). Kel-Tešup son of Pa- . . . / Ḫ(u?-tiya?) obtains from Takuya son of (Umpin)-api? structures, a threshing floor, and orchard land in Ḫurāṣina-ṣeḫru. (Takuya declares he has received payment) from Kel-Tešup.

JEN 791 (*JEN*u 70a; Rm. 15) (*ṭuppi*) *šupeʾʾulti*. Teḫip-Tilla son of Puḫi-šenni obtains from Ḫunniya (son of . . .) and Ḫizame (wife? of) Ak?- . . . -ya?[31] land by the (road to) Ulamme (in Nuzi, most probably) in exchange for land between the (*dimtu*?) of Arip-apu and the *dimtu* of Ziliya son of Tenteya (in Nuzi) and an additional payment of *mobilia*. Scribe: Urḫiya son of Keliya.

JEN 792 (*JEN*u 155; Rm. 15) *ṭuppi šupeʾʾulti*. Teḫip-Tilla son Puḫi-šenni obtains from Kintutti and Šekaru sons of x- . . . land by the road to Tarkulli (in Nuzi or Šinina)[32] in exchange for land in the *dimtu* of Te-x- . . . and an additional payment (of *mobilia*).

JEN 793 See *JEN* 706.

JEN 794 (*JEN*u 348a (+) 348b; Rm. 11) *ṭuppišu* (*sic*) *tamgurti*. Ḫilpiš-šuḫ son of Šuḫun-zirira and Zi- . . . -ta son of Zilip-Til(la, probably) confirm an agreement.[33] Scribe: Šušeya.

JEN 795 (*JEN*u 387; Rm. 16) (*ṭuppi šupeʾʾulti*). Teḫip-Tilla (son of Puḫi-šenni) obtains from Abutteya son of Kub(butu, very likely) and Ṣalmu son of Ay-abâš land and structures? in or near the *dimtu* of Tupki-Tilla (in Unap-še) in exchange for land in Unap-še. Scribe: Itḫ-apiḫe (son of Taya).

JEN 796 (*JEN*u 459(+)459B; Rm. 15[34]) *ṭuppi šupeʾʾulti*. Teḫip-Tilla (son of Puḫi-šenni) obtains from Pal-Tilla (son of . . .) structures (in? the town of Arr)apḫa? in exchange for structures. Scribe: . . . -x-ni.[35]

JEN 797 (*JEN*u 596; Rm. 15) (*ṭuppi šupeʾʾulti*). Teḫ(ip-Tilla, probably and, if so, he is the son of Puḫi-šenni) obtains from . . . -x son of Tup-ki?- . . . (structures in exchange for) structures. Scribe: Itḫ-apiḫe son of Taya.

JEN 798 (*JEN*u 359+538; Rm. 16[36]) *ṭuppi šupeʾʾulti*. Teḫip-Tilla son of Puḫi-šenni obtains from Šennaya, Taya, Ikkiri, Akap-ura, and

[31] If "*Ak- . . . -ya*" prove correct, the PN will have been "Akkuya," "Akku-teya," or the like.

[32] For the basis of this conclusion, see *THNT*, comment to *JEN* 792:9.

[33] The contents of the agreement are lost.

[34] Chiera's catalogue entry for this item mentions no room number. All other sources (including Chiera himself in an unpublished note) ascribe *JEN*u 459 to room 15. There are no data on *JEN*u 459B as a discrete item.

[35] For further on the identity of the scribe(s), see *THNT*, comment to *JEN* 796:14–15.

[36] Chiera's catalogue assigns both pieces to room 16. The card in the box originally containing *JEN*u 538 gives room 16 as the findspot for that piece. No other data are available.

Aril-lumti sons of Ḫašip-apu land (quite possibly in or near the *dimti piršanni* in Zizza) in exchange for land in the town of (Zizza, probably) and an additional payment of *mobilia.* (Scribe:) Uta-andul (son of Taya).

JEN 799 (*JEN*u 512; Rm. 16) *ṭuppi šupeʾʾulti.* Teḫip-Tilla son of Puḫi-šenni obtains from Šilwa-Tešup son of Abeya and Pal-teya (Šilwa-Tešup's brother) land in the *dimtu* of (Tupki-Tilla) by (Malašu) Stream (in Unap-še) in exchange for land by the (*dimtu* of . . . -x-ya,[37] probably in Unap-še) and an additional payment of *mobilia.* Scribe: Itḫ-apiḫe son of Taya.

JEN 800 (*JEN*u 321; Rm. 15) A list of field holdings in various towns. These include (but are not necessarily limited to) Zalmi?, Az?- / Ḫe?- . . . , Artiḫi, Ḫušri, Apena, Ipḫušše (*sic*), Palaya, Ša-ku?-mi?, and Nuzi.

JEN 801 See *JEN* 869.

JEN 802 (*JEN*u 529a; Rm. 16[38]) *ṭuppi šupeʾʾulti.* Teḫip-Tilla son of Puḫi-šenni obtains from Apen-atal son of Taya and Attilammu son of Taya land in Nuzi by the road to Anzugalli in exchange for land by the road to Apena in Nuzi. Scribe: Balṭu-kašid son of Apil-Sin.

JEN 803 (*JEN*u 743; Rm. 16) *ṭuppi šupeʾʾulti.* Teḫip-Tilla (son of Puḫi-šenni) obtains from Zike son of x-ur-nuri land in exchange for land in the *dimtu* of Akapaḫi, probably, and an additional payment (of *mobilia*). Scribe: Waqar-bêli son of Taya.

JEN 804 (*JEN*u 976; Rm. ?) *ṭuppi šupeʾʾulti.* Teḫip-Tilla son of (Puḫi-šenni) obtains from (Akap-tae?) son of Šeḫel-Tešup land by the road to (the *dimtu*? of Bê)l-abi (in any case, in Nuzi probably) in exchange for land at least part of which is in or near the *dimtu* of Bêl-abi (in Nuzi). Scribe: Taya? (if so, he is the son of Apil-Sin).

JEN 805 (*JEN*u 762; Rm. 16) *ṭuppi šupeʾʾulti.* Teḫip-Tilla son of Puḫi-šenni obtains from Ḫupita son of Keliya land by the Nirašši Canal, by the road to Atakkal (in Nuzi) in exchange for land in the *dimtu* of Kinzuya (probably in Nuzi) and an additional payment of *mobilia.* Scribe: Taya son of Apil-Sin.

JEN 806 (*JEN*u 900 = A11958; Rm. 15) *ṭuppi šupeʾʾulti.* Teḫip-Tilla son of Puḫi-šenni obtains from Zike son of Kurruḫiya, Enna-mati son of Šennakka, and Ḫešalla son of Zume land by the *dimtu* of Kukkuya by the road to Ulamme (in Unap-še) in exchange for land by the *dimtu* of Teḫup-šenni by the road to Kipri (in Kipri itself) and an

[37] For further on this GN, see *THNT*, comment to *JEN* 799:11.

[38] The card in the box with this item and Lacheman's papers agree on this room assignment. Chiera's catalogue links *JEN*u 529 (not 529a) with room 15. No contradiction necessarily results.

additional payment of *mobilia*. In an atypical clause, it is stated that the three joint parties, in fact, received the *mobilia* promised to them as part of the exchange. Scribe: Iškur-andul son of Ziniya.

JEN 807 (*JEN*u 856; Rm. 4) (*ṭuppi šupeᵓᵓulti*). Mušeya son of Ḫašiya obtains from Ḫitippa son of Šêlebu and Ippalalu son of Šêlebu land in exchange for land. Scribe: Adad-nāṣir.

JEN 808 (*JEN*u 998; Rm. 16) *ṭuppi šupeᵓᵓulti*. Teḫip-Tilla son of Puḫi-šenni obtains from Ar-Tešup son of Ipša-ḫalu, Ḫanaya (son of Ar-Tešup, probably), and Ḫulukka (son of Ar-Tešup, possibly) land by the *dimtu* of Zaziya? (in Unap-še, in any case) in exchange for land by the *dimtu*? of . . . and an additional payment of *mobilia*. Scribe: (. . . son of) Taya.

JEN 809 (*JEN*u 1004; Rm. 16) *ṭuppi šupeᵓᵓulti*. Teḫip-Tilla son of Puḫi-šenni obtains from Akalaya and Kittu (and another?) land in (Ar)ti(ḫi)? in exchange for (land) . . . and an additional payment (of *mobilia*). Scribe: Itḫ-apiḫe son of Taya.

JEN 810 (*JEN*u 41; Rm. 16) *ṭuppi šupeᵓᵓulti*. Enna-mati son of Teḫip-Tilla obtains from . . . , (. . . ?-)x-li-Tešup and . . . ? sons of Kuari and x- . . . -ši?-ya (son of . . .) land . . . (in exchange for land, probably in Turša) and an additional payment of *mobilia*. Scribe: Zunzu (son of Intiya).

JEN 811 (*JEN*u 350; Rm. 16[39]) *ṭuppi šupeᵓᵓulti*. Enna-mati son of Teḫip-Tilla obtains from Âtanaḫ and Nizuk sons of Al- . . . -x?-ni? orchard land and a *kuppu*-structure in Turša in exchange for *ḫawalḫu*-land, also called orchard land, in Turša, by the road to Nu?(zi?) and an additional payment of *mobilia*. Scribe: Zunzu son of Intiya.

JEN 812 (*JEN*u 533; Rm. 15) *ṭuppi šupeᵓᵓulti* involving an exchange of persons. Enna-mati son of Teḫip-Tilla obtains from Warad-kenūni son of Ay-abâš a slave from the land of the Lullubians in exchange for a slave from the land of the Lullubians. Neither slave bears a patronymic. Scribe: Enna-mati son of Šamaš-ilu-ina-mâti.

JEN 813 (*JEN*u 381;[40] Rm. 16) *ṭuppi šupeᵓᵓulti*. Teḫip-Tilla son of Puḫi-šenni obtains from Šer-x- . . . and x- . . . sons of It?- . . . land (in Unap-še? and?) in? the town of ZA- . . . ? in exchange for land in or near the *dimtu* of Ku(kkuya? and, if so, in Unap-še; by the . . .)

[39] The card in the box with *JEN*u 350 and Chiera's catalogue data for *JEN*u 350 assign that tablet to room 16. The card for *JEN*u 911 assigns that item also to room 16. According to Porada's notes, the latter item comes from room 15.

[40] For further on this tablet, see above, Register of Tablets, n. 11.

Canal. Scribe: Itḫ-apiḫe (son of Taya). This tablet also appears as *JEN* 879.

JEN 814 (*JEN*u 736; Rm. 15) *ṭuppi šupe*ʾʾ*ulti*. Enna-mati son of Teḫip-Tilla obtains from (probably, Elḫ)ip-šarri son of Taya land in exchange for land and an additional payment of *mobilia*. Scribe: Zunzu son of Intiya.

JEN 815 (*JEN*u 824; Rm. 16) *ṭuppi šupe*ʾʾ*ulti*. Enna-mati son of Teḫip-Tilla obtains from Našwi? son of x-x-attu land in Nuzi, part of which is by the *dimtu* of . . . and part by the Akip-Tešup Canal in exchange for land in Nuzi between the *dimtu* of . . . -RI and that of Zi-x-ya? and an additional payment of *mobilia*. Scribe: Uta-andul son of Taya.

JEN 816 (*JEN*u 215; Rm. 13) (*ṭuppi*) *šupe*ʾʾ*ulti*. Tarmi-Tilla son of Šurki-Tilla obtains from Wur-Tešup son of Akip-tašenni *paiḫu*-land in exchange for *paiḫu*-land in the heart of Nuzi. Scribe: Turar-Tešup son of Itḫ-apiḫe.

JEN 817 (*JEN*u 629; Rm. 11) (*ṭuppi šupe*ʾʾ*ulti*). Kel-Tešup (son of Ḫutiya) obtains from Eḫli-Tešup (son of?) Mat-Tešup land in the *dimtu* of Kizzuk, by the *dimtu* of . . . in exchange for land in Šurini, by the road to Apzaḫullušše and an additional payment of *mobilia*. Scribe: Šar-Tešup (son of Pureya, probably, less likely the son of Ḫašip-. . .).

JEN 818 (*JEN*u 802; Rm. ?[41]) (*ṭuppi šupe*ʾʾ*ulti*). Kel-Tešup son of Ḫutiya obtains from Kuparša son of Urkutu land by the road to the town of x- . . . by a canal in exchange for (land) and an additional payment of *mobilia*. Scribe: Šar-Tešup (probably son of Pureya, less likely the son of Ḫašip-. . .). This tablet also appears as *JEN* 875.

JEN 819 (*JEN*u 239 = A11911; Rm. 16) A receipt. Probably a receipt of *mobilia* perhaps concluding a transaction. (Mu?)š-Tešup (son of? / and? [the latter is more likely]) Pui-tae obtain *mobilia* from Pakla-piti (son of Enna-mati, probably).

JEN 820 (*JEN*u 118; Rm. 13) (personal *ṭuppi tidennūti* [probably, but a personal *tidennūtu* transaction in any case]). Tarmi-Tilla (son of Šurki-Tilla) receives from Akkul-enni (son of . . .) his services for a loan of *mobilia*.

JEN 821 See *JEN* 822.

[41] Chiera's catalogue assigns this tablet to a specific room other than 13, 15, and 16. There are no other data available on the findspot of this text.

JEN 822 (*JEN*u 632; Rm. ?[42]) *ṭuppi tidennūti* based on real estate. Ḫui-te (son of Mušeya) receives from Šešerpa son of Itḫ-apu land by the road to the town of . . . -puša (probably in Ḫurāṣina-ṣeḫru) for a loan of (*mobilia*). Scribe: x- . . . (Iriri is a good possibility).

JEN 823 (*JEN*u 818; Rm. 4) *ṭuppi tidennūti* based on real estate. Taya son of Qîšteya receives from Šešerpa son of Itḫ-apu land in Ḫurāṣina-ṣeḫru for a loan of *mobilia*. Scribe: Šamaš-bārī.

JEN 824 (*JEN*u 791; Rm. 1) *ṭuppi tidennūti* based on real estate. Ḫui-te son of Mušeya receives from Šešerpa son of Itḫ-apu land in Ḫurāṣina-ṣeḫru for a loan of *mobilia*. Scribe: Iriri.

JEN 825 (*JEN*u 979; Rm. 1) *ṭuppi tidennūti* based on real estate. Taya son of Qîšteya receives from Ḫaniu and Šešerpa sons of Itḫ-apu land in the town of (Ḫurāṣina-ṣeḫru, probably) for a loan of *mobilia*. Scribe: Šamaš-bārī.

JEN 826 (*JEN*u 119; Rm. 13) *ṭuppi tidennūti* based on real estate. (Tarmi-Tilla?, and, if so, then he is the son of Šurki-Tilla) receives from Ziliya son of . . . land for a loan of *mobilia*. Scribe: Turar-Tešup son of Itḫ-apiḫe.

JEN 827 (*JEN*u 295; Rm. ?[43]) *ṭuppi tidennūti* based on real estate. X-miya son of Puḫi receives from Zilip-Tilla (son of . . .) land, part of which is located (by the roa)d? to Āl-ilani for a loan of *mobilia*.

JEN 828 (*JEN*u 858; Rm. 11) A catalogue. It appears to be a type of cadastre. Responsibility for bearing the *ilku* for certain land is (re?)assigned or confirmed to specific individuals.

JEN 829 (*JEN*u 627; Rm. 13) (*lišānšu*) relating to a personal *tidennūtu*. Wunni (son of . . .) declares he has gotten a loan of *mobilia* from Paikku and has entered his (namely, Paikku's) service in return. Scribe: Arip-šarri.

JEN 830 (*JEN*u 972; Rm. ?[44]) *ṭuppi tidennūti* based on real estate. Ḫui-te son of Mušeya receives from Šaḫlu-Tešup and Waḫr-api sons of Mušeya land in the *dimtu* of . . . -x- . . . -(y)a? in Ḫurāṣina-ṣeḫru for a loan of *mobilia*. Scribe: Iriri.

[42] The card in the box with this tablet and Lacheman's papers both note the findspot of this item as room 16. Given the identities of the principal parties to the transaction here described, this findspot is most unlikely. Chiera's catalogue, in fact, assigns this tablet to a specific room other than 13, 15, or 16.

[43] The card in the box with this tablet and Lacheman's notes both assign this tablet to room 1. Chiera's catalogue links this item to room 14.

[44] Chiera's catalogue assigns to this tablet a findspot other than room 13, 15, or 16. No other source deals with the findspot of this document.

JEN 831 (*JEN*u 799; Rm. 1) *ṭuppi tidennūti* based on real estate. Šaḫlu-te son of Mušeya receives from Waratteya son of Še?-x-e-a land in Ḫurāṣina-ṣeḫru for a loan of *mobilia*. Scribe: Eḫlip-apu.

JEN 832 (*JEN*u 775; Rm. 1) (*ṭuppi tidennūti*) based on real estate. Ḫui-te son of Mušeya receives from Taika (son of . . .) land (in) Ḫurāṣina-ṣeḫru for a loan of *mobilia*. Scribe: Aittara, probably.

JEN 833 (*JEN*u 792; Rm. 1) (*ṭuppi tidennūti*) based on real estate. Ḫui-te son of Mušeya receives from Šumu-dârī (son of Nûriya, probably) land (near?) the town of Nanu (in) Ḫurāṣina-ṣeḫru. Scribe: Iriri.

JEN 834 (*JEN*u 829; Rm. 15) *ṭuppi tidennūti* based on real estate. Tarmiya (son of . . .) receives land from Keliya and U-x- . . . (sons of?) X-altuya, through, it seems, the mediation of Tae, for a loan of *mobilia*. Scribe: Zike.

JEN 835 (*JEN*u 851; Rm. ?[45]) (*ṭuppi*) *tidennūti* based on real estate. Iššukkal s(on? of?) . . . -din? receives from Ḫilpiš-šuḫ son of Šuḫun-zirira land in the *dimtu* of (K)izzuk or (N)izuk for a loan of *mobilia*. Scribe: Ma-x-piya.

JEN 836 (*JEN*u 958; Rm. 16) (*ṭuppi tidennūti*) based on real estate. (Teḫip-Tilla son of Puḫi-šenni, probably) receives from . . . -x-ḫe?-ka?-RI land for a loan of *mobilia*. Scribe: Ariḫ-ḫamanna son of Ḫutiya.

JEN 837/838 (*JEN*u 546; Rm. 13) (*ṭuppi šupeʾʾulti*). Tarmi-Tilla (son of Šurki-Tilla) obtains from Turar-(Tešup, probably) structures (probably *kuppātu*) in? Nu(zi)? in exchange for *kuppātu*-structures.

JEN 839 (*JEN*u 7; Rm. 13) *lišānšu* relating to a *tidennūtu* based on real estate. Wantiya declares that Ḫuratta has received from Wantiya land for a loan of *mobilia*. Scribe: Arip-šarri.

JEN 840 (*JEN*u 924; Rm. 13) *ṭuppi tidennūti* based on real estate. Ḫutarrapḫe son of Tišam-mušni receives from Tupki-šenni son of Kerar-Tilla and Azuli wife of Kerar-Tilla land in Nuzi for a loan of *mobilia*. Scribe: Tarmi-Tešup son of Itti-šarri.

JEN 841 (*JEN*u 439; Rm. 16) *ṭuppi* (*mārūti*). Teḫip-Tilla son of Puḫi-šenni obtains from Arip-apu son of (A)r?pazzaḫ land, some by Malašu Stream by the *dimtu* of Tur-šenni (in Unap-še) and some by the *dimtu* of Ukin-zaḫ (most likely in Unap-še). Scribe: Muš-teya son of Sin-ibnī.

[45] Chiera's catalogue associates this tablet with a room other than 13, 15, or 16. The card in the box with this item identifies the findspot as room 16. Given the involvement of Ḫilpiš-šuḫ son of Šuḫun-zirira in this transaction, Chiera's datum is to be preferred.

JEN 842 (*JEN*u 1028; Rm. ?) *ṭuppi mārūti*. Ḫui-te son of Mušeya obtains from Naik-kemar son of Ak-apiḫe a threshing floor by the road to Akmašar in Ḫurāṣina-ṣeḫru. Scribe: Iriri.

JEN 843 (*JEN*u 233; Rm. 16) (*ṭuppi mārūti*, possibly). Teḫip-Tilla (son of Puḫi-šenni obtains from . . .). Scribe: Attilammu.

JEN 844 (*JEN*u 668; Rm. 16) (Personal *ṭuppi tidennūti*, possibly. Teḫip-Tilla son of Puḫi-šenni [the probable lender if this is a *ṭuppi tidennūti*] receives from . . . the services of . . . for a loan of *mobilia*.) Scribe: Itḫ-apiḫe (son of Taya).

JEN 845 (*JEN*u 10; Rm. 13) *umma*. Ziliya (probably), Šukriya (probably), Teḫip-šarri, and Šilaḫi sons of Šilwa-Tešup state that they have sold a female slave to Ḫut-arrapḫe son of Tišam-mušni for *mobilia* and, in fact, have received the *mobilia*. Scribe: Šimânni(-Adad son of ^{d}AK.DINGIR.RA).

JEN 846 (*JEN*u 648; Rm. 16) Record of litigation. Teḫip-Tilla son of Puḫi-šenni defeats Ikki-teya son of Milkuya?. The latter had stolen livestock from the former (and is made to restore similar goods to the former). Scribe: Ḫutiya son of Uta-mansi.

JEN 847 (*JEN*u 663; Rm. 16) Record of litigation. Teḫip-Tilla (son of Puḫi-šenni) defeats Šummiya, his shepherd. The latter (may have stolen wool from the former and) is made to return wool? to Teḫip-Tilla.

JEN 848 (*JEN*u 623; Rm. 16) Record of litigation. Enna-mati son of Teḫip-Tilla defeats Zike son of Kakkuzzi regarding land (in) the *dimtu* of Kinzuya. (The latter had claimed rightful occupancy of that land based on a prior) *šupeʾʾultu* transaction with Teḫip-Tilla (father of Enna-mati). (Zike) pays a penalty (to Enna-mati for illegal occupancy of the land).

JEN 849 (*JEN*u 1; Rm. 13) Record of litigation. Zike and Tarmi-Tilla sons of Šurki-Tilla defeat Akip-Tilla son of Šurki-Tilla. The former recover three females as a result. Scribe: Turar-Tešup son of Itḫ-apiḫe.

JEN 850 (*JEN*u 442; Rm. ?) Record of litigation. Teḫip-Tilla son of Puḫi-šenni defeats Teššuya son of Kinniya regarding (ownership of) a female slave. The former recovers (her).

JEN 851 (*JEN*u 768; Rm. 16[46]) *umma*. Four judges, namely, Paya, Ḫaiš-Tešup, Mat-Tešup son of Itḫ-apu, and Punniya state that, after testimony has been solicited, Enna-mati son of Teḫip-Tilla is adjudged to have defeated Nan-Tešup son of Ar-nupatašuk. Enna-

[46] This room number appears in Chiera's catalogue and Lacheman's papers. The card in the box with this item reads: 15/16.

mati correctly claimed (already) to have paid Nan-Tešup (as per a prior agreement). Scribe: Taya (son of Apil-Sin).

JEN 852 (*JEN*u 423; Rm. 11) Record of litigation. Mat-Tešup son of Ḫilpiš-šuḫ (defeats) Aittara son of Šuḫun-zirira. The latter had occupied a building of the former in Temtena. The dispute over this part of the family estate stemmed from the fact that Mat-Tešup's father and Aittara were brothers. Aittara pays a penalty to Mat-Tešup. Scribe: Šamaš-ûrâšu.

JEN 853 (*JEN*u 532; Rm. 15) Precise contents obscure. Takku (son of Enna-mati) seems to obtain livestock from Šurki-Tilla? (son of?) Itḫ-apiḫe?. Scribe: Turar-Tešup.

JEN 854 (*JEN*u 190; Rm. 16) A document once describing a transaction between two parties. Scribe: Nanna-adaḫ.

JEN 855 (*JEN*u 63; Rm. 15) *ṭuppi mārūti*. Teḫip-Tilla son of Puḫi-šenni obtains from Ḫanakka son of Akkuya land. Scribe: Ḫawi-. . . .

JEN 856 (*JEN*u 164; Rm. 12) Loan document. Tarmi-Tilla son of x-. . . -x lends *mobilia* to x-ur-nuzi? son of? . . . -ḫiti- . . . ?. Scribe: Turar-Tešup.

JEN 857 (*JEN*u 855; Rm. 4) Document relating to a real estate transaction. A threshing floor is mentioned. Aḫu-ekī? son of Taleya is one of the two principal parties.

JEN 858 (*JEN*u 298; Rm. 15) (*ṭuppi šupeʾʾulti*). Enna-mati (son of Teḫip-Tilla) obtains from Arik-kewar son of Itḫi- . . . land (in Nuzi?) in exchange for land (in Nuzi?) and an additional payment of *mobilia*.

JEN 859 (*JEN*u 710; Rm. 11) A document describing, perhaps, entry into servitude. Ipša-ḫalu is to be at the call of Kel-Tešup (son of Ḫutiya, probably).

JEN 860 (*JEN*u 813; Rm. ?) (Record of litigation, probably).[47] Ḫui-te (son of Mušeya, probably) defeats Naniya?. The dispute appears to center on title to land in Hurāṣina-seḫru?.

JEN 861 (*JEN*u 353;[48] Rm. 16) A list of eleven witnesses who assert, probably, that Ḫattue indeed got *mobilia* in return for harvest work.

JEN 862 (*JEN*u 652; Rm. 4) *umma*. Contents unclear. Five (witnesses) make a statement regarding the transfer? of silver from Kumpali (and/ [less likely] son of) Sin-uballiṭ to Ilim-x. Ilim-x undertakes not to litigate regarding the silver against Kumpali?.

[47] It is not entirely clear to me that the obverse and reverse as depicted are actually the obverse and reverse.

[48] On this item, see above, Register of Tablets, n. 10.

JEN 863 (*JEN*u 1136; Rm. 13[49]) *lišānšu* regarding real estate. X-mi-Tešup son of . . . -x- . . . -x makes a declaration regarding land (of?) Turar-Tešup (given to?) Teššuya.

JEN 864 (*JEN*u 637; Rm. 4[50]) Precise contents obscure. Transfer of barley seems to be involved. (Re?)payment of that barley to Tarmi-Tilla may also be mentioned. Scribe: X-x-a.

JEN 865 (*JEN*u 580: Rm. ?[51]) A type of deposition, perhaps. Itḫ-apu son of x- . . . and Zike? appear to be in dispute regarding the division (of property).

JEN 866 (*JEN*u 339;[52] Rm. 16) *umma*. X- . . . son of Kutukka makes a statement that he undertakes not to r(aise a claim?) regarding (alienated) land. Scribe: X-X-AN-. . . .

JEN 867 (*JEN*u 309; Rm. 15) (Contract of servitude, possibly); it is followed by a *lišānšu* regarding (sale? into slavery). Tulpun-naya (sells? herself? and?) her children into (slavery) to Teḫip-Tilla (son of Puḫi-šenni). Scribe: Taya (son of Apil-Sin).

JEN 868 (*JEN*u 631; Rm. ?[53]) *ṭuppi mārtūti*. Ḫašun-naya daughter of Teḫup?-šenni adopts Kelim-matka daughter of Aziku daughter of Akip-ta(šenni, probably) and marries her off. The text encompasses perhaps even more than a two-stage transaction. Scribe: Tarmi-Tešup son of Šarru-mālik.

JEN 869 (*JEN*u 229; Rm. 15) *ṭuppi* (*šupeʾʾulti*) involving an exchange of persons followed by a *lišānšu*. Teḫip-Tilla son of Puḫi-šenni obtains from Taena (son of . . . a slave) in exchange for a slave. Taena declares the exchange of slaves to have taken place. This tablet also appears as *JEN* 801.

JEN 870 (*JEN*u 811; Rm. 4) *ṭuppi mārūti* (genuine). Enna-mati son of BE- . . . -x is one of the principal parties. He is, it appears, adopted by a female. Scribe: Ḫutiya son of Iriri.

[49] This datum derives from Porada's notes.

[50] The *CAD* Nuzi file regarding this text records "no number." However, Chiera's catalogue does define the findspot. It is from a particular room other than 13, 15, or 16. This is seemingly confirmed by the card in the box with this tablet. It bears the unusual datum: "4 13". Room 4 is thus a likely locus for this text. Perhaps room 13 somehow became a candidate due to the presence of the PN, "Tarmi-Tilla." The archive of Tarmi-Tilla son of Šurki-Tilla was located in room 13.

[51] Chiera's catalogue assigns this tablet to room 15. The card in the box with this tablet and Lacheman's papers define the findspot as room 1.

[52] On the *JEN*u number of this tablet, see above, register of tablets, n. 8.

[53] The card in the box containing this item defines the findspot as room 16. Chiera's catalogue links it to a specific room other than 13, 15, or 16.

JEN 871 (*JEN*u 679; Rm. 11) Precise contents unclear. In part, at least, Kel-Tešup (son of Ḫutiya purchases? from) Ekeke son of Zanunu a door. Scribe: Tupki-Tilla.

JEN 872 (*JEN*u 220 = A11906; Rm. 12) A list. Thirty-seven or thirty-eight men are named. They are sent? to measure land.

JEN 873 (*JEN*u 84; Rm. 16) Record of litigation. Enna-mati (son of Teḫip-Tilla defeats) the female, Puḫuya (daughter? of . . .), in a case pertaining to (the legal disposition? of) her? offspring. As an end result, Enna-mati obtains personnel. Scribe: Nanna-adaḫ.

JEN 874 (*JEN*u 143; Rm. 11) A record of litigation, probably. Našwi appears to be one of the litigants, the defeated party, it seems.

JEN 875 See *JEN* 818.

JEN 876 (*JEN*u 893; Rm. 11) A list. Disbursements of grain, mostly barley but some emmer, (from?) Turar?- . . . to males identified by PN but not by patronymic.

JEN 877 See *JEN* 753.

JEN 878 (*JEN*u 189; Rm. 16) Precise contents obscure. A transaction involving two parties.

JEN 879 See *JEN* 813.

JEN 880 (*JEN*u 859; Rm. 11) *ṭuppi Šimuti* (*sic*). A will of Mat-Tešup son of Ḫilpiš-šuḫ dealing with his wife, Allaiše daughter of Naik-kemar and with his son, Nizuk. Scribe: Šušeya.

JEN 881 (*JEN*u 620; Rm. ?[54]) *ṭuppi šupe*ʾʾ*ulti*. Kel-Tešup son of Ḫutiya obtains from Akiya son of Šekaru a structure or structures, a cistern, and land in the heart of the t(own? of . . .), in the *dimtu* of Turumiṣru?? in exchange for land by a stream and an additional payment of *mobilia*. Scribe: Šar-Tešup son of Pureya.

[54] The card in the same box with this tablet and Chiera's catalogue both identify the document as coming from room 15. Given the identity of the principal parties to the transaction described in the text, this ascription is very doubtful. In an unpublished note, Lacheman already asserted either that the tablet did not or could not come from room 15.

674

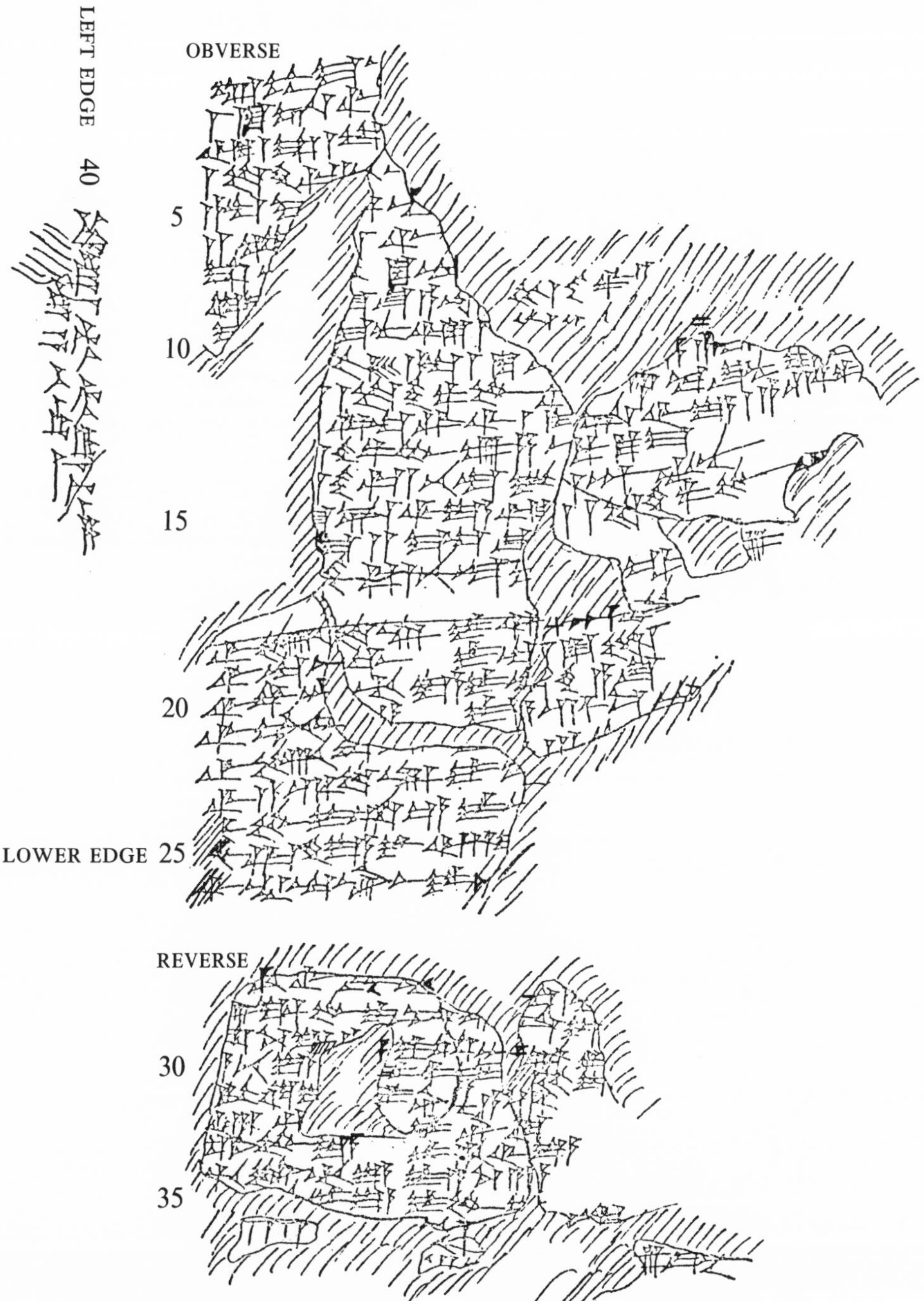

*
Rest of reverse destroyed

*Additional text; see *THNT*.

675

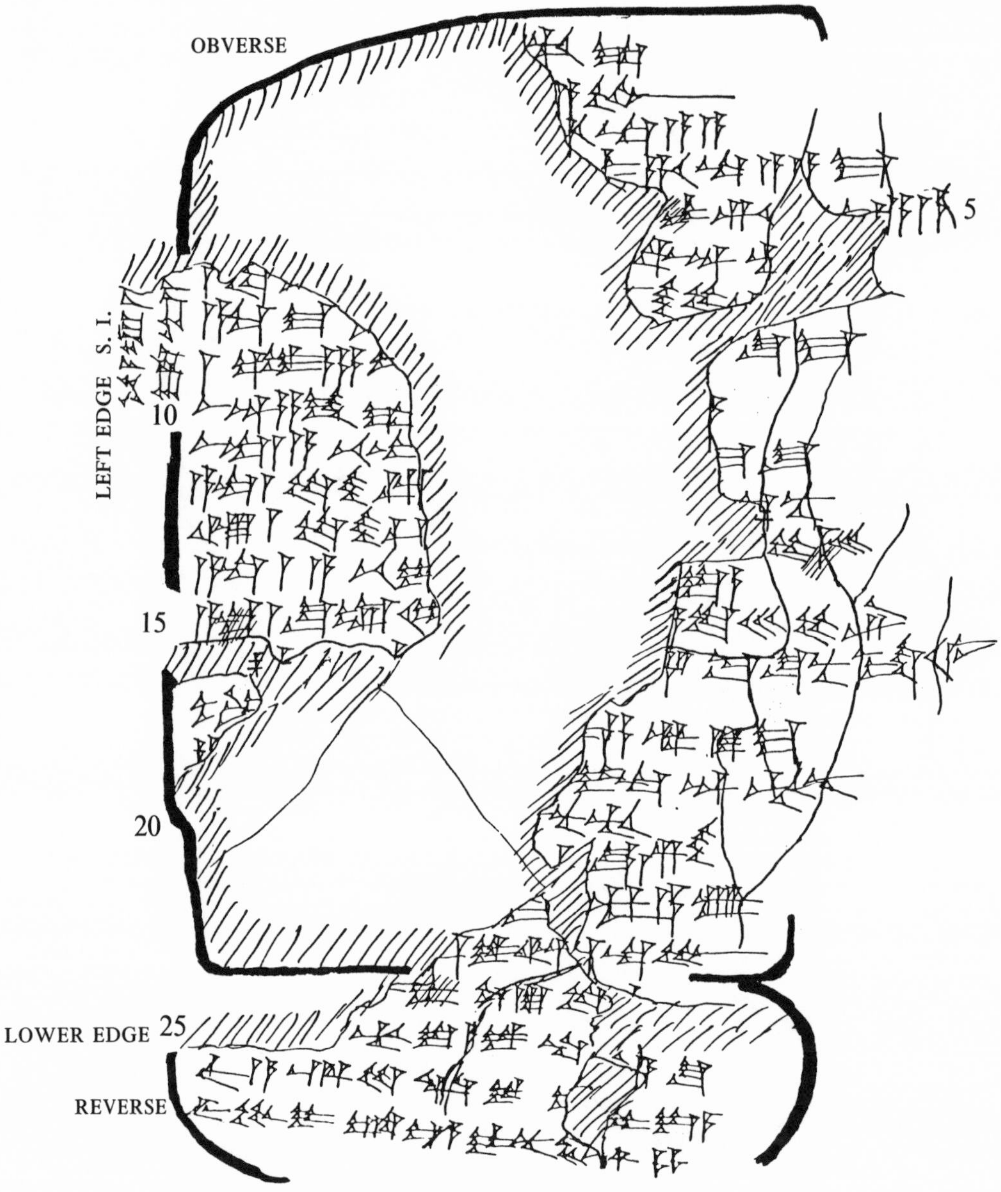

675

REVERSE (CONT'D)

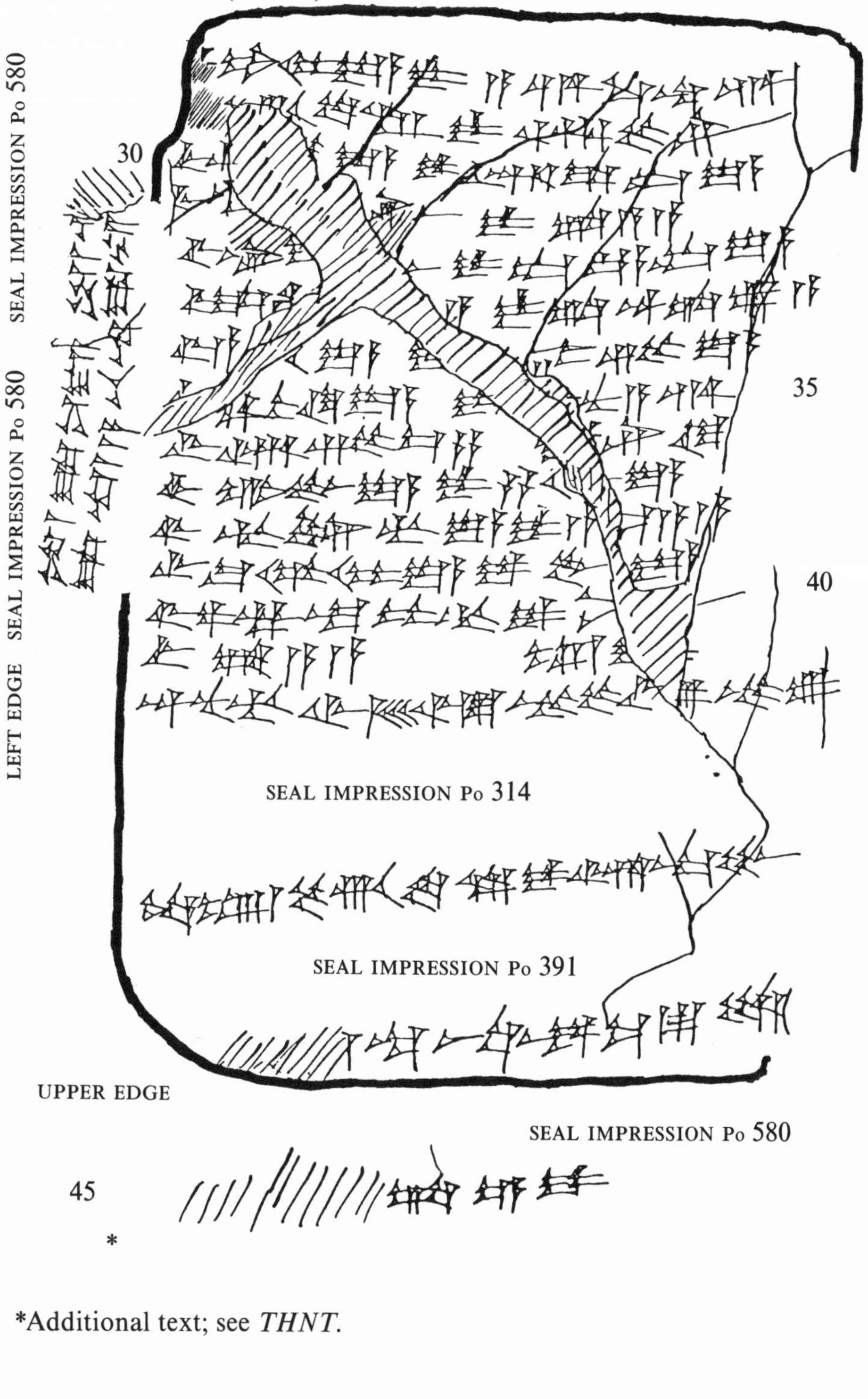

*Additional text; see *THNT*.

676

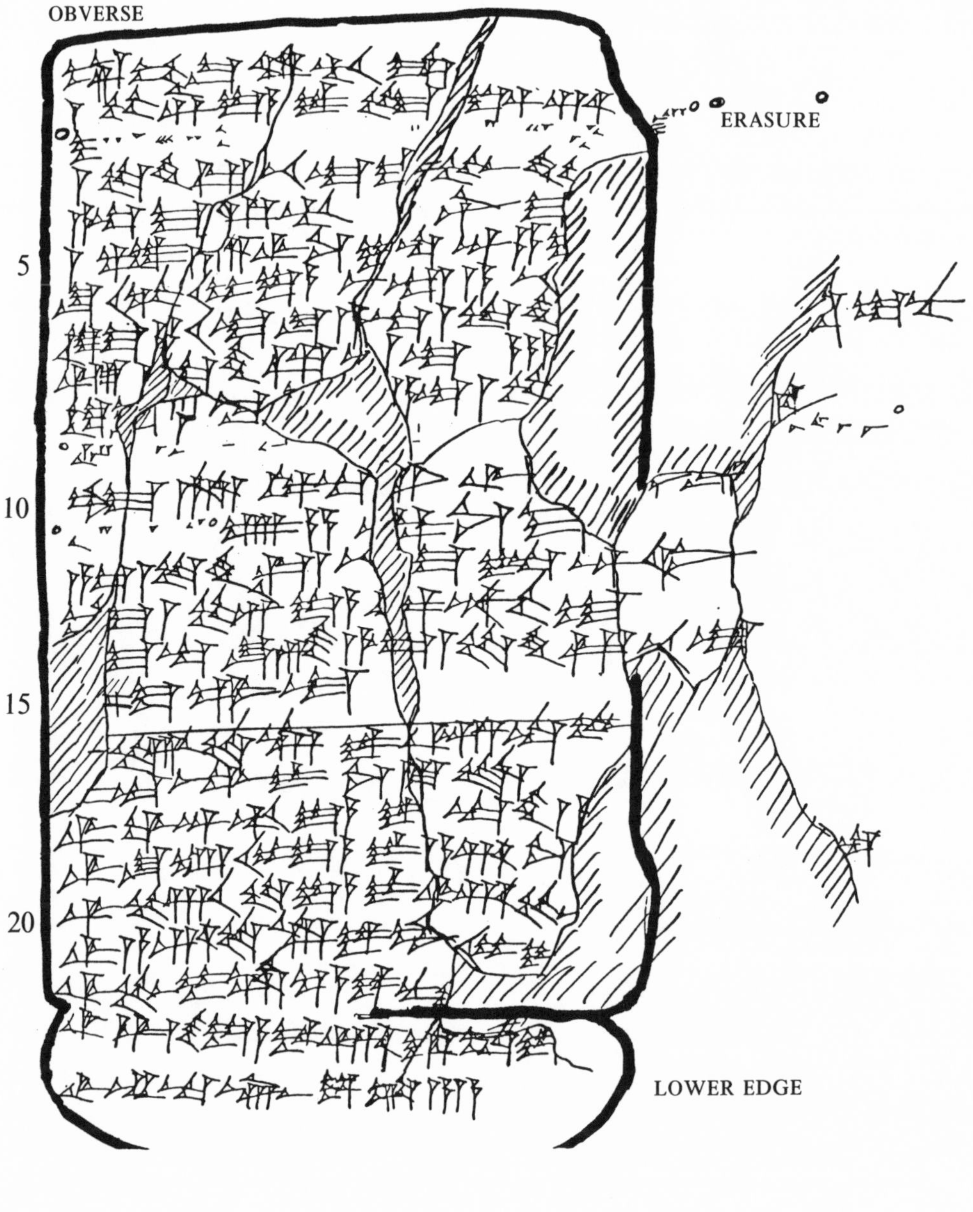

676

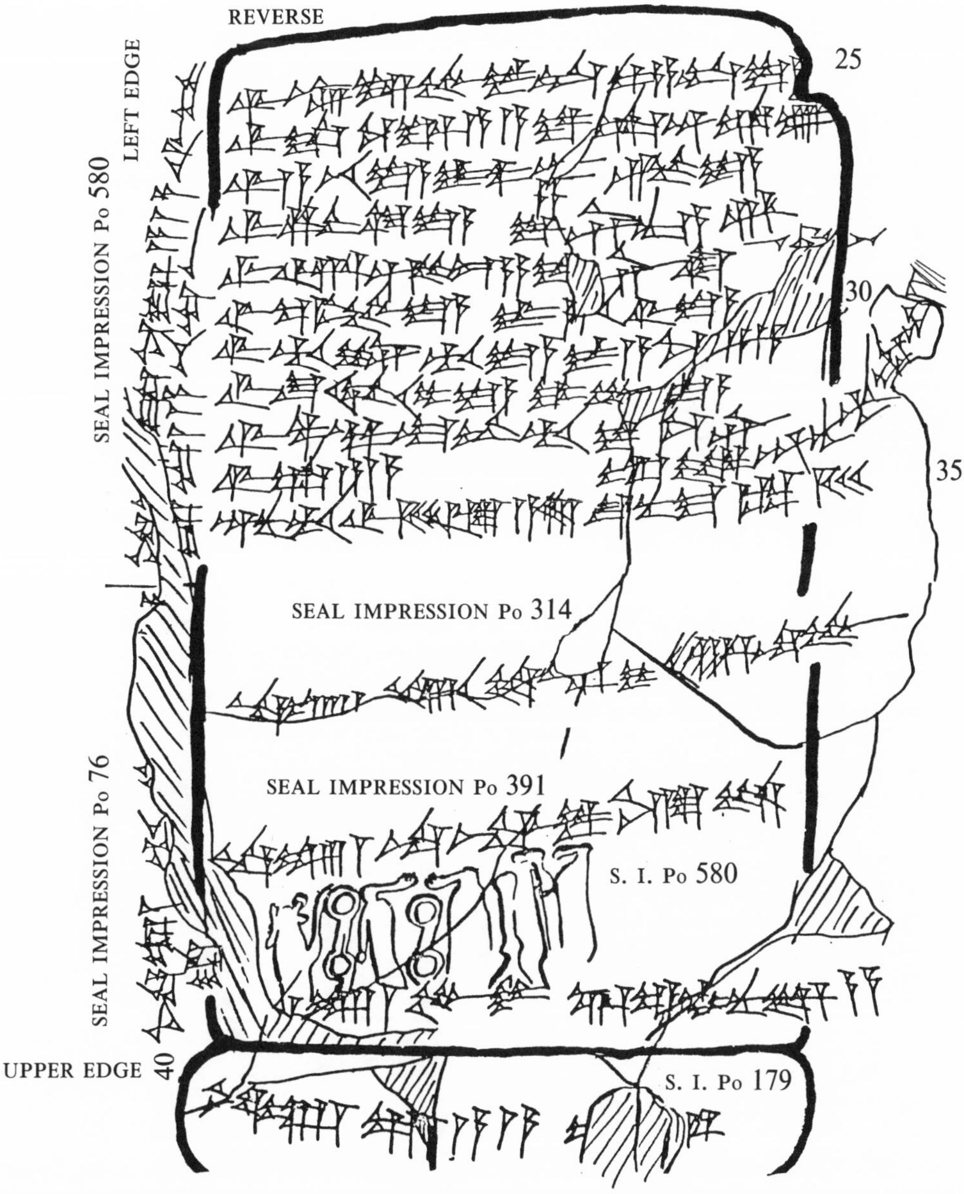
REVERSE
LEFT EDGE
SEAL IMPRESSION Po 580
25
30
35
SEAL IMPRESSION Po 314
SEAL IMPRESSION Po 391
SEAL IMPRESSION Po 76
S. I. Po 580
UPPER EDGE
40
S. I. Po 179

677

OBVERSE

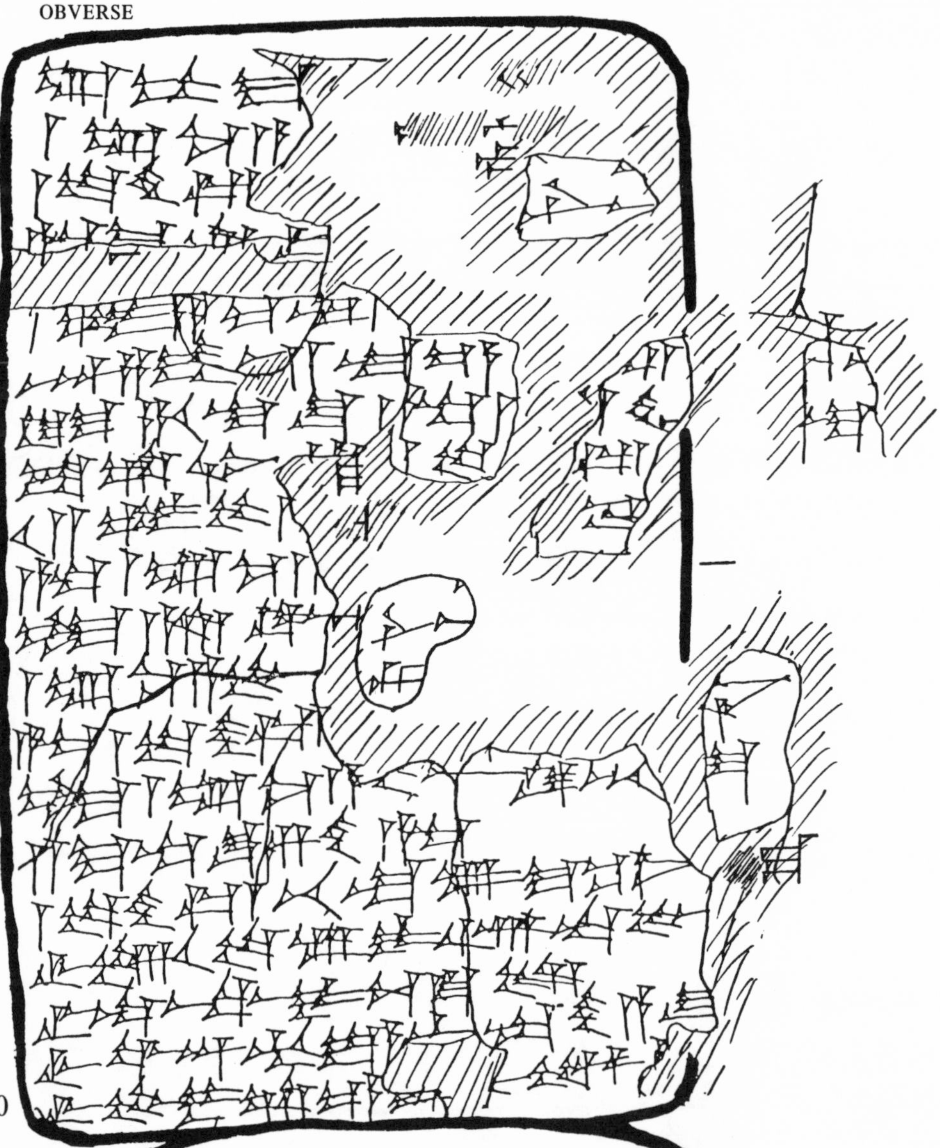

LOWER EDGE

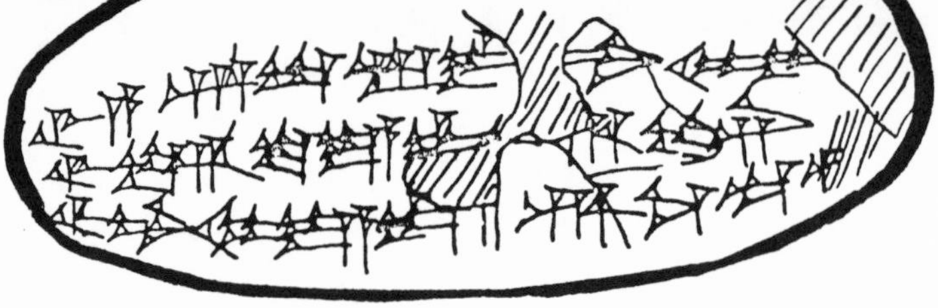

677

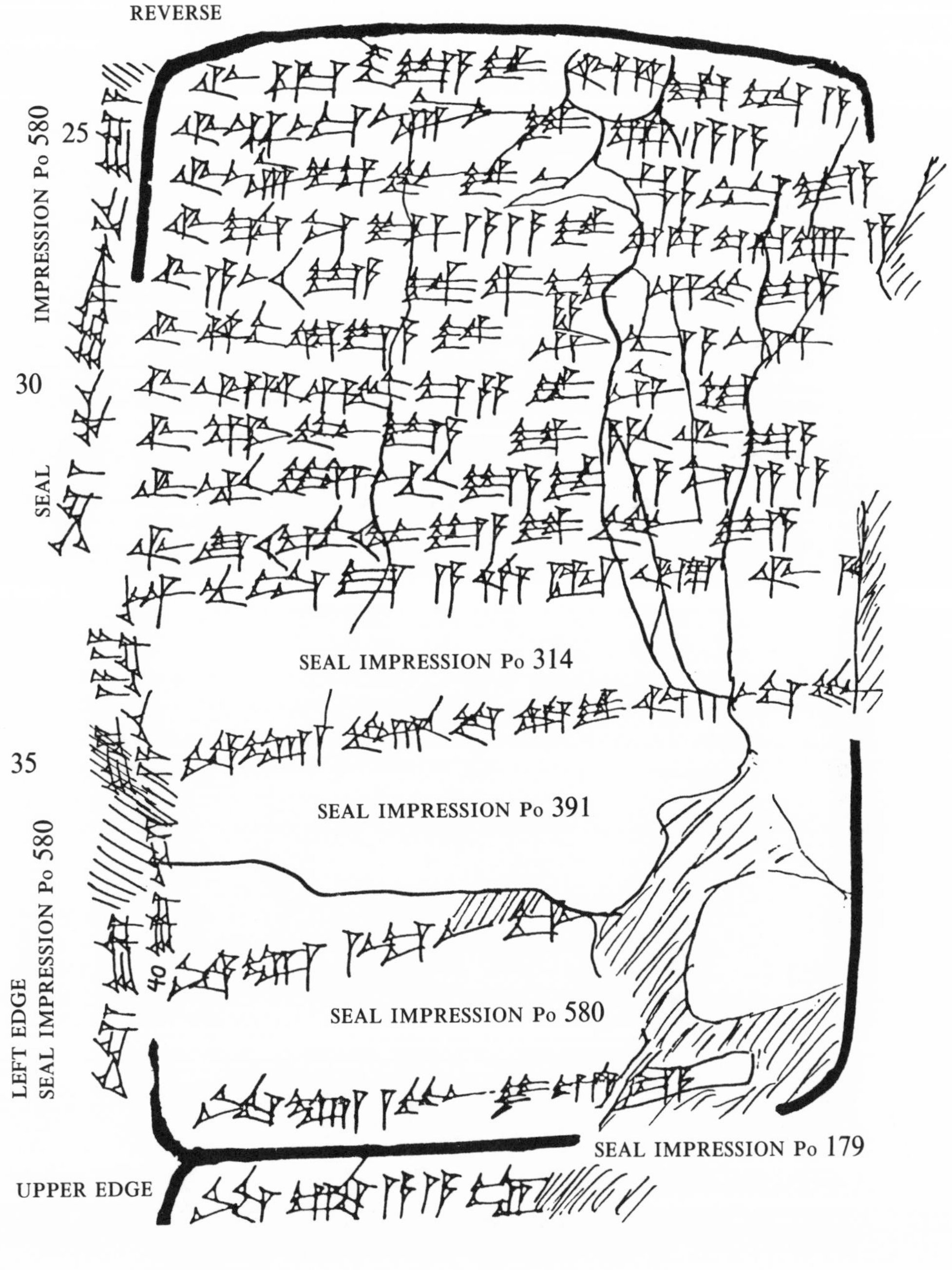
REVERSE
SEAL IMPRESSION Po 580
SEAL IMPRESSION Po 314
SEAL IMPRESSION Po 391
SEAL IMPRESSION Po 580
LEFT EDGE
SEAL IMPRESSION Po 580
SEAL IMPRESSION Po 179
UPPER EDGE

678

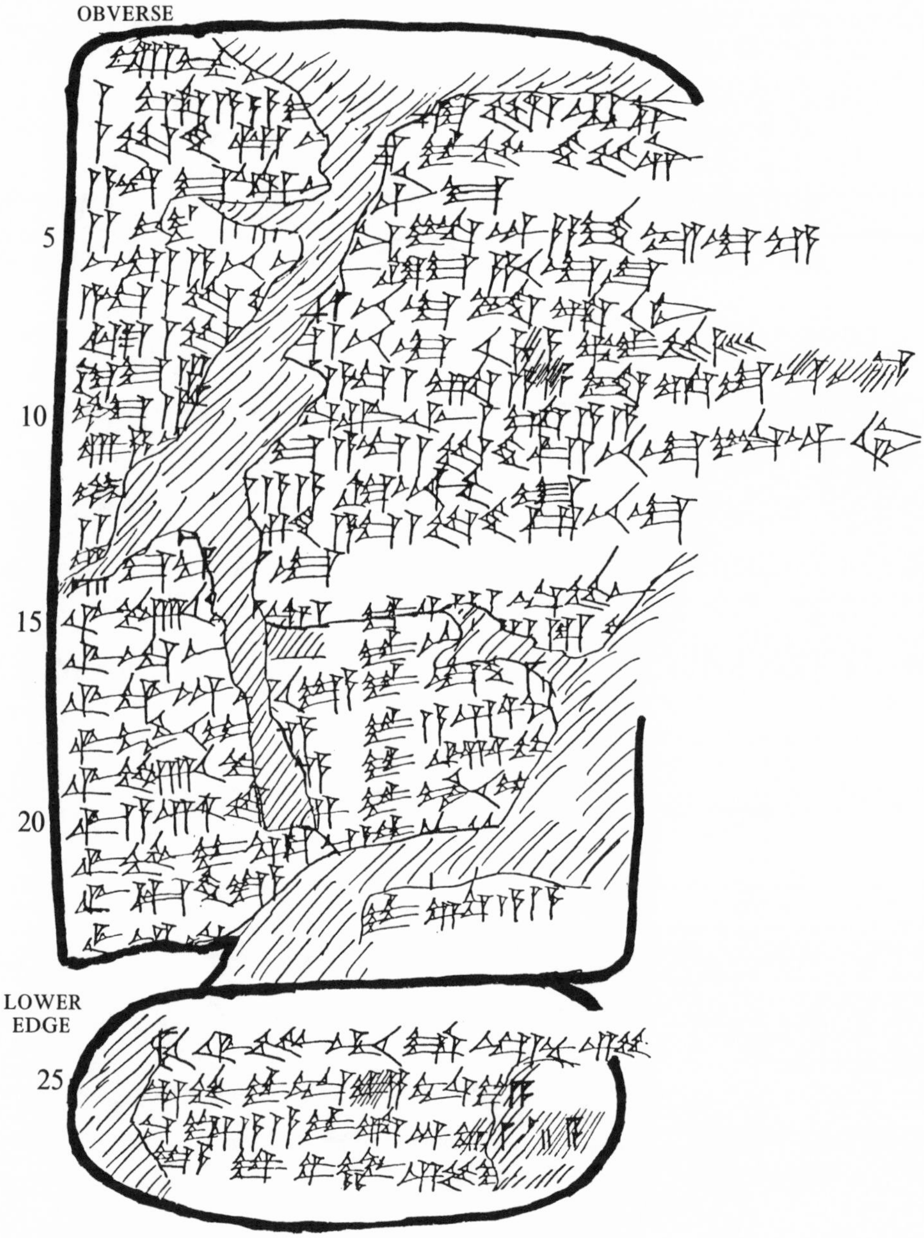

678

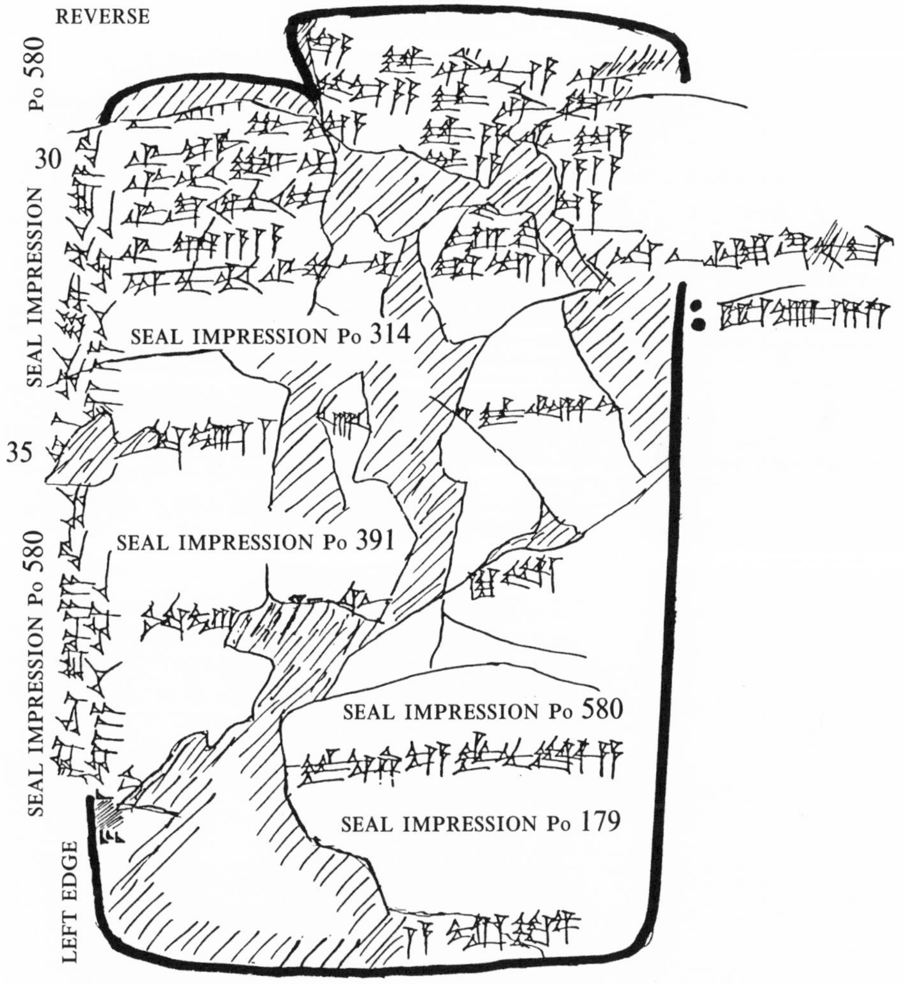
REVERSE
Po 580
30
SEAL IMPRESSION
SEAL IMPRESSION Po 314
35
SEAL IMPRESSION Po 391
SEAL IMPRESSION Po 580
SEAL IMPRESSION Po 580
SEAL IMPRESSION Po 179
LEFT EDGE

679

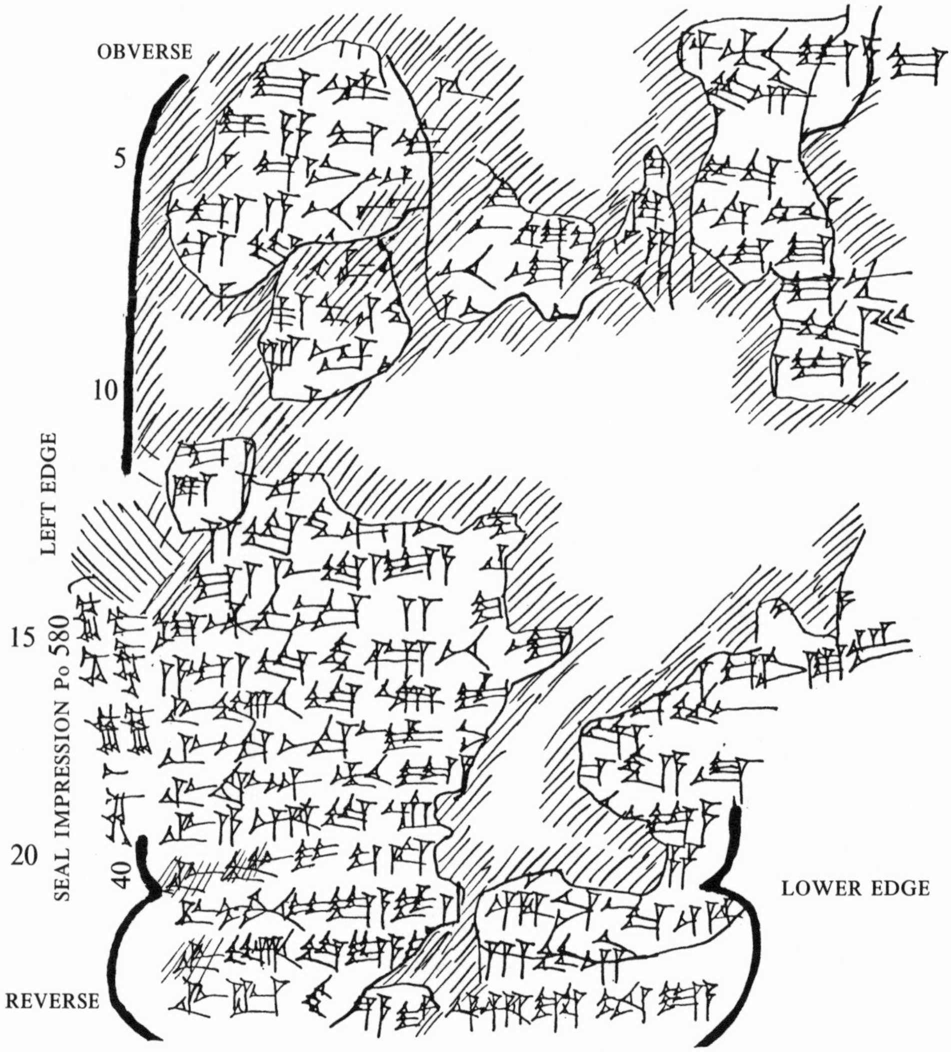
OBVERSE
5
10
LEFT EDGE
15
SEAL IMPRESSION Po 580
20
40
LOWER EDGE
REVERSE

679

REVERSE (CONT'D)

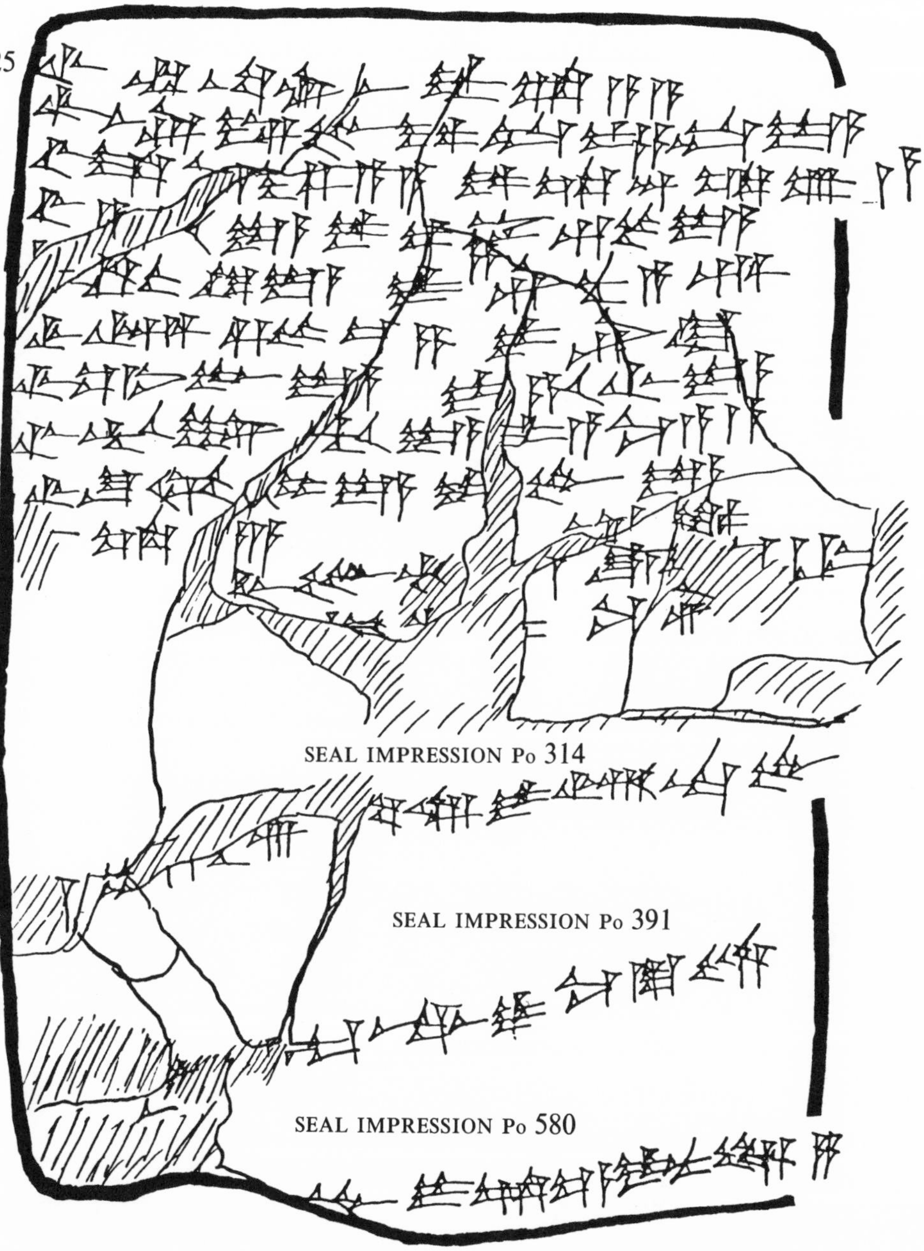

680

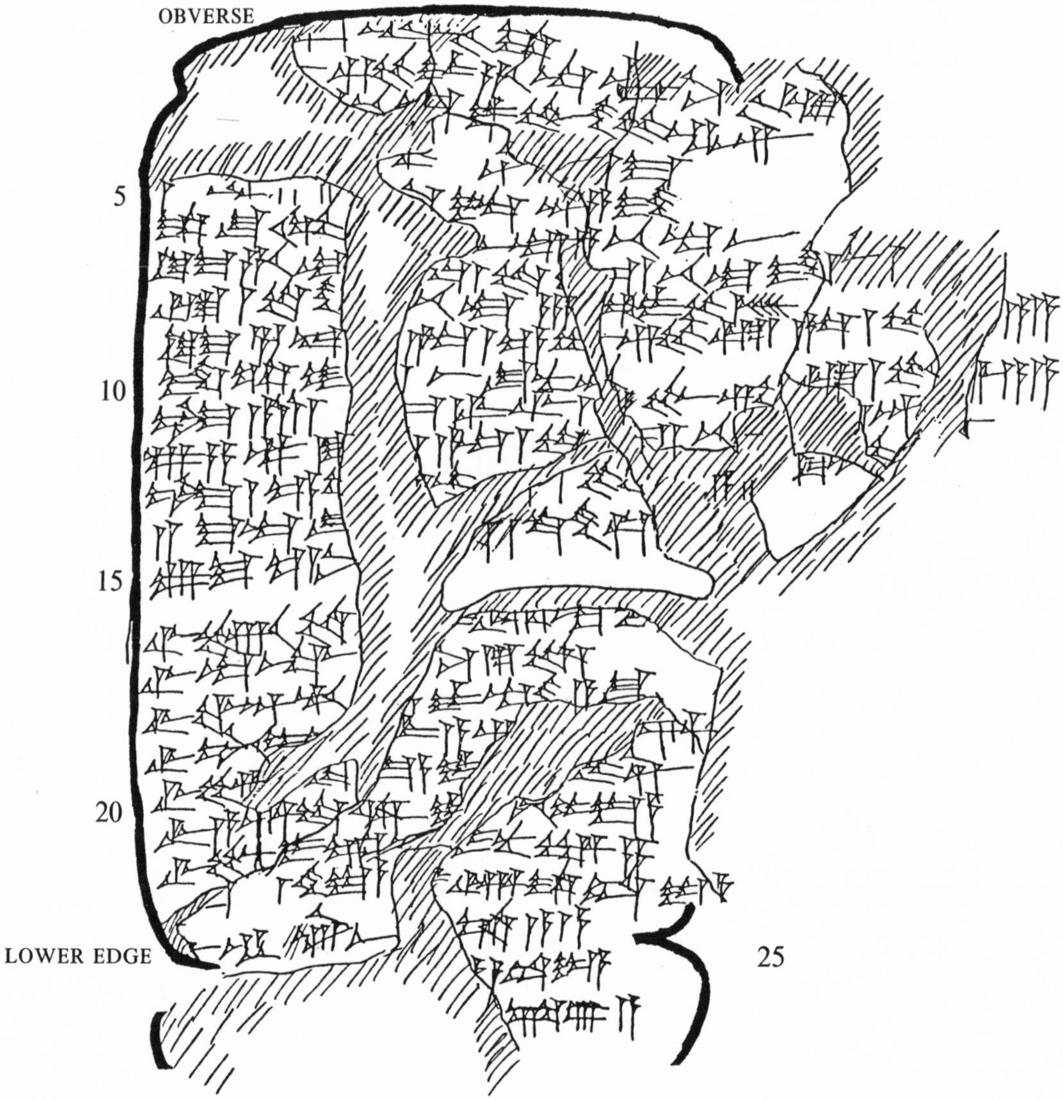

680

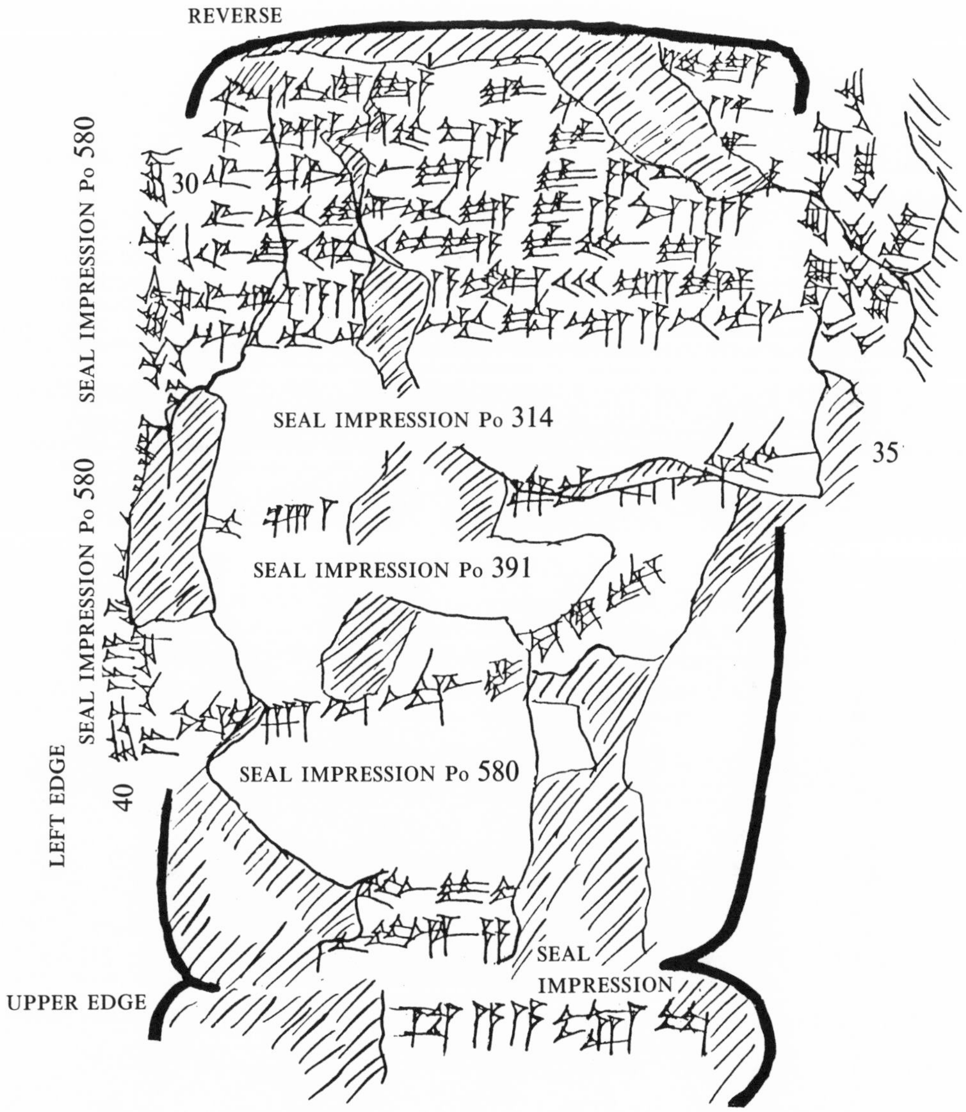
REVERSE
SEAL IMPRESSION Po 580
30
SEAL IMPRESSION Po 314
35
SEAL IMPRESSION Po 580
SEAL IMPRESSION Po 391
SEAL IMPRESSION Po 580
SEAL IMPRESSION Po 580
LEFT EDGE
40
SEAL IMPRESSION
UPPER EDGE

681

OBVERSE

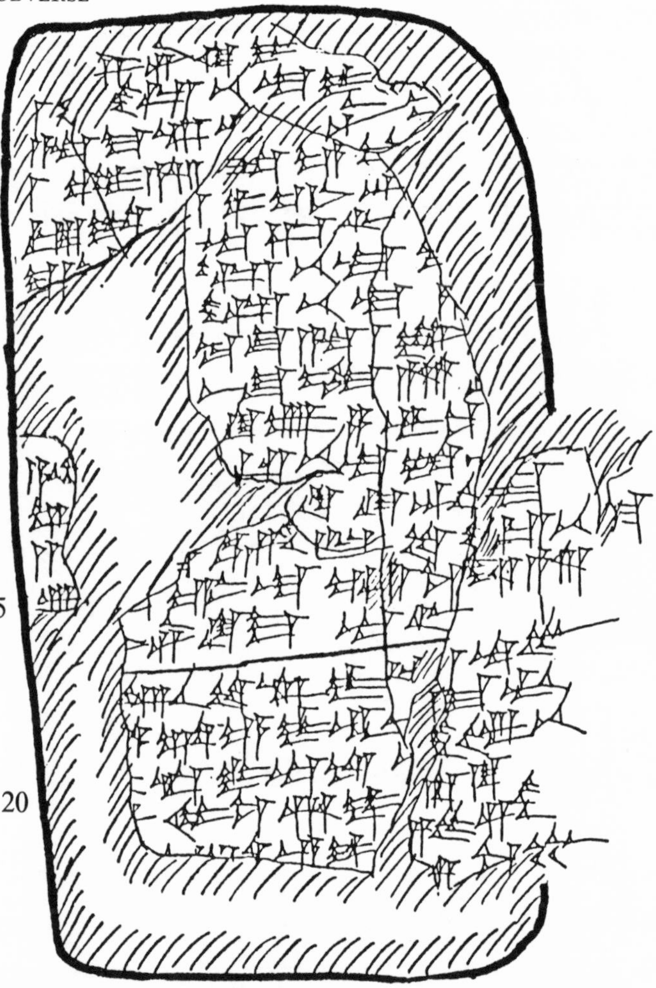

*

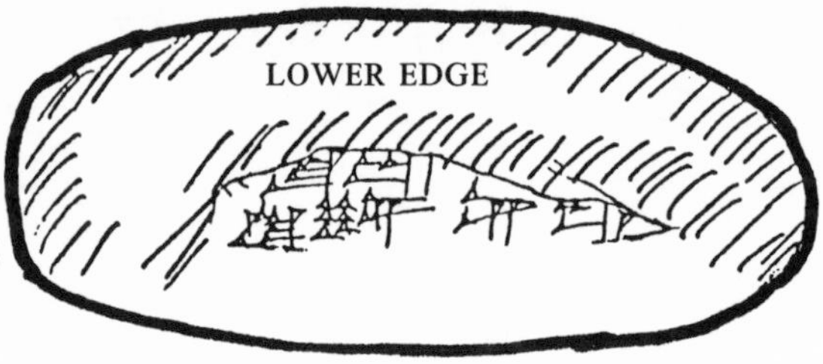

*Additional text; see *THNT*.

681

REVERSE

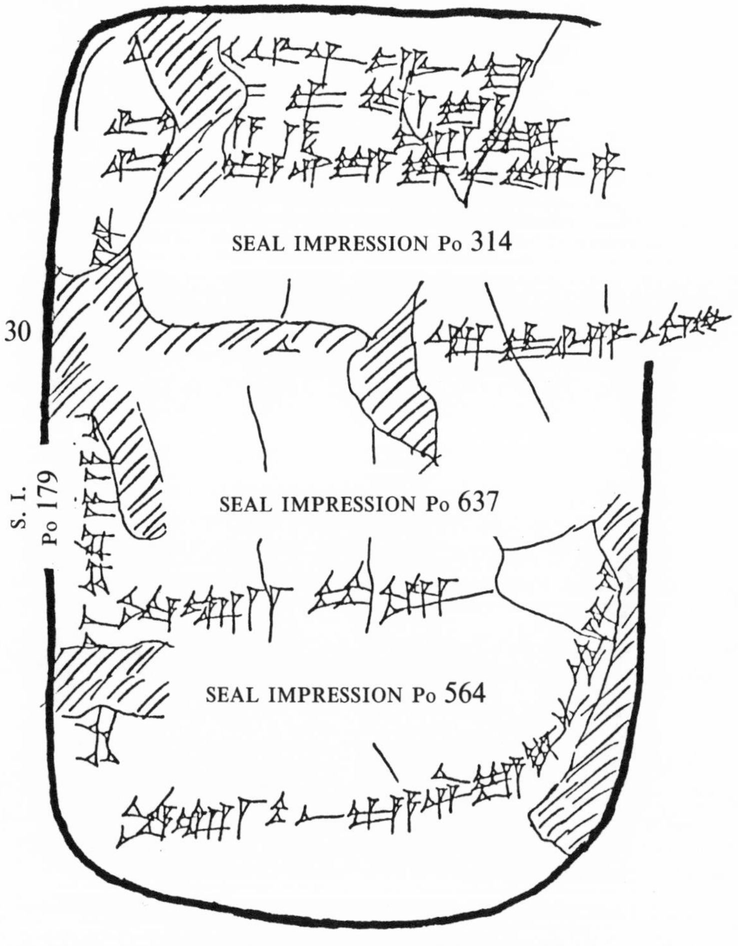
SEAL IMPRESSION Po 314
30
S. I. Po 179
SEAL IMPRESSION Po 637
SEAL IMPRESSION Po 564

682

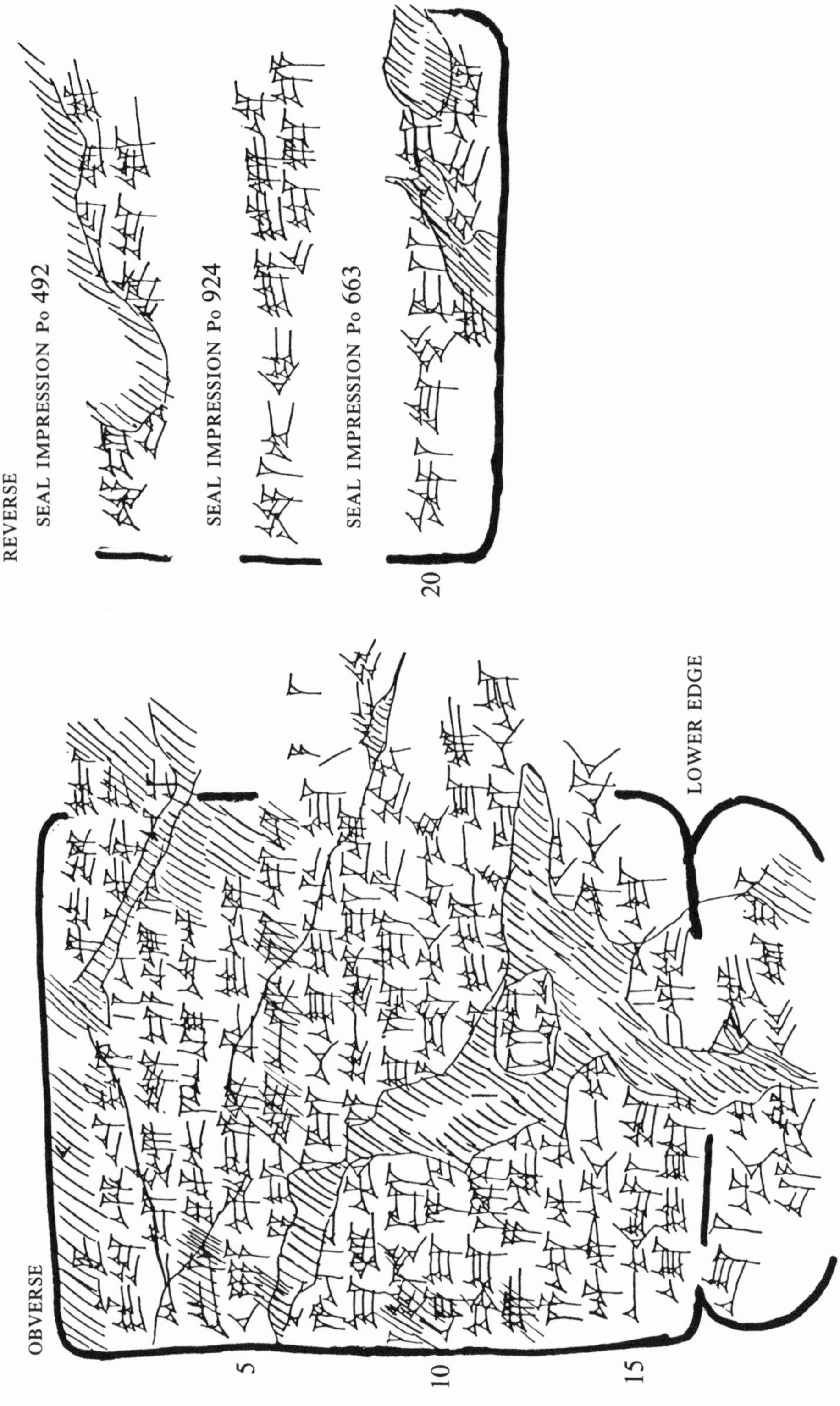
OBVERSE
LOWER EDGE
REVERSE
SEAL IMPRESSION Po 492
SEAL IMPRESSION Po 924
SEAL IMPRESSION Po 663

683

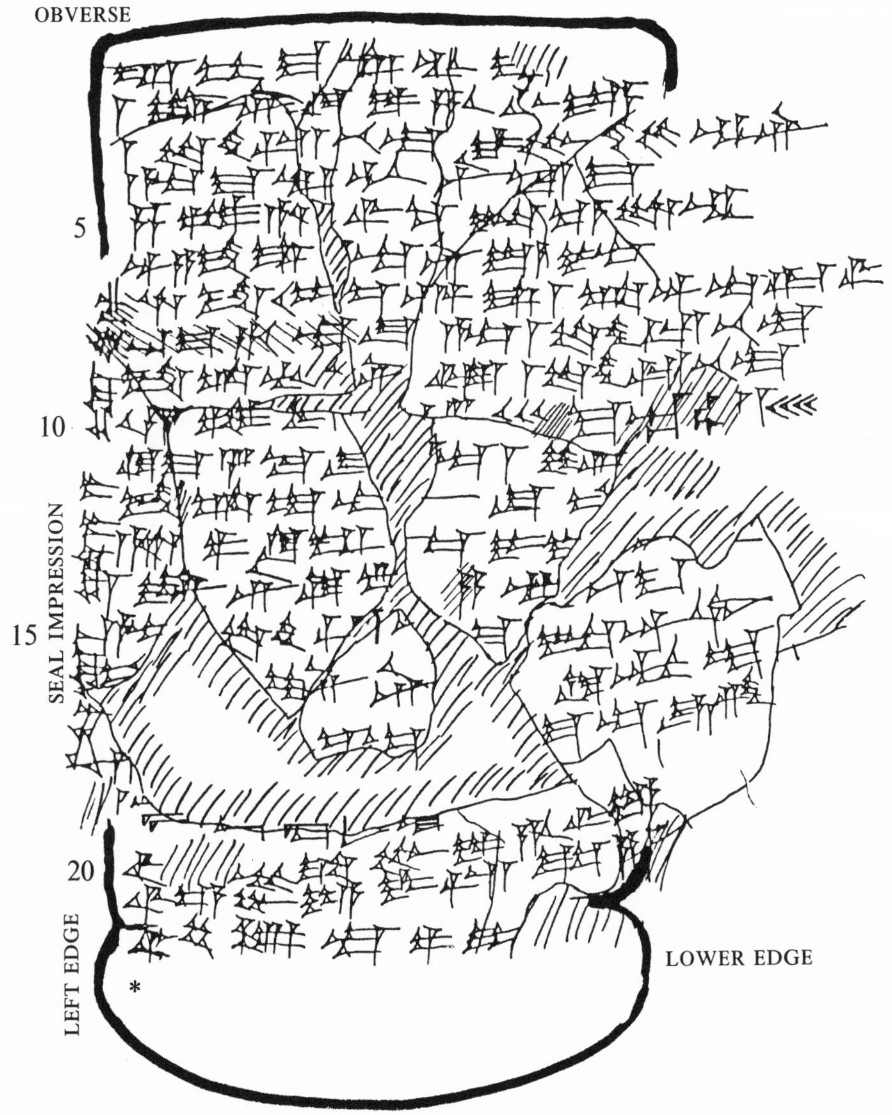

*Additional text; see *THNT*.

683

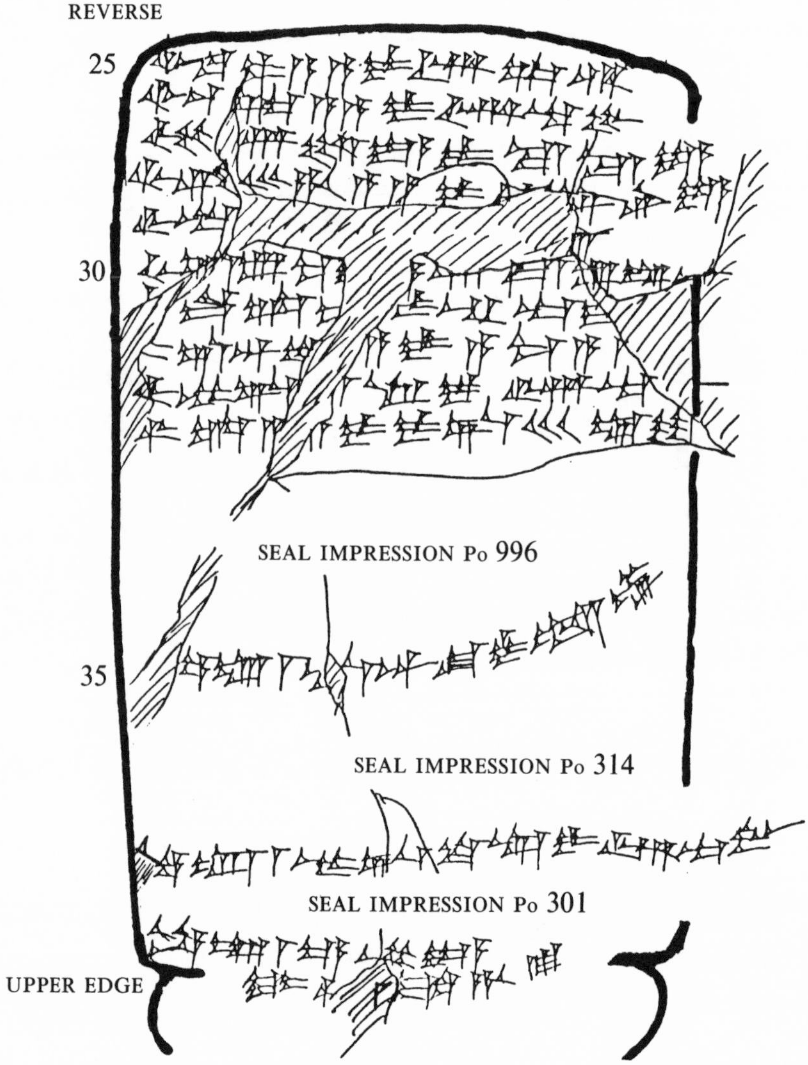
REVERSE
25
30
SEAL IMPRESSION Po 996
35
SEAL IMPRESSION Po 314
SEAL IMPRESSION Po 301
UPPER EDGE

684

OBVERSE

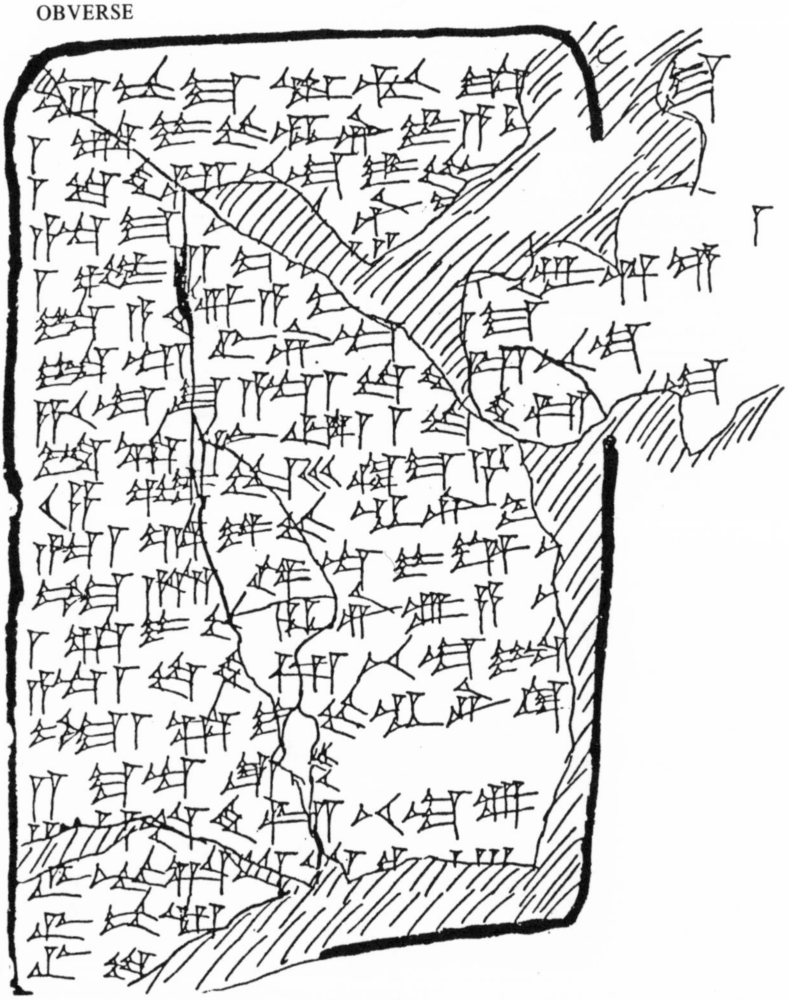

684

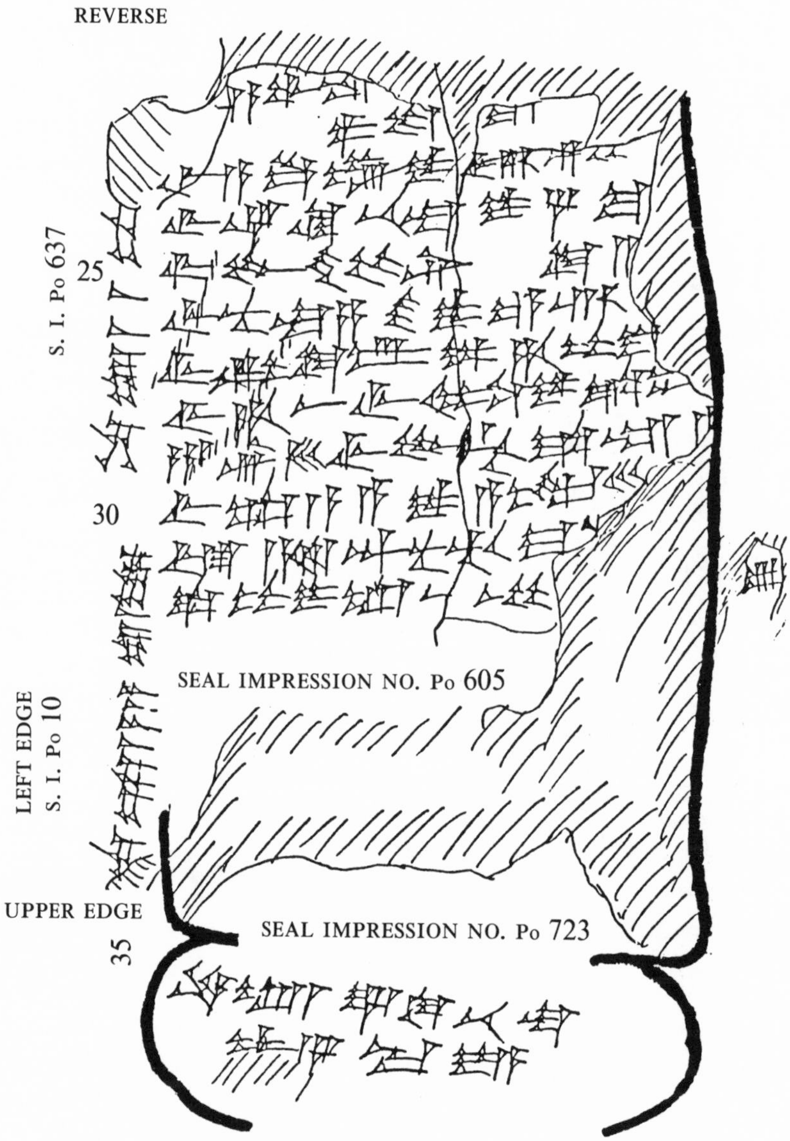
REVERSE
S. I. Po 637
25
30
SEAL IMPRESSION NO. Po 605
LEFT EDGE
S. I. Po 10
UPPER EDGE
35
SEAL IMPRESSION NO. Po 723

685

OBVERSE

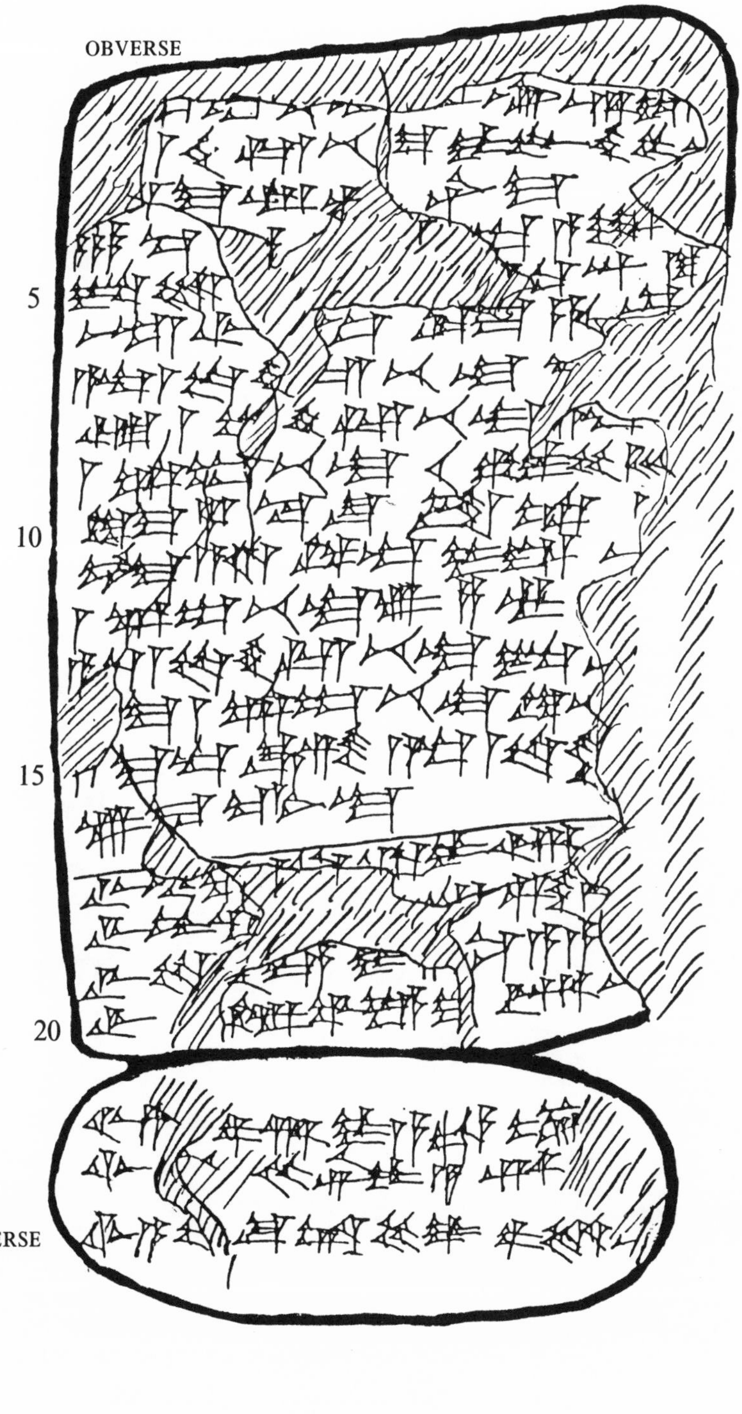

REVERSE

685

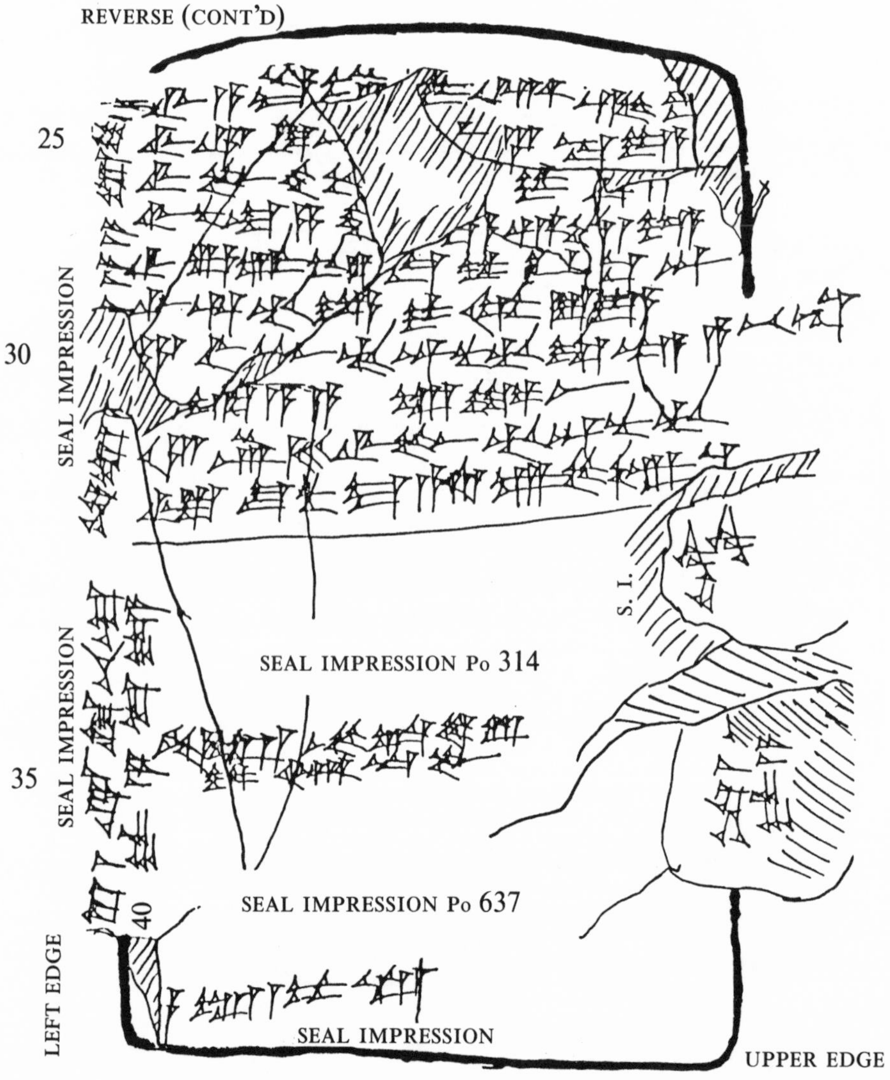
REVERSE (CONT'D)
25
30
35
40
SEAL IMPRESSION
SEAL IMPRESSION
S. I.
SEAL IMPRESSION Po 314
SEAL IMPRESSION Po 637
LEFT EDGE
SEAL IMPRESSION
UPPER EDGE

686

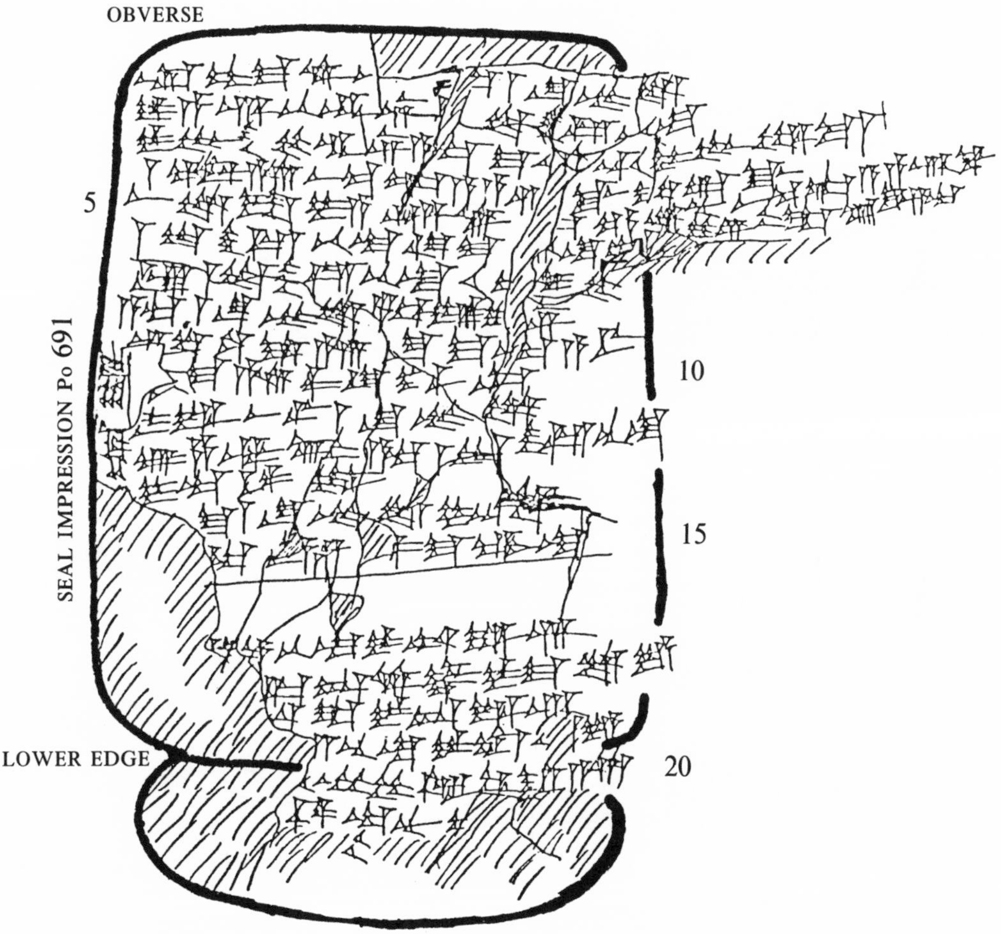

686

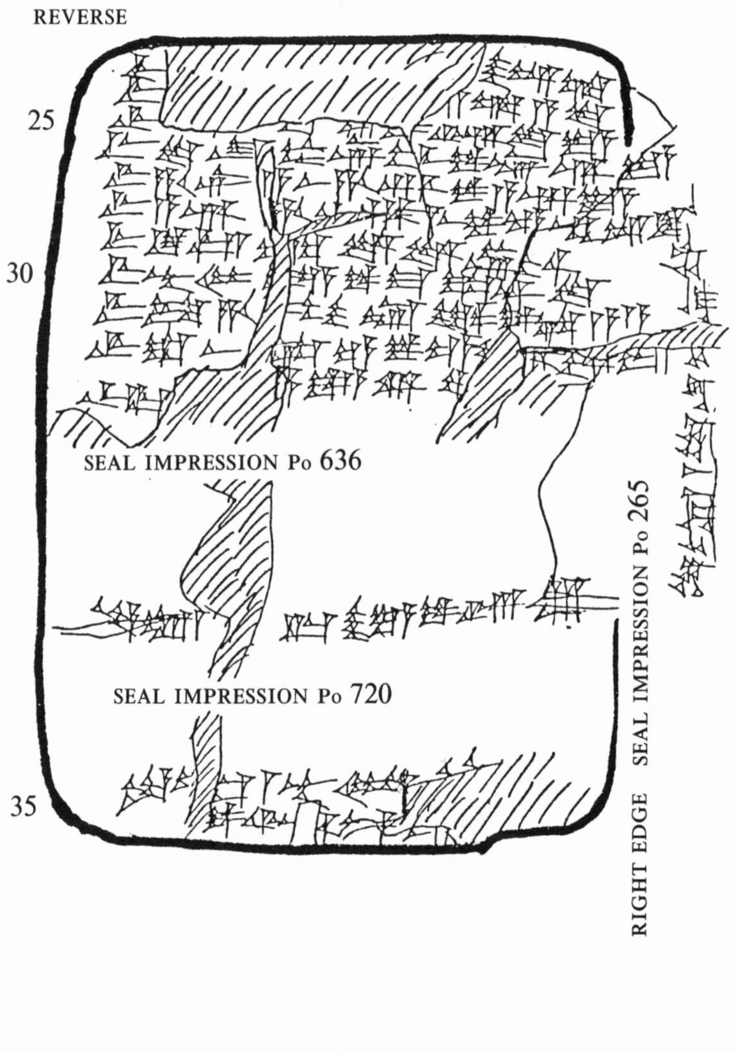
REVERSE
25
30
SEAL IMPRESSION Po 636
SEAL IMPRESSION Po 720
35
RIGHT EDGE SEAL IMPRESSION Po 265

687

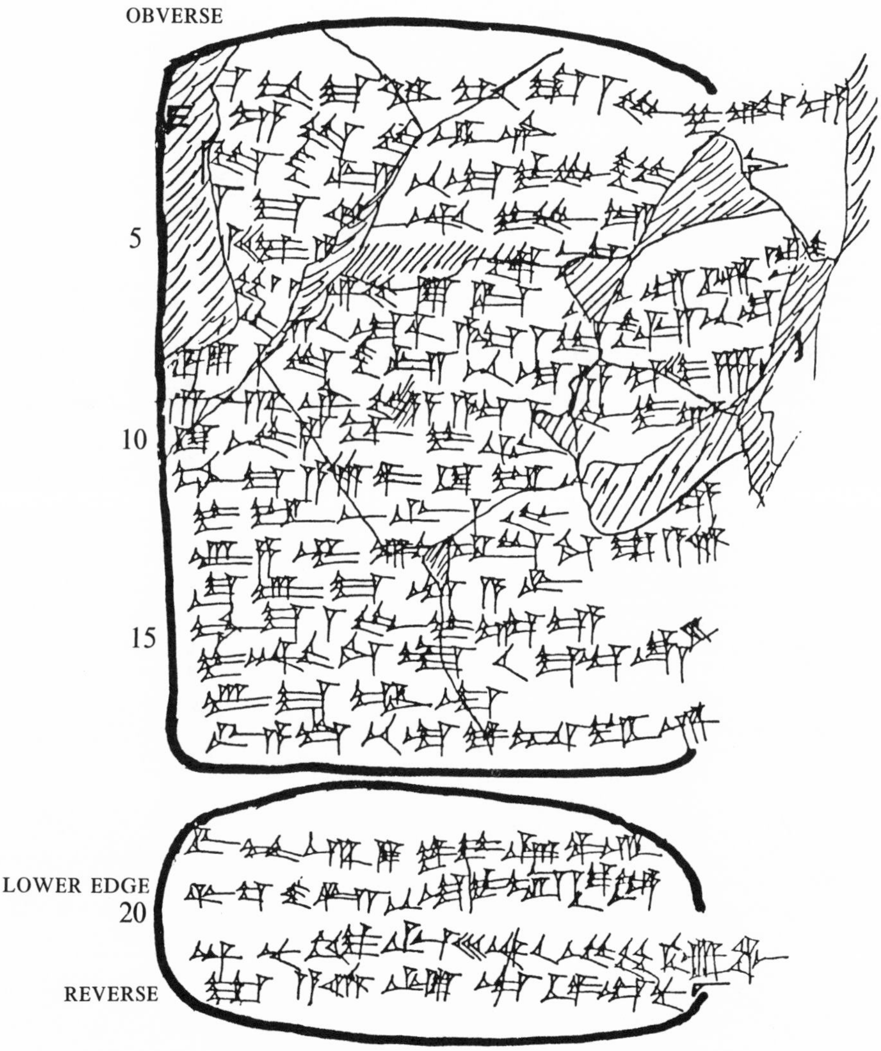

687

REVERSE (CONT'D)

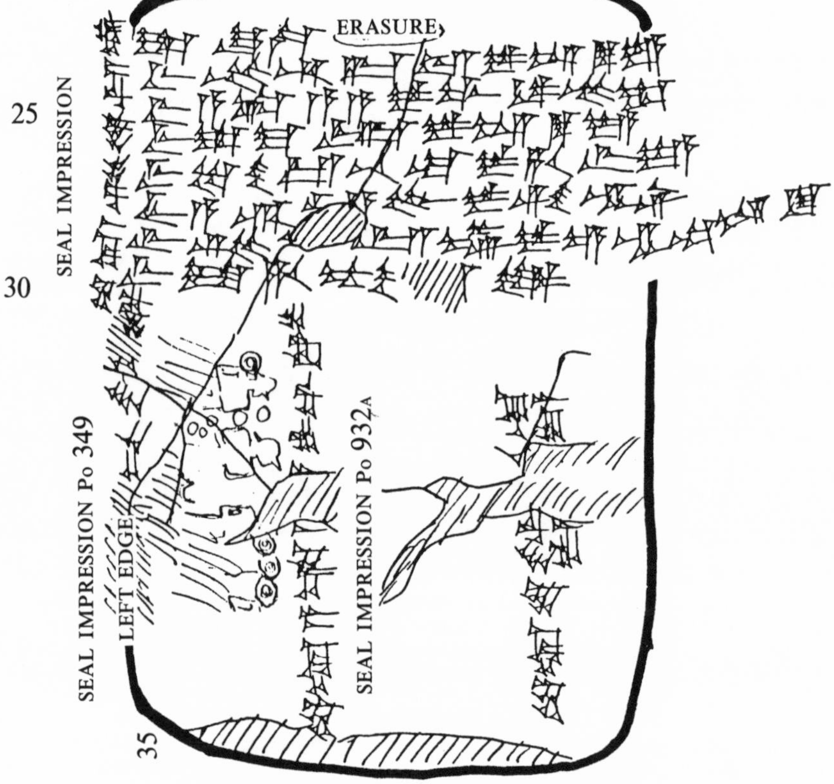

688

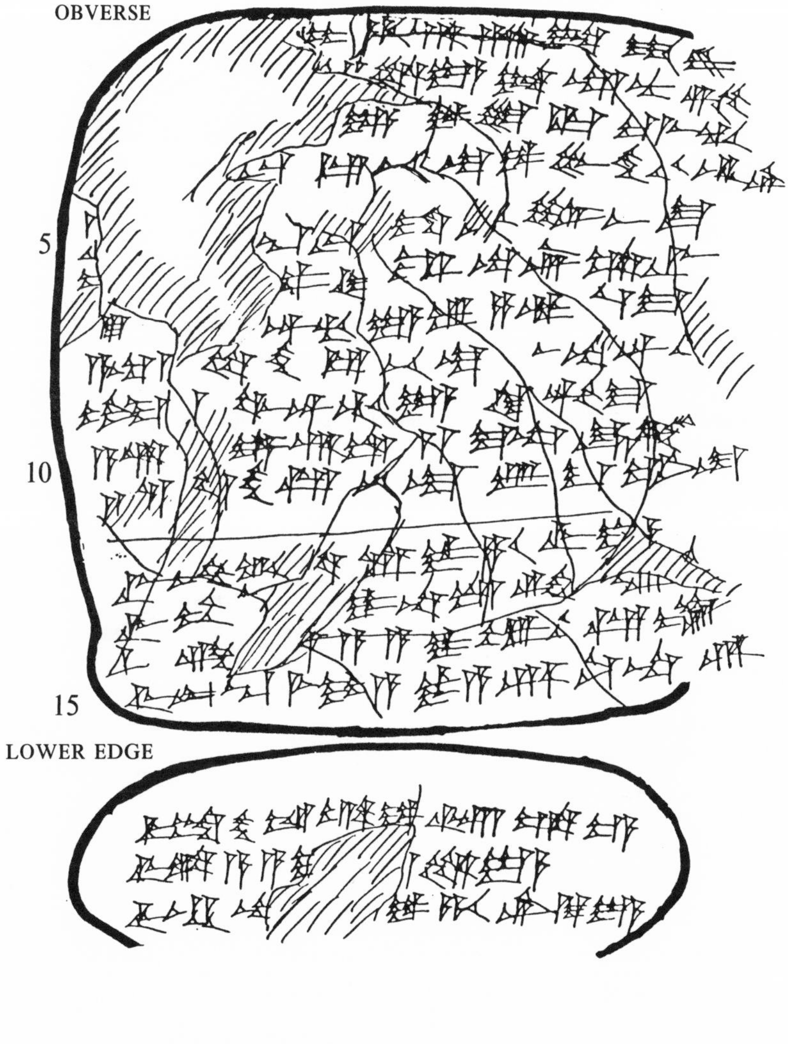

688

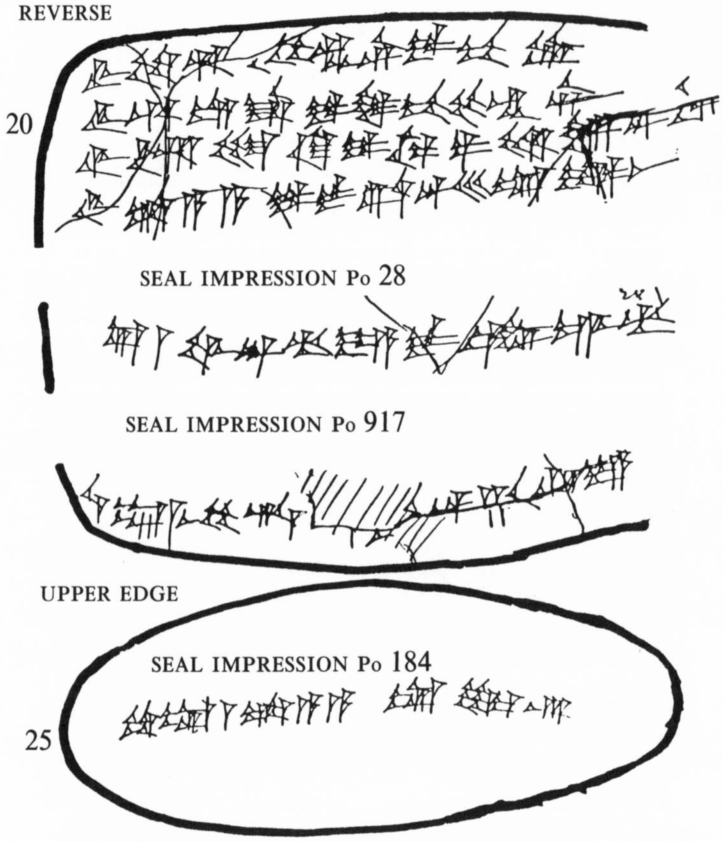
REVERSE
20
SEAL IMPRESSION Po 28
SEAL IMPRESSION Po 917
UPPER EDGE
SEAL IMPRESSION Po 184
25

689

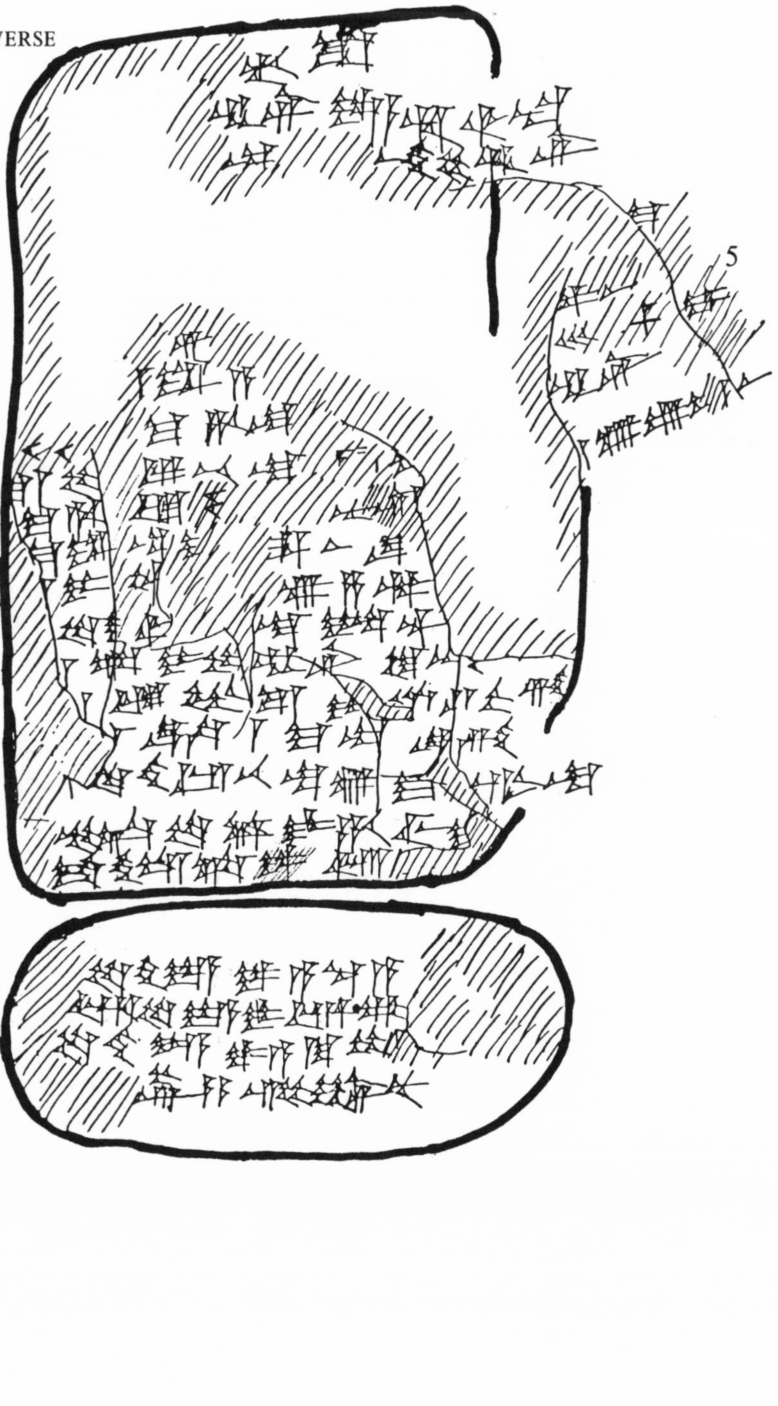

689

REVERSE

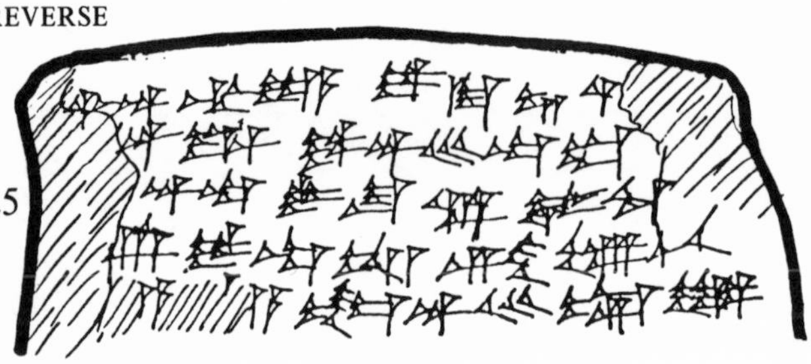

SEAL IMPRESSION Po 108

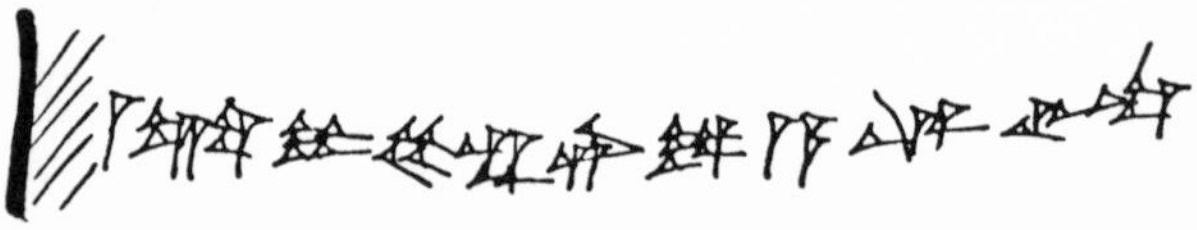

SEAL IMPRESSION Po 917

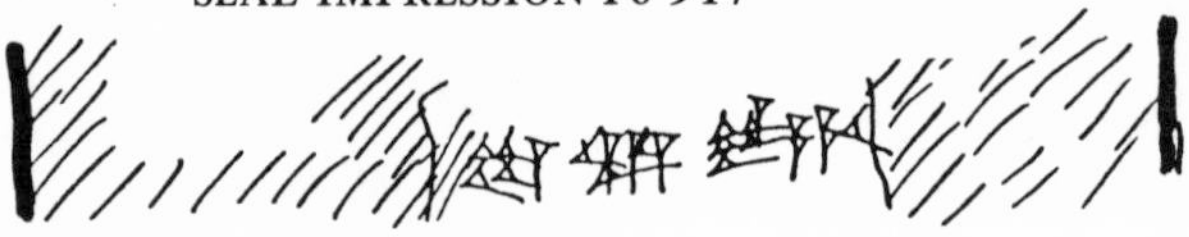

SEAL IMPRESSION

690

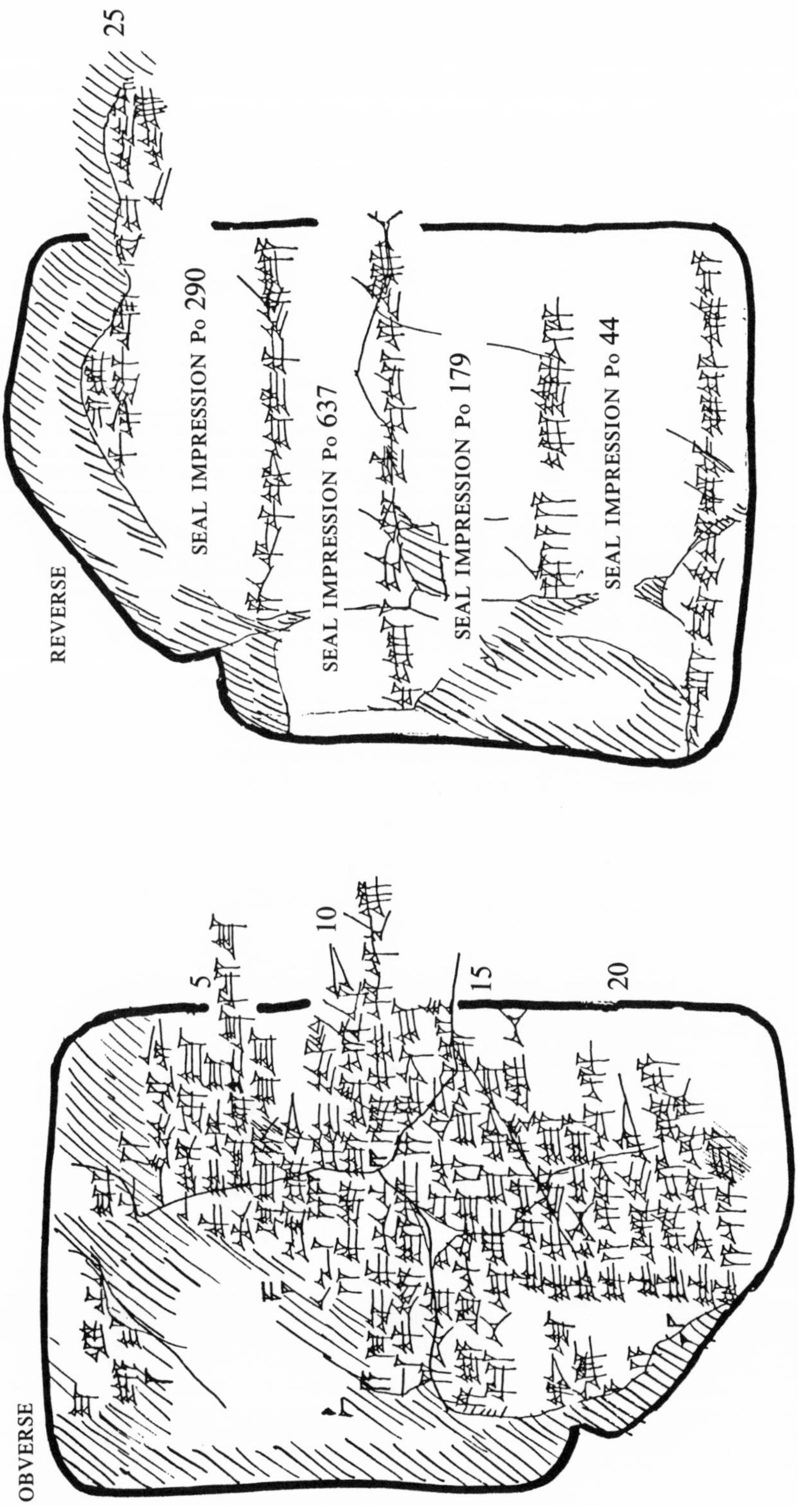

Rest of obverse, beginning of reverse destroyed

691

OBVERSE

*

*Additional text; see *THNT*.

691

REVERSE

SEAL IMPRESSION

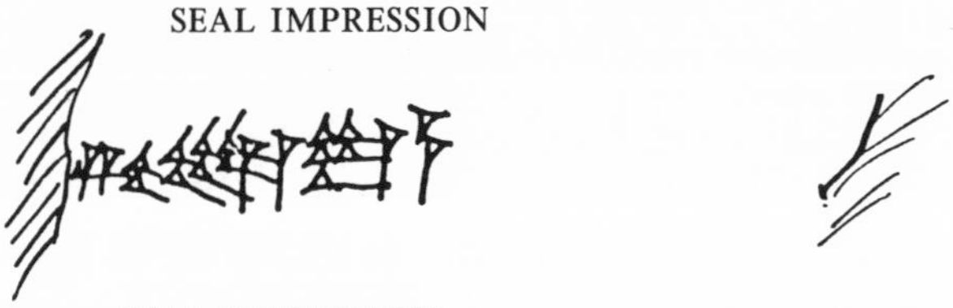

SEAL IMPRESSION

SEAL IMPRESSION

UPPER EDGE SEAL IMPRESSION

692

OBVERSE

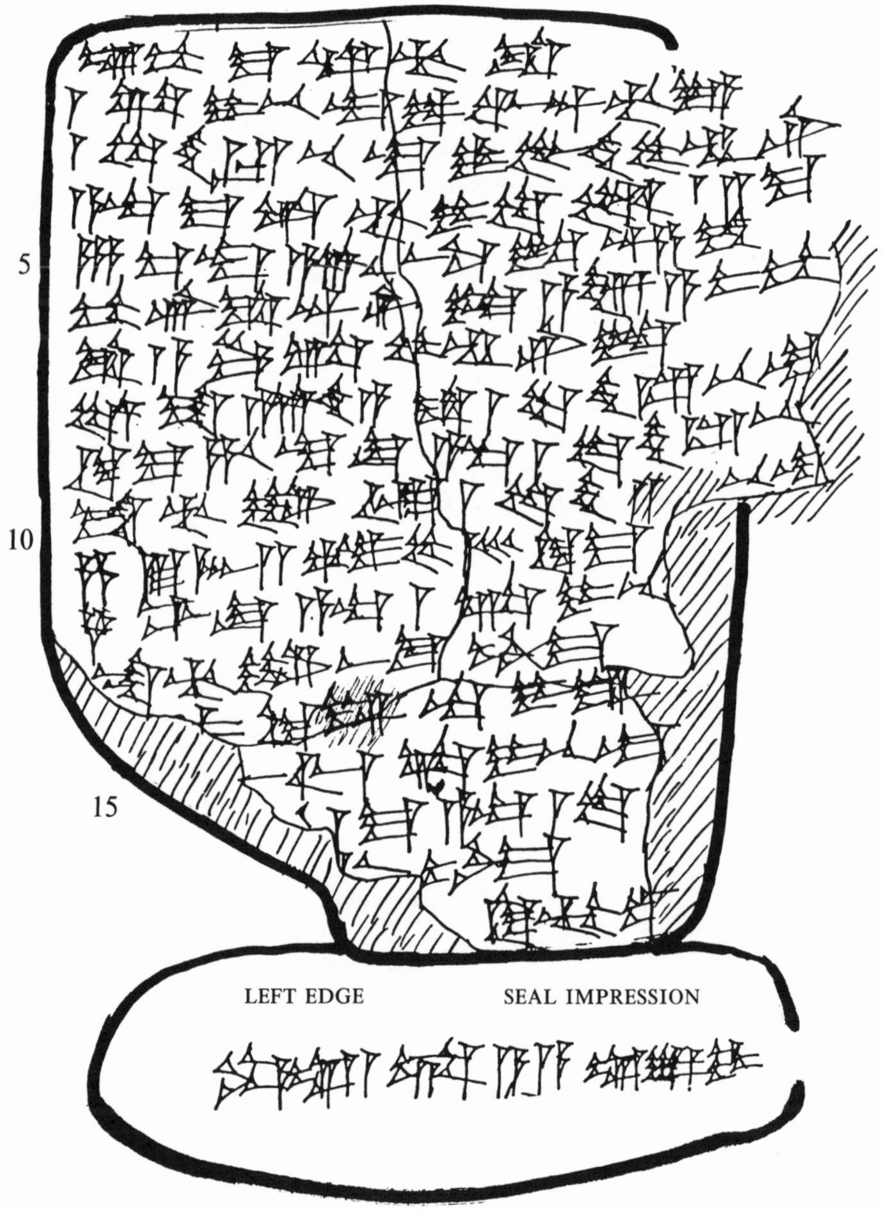

692

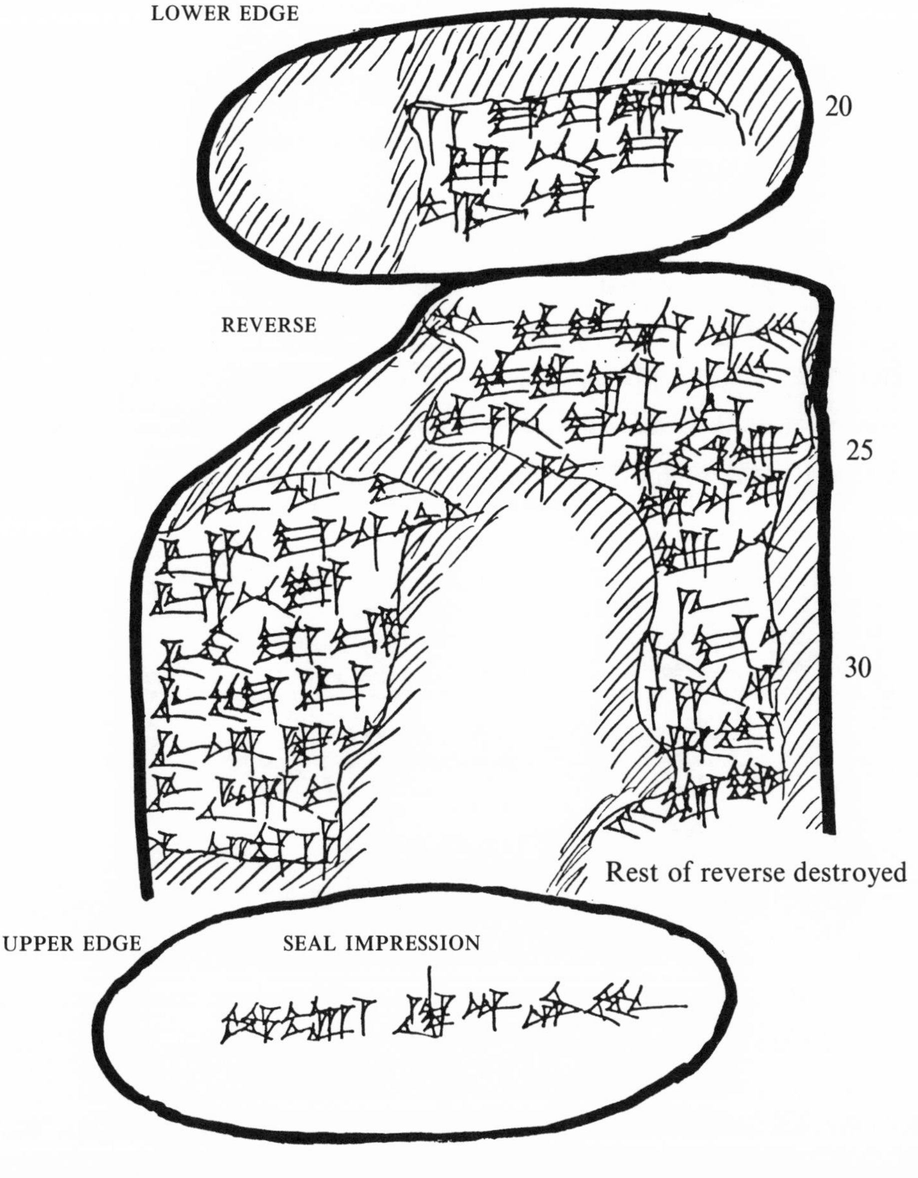
LOWER EDGE
20
REVERSE
25
30
Rest of reverse destroyed
UPPER EDGE
SEAL IMPRESSION

693

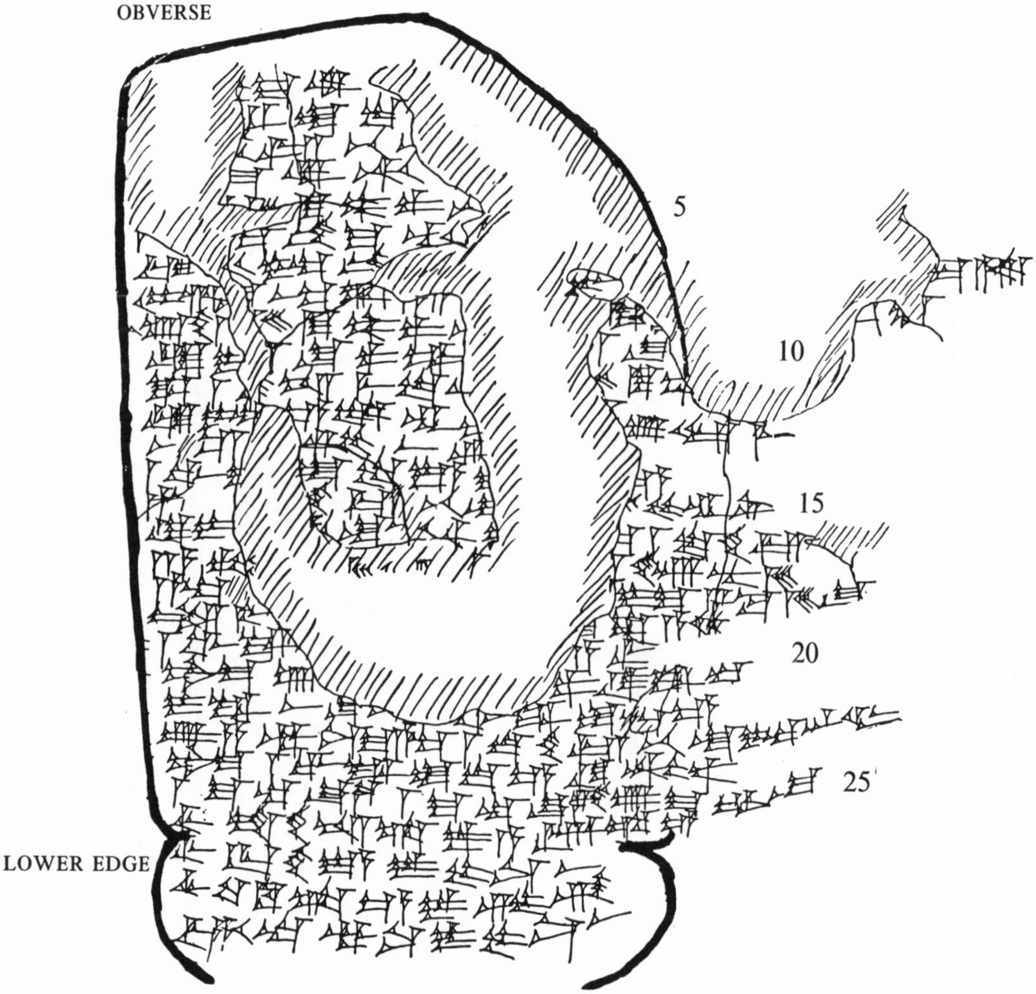

693

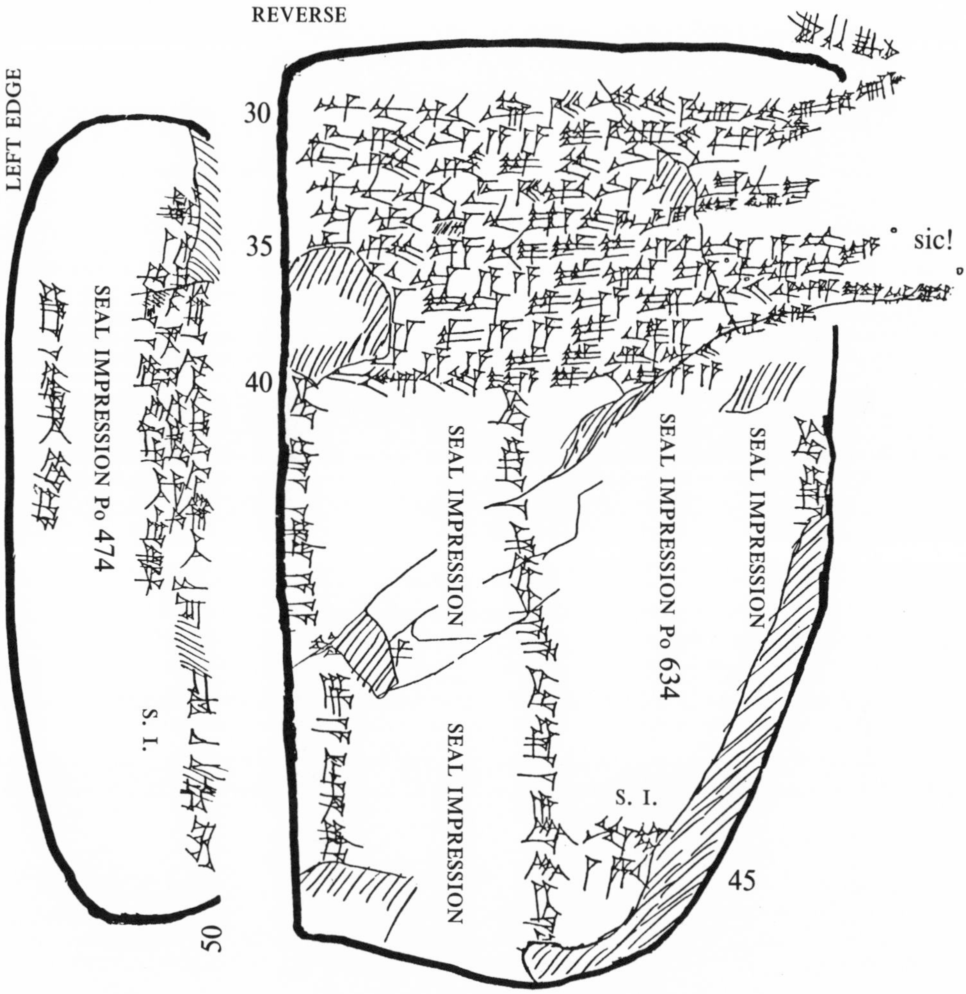
REVERSE
LEFT EDGE
30
35
40
45
50
sic!
SEAL IMPRESSION Po 474
S. I.
SEAL IMPRESSION
SEAL IMPRESSION Po 634
SEAL IMPRESSION
SEAL IMPRESSION
S. I.

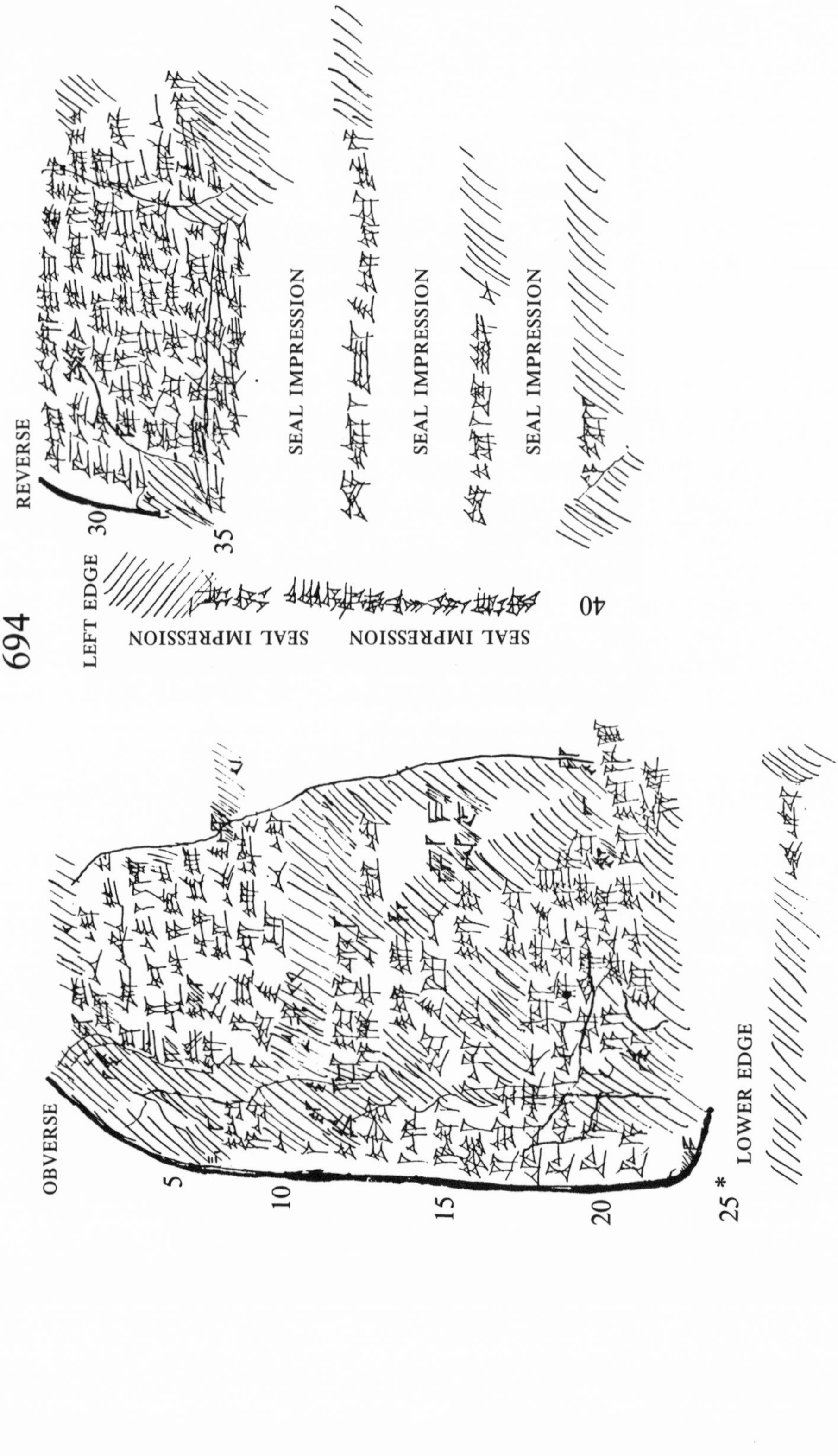

*Additional text; see *THNT*.

695

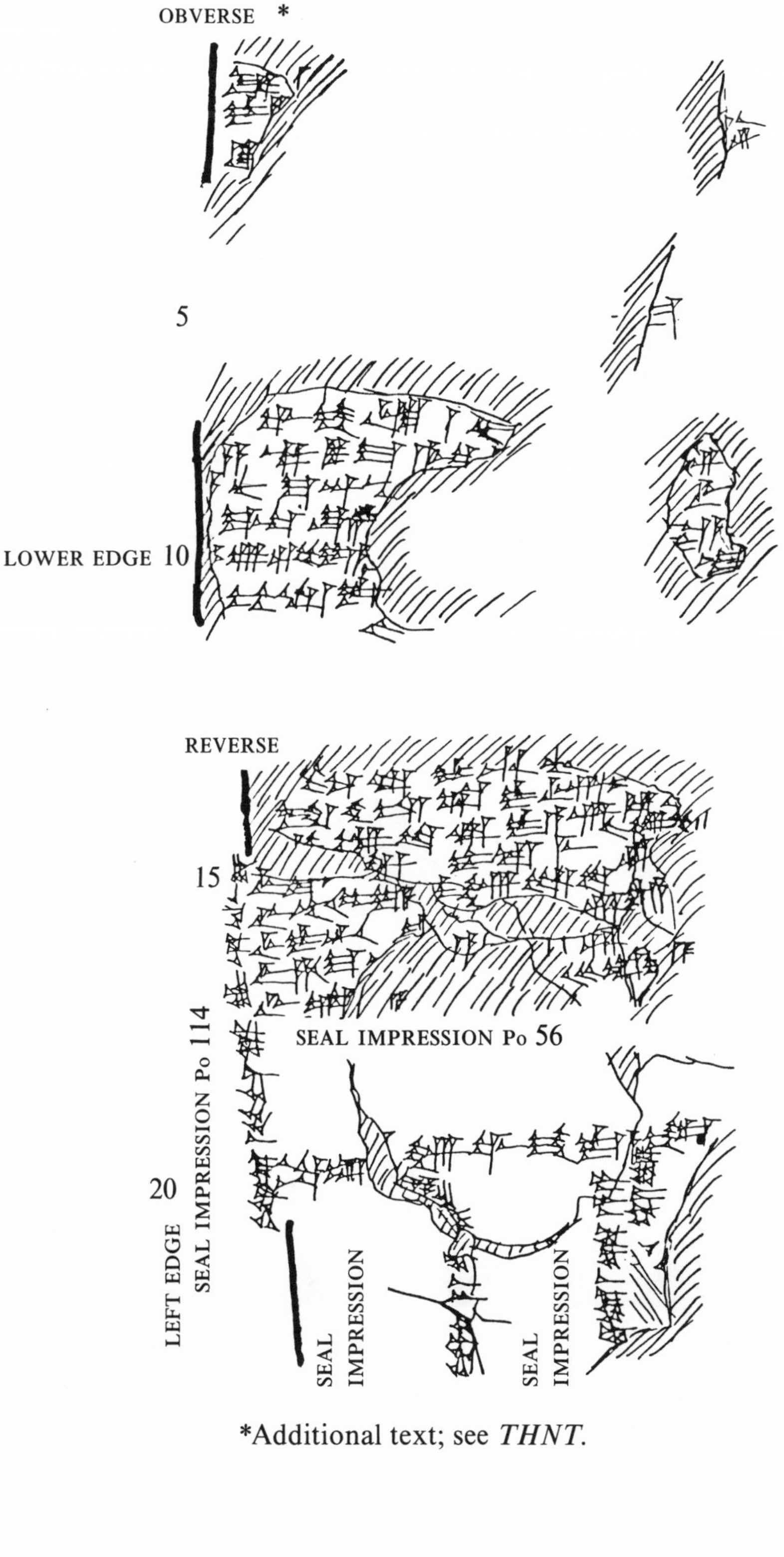

*Additional text; see *THNT*.

696

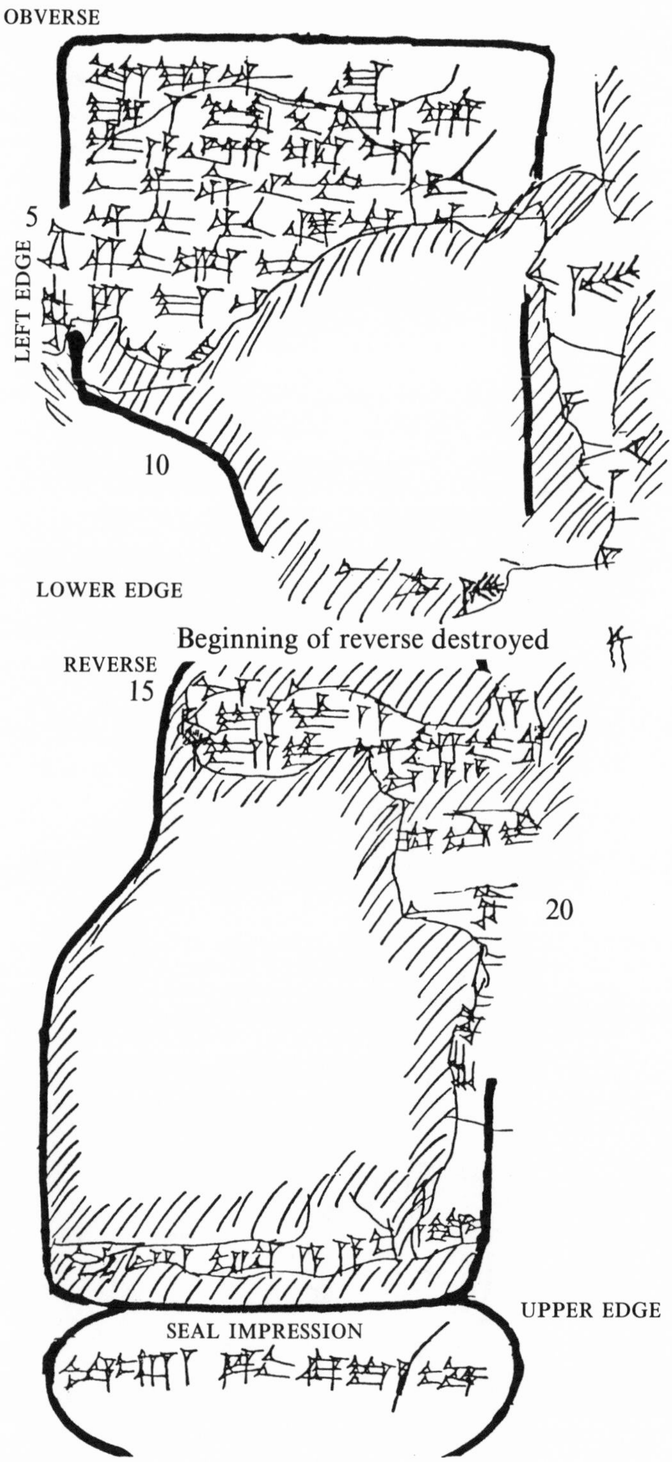
OBVERSE
LEFT EDGE
LOWER EDGE
Beginning of reverse destroyed
REVERSE
UPPER EDGE
SEAL IMPRESSION

697

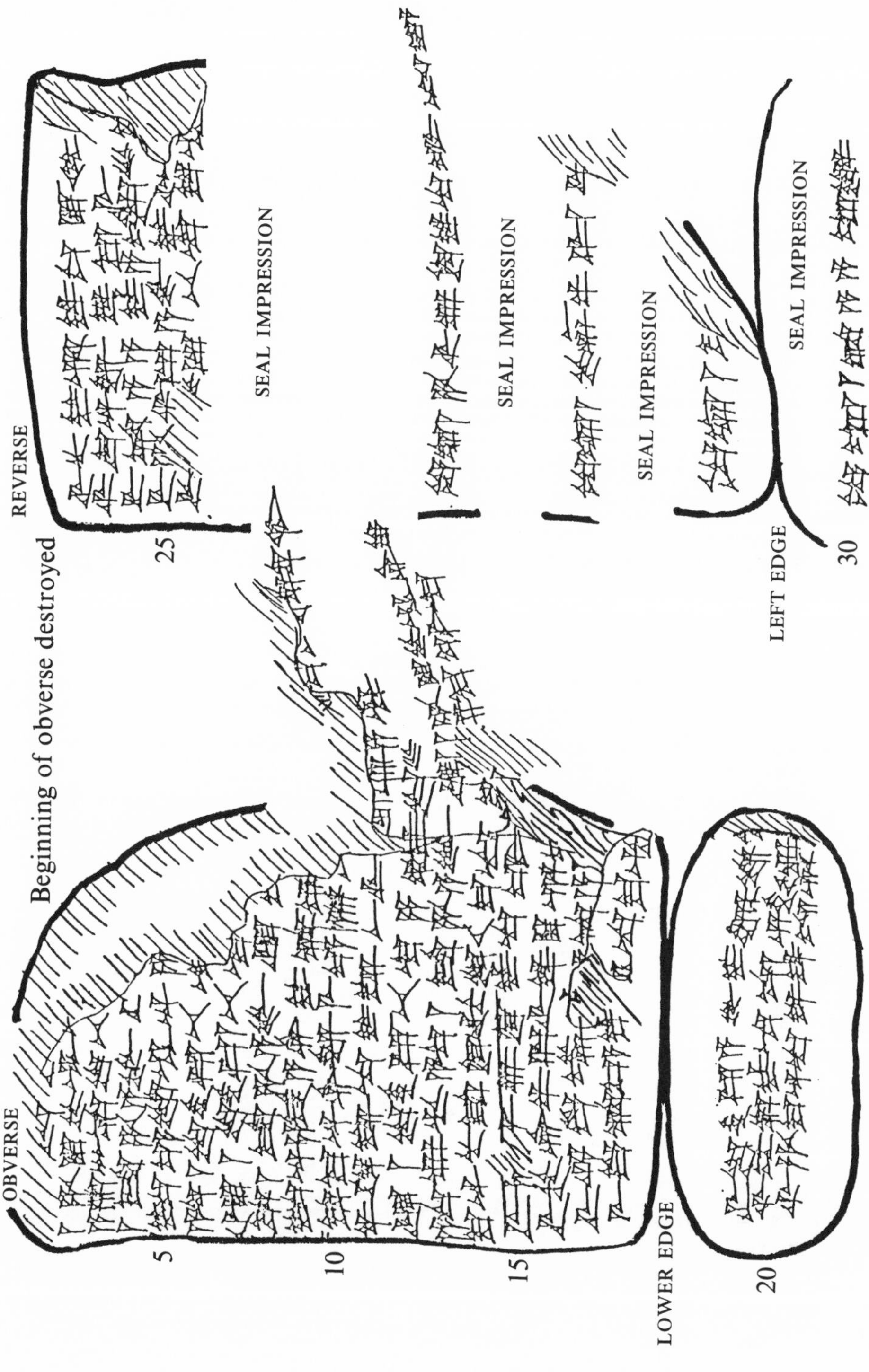
Beginning of obverse destroyed
OBVERSE
LOWER EDGE
REVERSE
SEAL IMPRESSION
SEAL IMPRESSION
SEAL IMPRESSION
SEAL IMPRESSION
LEFT EDGE
5
10
15
20
25
30

698

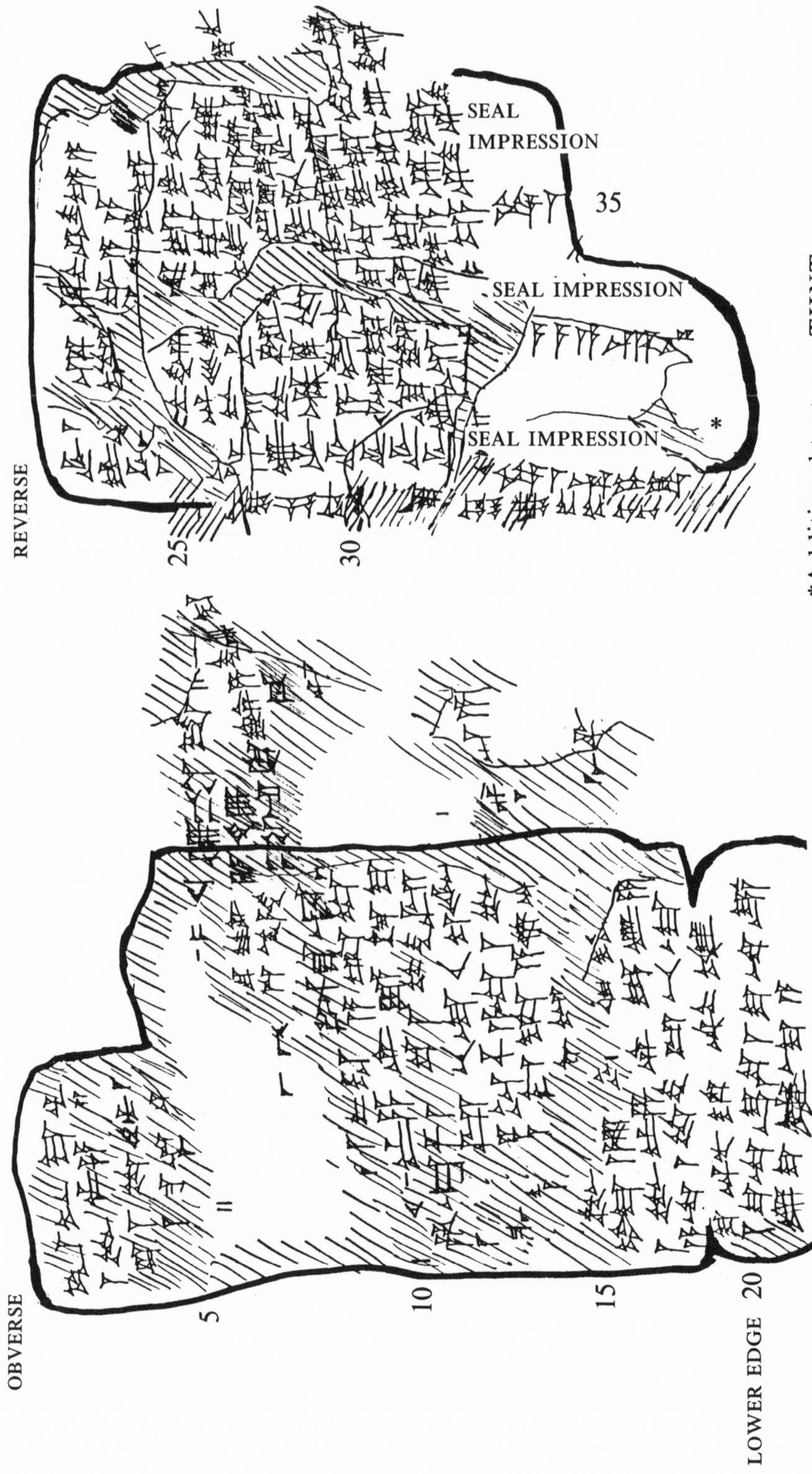

*Additional text; see *THNT.*

699

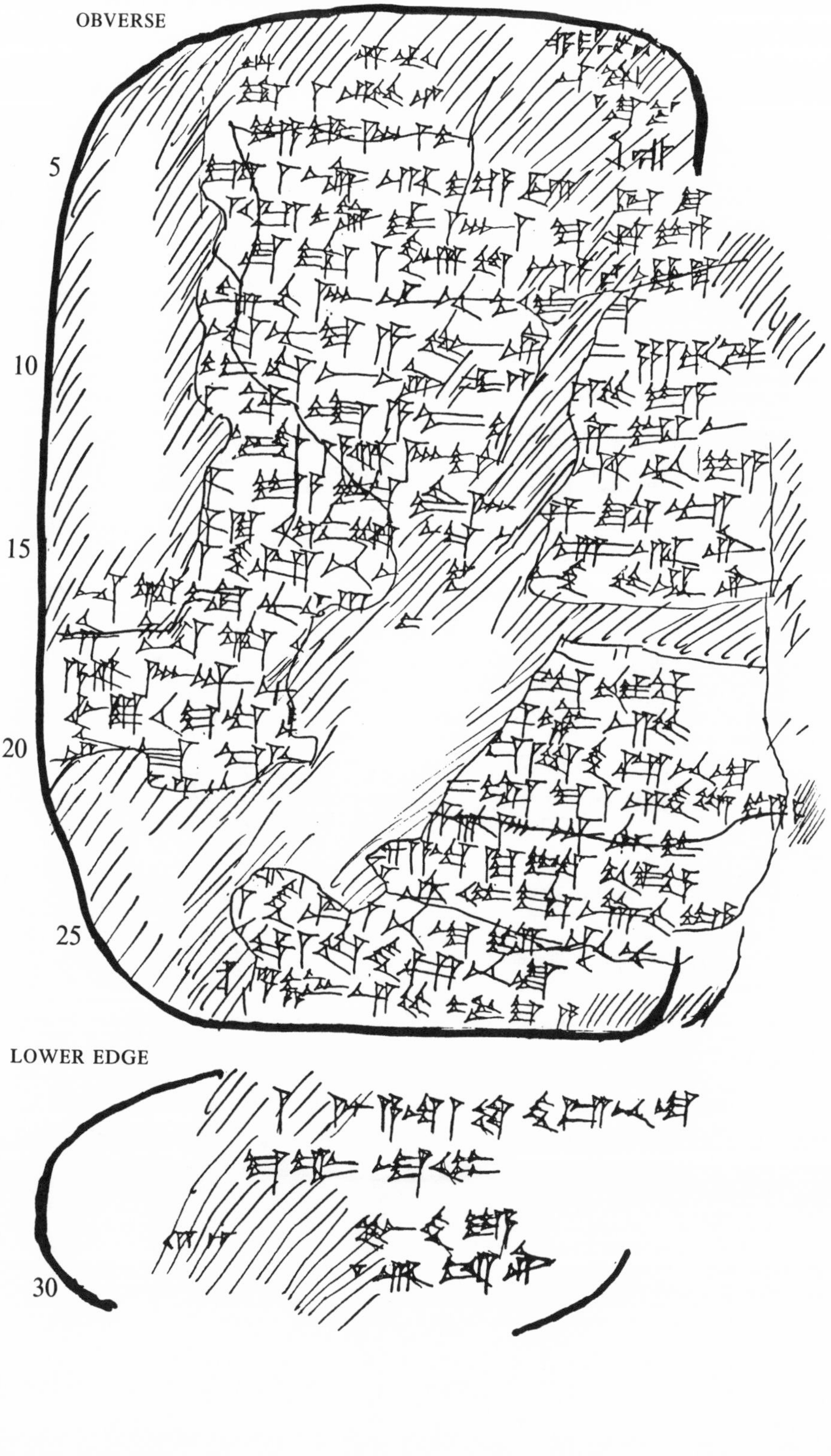

699

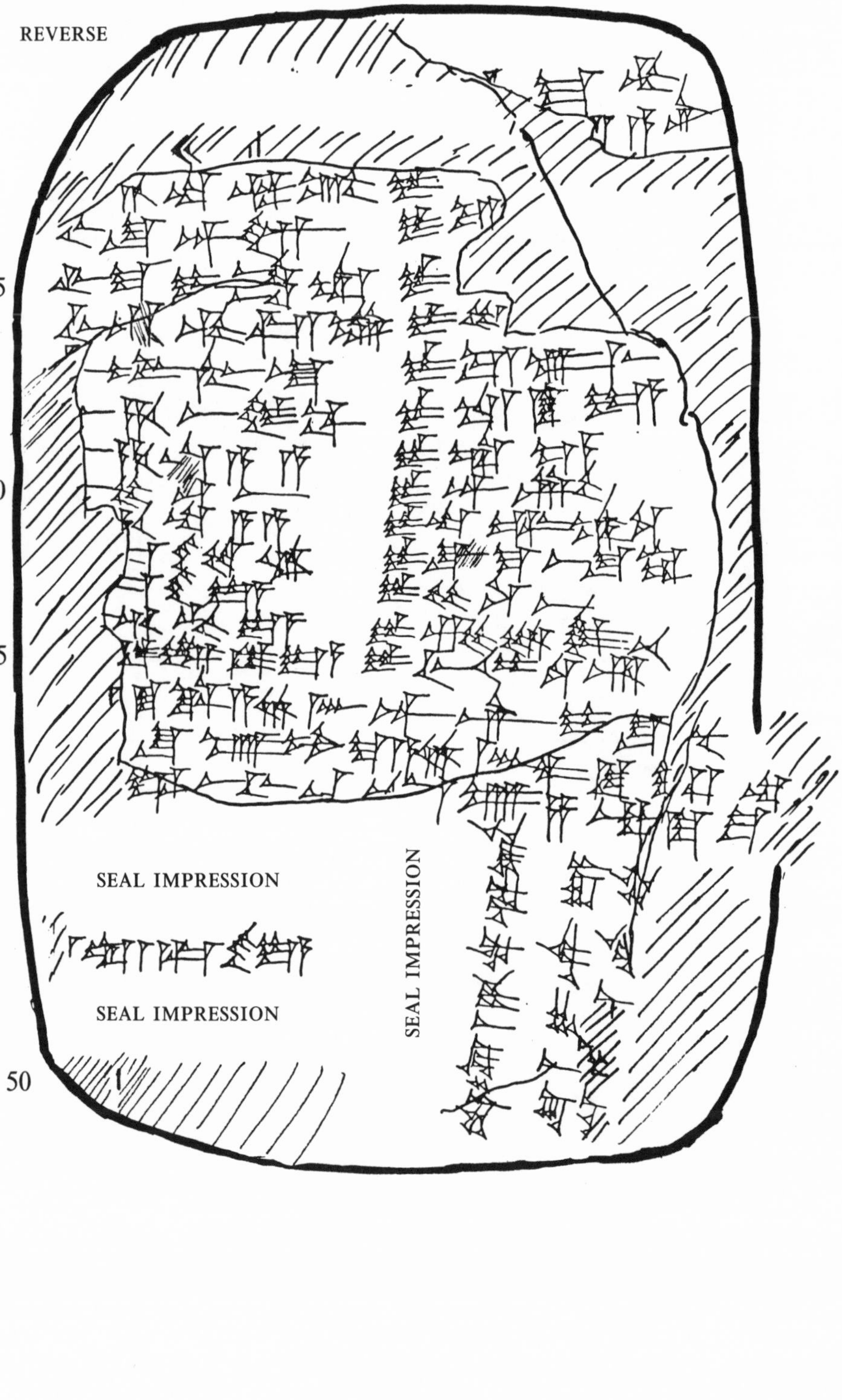

700

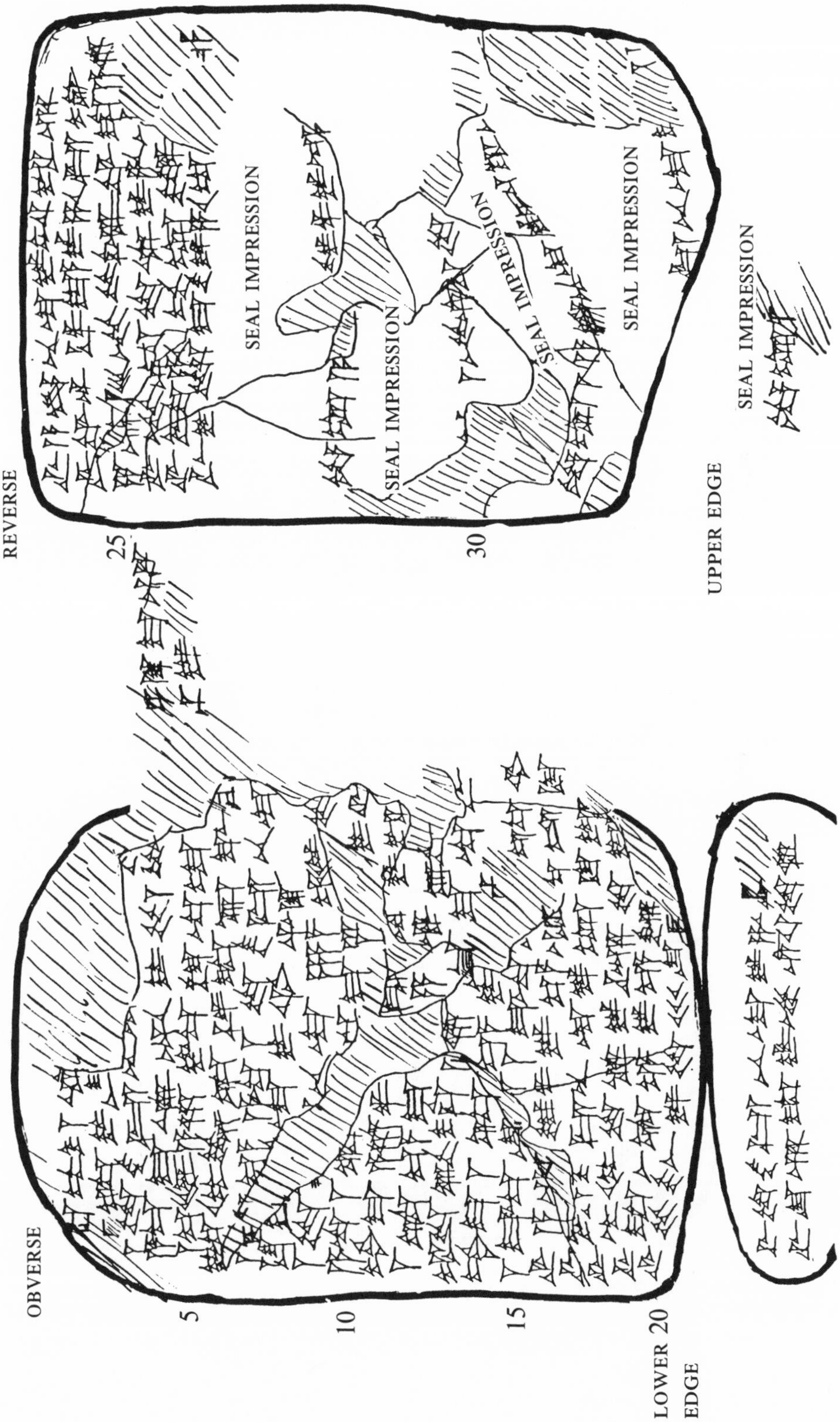
OBVERSE
LOWER EDGE
REVERSE
UPPER EDGE
SEAL IMPRESSION
SEAL IMPRESSION
SEAL IMPRESSION
SEAL IMPRESSION
SEAL IMPRESSION

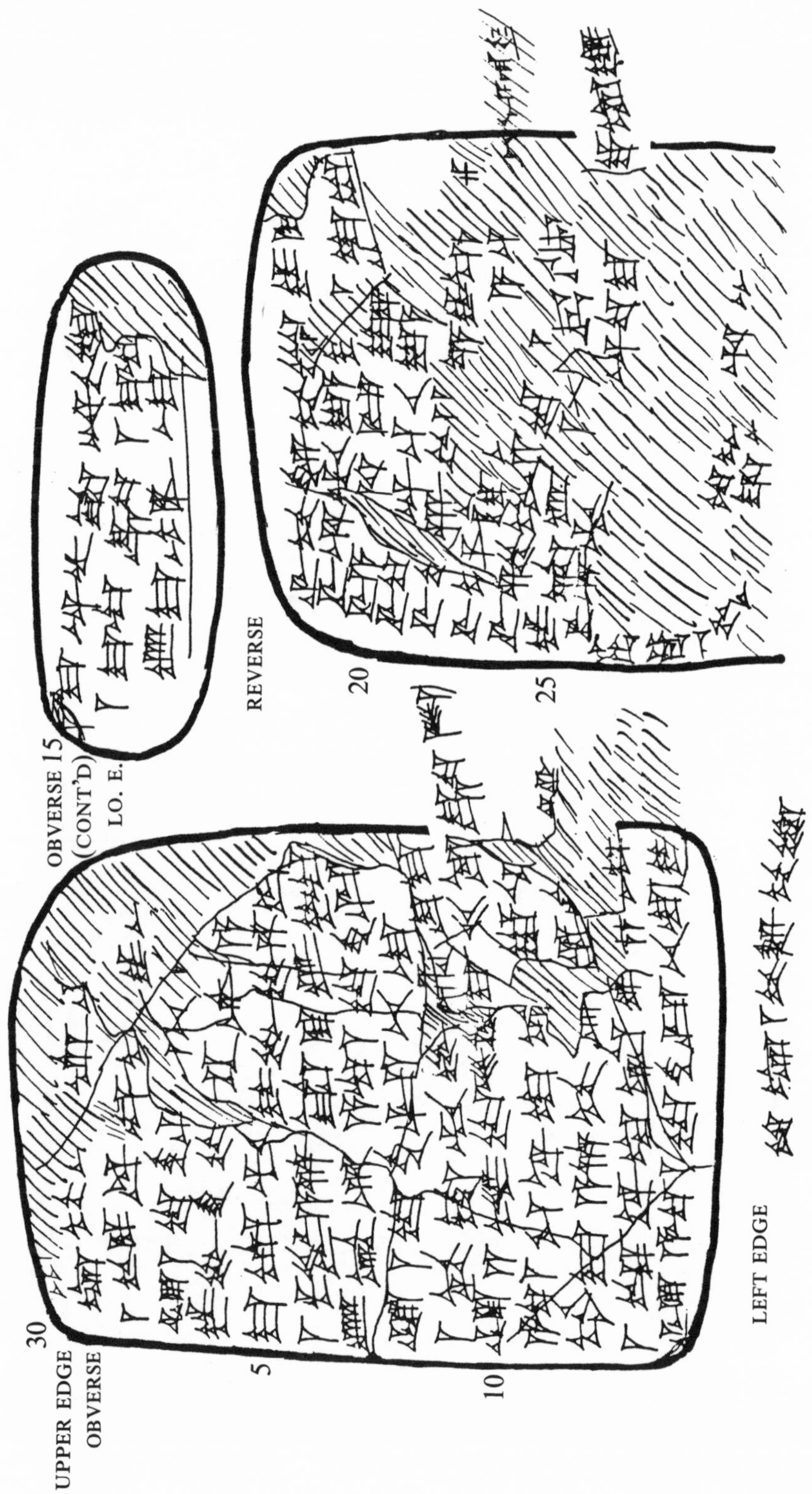
701
UPPER EDGE
OBVERSE
30
5
10
OBVERSE 15 (CONT'D)
LO. E.
REVERSE
20
25
LEFT EDGE

702

OBVERSE

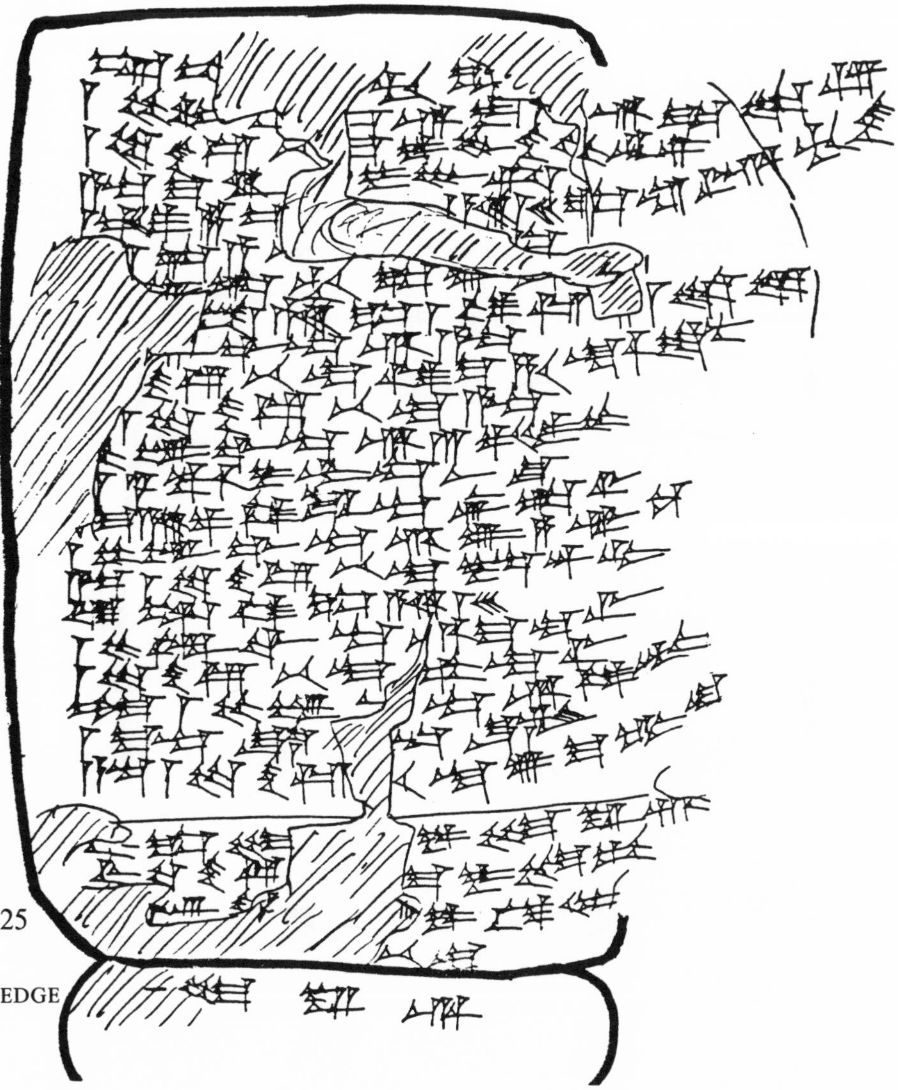

LOWER EDGE

702

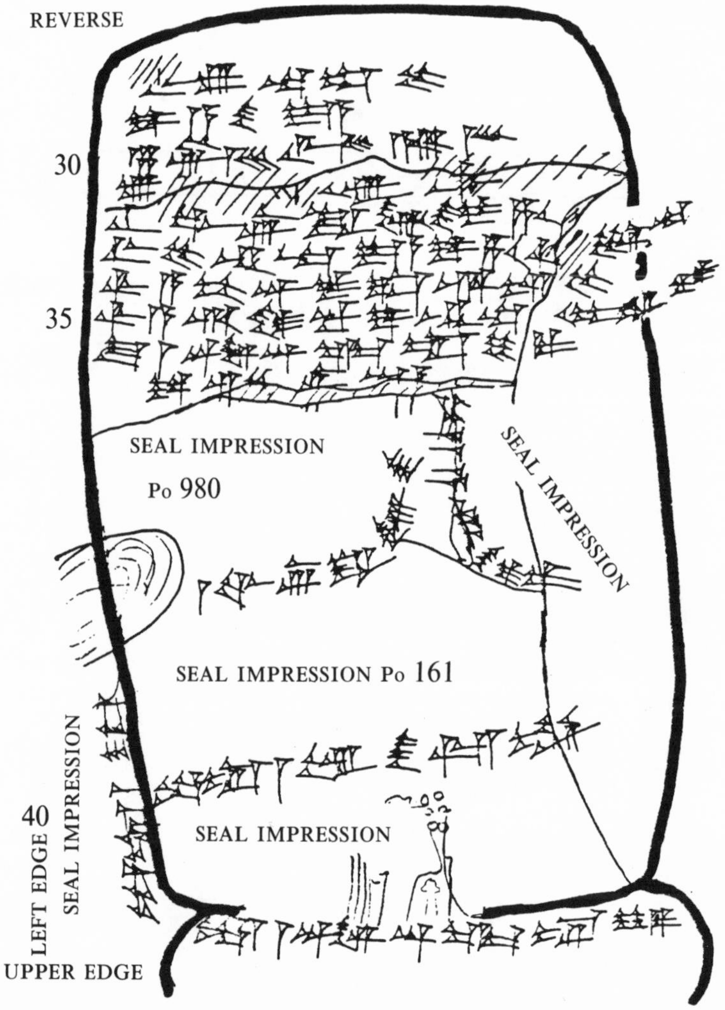
REVERSE
SEAL IMPRESSION
Po 980
SEAL IMPRESSION
SEAL IMPRESSION Po 161
SEAL IMPRESSION
LEFT EDGE
SEAL IMPRESSION
UPPER EDGE

703

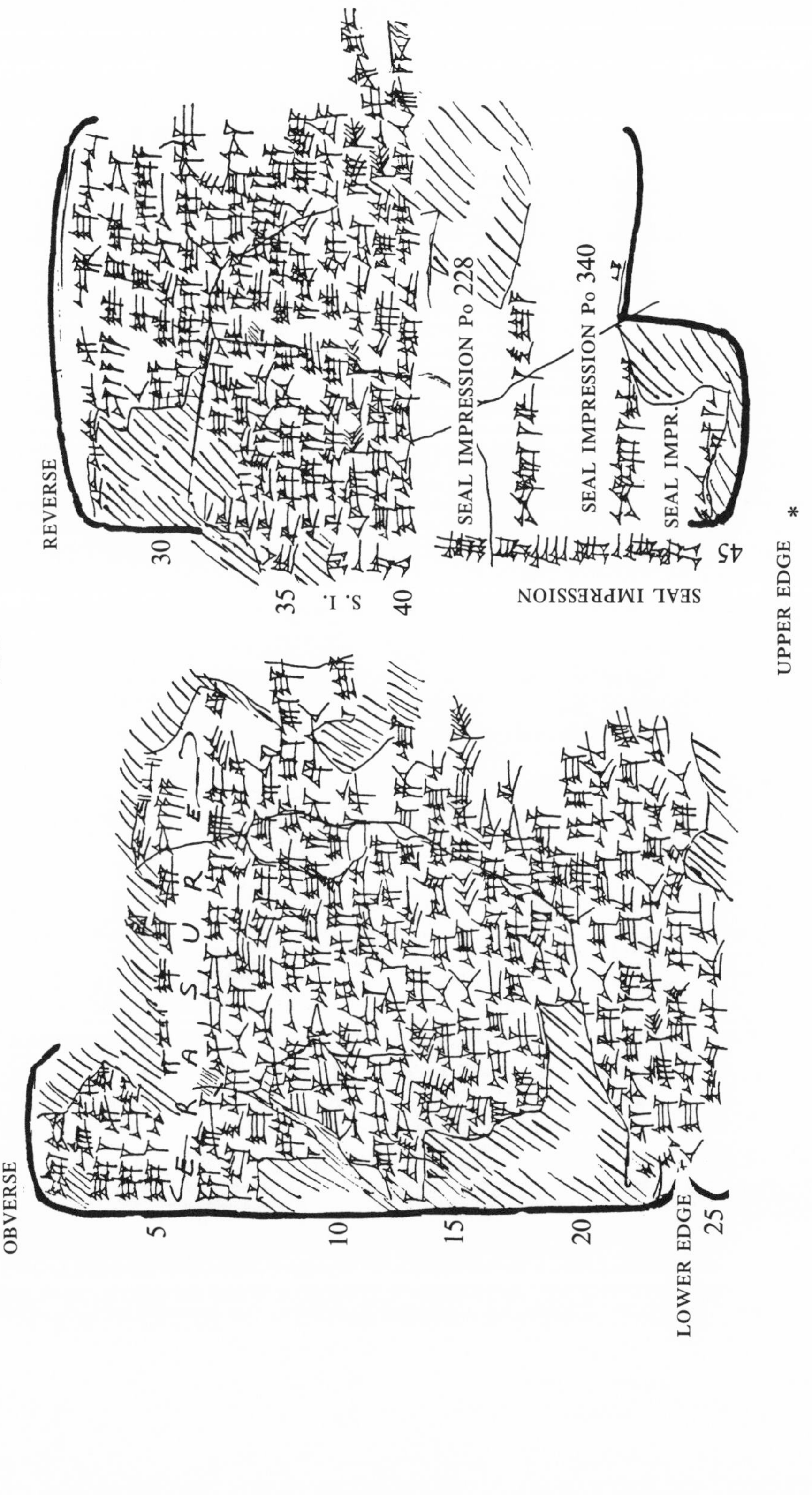

*Additional text; see *THNT*.

704

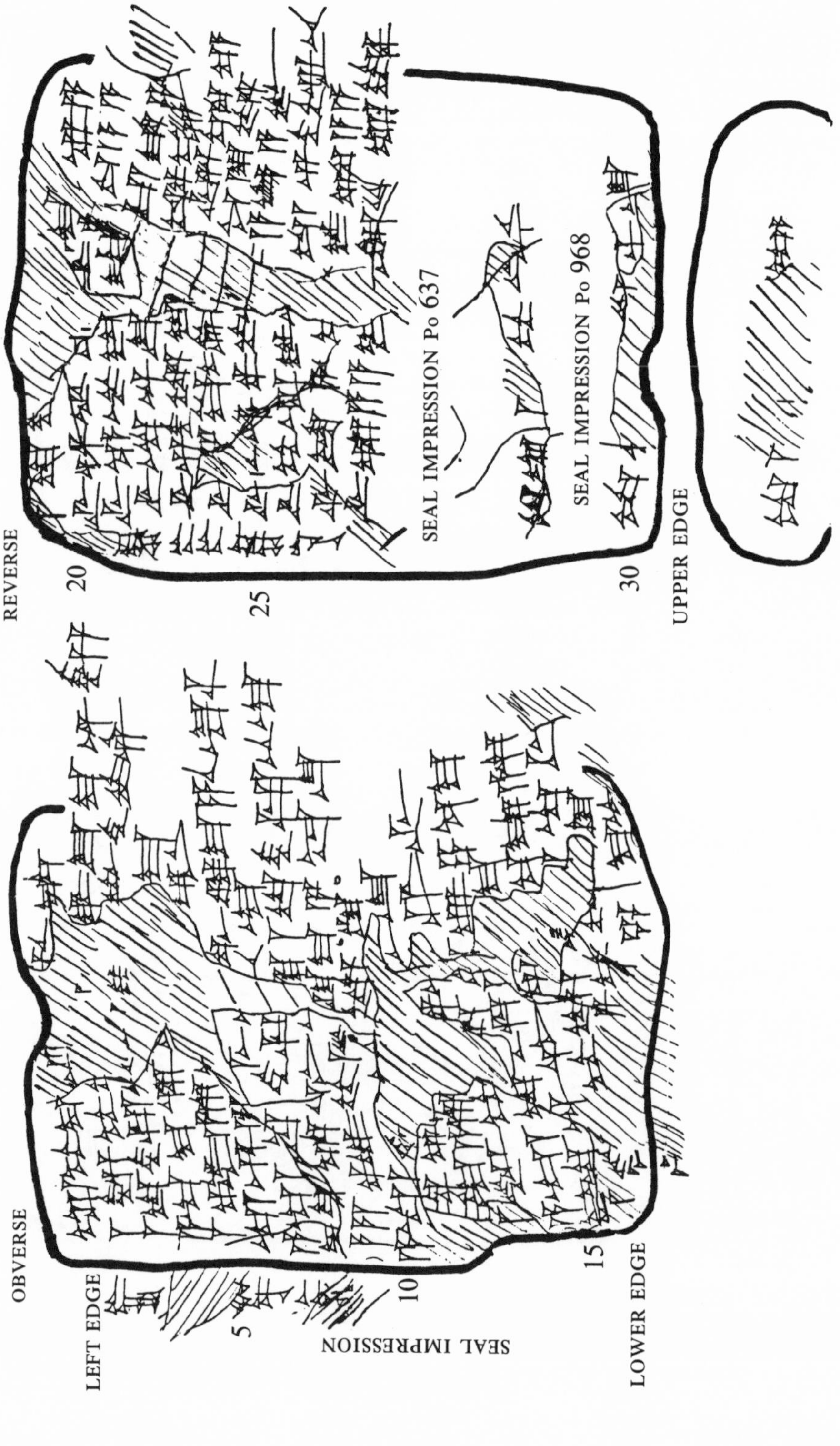
REVERSE
SEAL IMPRESSION Po 637
SEAL IMPRESSION Po 968
UPPER EDGE
OBVERSE
LEFT EDGE
SEAL IMPRESSION
LOWER EDGE

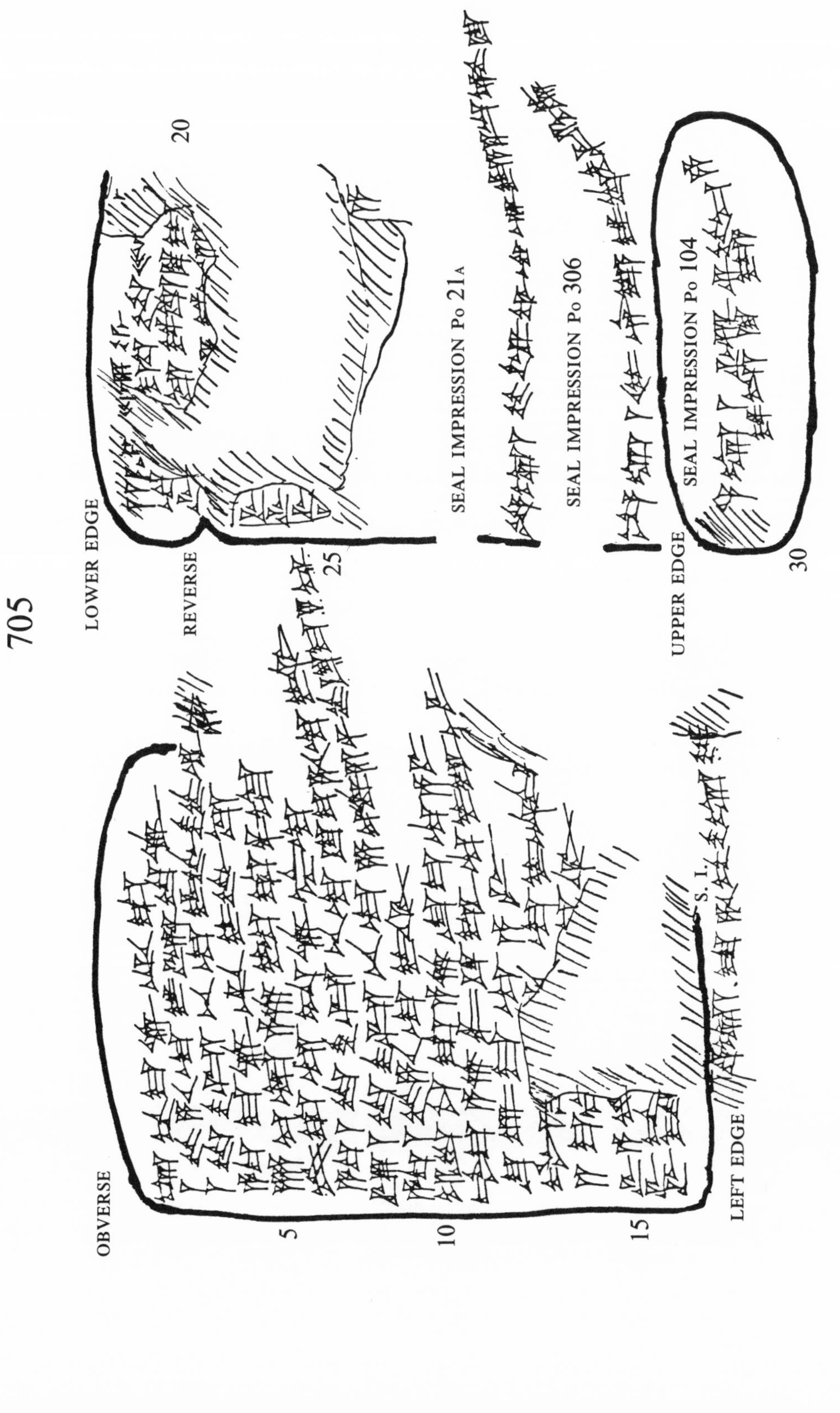
705
OBVERSE
LEFT EDGE
S. I.
LOWER EDGE
REVERSE
UPPER EDGE
SEAL IMPRESSION Po 21A
SEAL IMPRESSION Po 306
SEAL IMPRESSION Po 104

706 (= 793)*

OBVERSE

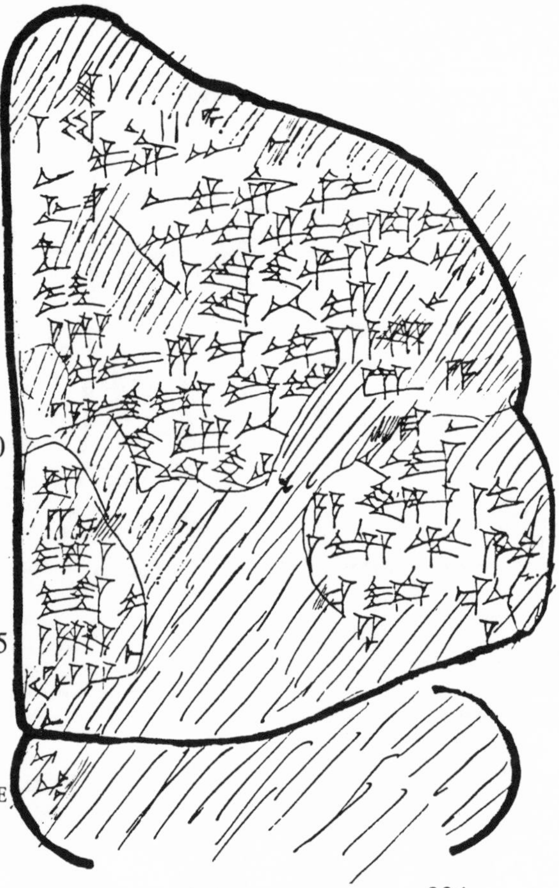

LOWER EDGE

REVERSE

SEAL IMPRESSION Po 924

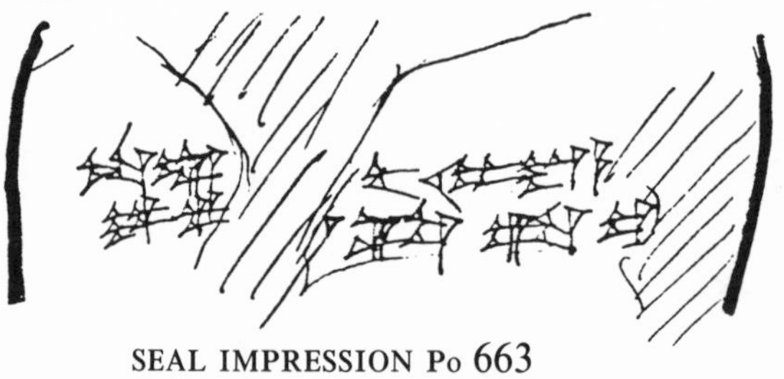

SEAL IMPRESSION Po 663

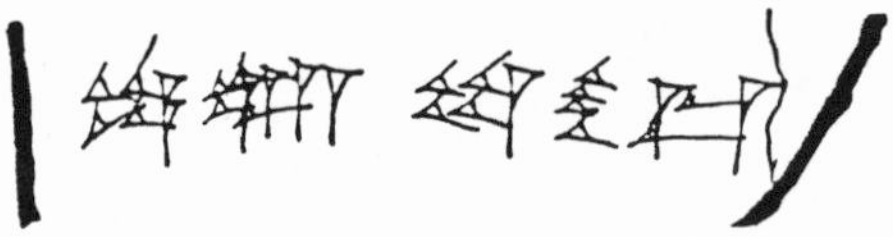

SEAL IMPRESSION Po 492

Rest of reverse destroyed

*706 is the better of the two copies. See comments to this text in *THNT*.

707

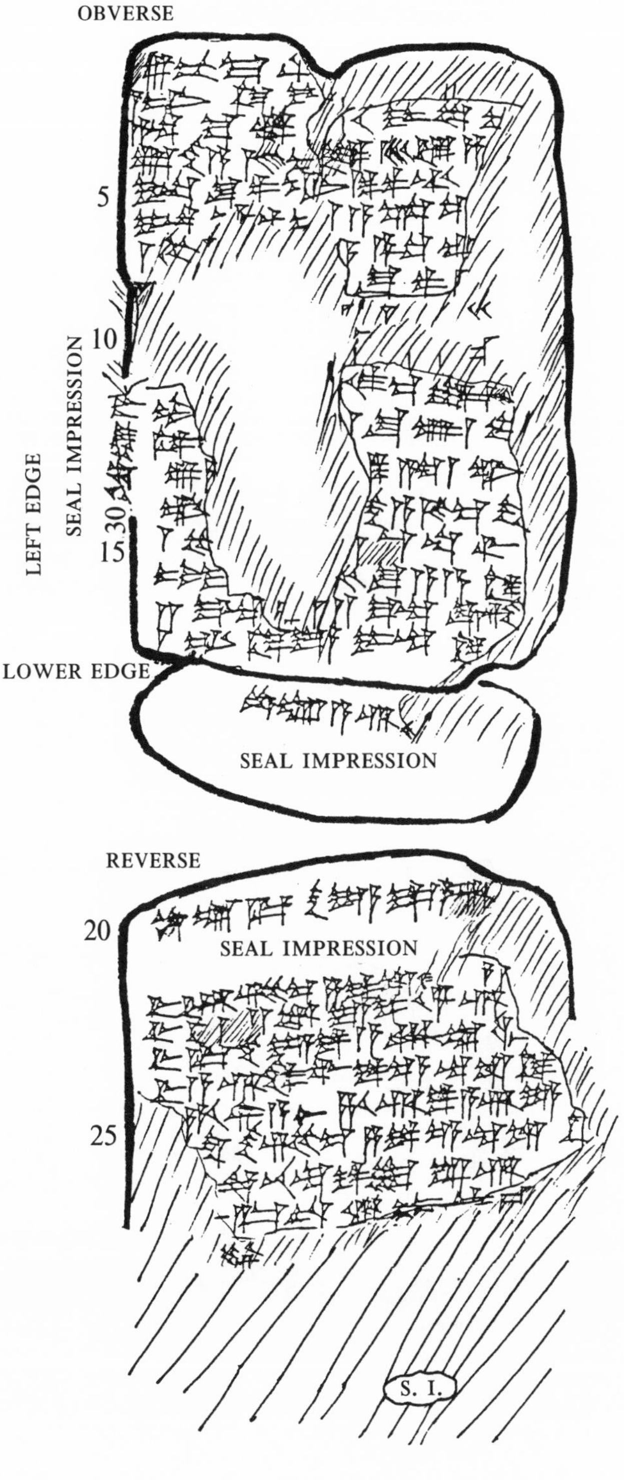
OBVERSE
LEFT EDGE
SEAL IMPRESSION
LOWER EDGE
SEAL IMPRESSION
REVERSE
SEAL IMPRESSION
S. I.

708

OBVERSE Beginning of obverse destroyed

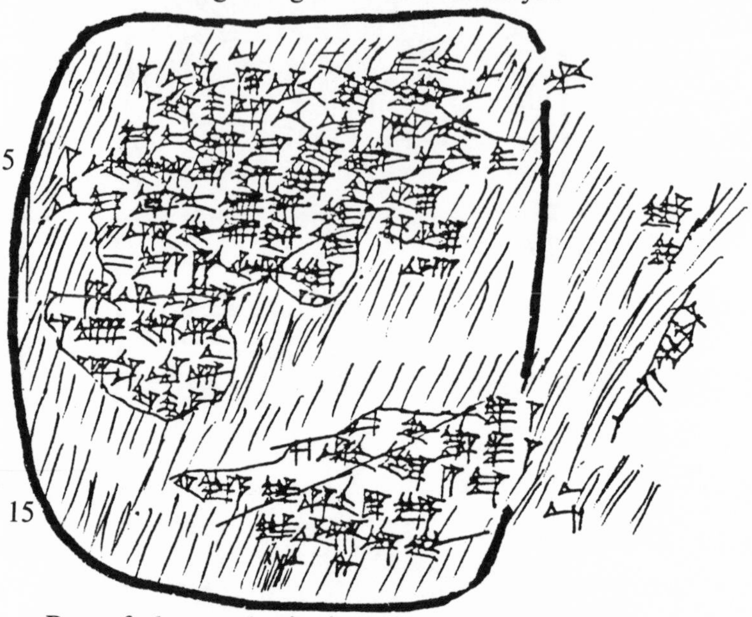

Rest of obverse, beginning of reverse destroyed

REVERSE

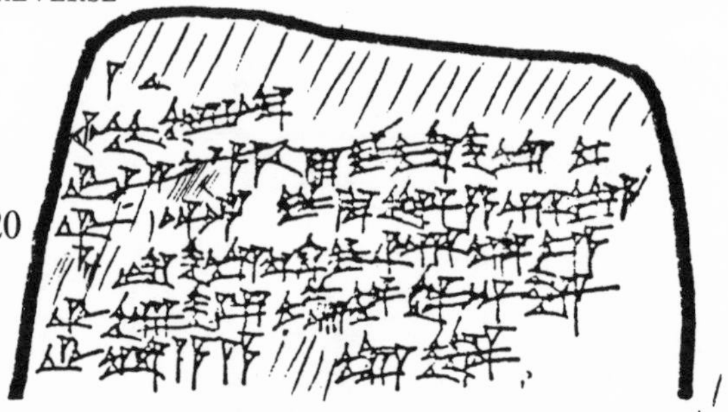

SEAL IMPRESSION Po 47

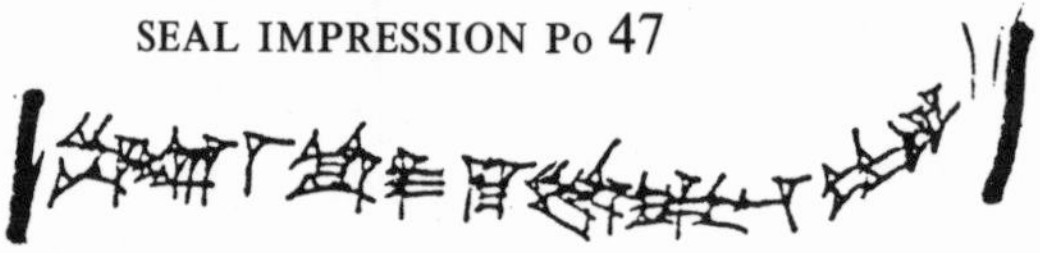

SEAL IMPRESSION

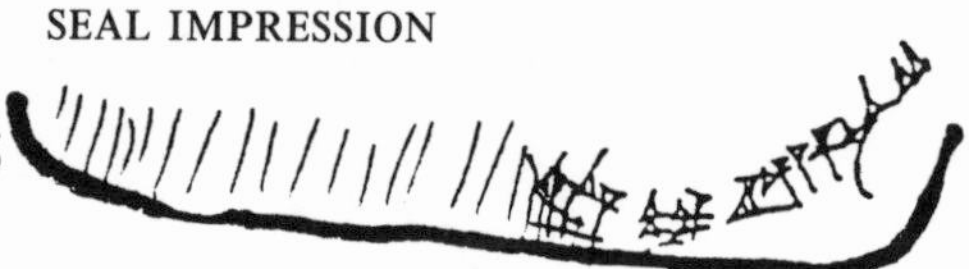

Rest of reverse destroyed

709

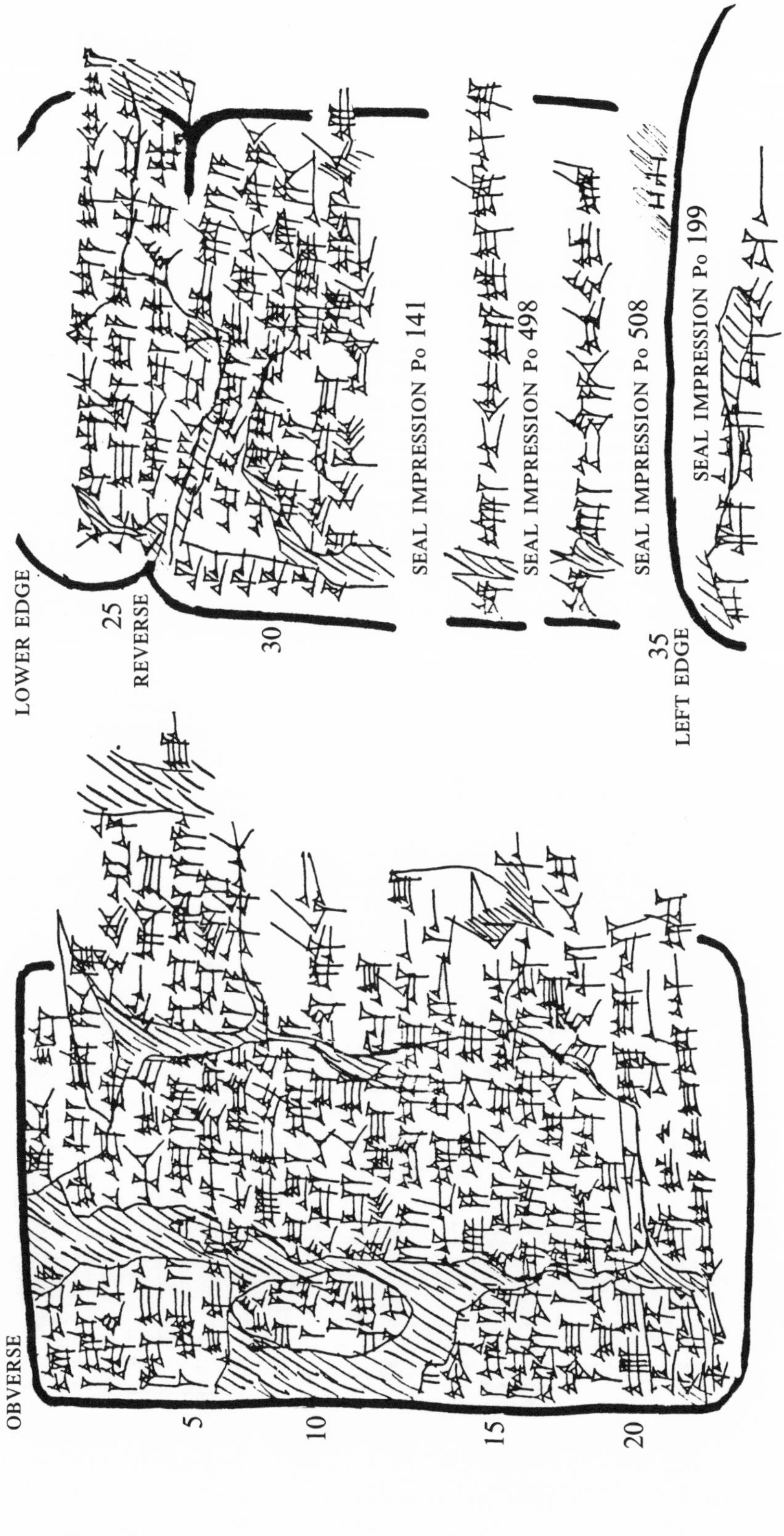
OBVERSE
LOWER EDGE
REVERSE
LEFT EDGE
SEAL IMPRESSION Po 141
SEAL IMPRESSION Po 498
SEAL IMPRESSION Po 508
SEAL IMPRESSION Po 199

710

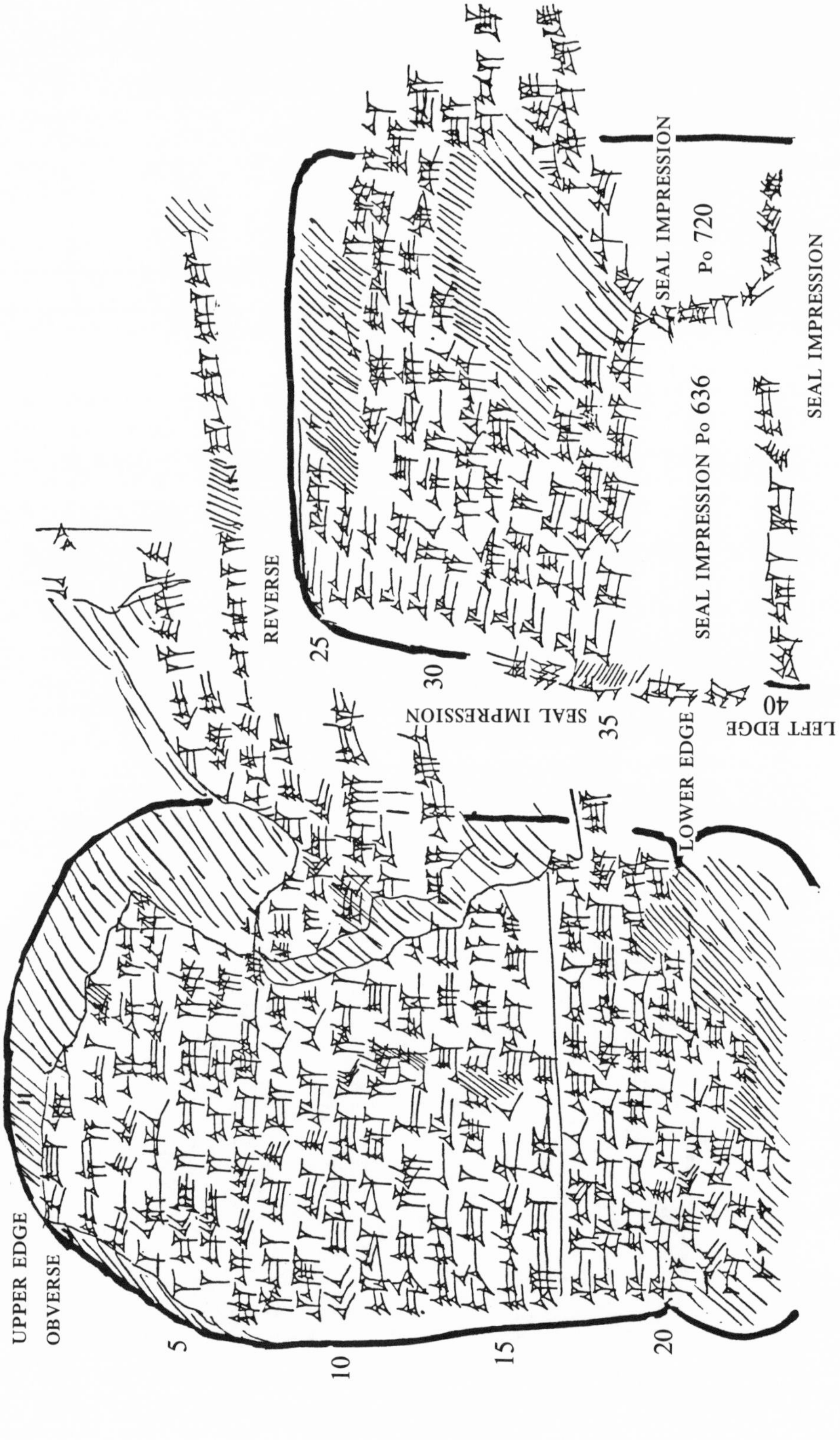
UPPER EDGE
OBVERSE
REVERSE
SEAL IMPRESSION
LOWER EDGE
LEFT EDGE
SEAL IMPRESSION Po 636
SEAL IMPRESSION
Po 720
SEAL IMPRESSION

711

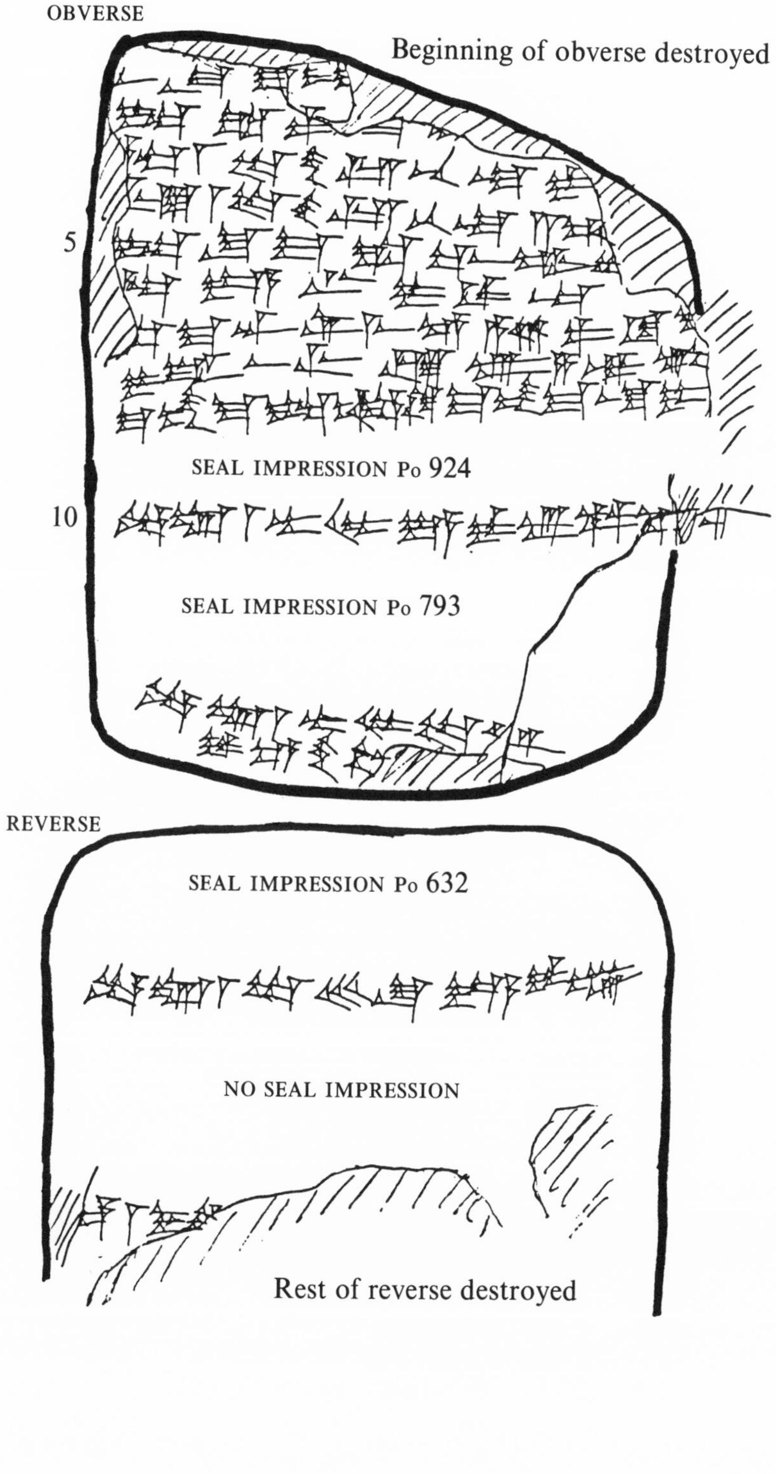
OBVERSE
Beginning of obverse destroyed
SEAL IMPRESSION Po 924
SEAL IMPRESSION Po 793
REVERSE
SEAL IMPRESSION Po 632
NO SEAL IMPRESSION
Rest of reverse destroyed

712 (= 753 = 877)*

OBVERSE Beginning of Obverse destroyed

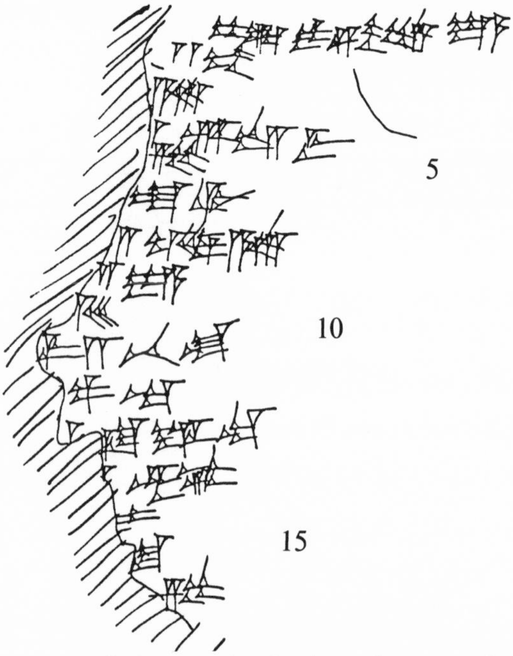

Rest of obverse, beginning of reverse destroyed

REVERSE

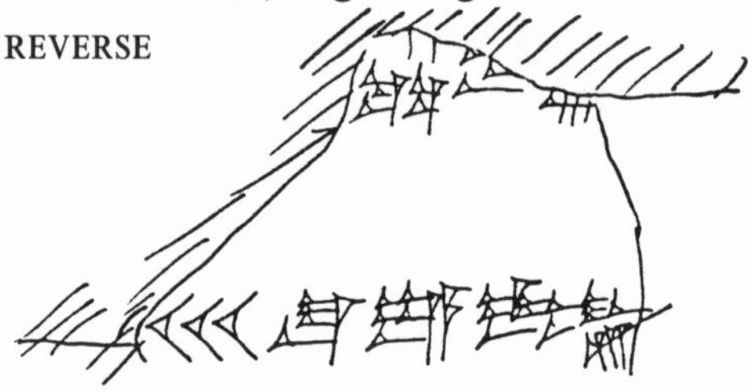

SEAL IMPRESSION Po 632

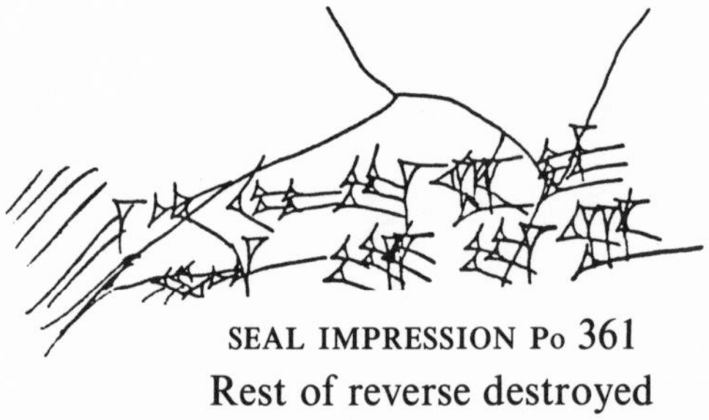

SEAL IMPRESSION Po 361

Rest of reverse destroyed

*753 is the best of the three copies.
See comments to that text in *THNT*.

713

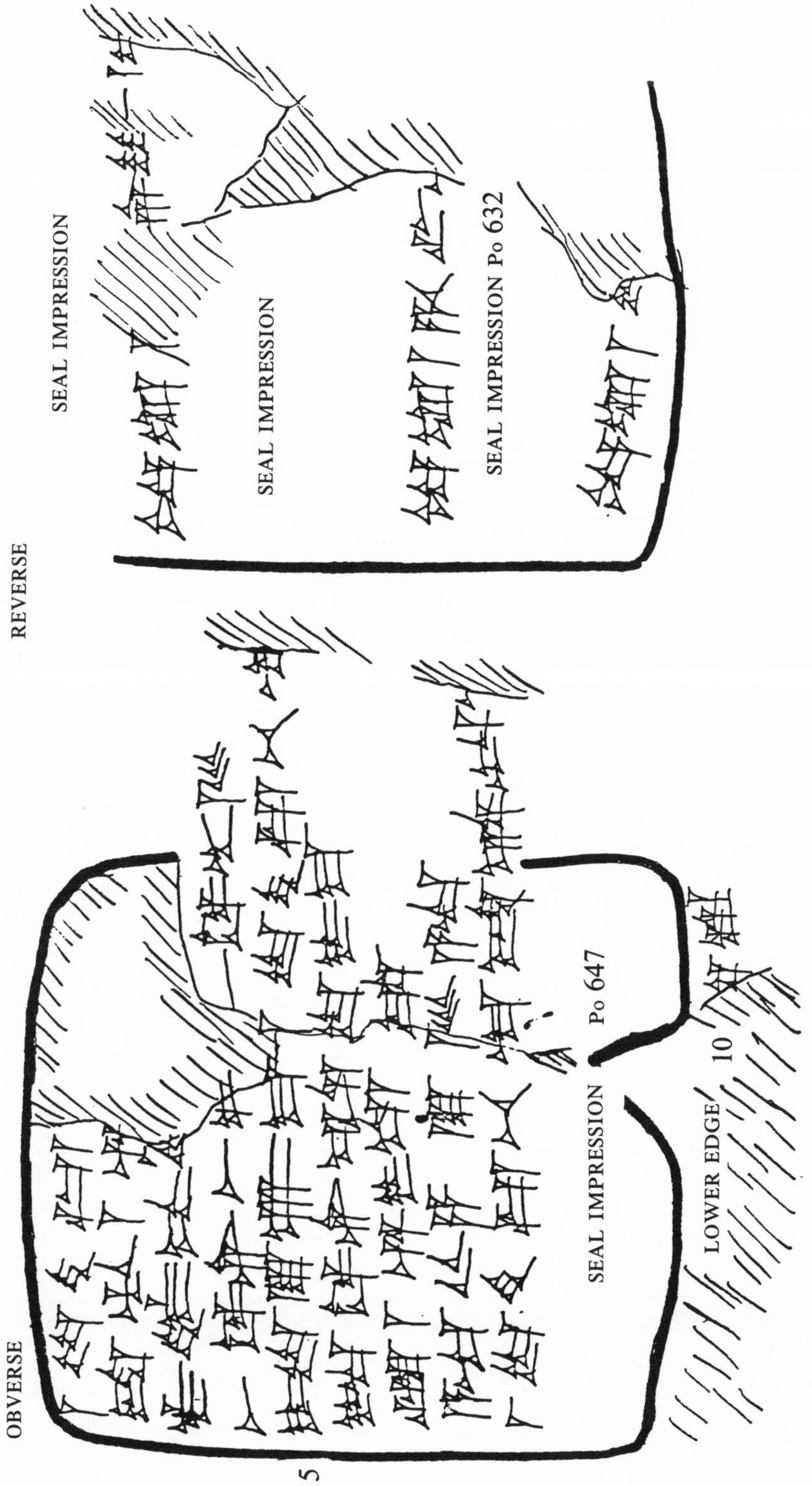
OBVERSE
REVERSE
SEAL IMPRESSION
SEAL IMPRESSION
SEAL IMPRESSION Po 632
SEAL IMPRESSION Po 647
LOWER EDGE

714

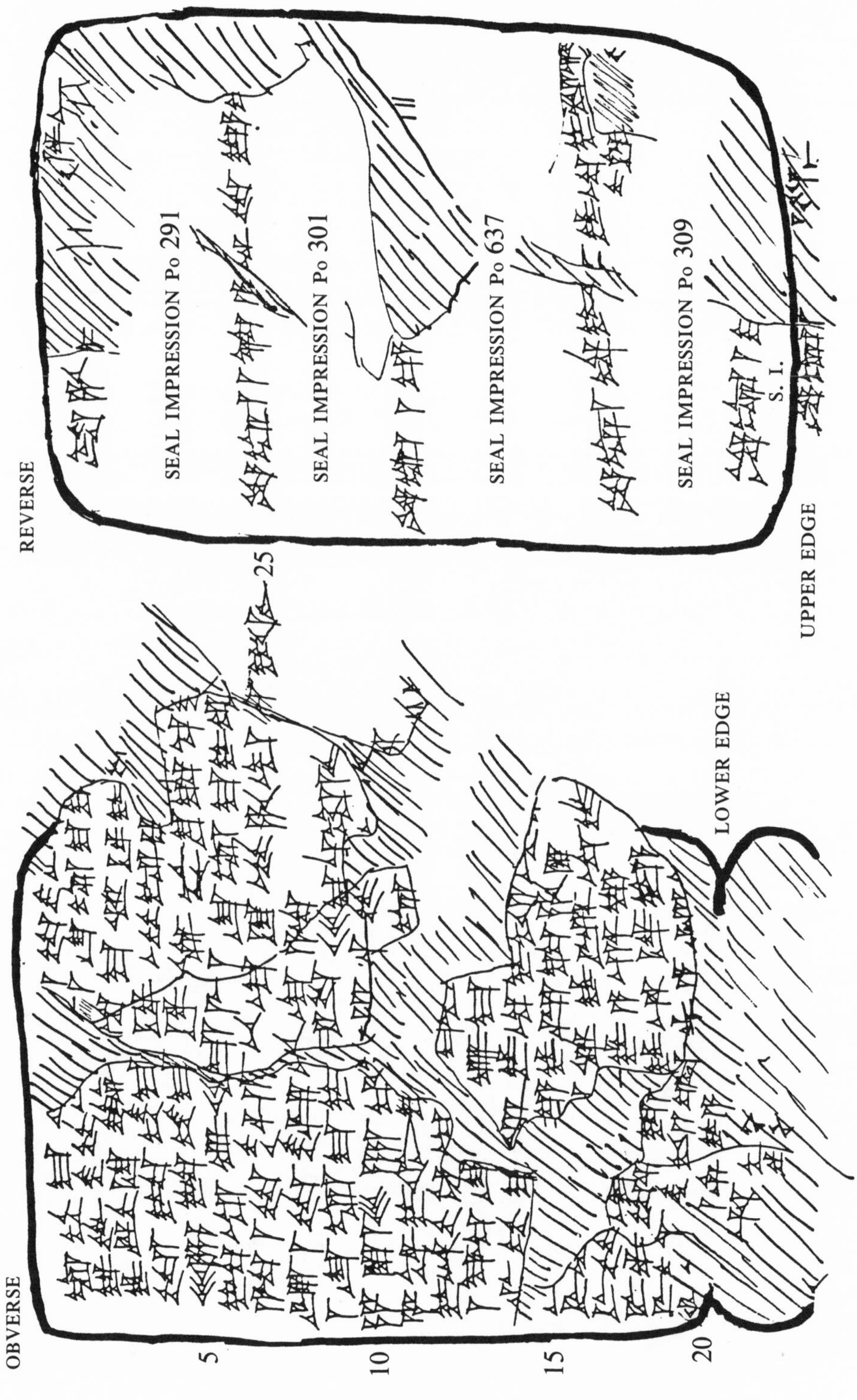
OBVERSE
LOWER EDGE
REVERSE
SEAL IMPRESSION Po 291
SEAL IMPRESSION Po 301
SEAL IMPRESSION Po 637
SEAL IMPRESSION Po 309
S. I.
UPPER EDGE

715

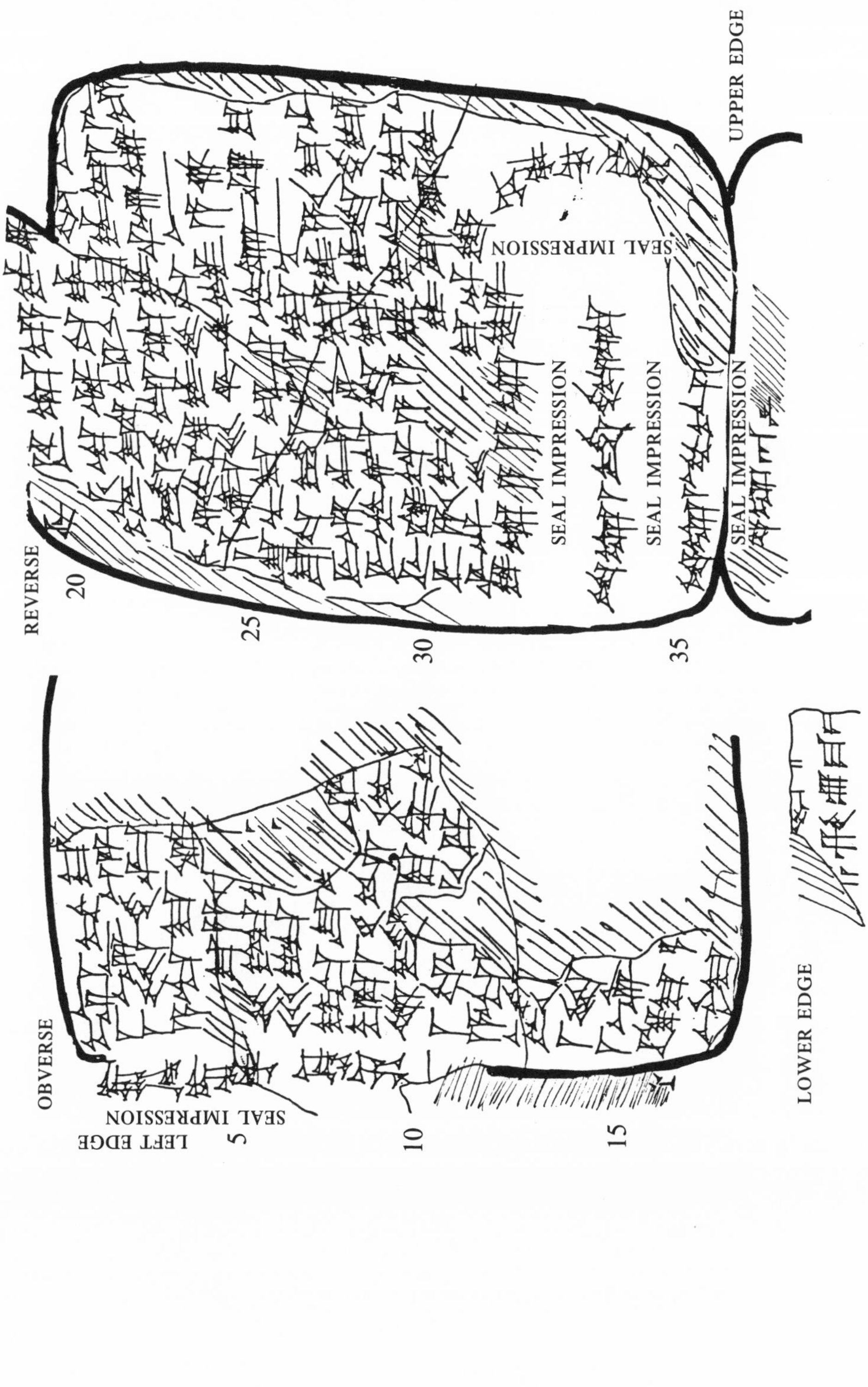
OBVERSE
LEFT EDGE
SEAL IMPRESSION
5
10
15
LOWER EDGE
REVERSE
20
25
30
35
SEAL IMPRESSION
SEAL IMPRESSION
SEAL IMPRESSION
SEAL IMPRESSION
UPPER EDGE

716

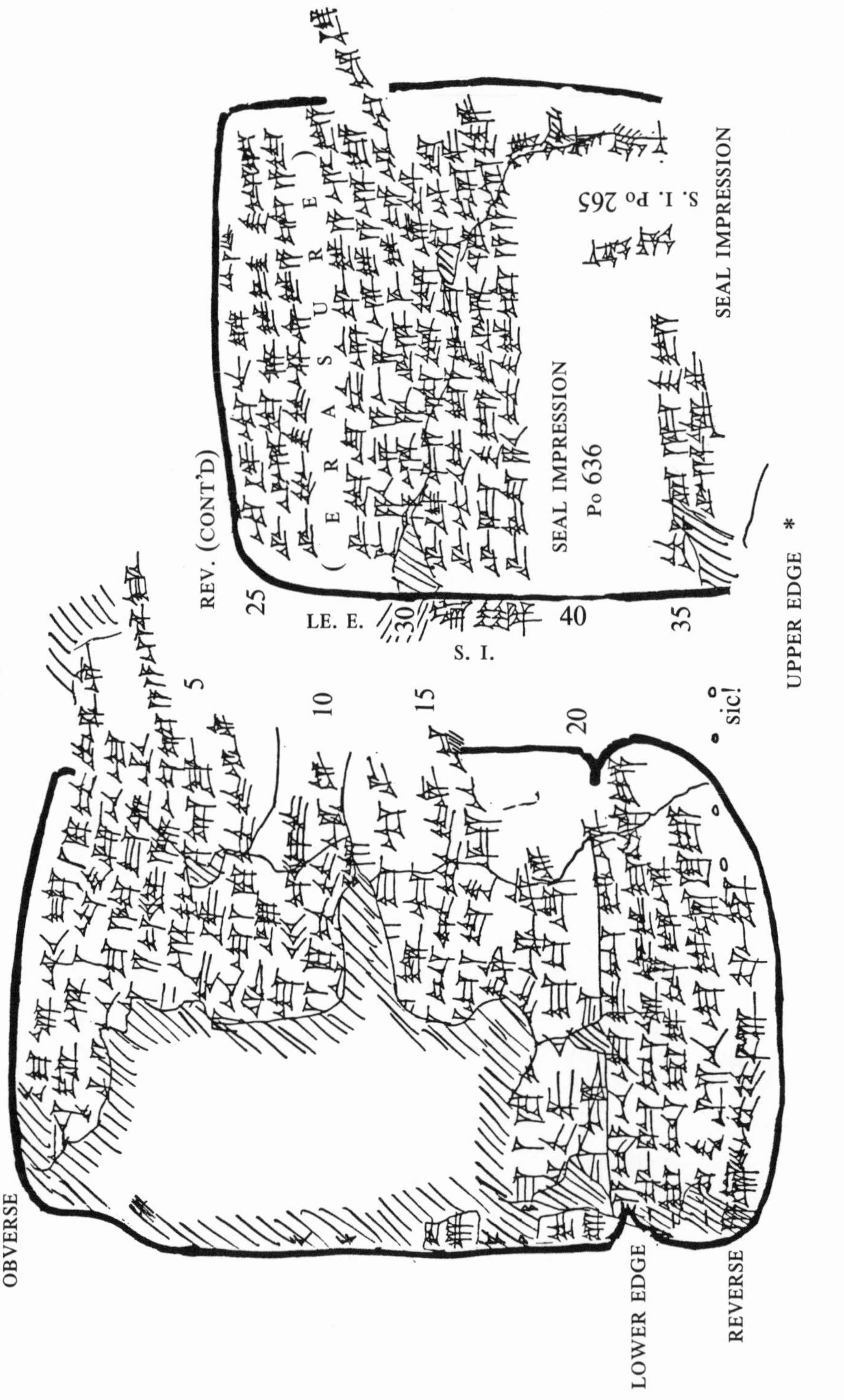

*Additional text; see *THNT*.

717

OBVERSE

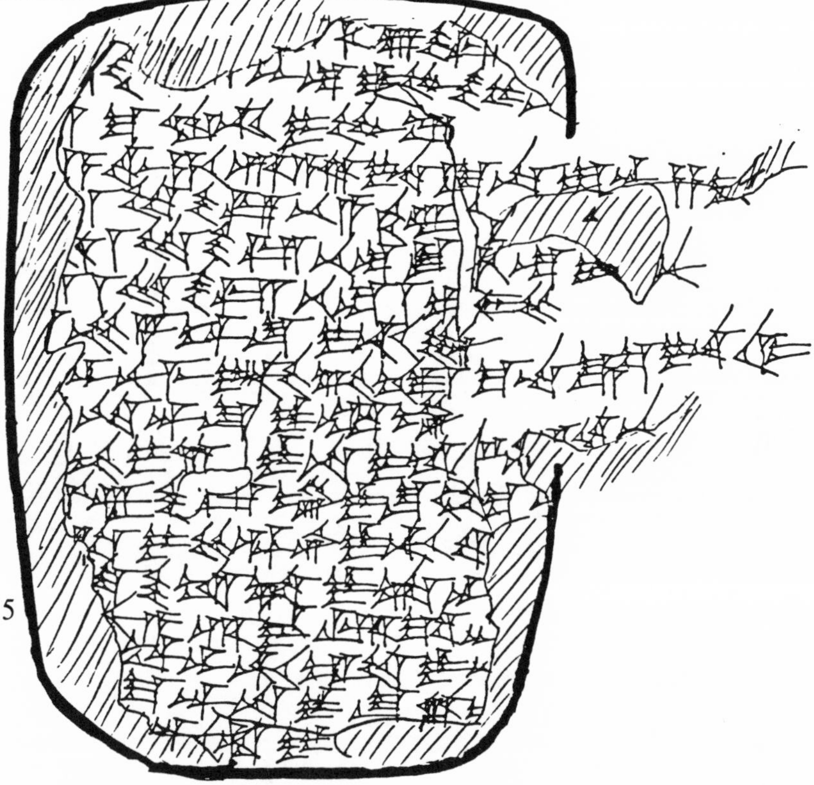

REVERSE

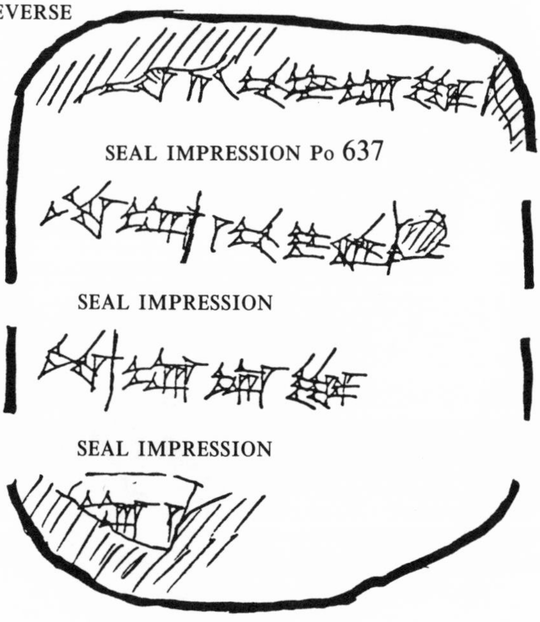

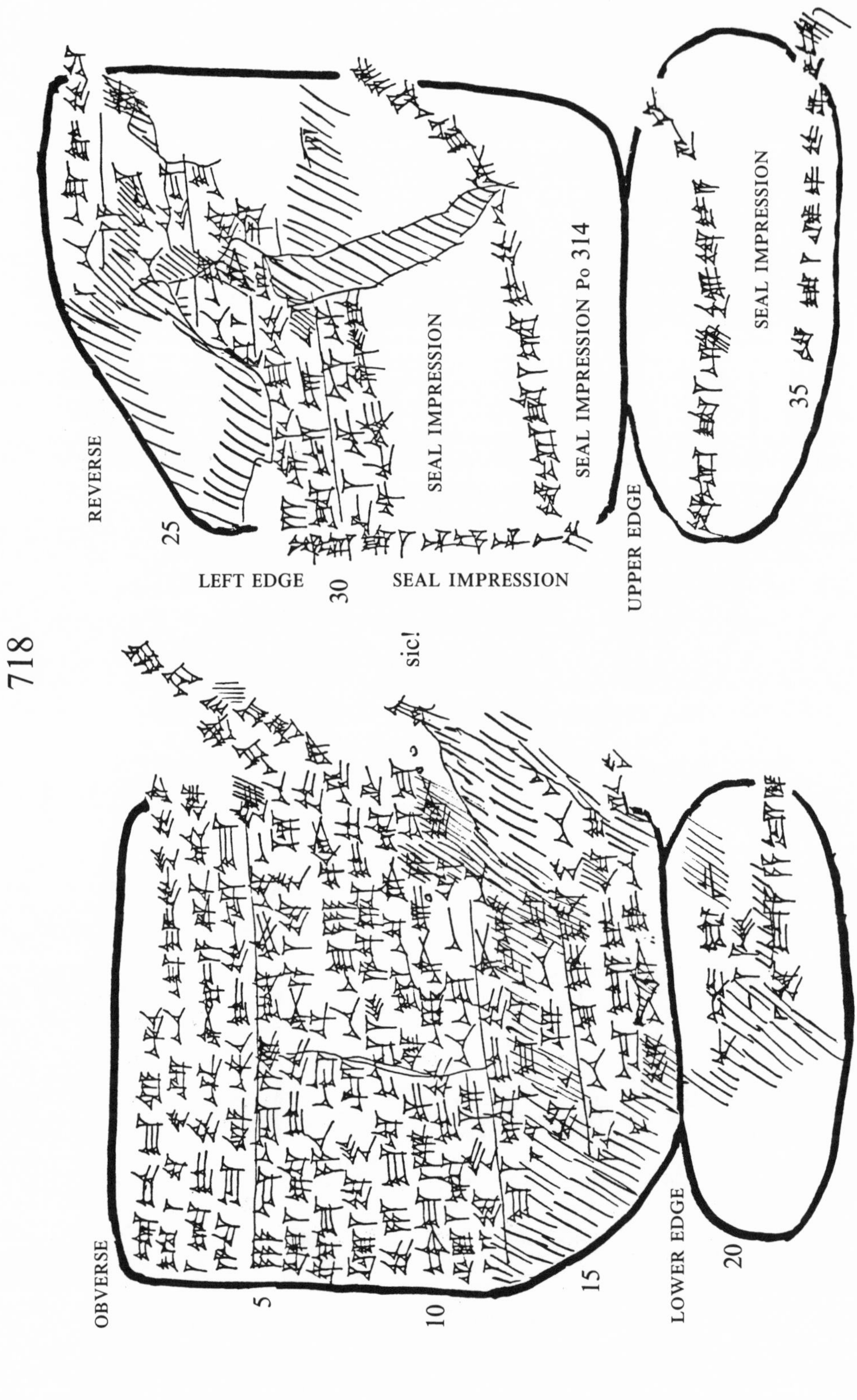
718
OBVERSE
5
10
15
LOWER EDGE
20
sic!
REVERSE
25
LEFT EDGE
30
SEAL IMPRESSION
SEAL IMPRESSION
SEAL IMPRESSION Po 314
UPPER EDGE
SEAL IMPRESSION
35

719

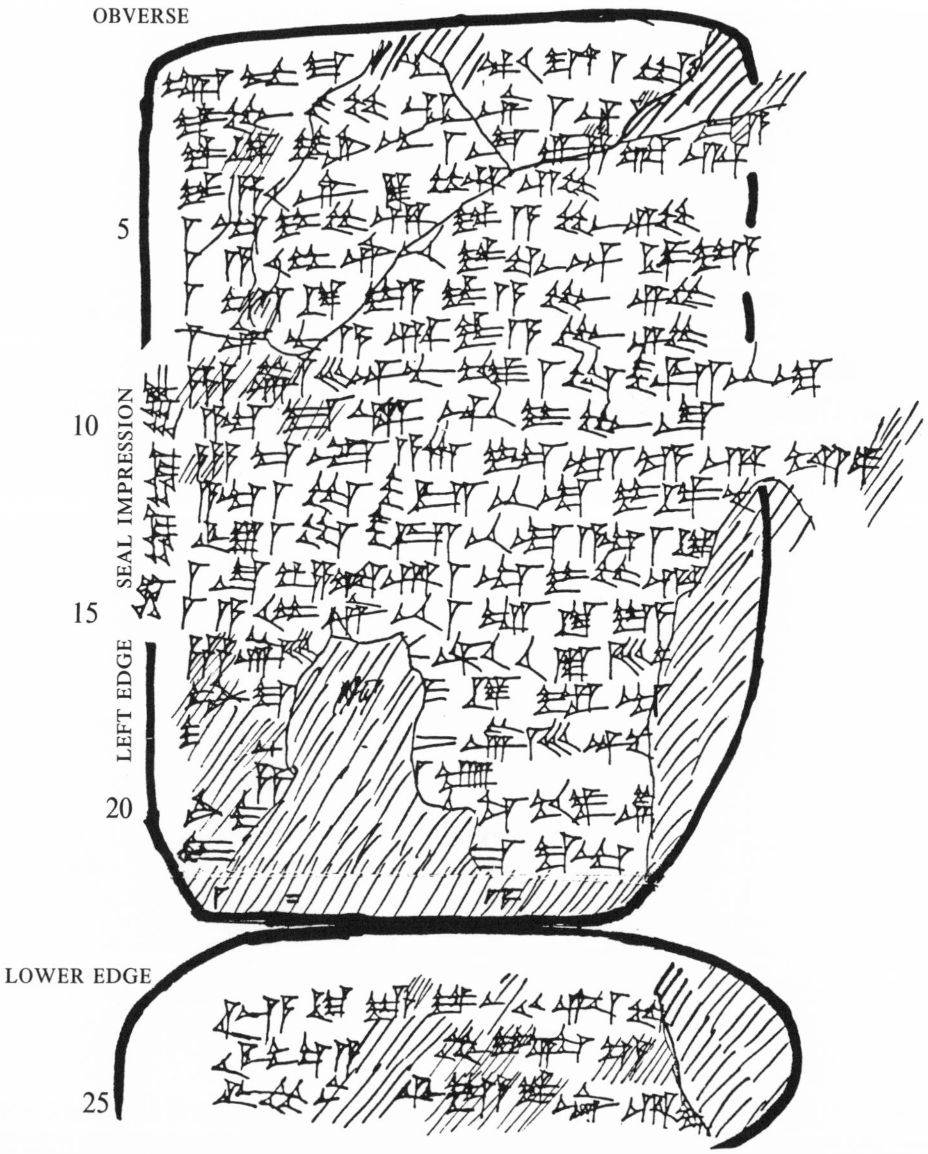

719

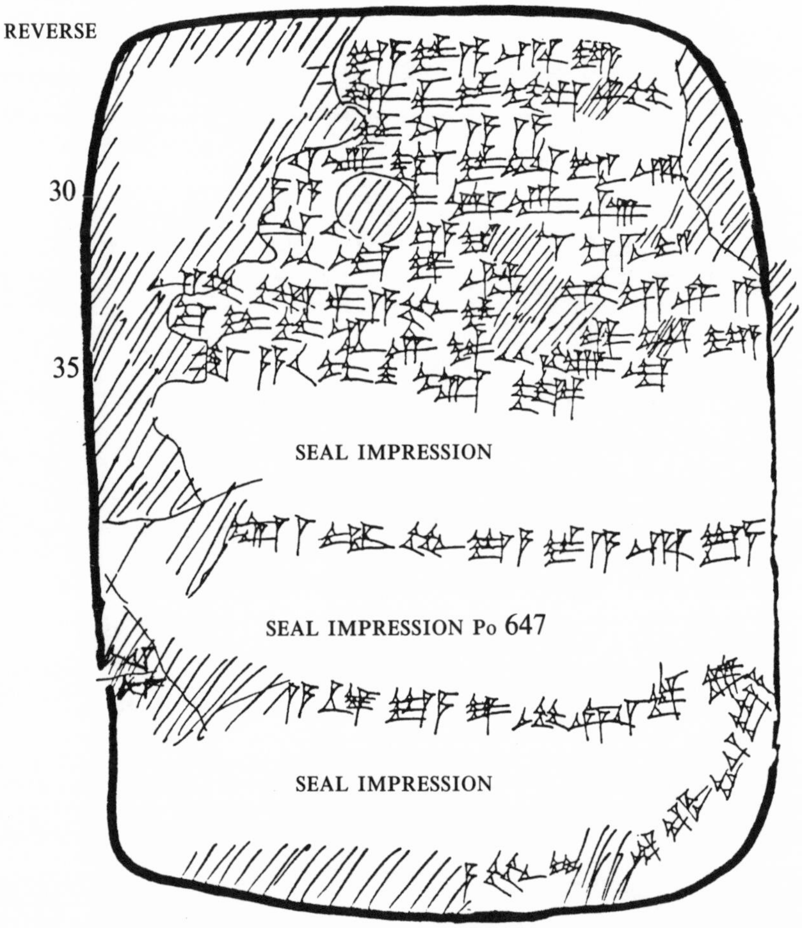
REVERSE
30
35
SEAL IMPRESSION
SEAL IMPRESSION Po 647
SEAL IMPRESSION

720

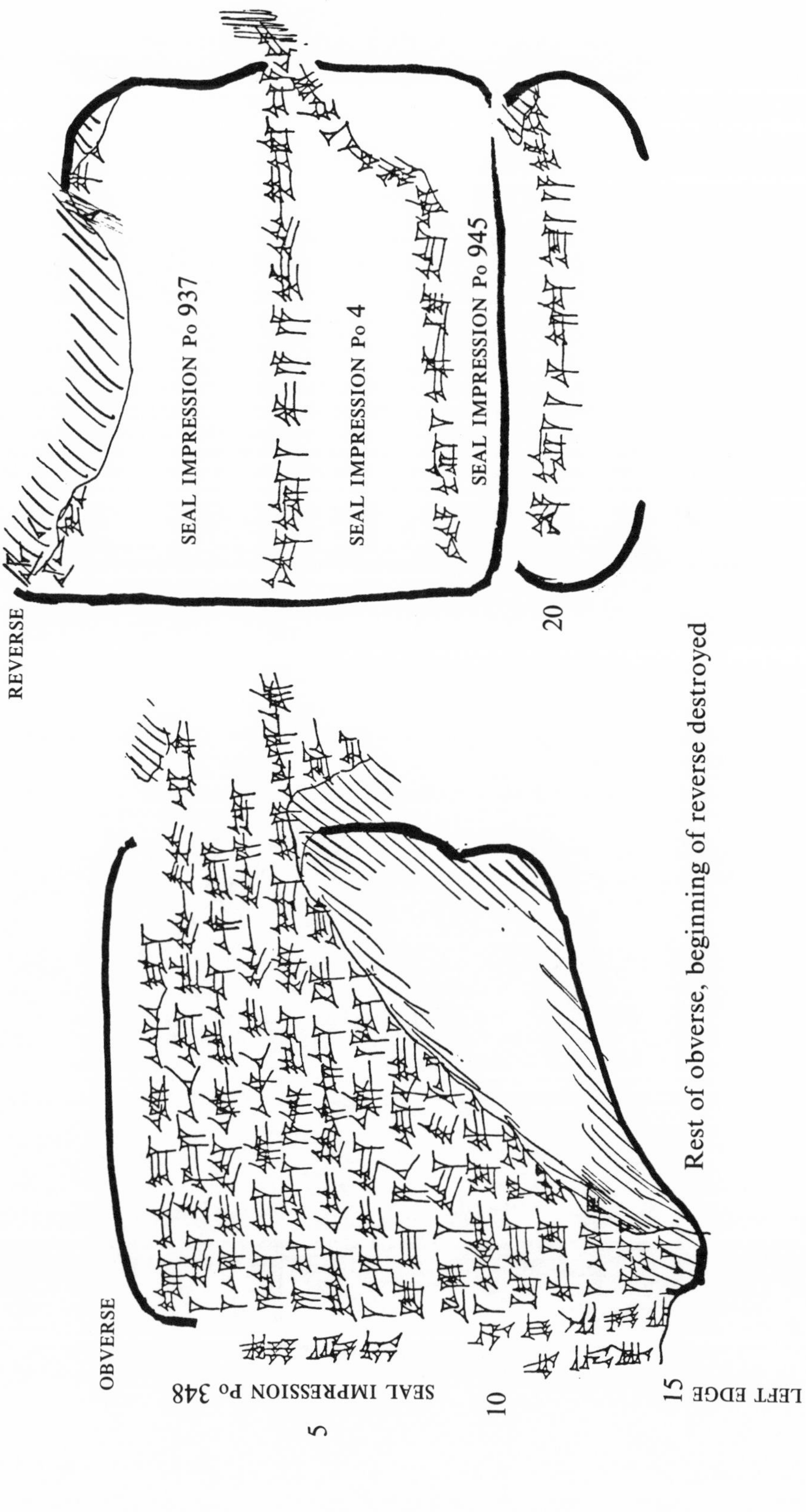

Rest of obverse, beginning of reverse destroyed

721

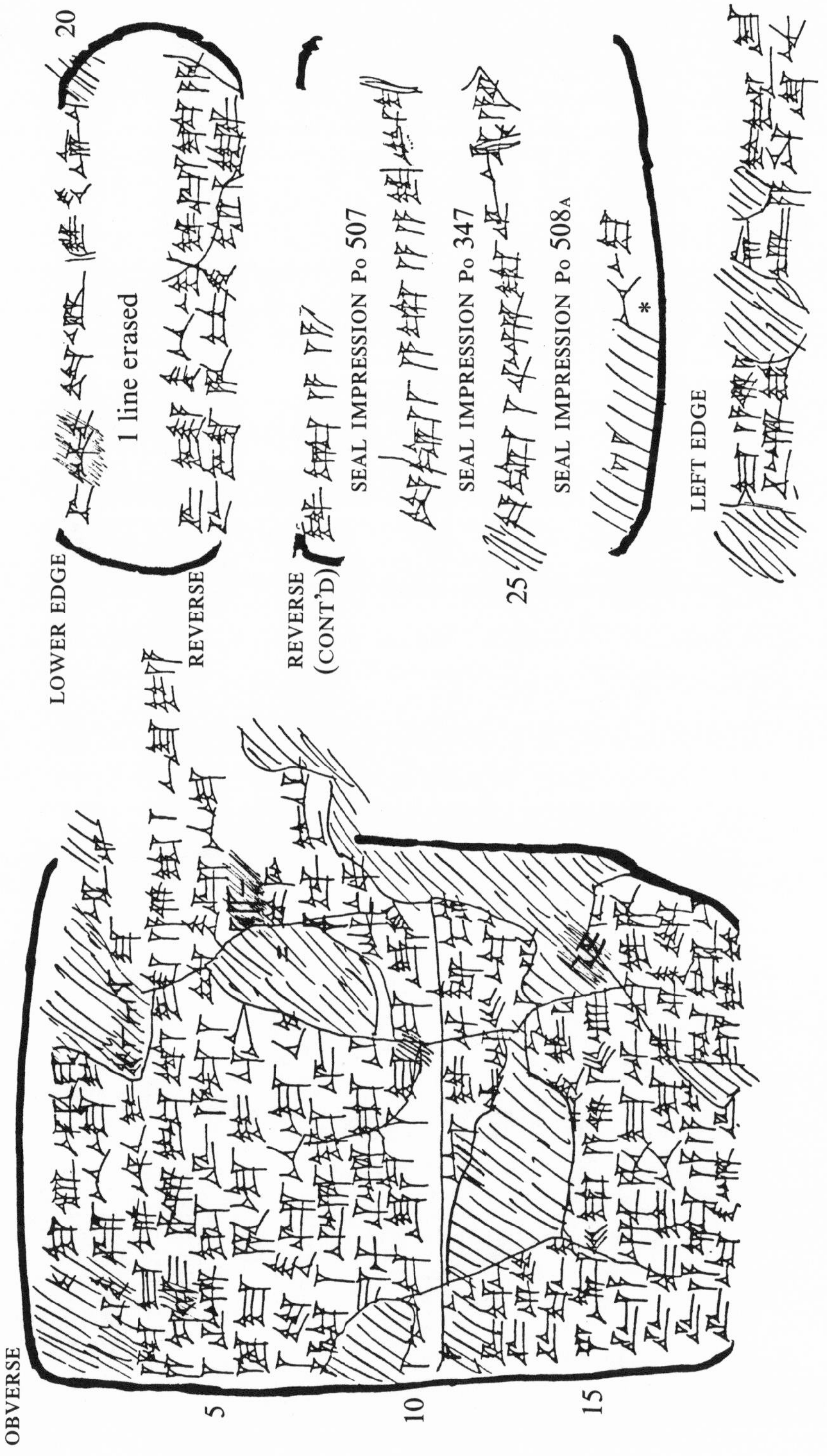

*Additional text; see *THNT*.

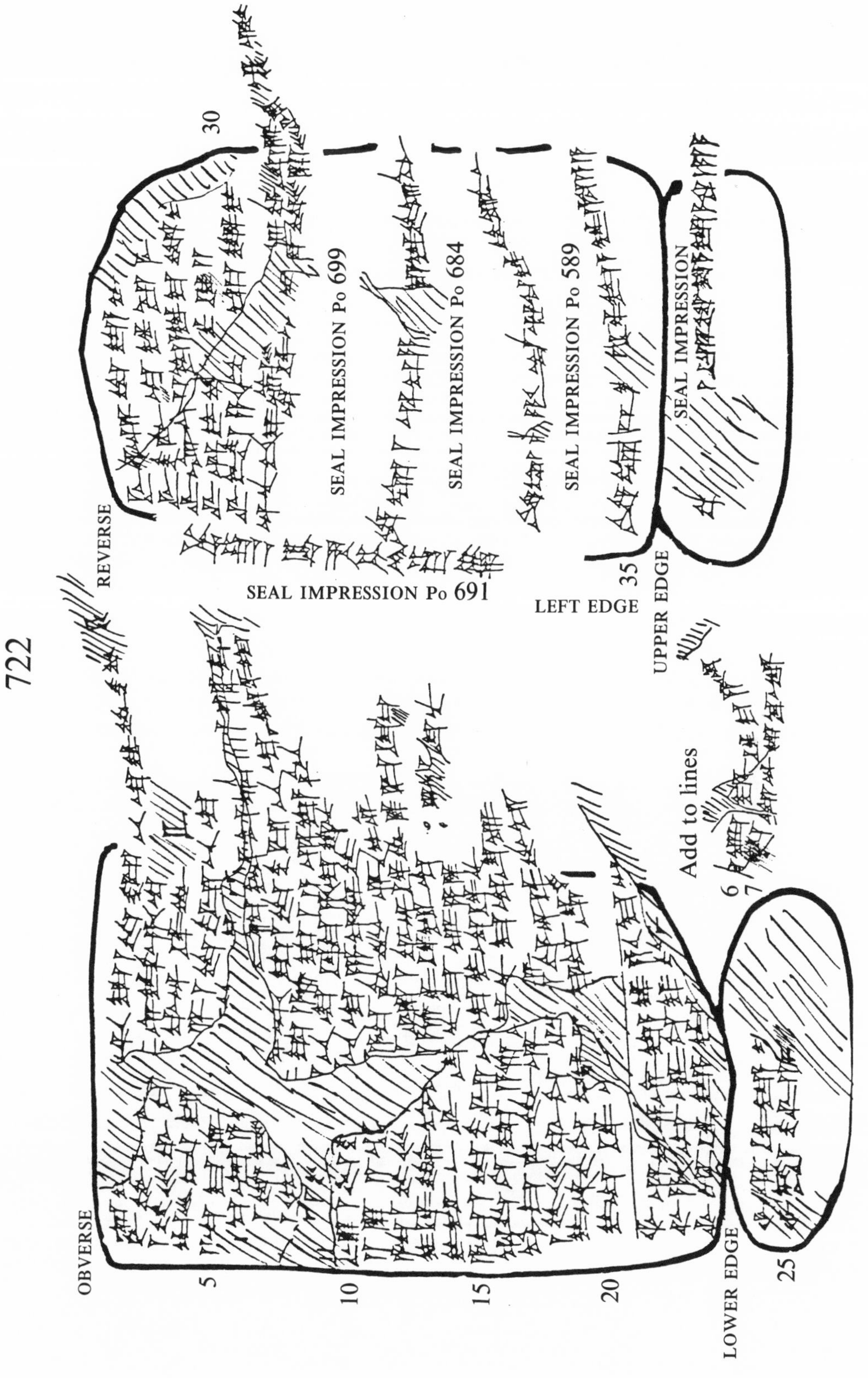
722
OBVERSE
LOWER EDGE
REVERSE
SEAL IMPRESSION Po 691
SEAL IMPRESSION Po 699
SEAL IMPRESSION Po 684
SEAL IMPRESSION Po 589
SEAL IMPRESSION
LEFT EDGE
UPPER EDGE
Add to lines
6
7

723

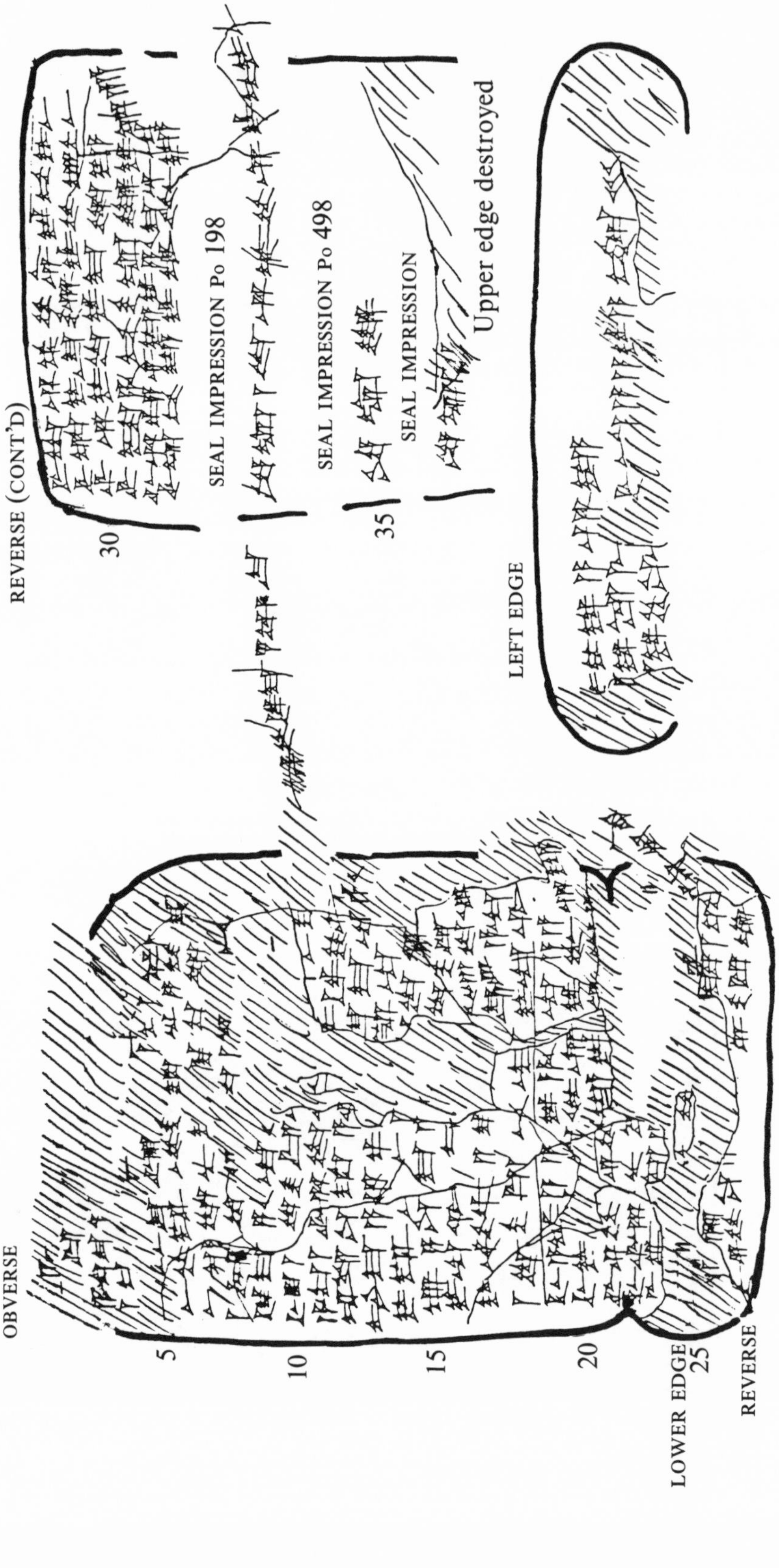
OBVERSE
5
10
15
20
LOWER EDGE
25
REVERSE
REVERSE (CONT'D)
30
SEAL IMPRESSION Po 198
SEAL IMPRESSION Po 498
35
SEAL IMPRESSION
Upper edge destroyed
LEFT EDGE

724

OBVERSE

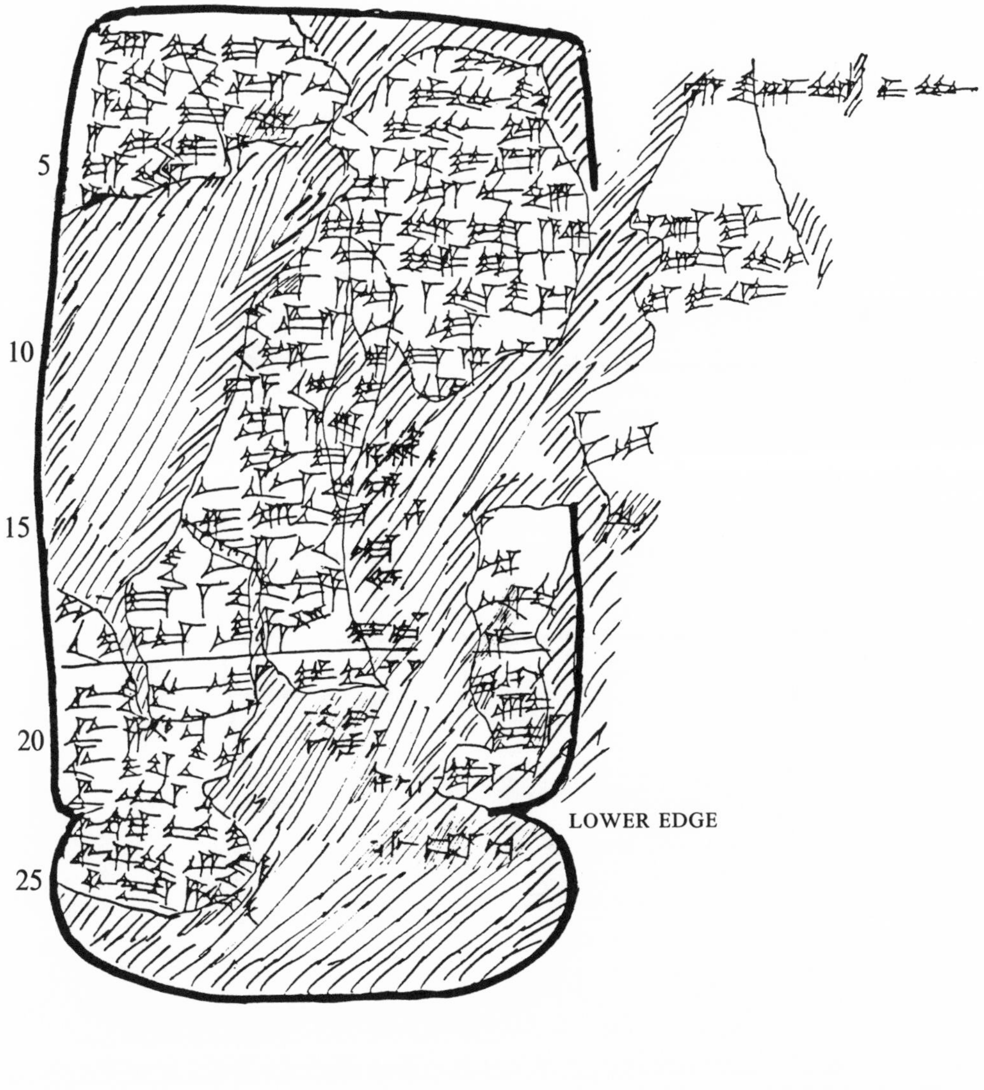

724

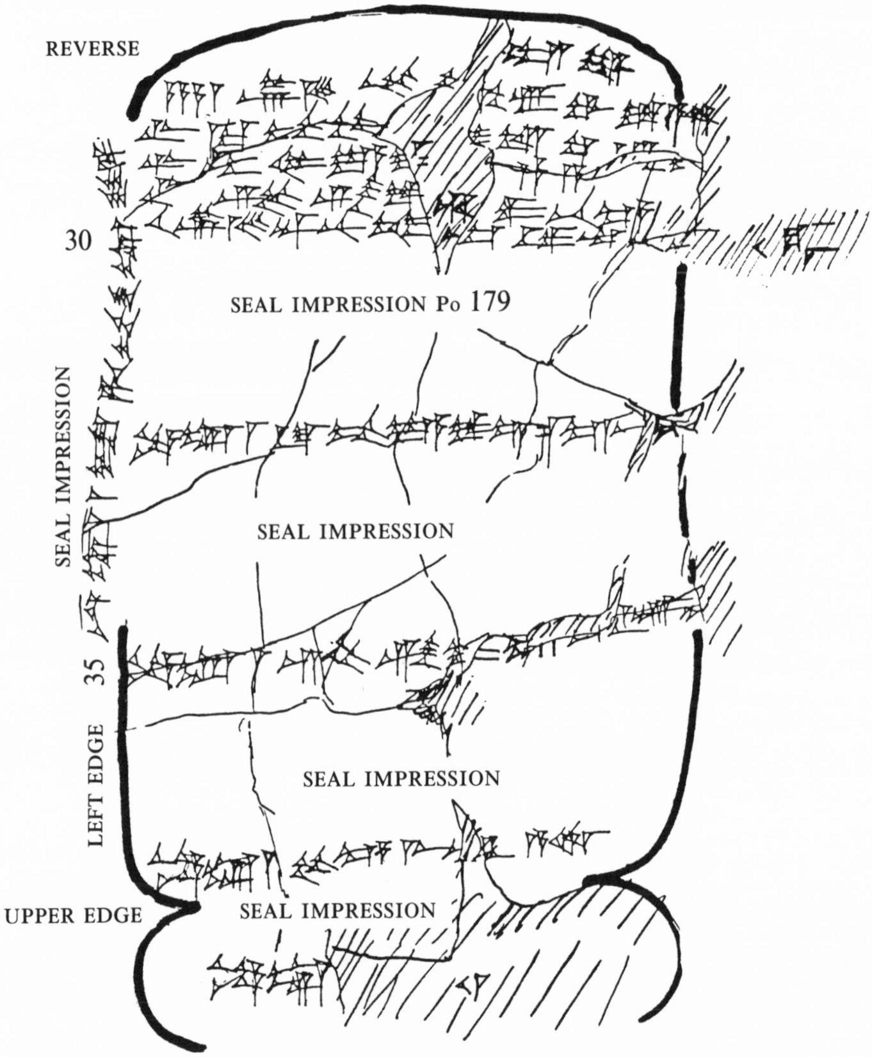
REVERSE
30
SEAL IMPRESSION Po 179
SEAL IMPRESSION
SEAL IMPRESSION
35
LEFT EDGE
SEAL IMPRESSION
UPPER EDGE
SEAL IMPRESSION

725

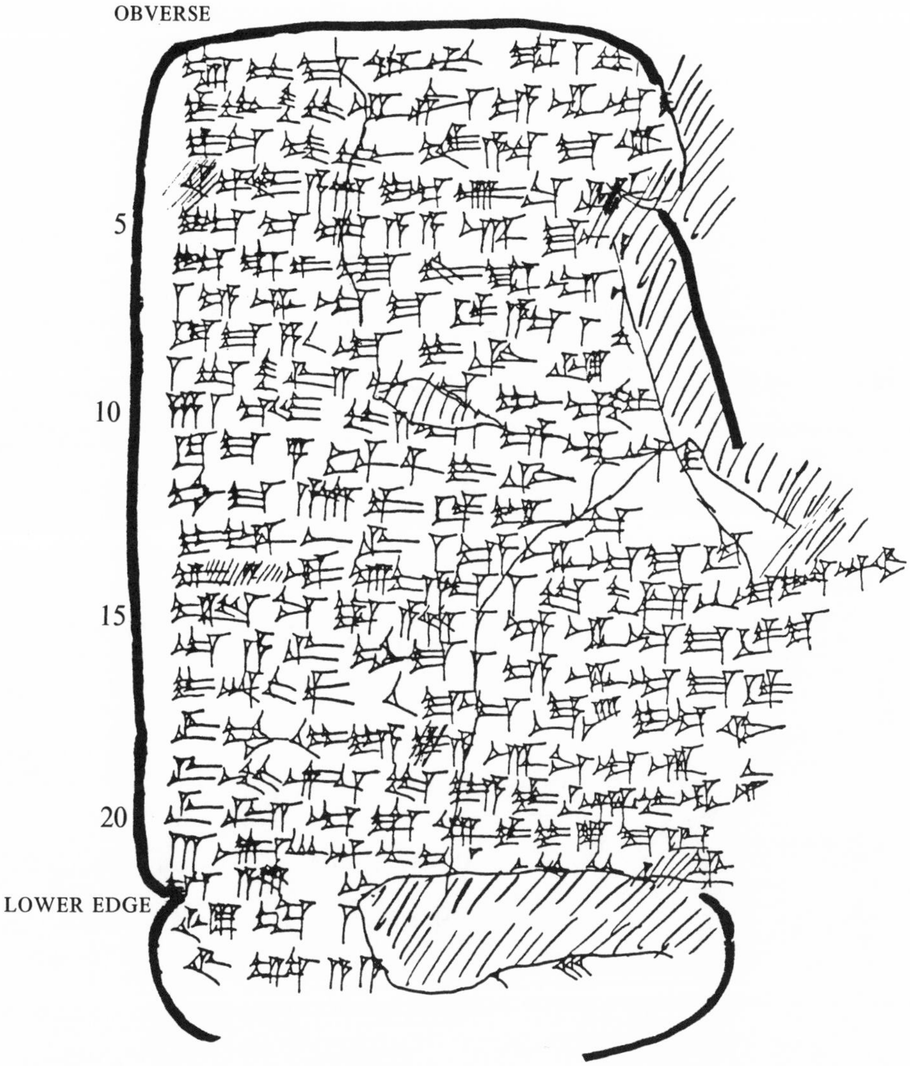

725

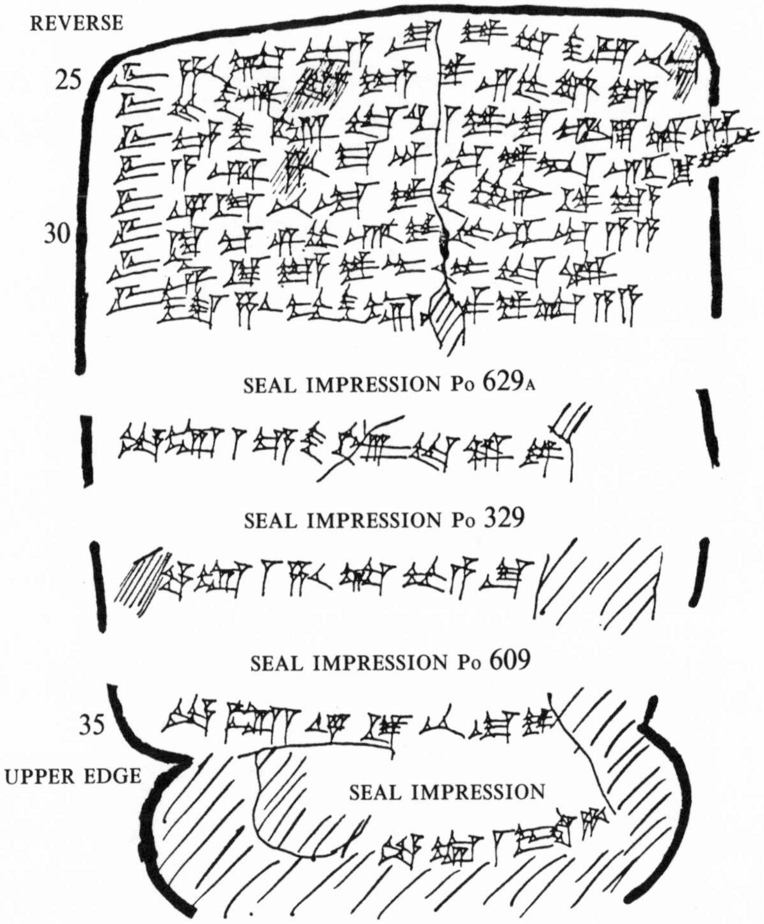
REVERSE
25
30
SEAL IMPRESSION Po 629A
SEAL IMPRESSION Po 329
SEAL IMPRESSION Po 609
35
UPPER EDGE
SEAL IMPRESSION

726

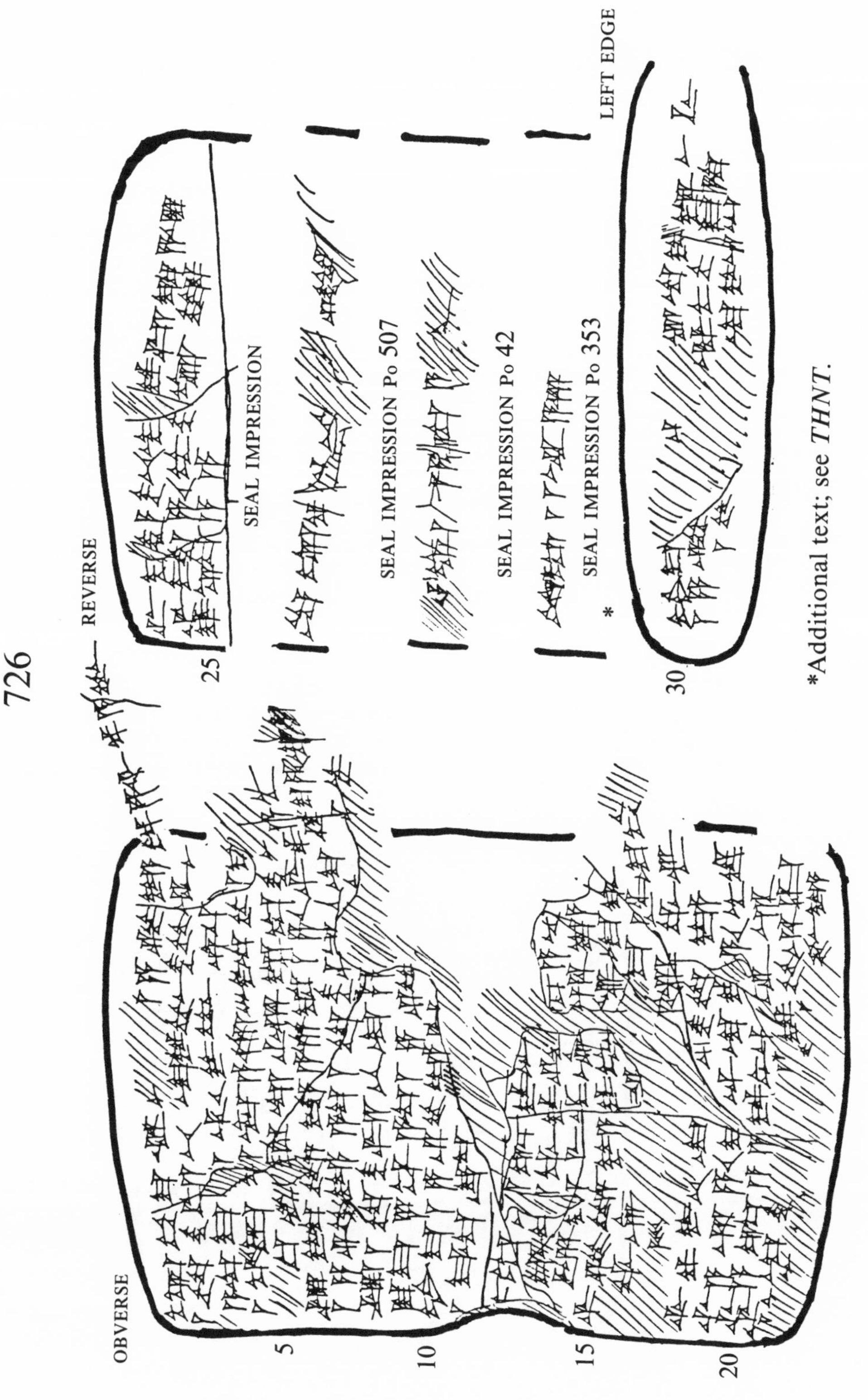

*Additional text; see *THNT*.

727

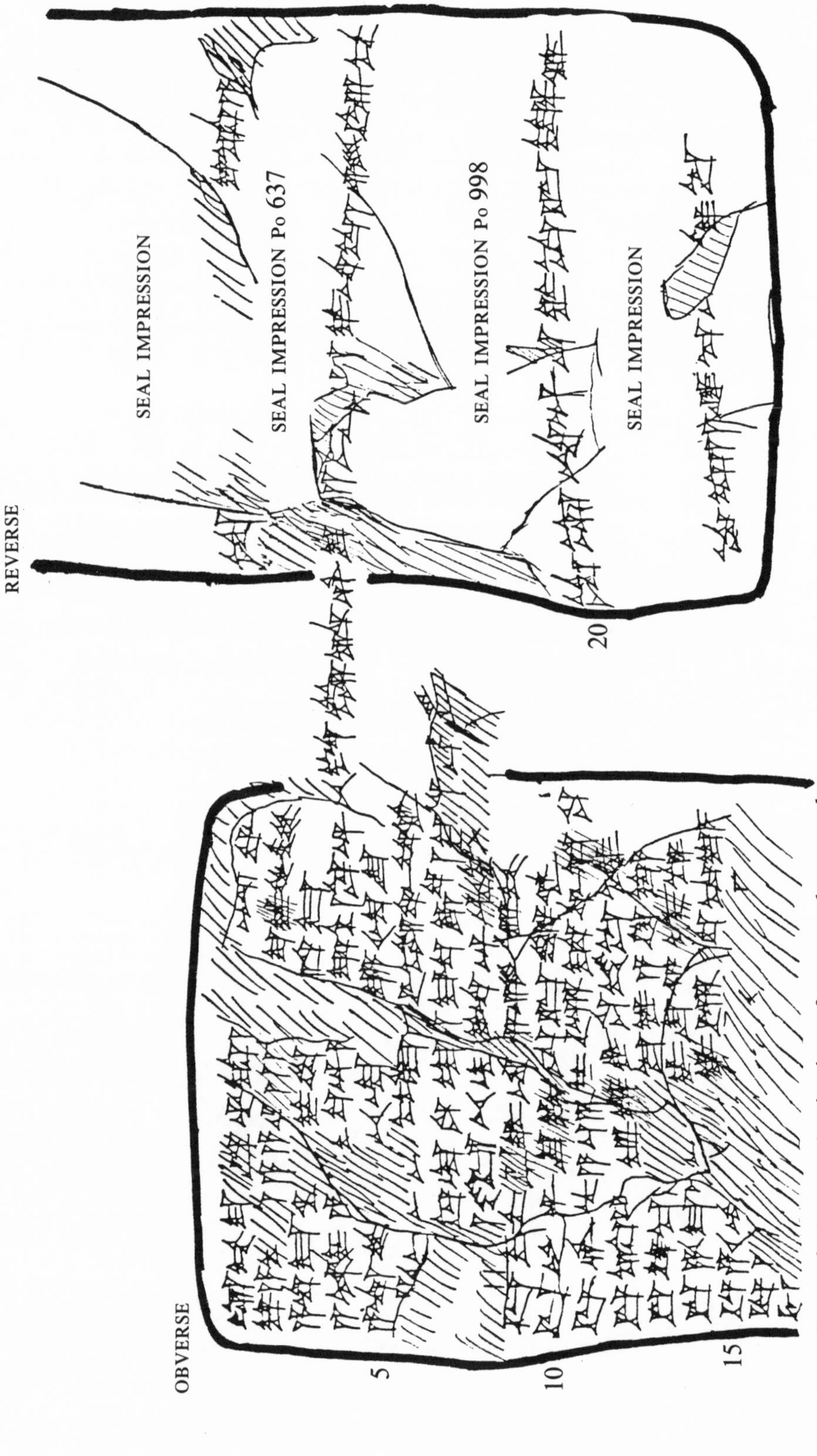

Rest of obverse, beginning of reverse destroyed

728

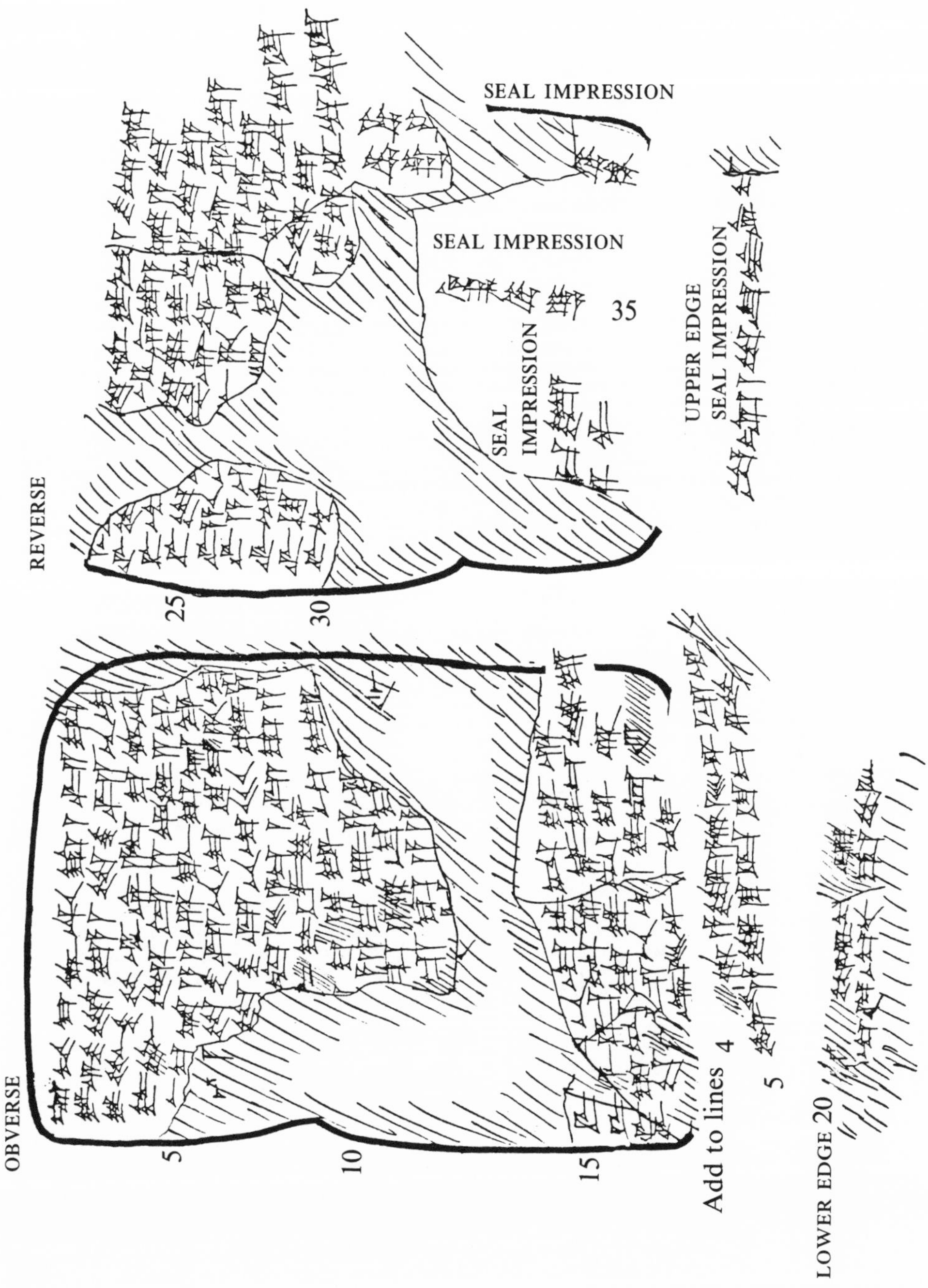
OBVERSE
REVERSE
SEAL IMPRESSION
SEAL IMPRESSION
SEAL IMPRESSION
UPPER EDGE
SEAL IMPRESSION
Add to lines 4
5
LOWER EDGE 20

729

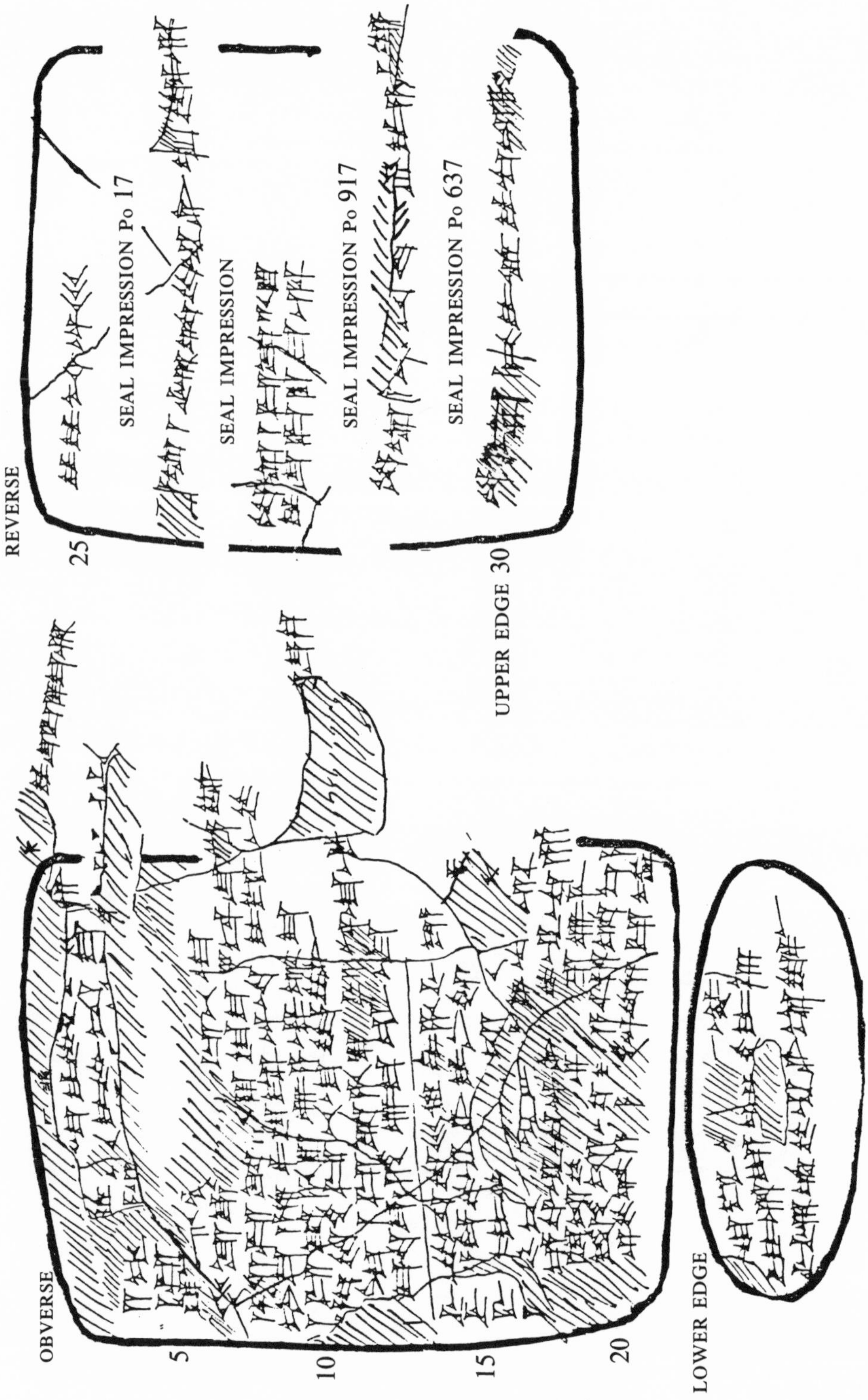
OBVERSE
LOWER EDGE
REVERSE
SEAL IMPRESSION Po 17
SEAL IMPRESSION
SEAL IMPRESSION Po 917
SEAL IMPRESSION Po 637
UPPER EDGE

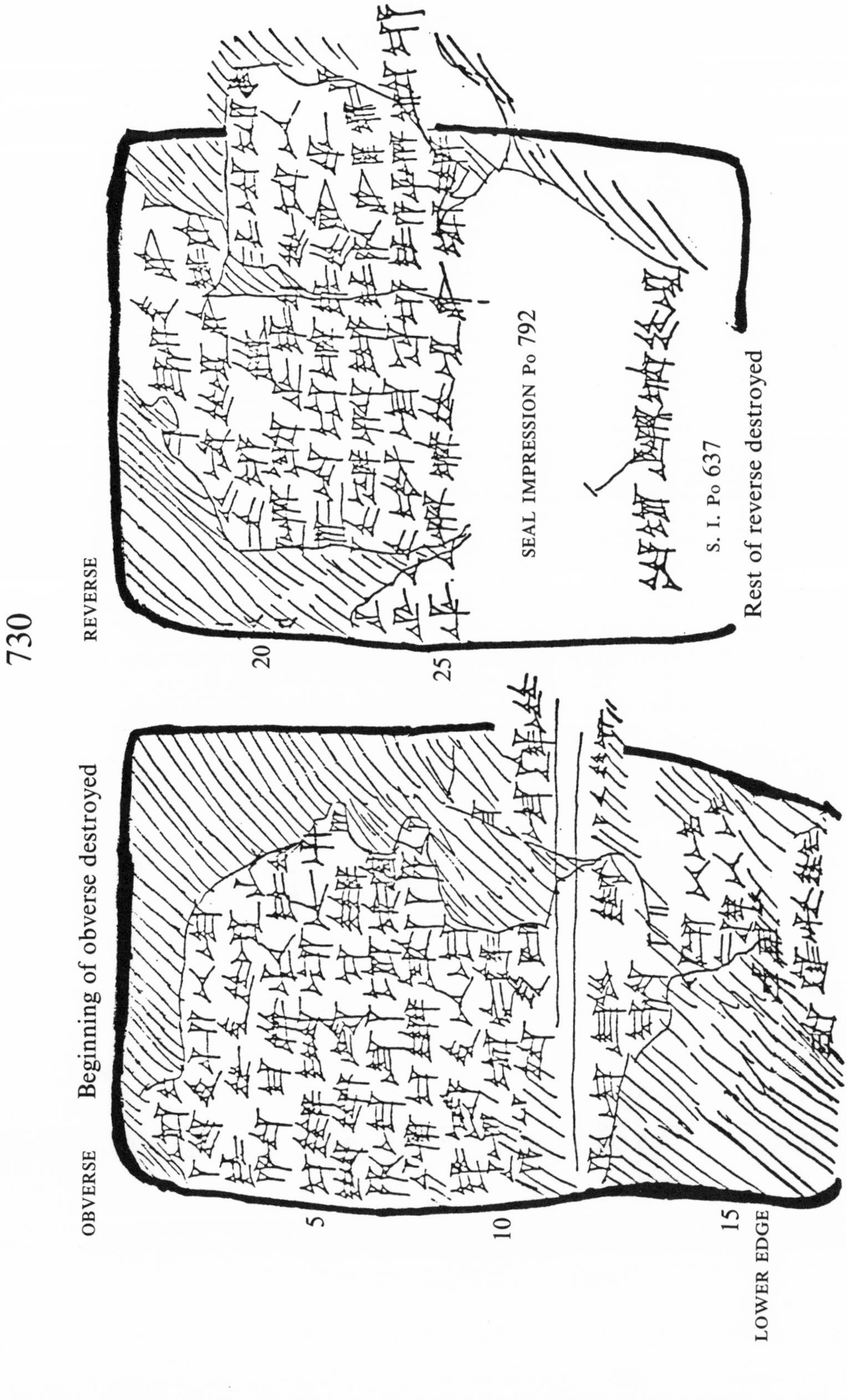
730
OBVERSE
Beginning of obverse destroyed
LOWER EDGE
REVERSE
SEAL IMPRESSION Po 792
S. I. Po 637
Rest of reverse destroyed

731

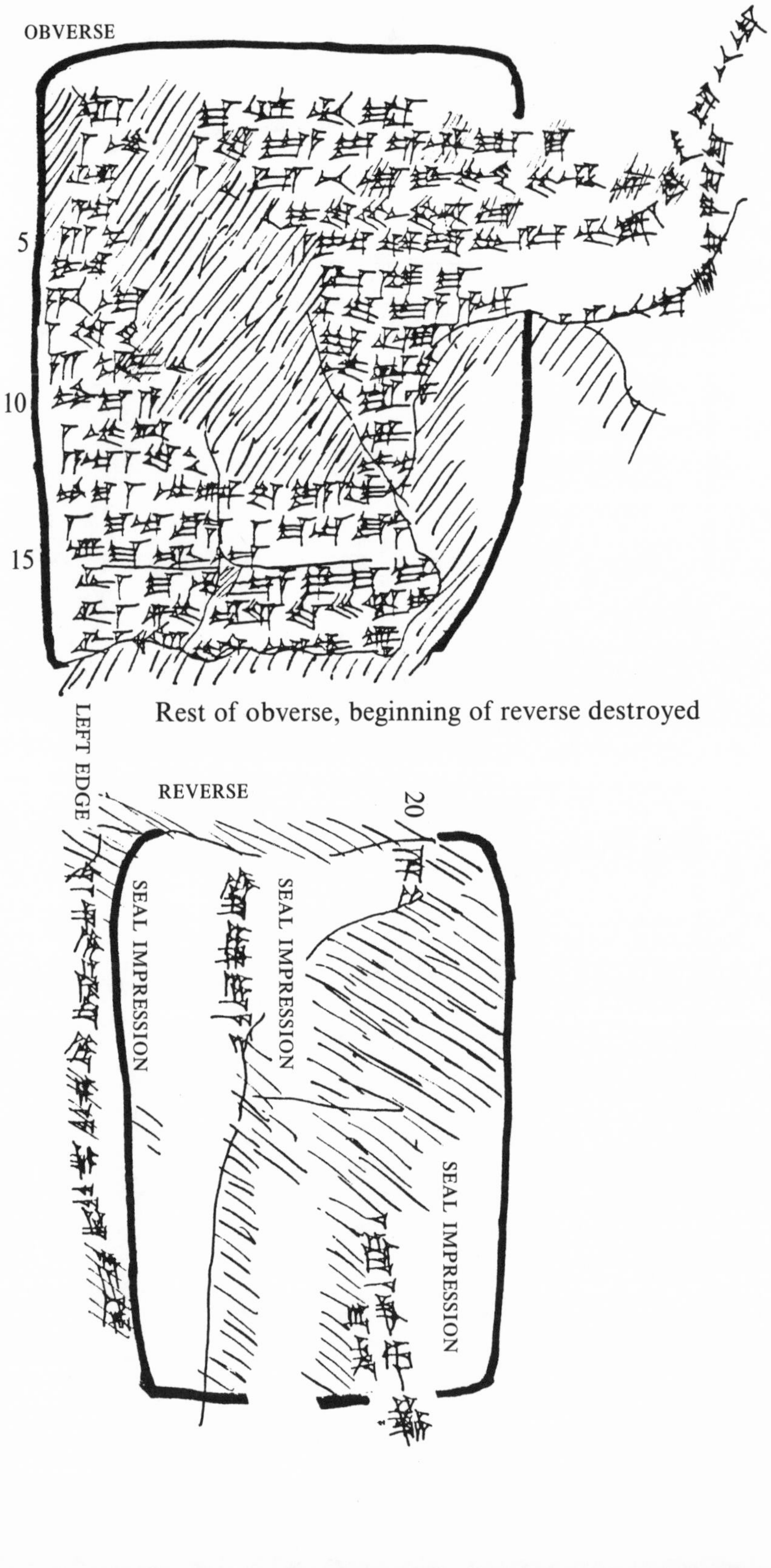
OBVERSE
Rest of obverse, beginning of reverse destroyed
LEFT EDGE
REVERSE
SEAL IMPRESSION
SEAL IMPRESSION
SEAL IMPRESSION

732

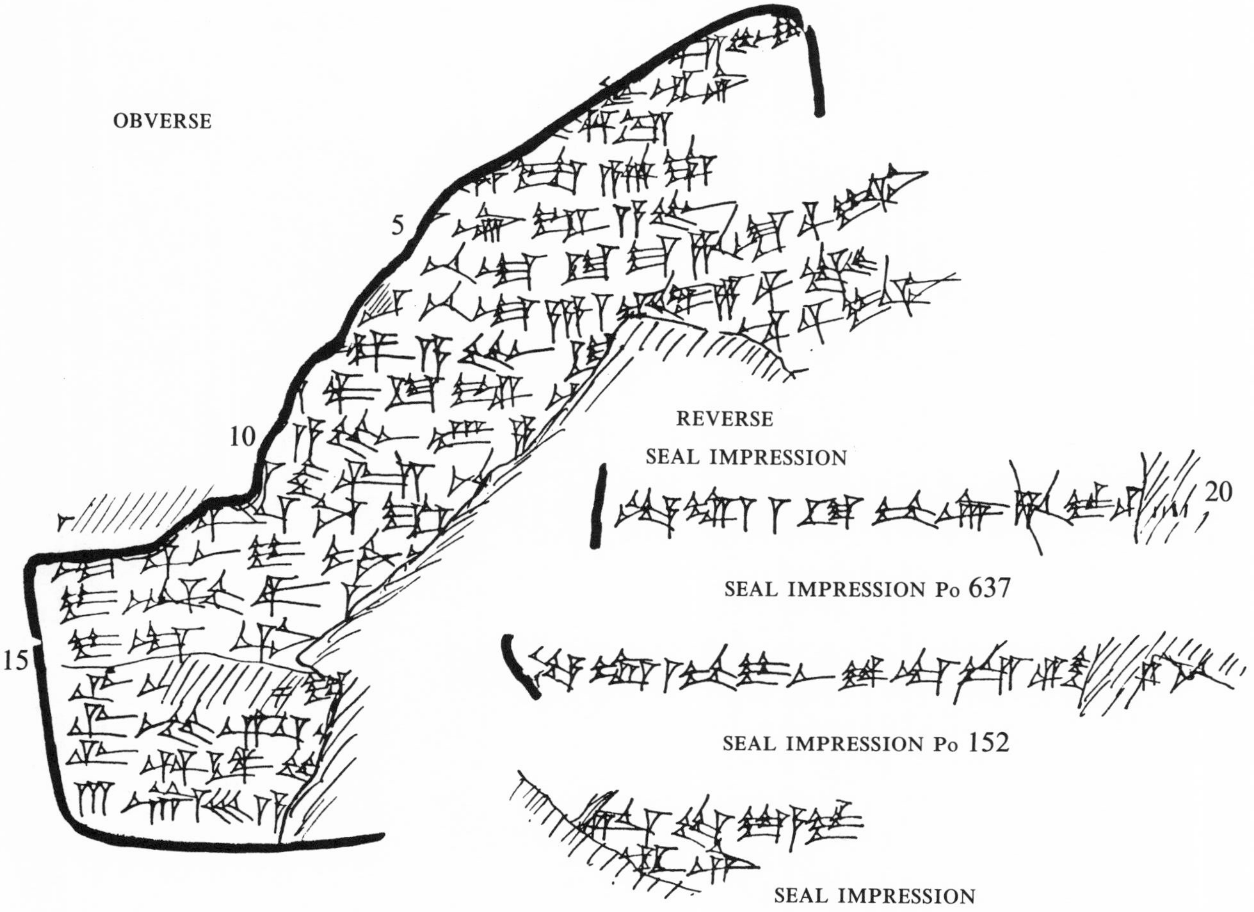

*Additional text; see *THNT*.

733

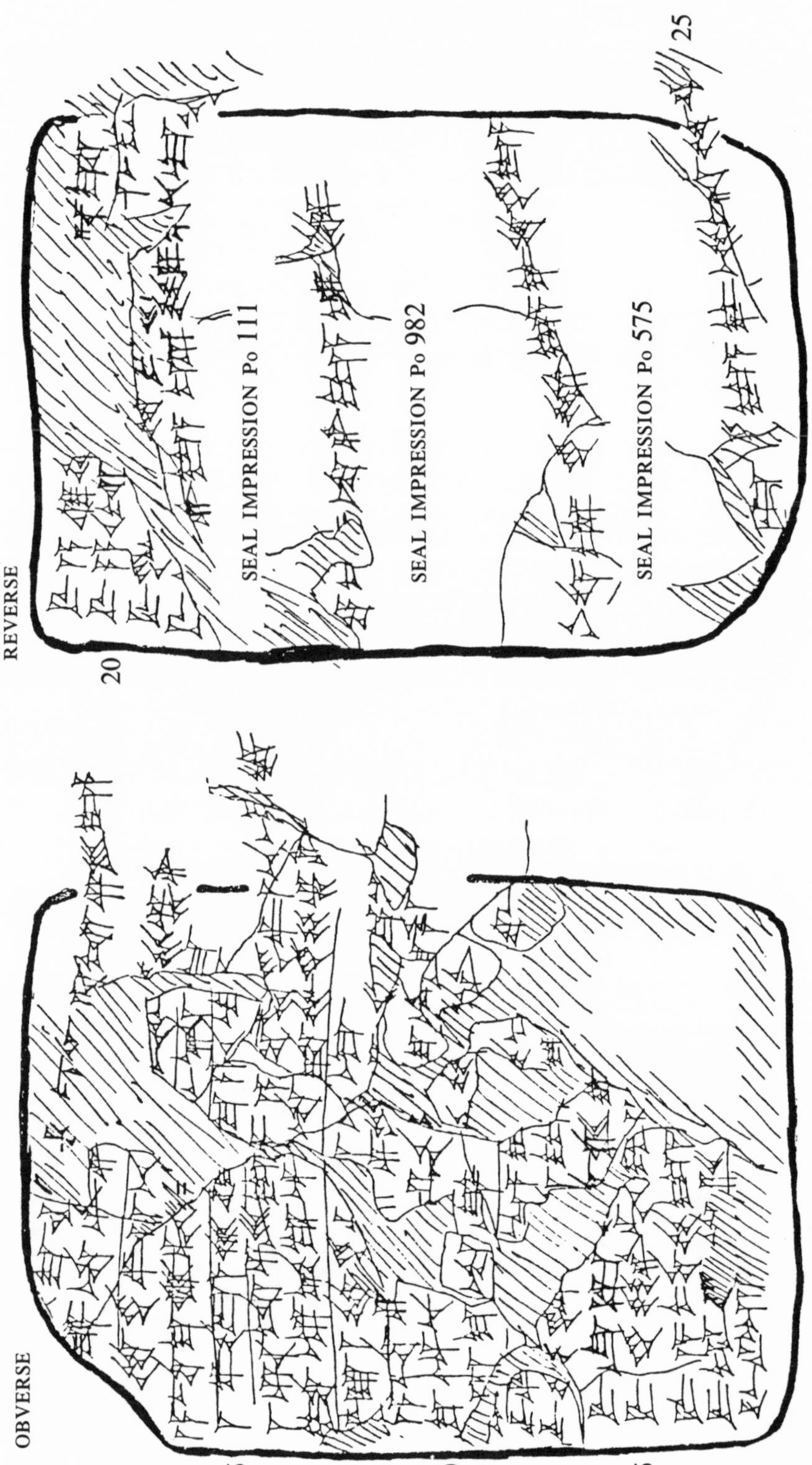
OBVERSE
REVERSE
SEAL IMPRESSION Po 111
SEAL IMPRESSION Po 982
SEAL IMPRESSION Po 575

734

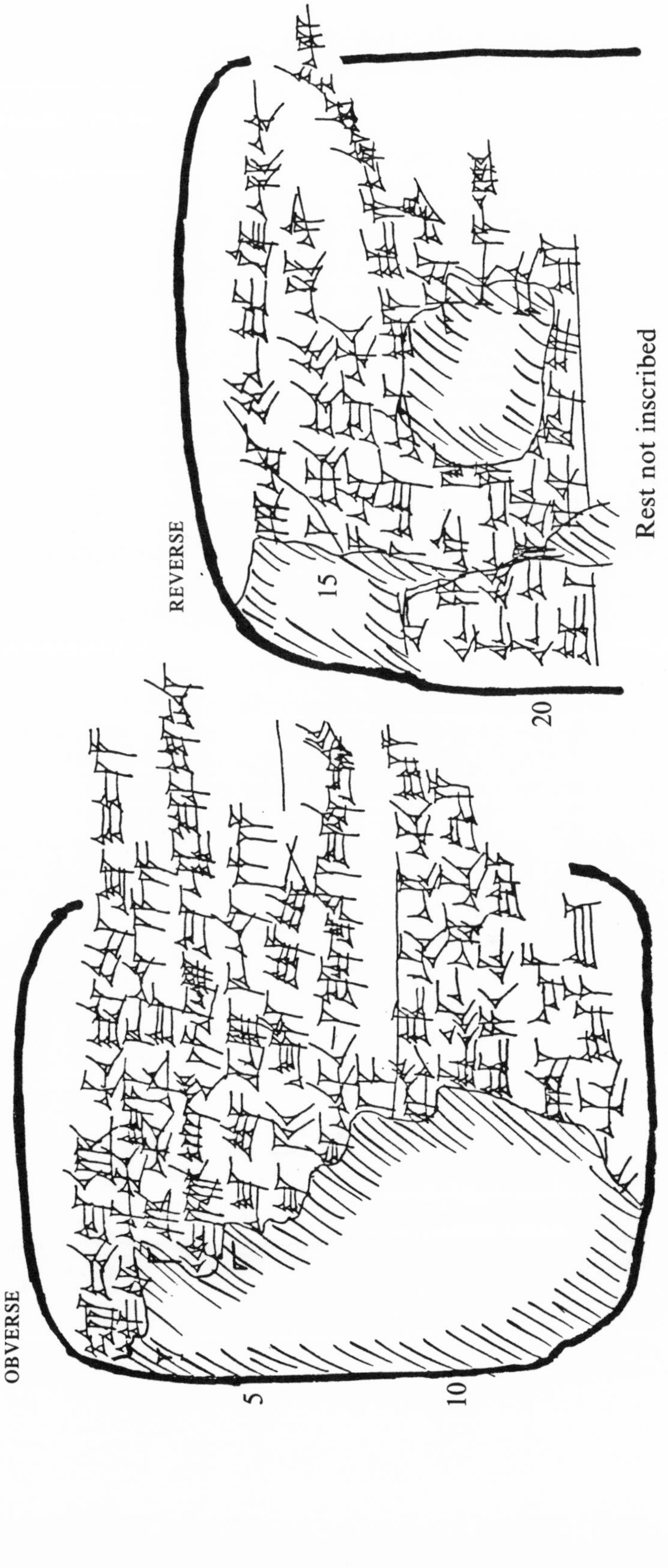

735

OBVERSE

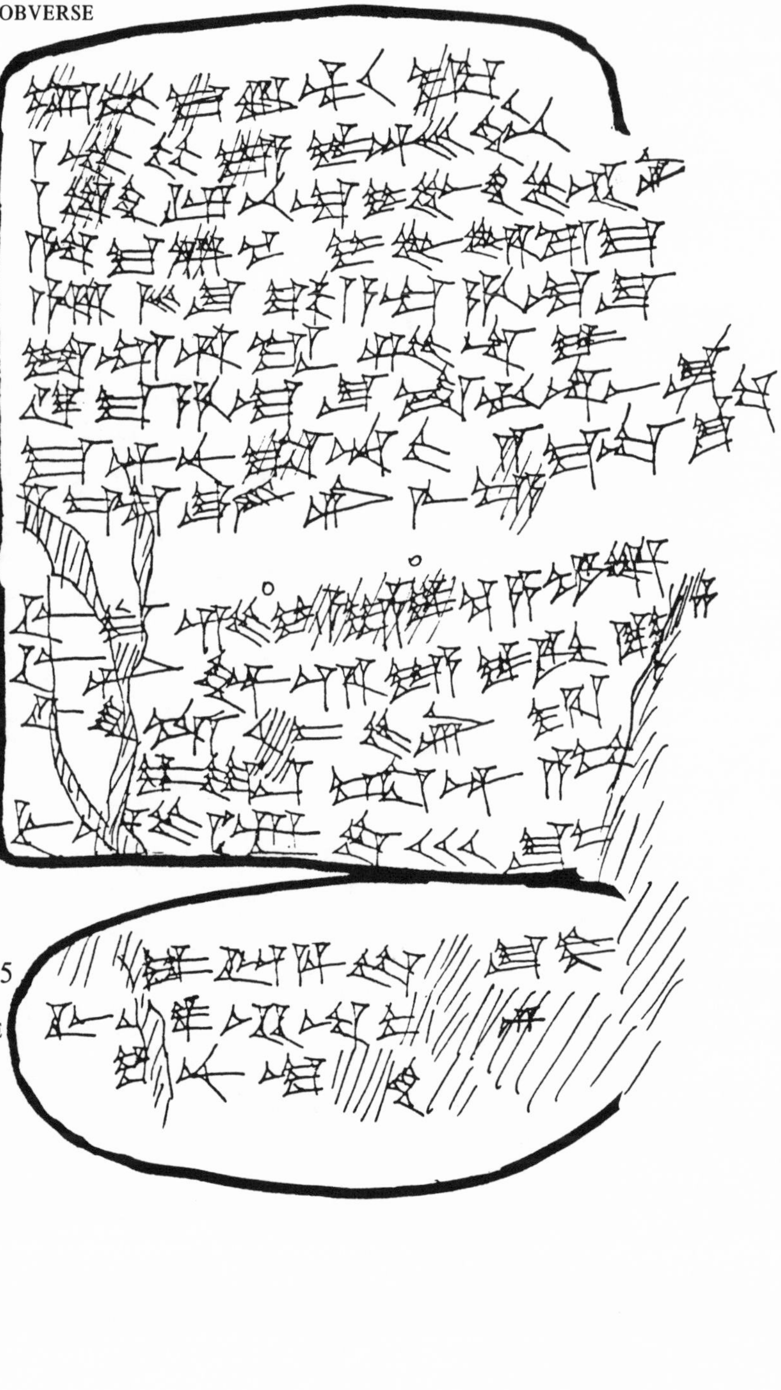

LOWER EDGE

735

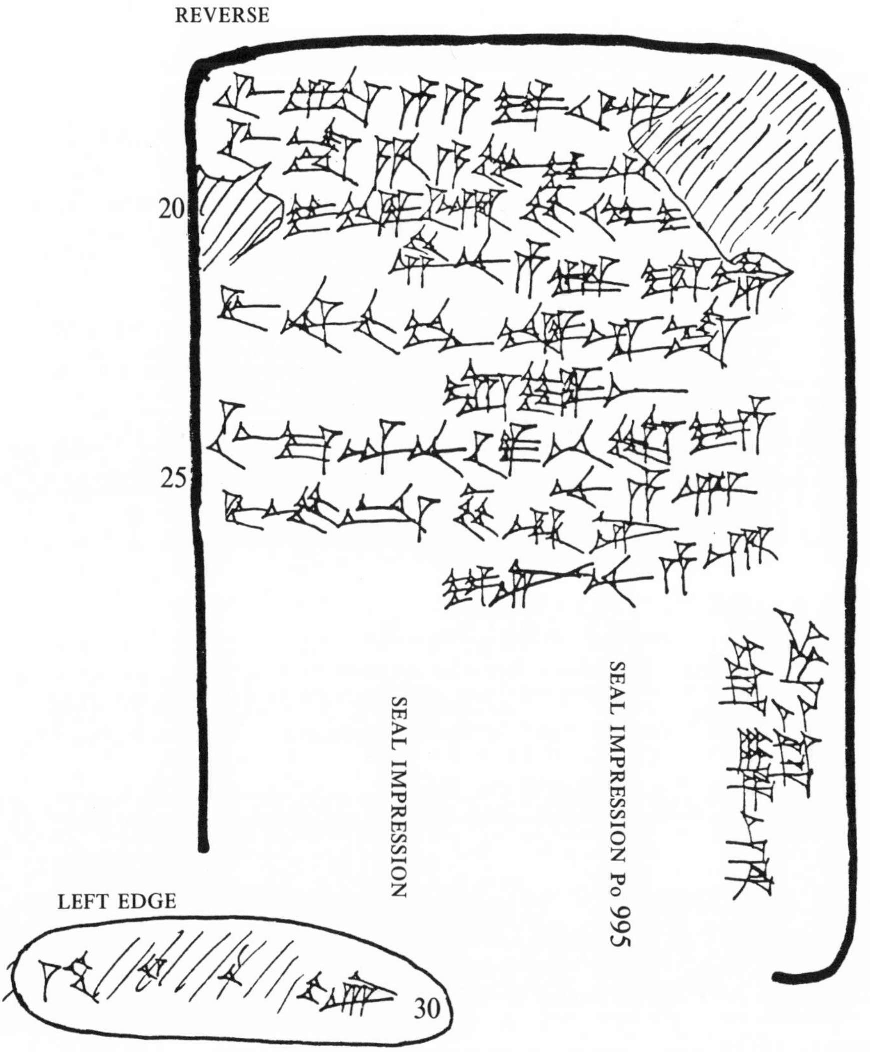

736

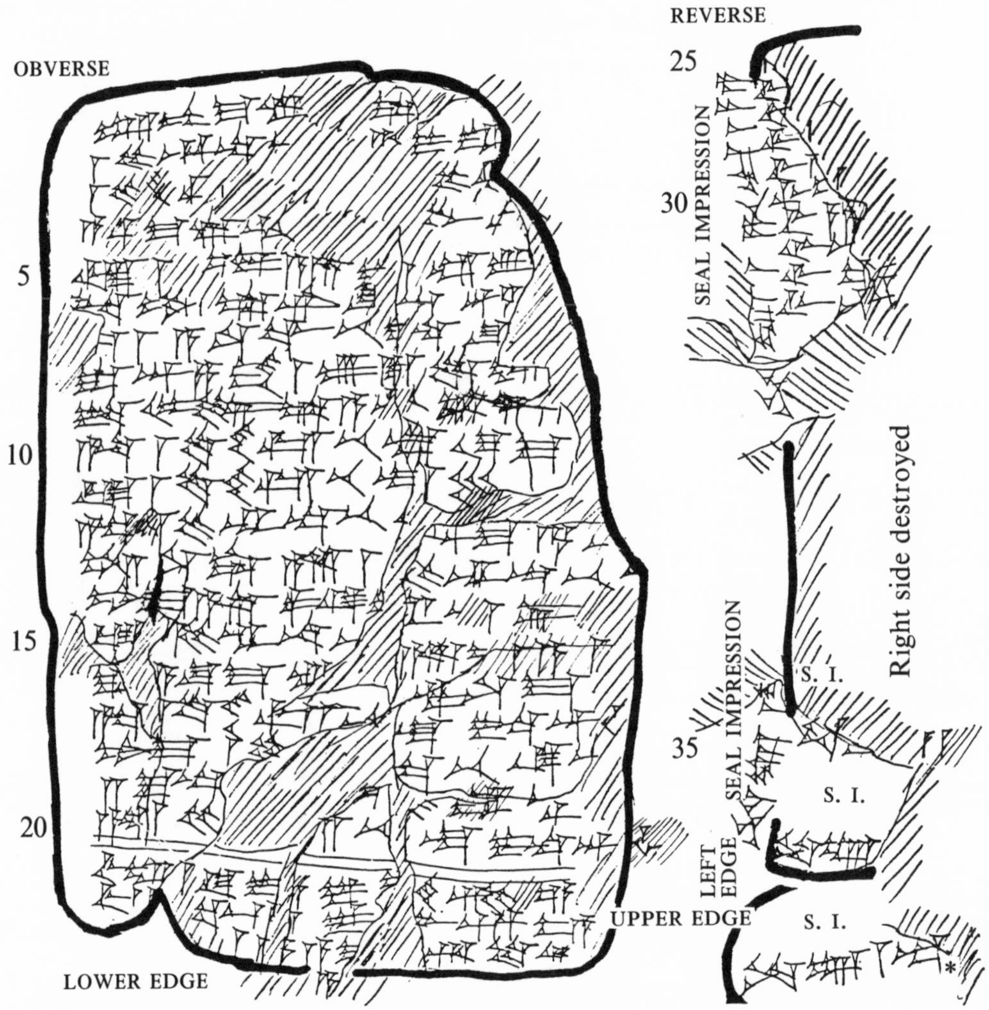

*Additional text; see *THNT*.

737

OBVERSE

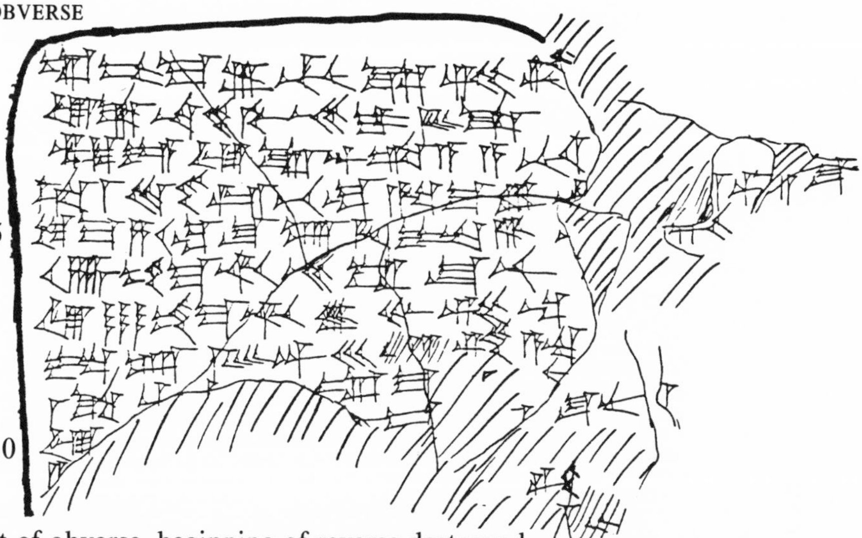

Rest of obverse, beginning of reverse destroyed

REVERSE

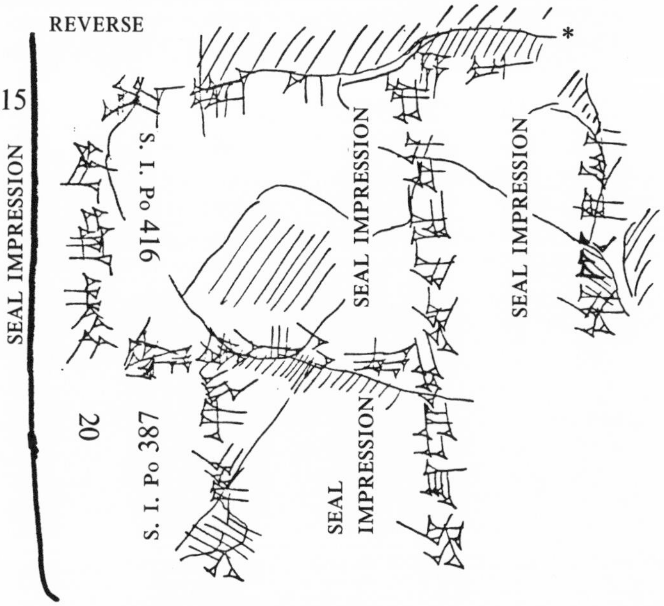

UPPER EDGE

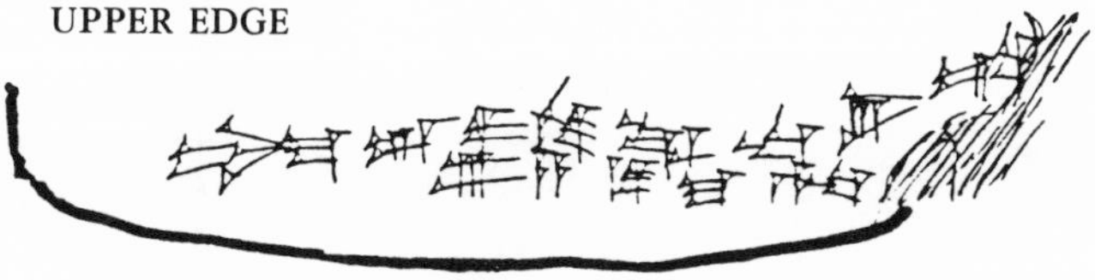

*Additional text; see *THNT*.

738

OBVERSE

Beginning of obverse destroyed

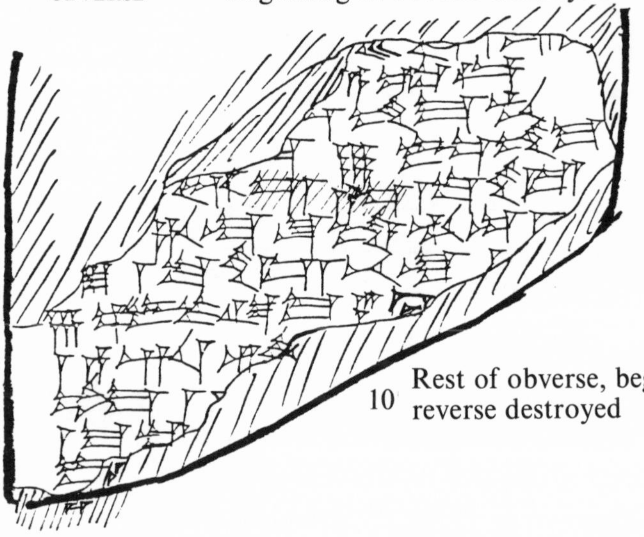

Rest of obverse, beginning of reverse destroyed

REVERSE

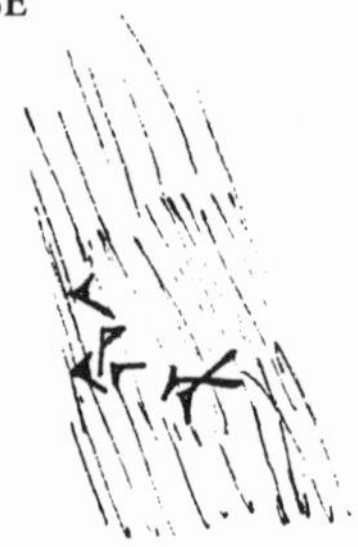

SEAL IMPRESSION

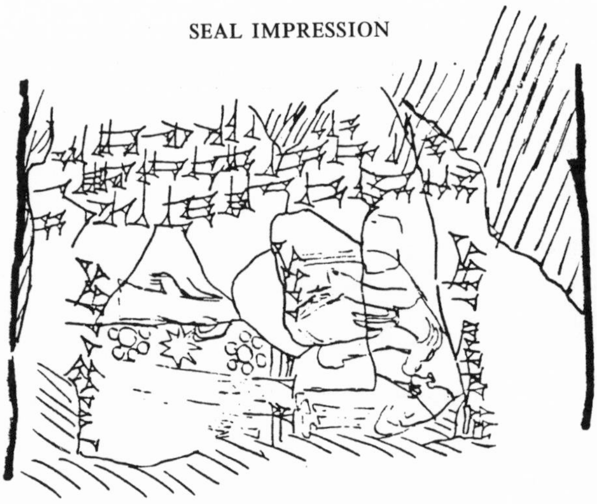

739

OBVERSE

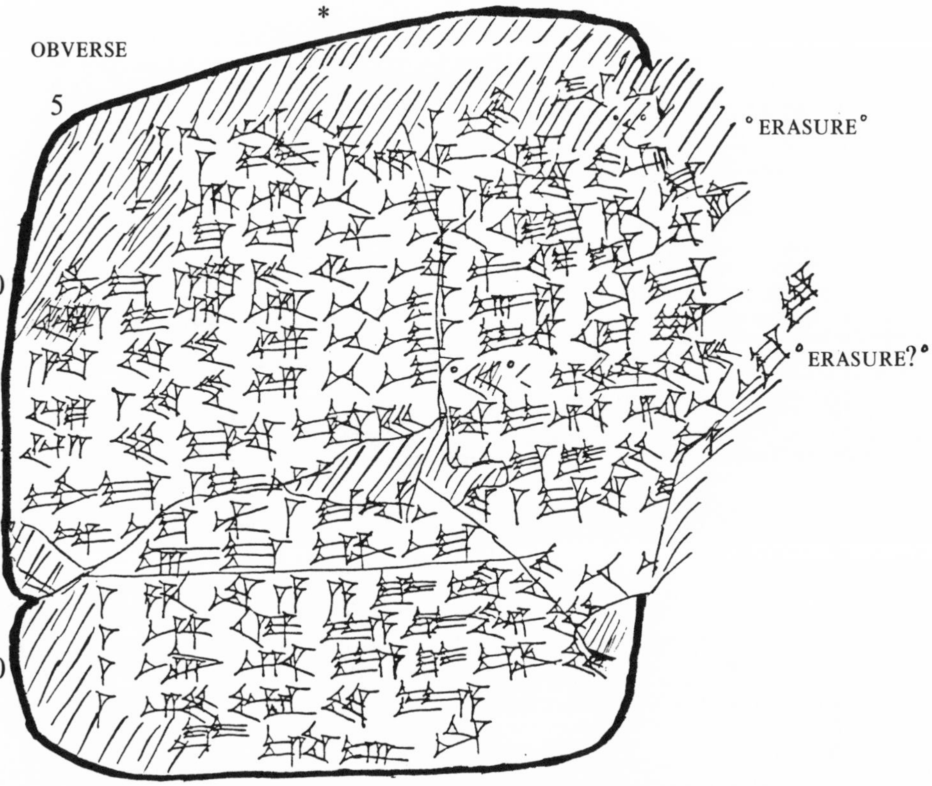

REVERSE

Beginning of reverse destroyed

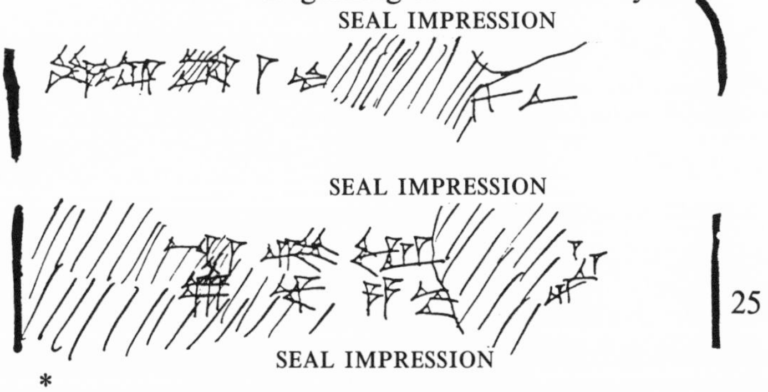

Rest of reverse destroyed

*Additional text; see *THNT*.

740

OBVERSE

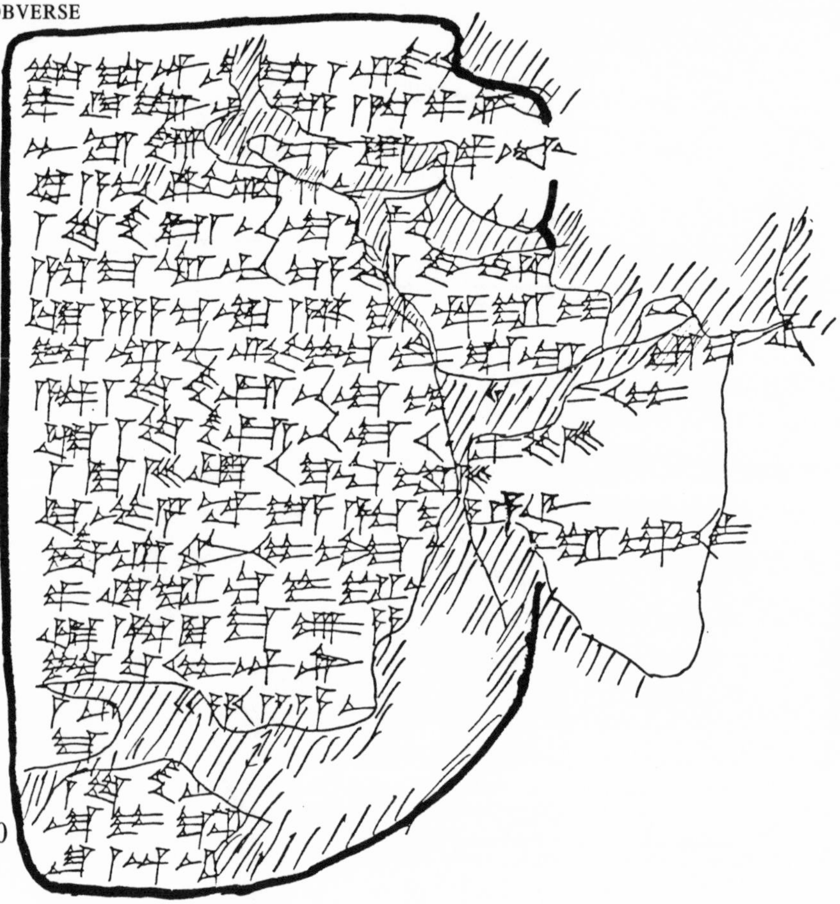

REVERSE

SEAL IMPRESSION Po 924

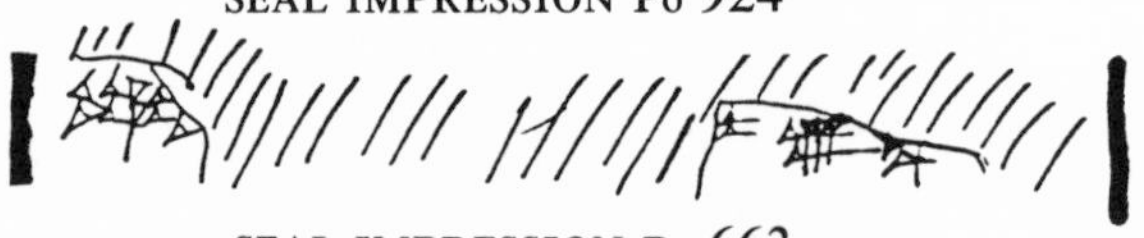

SEAL IMPRESSION Po 663

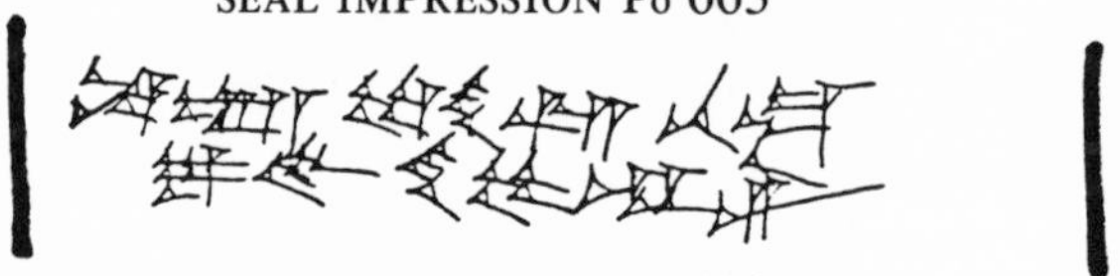

SEAL IMPRESSION Po 492

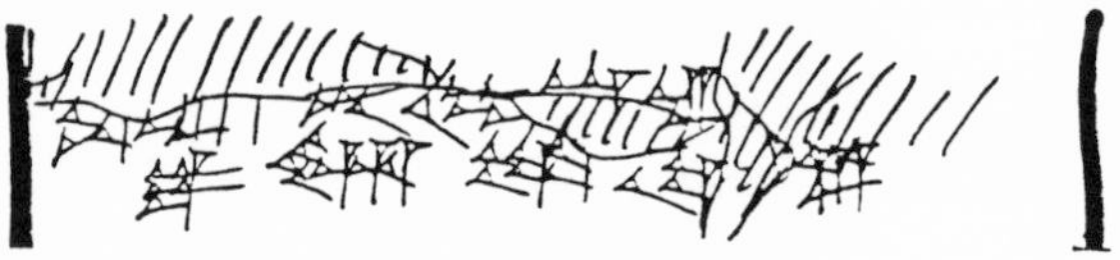

741

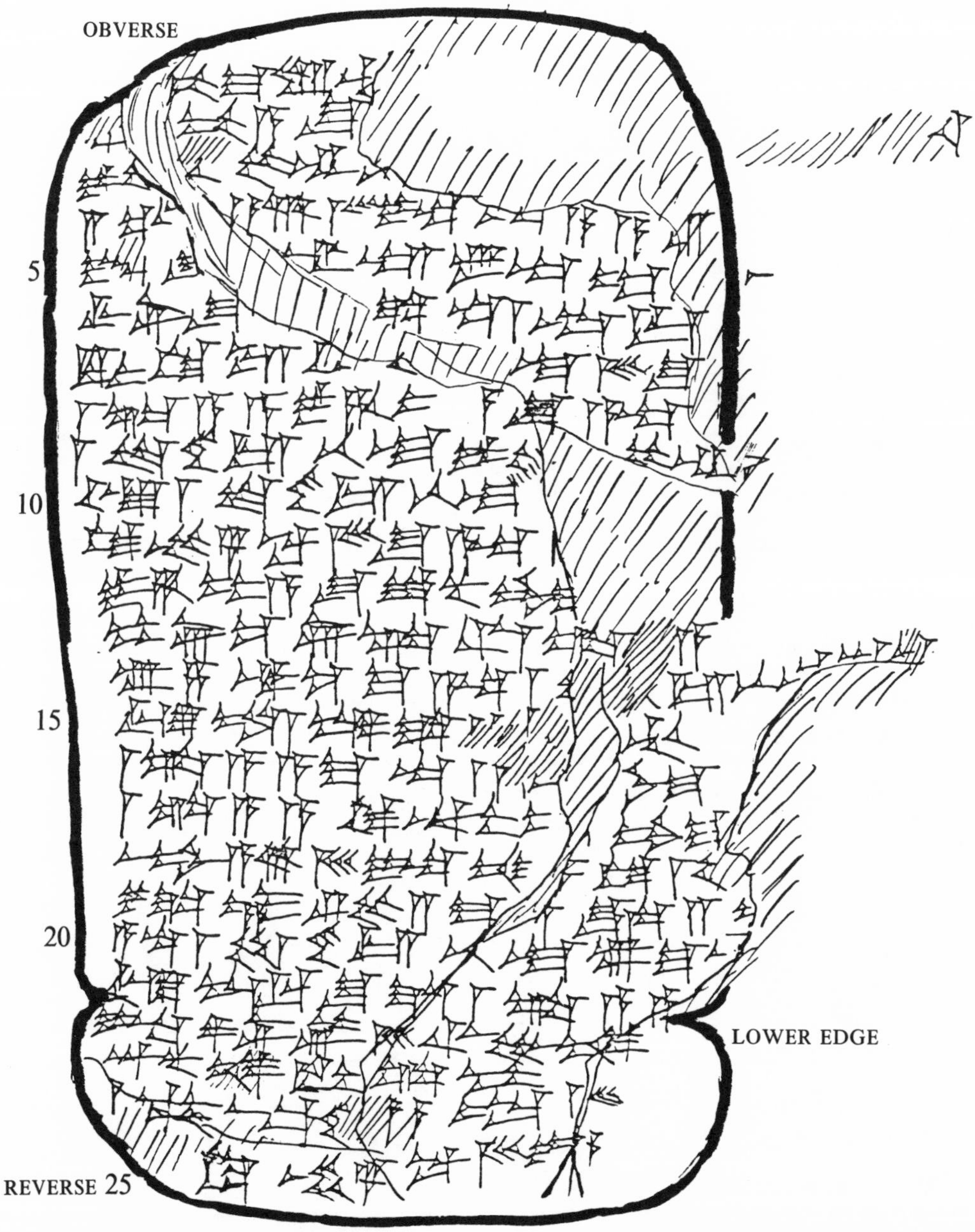

741

REVERSE (CONT'D)

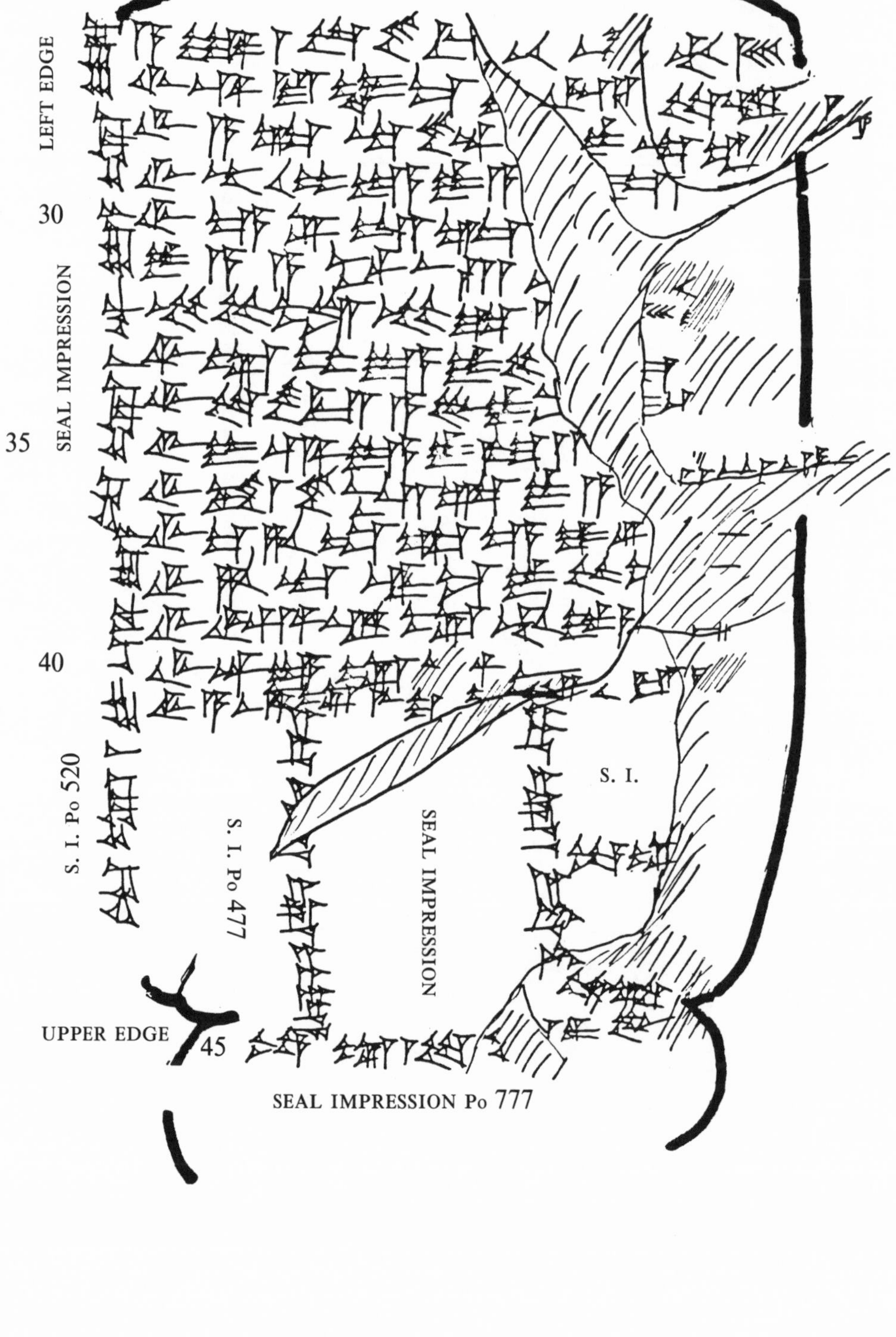

742

OBVERSE

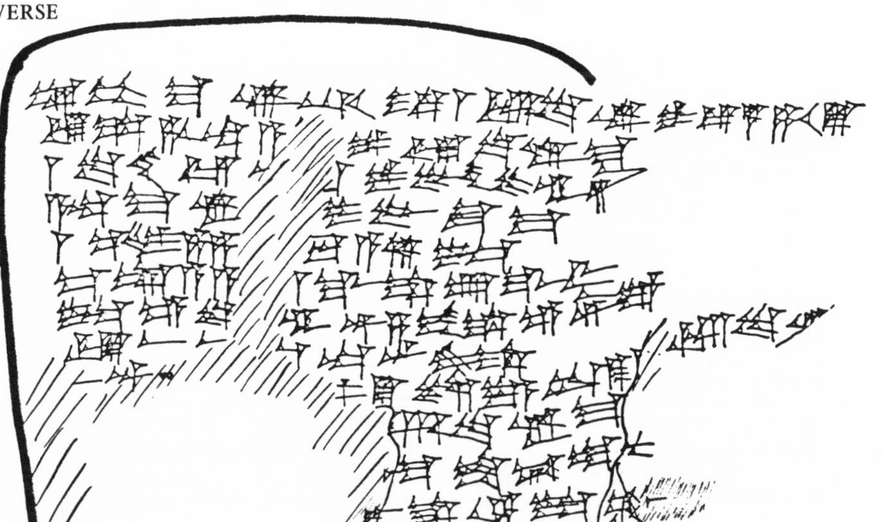

LOWER EDGE

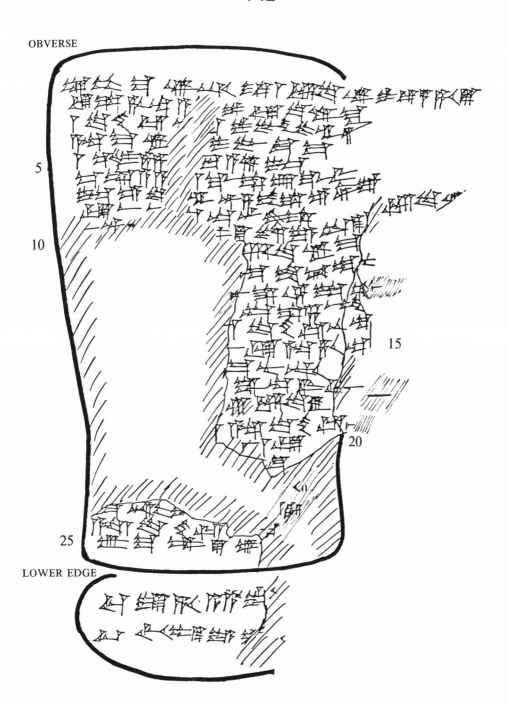

742

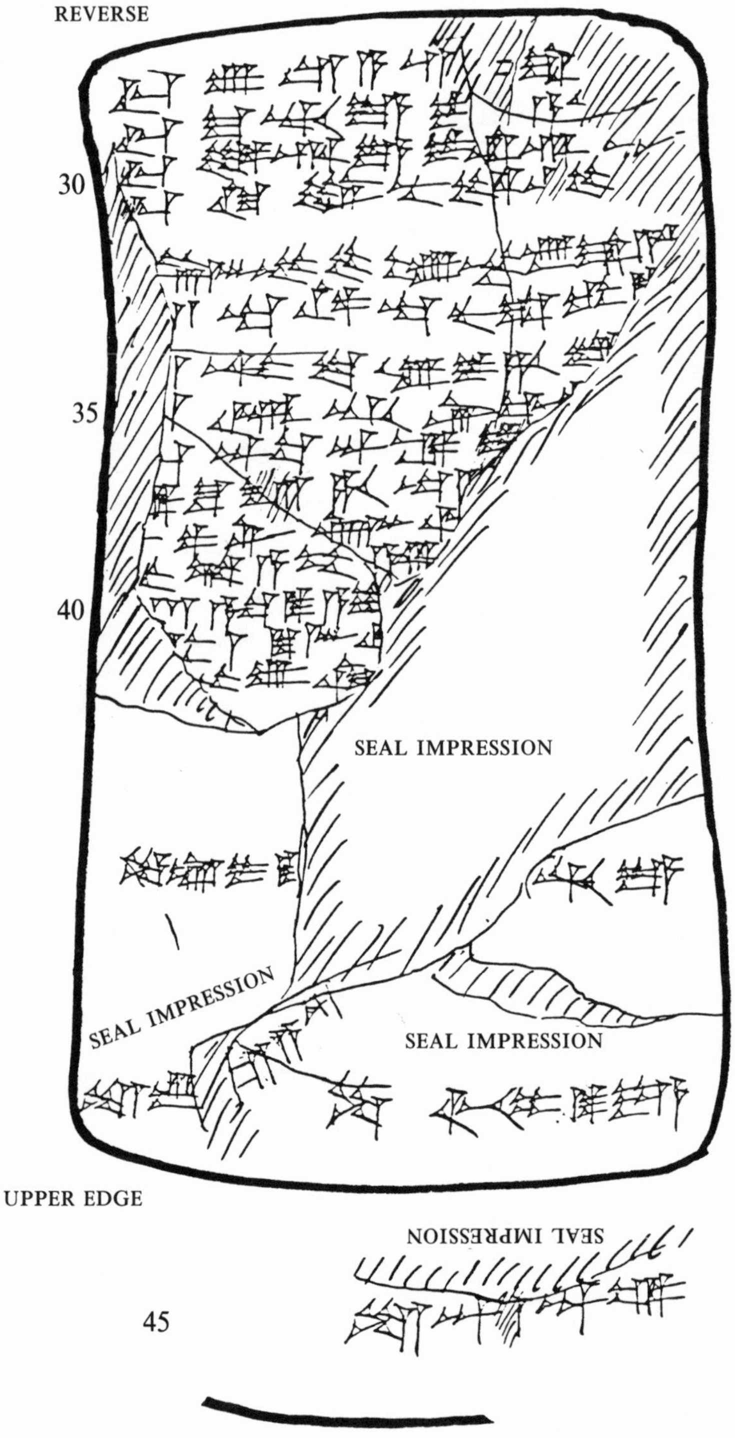
REVERSE
SEAL IMPRESSION
SEAL IMPRESSION
SEAL IMPRESSION
UPPER EDGE
SEAL IMPRESSION

743

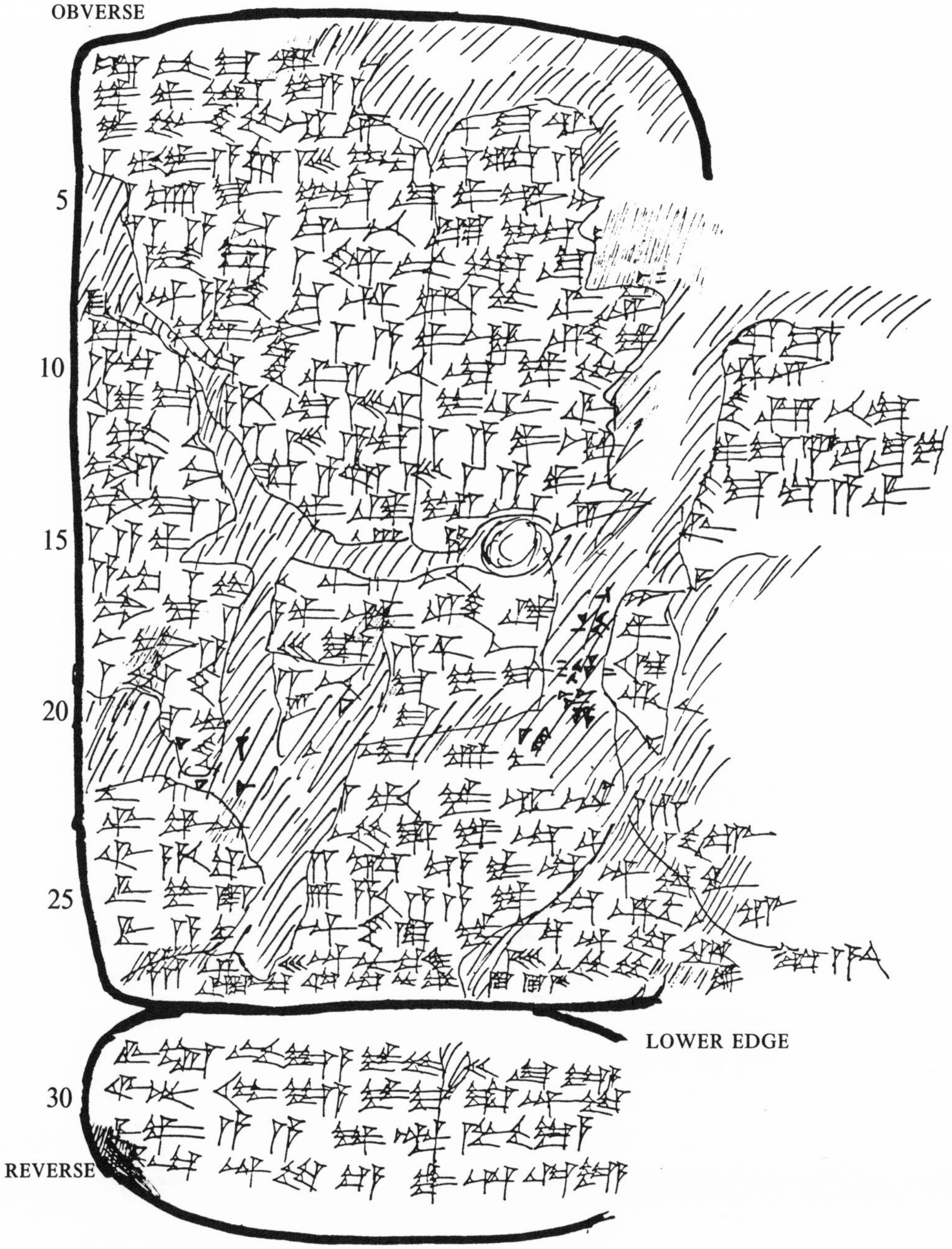

743

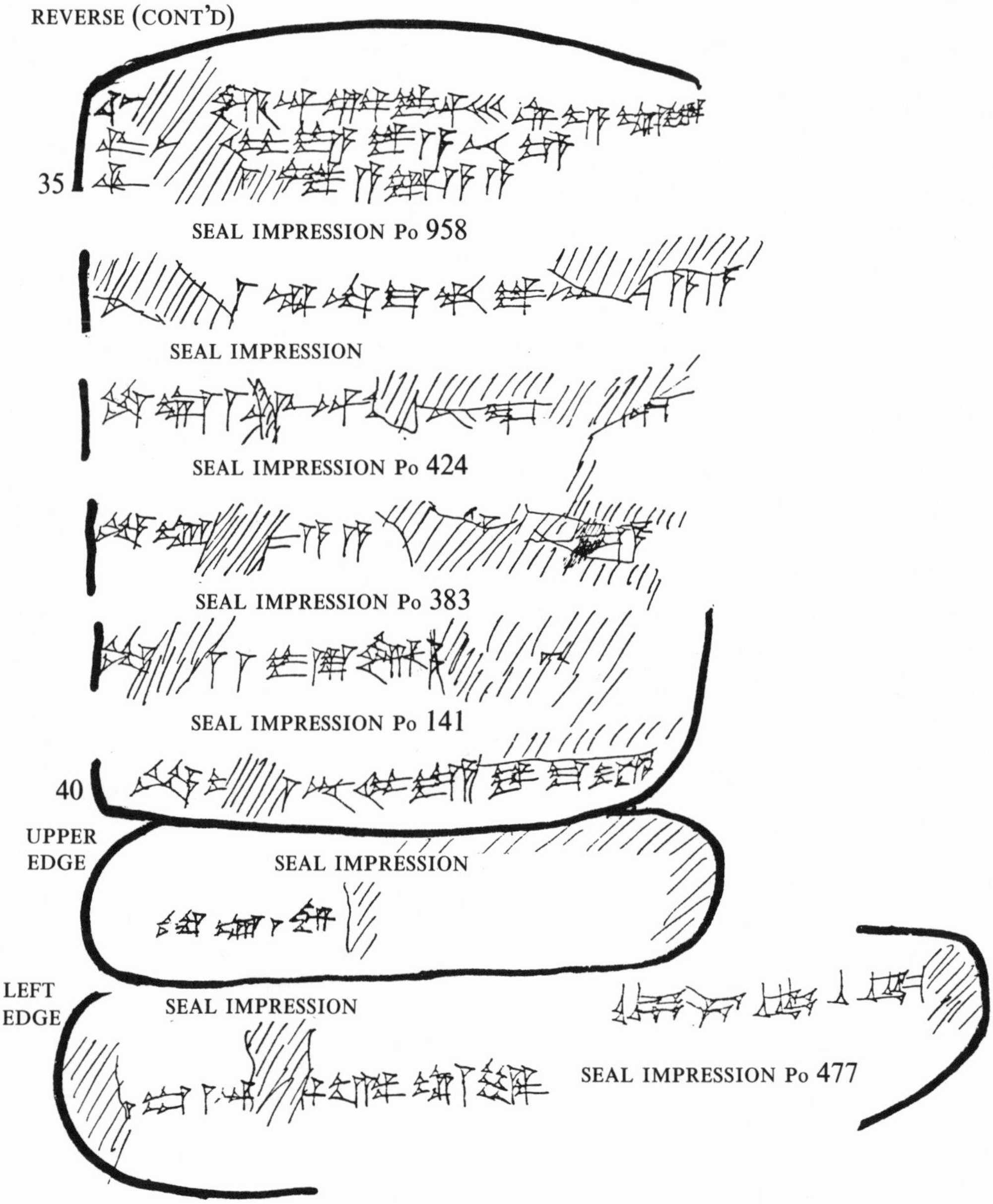
REVERSE (CONT'D)
35
SEAL IMPRESSION Po 958
SEAL IMPRESSION
SEAL IMPRESSION Po 424
SEAL IMPRESSION Po 383
SEAL IMPRESSION Po 141
40
UPPER EDGE
SEAL IMPRESSION
LEFT EDGE
SEAL IMPRESSION
SEAL IMPRESSION Po 477

744

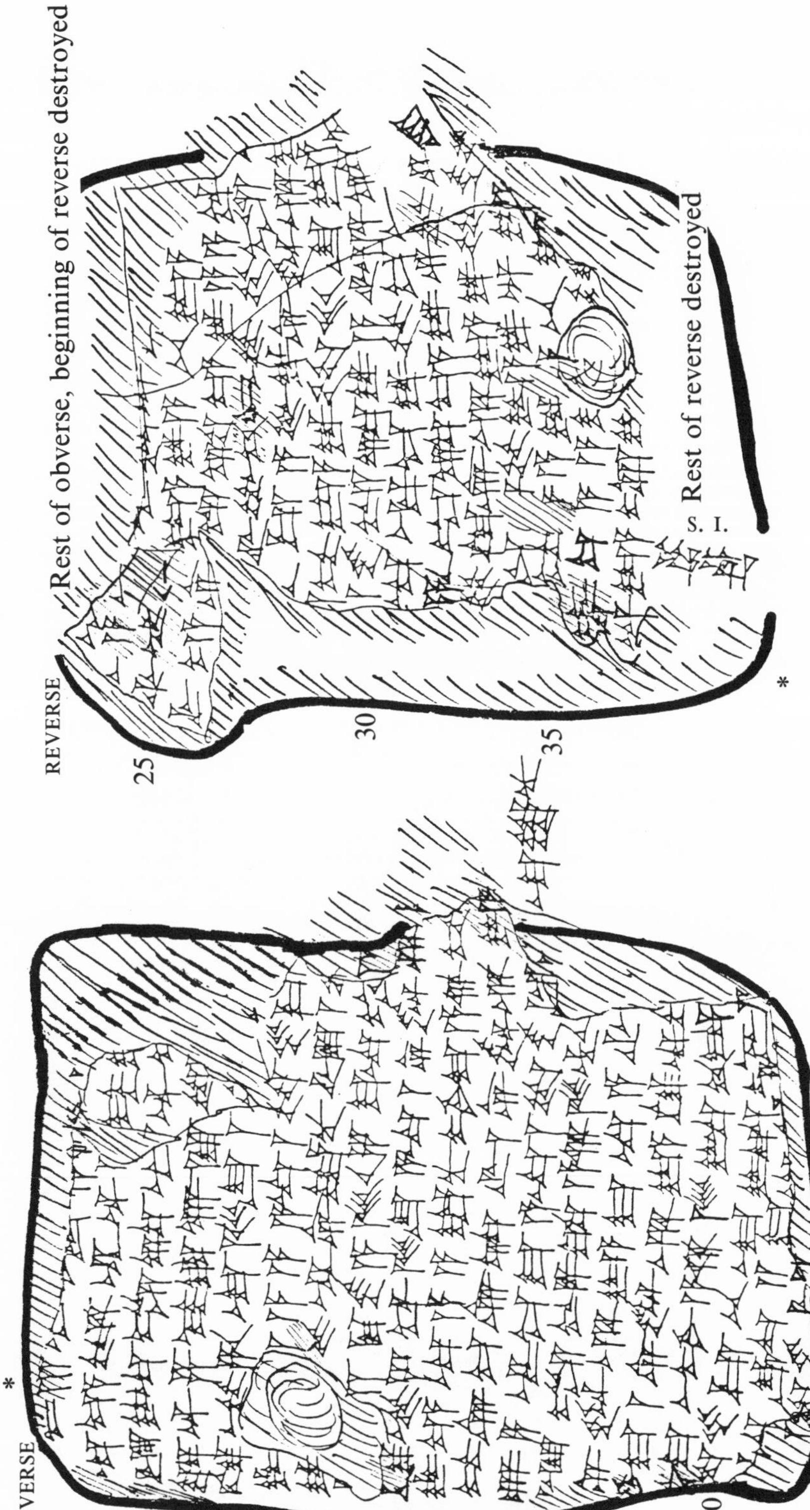

*Additional text; see *THNT*.

745

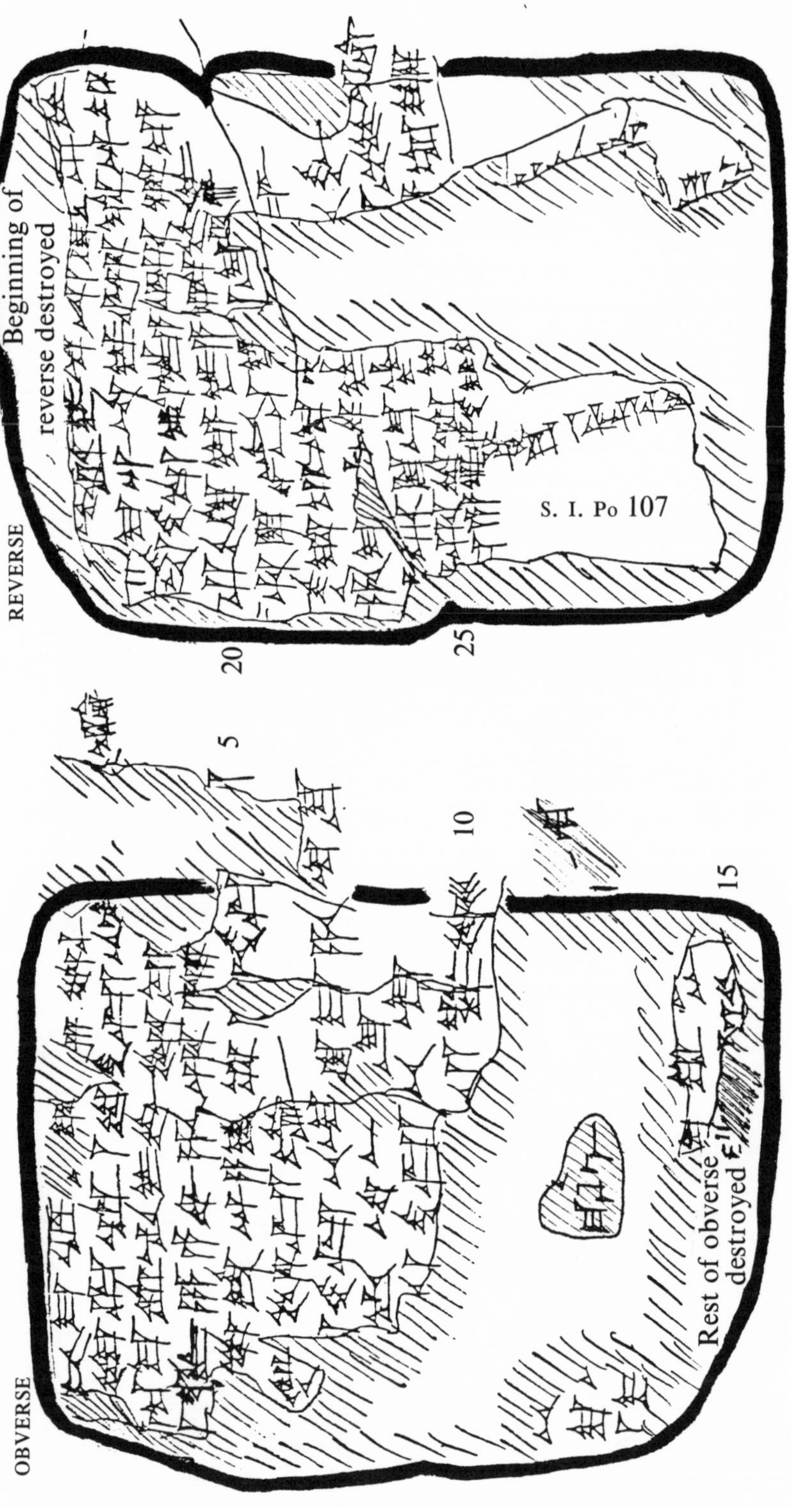
OBVERSE
REVERSE
Beginning of reverse destroyed
Rest of obverse destroyed
S. I. Po 107

746

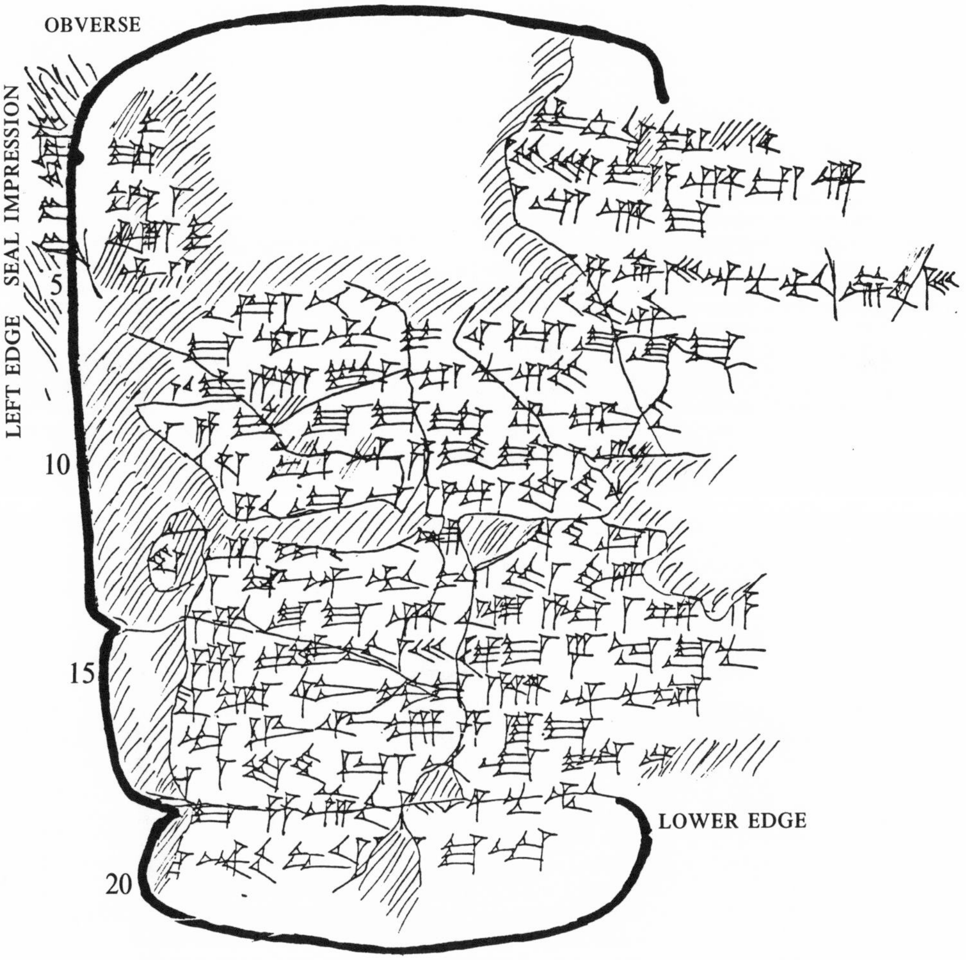

746

REVERSE

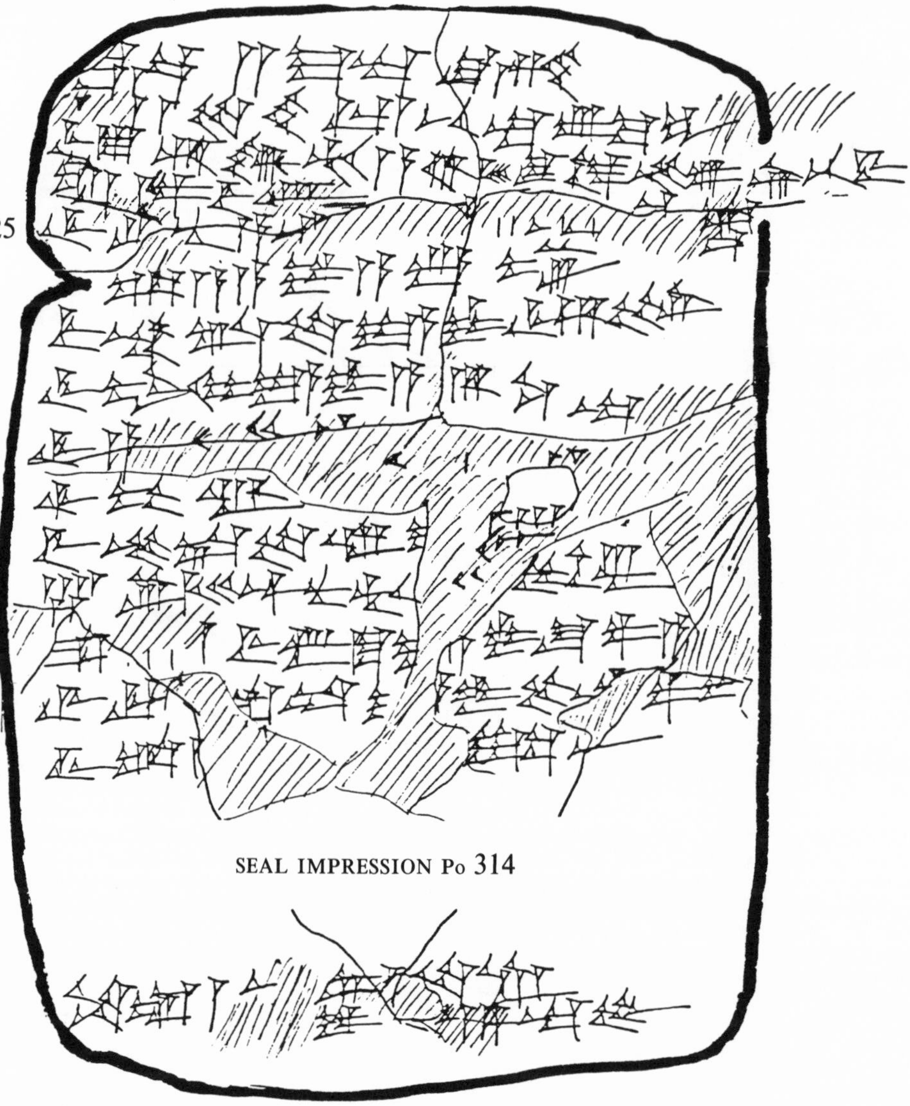

747

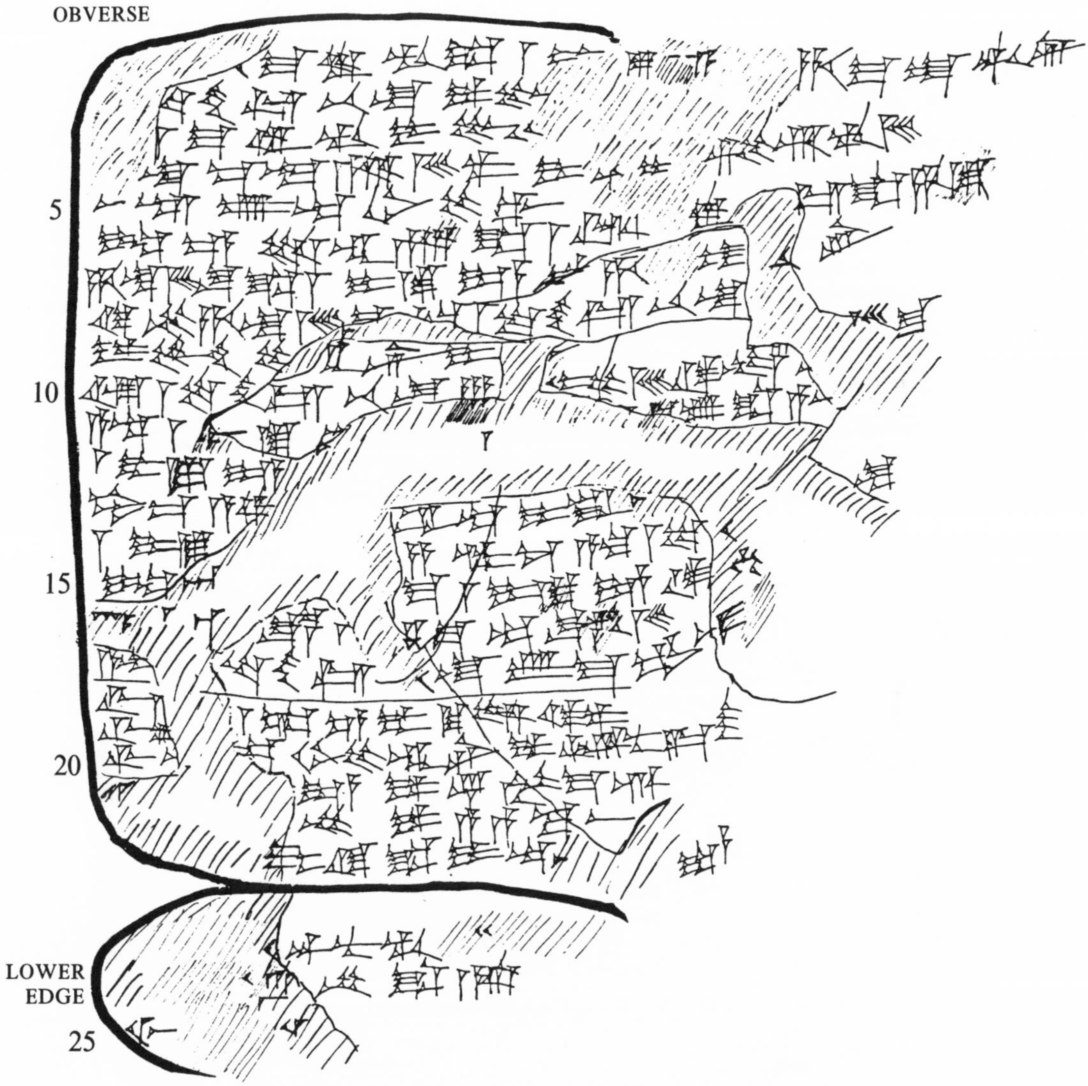

747

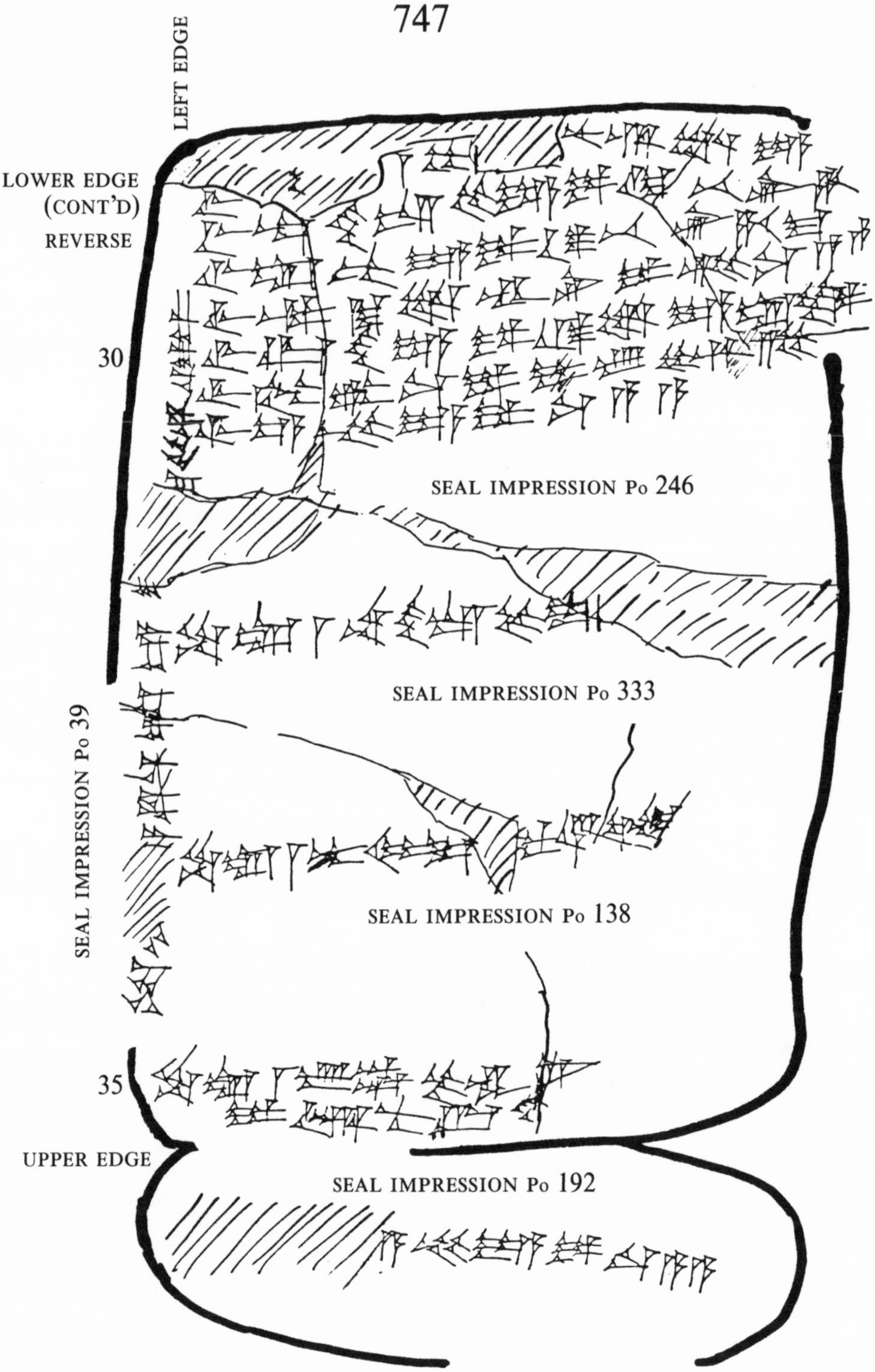
LEFT EDGE
LOWER EDGE (CONT'D)
REVERSE
30
SEAL IMPRESSION Po 246
SEAL IMPRESSION Po 333
SEAL IMPRESSION Po 39
SEAL IMPRESSION Po 138
35
UPPER EDGE
SEAL IMPRESSION Po 192

748

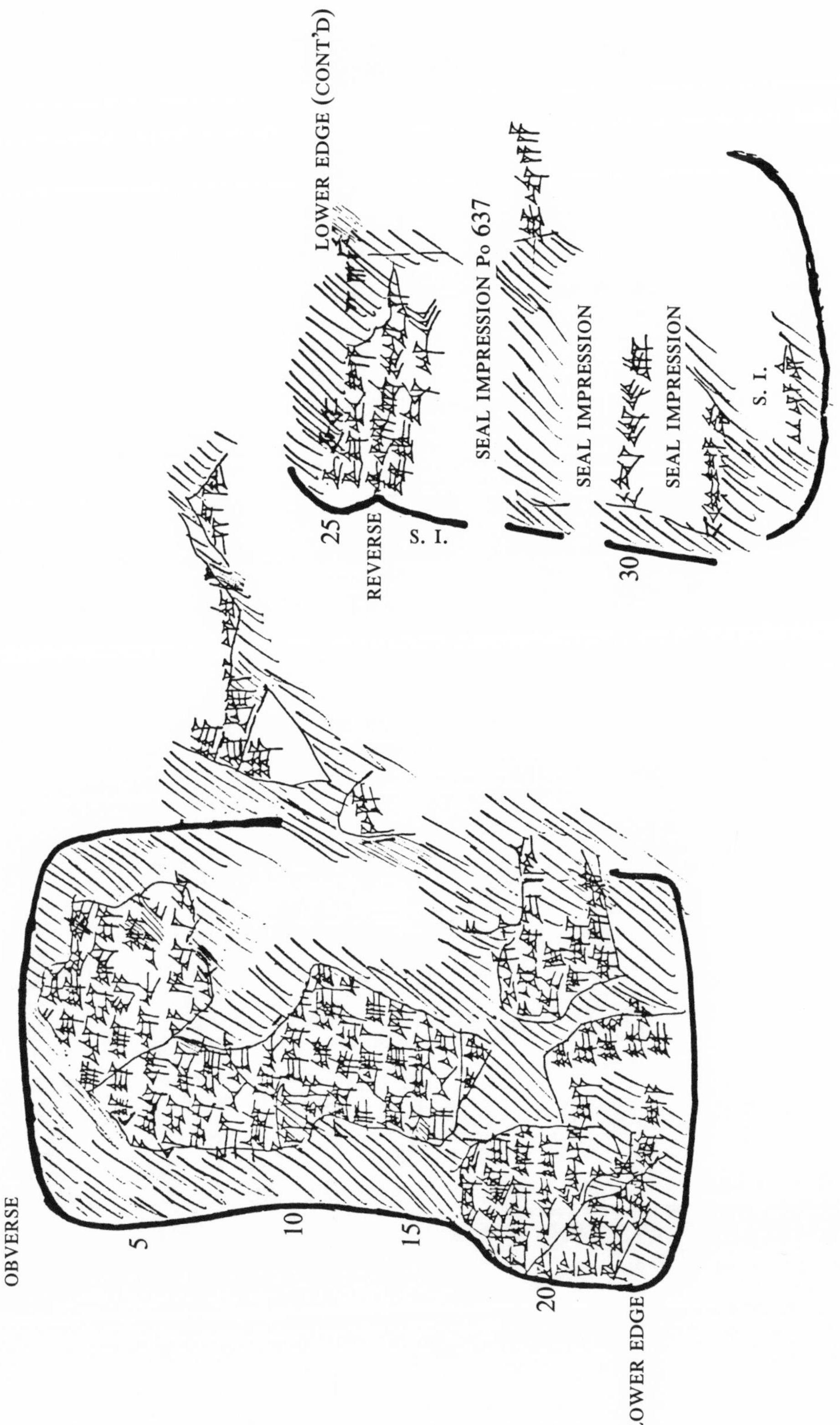
OBVERSE
5
10
15
20
LOWER EDGE
LOWER EDGE (CONT'D)
25
REVERSE
S. I.
SEAL IMPRESSION Po 637
SEAL IMPRESSION
30
SEAL IMPRESSION
S. I.

749

Beginning of obverse destroyed

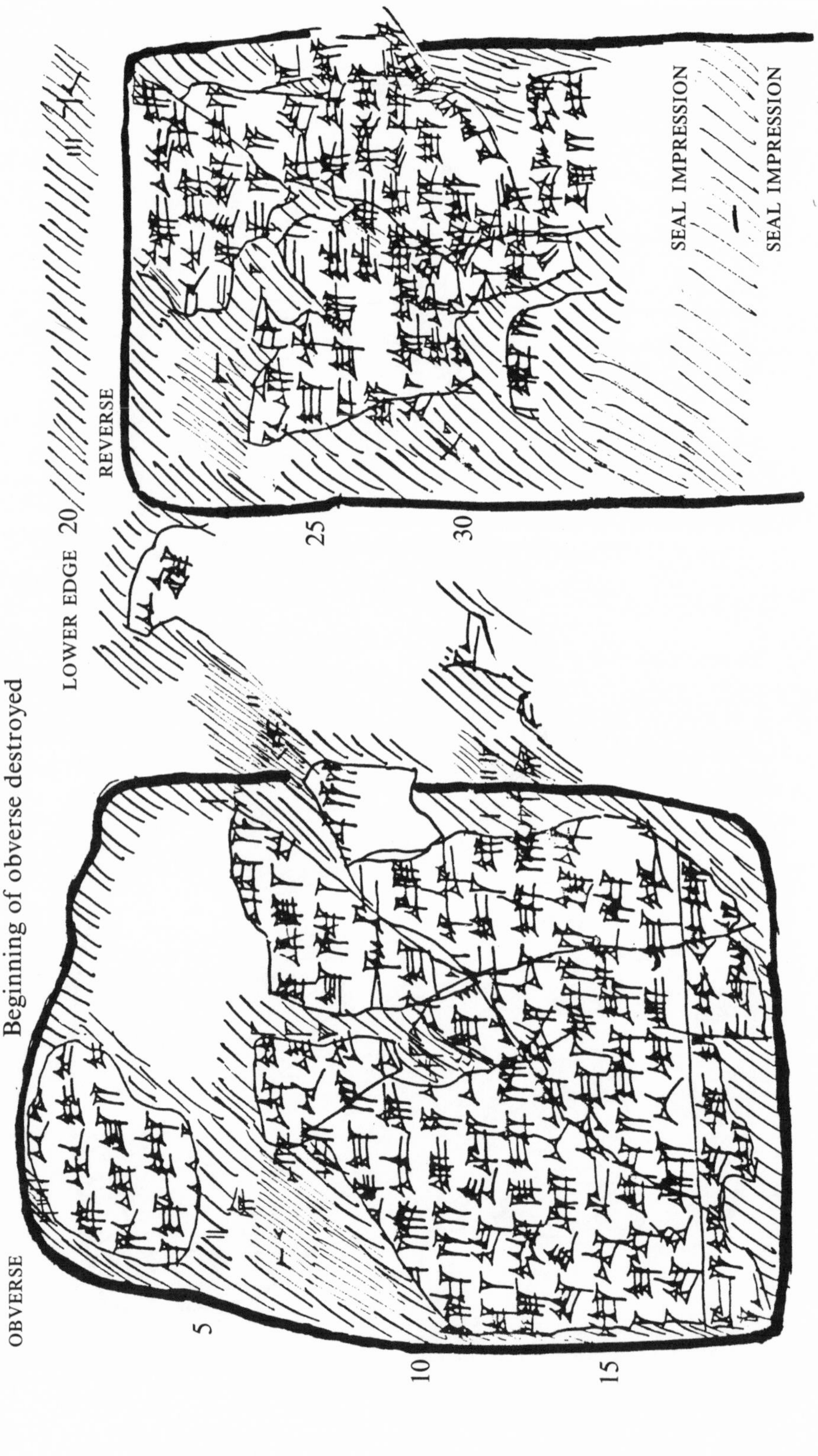

750

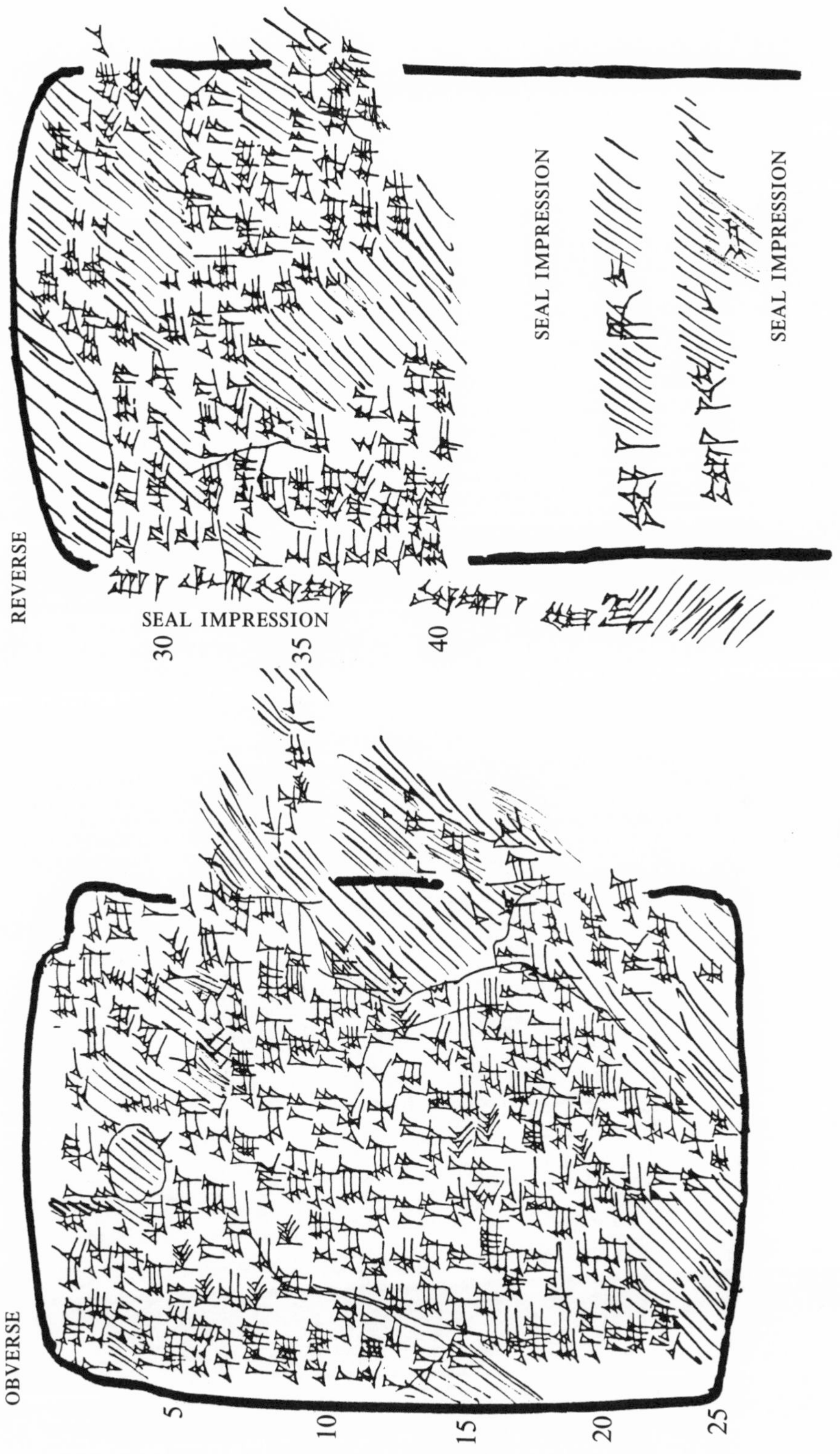
OBVERSE
5
10
15
20
25
REVERSE
SEAL IMPRESSION
30
35
40
SEAL IMPRESSION
SEAL IMPRESSION

751

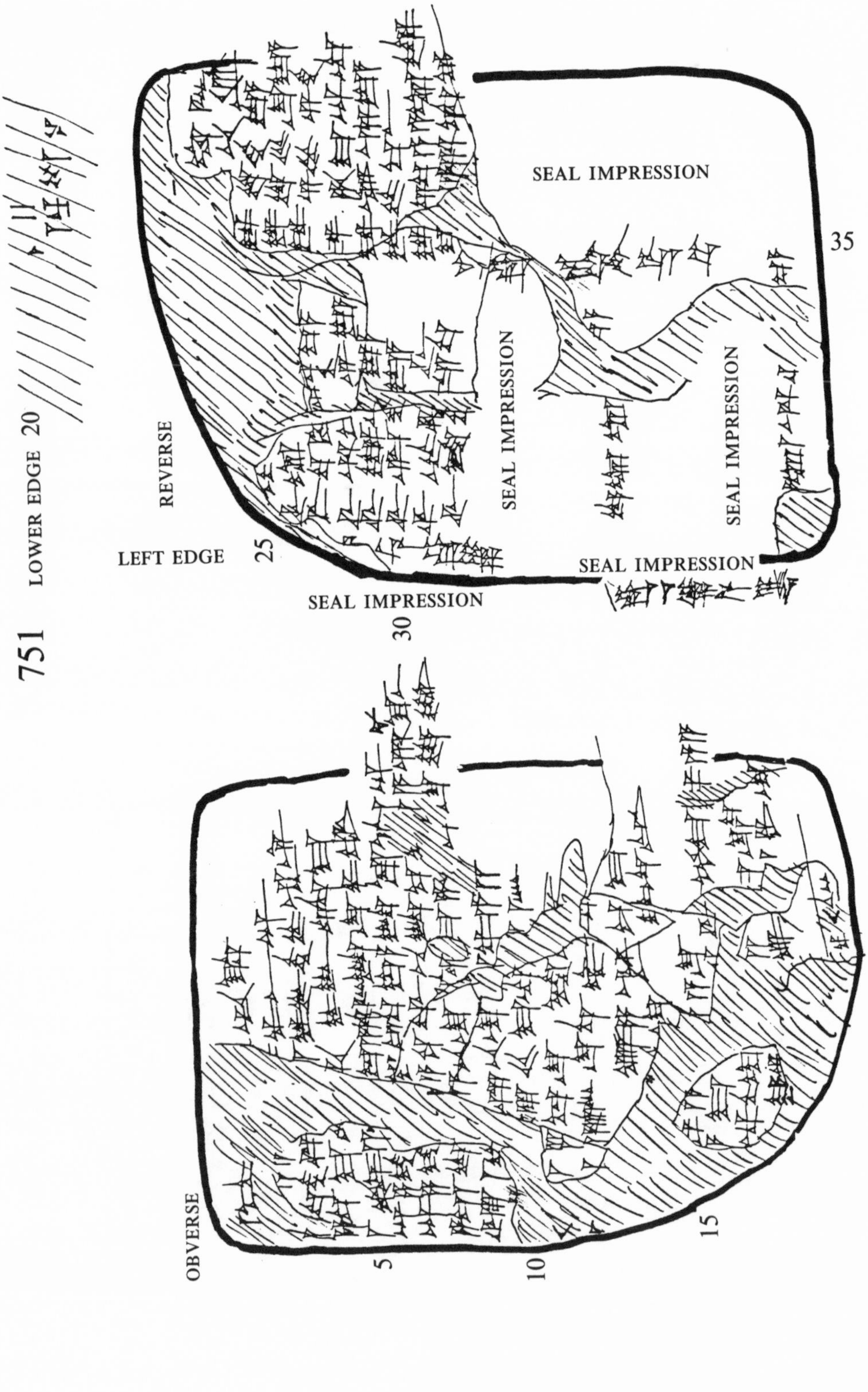
LOWER EDGE 20
REVERSE
LEFT EDGE
25
SEAL IMPRESSION
SEAL IMPRESSION
SEAL IMPRESSION
SEAL IMPRESSION
SEAL IMPRESSION
30
35
OBVERSE
5
10
15

752

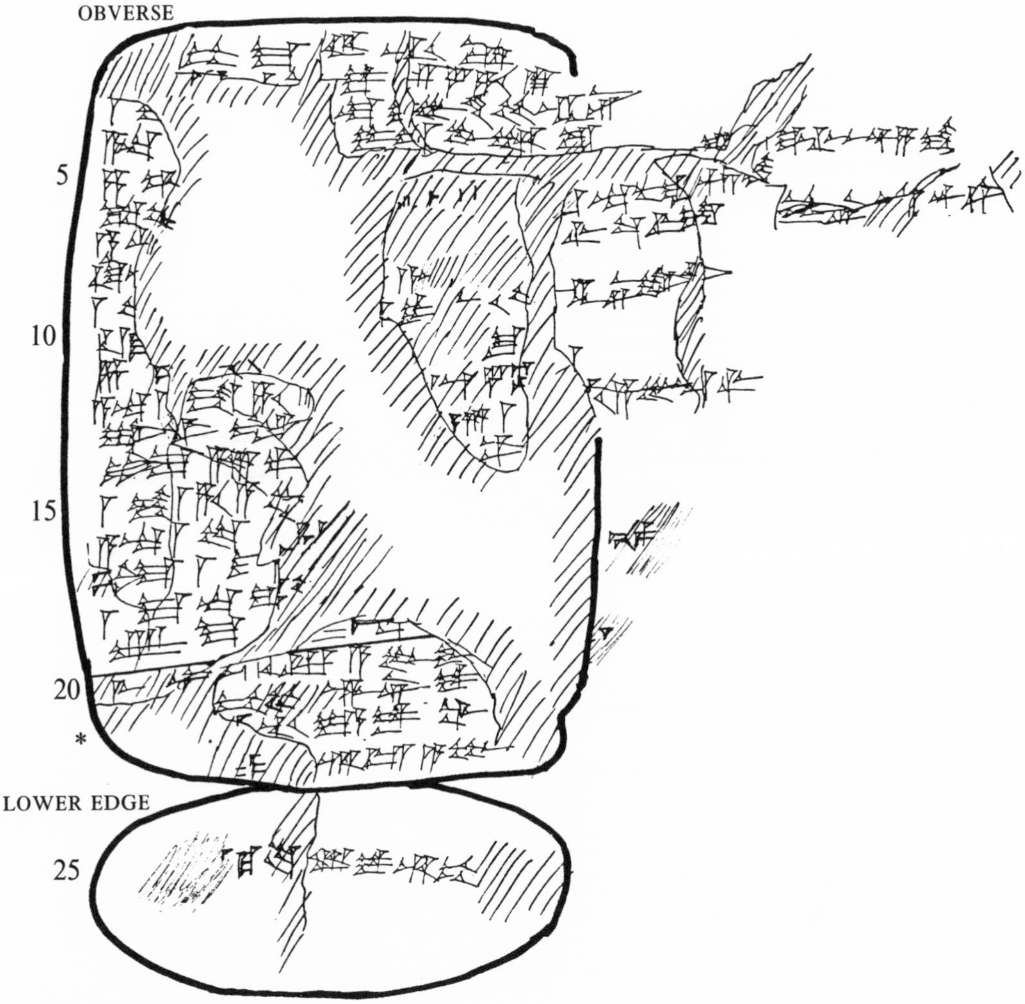

*Additional text; see *THNT*.

752

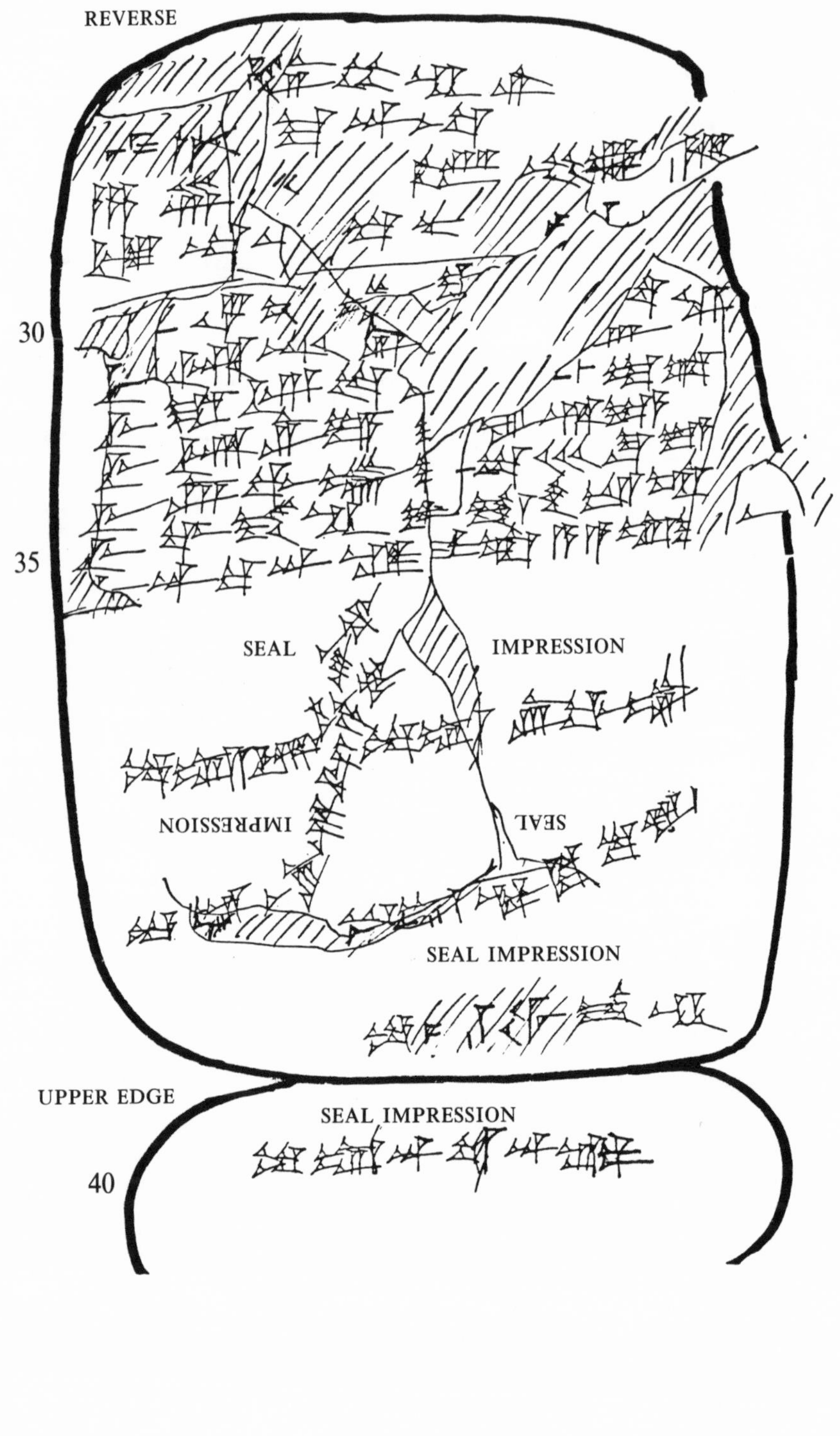
REVERSE
30
35
SEAL IMPRESSION
IMPRESSION SEAL
SEAL IMPRESSION
UPPER EDGE
SEAL IMPRESSION
40

753 (= 712 = 877)*

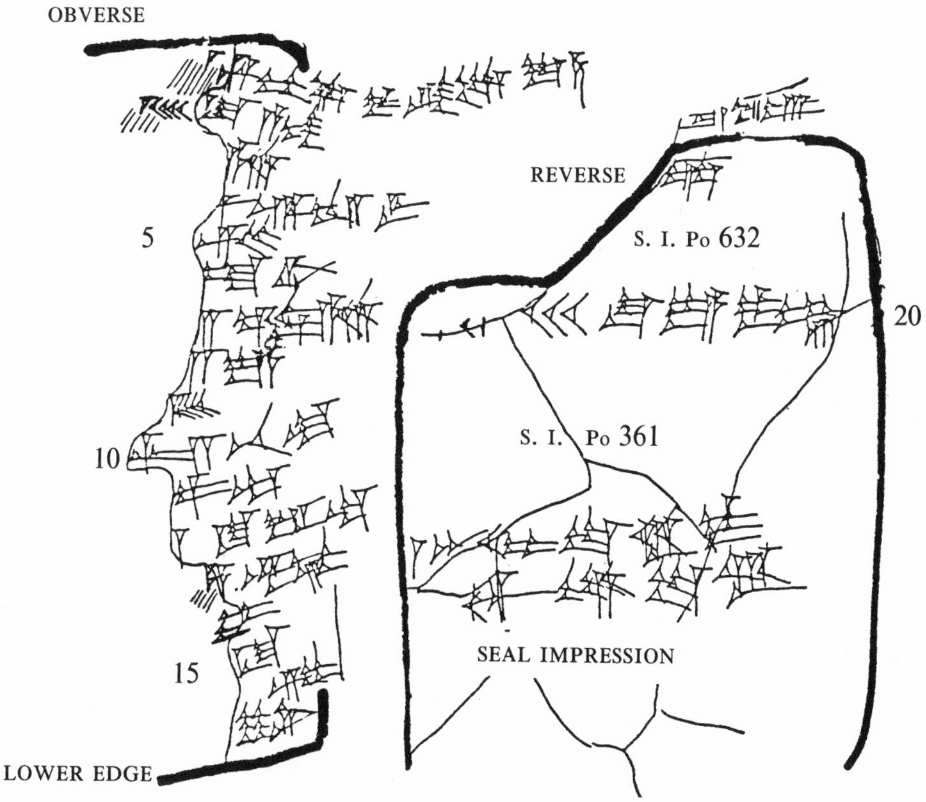

*753 is the best of the three copies. See comments to this text in *THNT*.

754

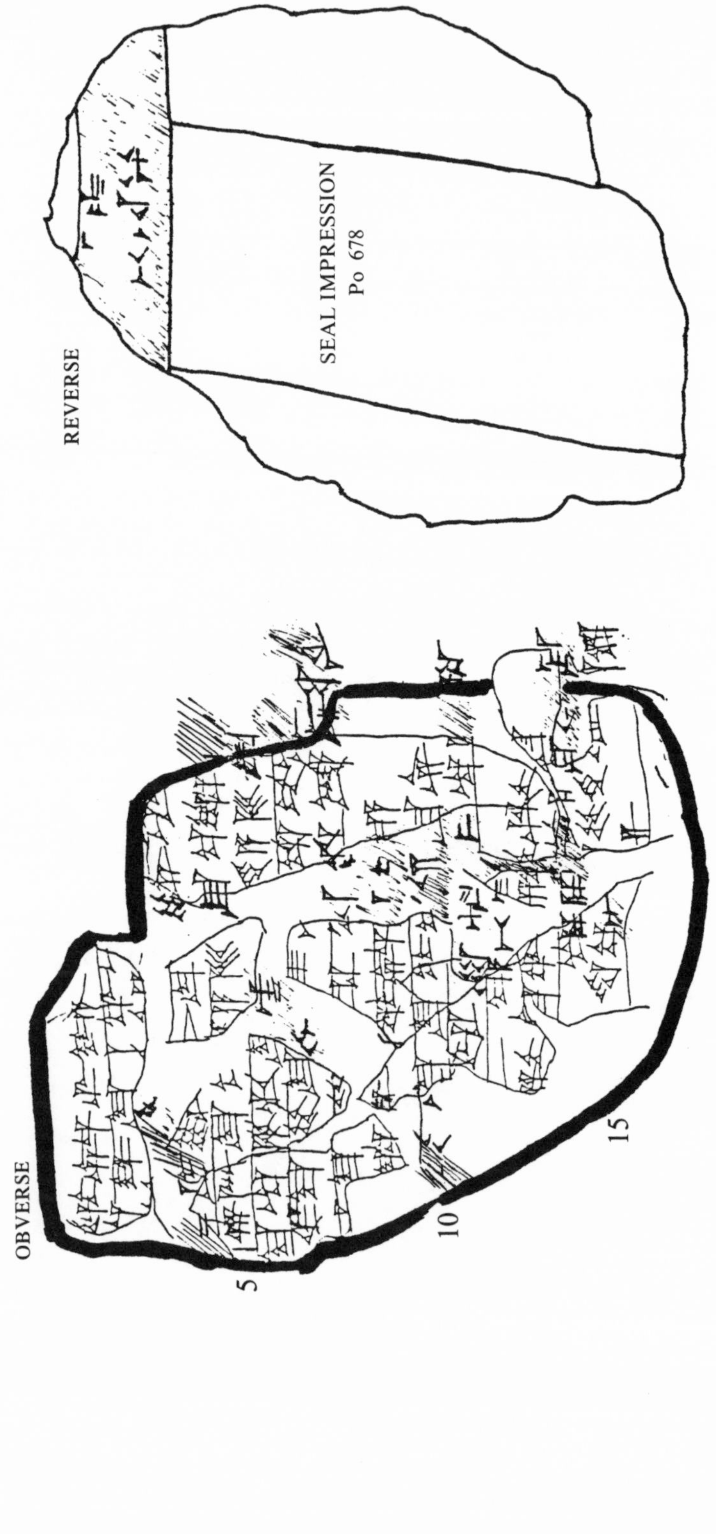

755

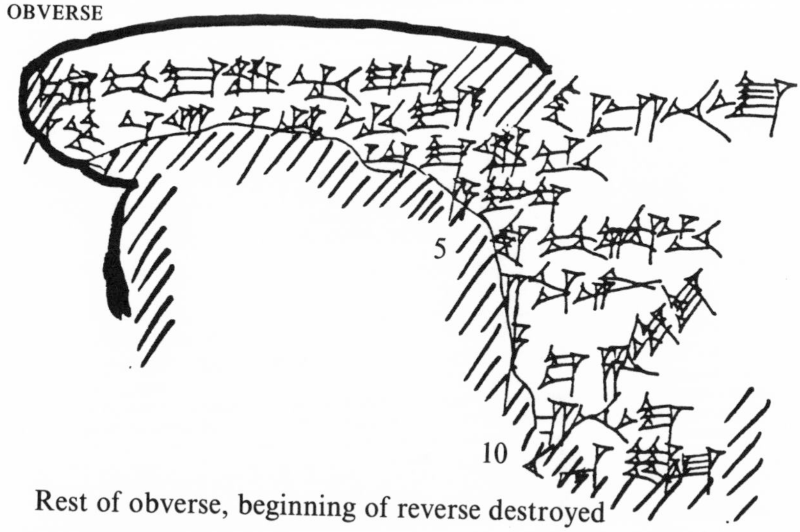

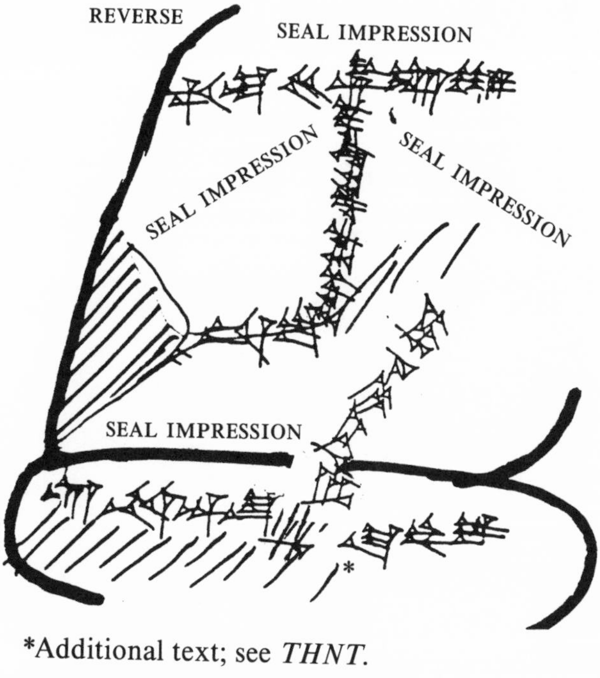

*Additional text; see *THNT*.

756

Beginning of obverse destroyed

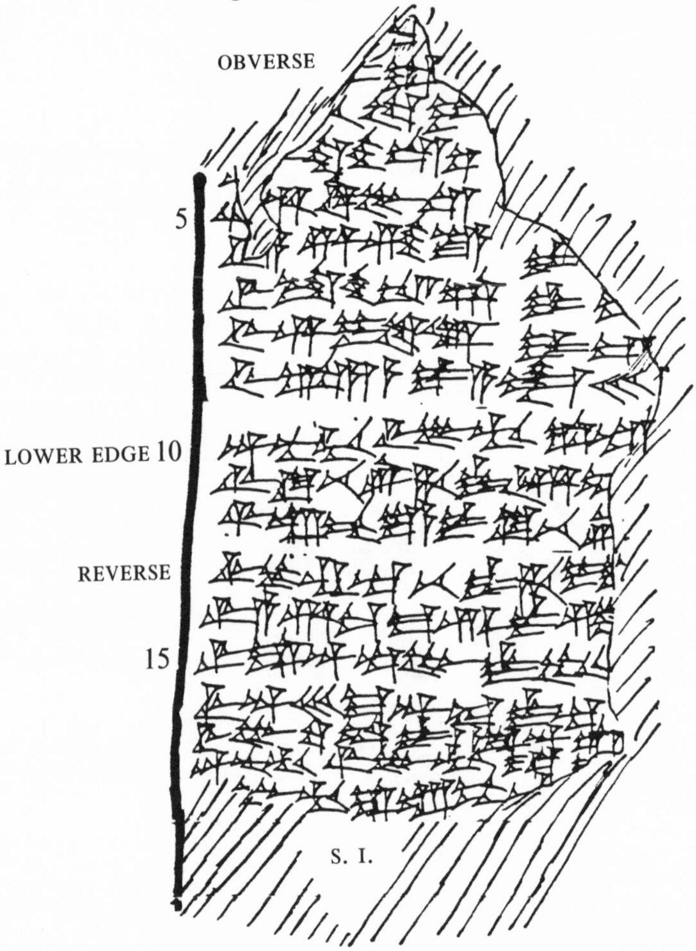

757

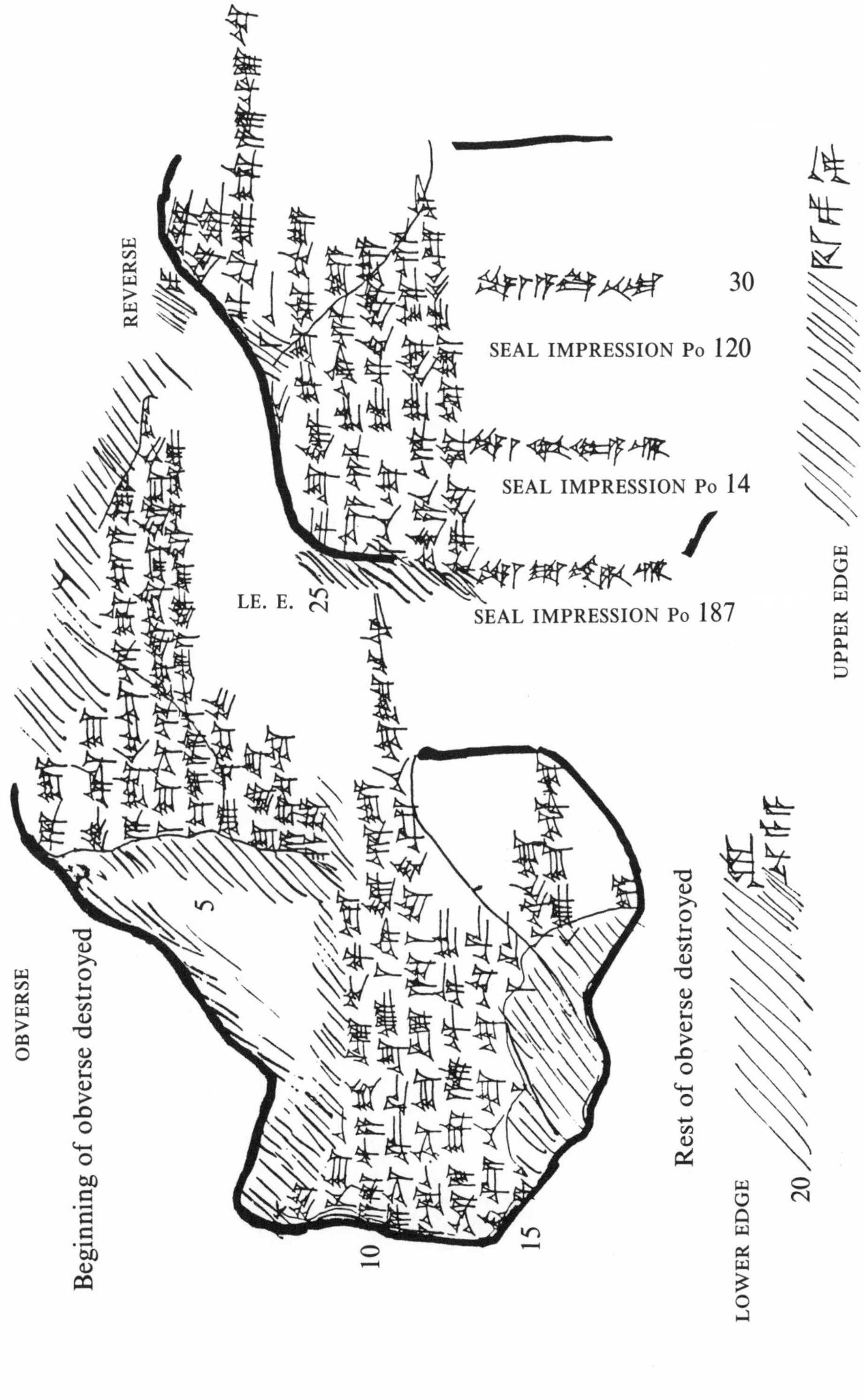
OBVERSE
Beginning of obverse destroyed
Rest of obverse destroyed
REVERSE
LE. E.
SEAL IMPRESSION Po 120
SEAL IMPRESSION Po 14
SEAL IMPRESSION Po 187
UPPER EDGE
LOWER EDGE

758

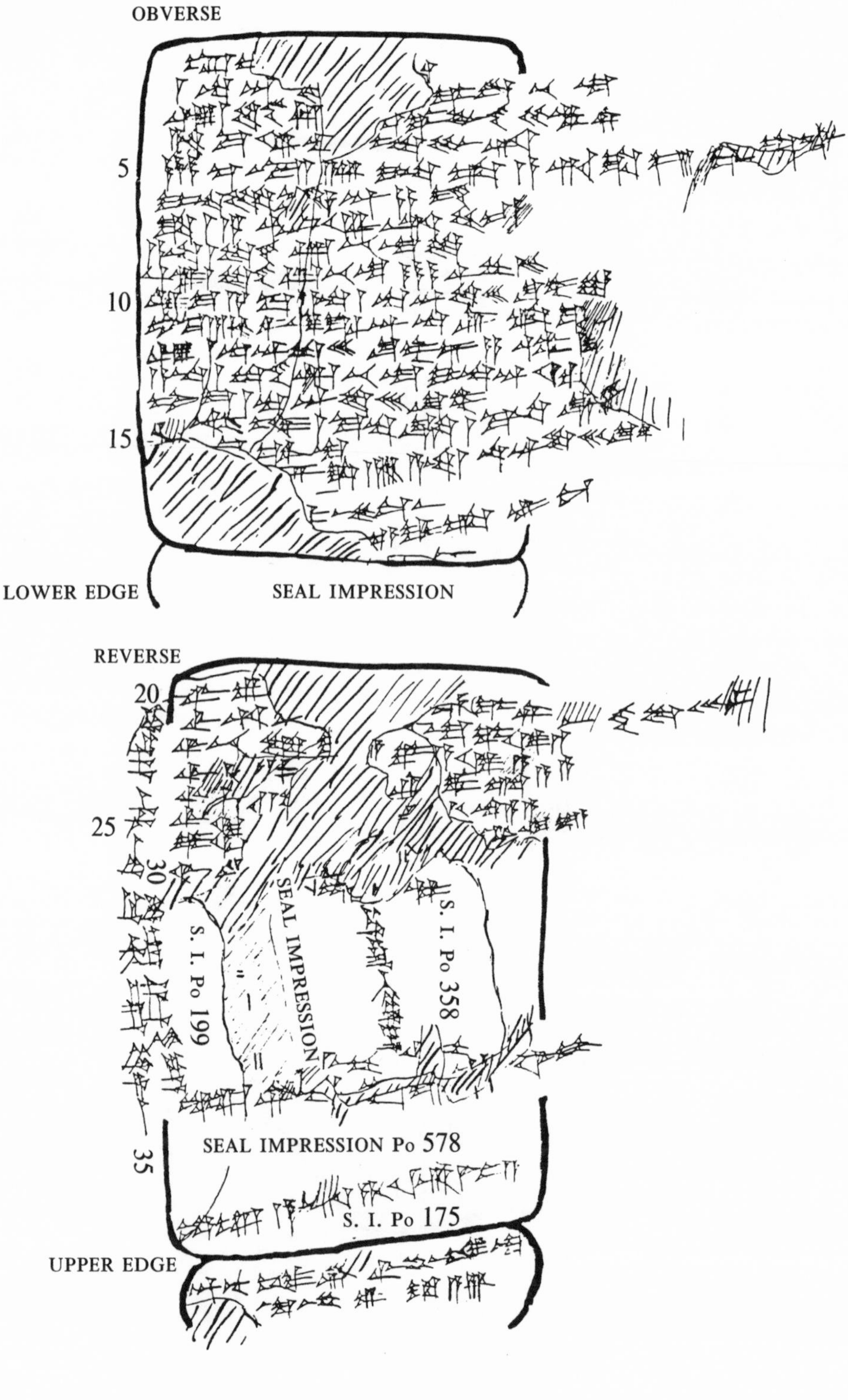
OBVERSE
LOWER EDGE
SEAL IMPRESSION
REVERSE
S. I. Po 199
SEAL IMPRESSION
S. I. Po 358
SEAL IMPRESSION Po 578
S. I. Po 175
UPPER EDGE

759

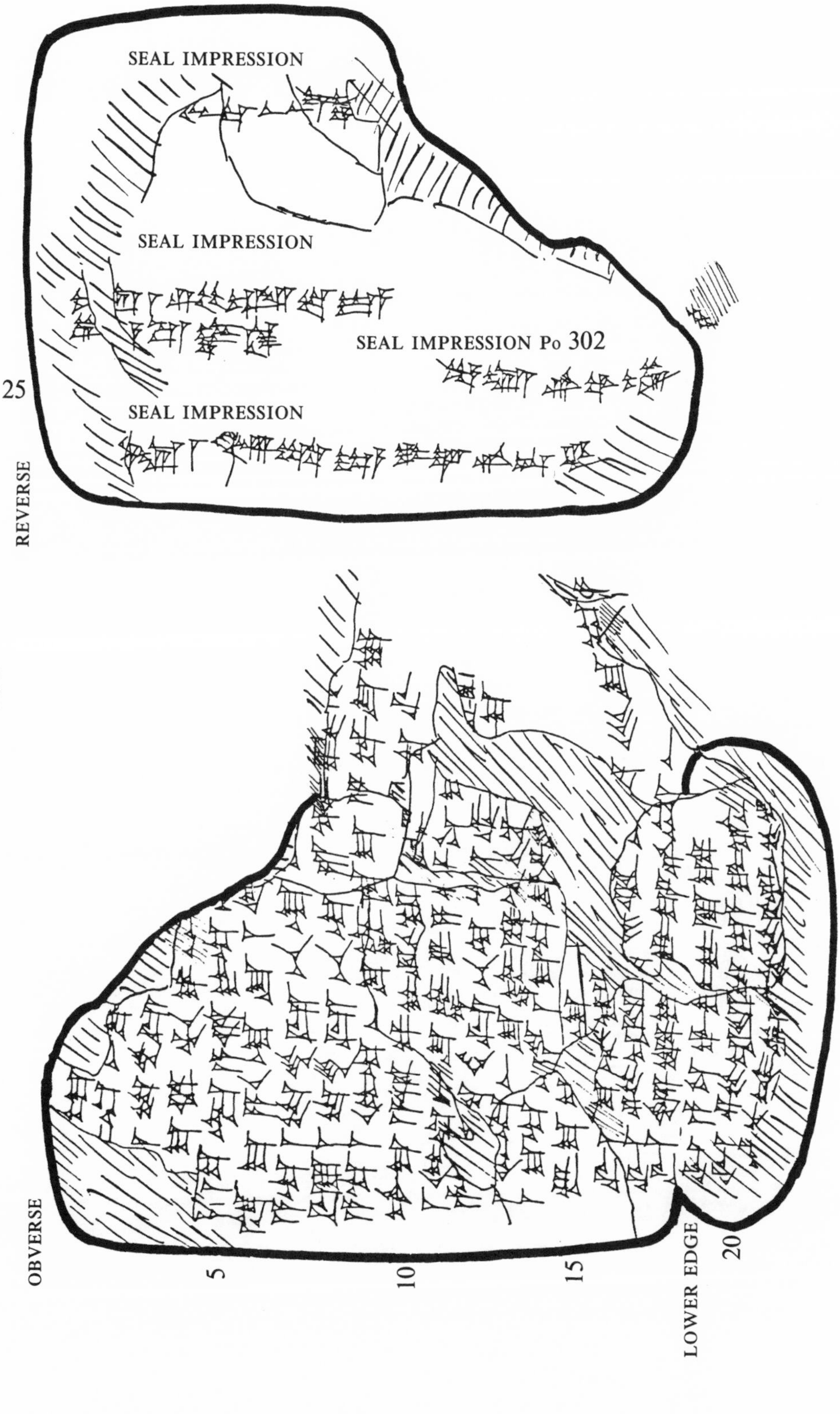
SEAL IMPRESSION
SEAL IMPRESSION
SEAL IMPRESSION Po 302
SEAL IMPRESSION
REVERSE
OBVERSE
LOWER EDGE

760

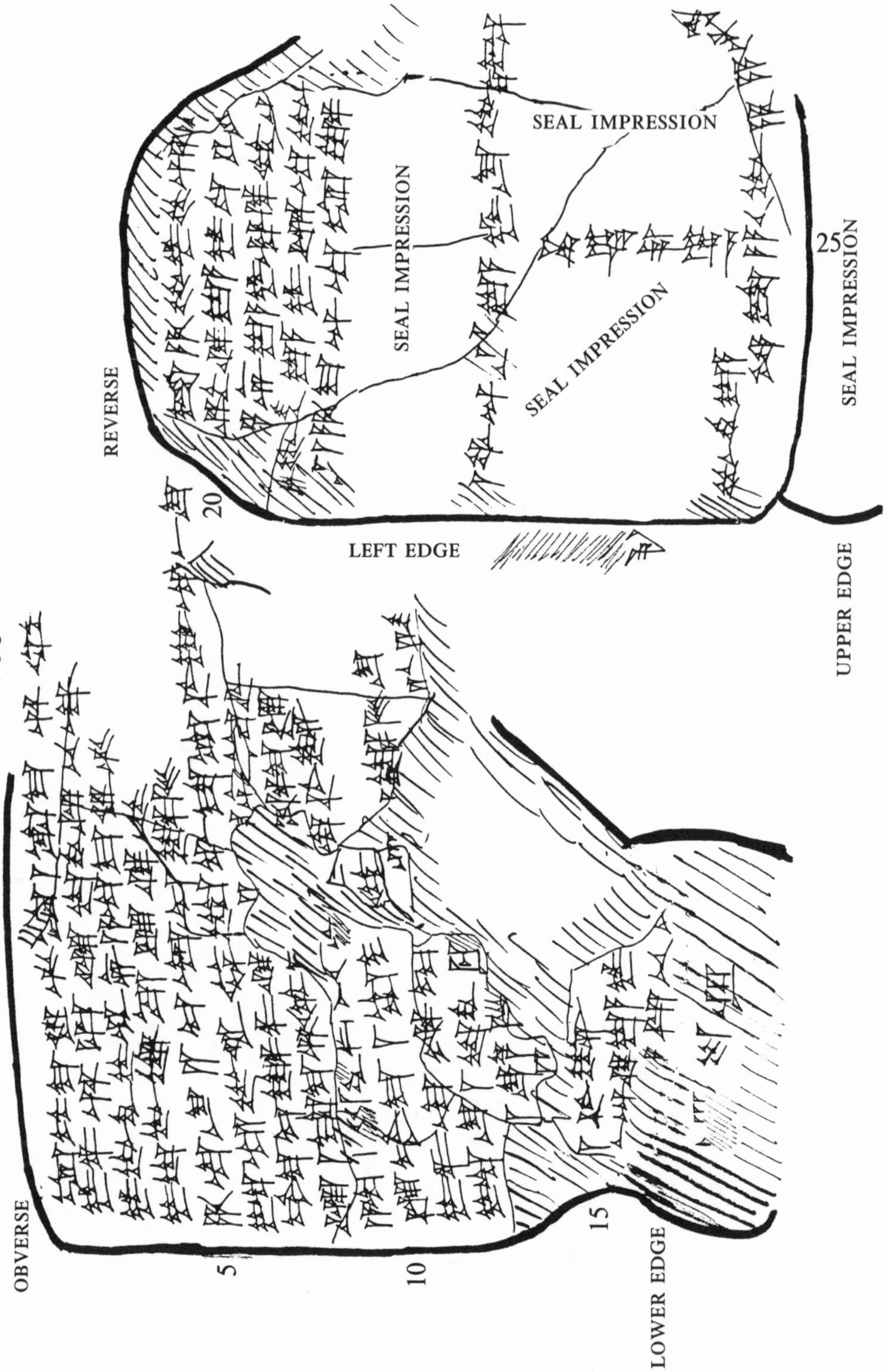
OBVERSE
LOWER EDGE
REVERSE
LEFT EDGE
UPPER EDGE
SEAL IMPRESSION
SEAL IMPRESSION
SEAL IMPRESSION
SEAL IMPRESSION

761

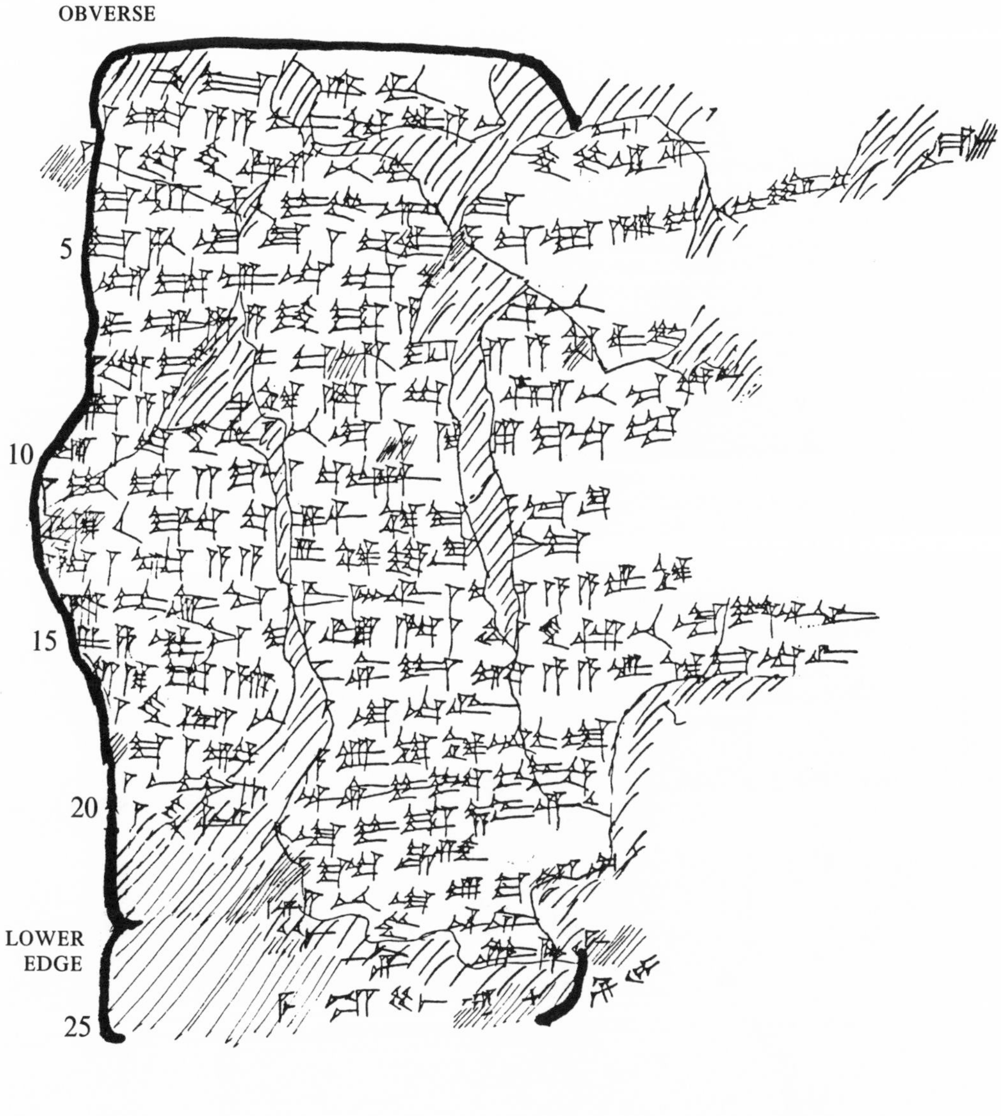

761

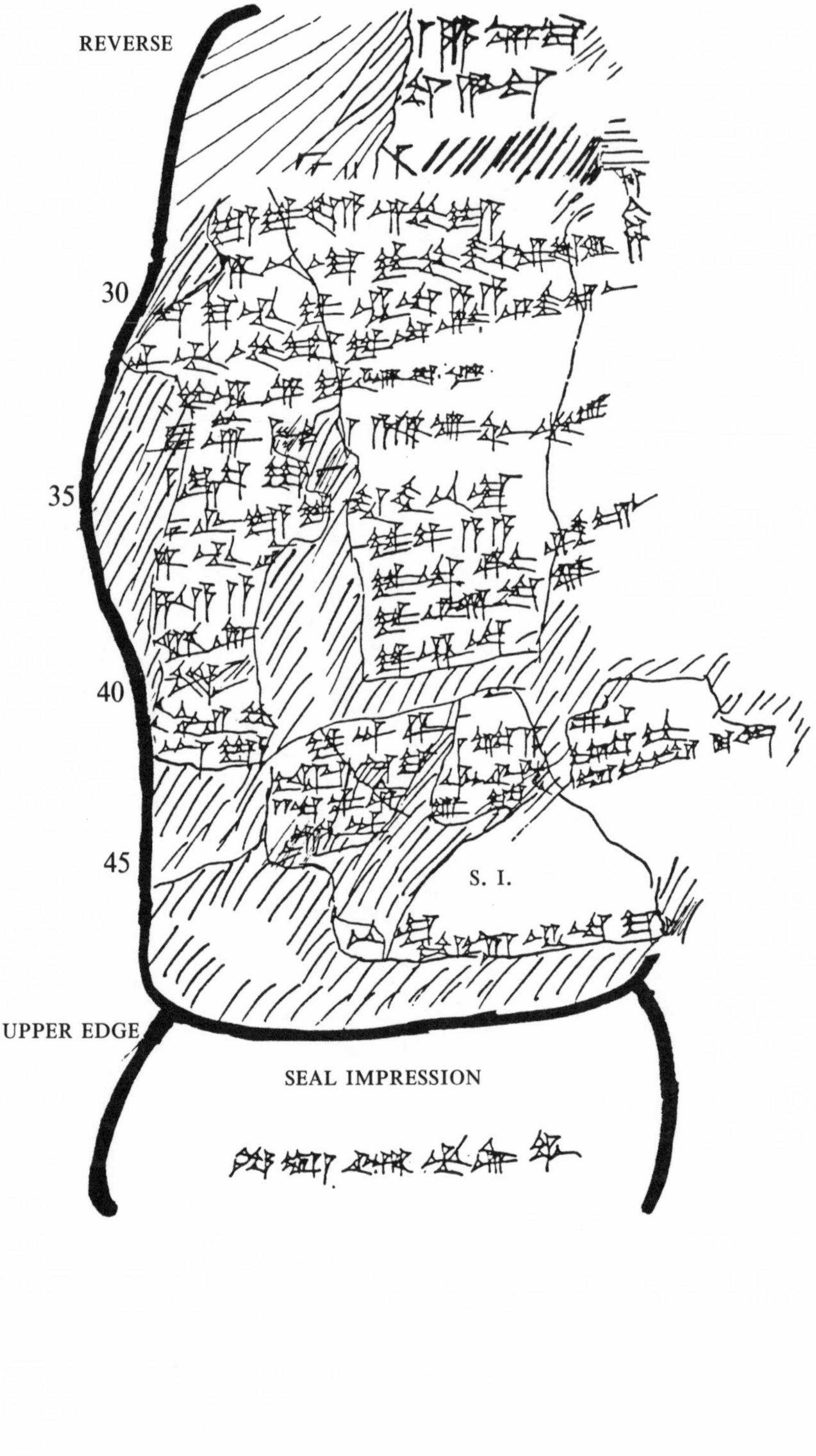

762

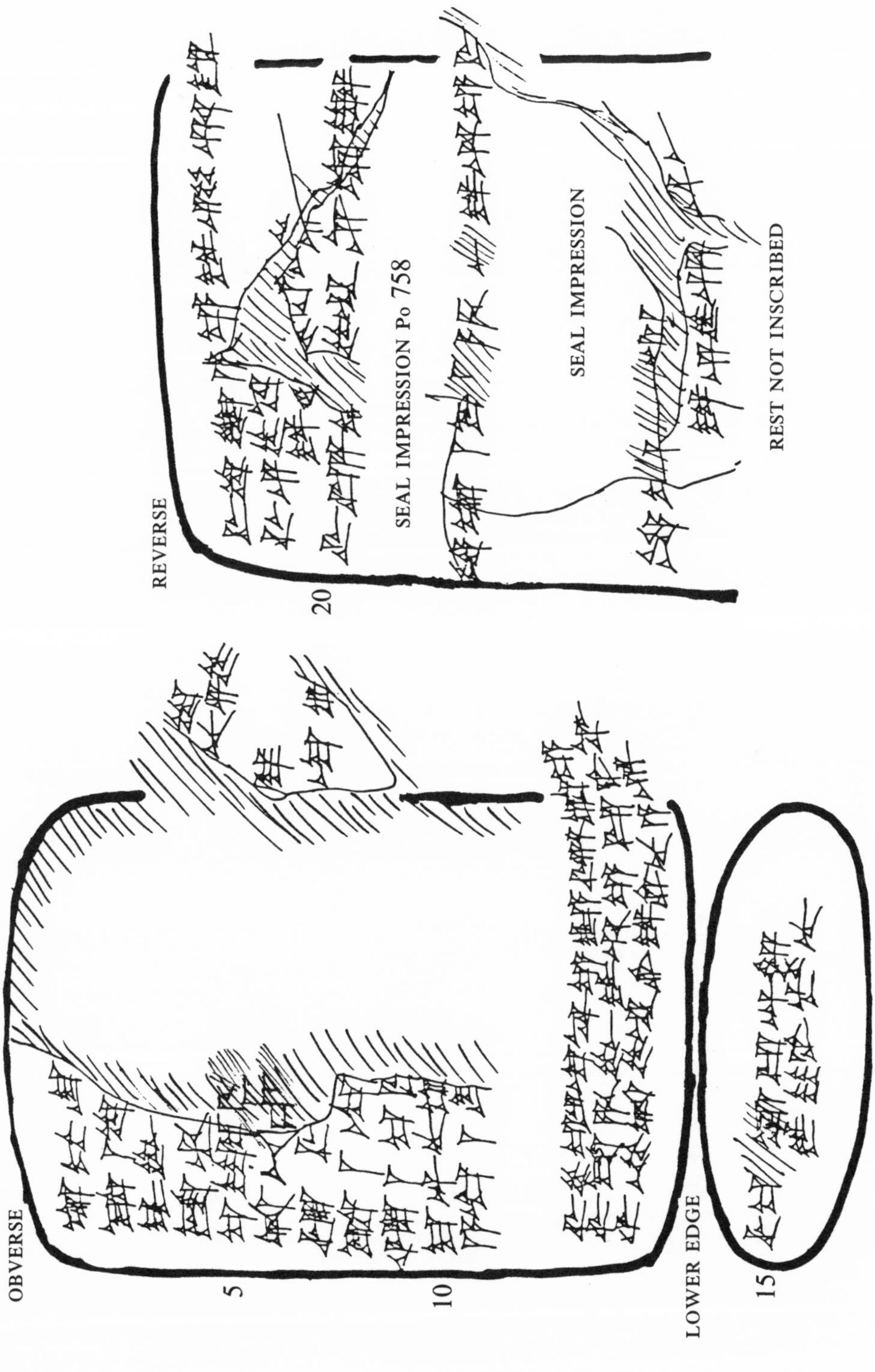
OBVERSE
5
10
LOWER EDGE
15
REVERSE
20
SEAL IMPRESSION Po 758
SEAL IMPRESSION
REST NOT INSCRIBED

763

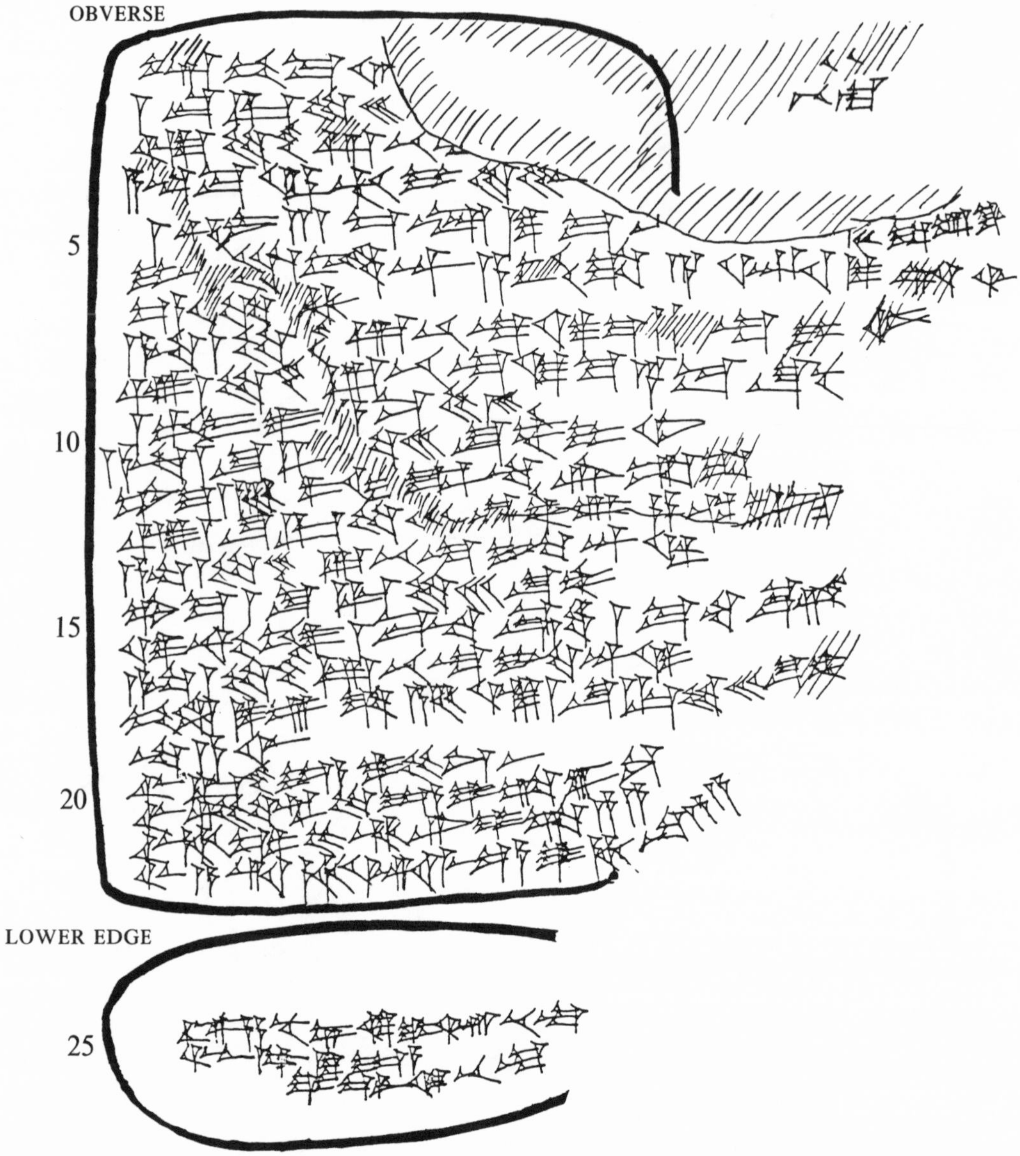

763

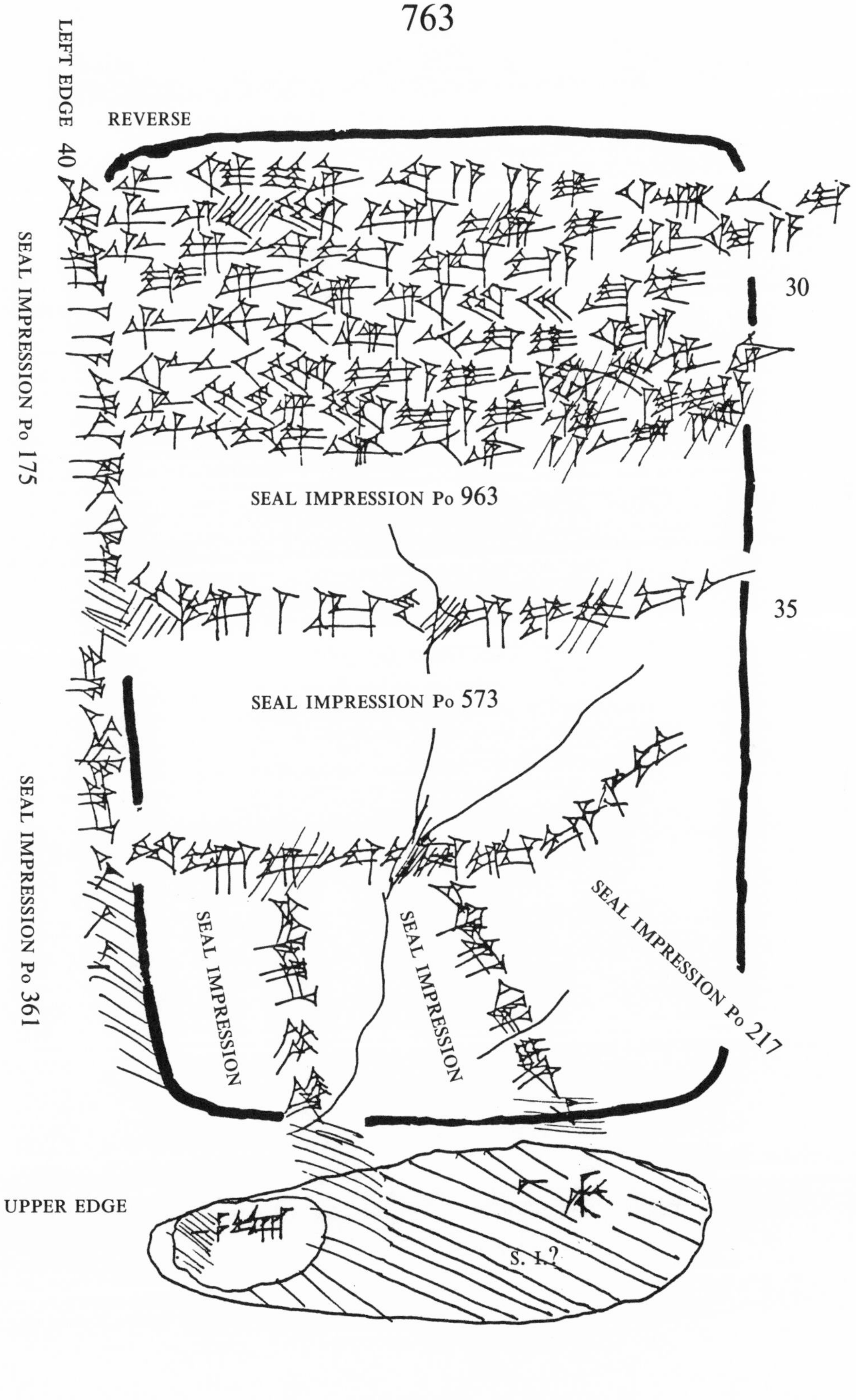
LEFT EDGE 40
REVERSE
30
35
SEAL IMPRESSION Po 175
SEAL IMPRESSION Po 963
SEAL IMPRESSION Po 573
SEAL IMPRESSION Po 361
SEAL IMPRESSION
SEAL IMPRESSION
SEAL IMPRESSION Po 217
UPPER EDGE
S. I.?

764

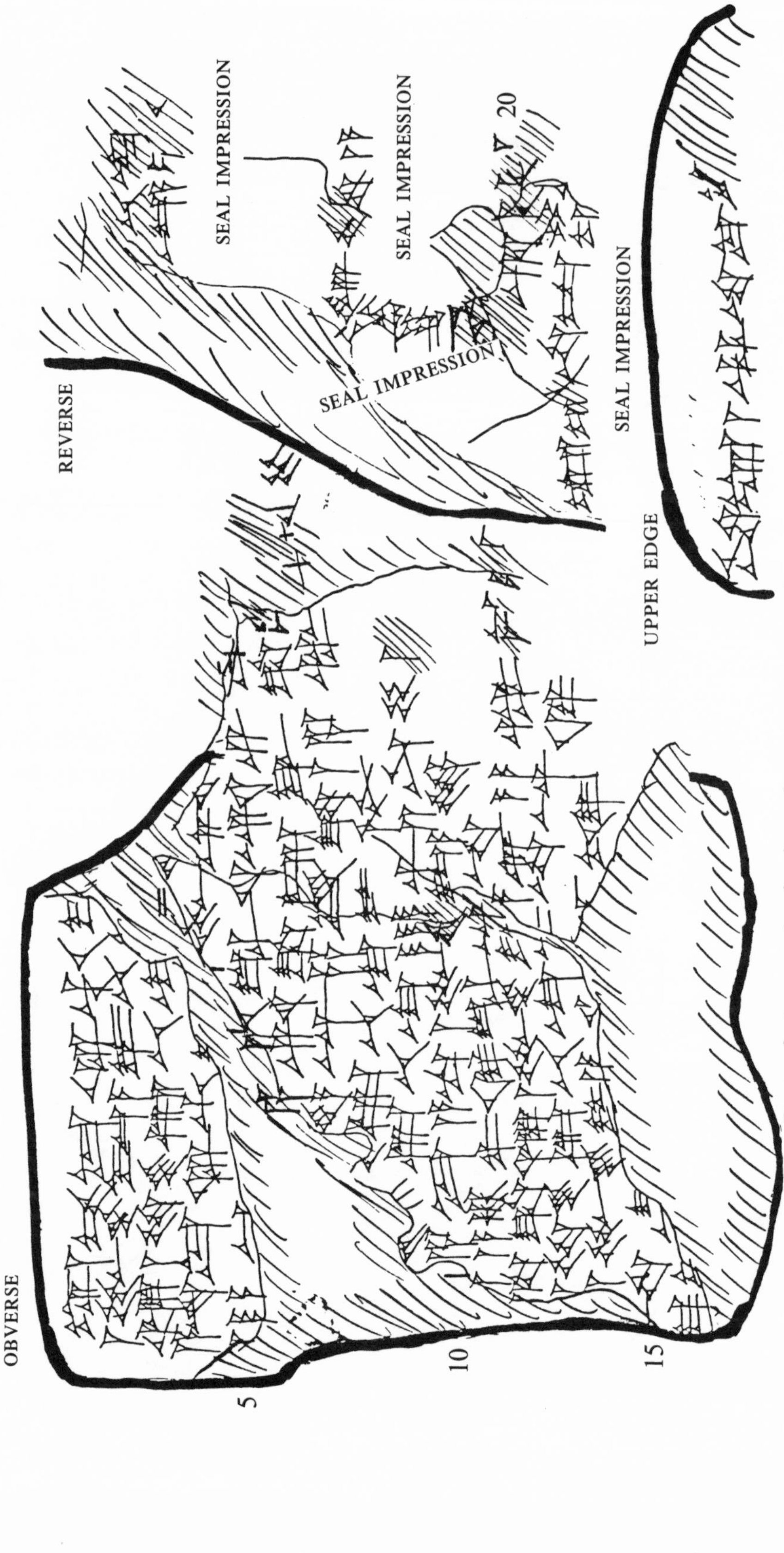

Rest of obverse, beginning of reverse destroyed

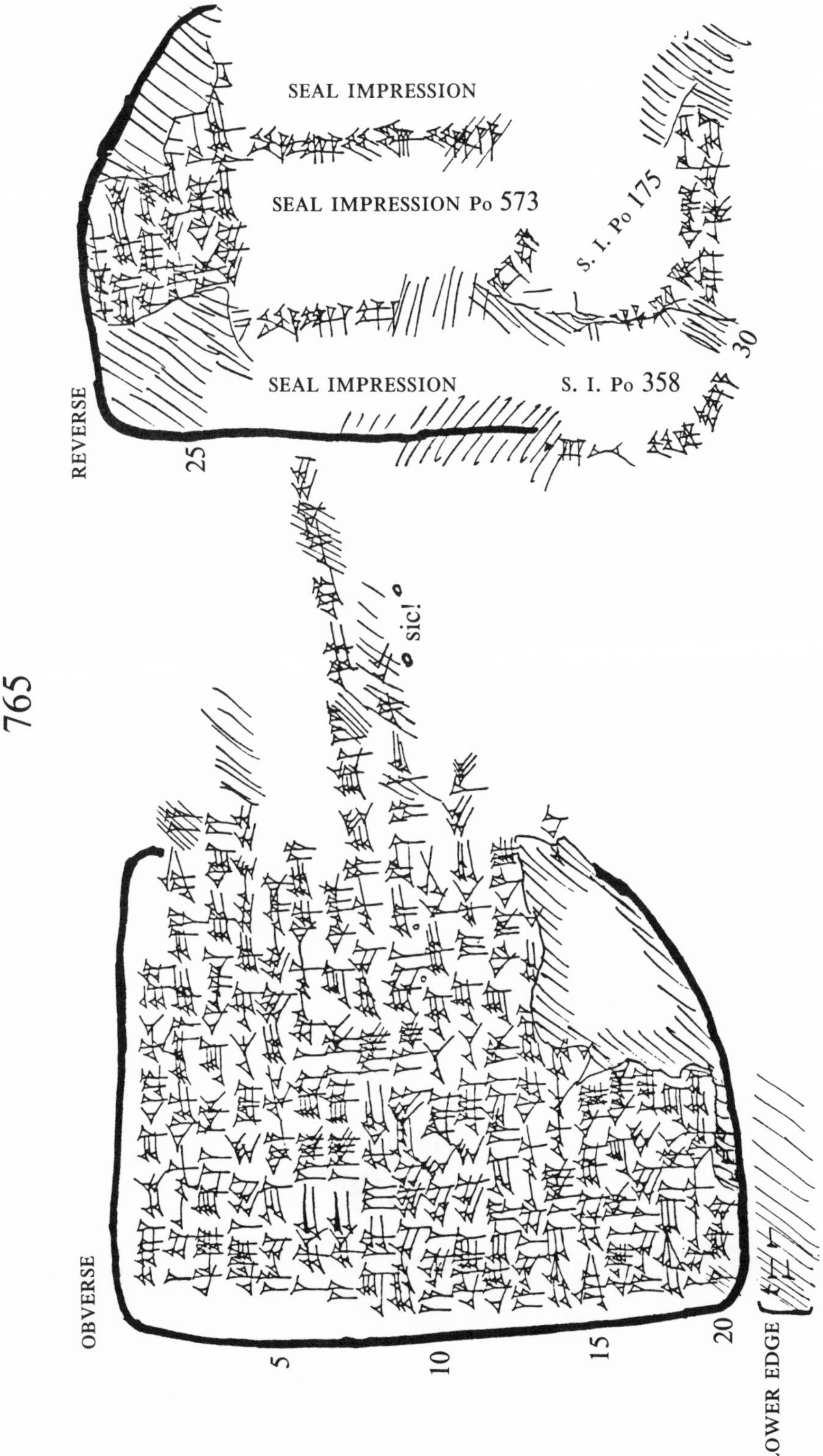
765
OBVERSE
REVERSE
LOWER EDGE
SEAL IMPRESSION
SEAL IMPRESSION Po 573
SEAL IMPRESSION
S. I. Po 175
S. I. Po 358
sic!
5
10
15
20
25
30

766

Beginning of obverse destroyed

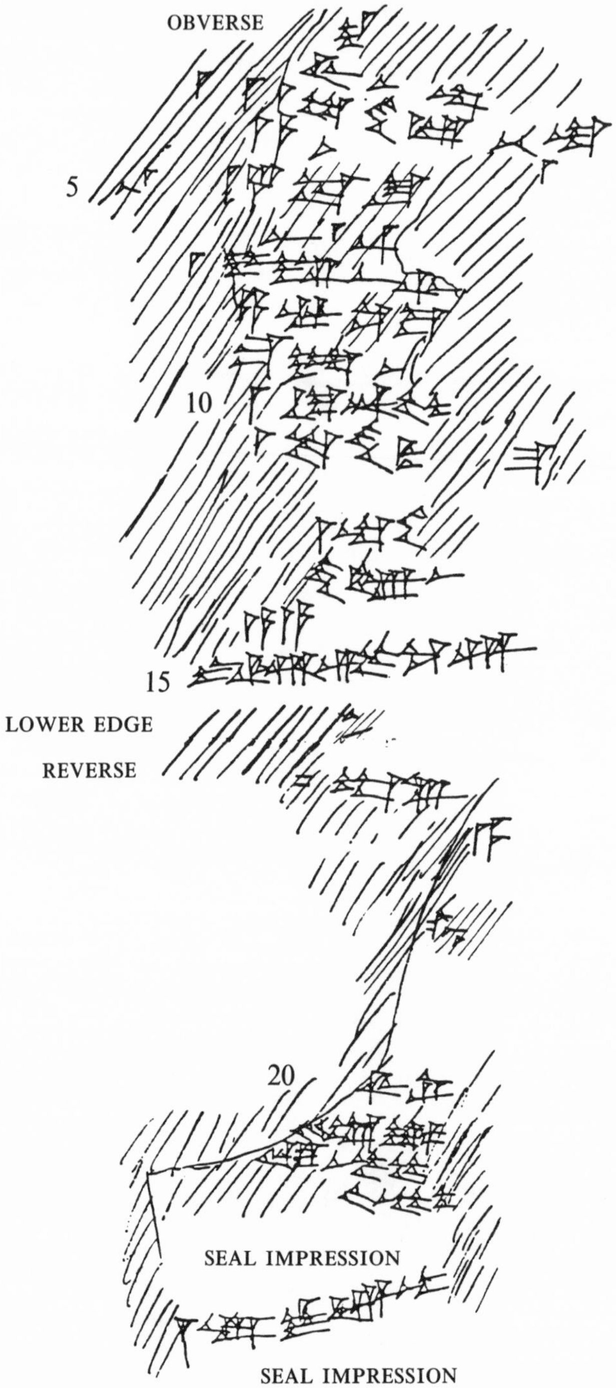

Rest of reverse destroyed

767

Beginning of obverse destroyed

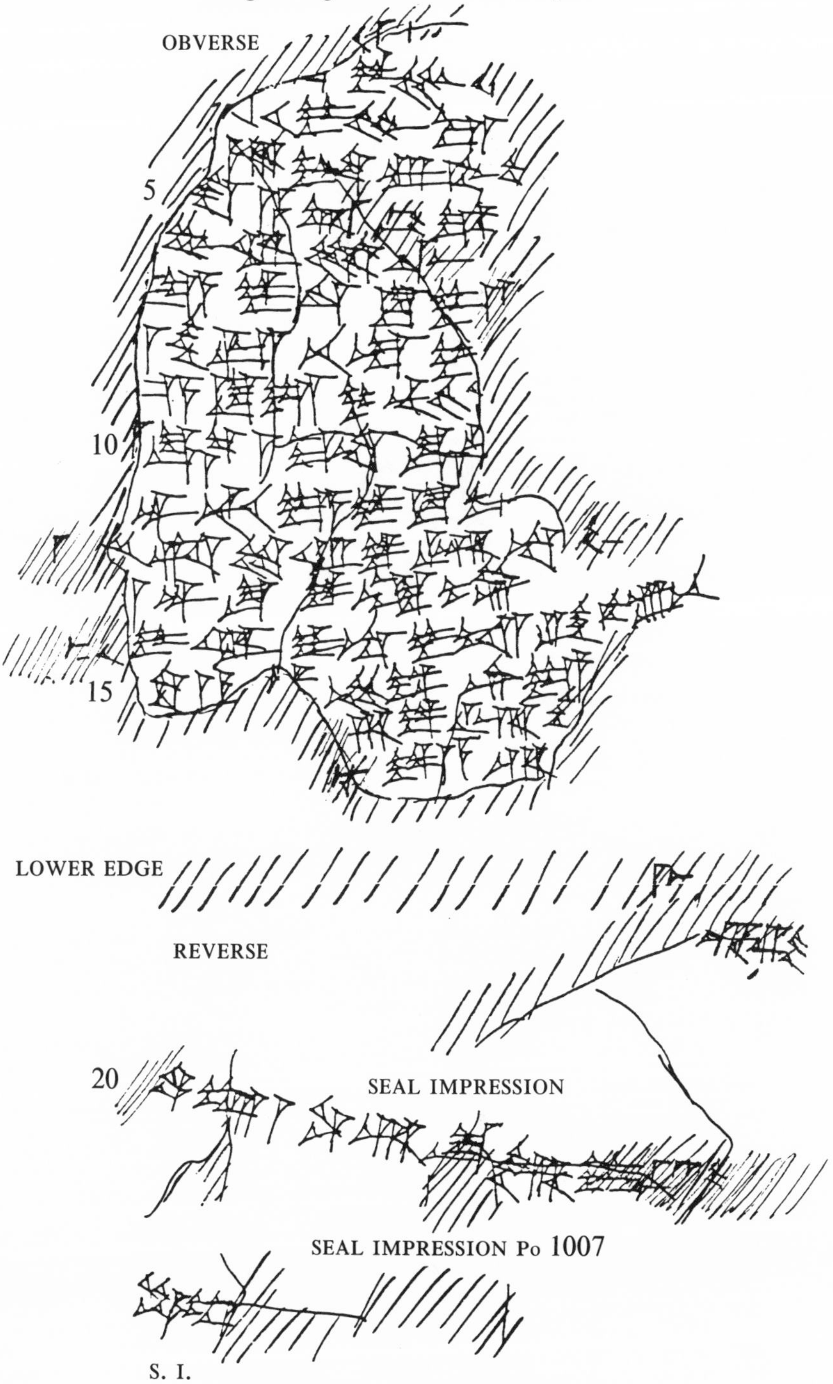

Rest of reverse destroyed

768

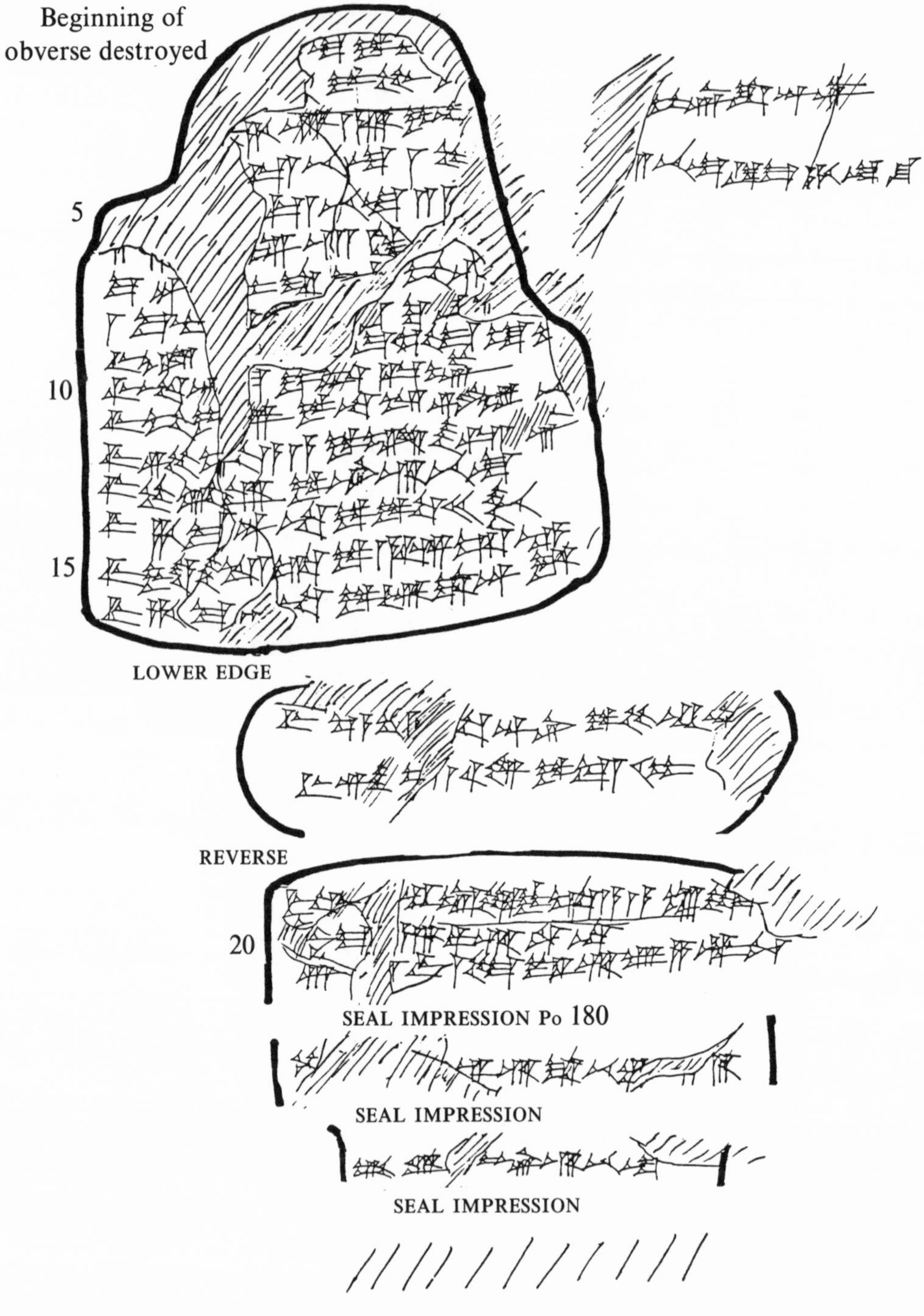
Beginning of obverse destroyed
5
10
15
LOWER EDGE
REVERSE
20
SEAL IMPRESSION Po 180
SEAL IMPRESSION
SEAL IMPRESSION

769

Beginning of obverse destroyed

OBVERSE

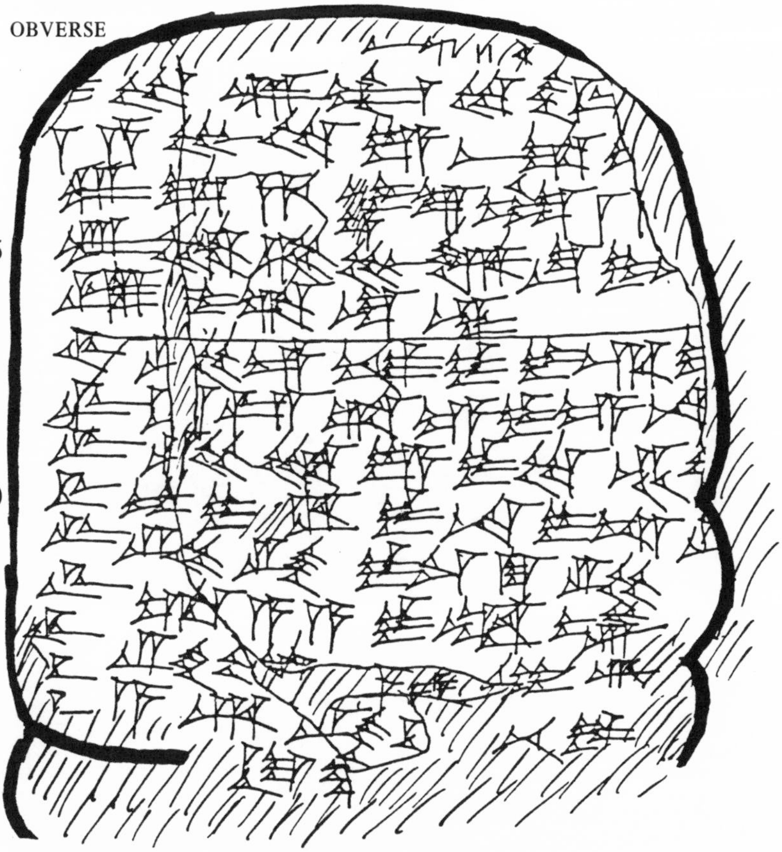

REVERSE

SEAL IMPRESSION Po 408

SEAL IMPRESSION Po 123

770

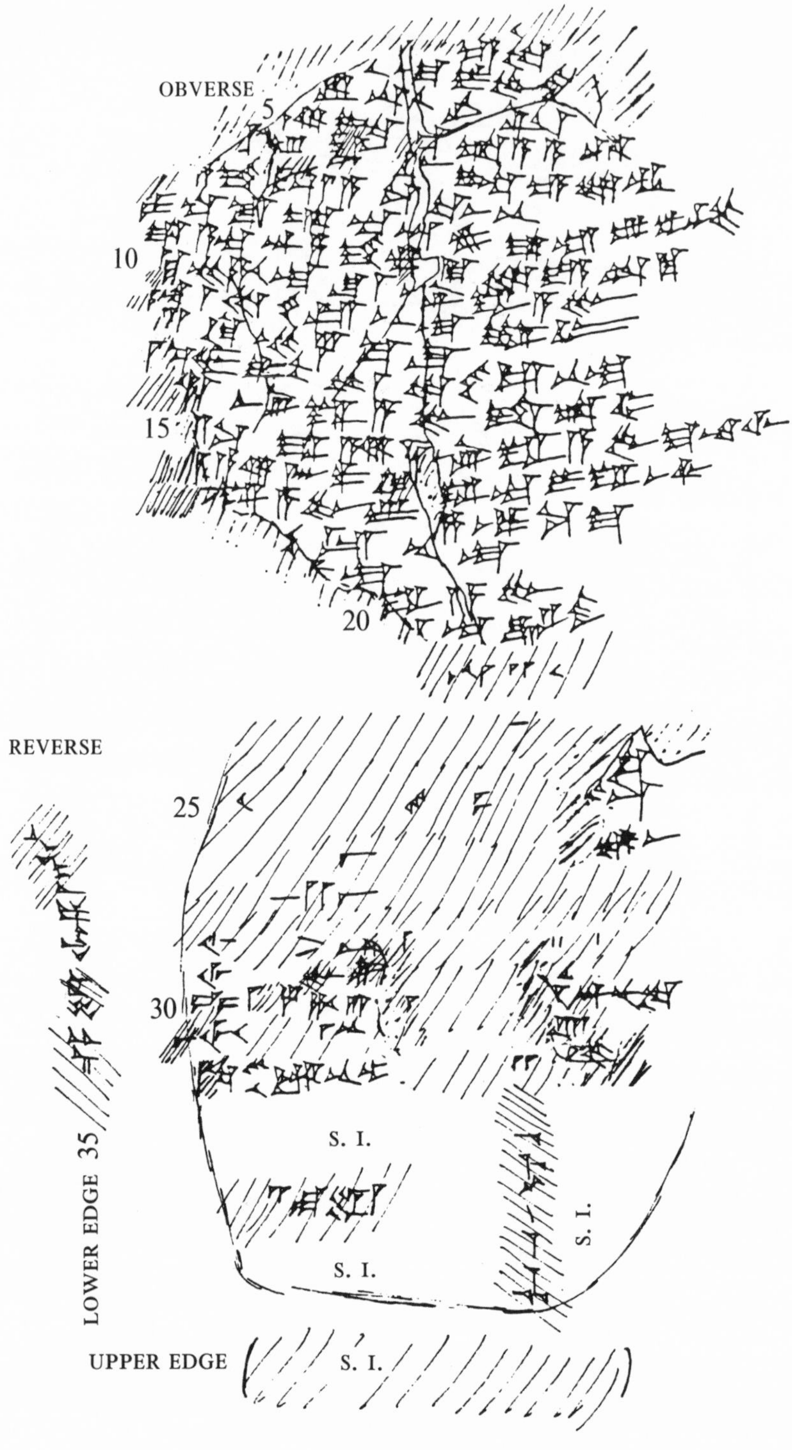
OBVERSE
5
10
15
20
REVERSE
25
30
LOWER EDGE 35
S. I.
S. I.
S. I.
UPPER EDGE
S. I.

771

Beginning of obverse destroyed

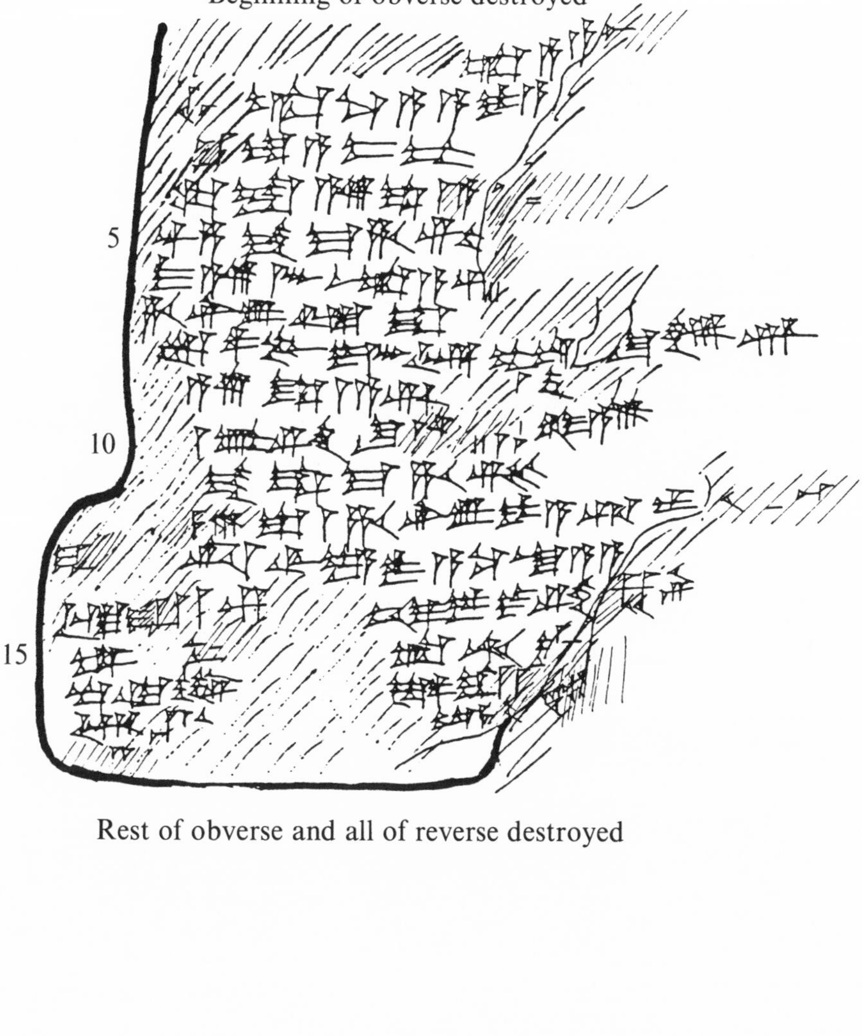

Rest of obverse and all of reverse destroyed

772

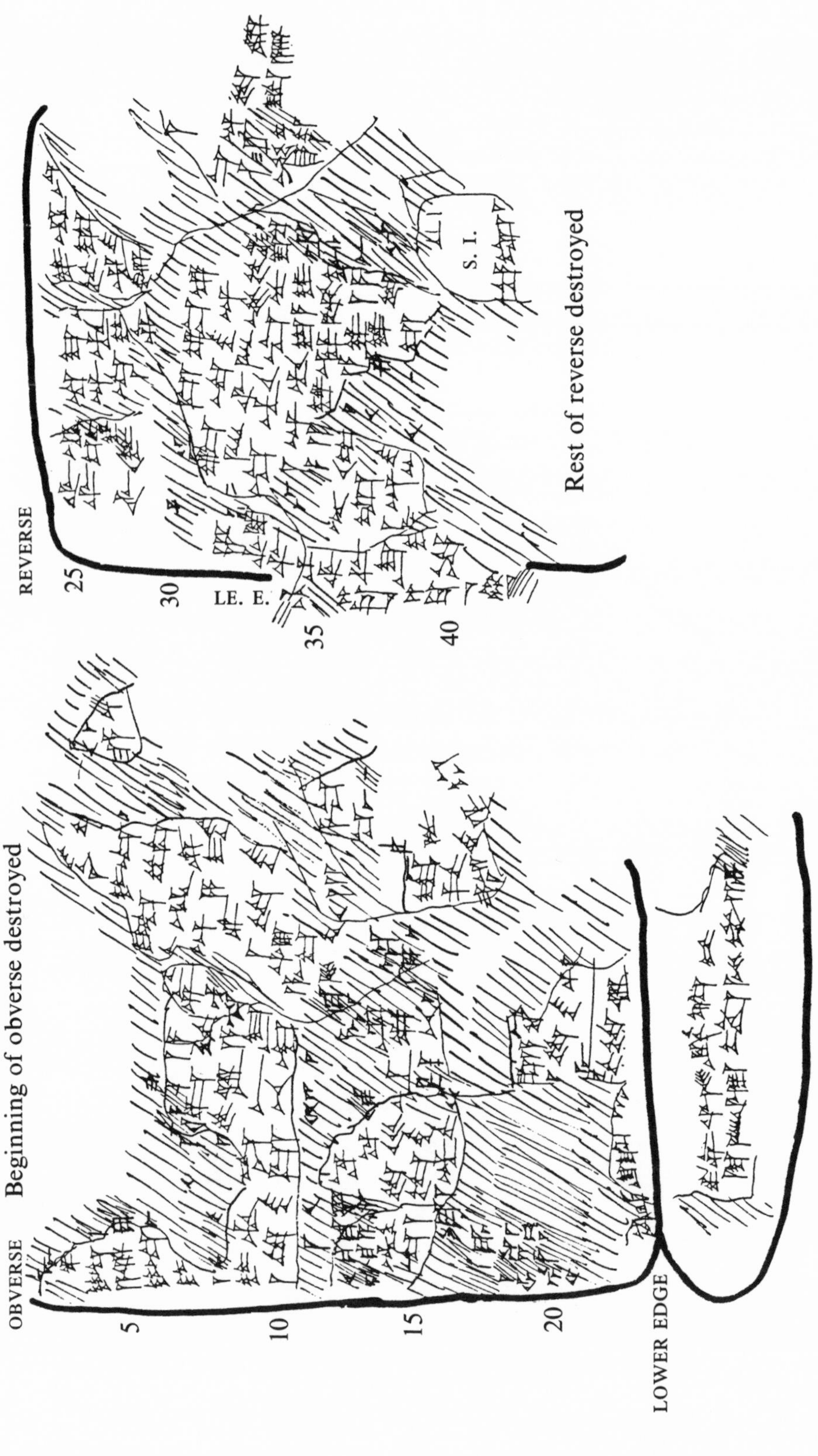
OBVERSE
Beginning of obverse destroyed
5
10
15
20
LOWER EDGE
REVERSE
25
30
LE. E.
35
40
S. I.
Rest of reverse destroyed

773

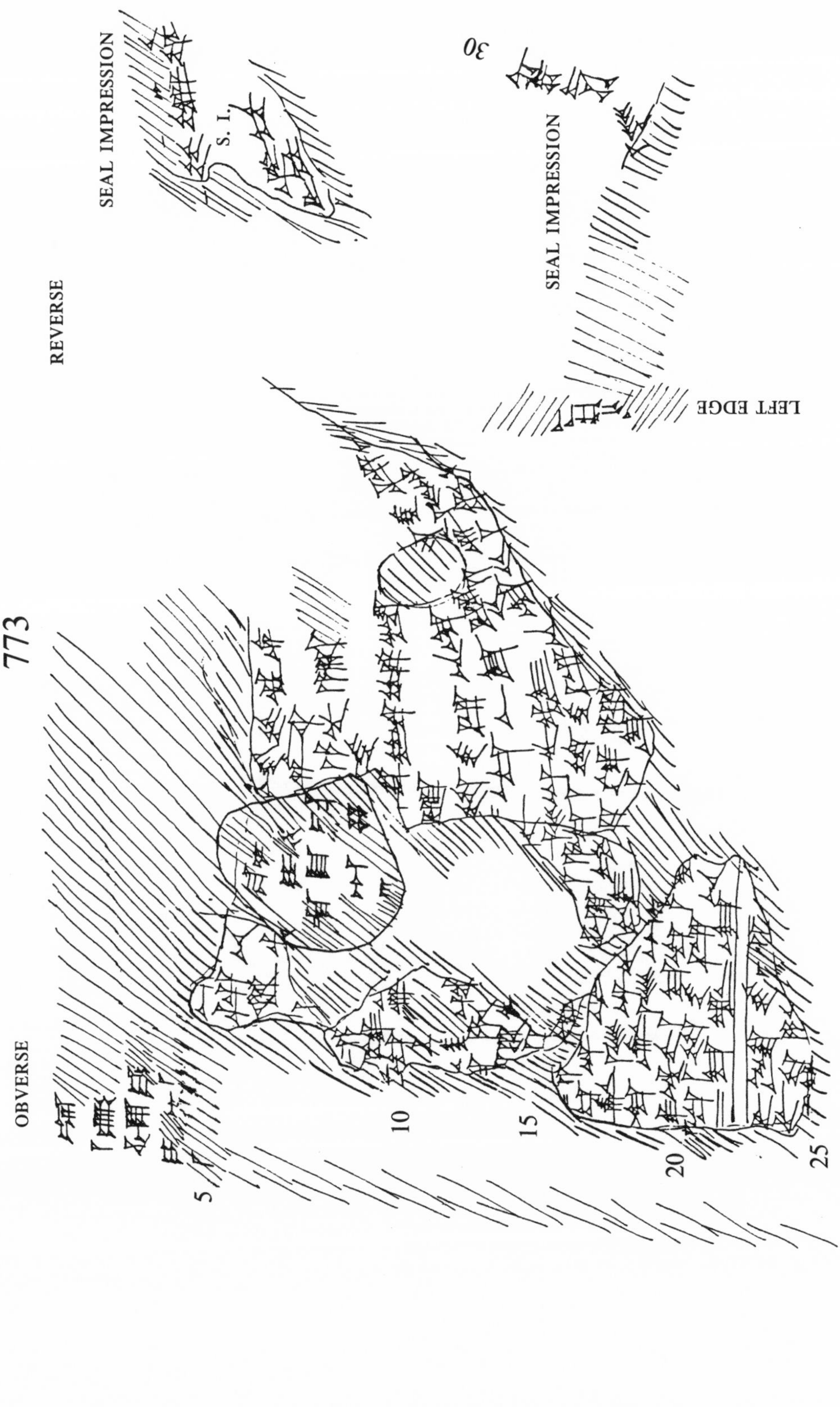

Rest of obverse, beginning of reverse destroyed

774

OBVERSE

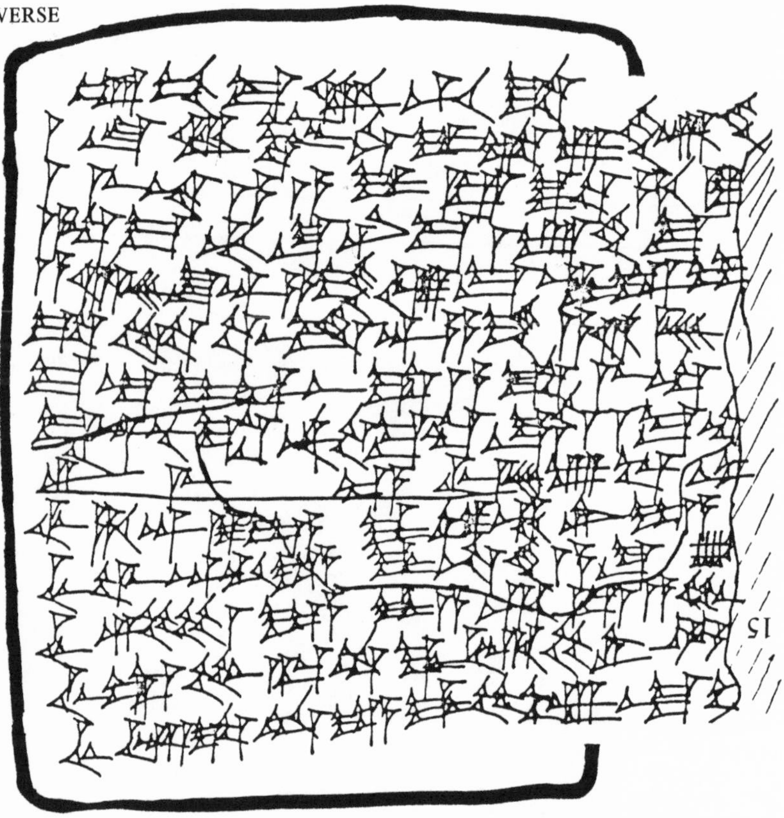

Beginning of reverse destroyed

S. I.

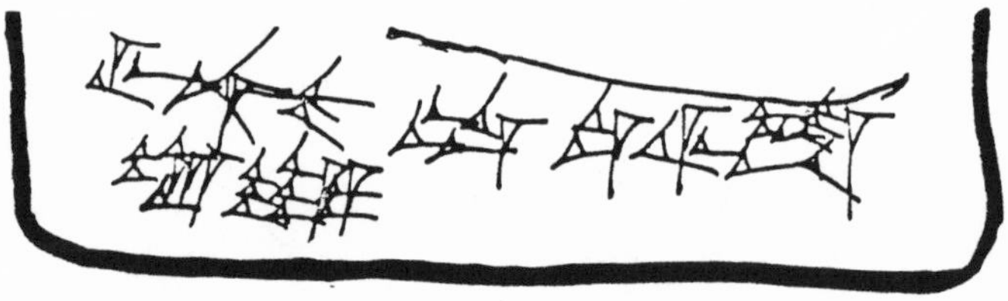

775

OBVERSE

Beginning of obverse destroyed

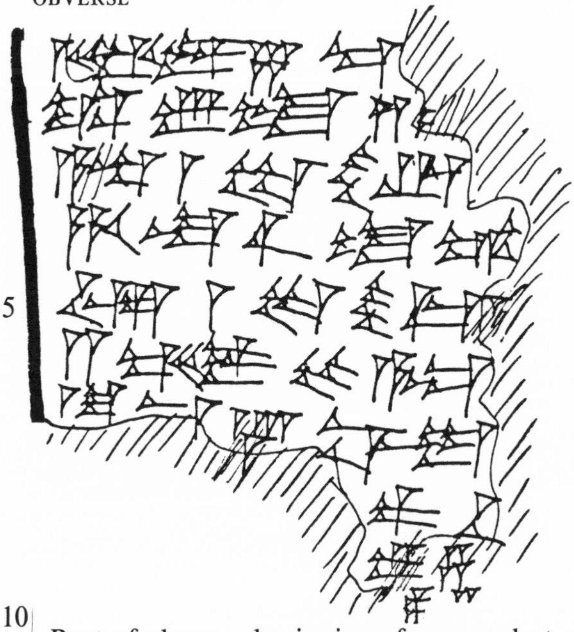

Rest of obverse, beginning of reverse destroyed

REVERSE

SEAL IMPRESSION Po 361

SEAL IMPRESSION Po 924

SEAL IMPRESSION

Rest of reverse destroyed

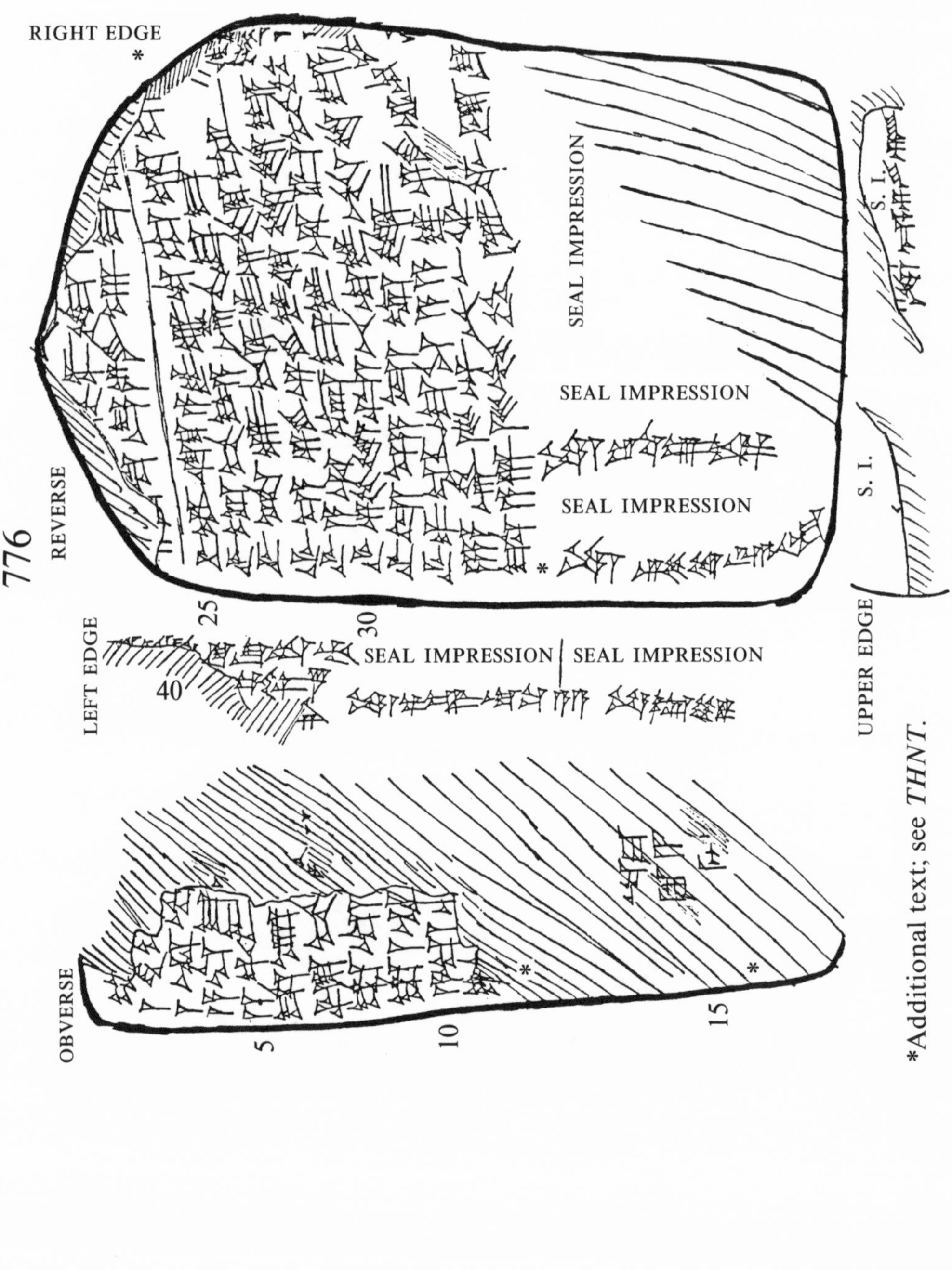

*Additional text; see *THNT*.

777

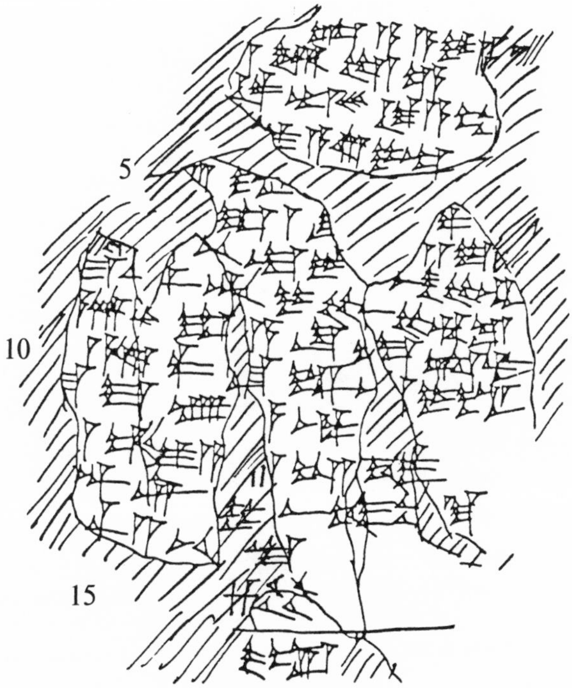

SEAL IMPRESSION

Rest destroyed

778

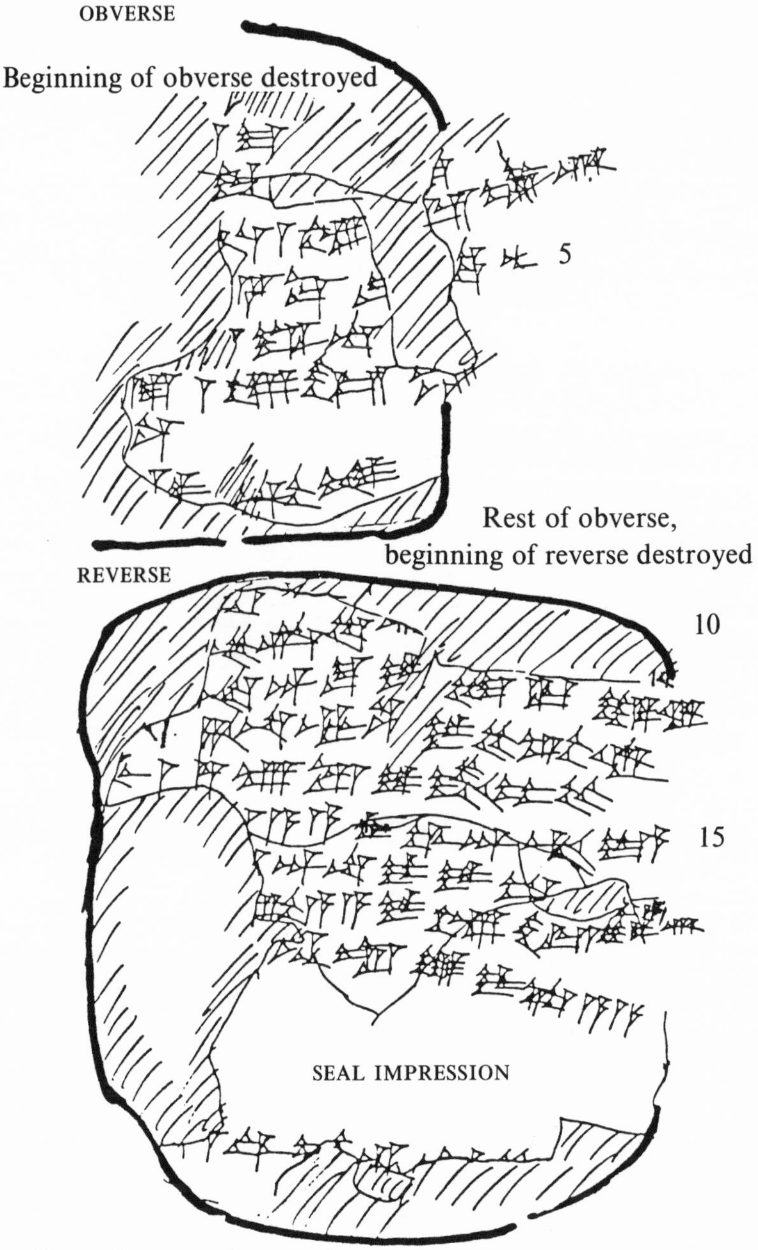

Rest of reverse destroyed

779

OBVERSE

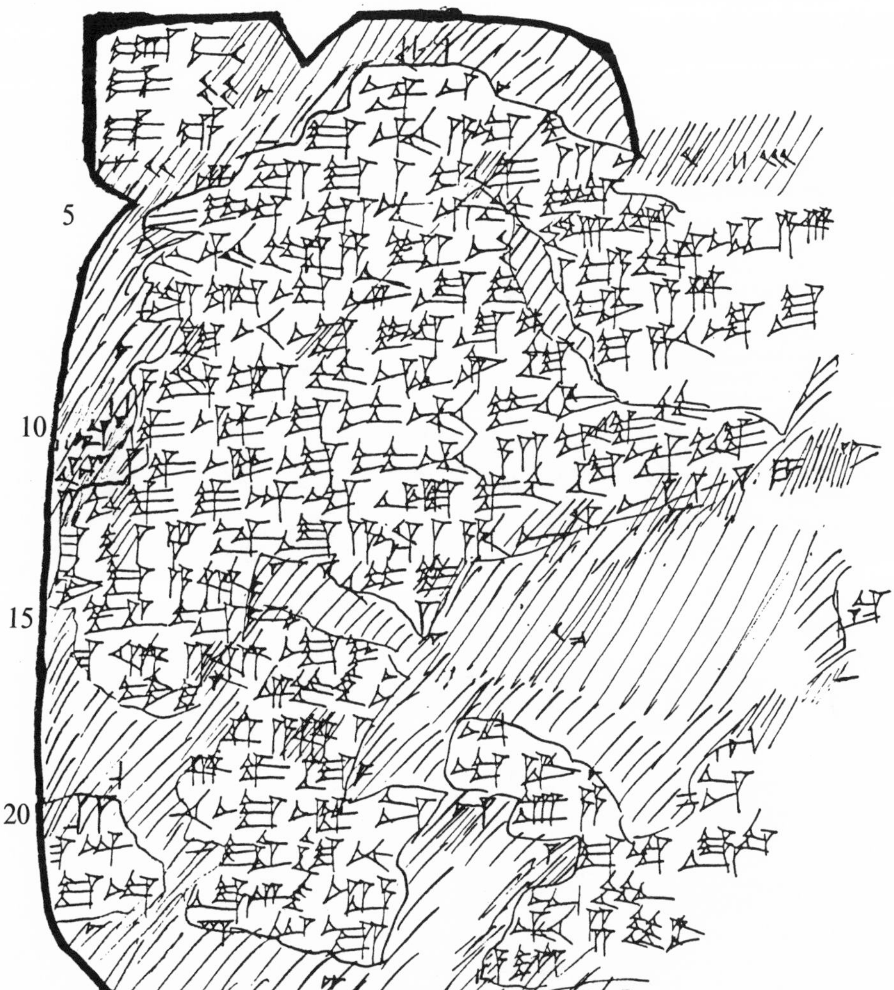

LOWER EDGE

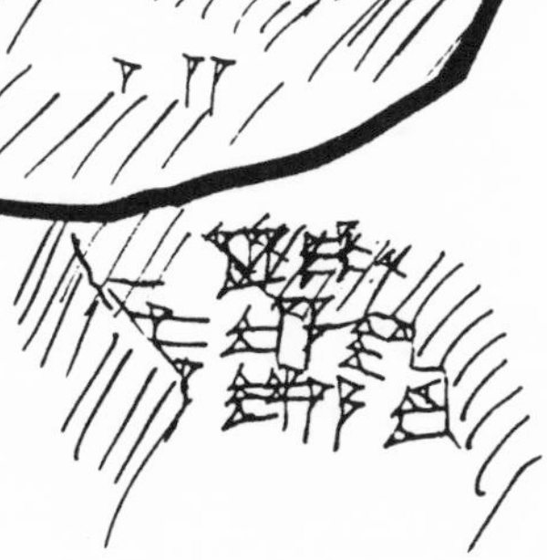

779

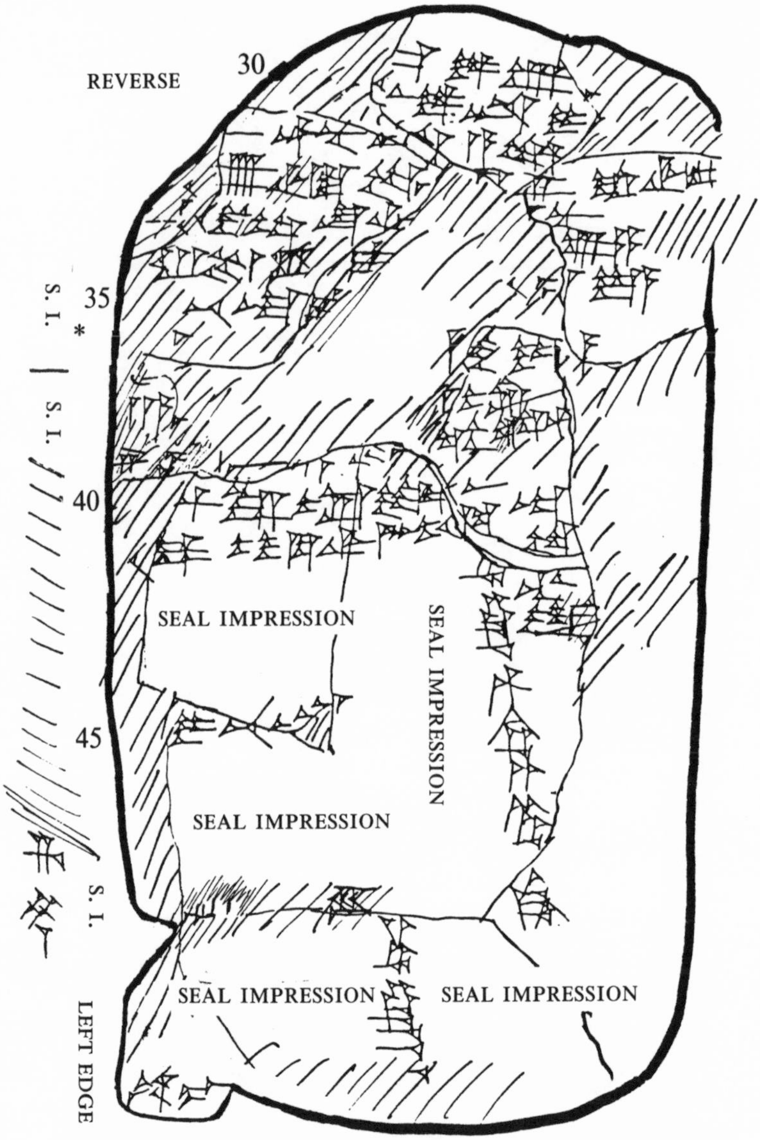

*Additional text; see *THNT*.

780

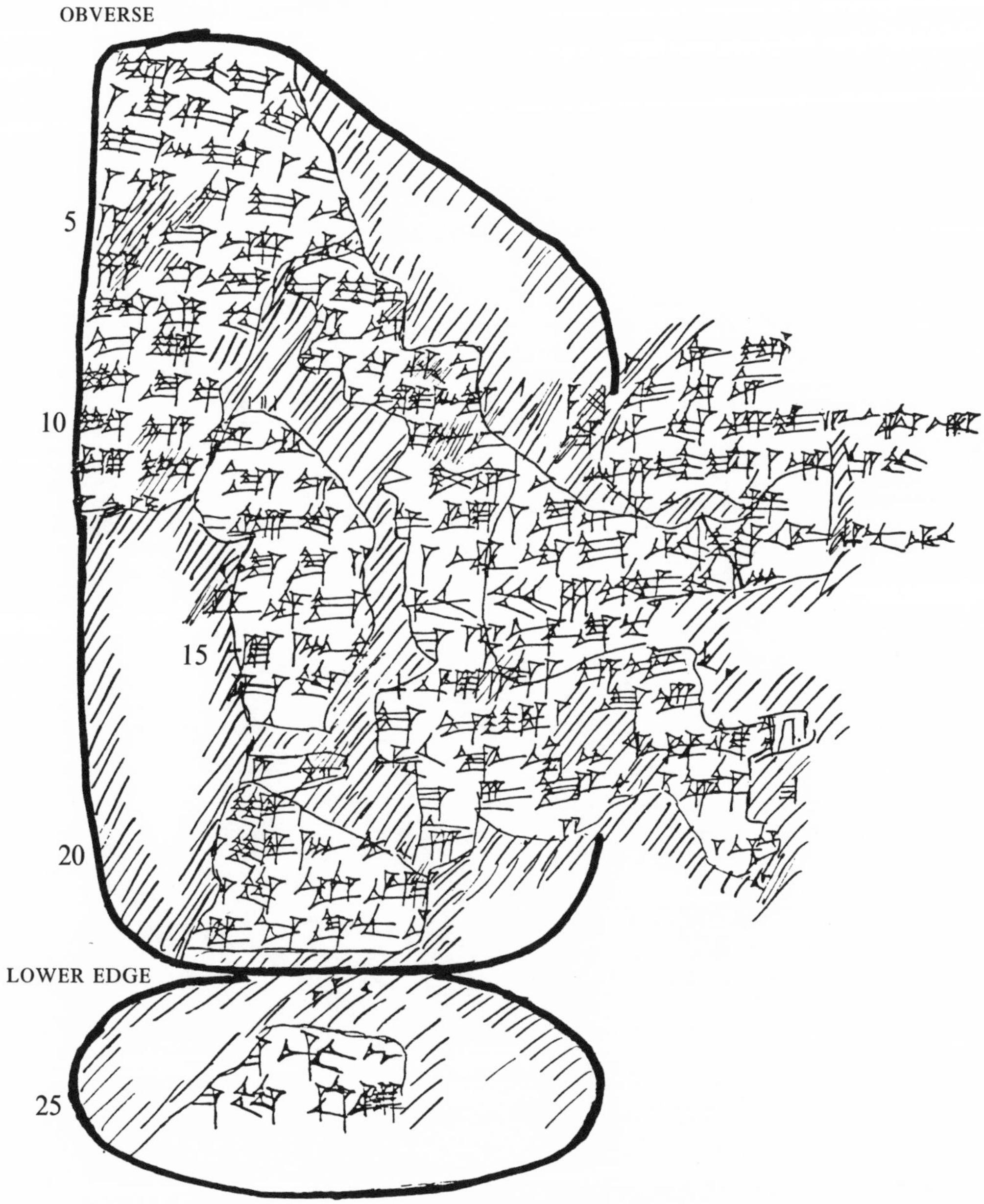

780

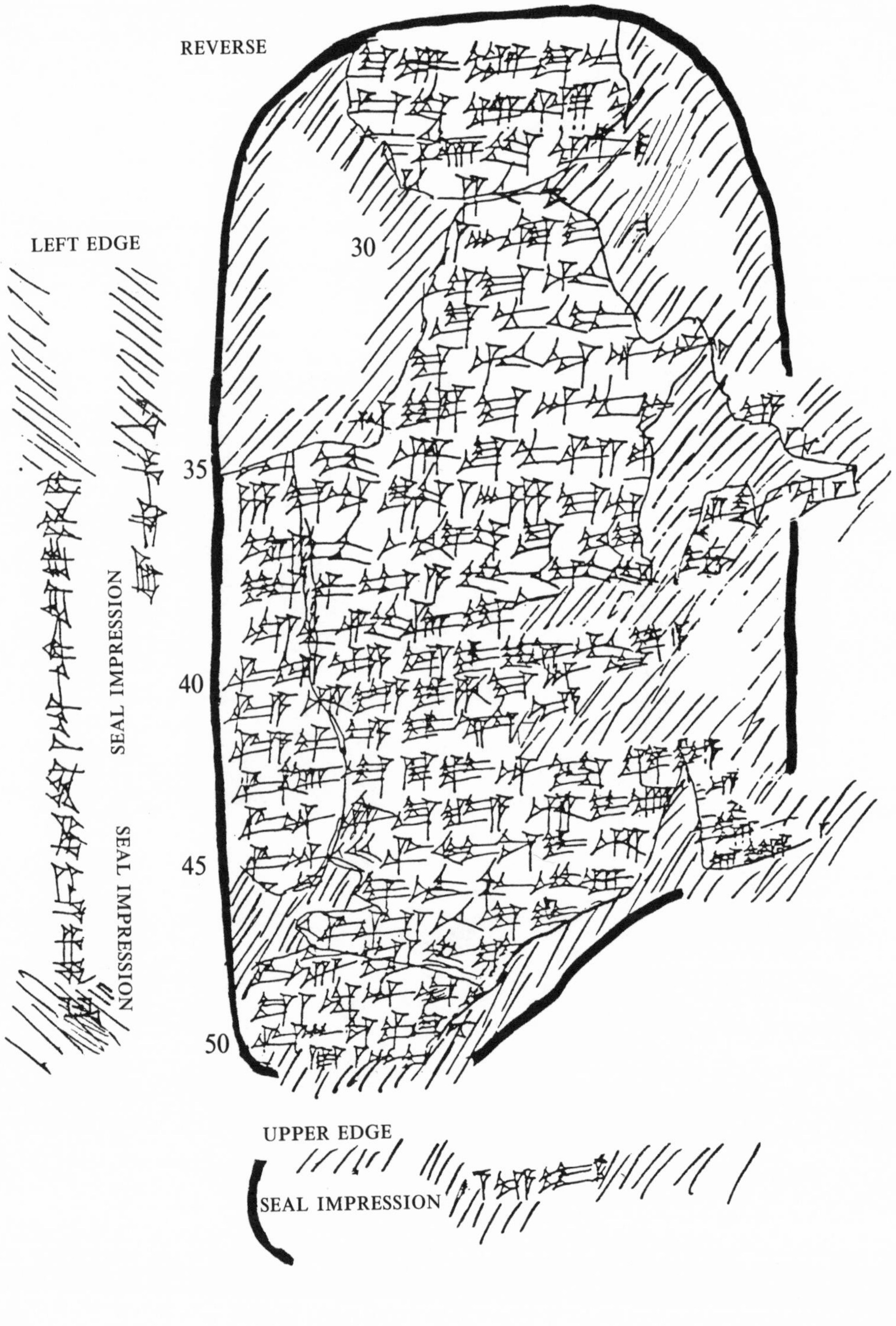
REVERSE
LEFT EDGE
30
35
40
45
50
SEAL IMPRESSION
SEAL IMPRESSION
UPPER EDGE
SEAL IMPRESSION

781

OBVERSE

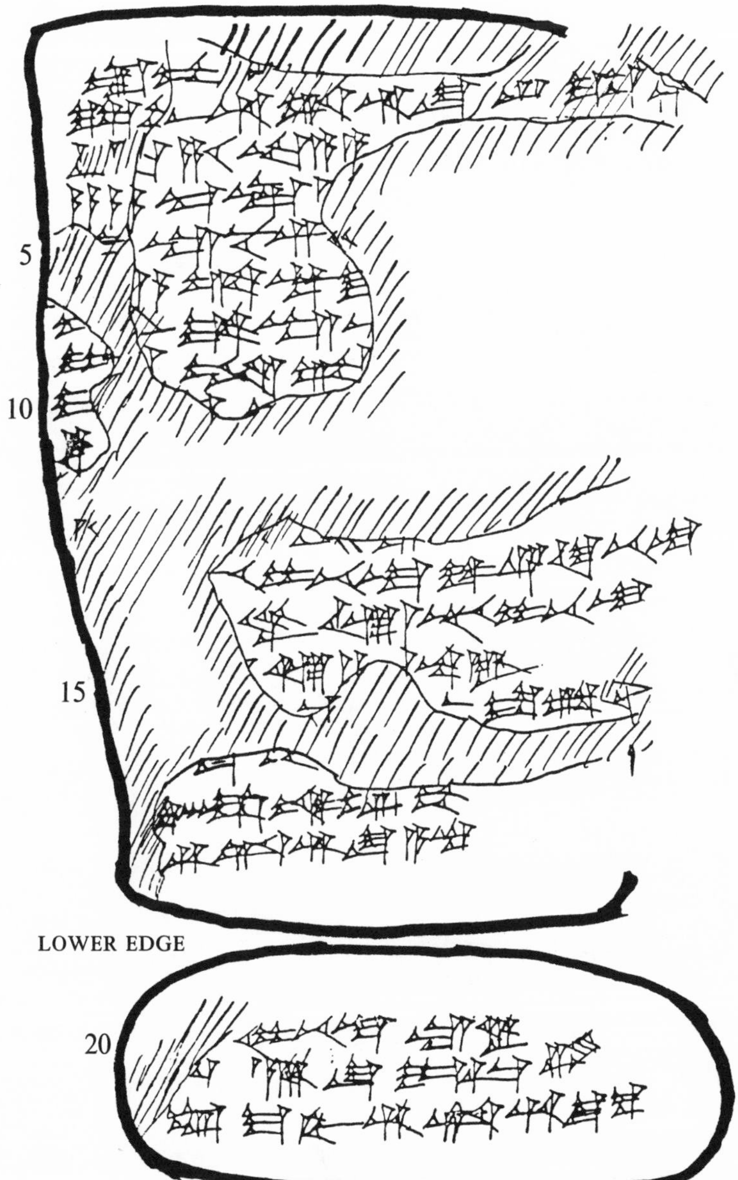

LOWER EDGE

781

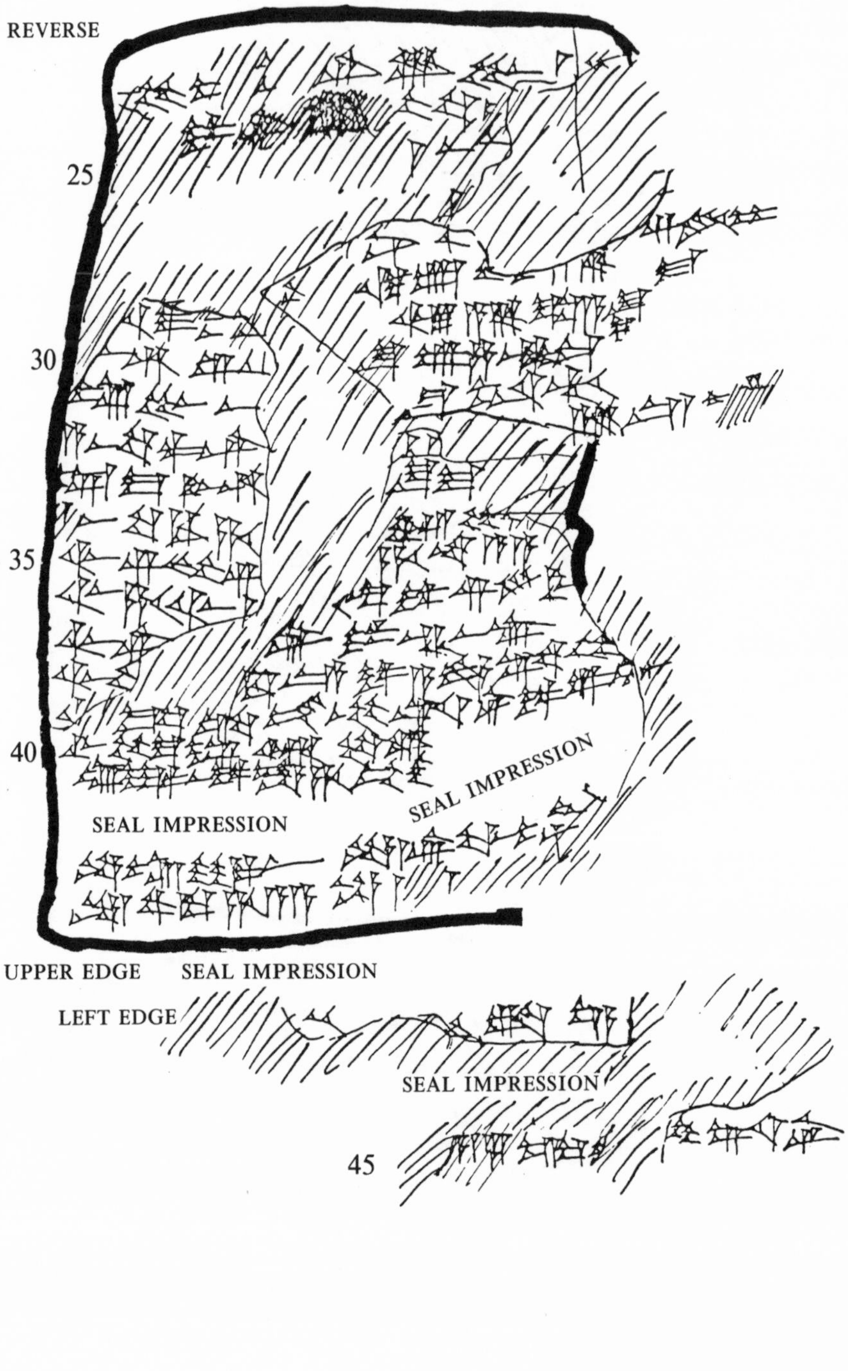
REVERSE
SEAL IMPRESSION
SEAL IMPRESSION
UPPER EDGE
SEAL IMPRESSION
LEFT EDGE
SEAL IMPRESSION

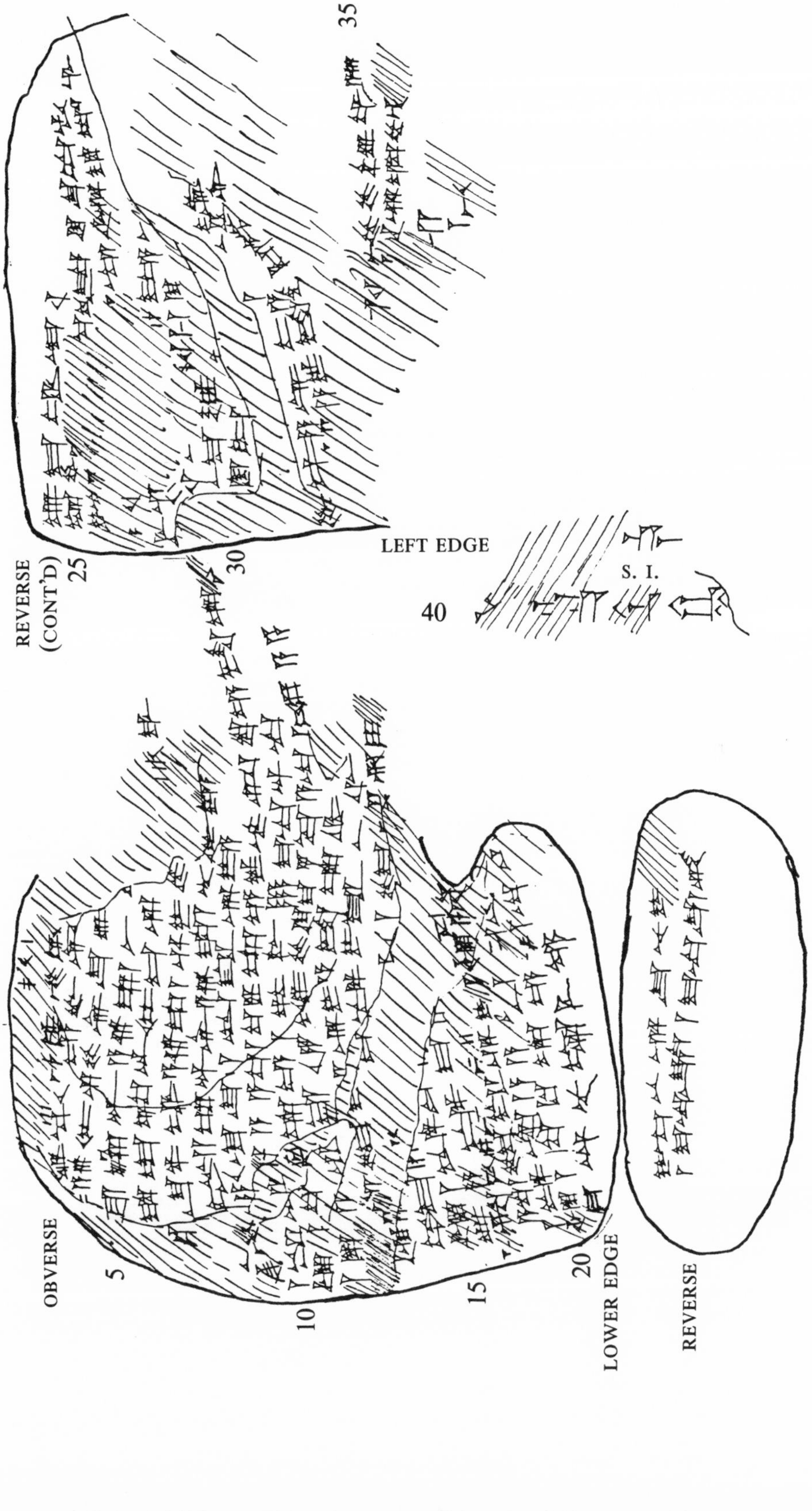
782
OBVERSE
LOWER EDGE
REVERSE
REVERSE (CONT'D)
LEFT EDGE
S. I.

783

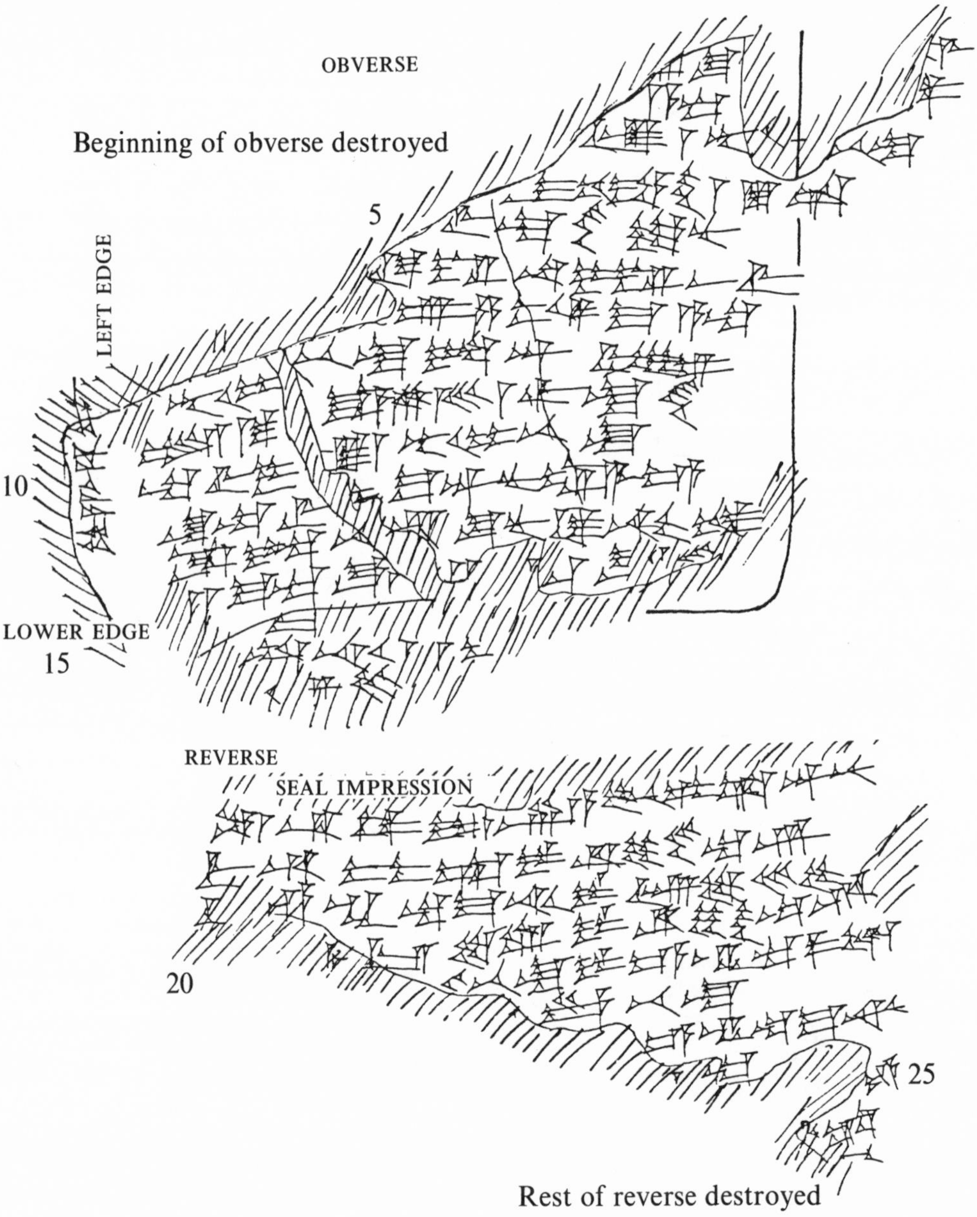
OBVERSE
Beginning of obverse destroyed
LEFT EDGE
LOWER EDGE
REVERSE
SEAL IMPRESSION
Rest of reverse destroyed

784

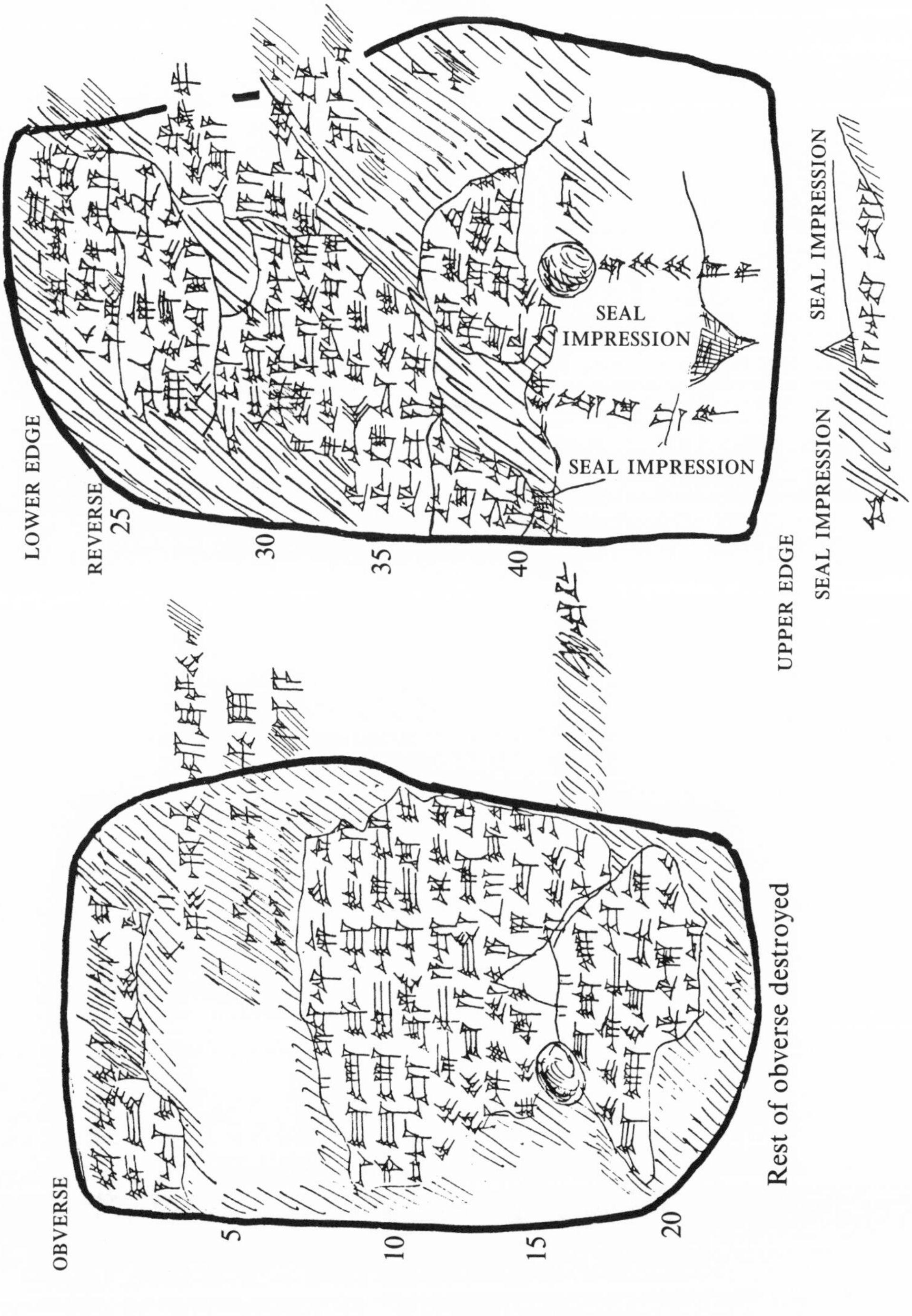
LOWER EDGE
REVERSE
25
30
35
40
SEAL IMPRESSION
SEAL IMPRESSION
SEAL IMPRESSION
UPPER EDGE
SEAL IMPRESSION
SEAL IMPRESSION
OBVERSE
5
10
15
20
Rest of obverse destroyed

785

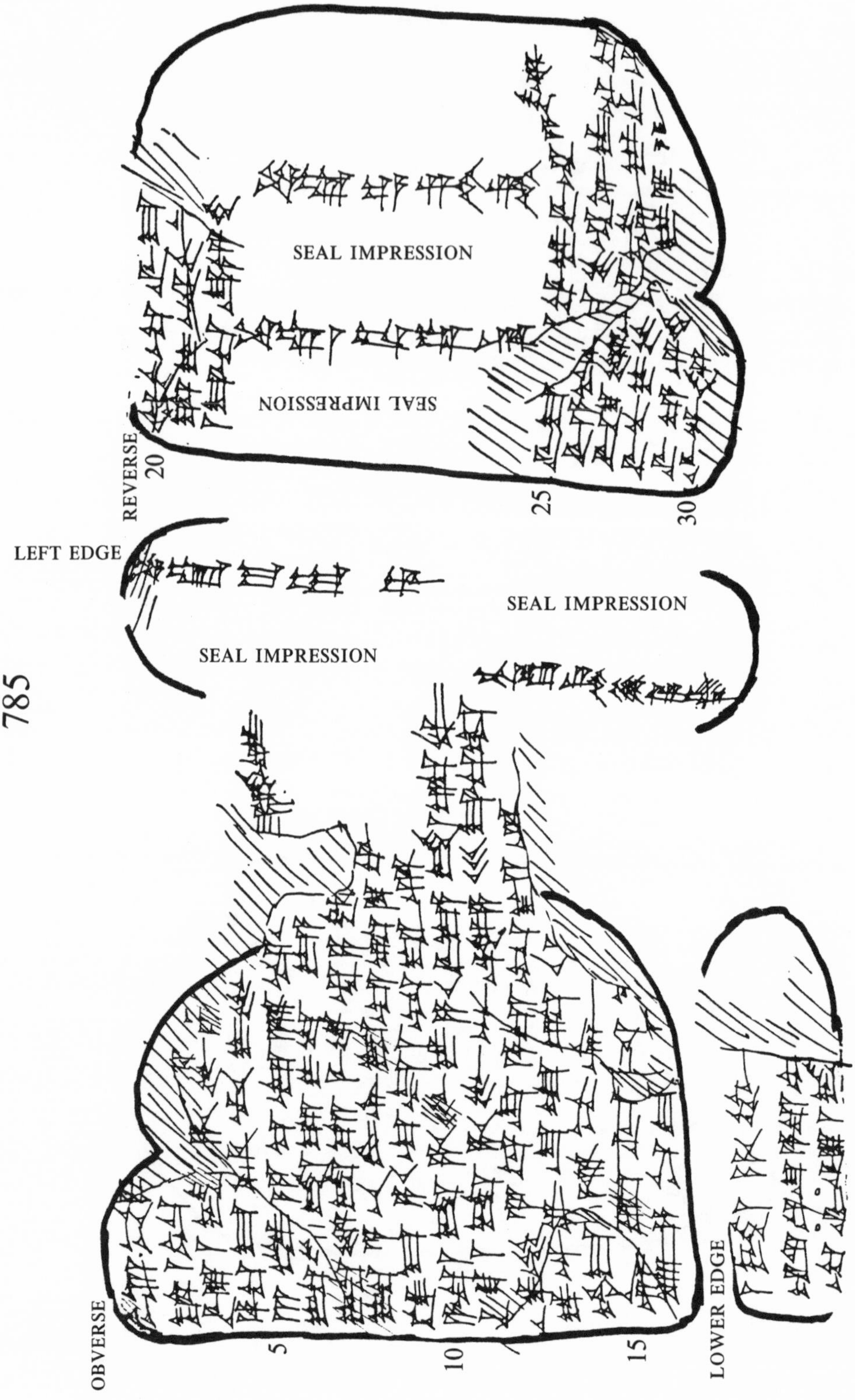
OBVERSE
5
10
15
LOWER EDGE
REVERSE
20
25
30
SEAL IMPRESSION
SEAL IMPRESSION
LEFT EDGE
SEAL IMPRESSION
SEAL IMPRESSION

786

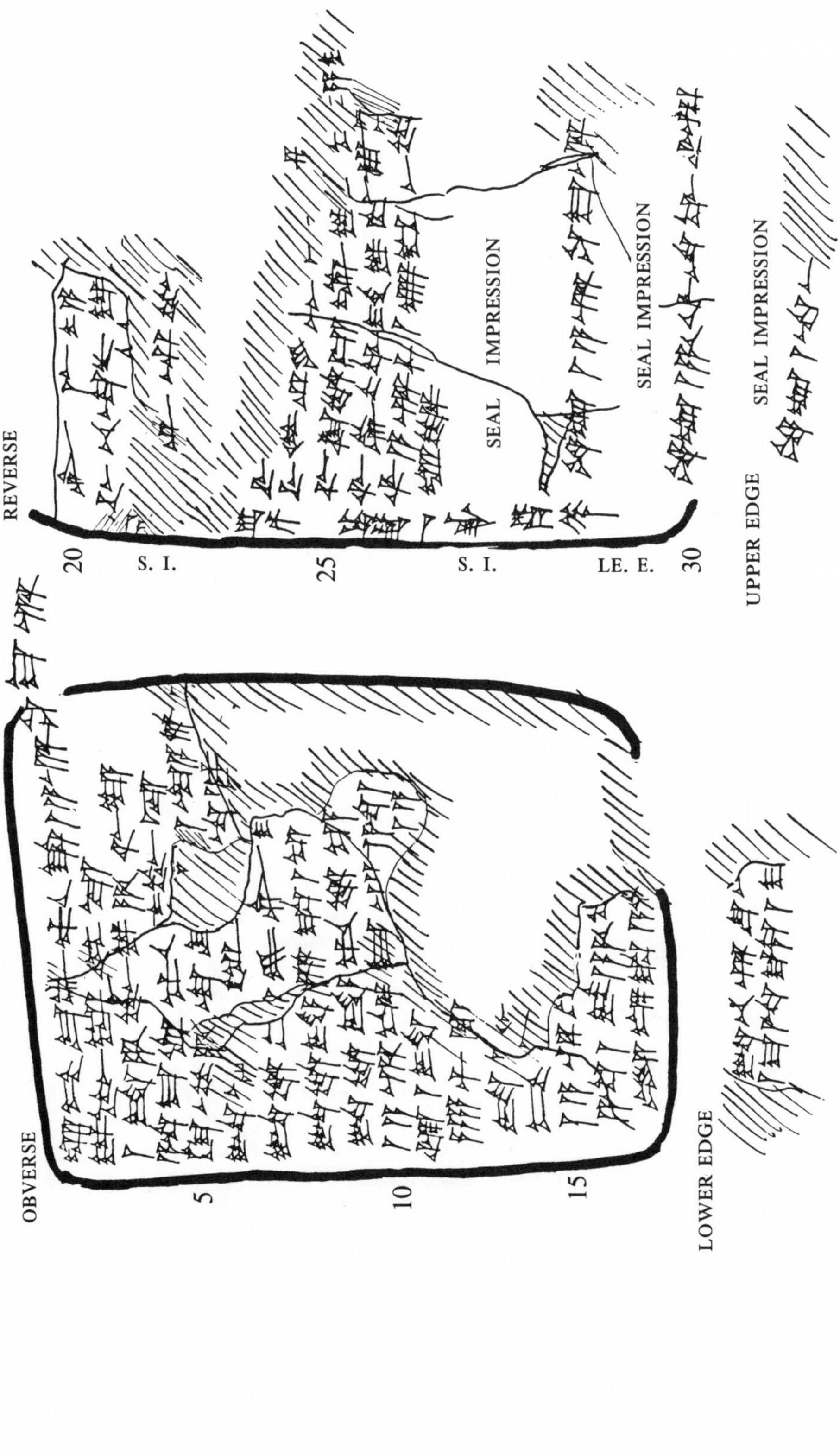
OBVERSE
LOWER EDGE
REVERSE
S. I.
S. I.
LE. E.
UPPER EDGE
SEAL IMPRESSION
SEAL IMPRESSION
SEAL IMPRESSION

787

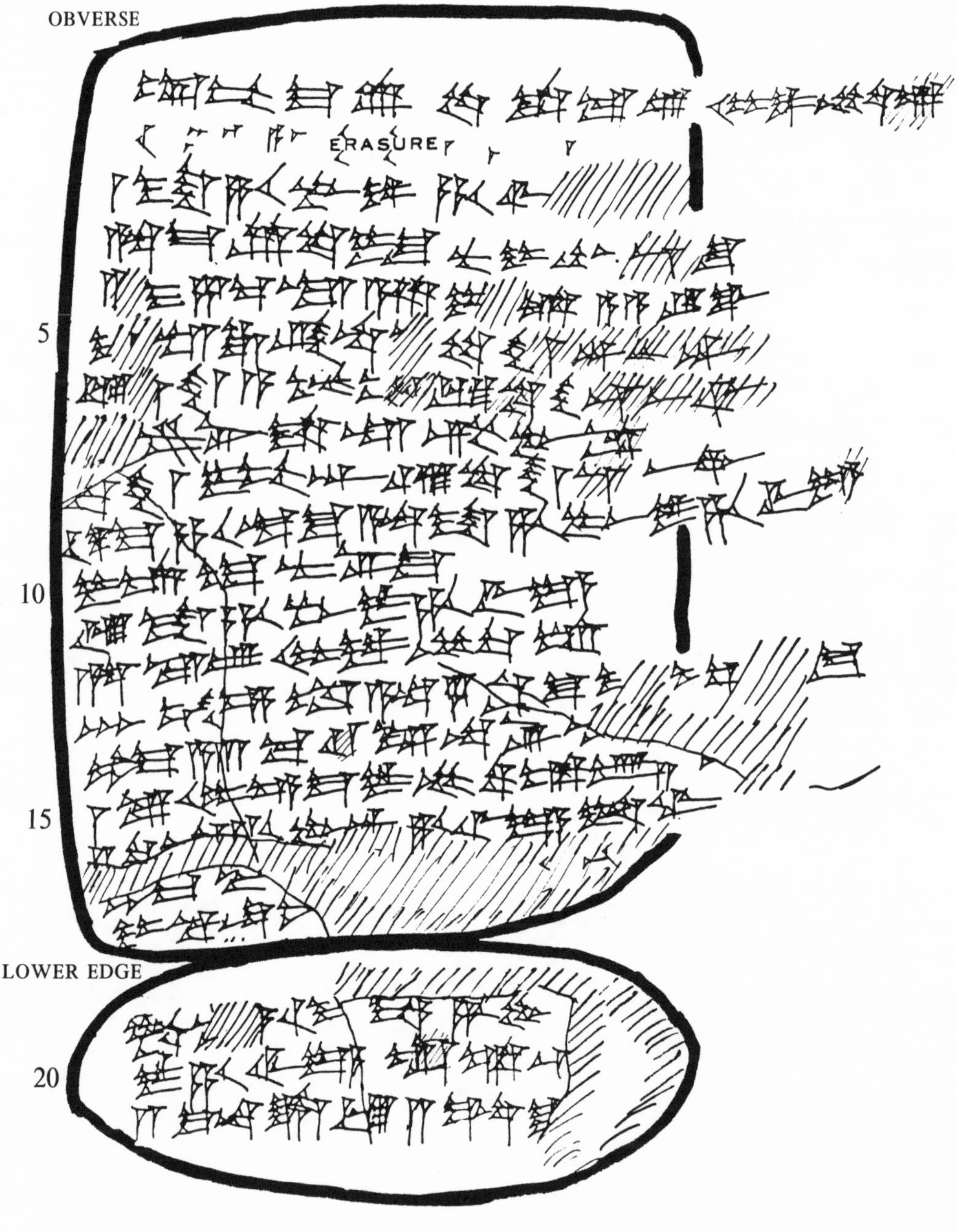

787

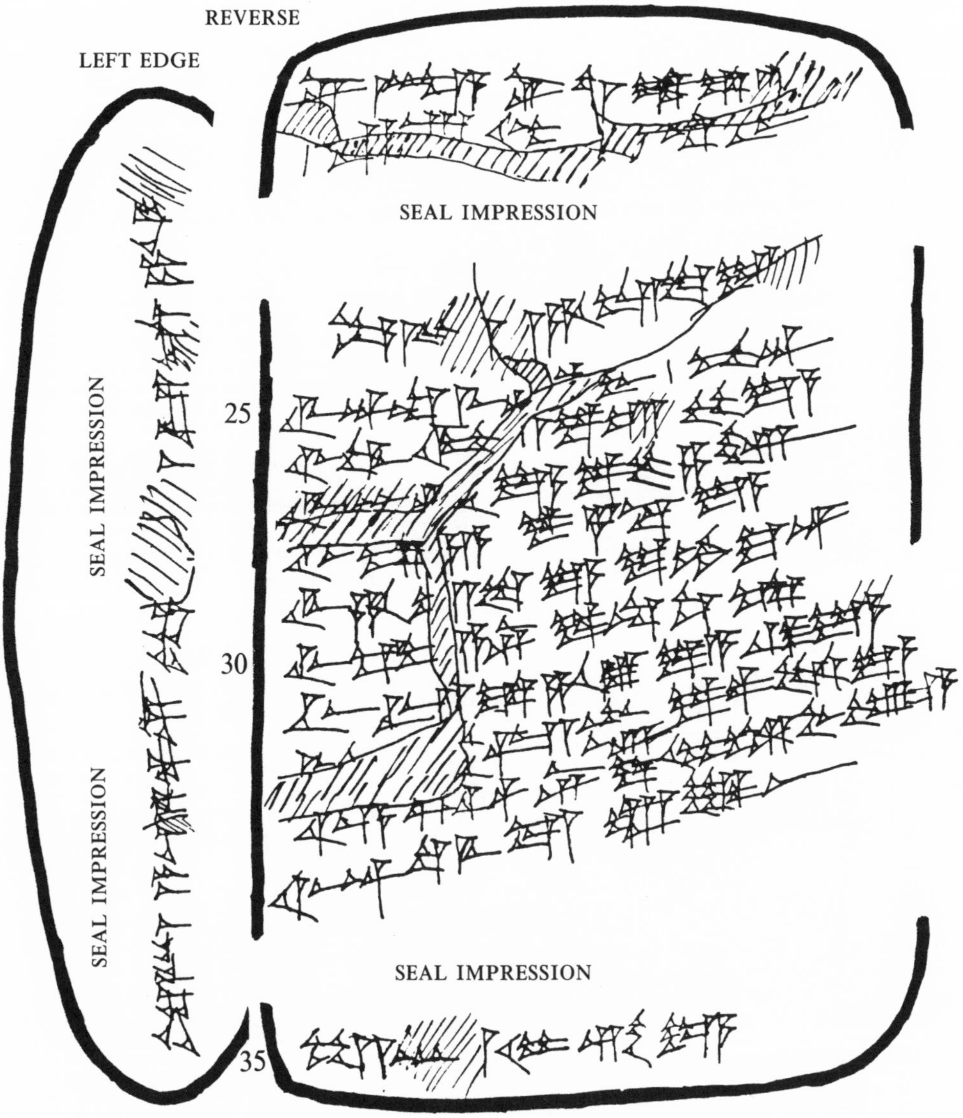
REVERSE
LEFT EDGE
SEAL IMPRESSION
SEAL IMPRESSION
SEAL IMPRESSION
SEAL IMPRESSION
25
30
35

788

OBVERSE

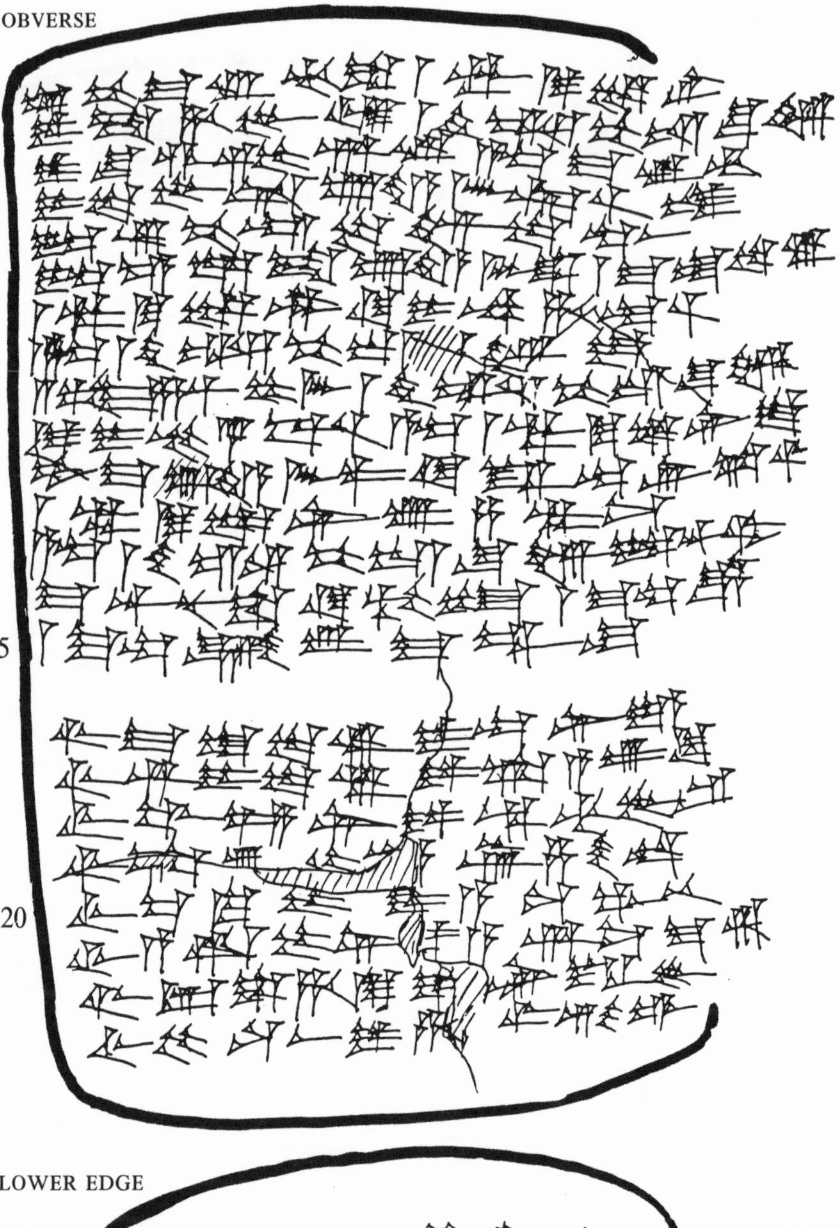

LOWER EDGE

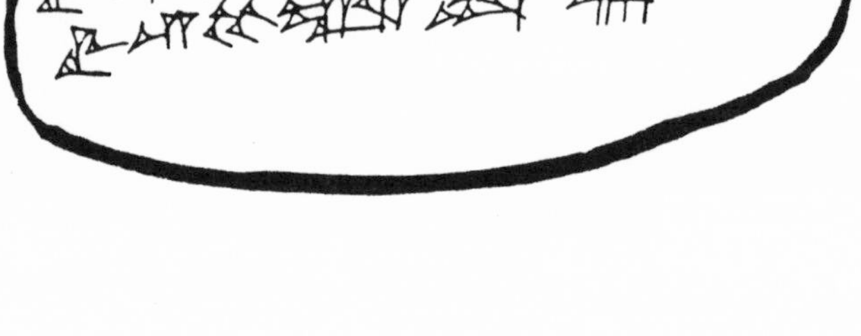

788

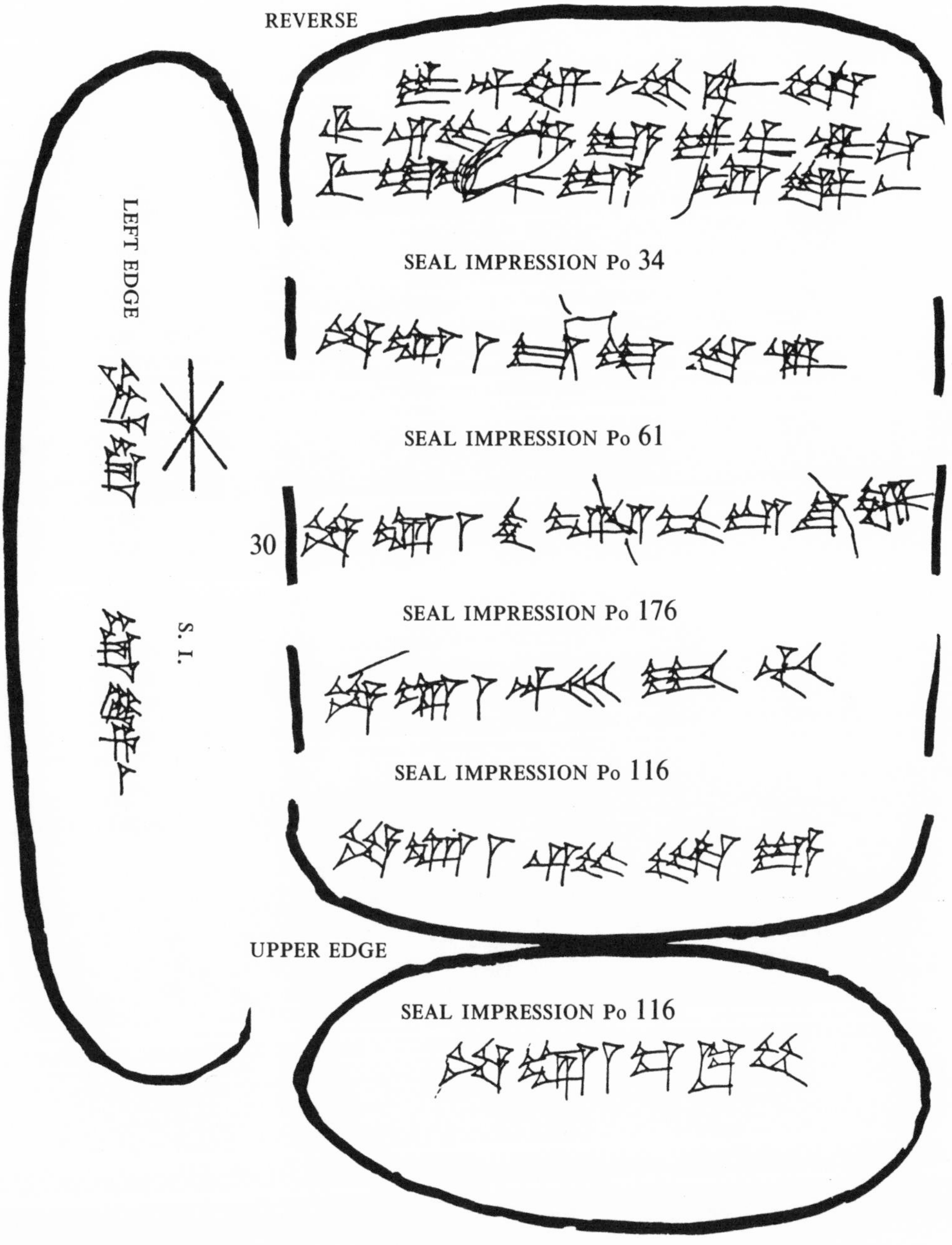
REVERSE
LEFT EDGE
SEAL IMPRESSION Po 34
SEAL IMPRESSION Po 61
30
S. I.
SEAL IMPRESSION Po 176
SEAL IMPRESSION Po 116
UPPER EDGE
SEAL IMPRESSION Po 116

789

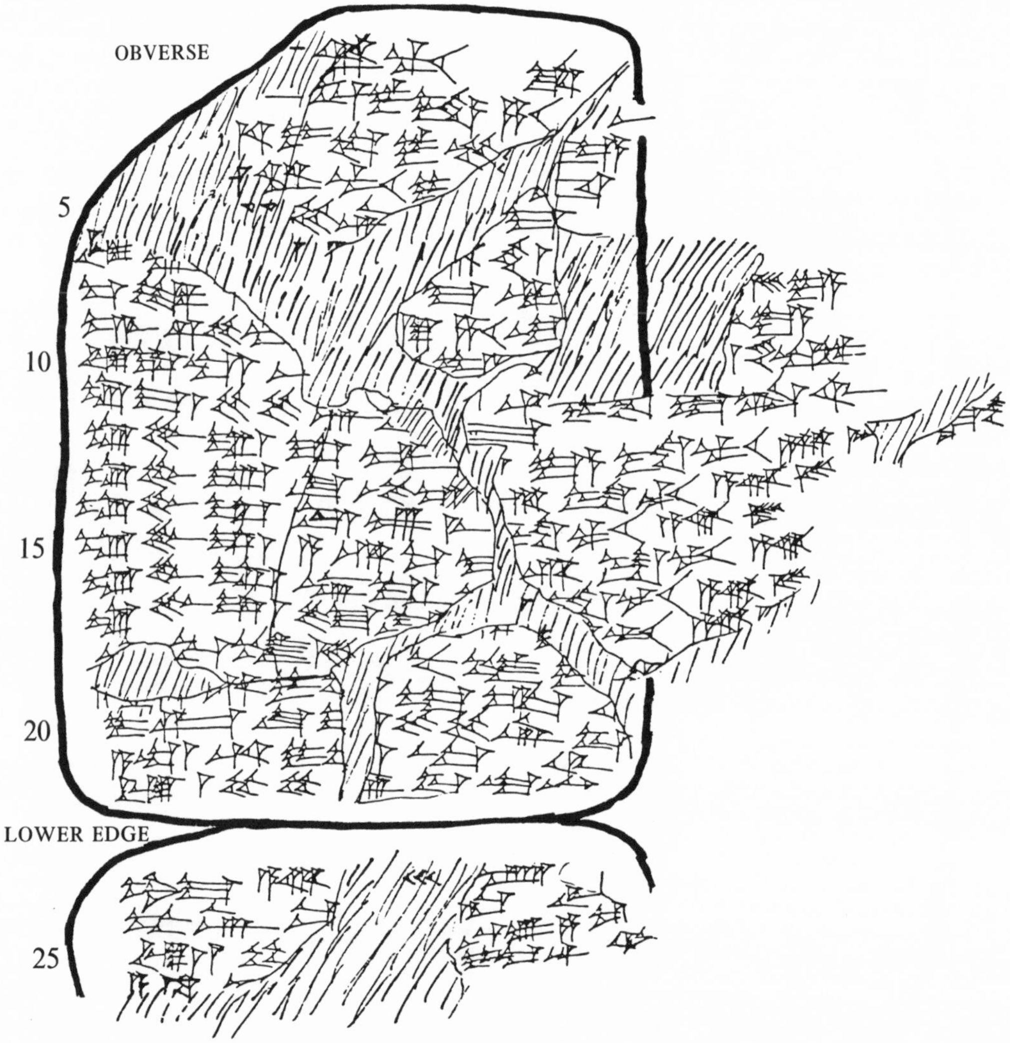

789

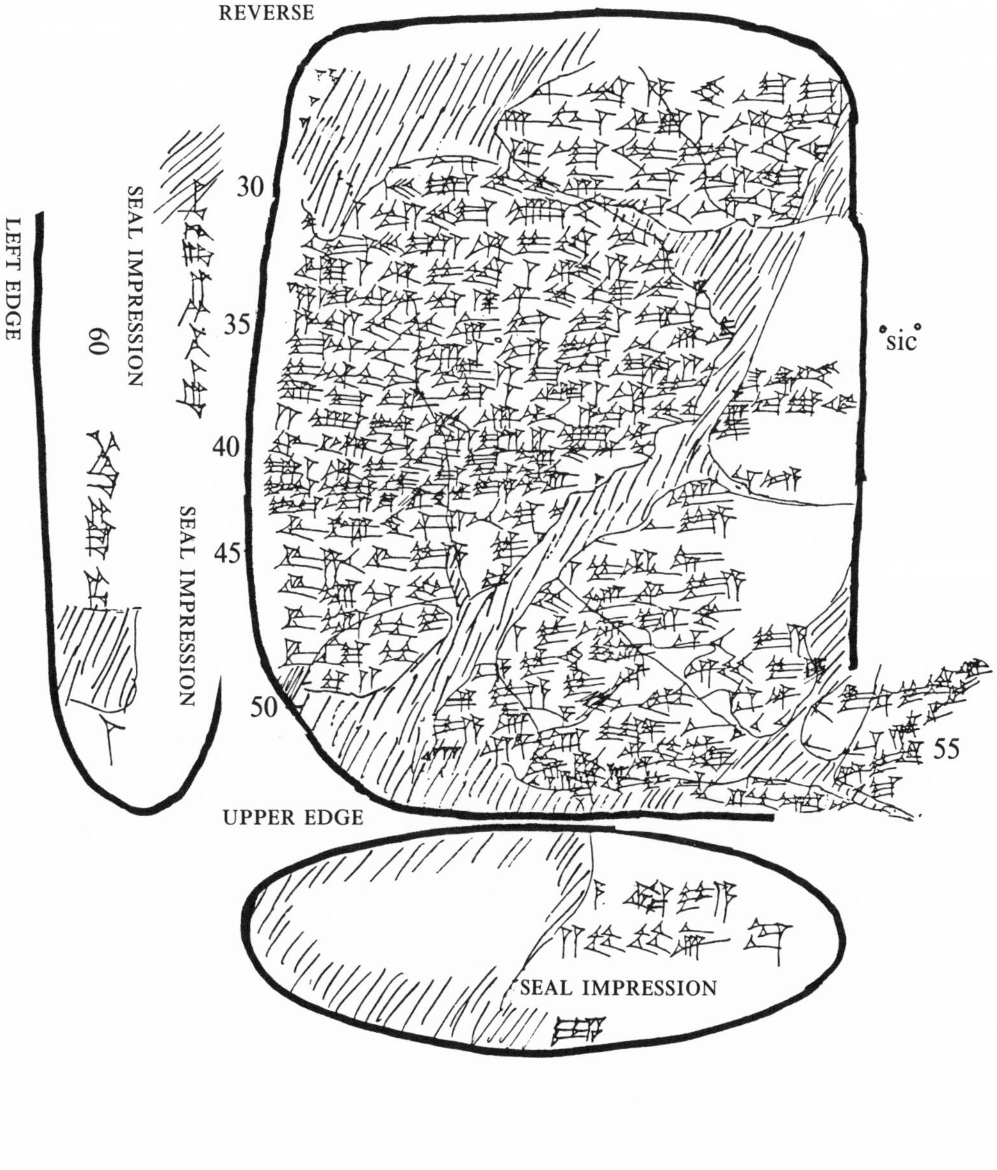
REVERSE
30
35
40
45
50
55
°sic°
SEAL IMPRESSION
60
LEFT EDGE
SEAL IMPRESSION
UPPER EDGE
SEAL IMPRESSION

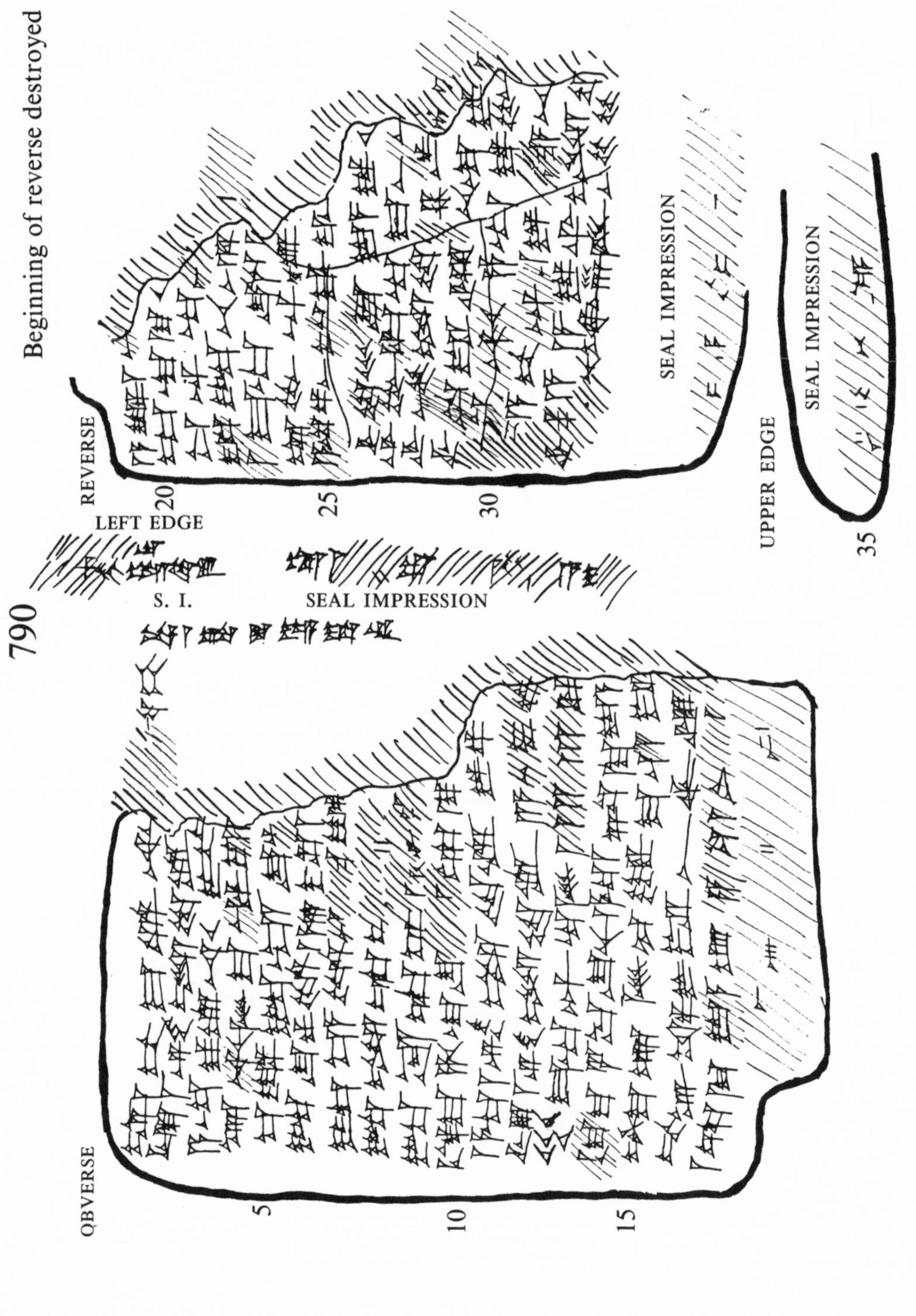
790
Beginning of reverse destroyed
REVERSE
20
25
30
SEAL IMPRESSION
UPPER EDGE
SEAL IMPRESSION
35
LEFT EDGE
S. I.
SEAL IMPRESSION
OBVERSE
5
10
15

791

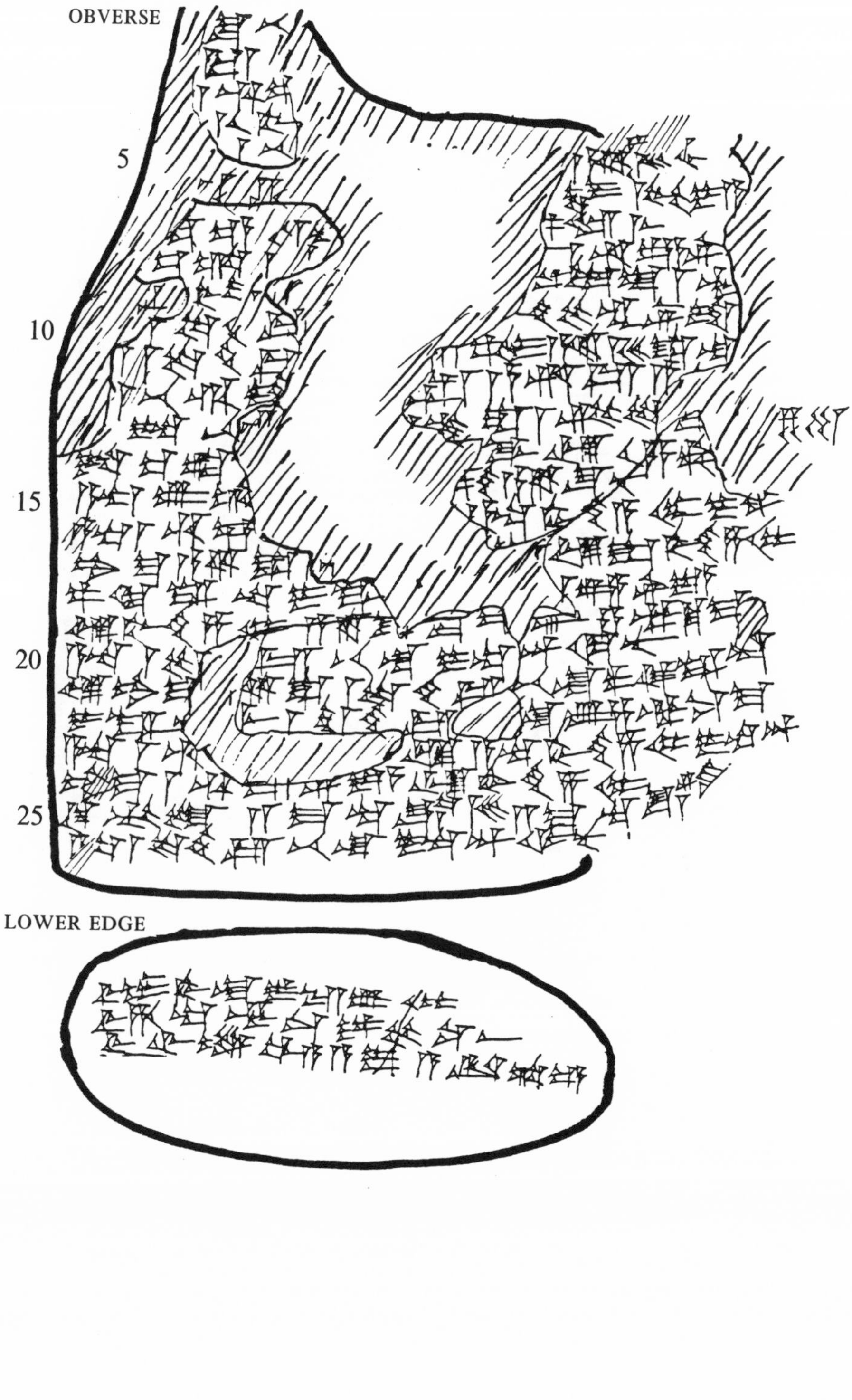

791

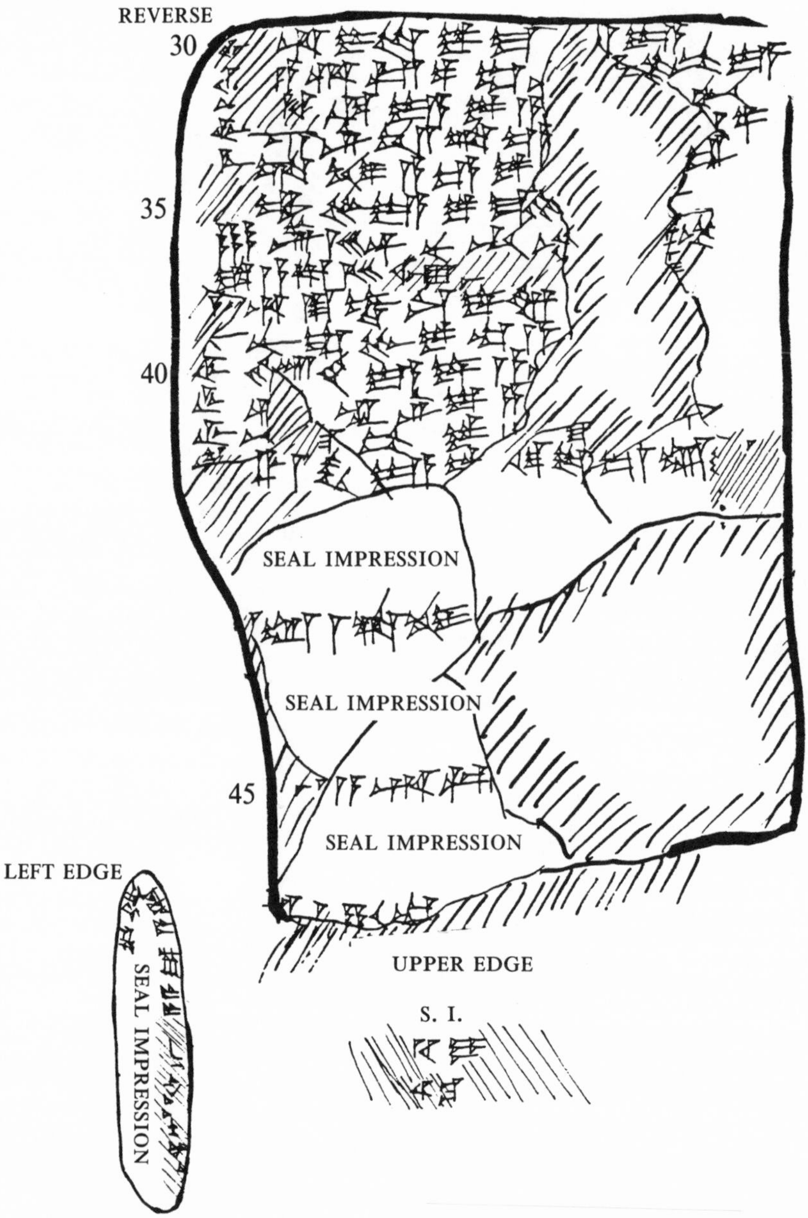
REVERSE
30
35
40
SEAL IMPRESSION
SEAL IMPRESSION
45
SEAL IMPRESSION
LEFT EDGE
SEAL IMPRESSION
UPPER EDGE
S. I.

792

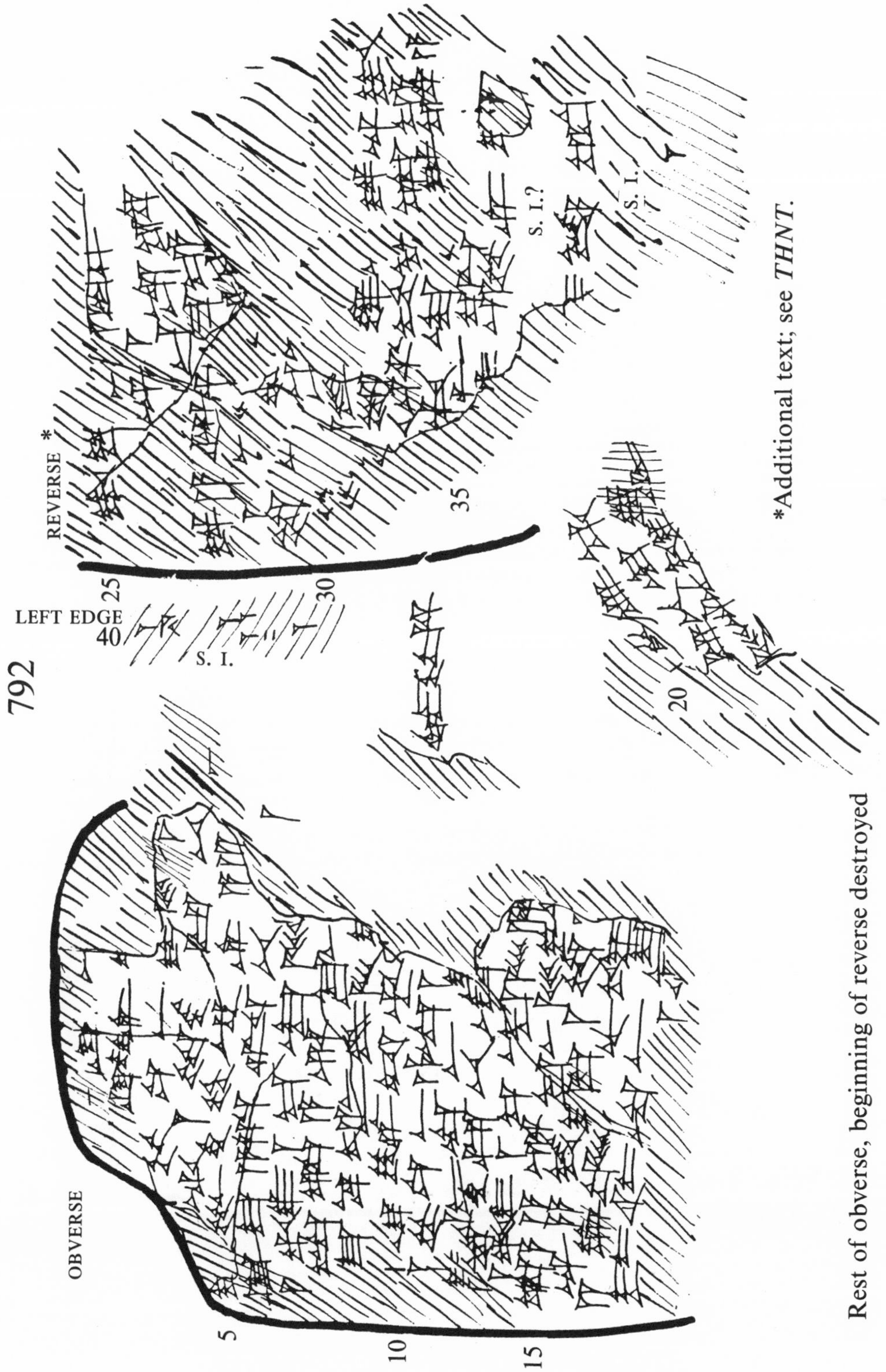

*Additional text; see *THNT.*

Rest of obverse, beginning of reverse destroyed

793 (= 706)*

OBVERSE

Beginning of obverse destroyed

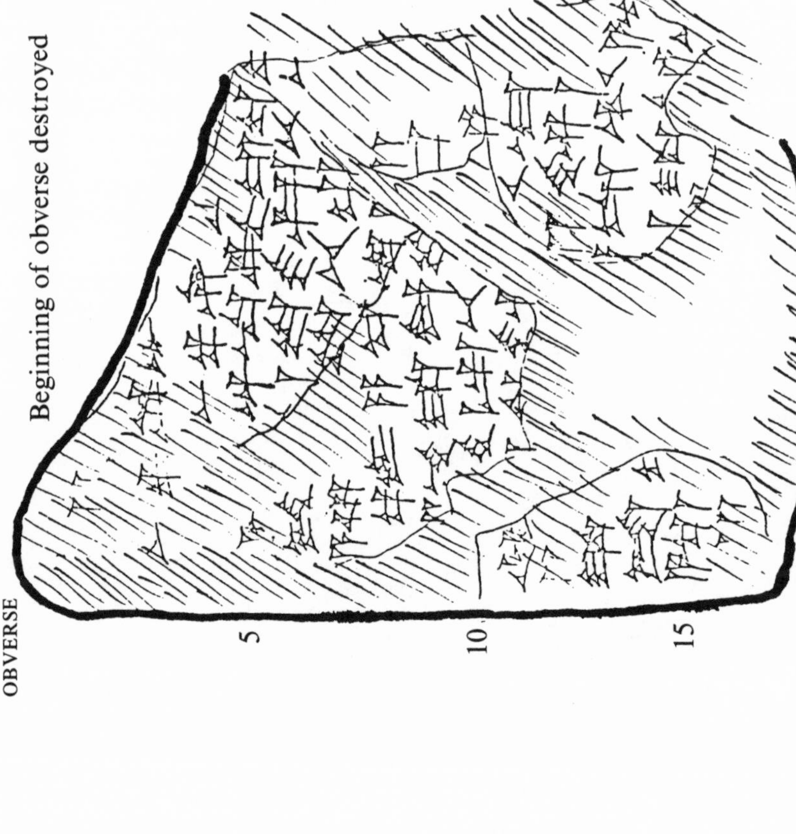

Rest of obverse, beginning of reverse destroyed

REVERSE

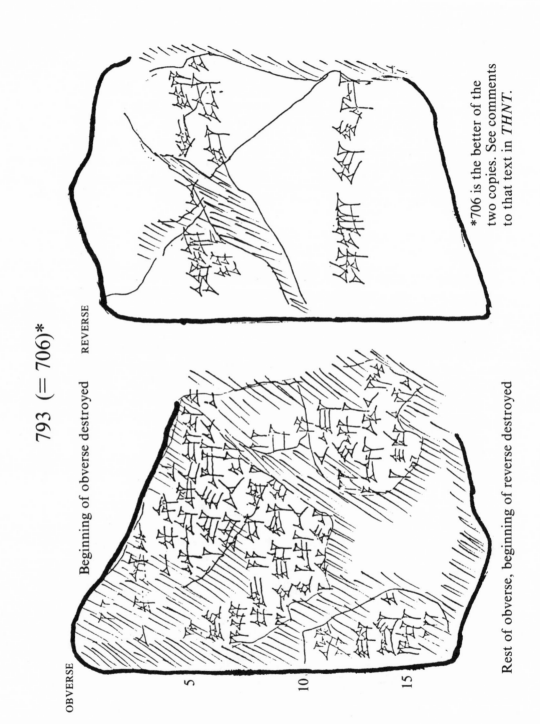

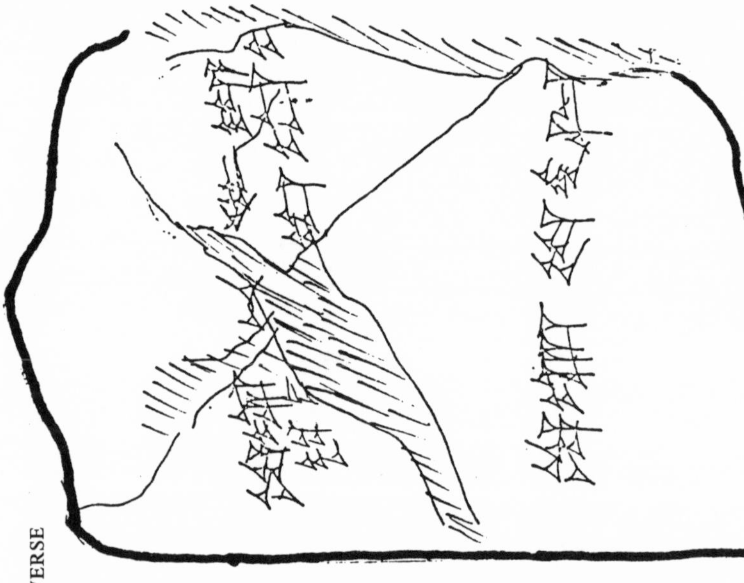

*706 is the better of the two copies. See comments to that text in *THNT*.

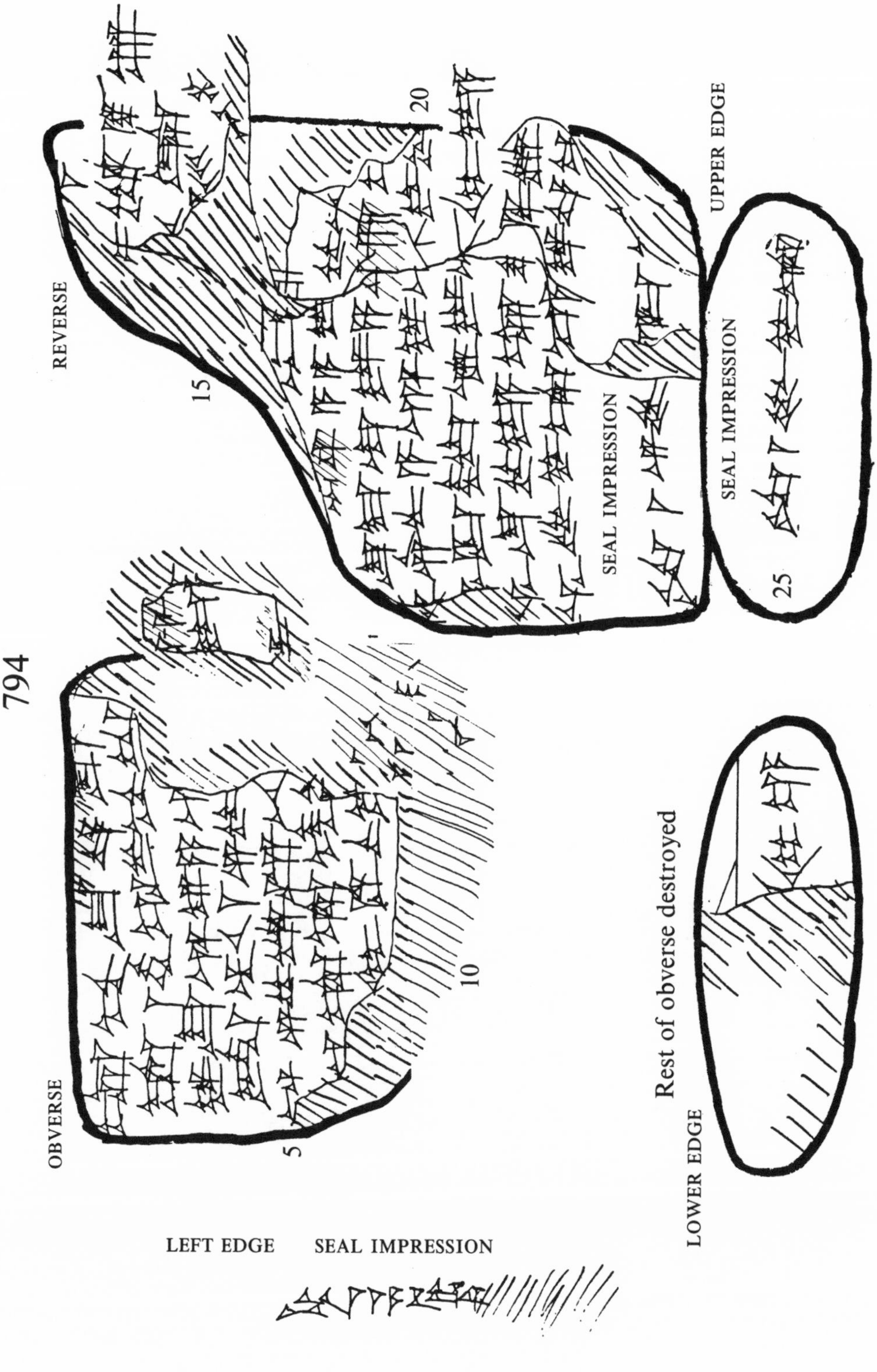
794
OBVERSE
5
10
REVERSE
15
20
SEAL IMPRESSION
UPPER EDGE
SEAL IMPRESSION
25
Rest of obverse destroyed
LOWER EDGE
LEFT EDGE
SEAL IMPRESSION

795

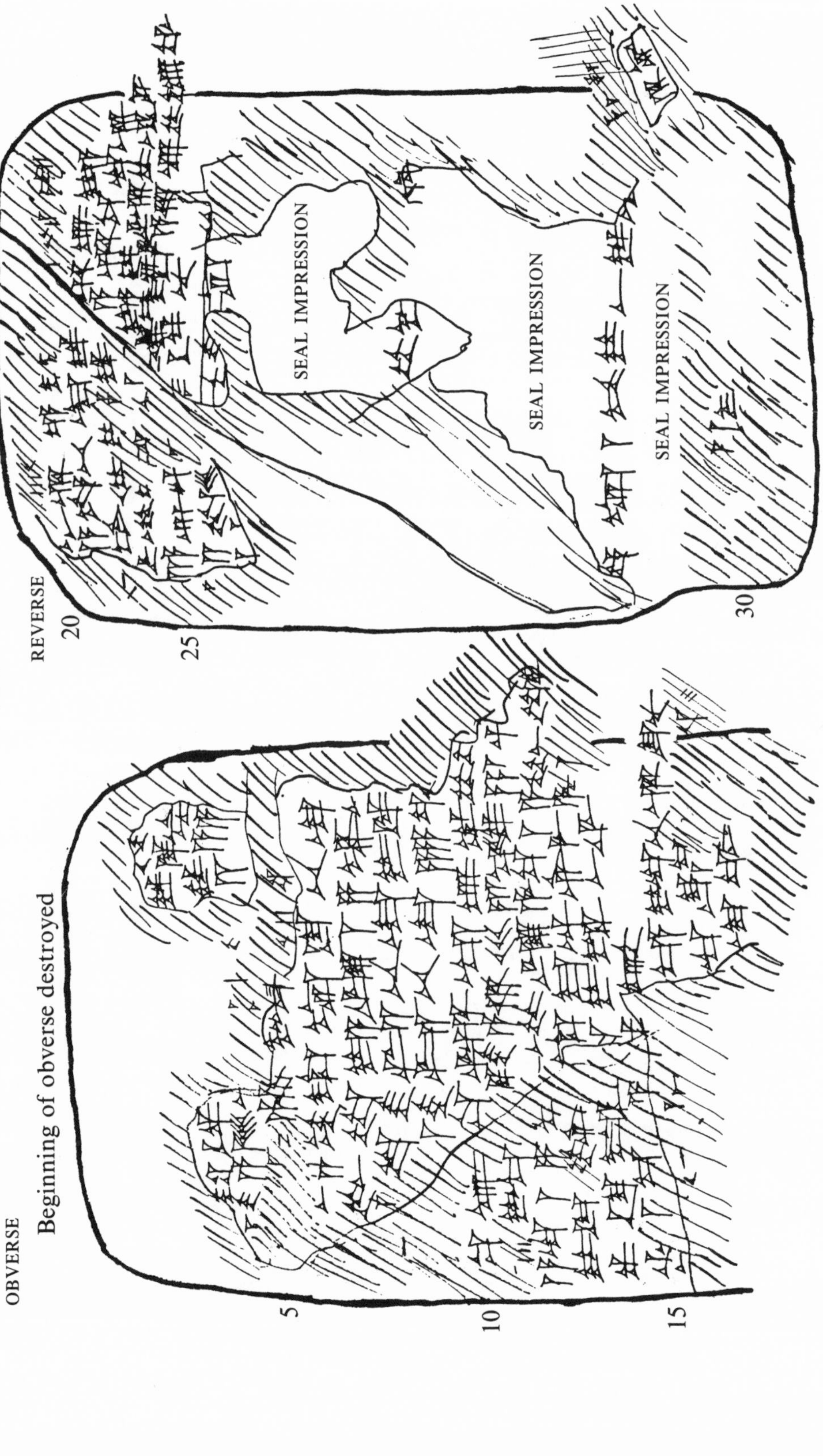
OBVERSE
Beginning of obverse destroyed
REVERSE
SEAL IMPRESSION
SEAL IMPRESSION
SEAL IMPRESSION

796

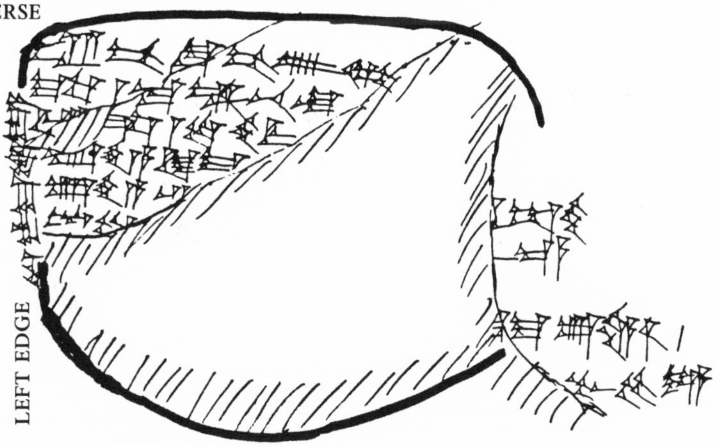

Rest of obverse destroyed

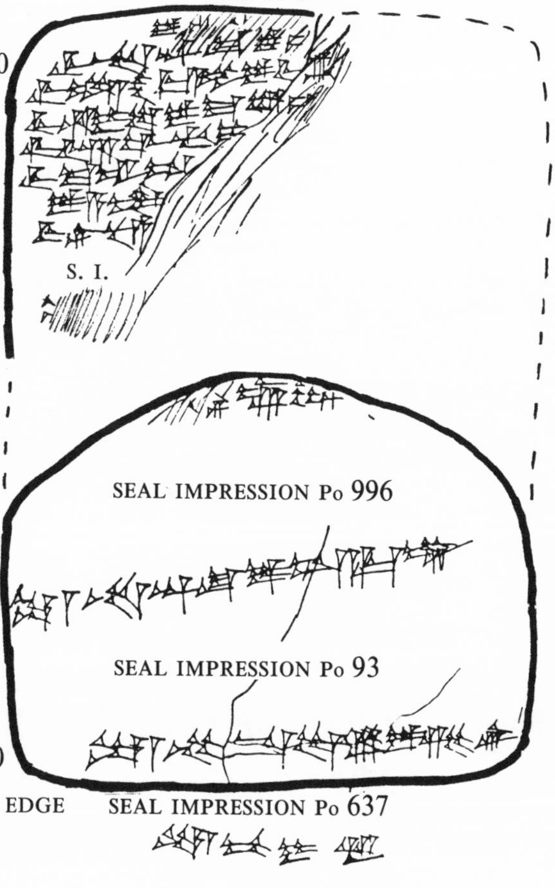

797

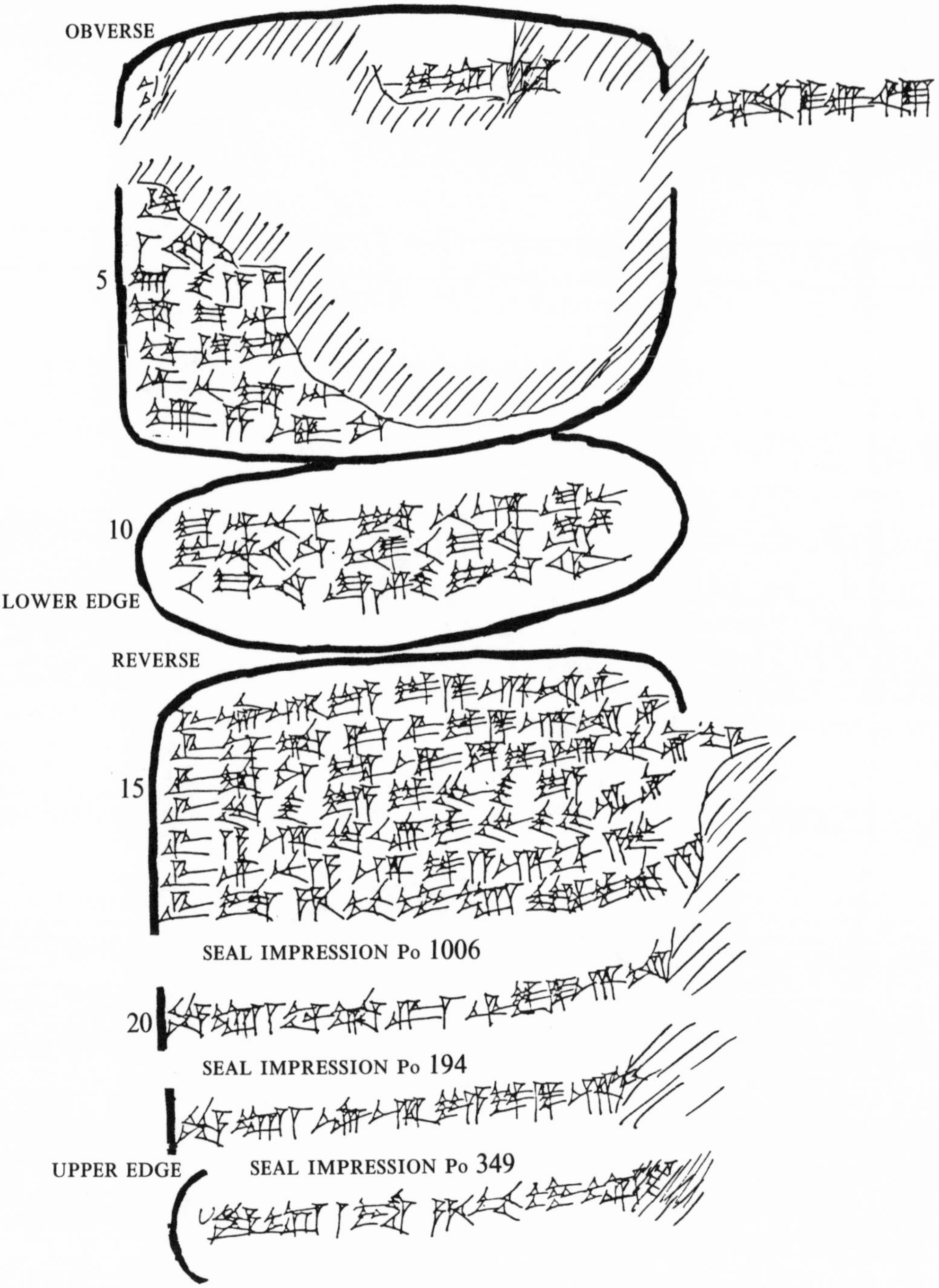
OBVERSE
5
10
LOWER EDGE
REVERSE
15
SEAL IMPRESSION Po 1006
20
SEAL IMPRESSION Po 194
UPPER EDGE
SEAL IMPRESSION Po 349

798

OBVERSE

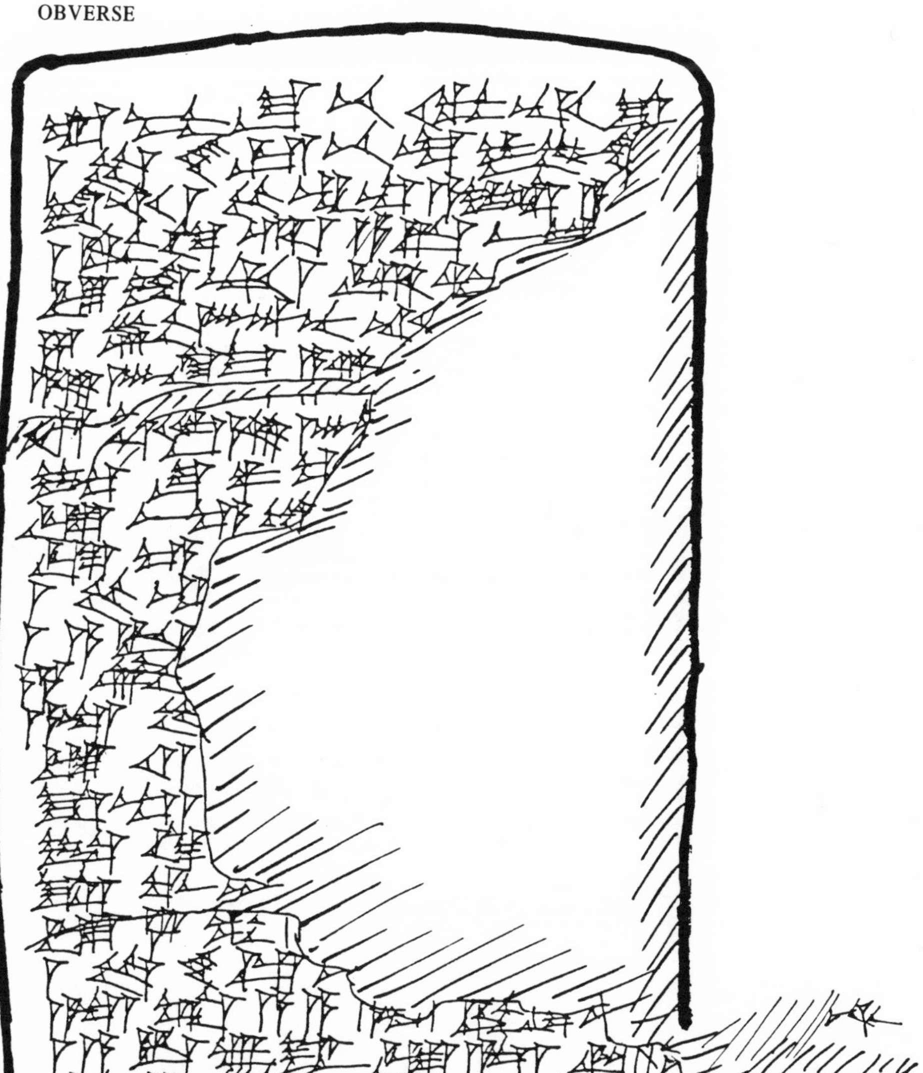

LOWER EDGE

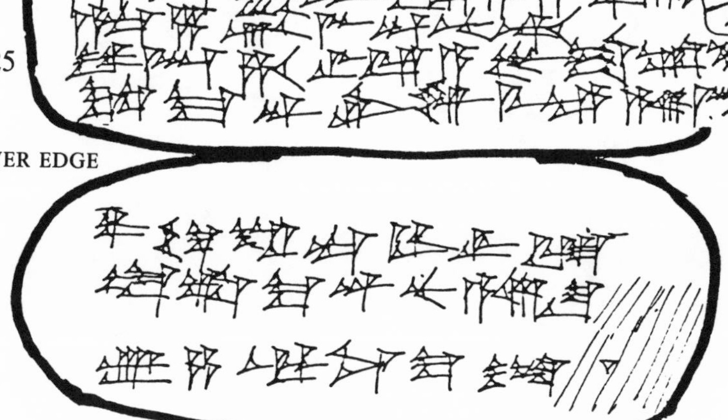

798

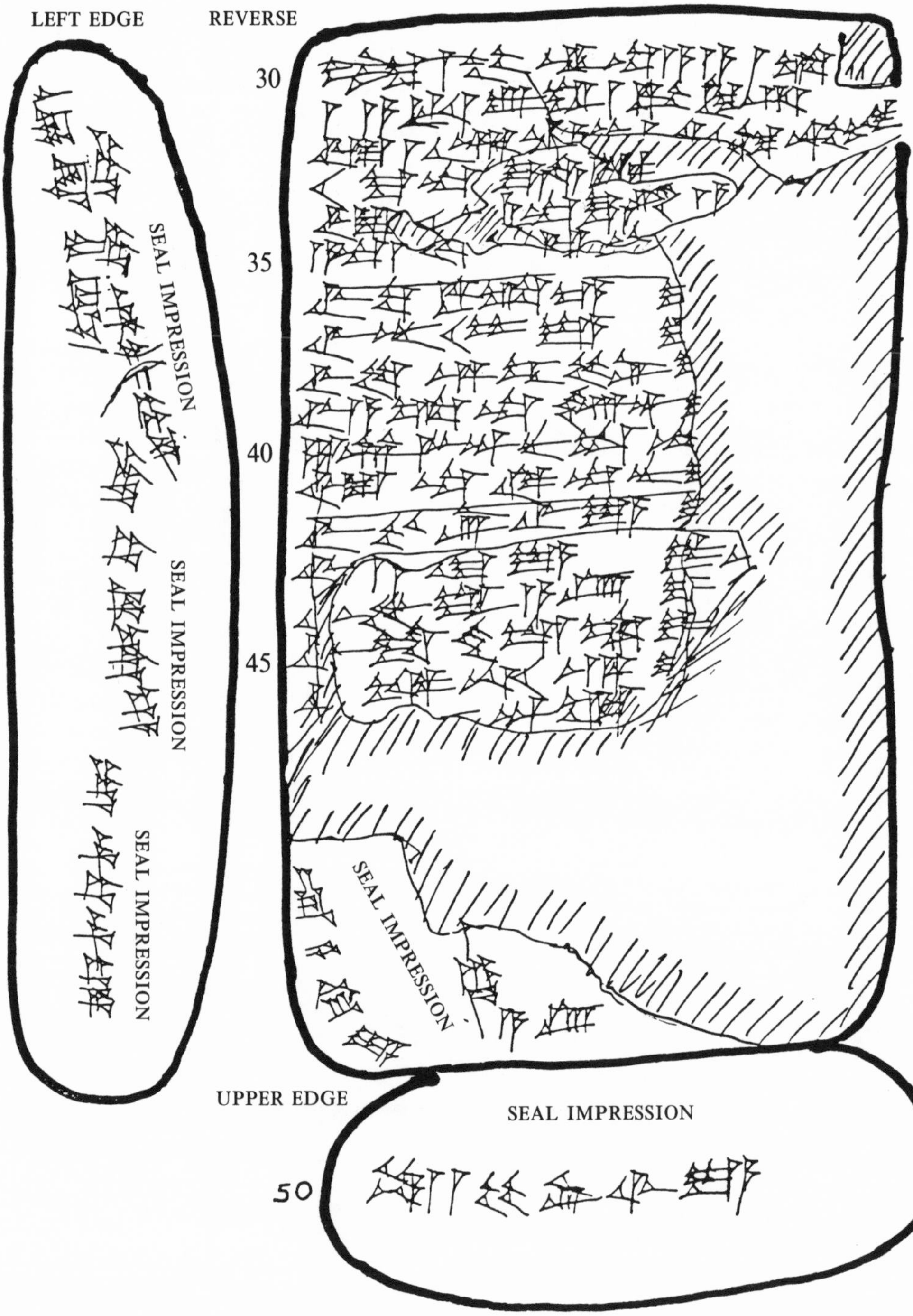
LEFT EDGE
REVERSE
30
35
40
45
SEAL IMPRESSION
SEAL IMPRESSION
SEAL IMPRESSION
SEAL IMPRESSION
UPPER EDGE
SEAL IMPRESSION
50

799

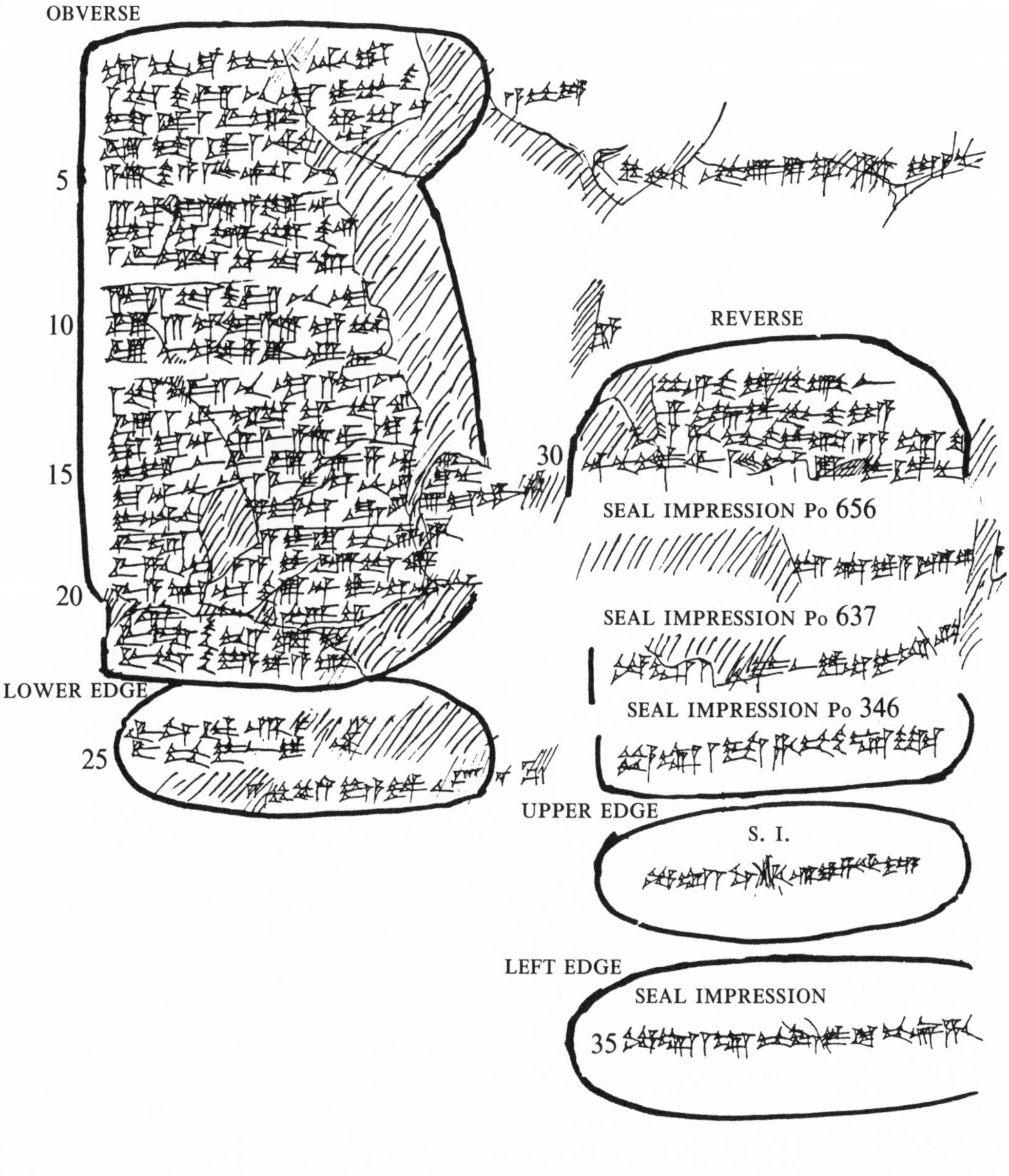
OBVERSE
LOWER EDGE
REVERSE
SEAL IMPRESSION Po 656
SEAL IMPRESSION Po 637
SEAL IMPRESSION Po 346
UPPER EDGE
S. I.
LEFT EDGE
SEAL IMPRESSION

800

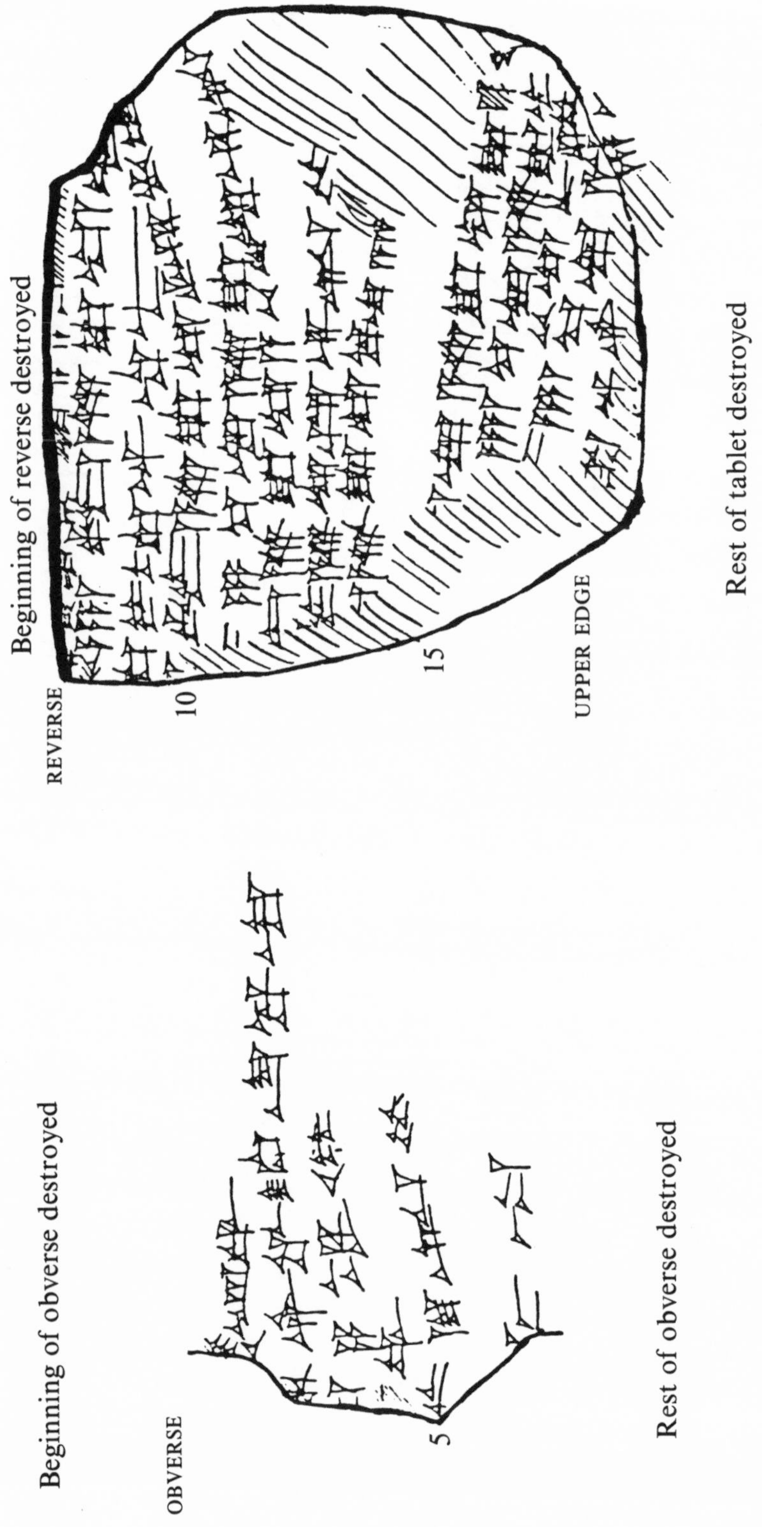
Beginning of obverse destroyed
OBVERSE
5
Rest of obverse destroyed
Beginning of reverse destroyed
REVERSE
10
15
UPPER EDGE
Rest of tablet destroyed

801 (= 869)*

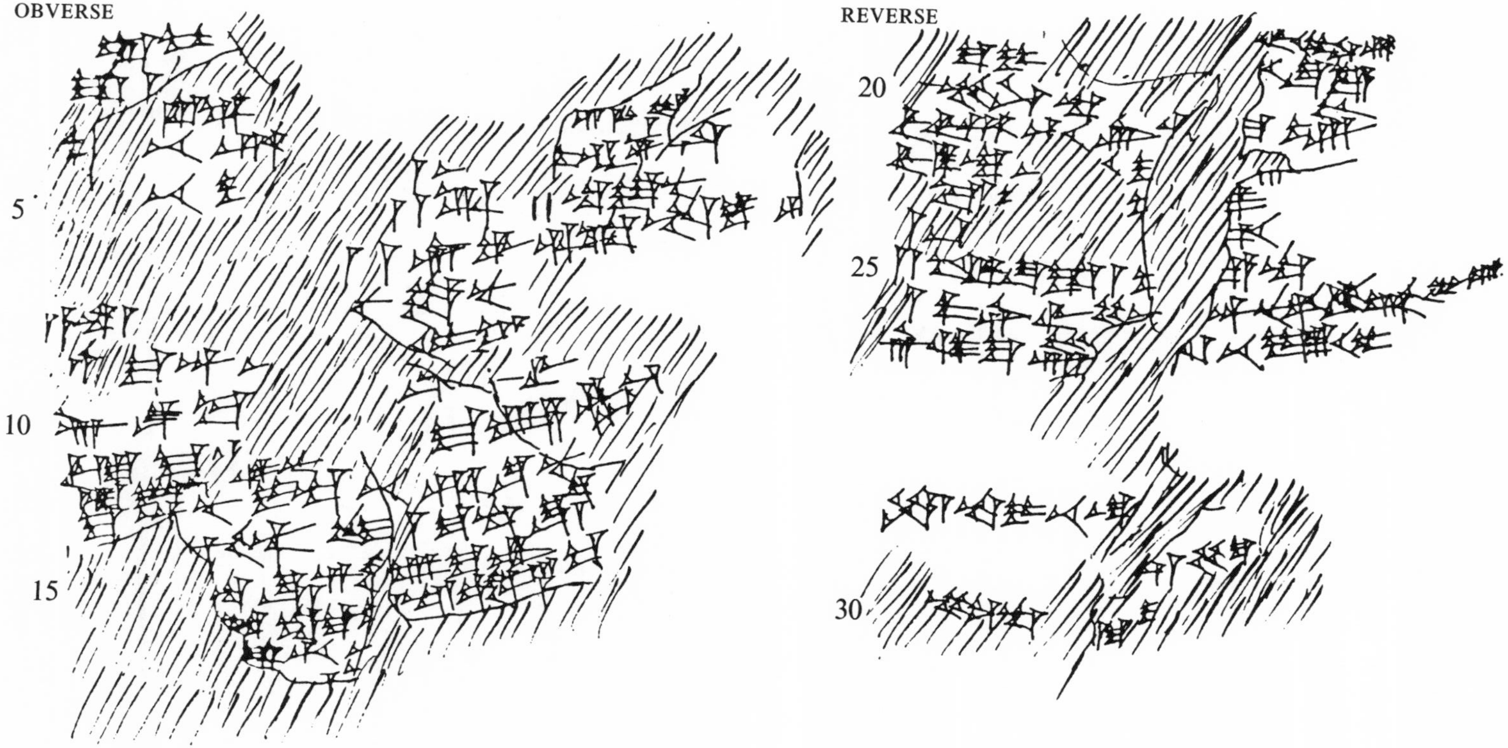

*869 is the better of the two copies. See comments to that text in *THNT*.

802

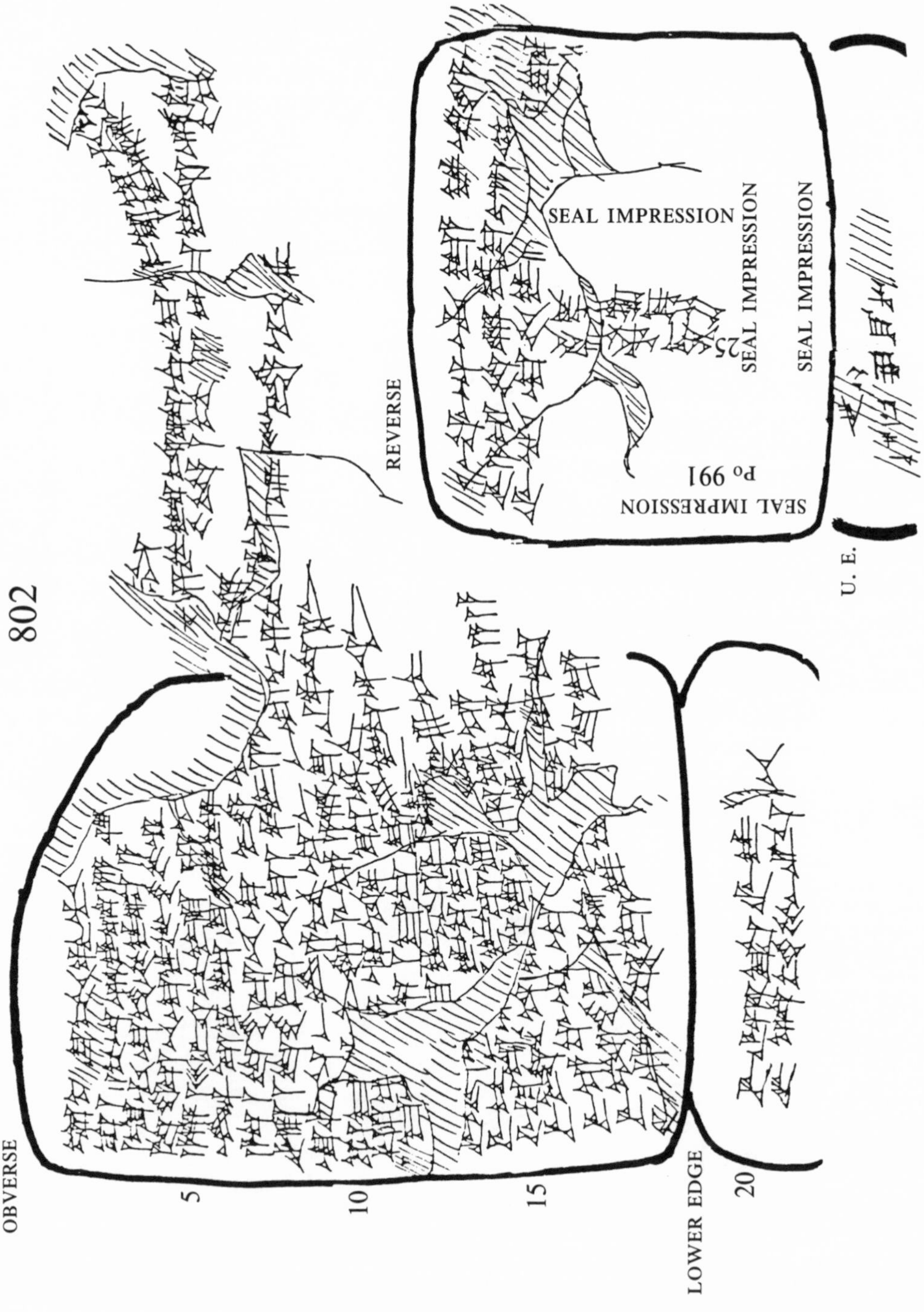
OBVERSE
5
10
15
LOWER EDGE
20
REVERSE
SEAL IMPRESSION
SEAL IMPRESSION
SEAL IMPRESSION
25
SEAL IMPRESSION
Po 991
U. E.

803

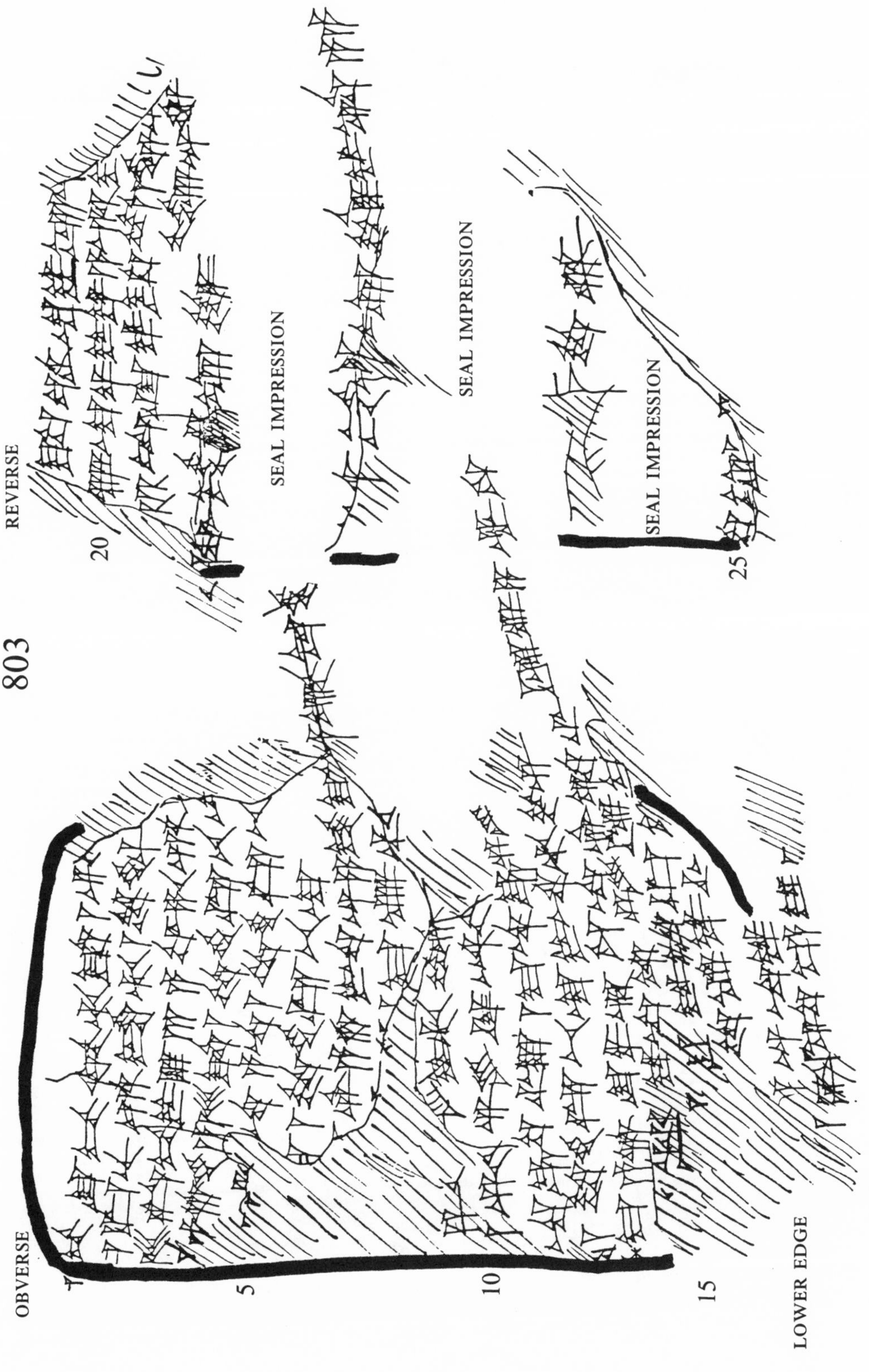
OBVERSE
REVERSE
SEAL IMPRESSION
SEAL IMPRESSION
SEAL IMPRESSION
LOWER EDGE

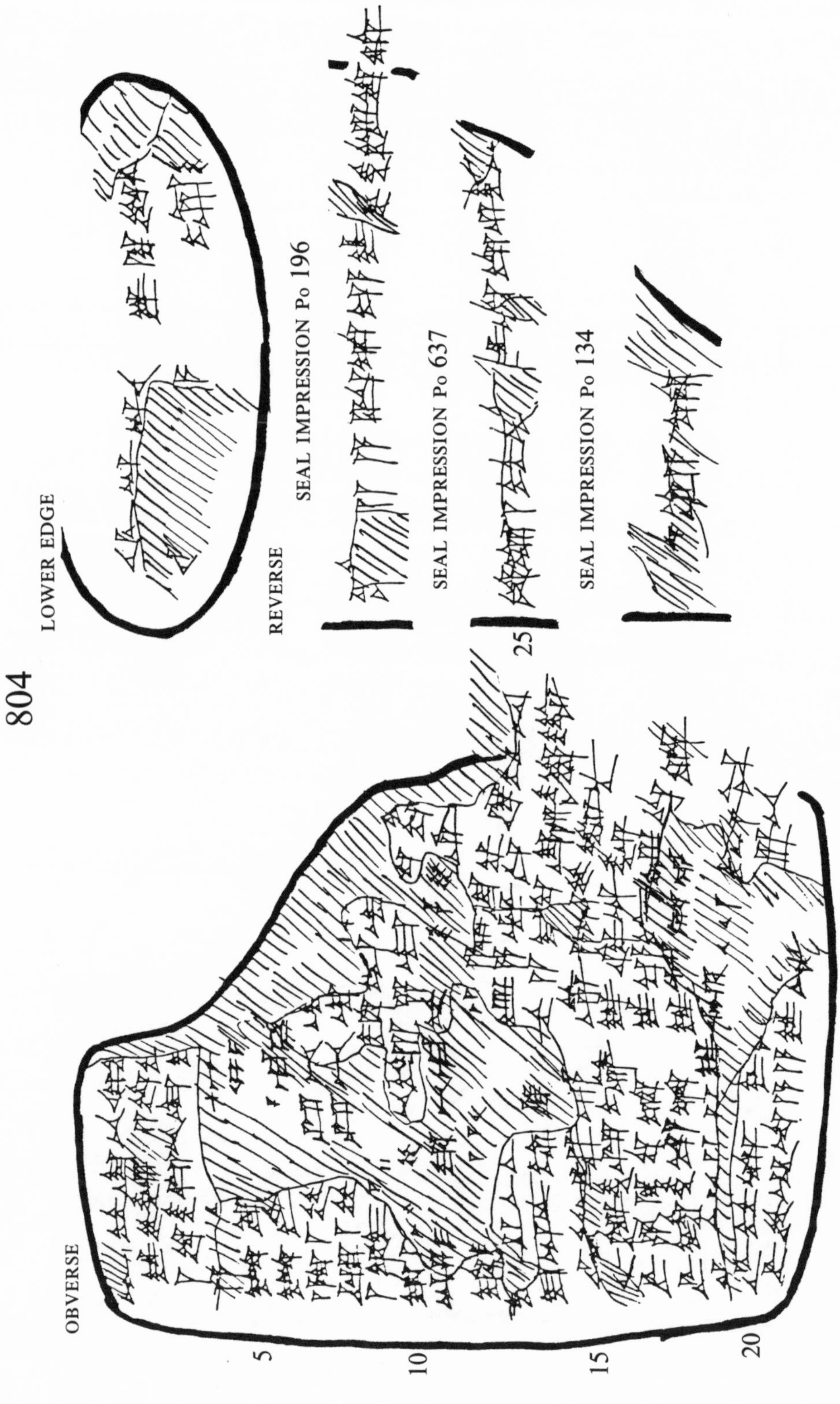
804
OBVERSE
LOWER EDGE
REVERSE
SEAL IMPRESSION Po 196
SEAL IMPRESSION Po 637
SEAL IMPRESSION Po 134

805

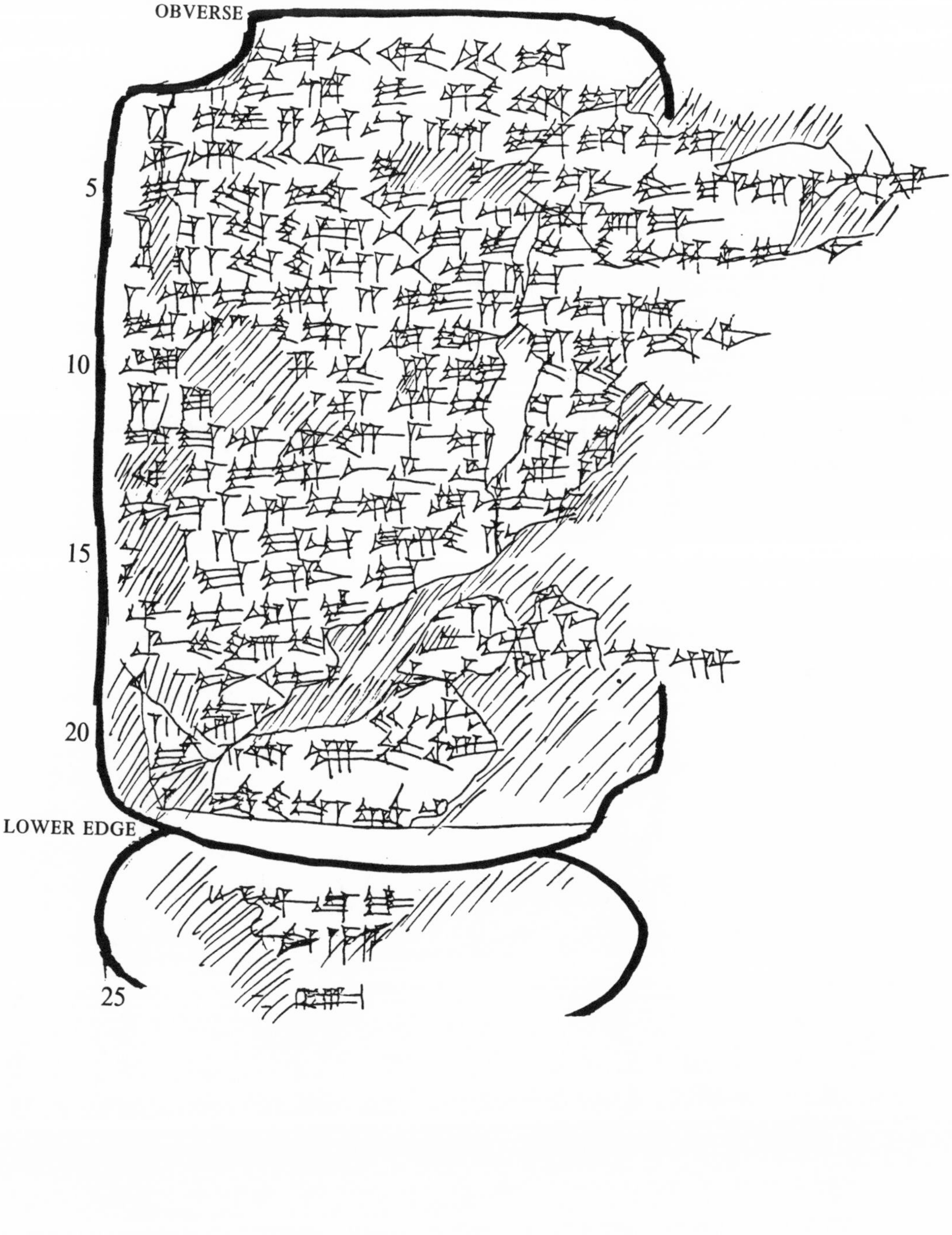

805

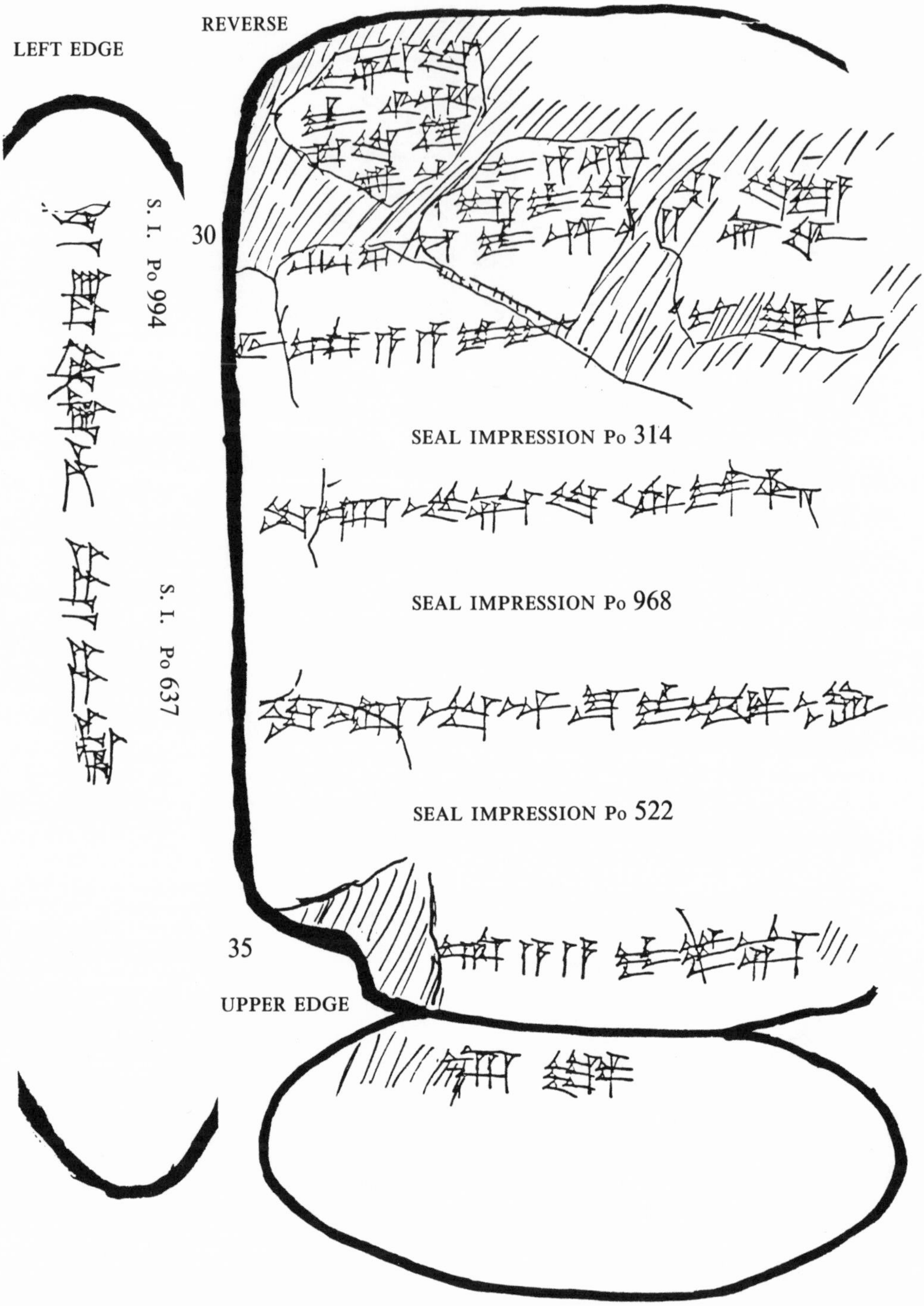
REVERSE
LEFT EDGE
S. I. Po 994
30
S. I. Po 637
SEAL IMPRESSION Po 314
SEAL IMPRESSION Po 968
SEAL IMPRESSION Po 522
35
UPPER EDGE

806

OBVERSE

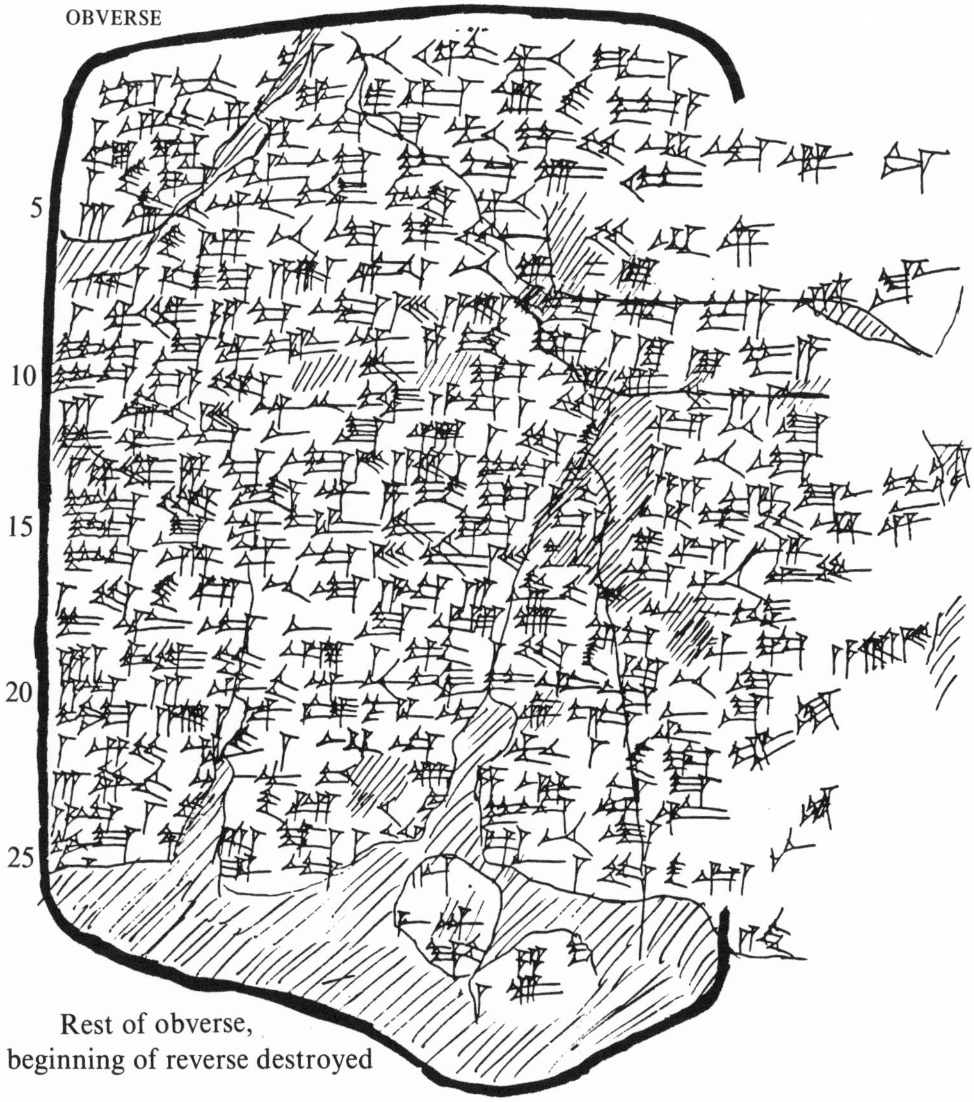

Rest of obverse, beginning of reverse destroyed

806

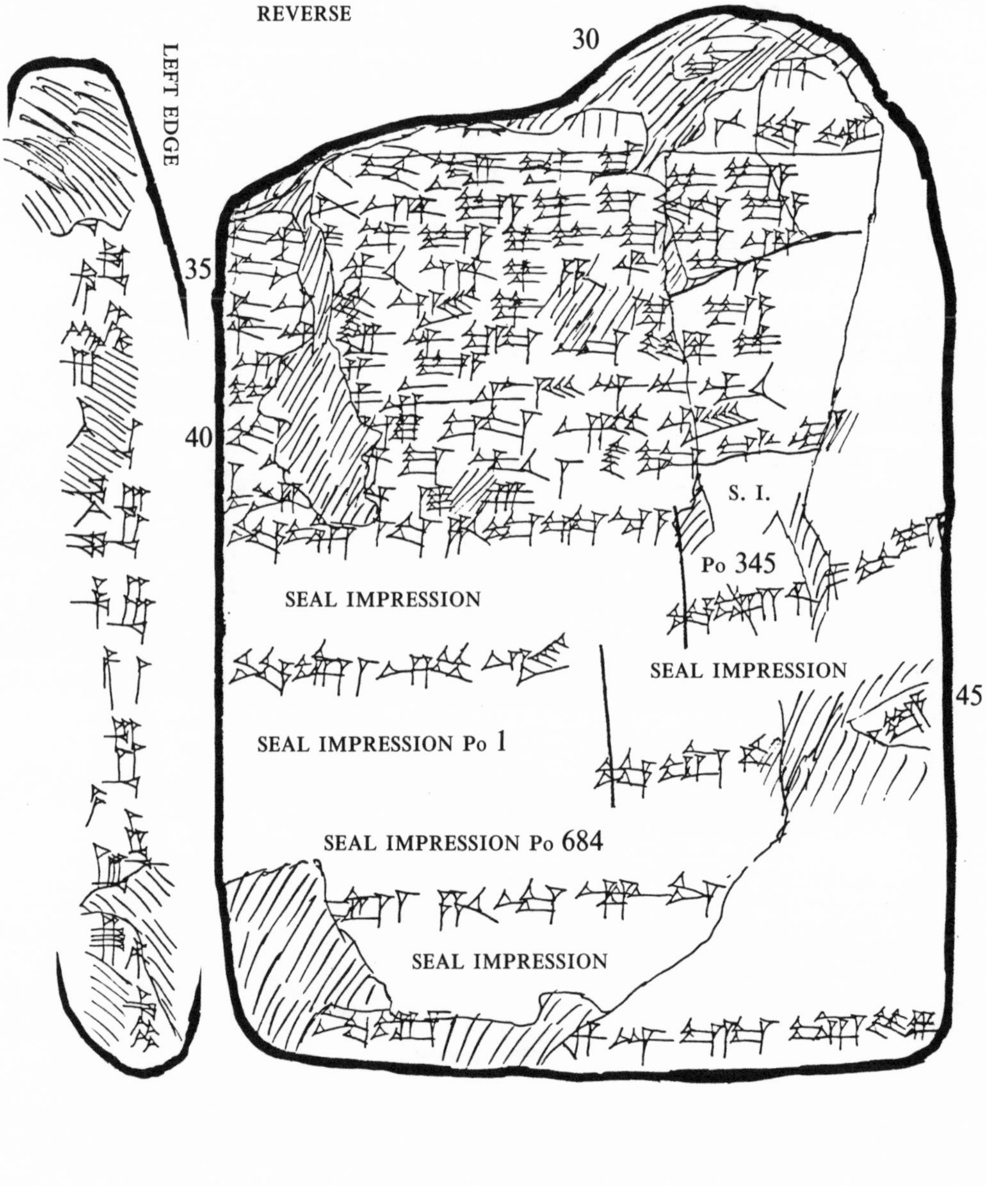
REVERSE
LEFT EDGE
30
35
40
S. I.
Po 345
SEAL IMPRESSION
SEAL IMPRESSION
45
SEAL IMPRESSION Po 1
SEAL IMPRESSION Po 684
SEAL IMPRESSION

807

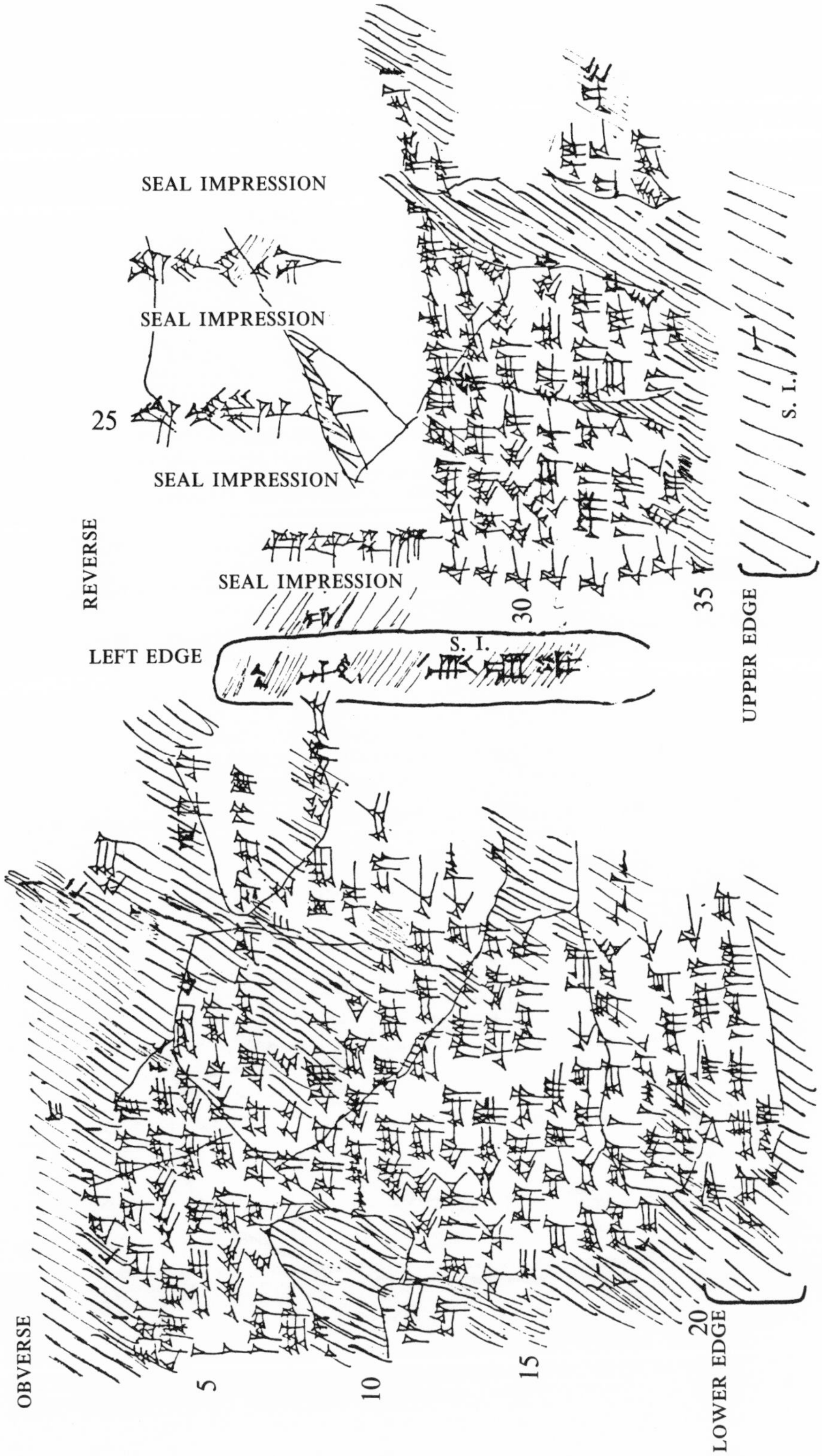
OBVERSE
LOWER EDGE
REVERSE
SEAL IMPRESSION
SEAL IMPRESSION
SEAL IMPRESSION
SEAL IMPRESSION
LEFT EDGE
S. I.
UPPER EDGE
S. I.

808

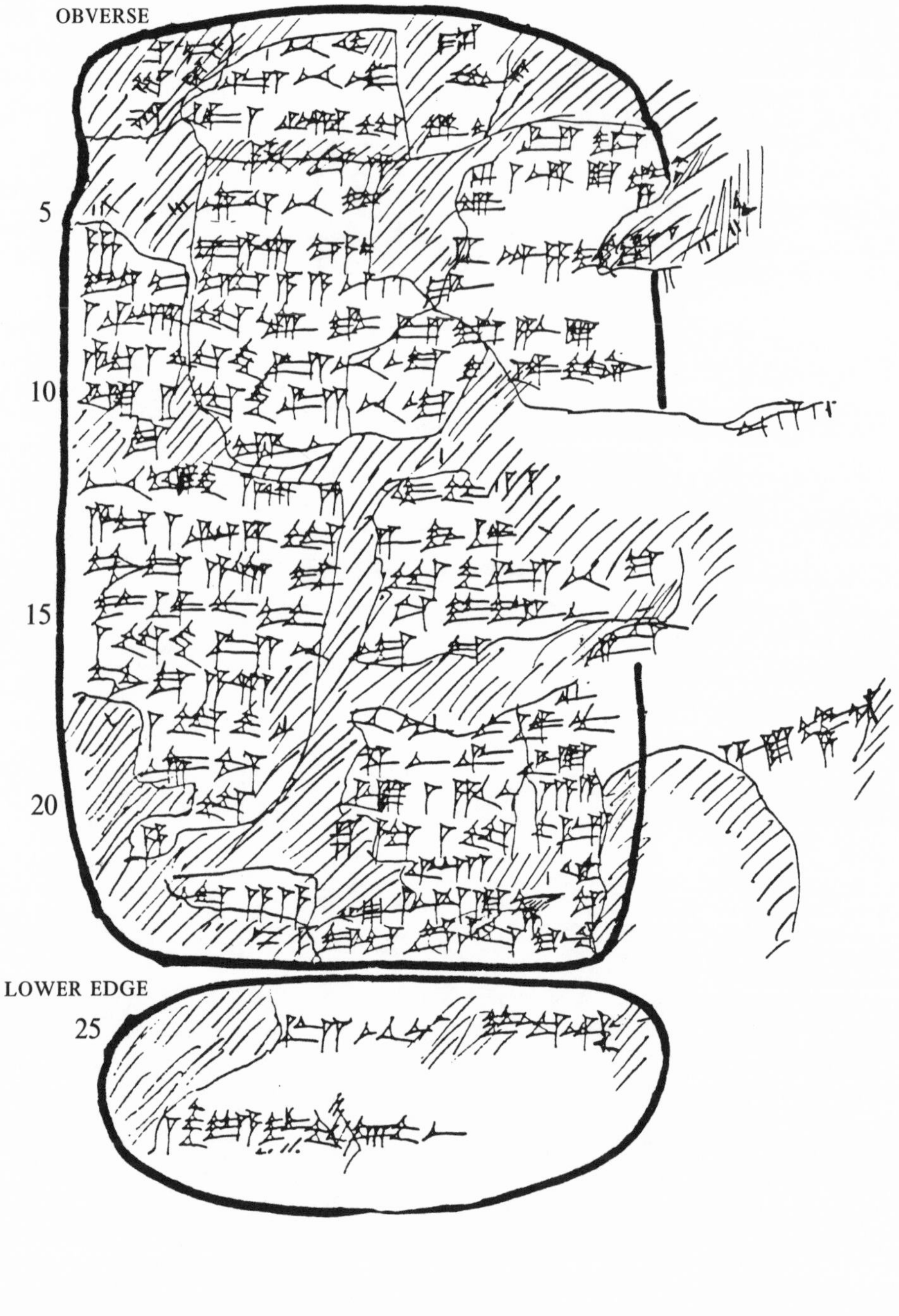

808

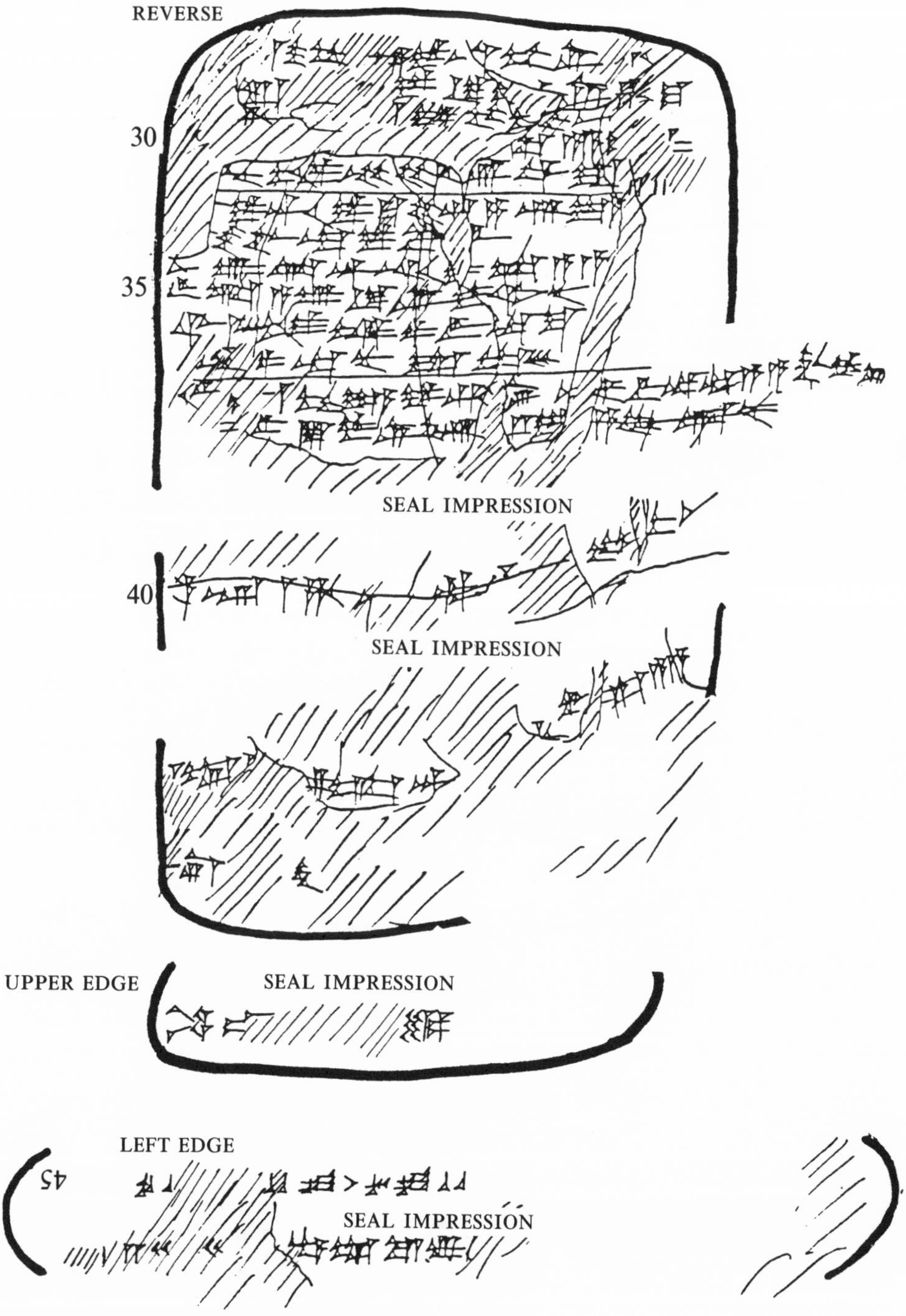
REVERSE
30
35
SEAL IMPRESSION
40
SEAL IMPRESSION
UPPER EDGE
SEAL IMPRESSION
LEFT EDGE
45
SEAL IMPRESSION

809

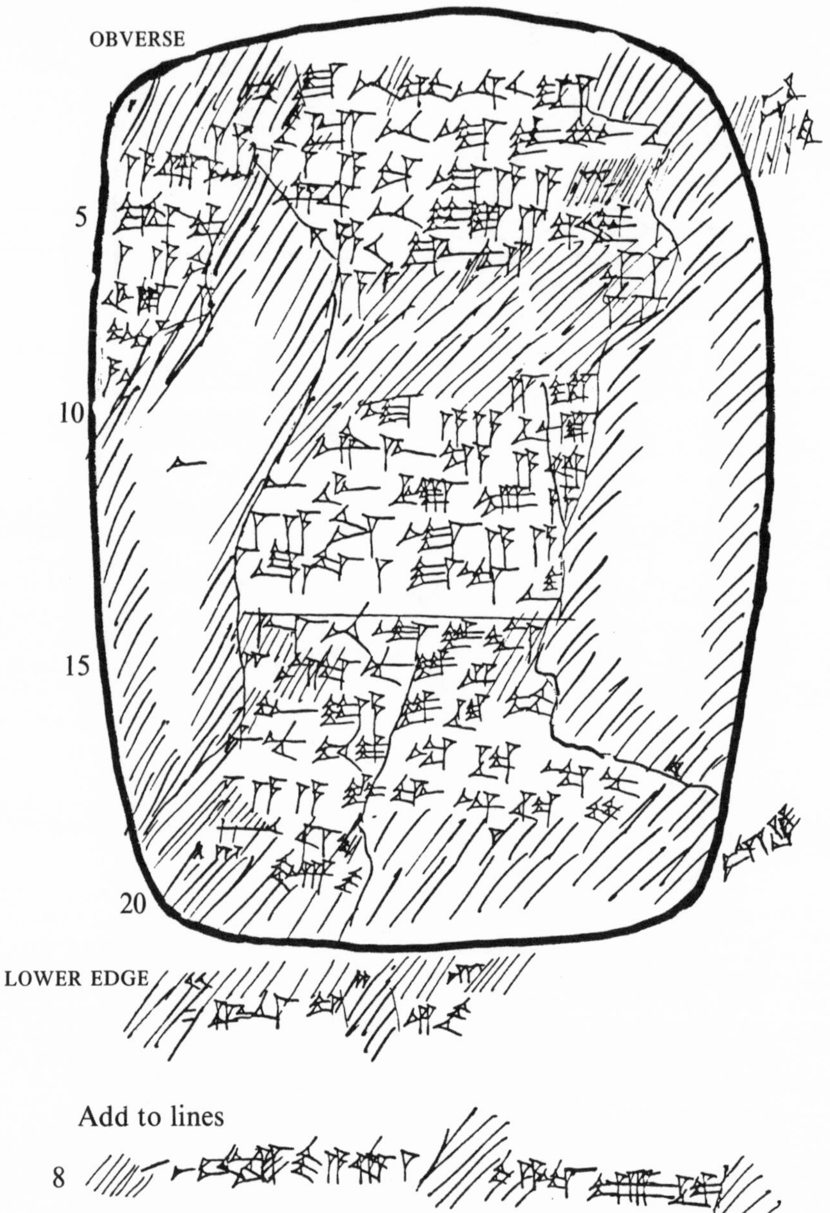

Add to lines

809

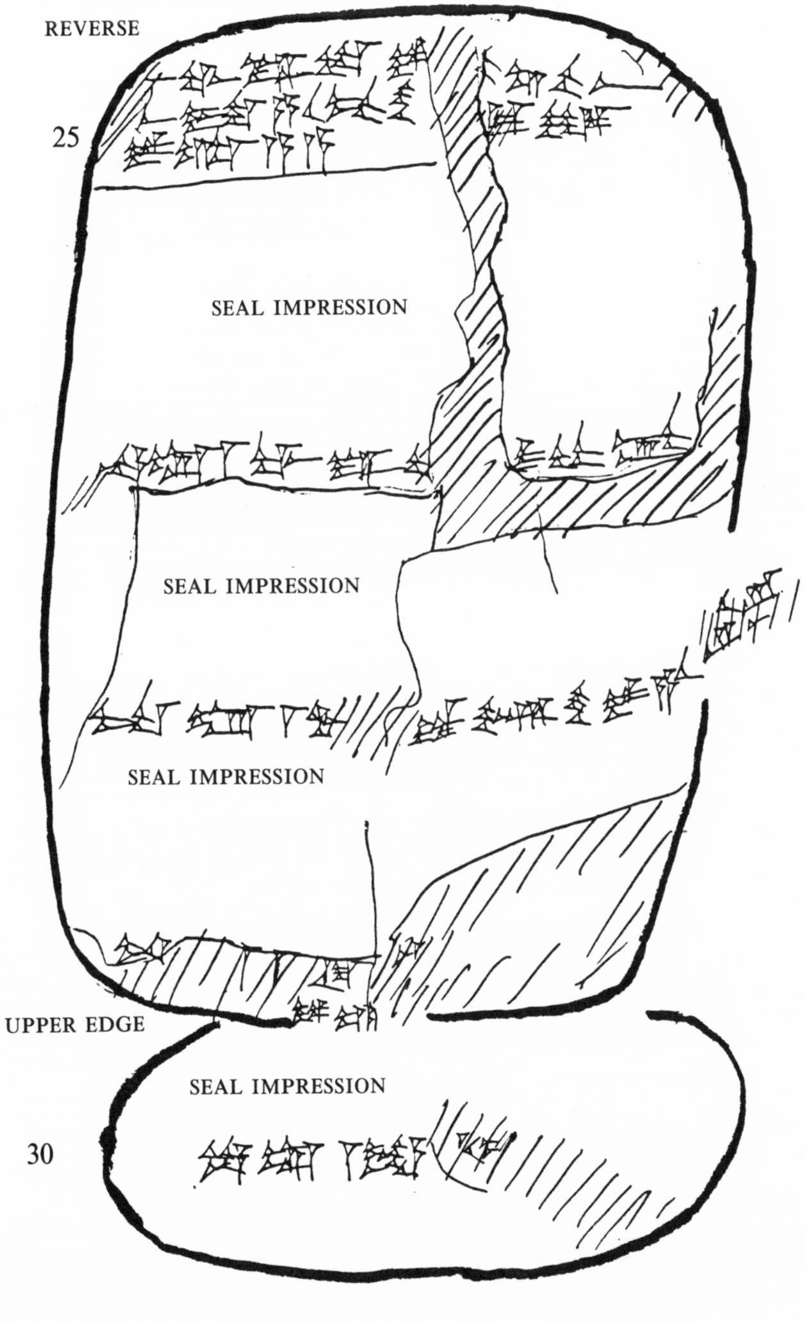
REVERSE
25
SEAL IMPRESSION
SEAL IMPRESSION
SEAL IMPRESSION
UPPER EDGE
SEAL IMPRESSION
30

810

OBVERSE

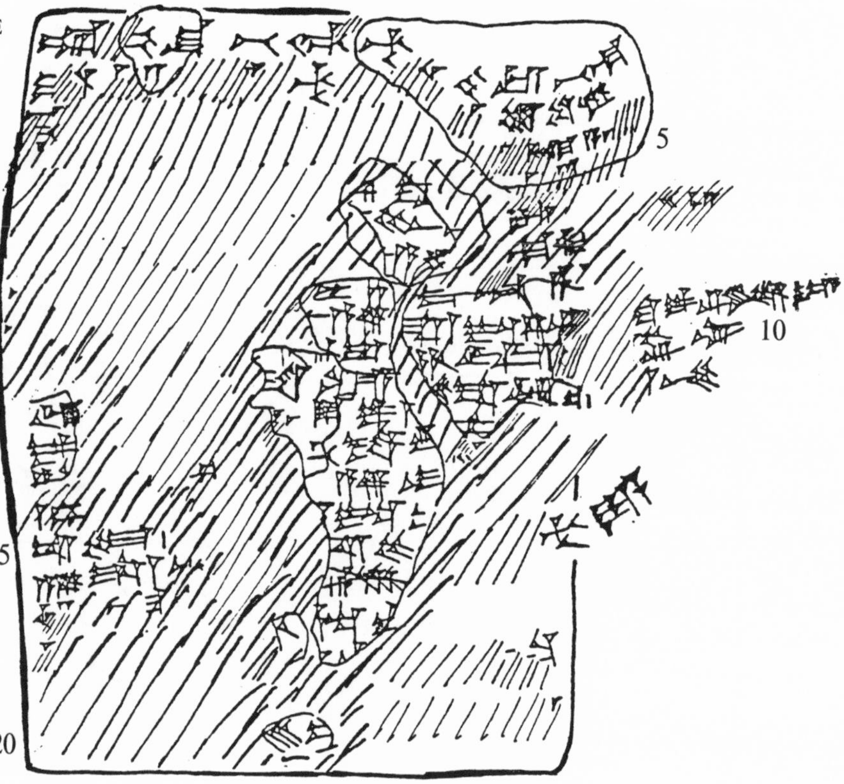

810

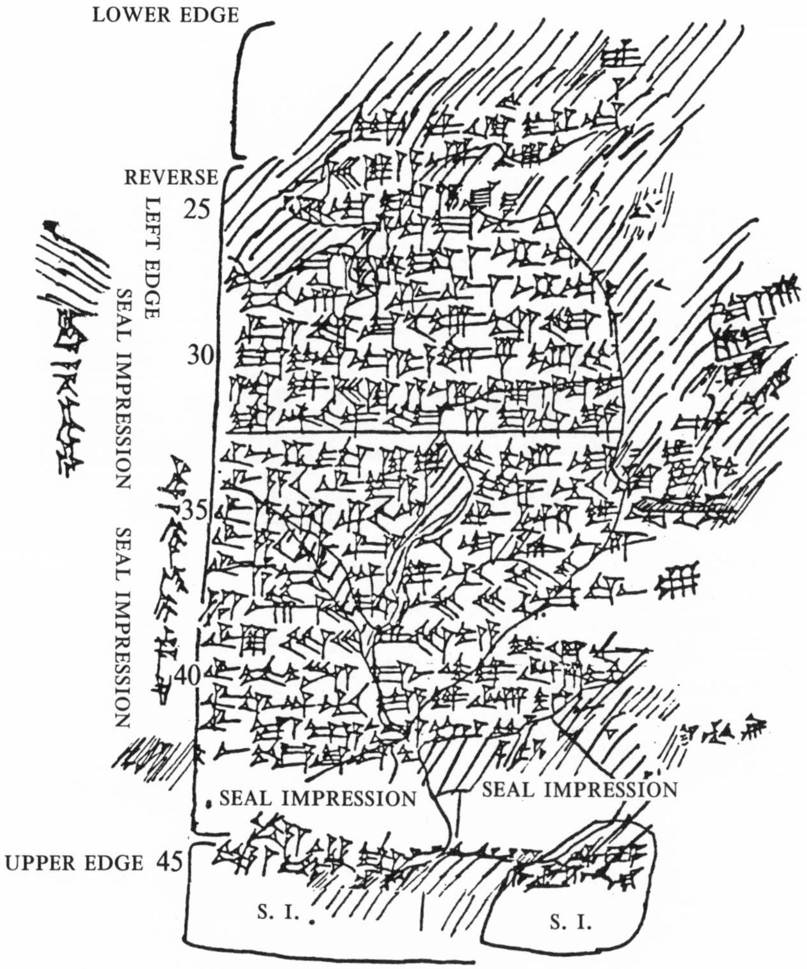
LOWER EDGE
REVERSE
25
LEFT EDGE
SEAL IMPRESSION
30
35
SEAL IMPRESSION
40
SEAL IMPRESSION
SEAL IMPRESSION
UPPER EDGE 45
S. I.
S. I.

811

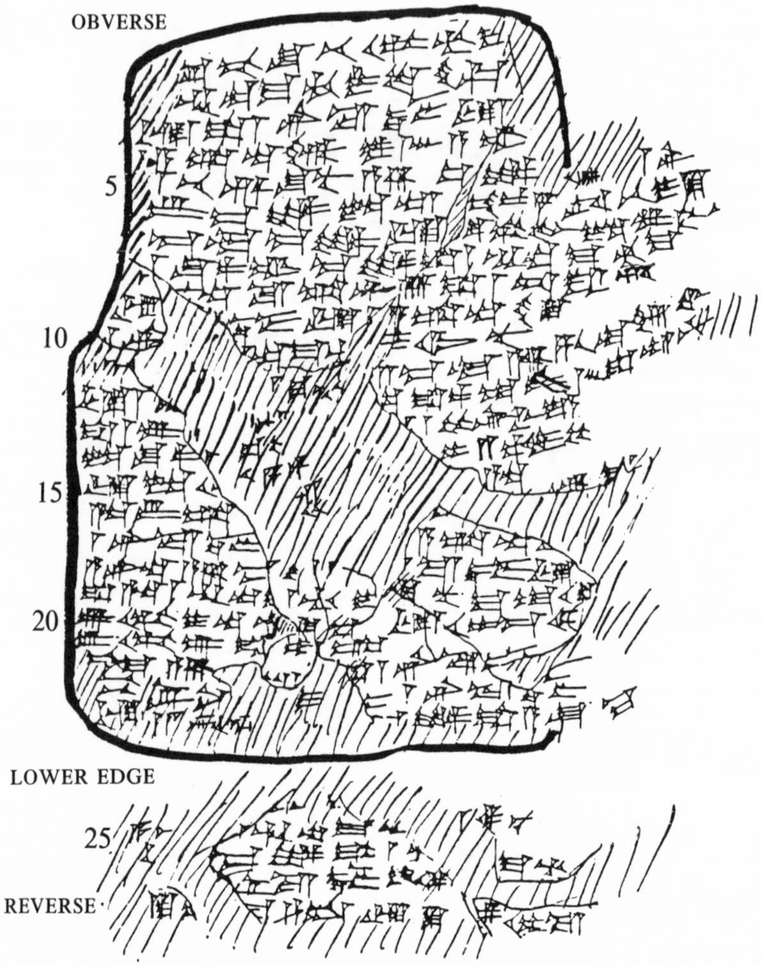
OBVERSE
5
10
15
20
LOWER EDGE
25
REVERSE

811

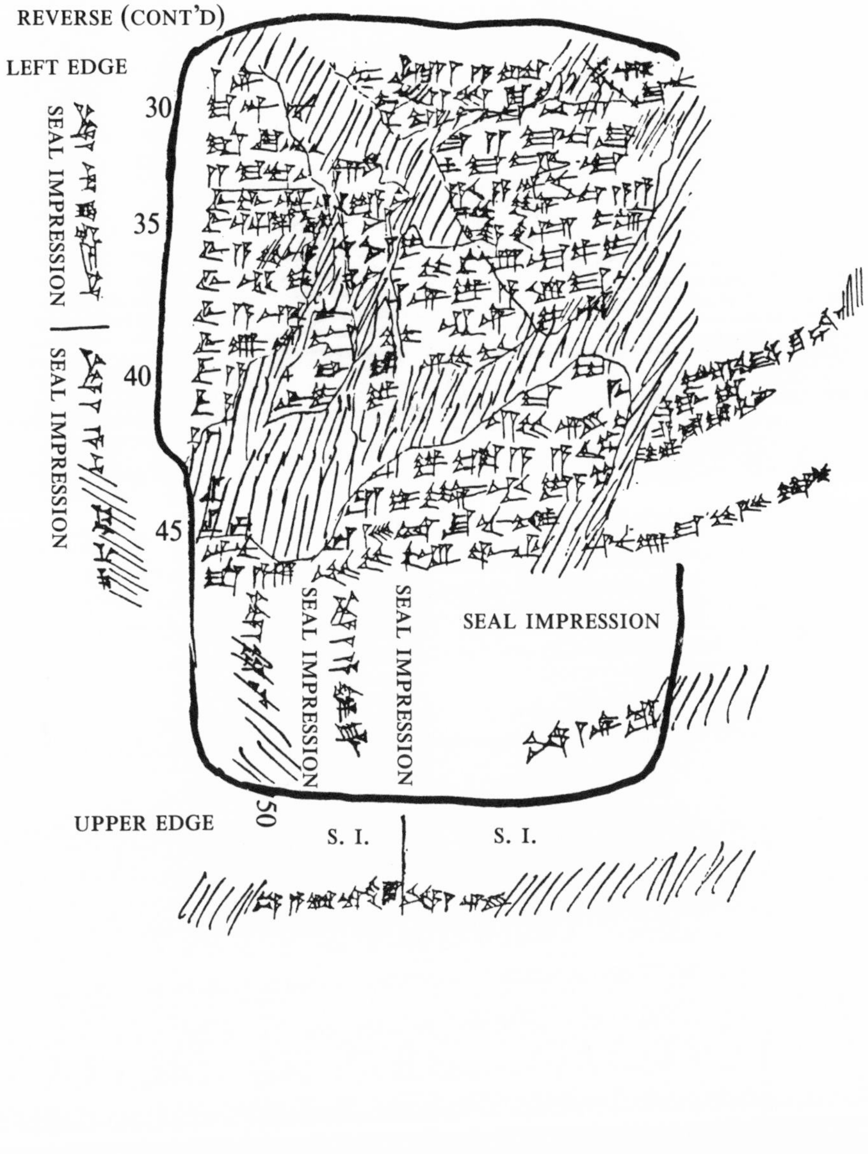
REVERSE (CONT'D)
LEFT EDGE
SEAL IMPRESSION
SEAL IMPRESSION
30
35
40
45
50
SEAL IMPRESSION
SEAL IMPRESSION
SEAL IMPRESSION
UPPER EDGE
S. I.
S. I.

812

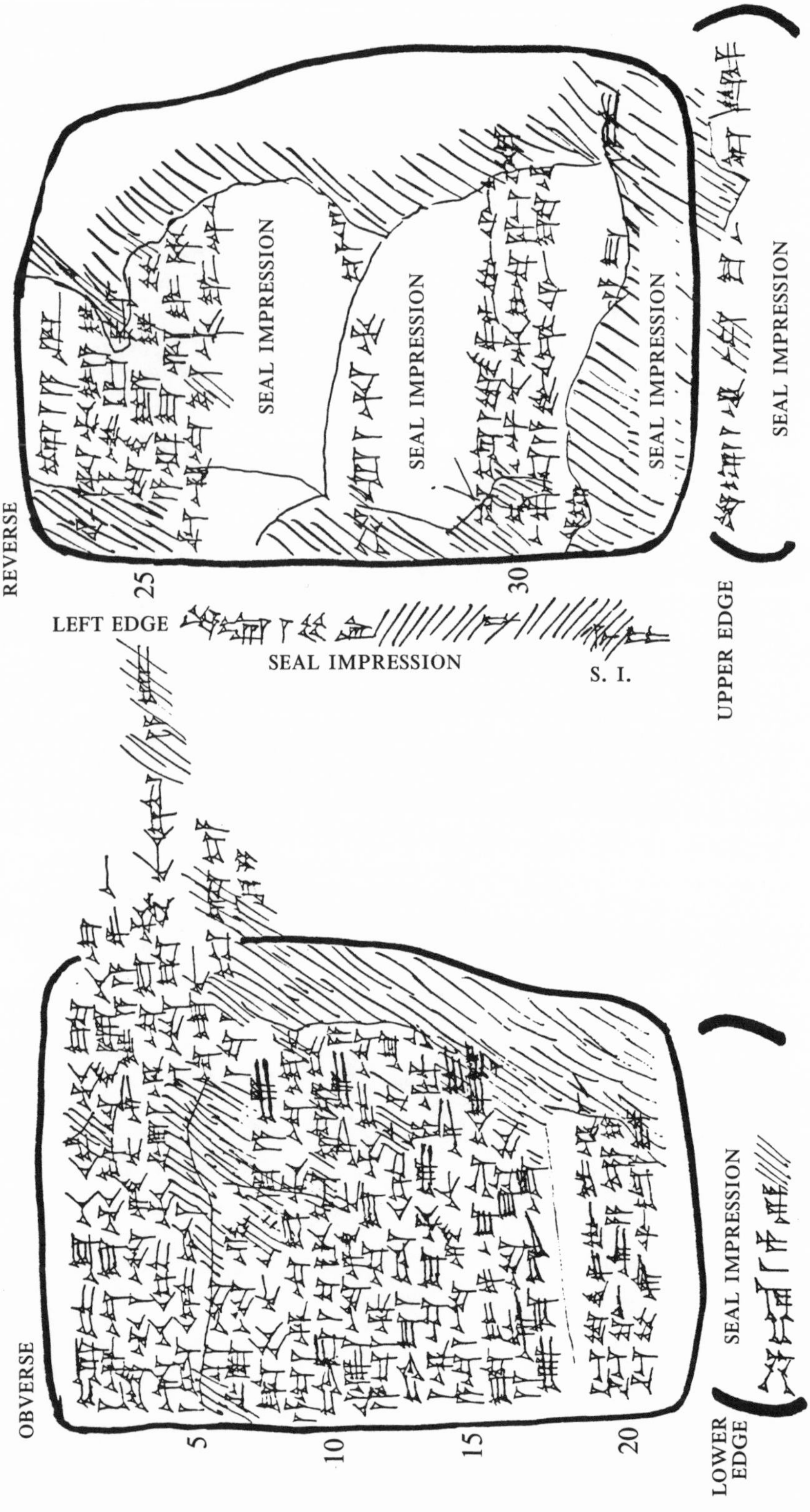
OBVERSE
5
10
15
20
LOWER EDGE
SEAL IMPRESSION
LEFT EDGE
SEAL IMPRESSION
S. I.
REVERSE
25
30
SEAL IMPRESSION
SEAL IMPRESSION
SEAL IMPRESSION
UPPER EDGE
SEAL IMPRESSION

813 (= 879)*

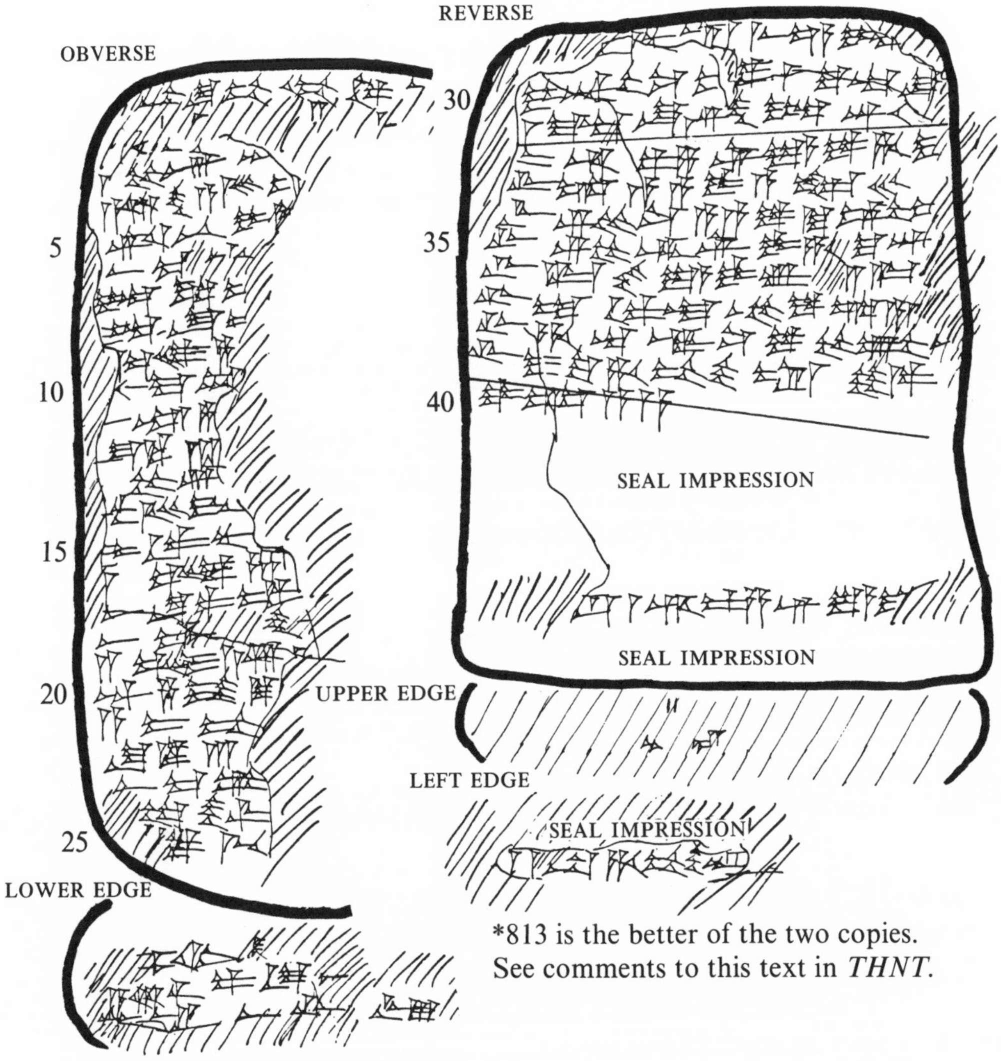

*813 is the better of the two copies. See comments to this text in *THNT*.

814

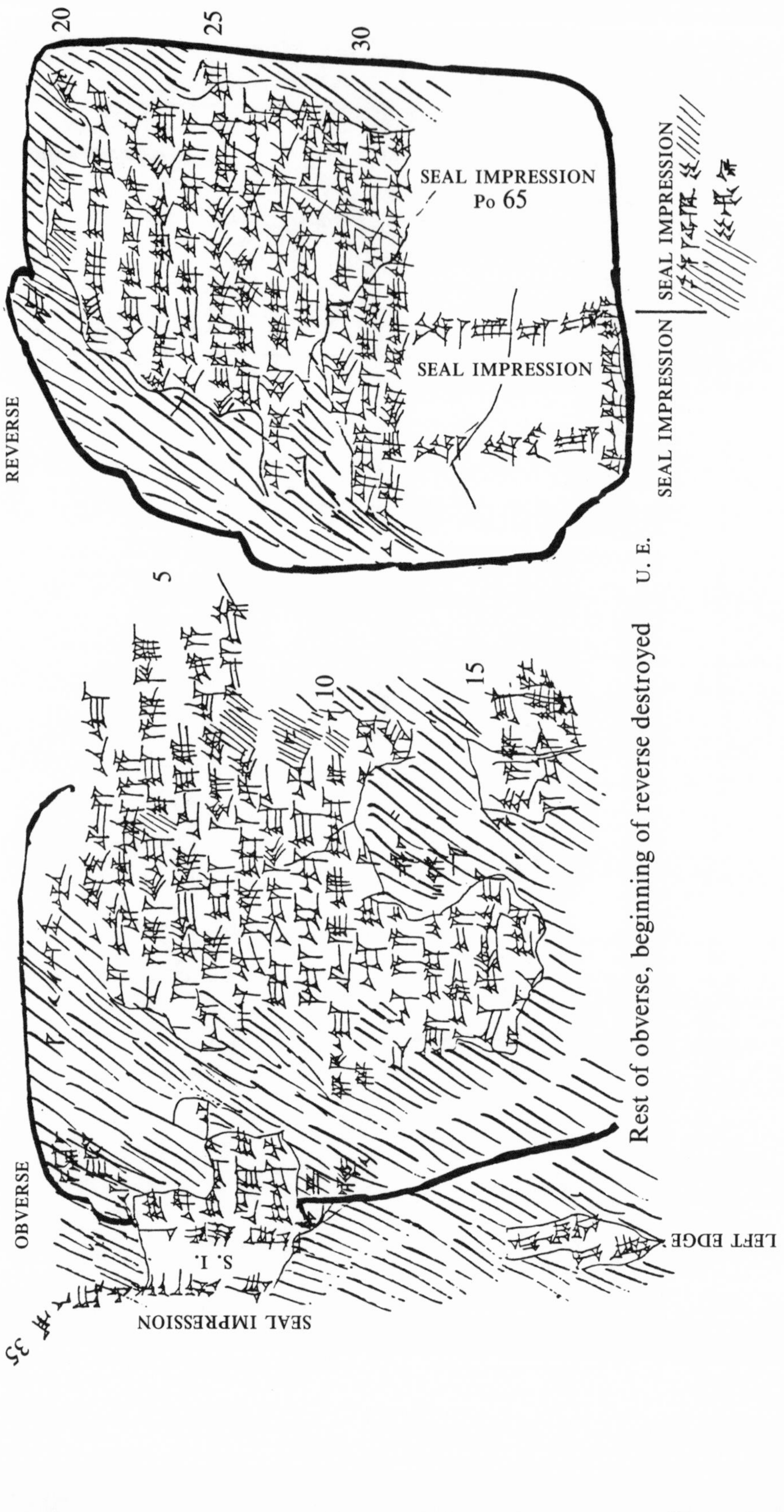
OBVERSE
REVERSE
SEAL IMPRESSION
Po 65
SEAL IMPRESSION
SEAL IMPRESSION
SEAL IMPRESSION
U. E.
Rest of obverse, beginning of reverse destroyed
S. I.
SEAL IMPRESSION
LEFT EDGE

815

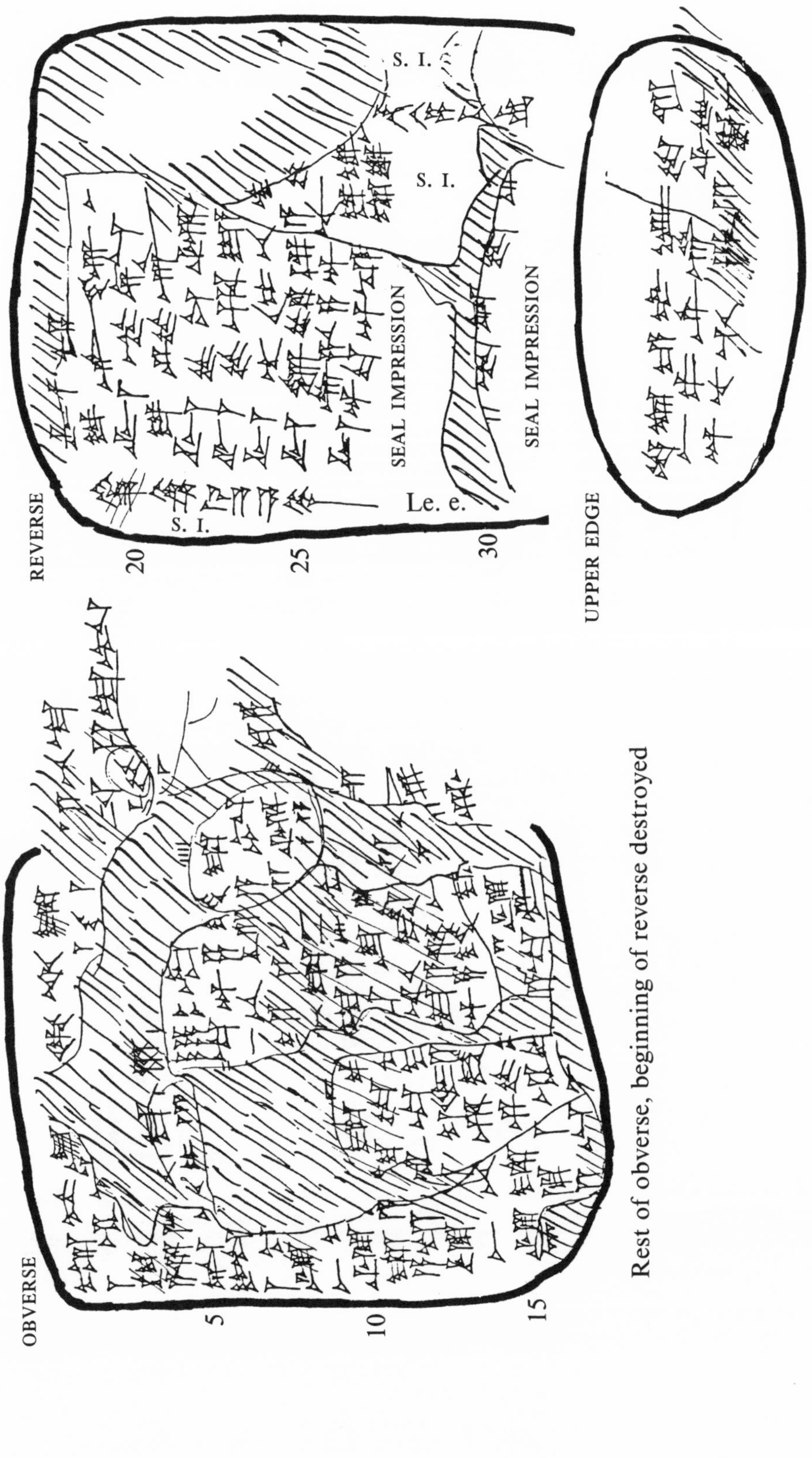
OBVERSE
REVERSE
S. I.
S. I.
S. I.
Le. e.
SEAL IMPRESSION
SEAL IMPRESSION
UPPER EDGE
Rest of obverse, beginning of reverse destroyed

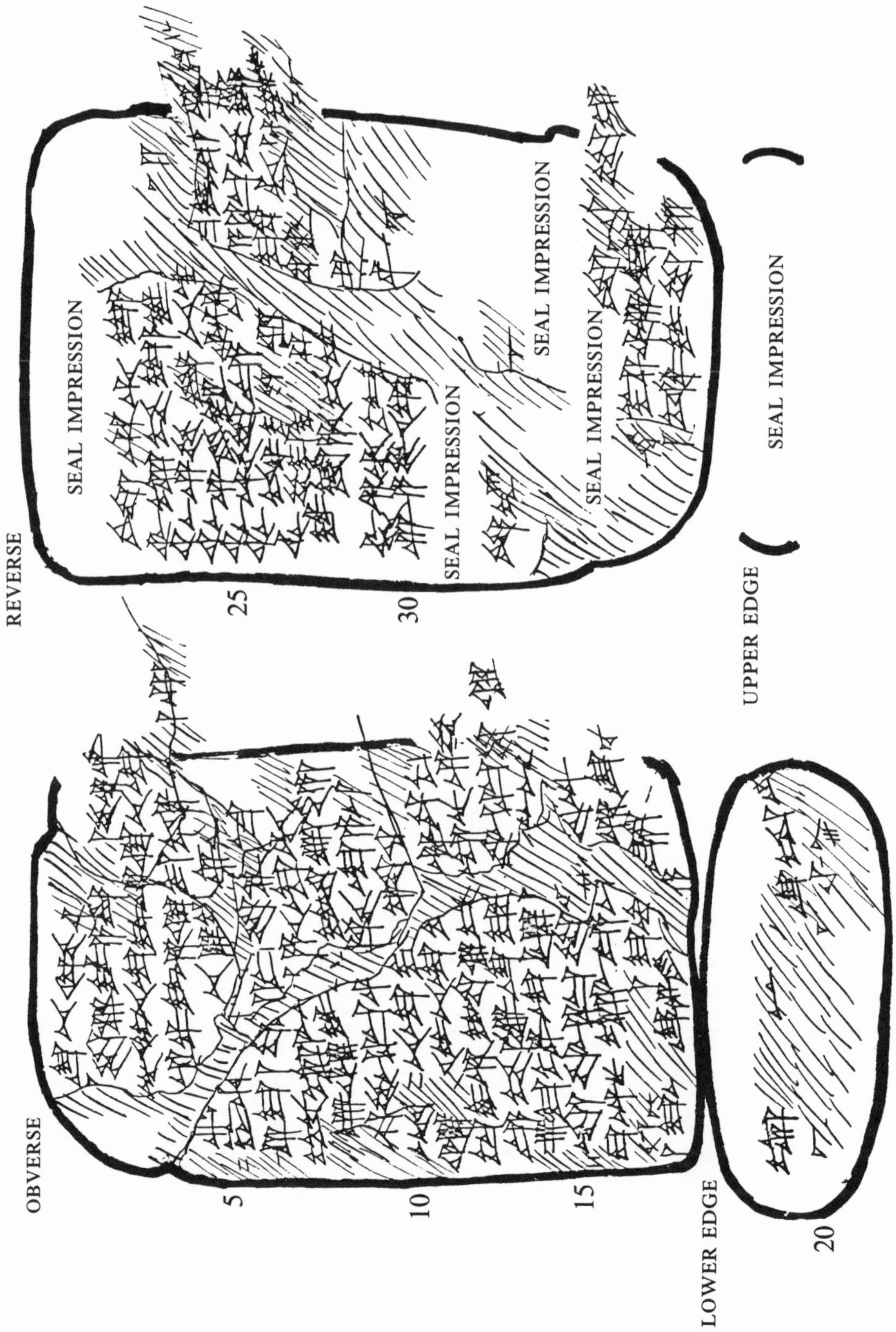
816
OBVERSE
5
10
15
LOWER EDGE
20
REVERSE
25
30
UPPER EDGE
SEAL IMPRESSION
SEAL IMPRESSION
SEAL IMPRESSION
SEAL IMPRESSION
SEAL IMPRESSION

817

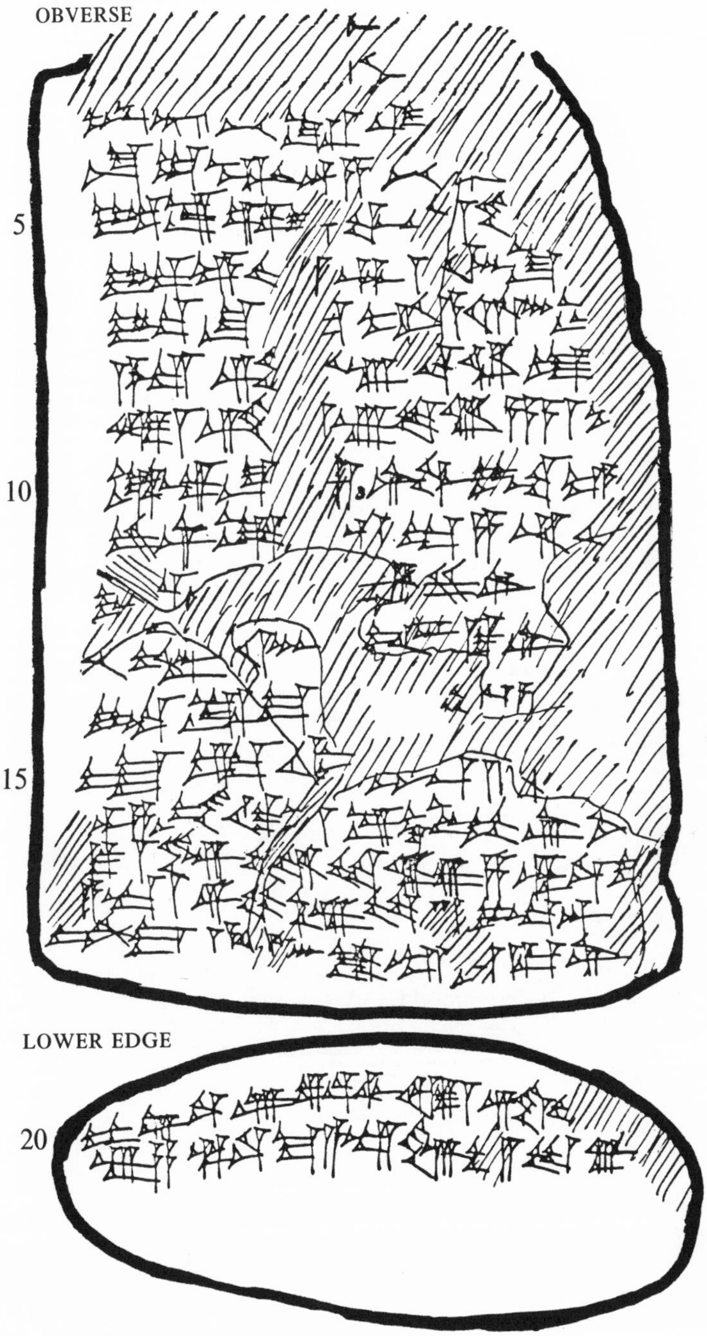

817

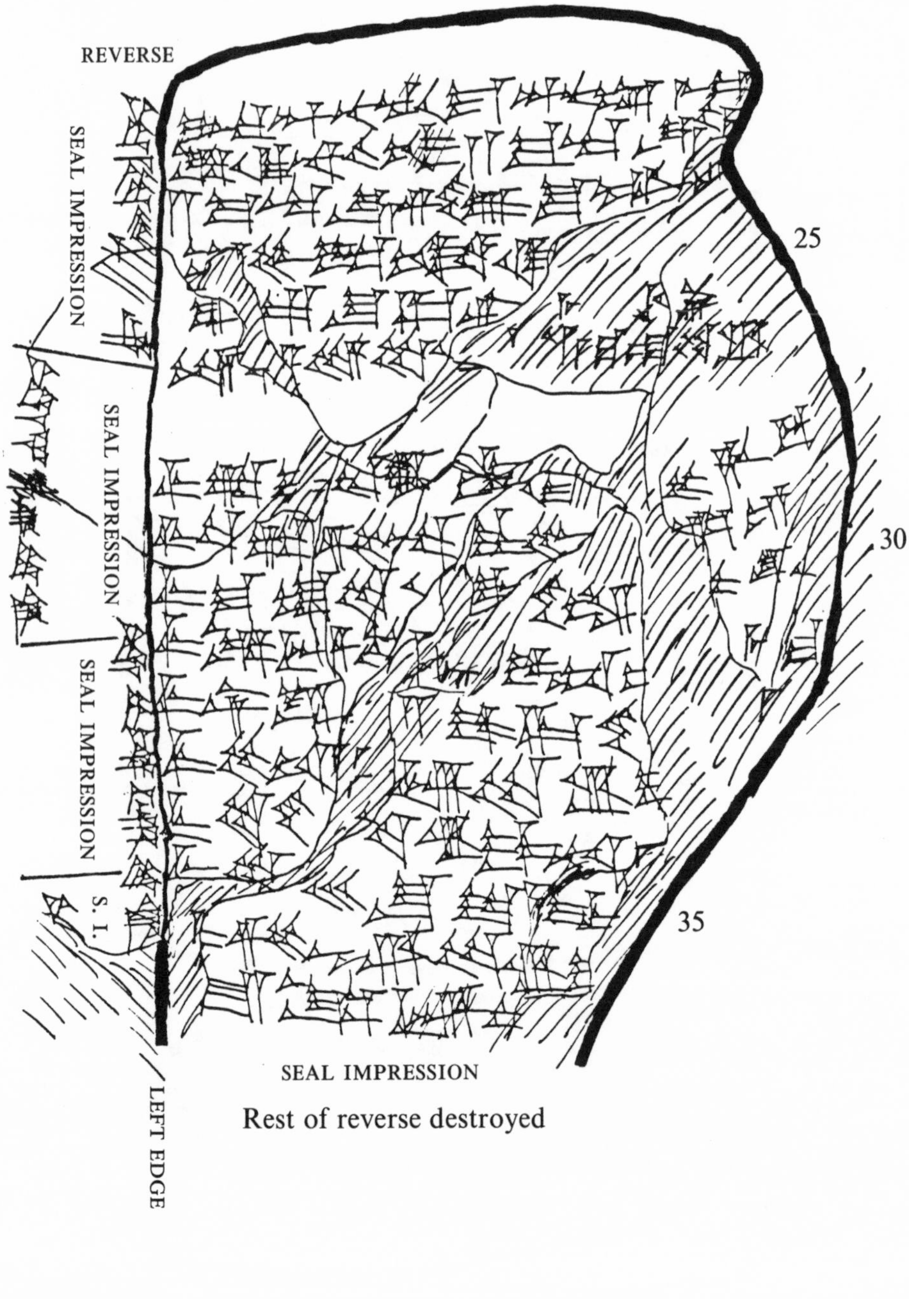

Rest of reverse destroyed

818 (= 875)*

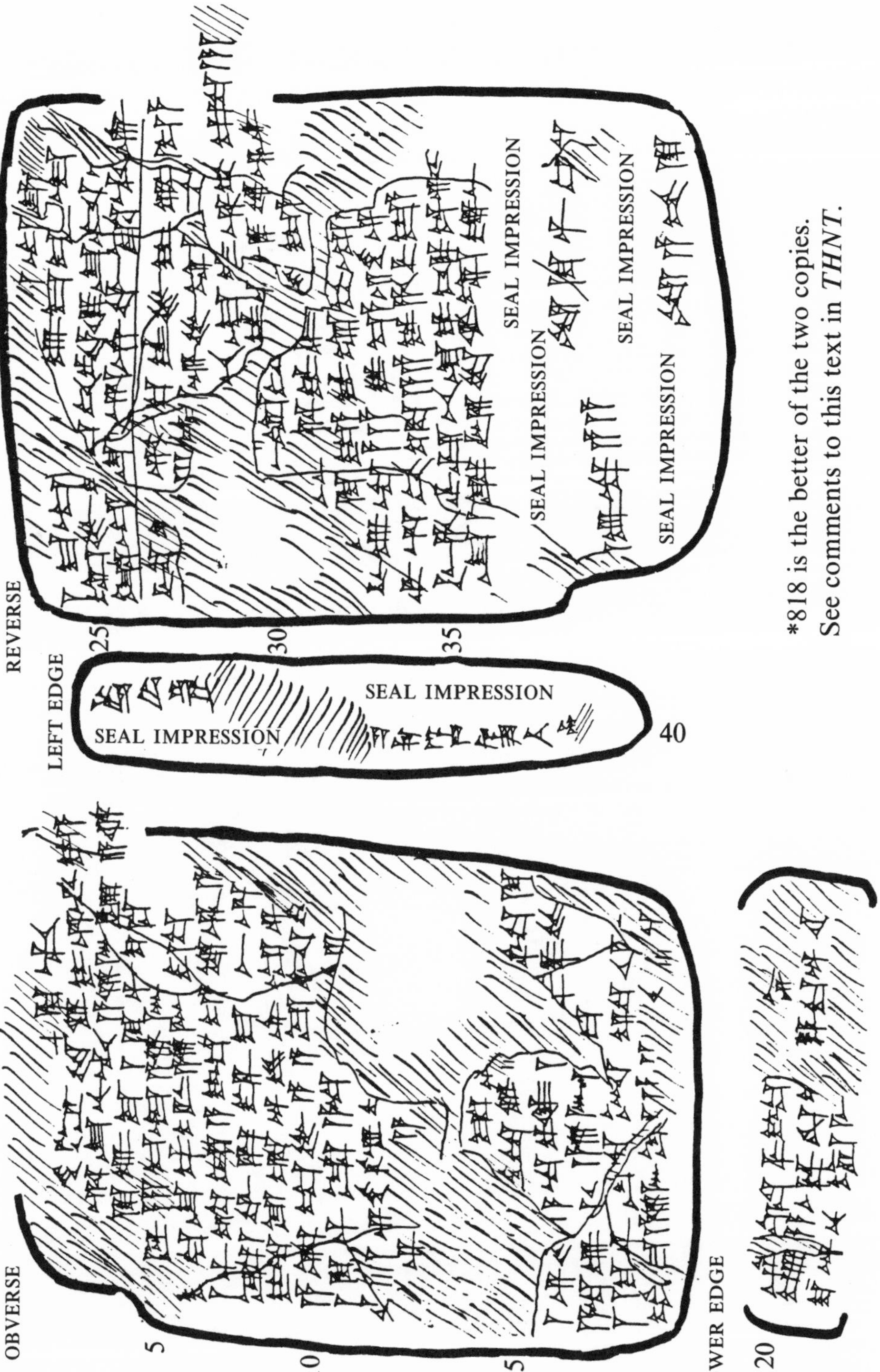

*818 is the better of the two copies.
See comments to this text in *THNT*.

819

OBVERSE

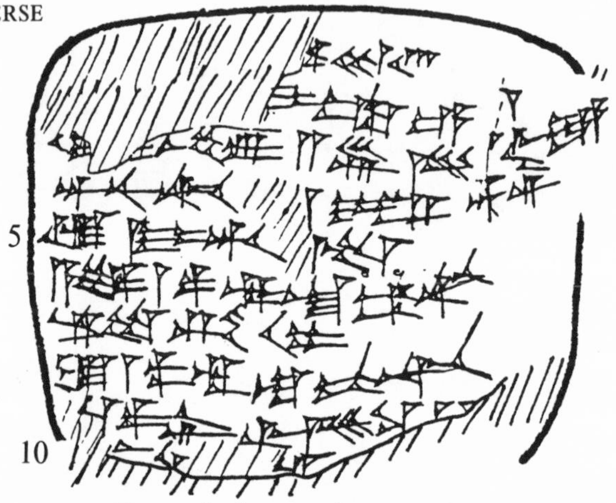

Rest of obverse destroyed

REVERSE

Beginning of reverse destroyed

820

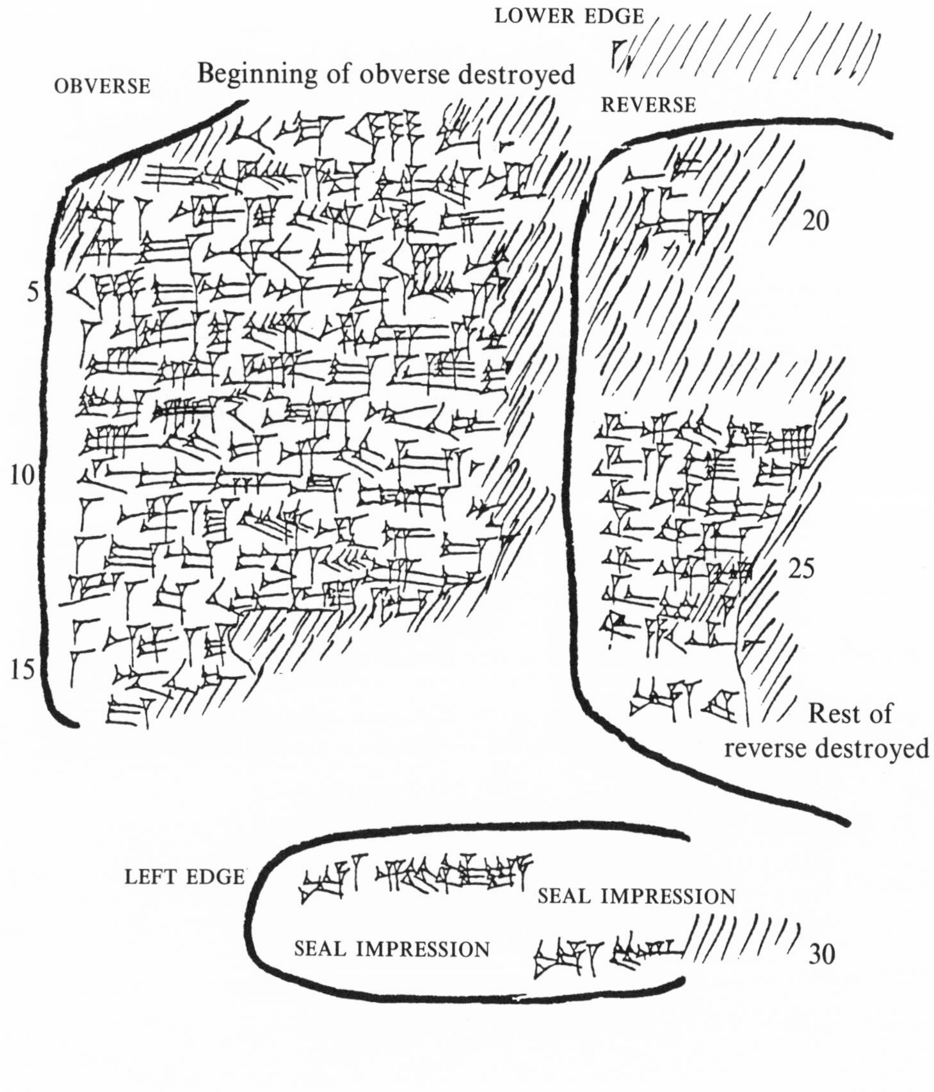
LOWER EDGE
OBVERSE
Beginning of obverse destroyed
REVERSE
5
10
15
20
25
Rest of reverse destroyed
LEFT EDGE
SEAL IMPRESSION
SEAL IMPRESSION
30

821 (= 822)*

OBVERSE

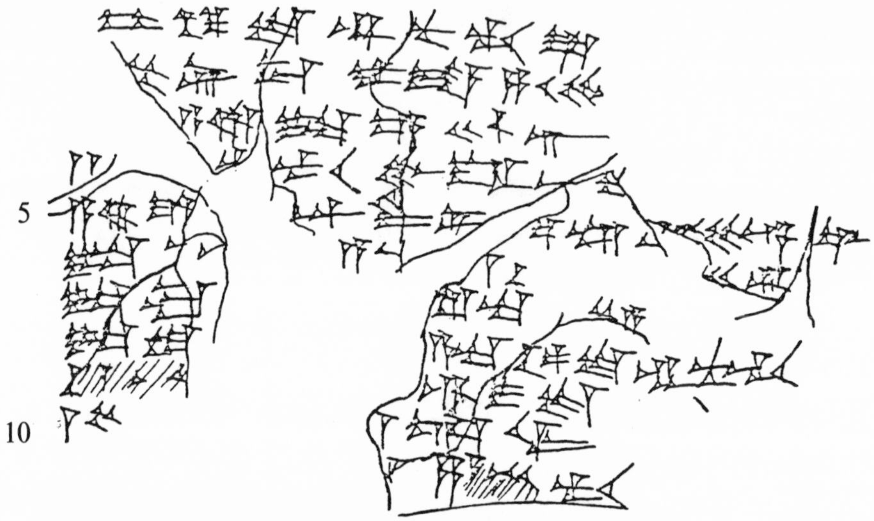

Rest of obverse, beginning of reverse destroyed

REVERSE

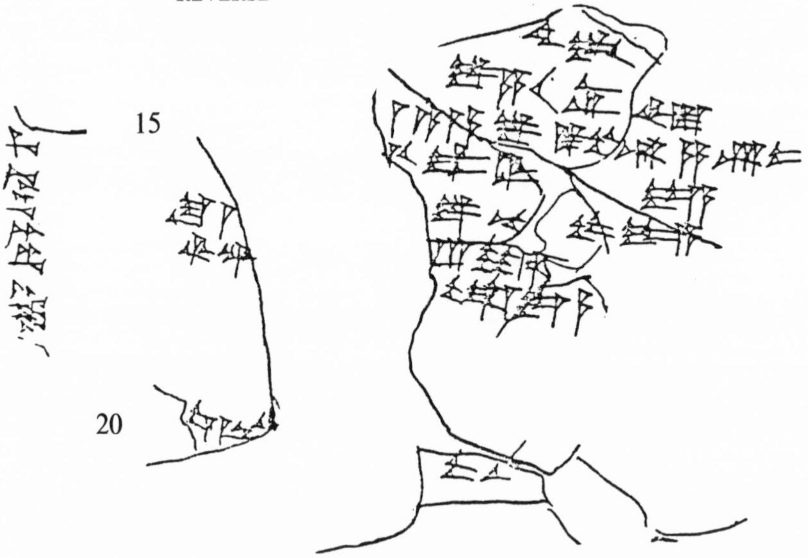

*822 is the better of the two copies. See comments to that text in *THNT*.

822 (= 821)*

OBVERSE

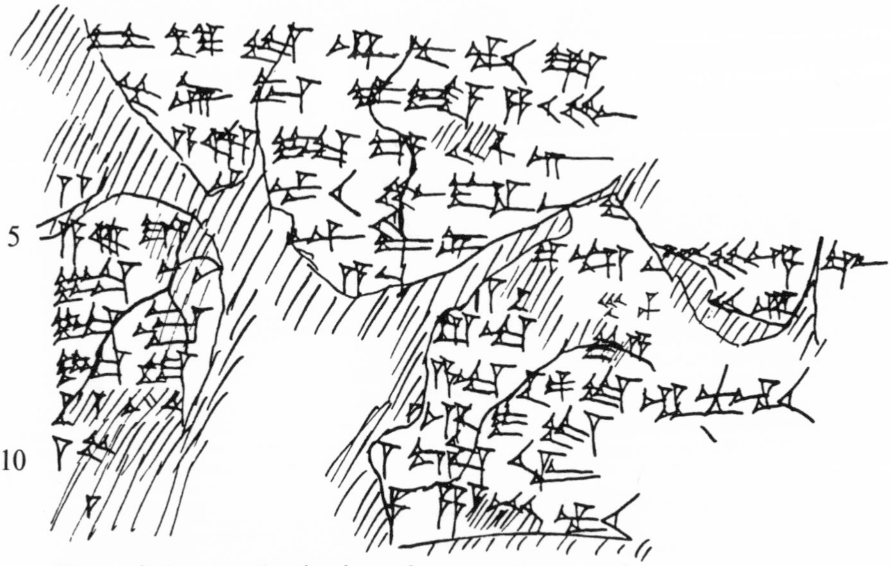

Rest of obverse, beginning of reverse destroyed

REVERSE

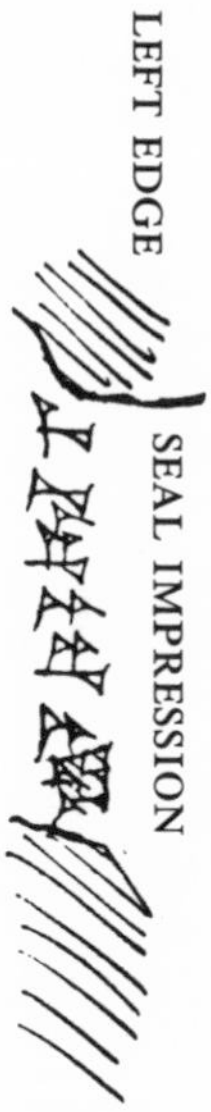

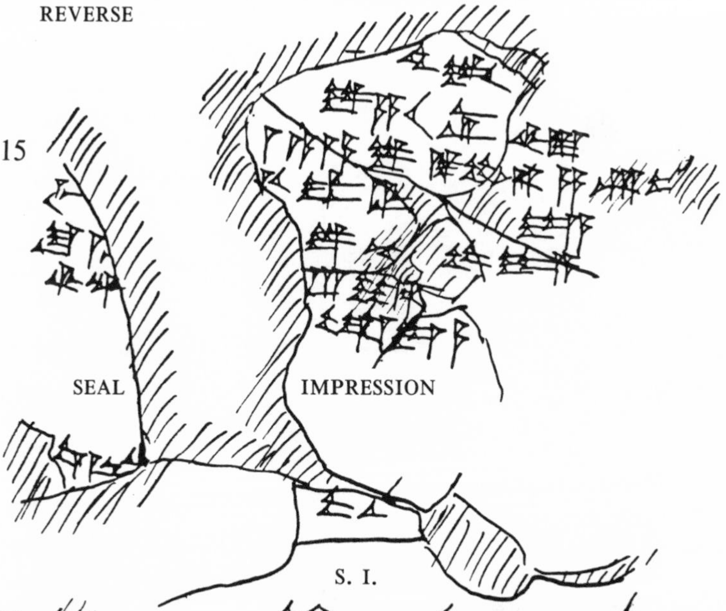

UPPER EDGE

*822 is the better of the two copies. See comments to this text in *THNT*.

823

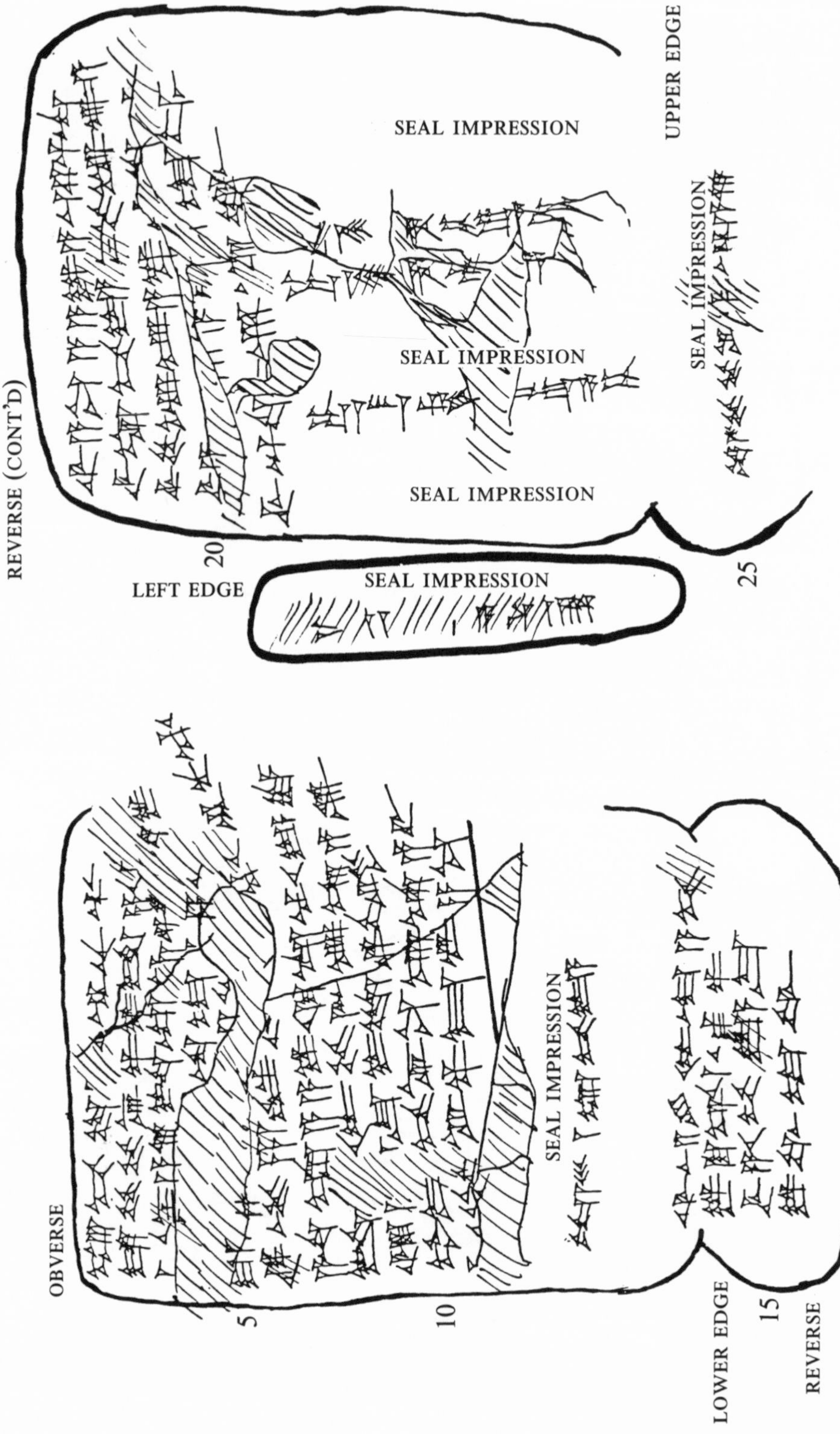
REVERSE (CONT'D)
SEAL IMPRESSION
SEAL IMPRESSION
SEAL IMPRESSION
UPPER EDGE
SEAL IMPRESSION
20
LEFT EDGE
SEAL IMPRESSION
25
OBVERSE
5
10
SEAL IMPRESSION
LOWER EDGE
15
REVERSE

824

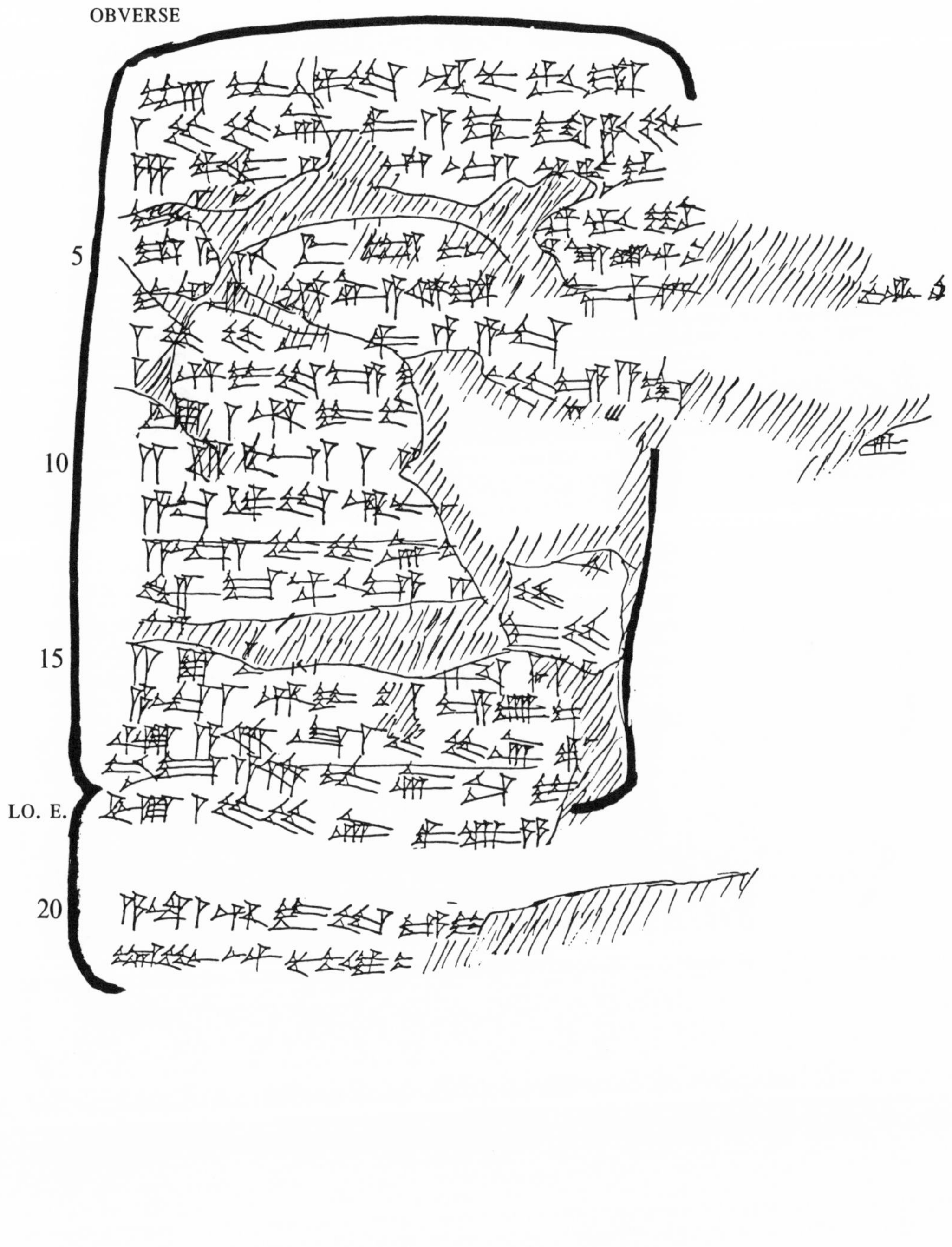

824

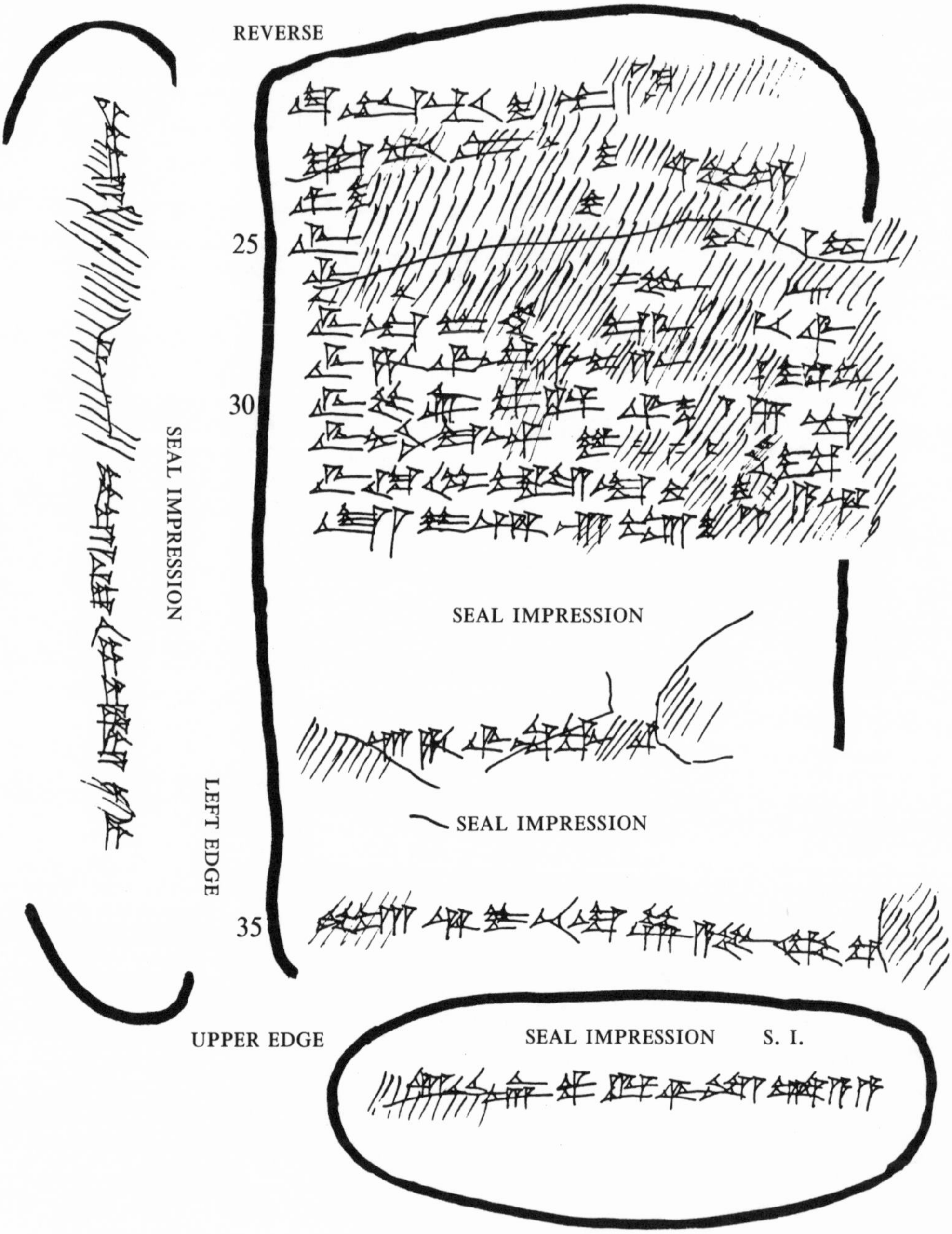
REVERSE
SEAL IMPRESSION
SEAL IMPRESSION
SEAL IMPRESSION
LEFT EDGE
UPPER EDGE
SEAL IMPRESSION
S. I.

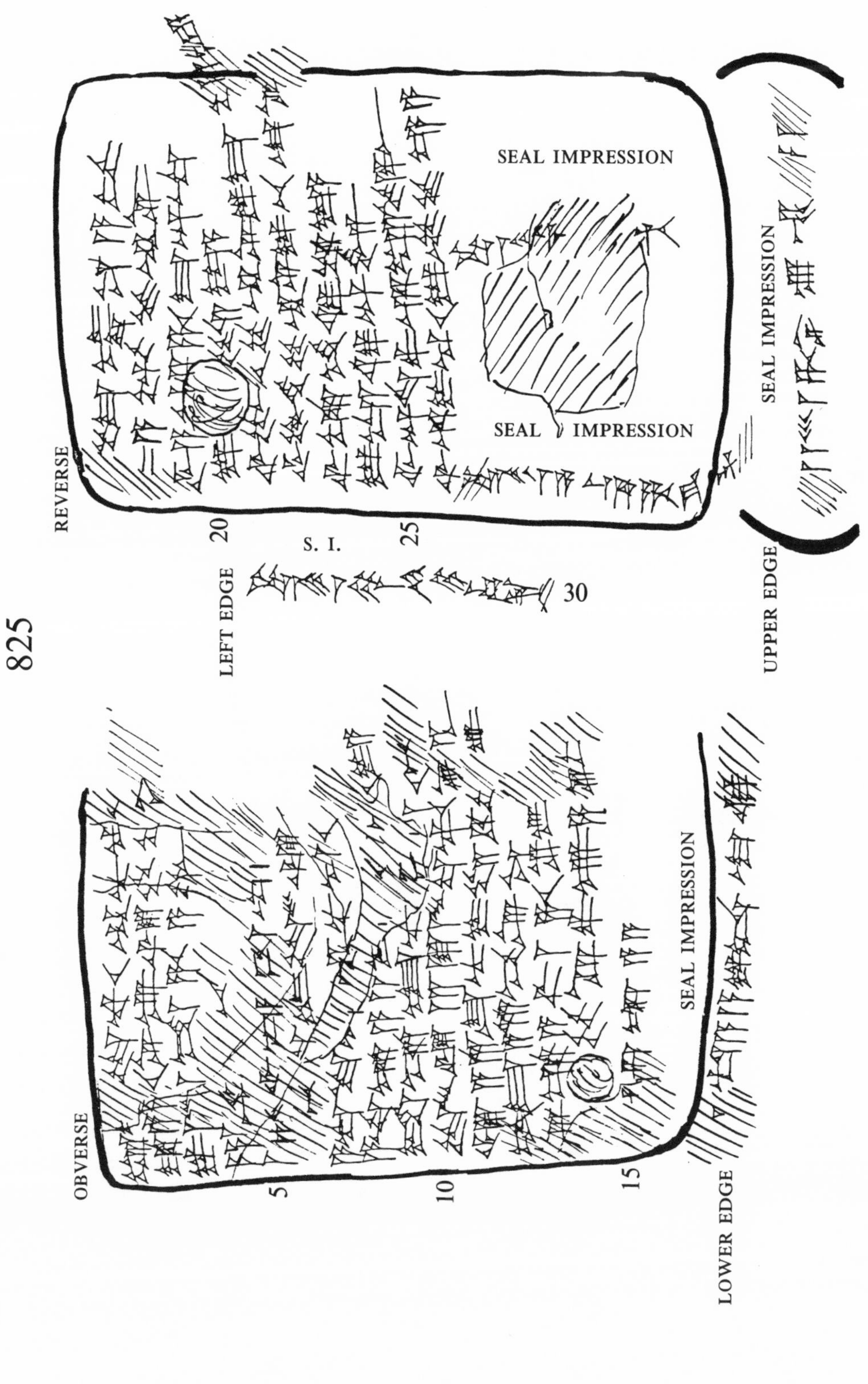
825
OBVERSE
REVERSE
LEFT EDGE
UPPER EDGE
LOWER EDGE
SEAL IMPRESSION
SEAL IMPRESSION
SEAL IMPRESSION
SEAL IMPRESSION
S. I.
5
10
15
20
25
30

826

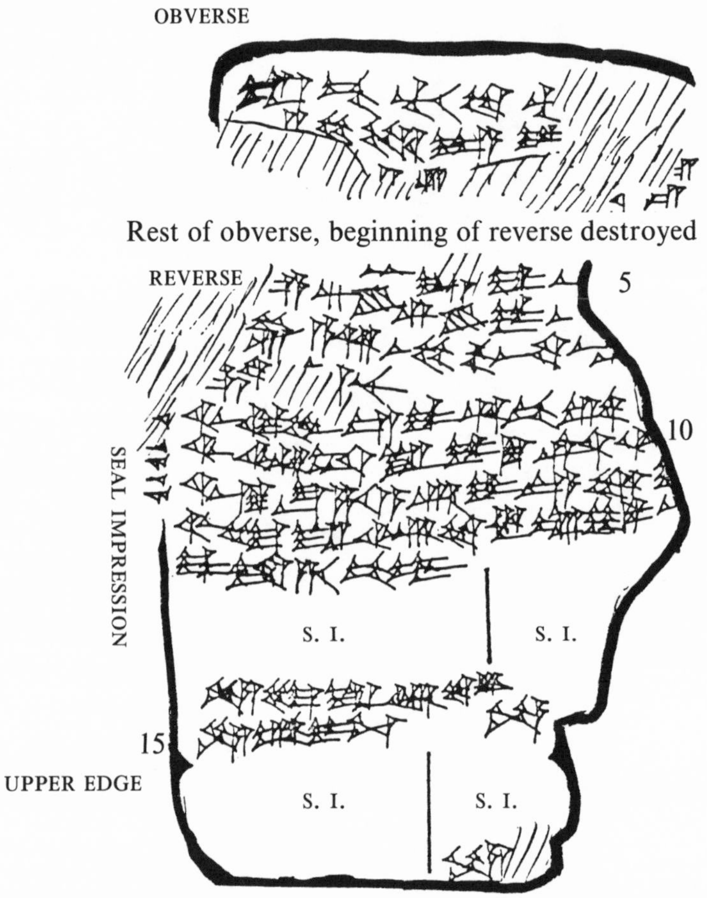
OBVERSE
Rest of obverse, beginning of reverse destroyed
REVERSE
5
10
SEAL IMPRESSION
S. I.
S. I.
15
UPPER EDGE
S. I.
S. I.

827

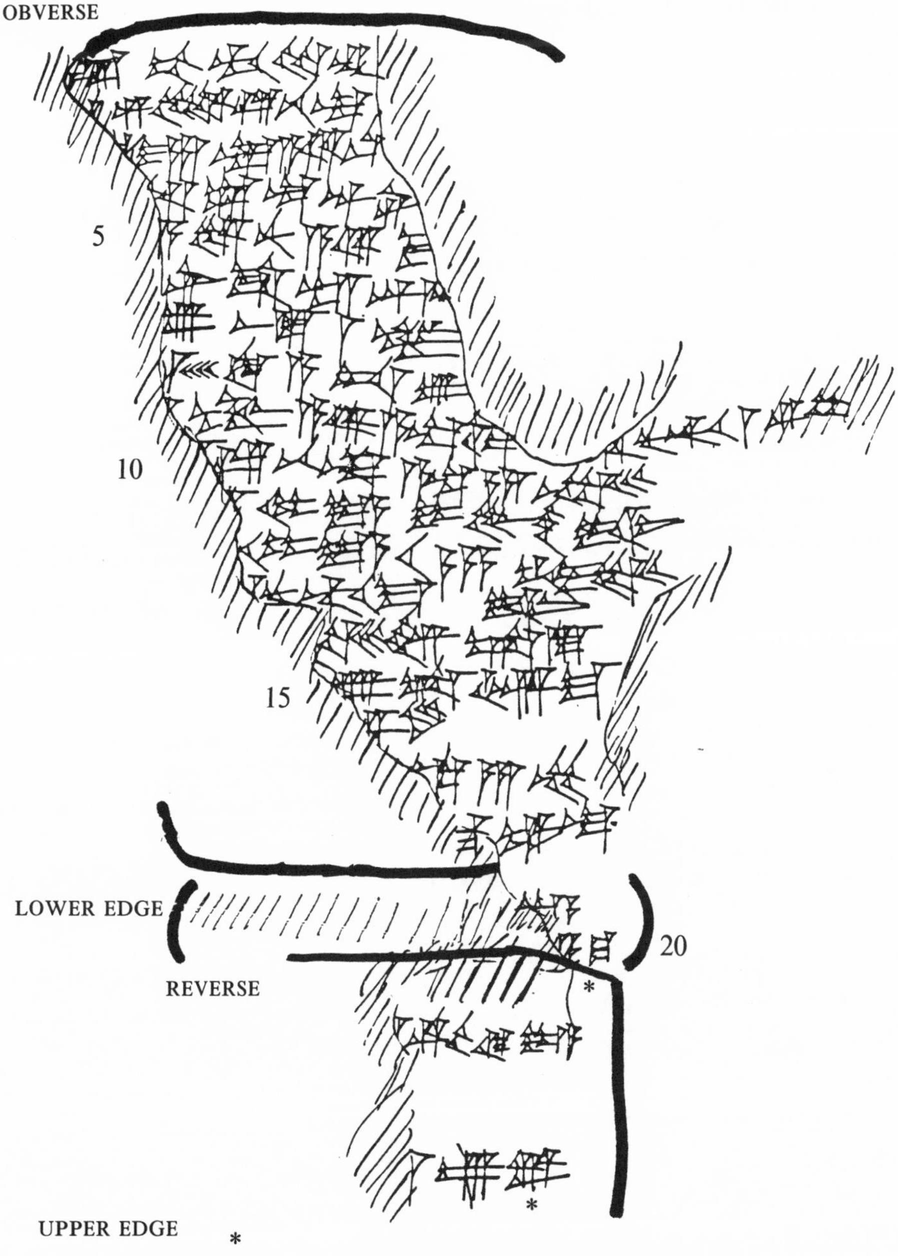

*Additional text; see *THNT*.

828

OBVERSE Beginning of obverse destroyed

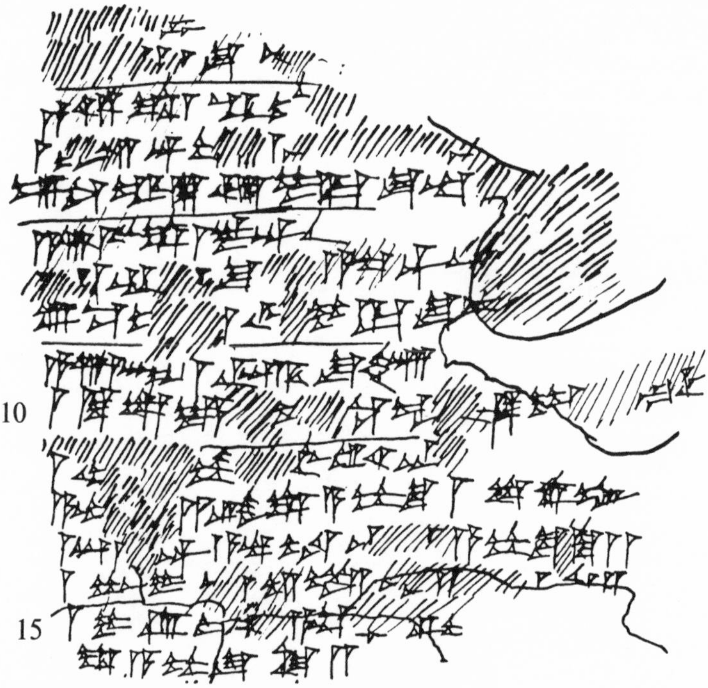

LOWER EDGE

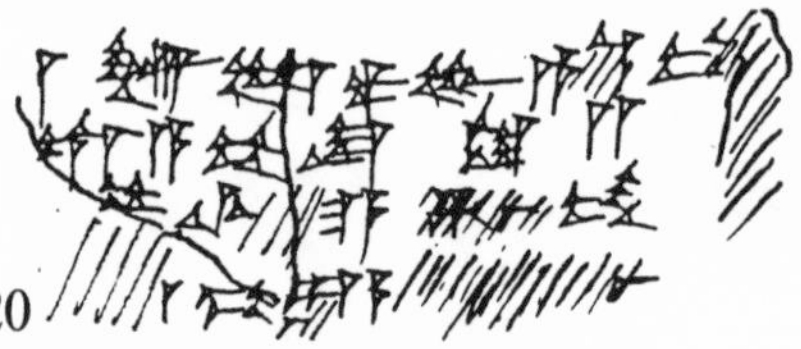

REVERSE

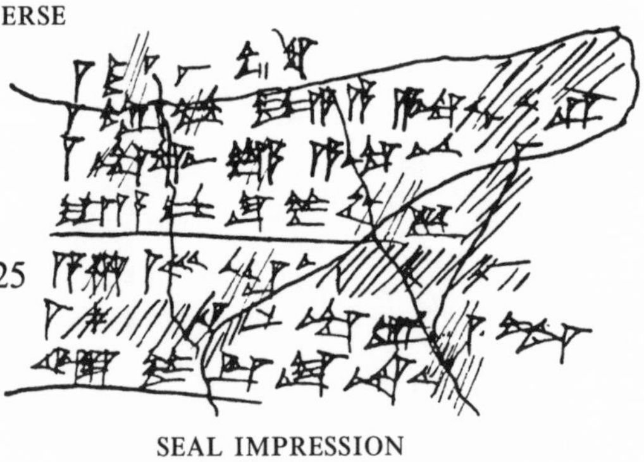

SEAL IMPRESSION

SEAL IMPRESSION

SEAL IMPRESSION

829

OBVERSE

LOWER EDGE

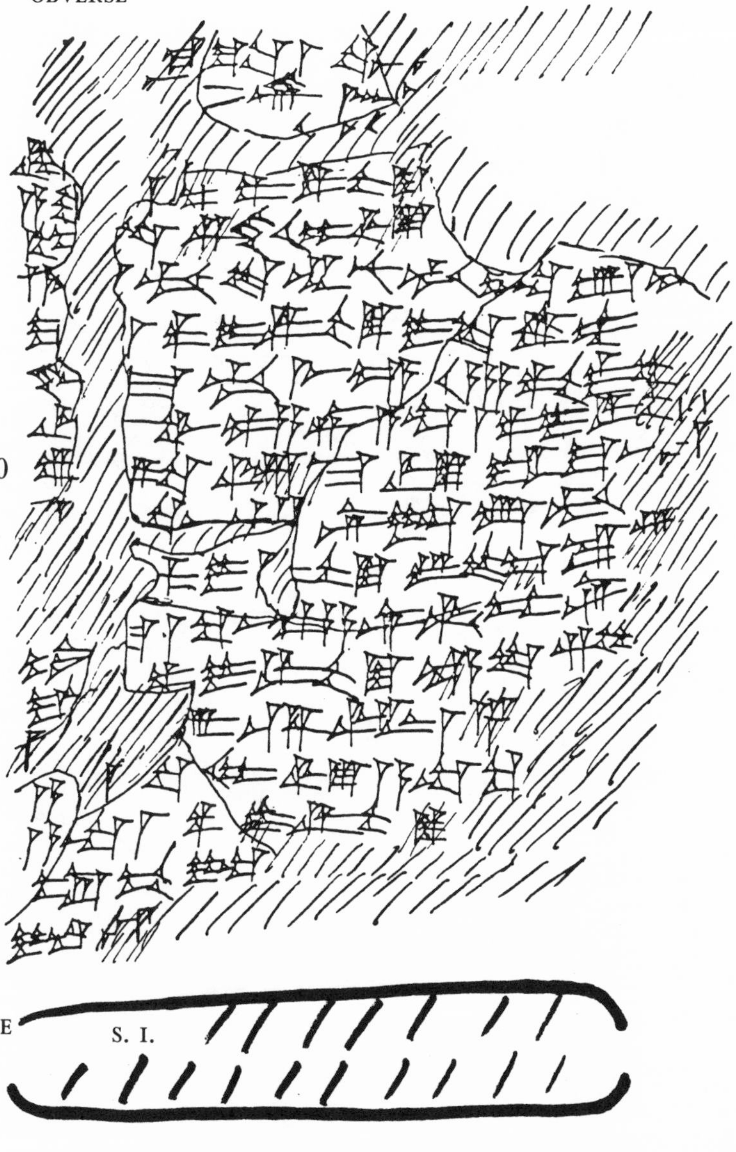

829

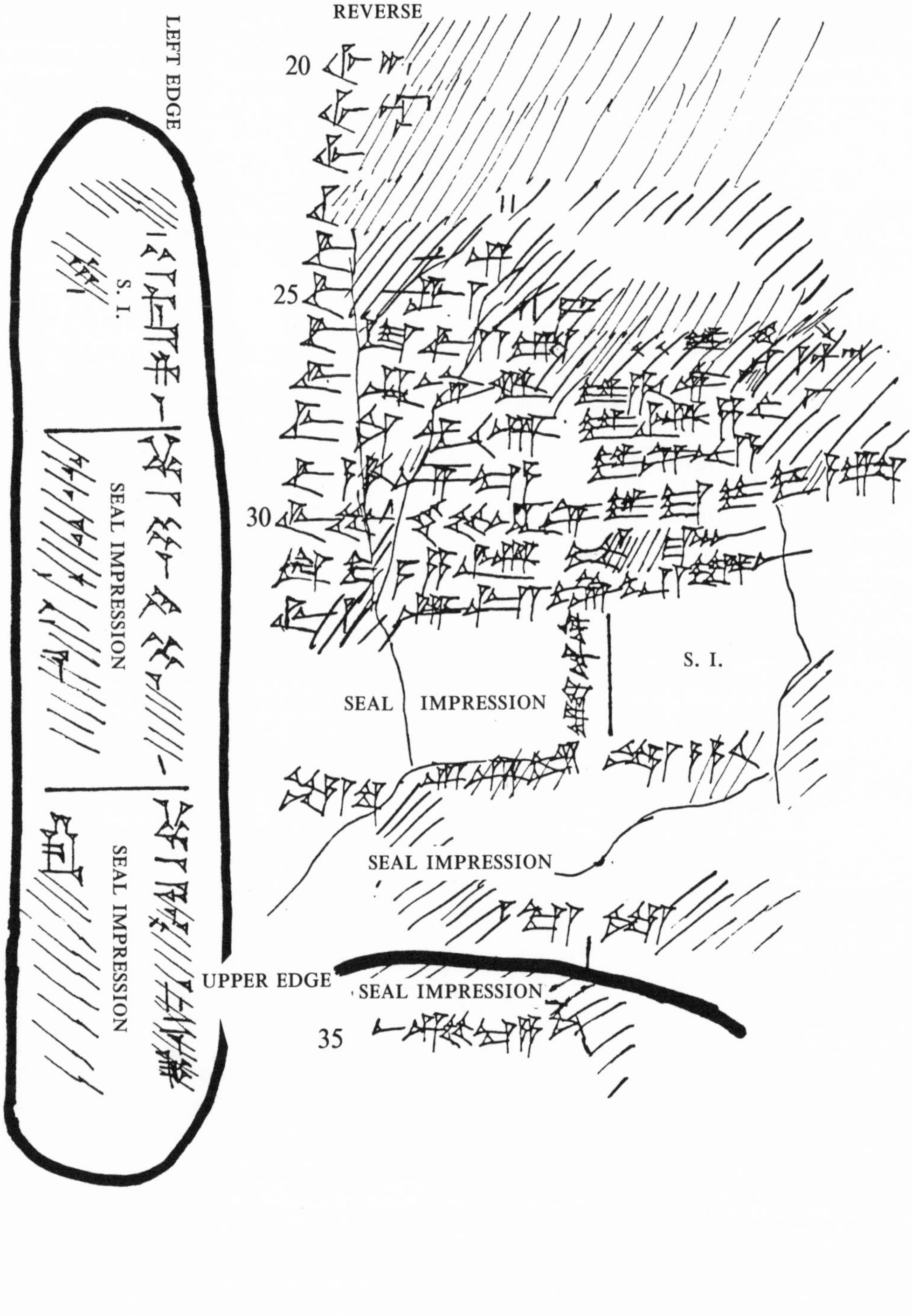
REVERSE
LEFT EDGE
20
25
30
35
S. I.
SEAL IMPRESSION
SEAL IMPRESSION
SEAL IMPRESSION
S. I.
SEAL IMPRESSION
UPPER EDGE
SEAL IMPRESSION

830

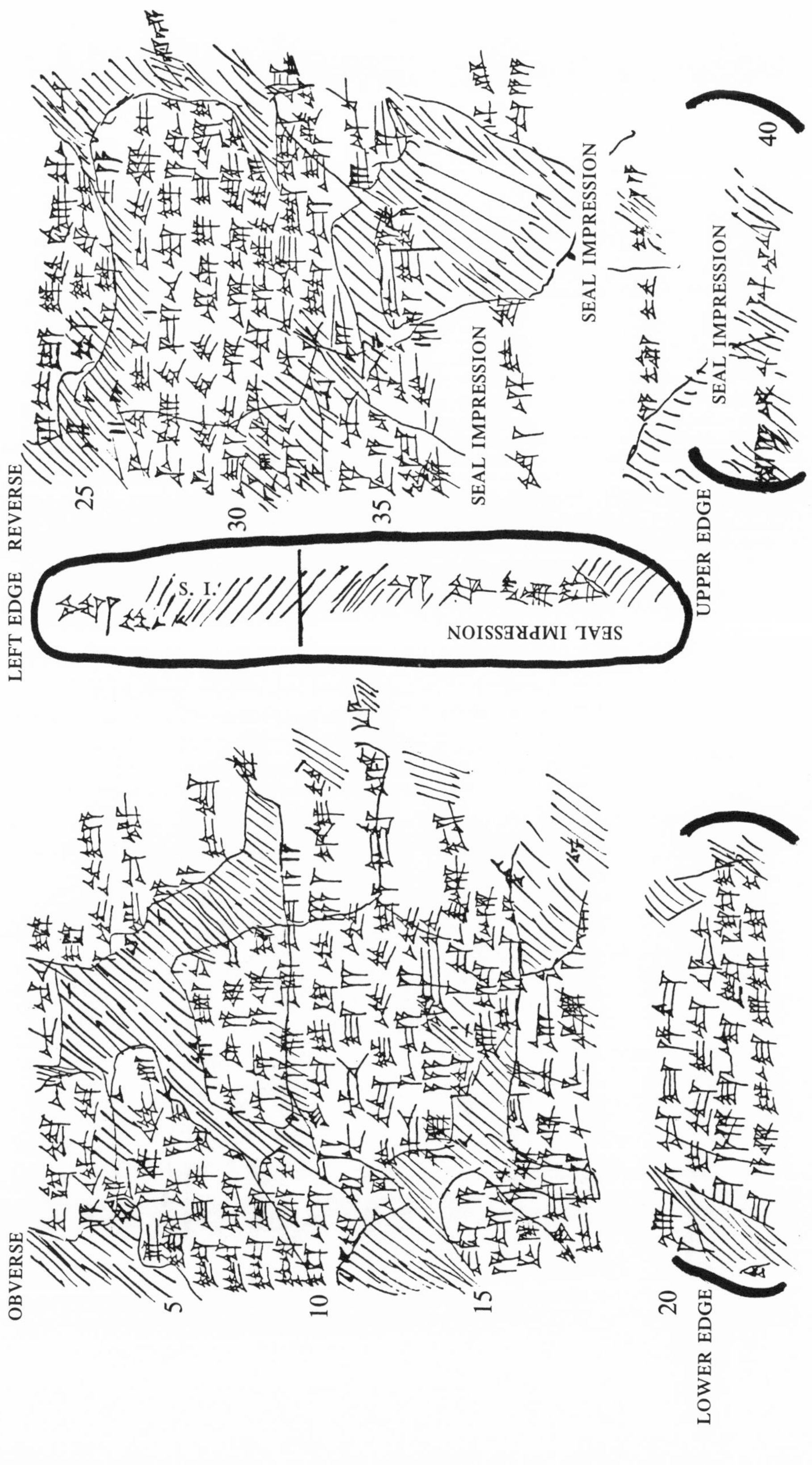
OBVERSE
LOWER EDGE
LEFT EDGE
REVERSE
UPPER EDGE
SEAL IMPRESSION
S. I.
SEAL IMPRESSION
SEAL IMPRESSION
SEAL IMPRESSION

831

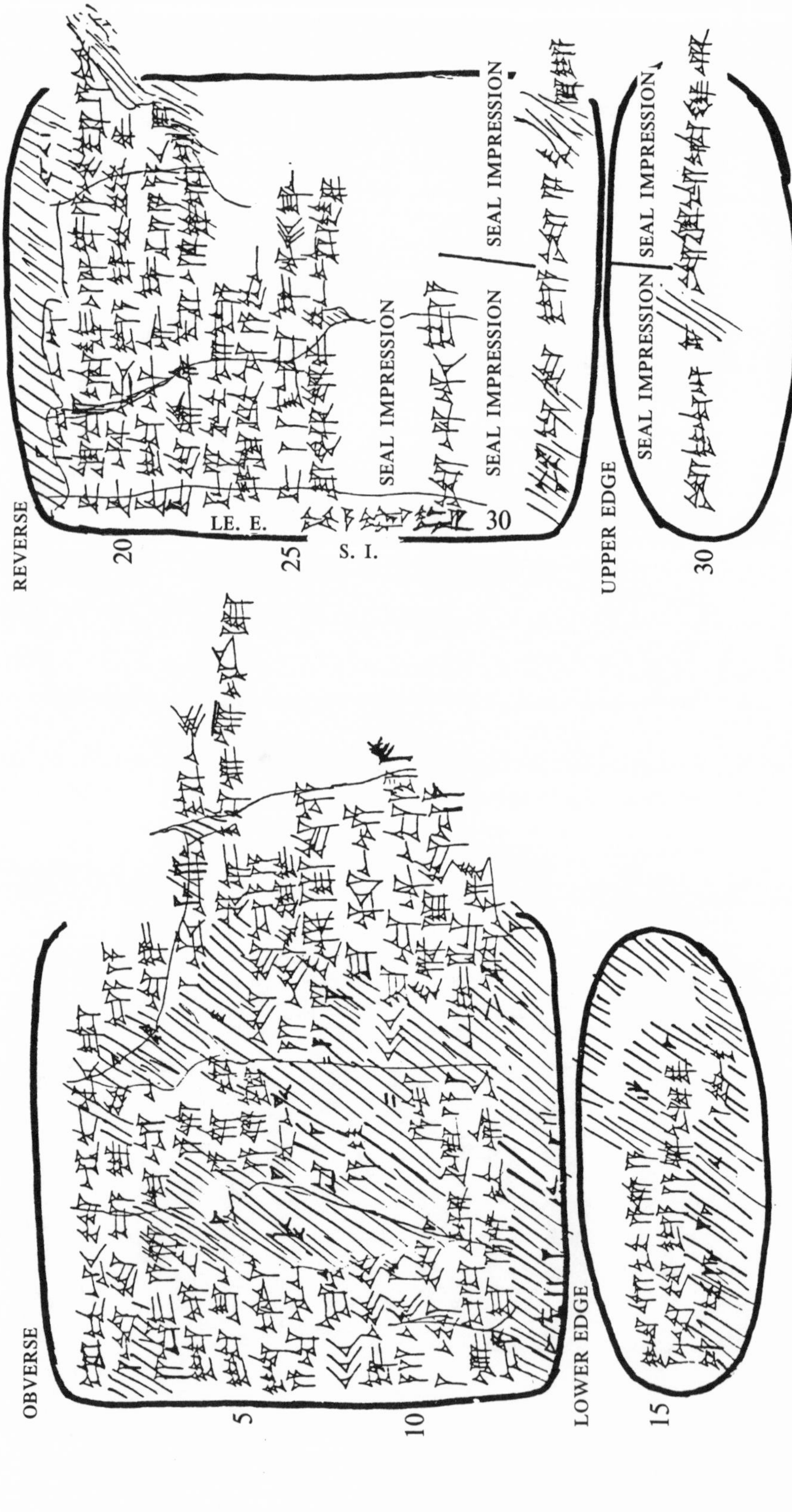
OBVERSE
5
10
LOWER EDGE
15
REVERSE
20
LE. E.
25
S. I.
SEAL IMPRESSION
SEAL IMPRESSION
SEAL IMPRESSION
30
UPPER EDGE
SEAL IMPRESSION
SEAL IMPRESSION
30

832

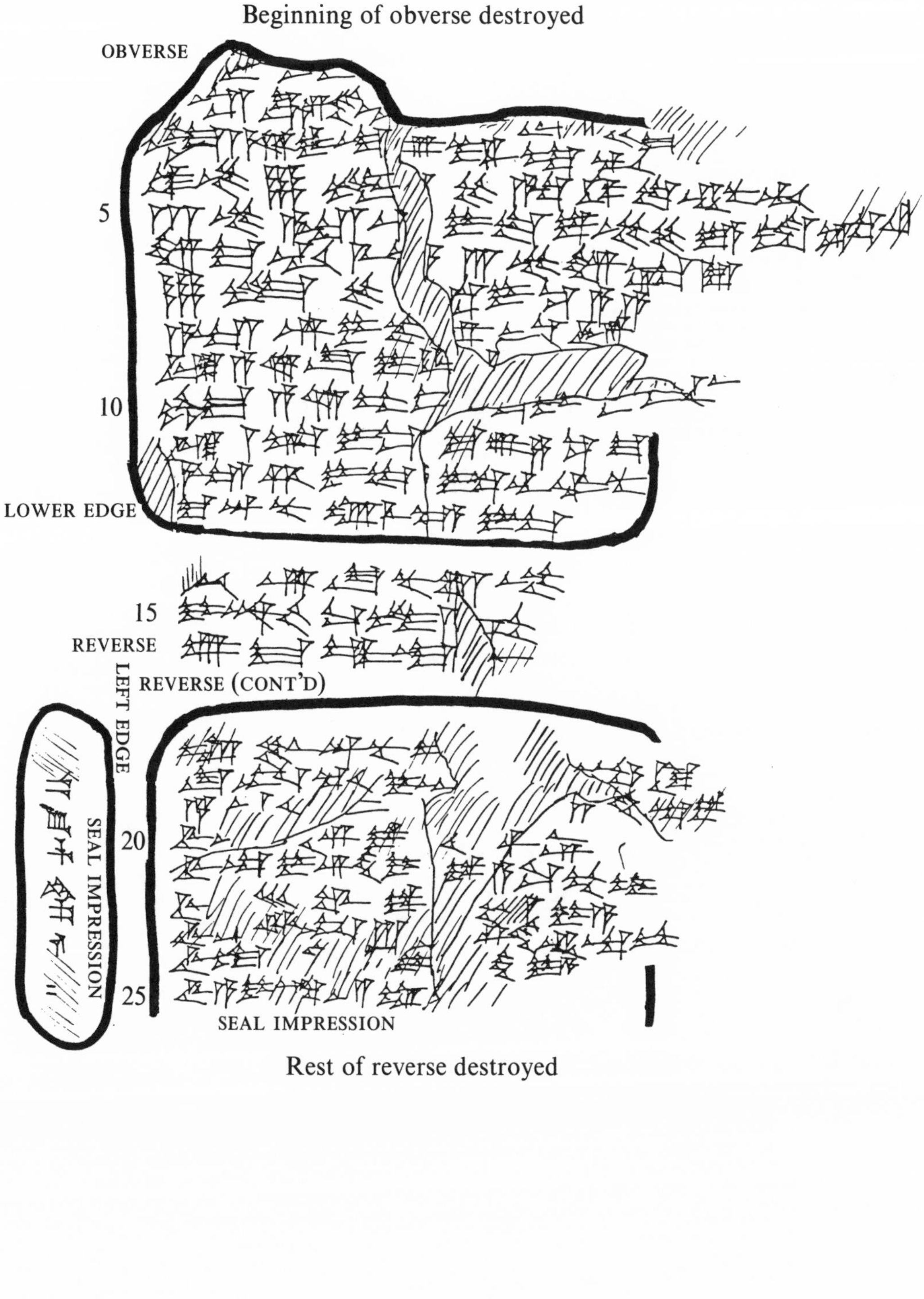
Beginning of obverse destroyed
OBVERSE
5
10
LOWER EDGE
15
REVERSE
LEFT EDGE
REVERSE (CONT'D)
SEAL IMPRESSION
20
25
SEAL IMPRESSION
Rest of reverse destroyed

833

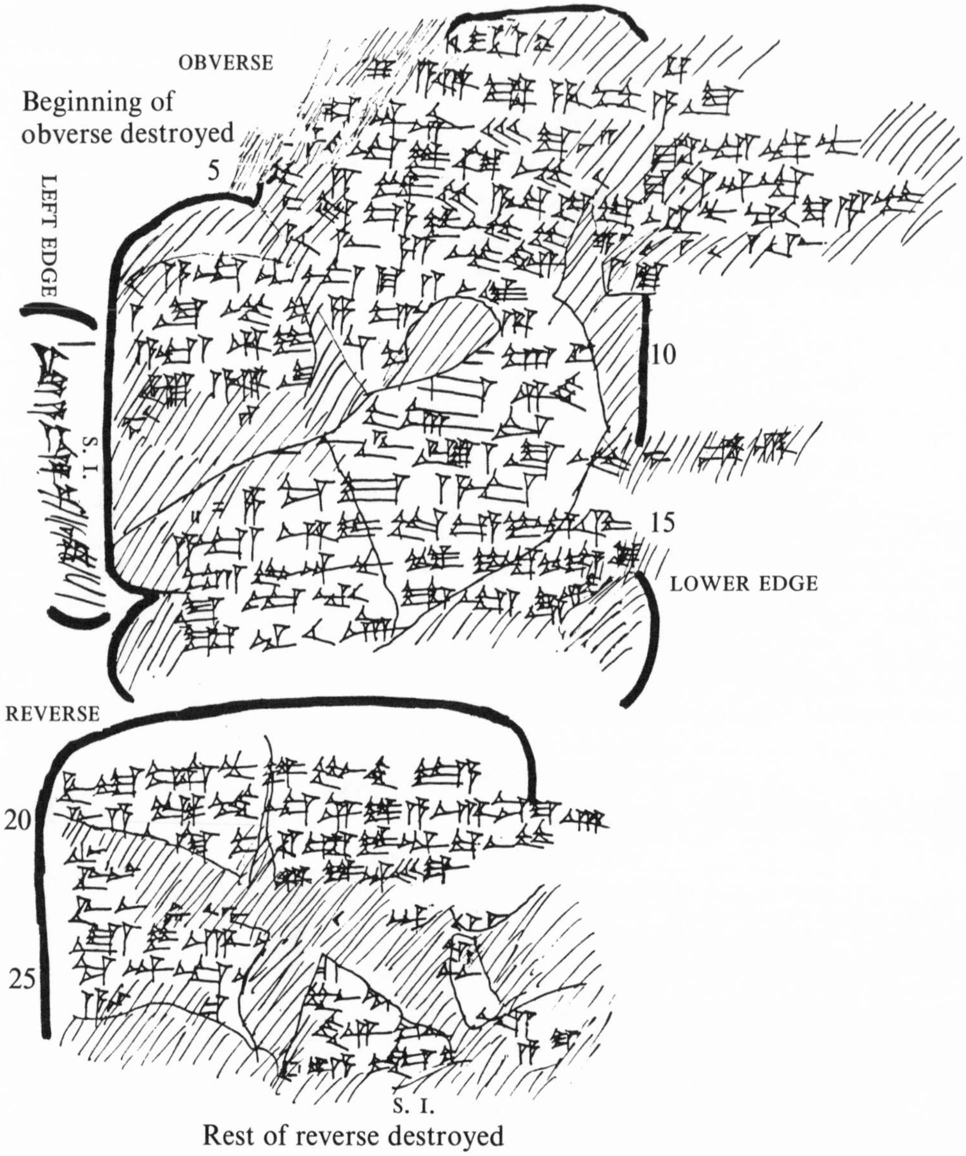
OBVERSE
Beginning of obverse destroyed
LEFT EDGE
S. I.
LOWER EDGE
REVERSE
S. I.
Rest of reverse destroyed

834

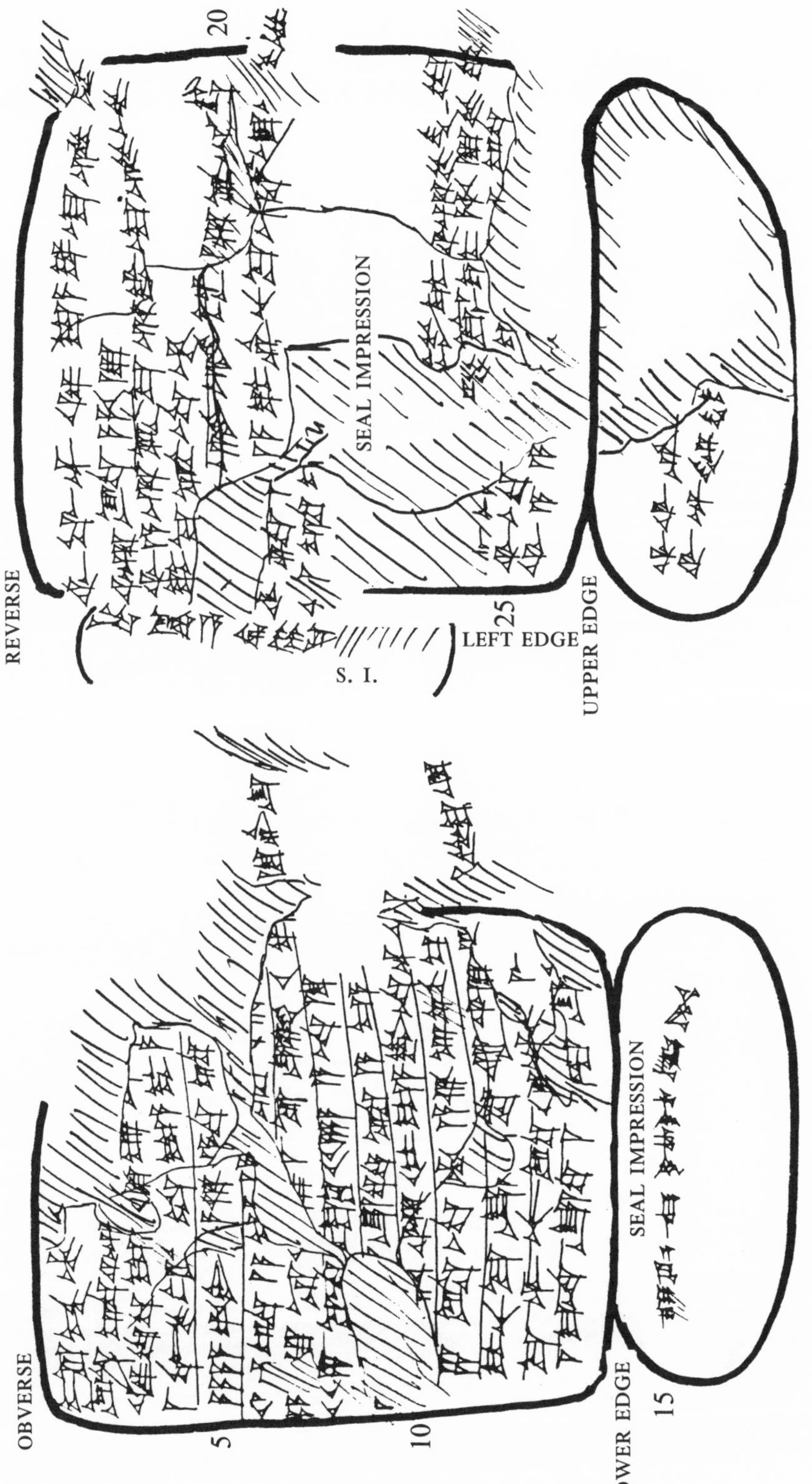
OBVERSE
5
10
LOWER EDGE
15
SEAL IMPRESSION
REVERSE
20
SEAL IMPRESSION
25
LEFT EDGE
S. I.
UPPER EDGE

835

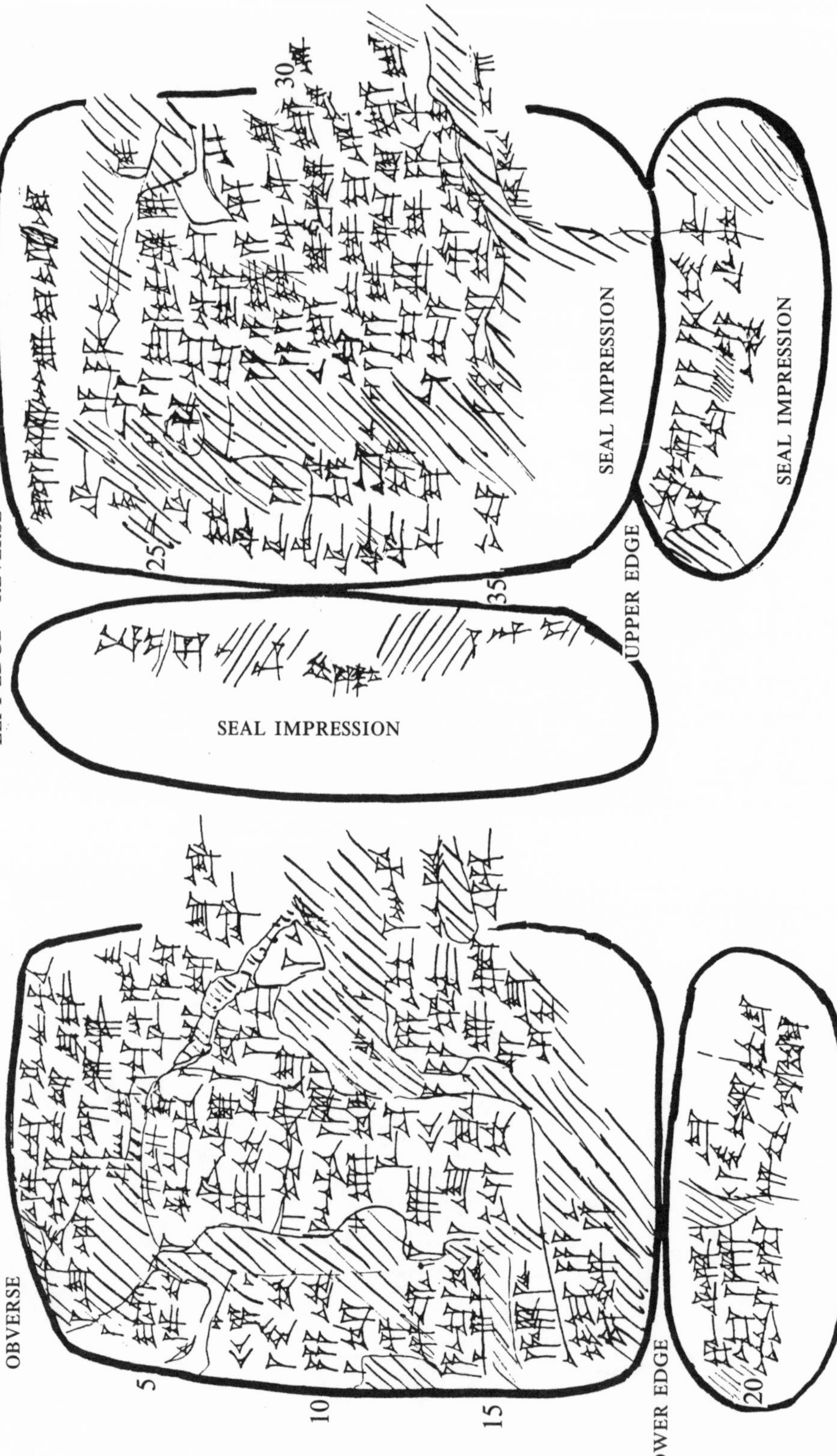
OBVERSE
LOWER EDGE
LEFT EDGE
REVERSE
UPPER EDGE
SEAL IMPRESSION
SEAL IMPRESSION
SEAL IMPRESSION

836

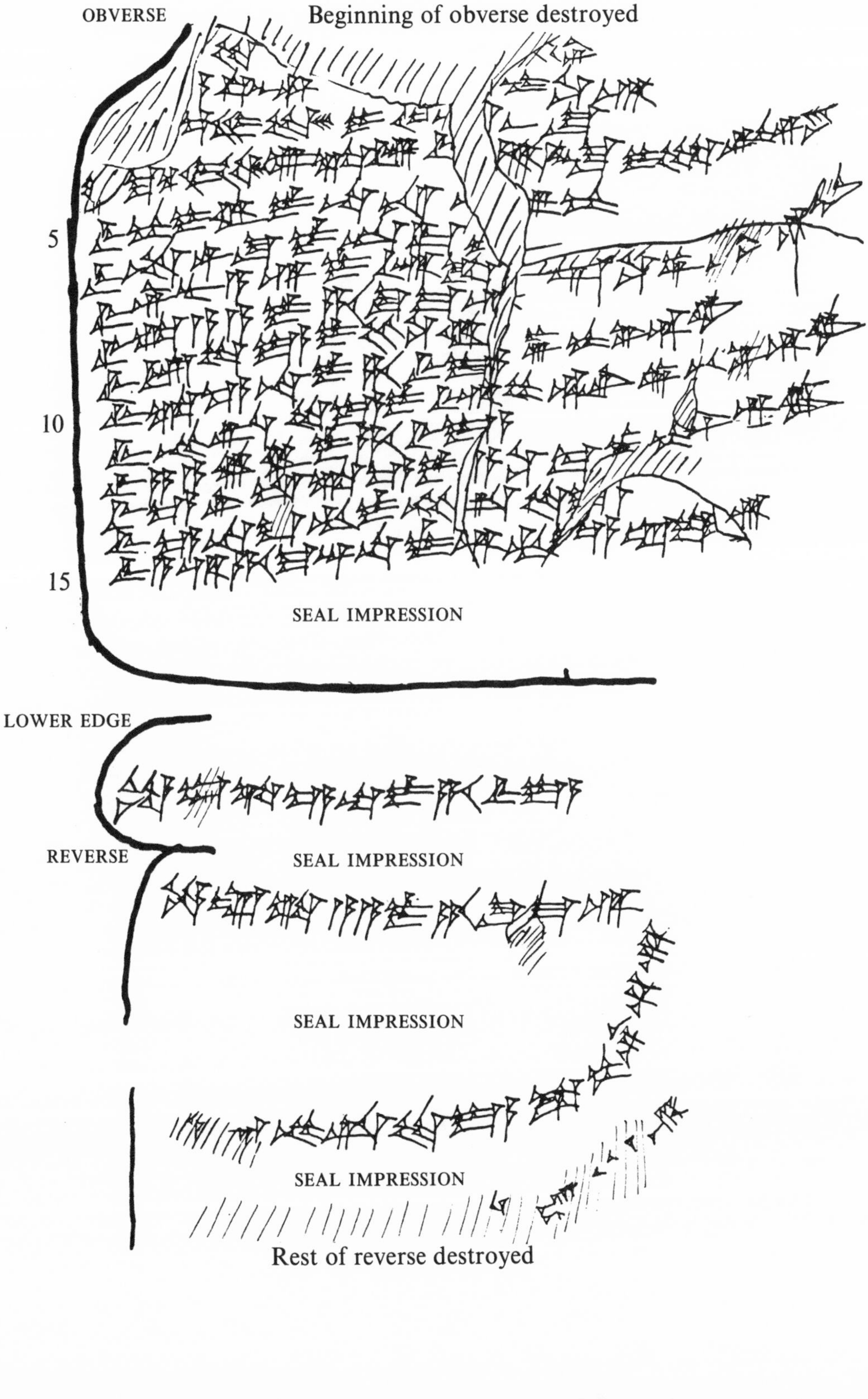
OBVERSE
Beginning of obverse destroyed
SEAL IMPRESSION
LOWER EDGE
REVERSE
SEAL IMPRESSION
SEAL IMPRESSION
SEAL IMPRESSION
Rest of reverse destroyed

837/838

OBVERSE

Beginning of obverse destroyed

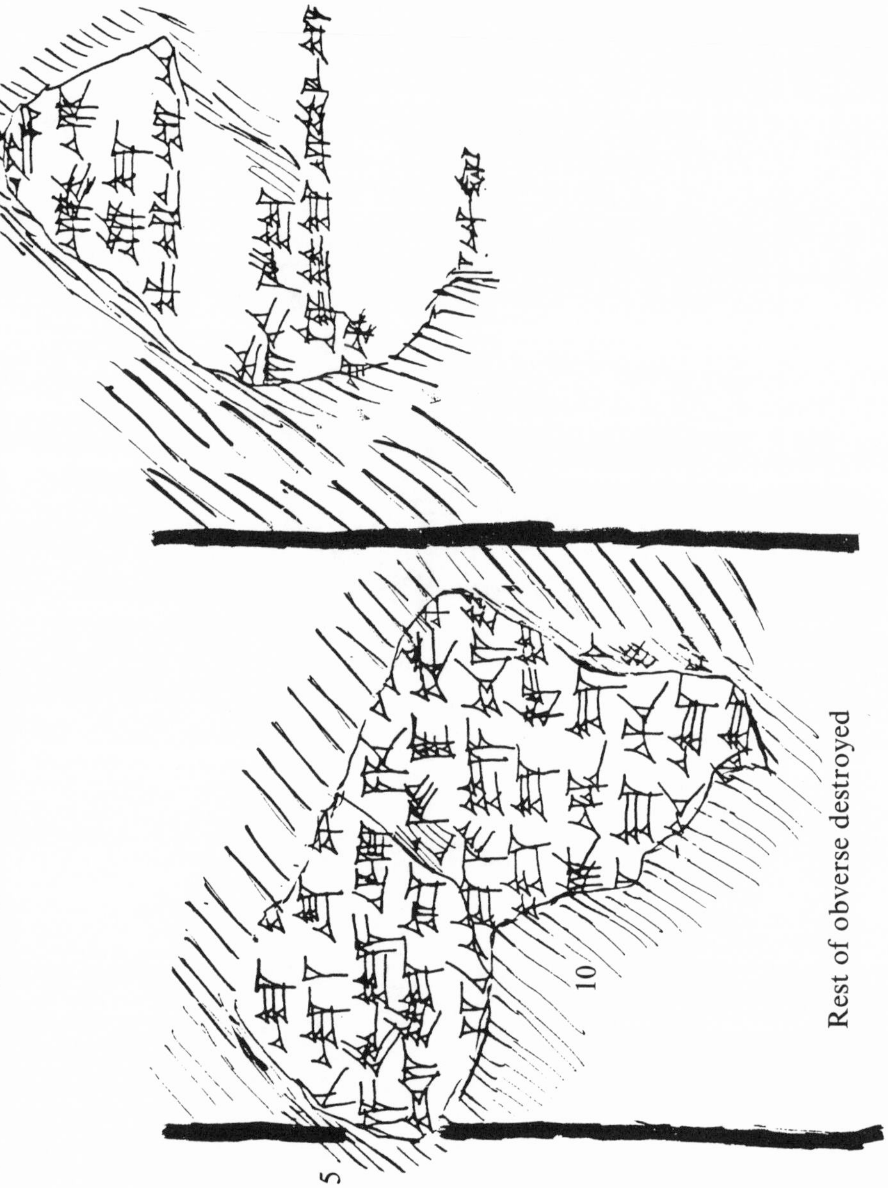

Rest of obverse destroyed

837/838

Beginning of reverse destroyed

REVERSE

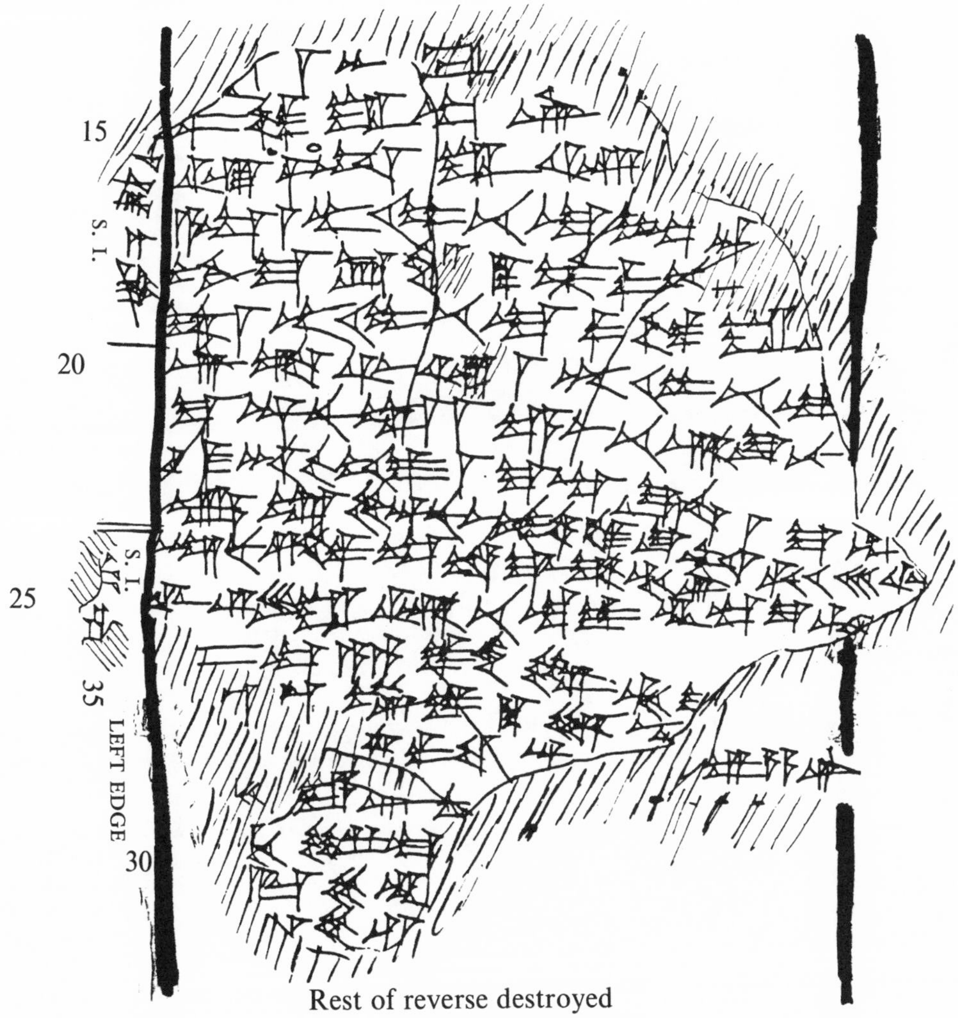

Rest of reverse destroyed

839

OBVERSE

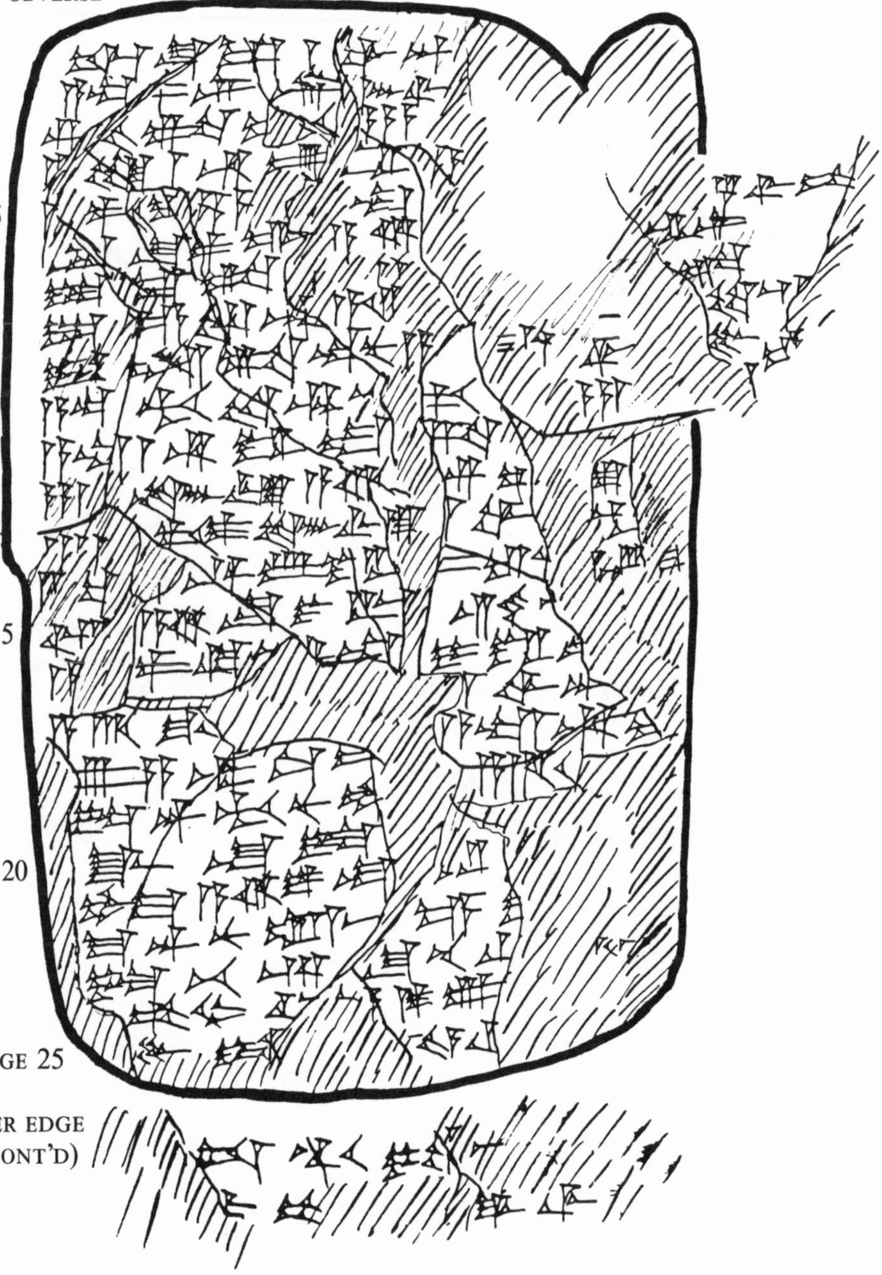

LOWER EDGE

LOWER EDGE (CONT'D)

839

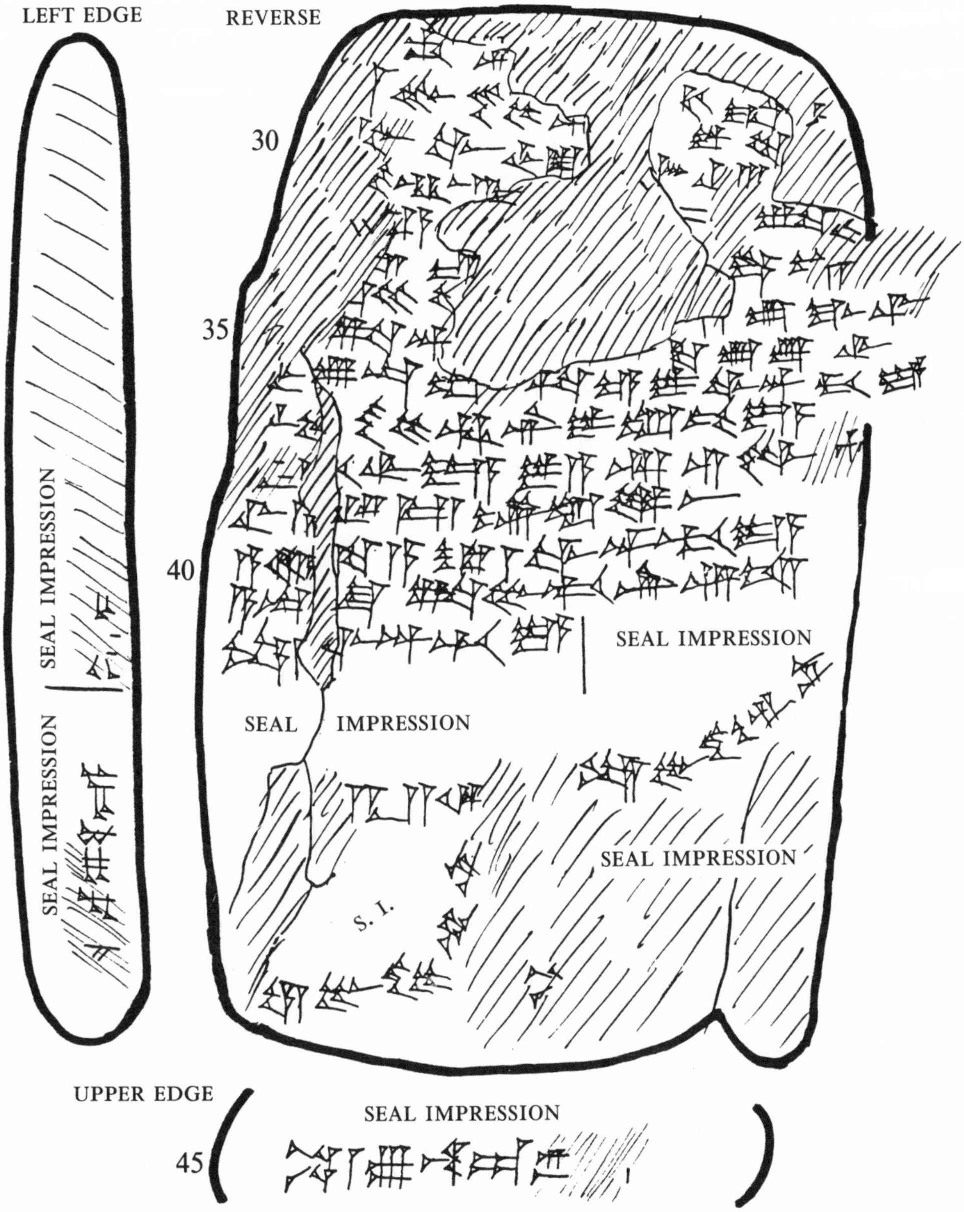
LEFT EDGE
REVERSE
30
35
40
SEAL IMPRESSION
SEAL IMPRESSION
SEAL IMPRESSION
SEAL IMPRESSION
SEAL IMPRESSION
S. I.
UPPER EDGE
SEAL IMPRESSION
45

840

OBVERSE

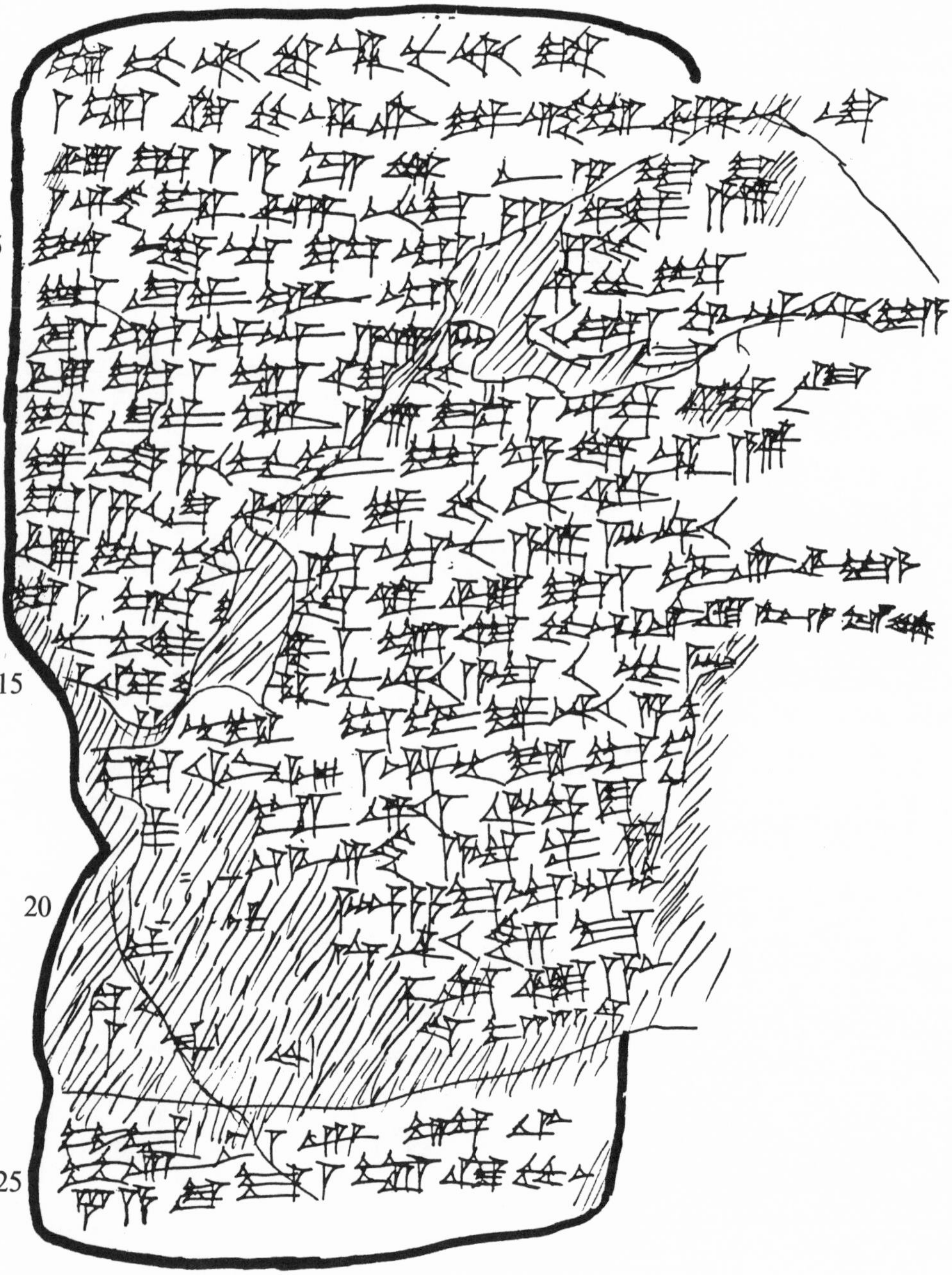

840

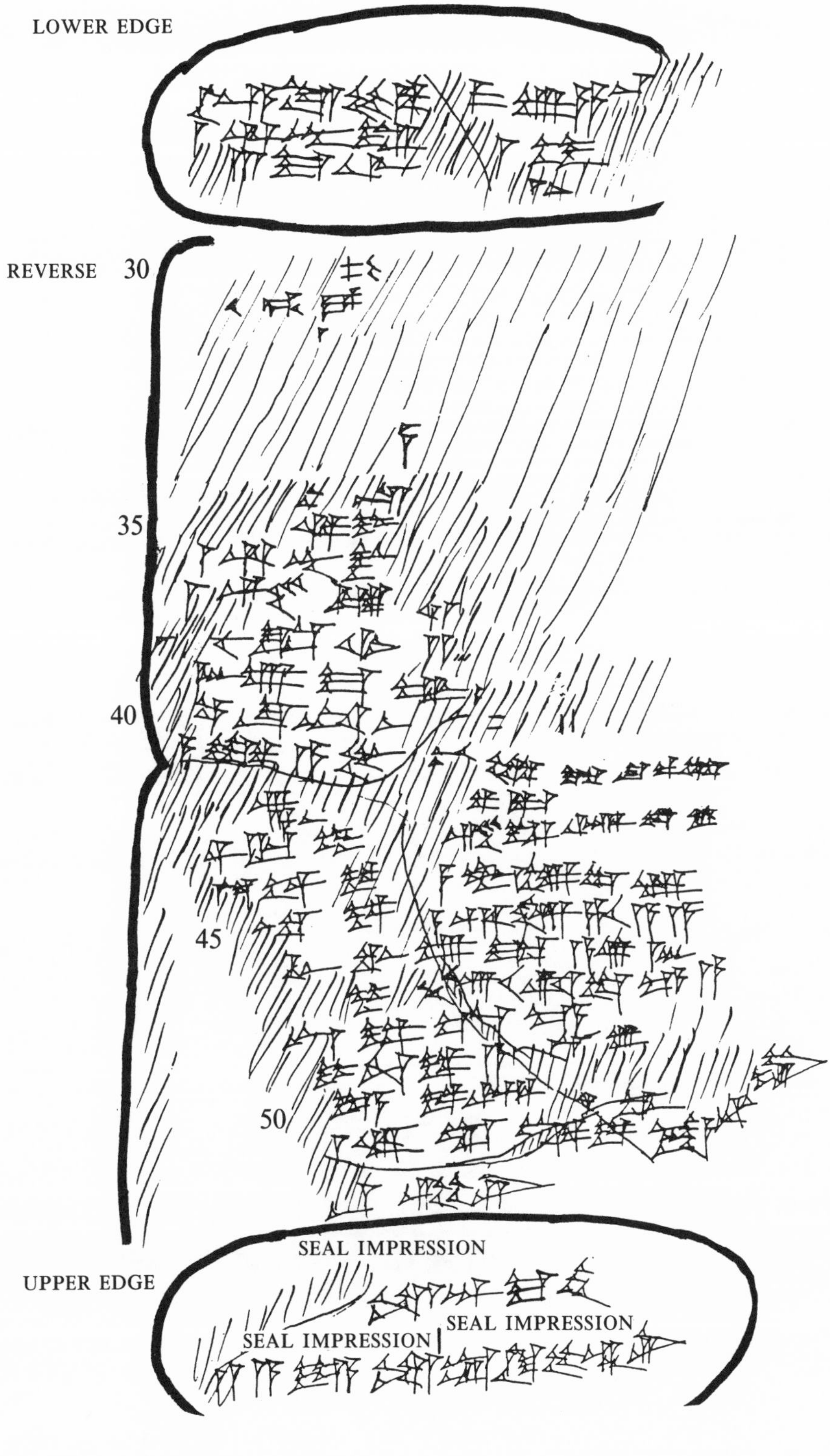
LOWER EDGE
REVERSE
30
35
40
45
50
SEAL IMPRESSION
UPPER EDGE
SEAL IMPRESSION
SEAL IMPRESSION

841

OBVERSE

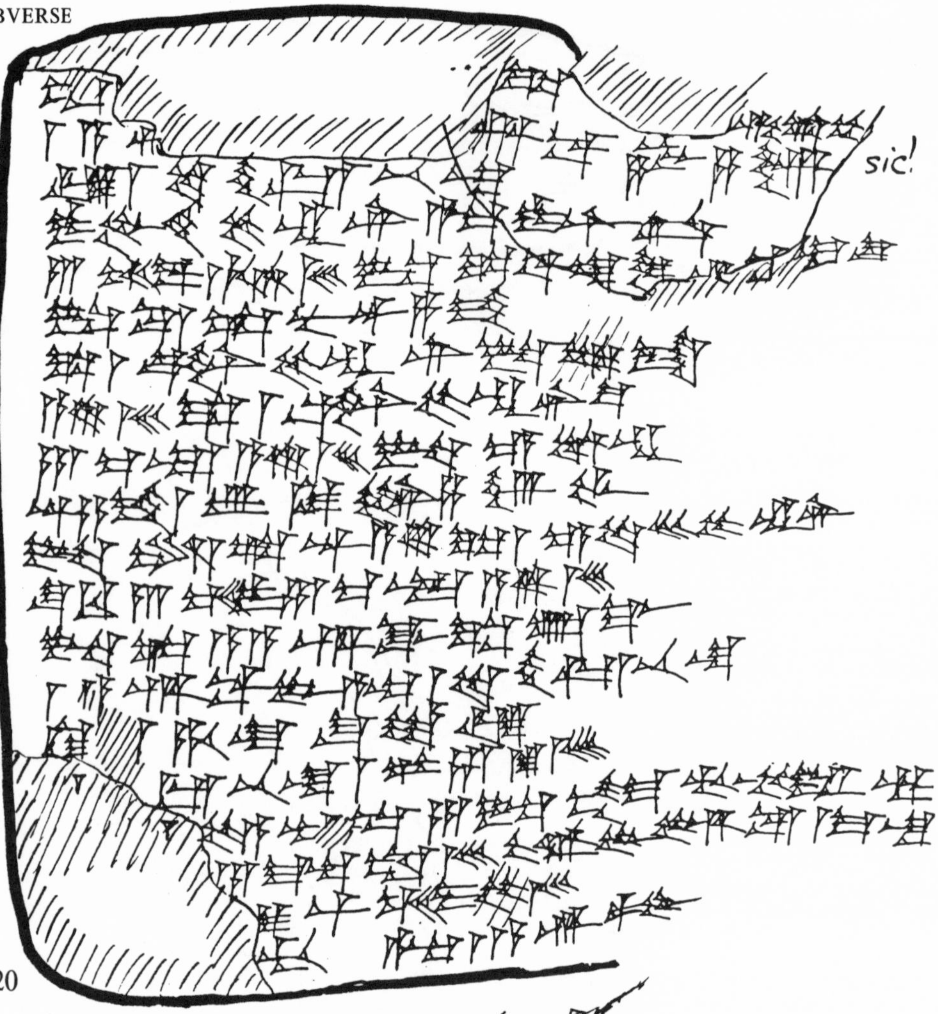

Add to lines 17
18

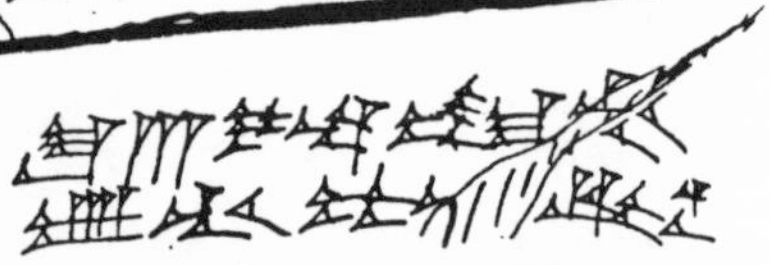

LOWER EDGE

REVERSE

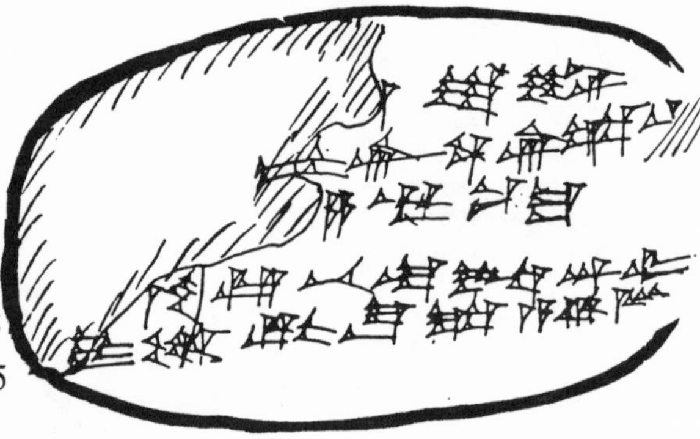

841

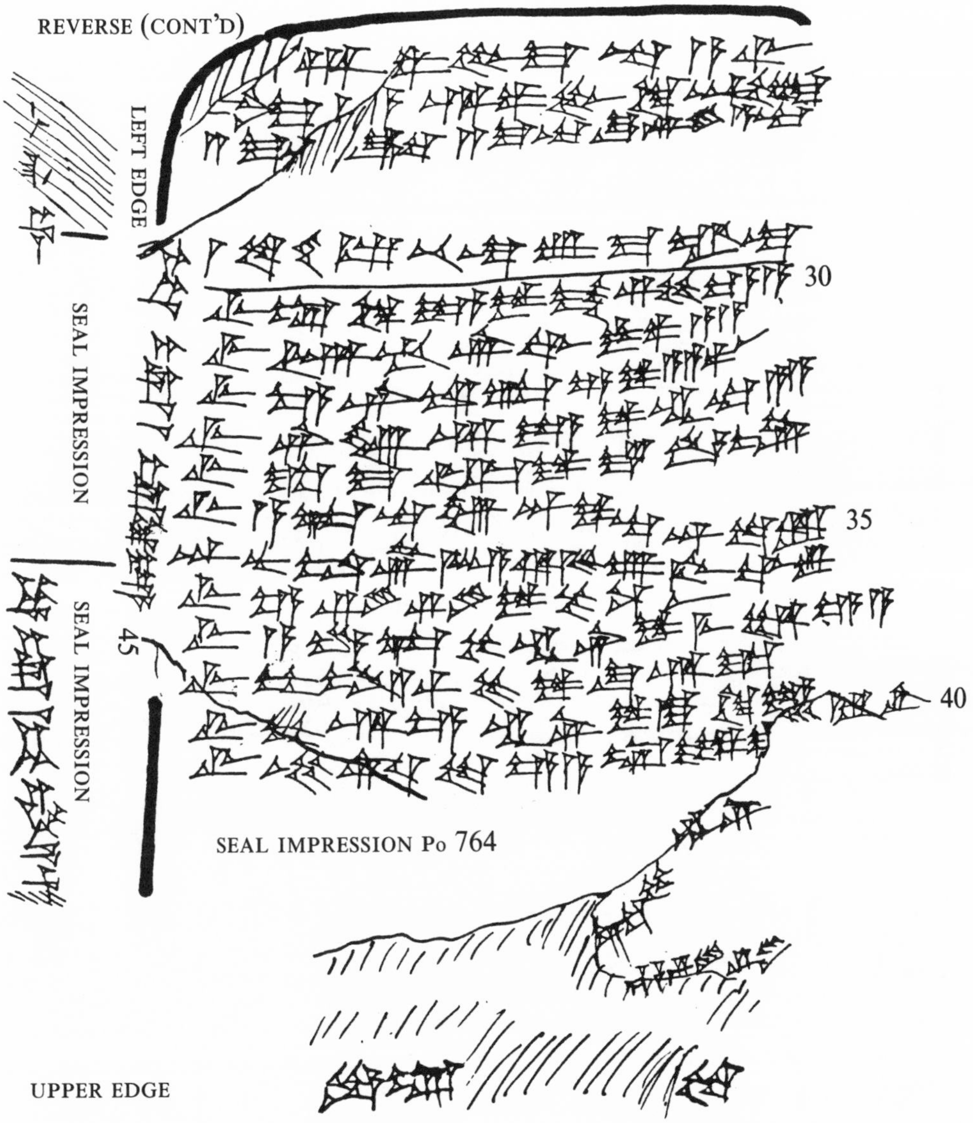
REVERSE (CONT'D)
LEFT EDGE
SEAL IMPRESSION
SEAL IMPRESSION
30
35
40
45
SEAL IMPRESSION Po 764
UPPER EDGE

842

OBVERSE

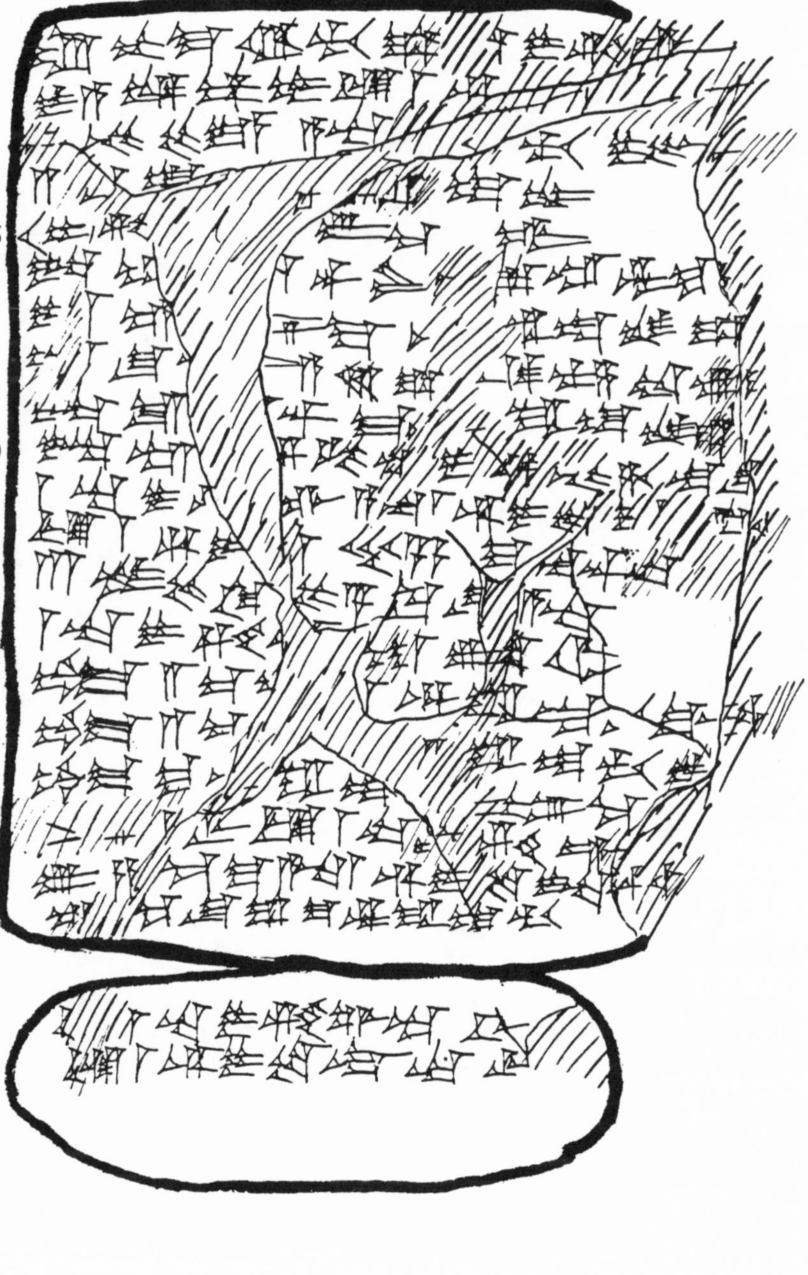

LOWER EDGE

842

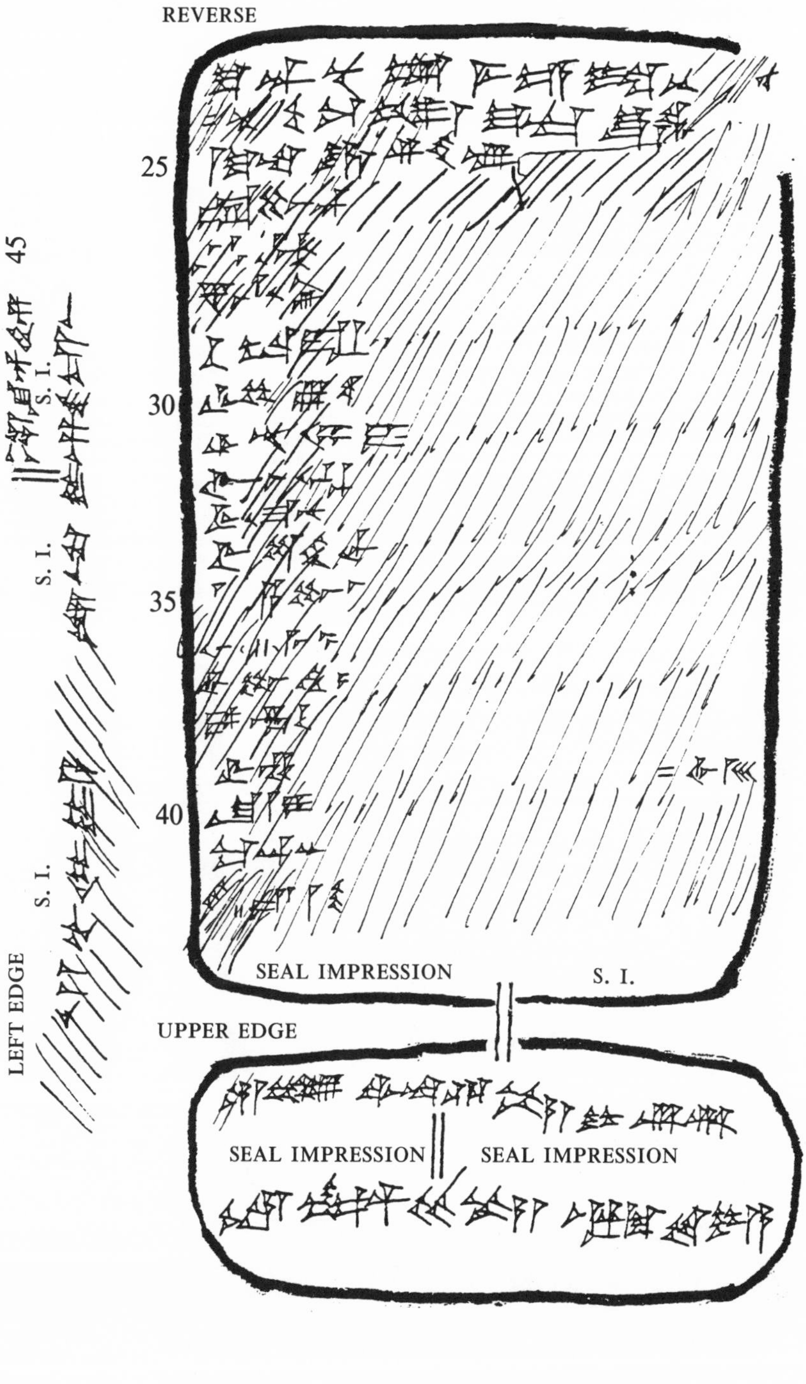
REVERSE
25
30
35
40
45
S. I.
S. I.
S. I.
LEFT EDGE
SEAL IMPRESSION
S. I.
UPPER EDGE
SEAL IMPRESSION
SEAL IMPRESSION

843

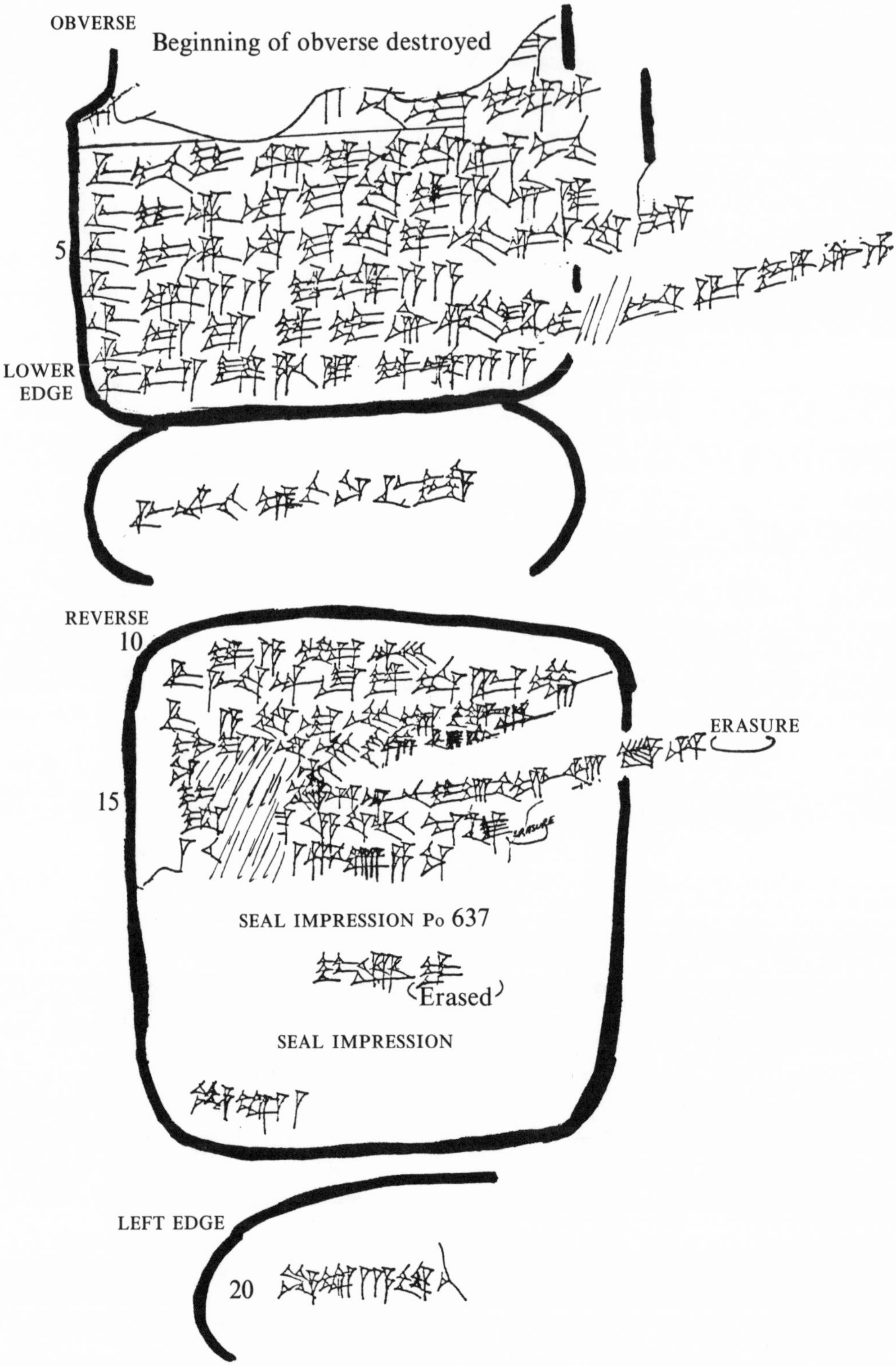
OBVERSE
Beginning of obverse destroyed
LOWER EDGE
REVERSE
ERASURE
ERASURE
SEAL IMPRESSION Po 637
(Erased)
SEAL IMPRESSION
LEFT EDGE

844

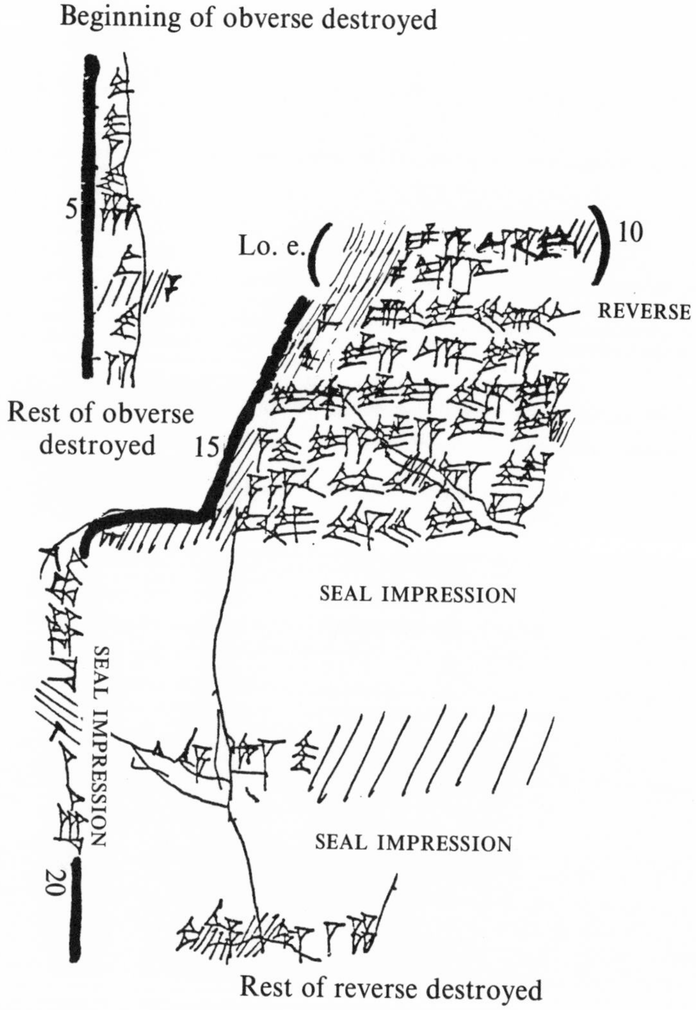
Beginning of obverse destroyed
5
Rest of obverse destroyed
Lo. e.
10
REVERSE
15
SEAL IMPRESSION
SEAL IMPRESSION
SEAL IMPRESSION
20
Rest of reverse destroyed

845

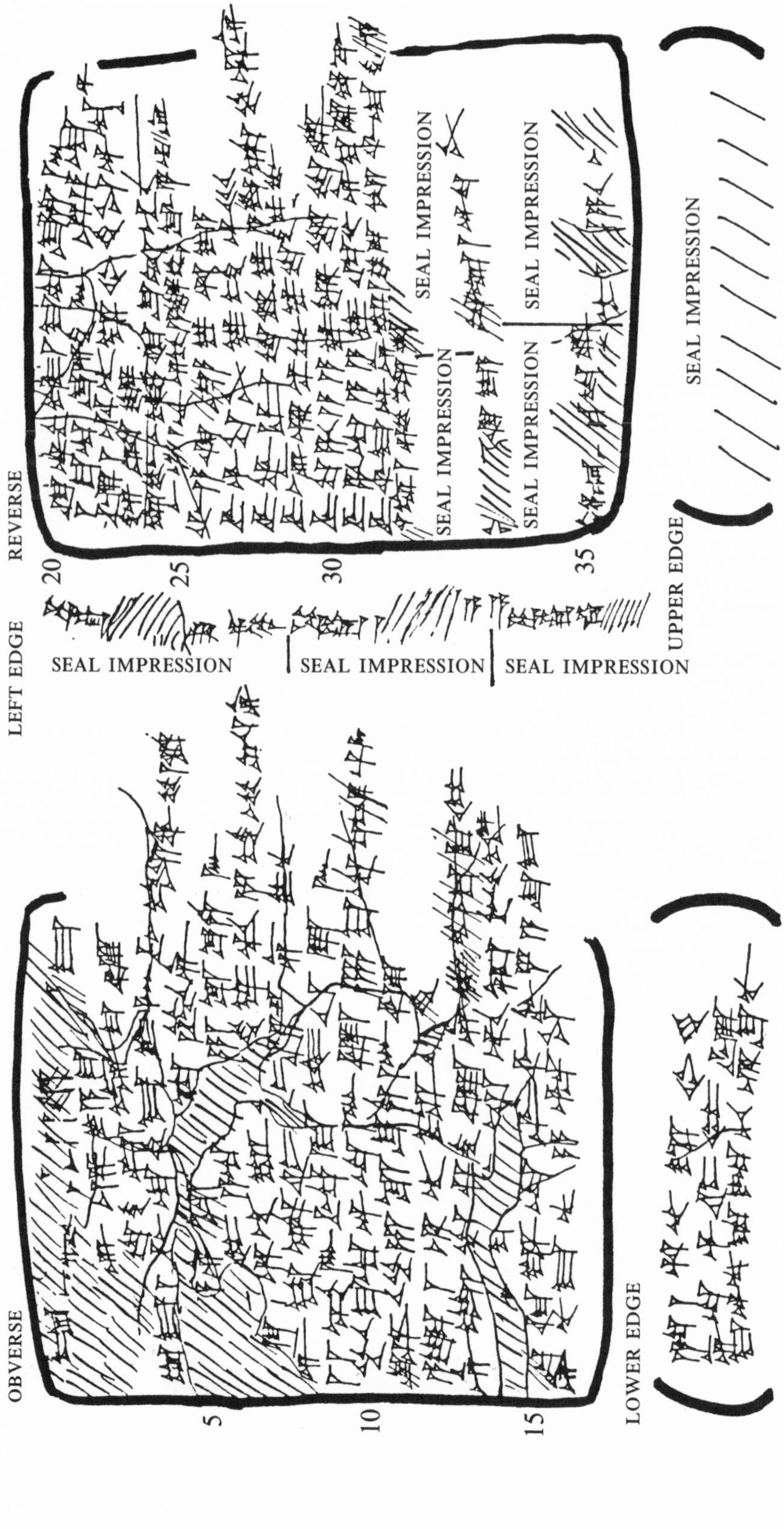
OBVERSE
5
10
15
LOWER EDGE
LEFT EDGE
SEAL IMPRESSION
SEAL IMPRESSION
SEAL IMPRESSION
REVERSE
20
25
30
35
SEAL IMPRESSION
SEAL IMPRESSION
SEAL IMPRESSION
SEAL IMPRESSION
SEAL IMPRESSION
UPPER EDGE
SEAL IMPRESSION

846

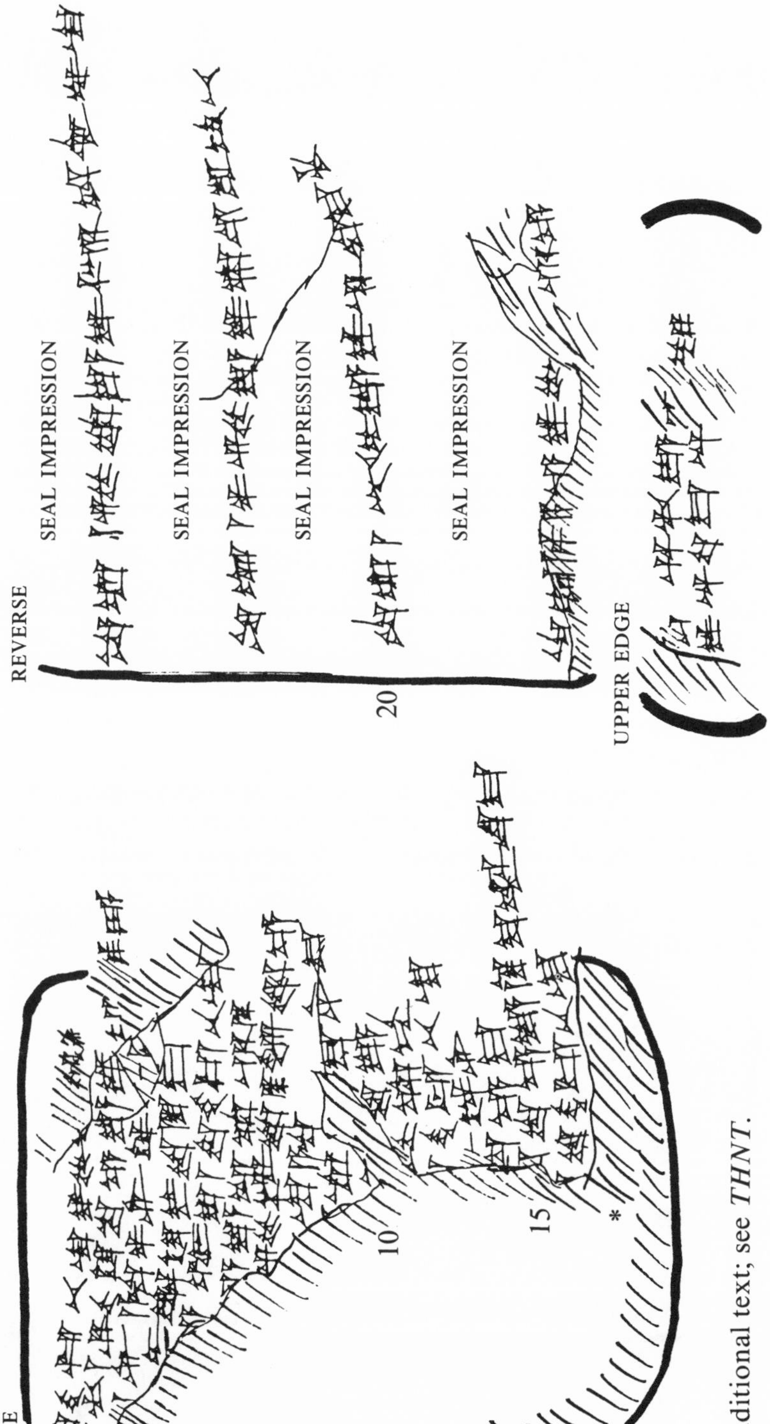

*Additional text; see *THNT*.

847

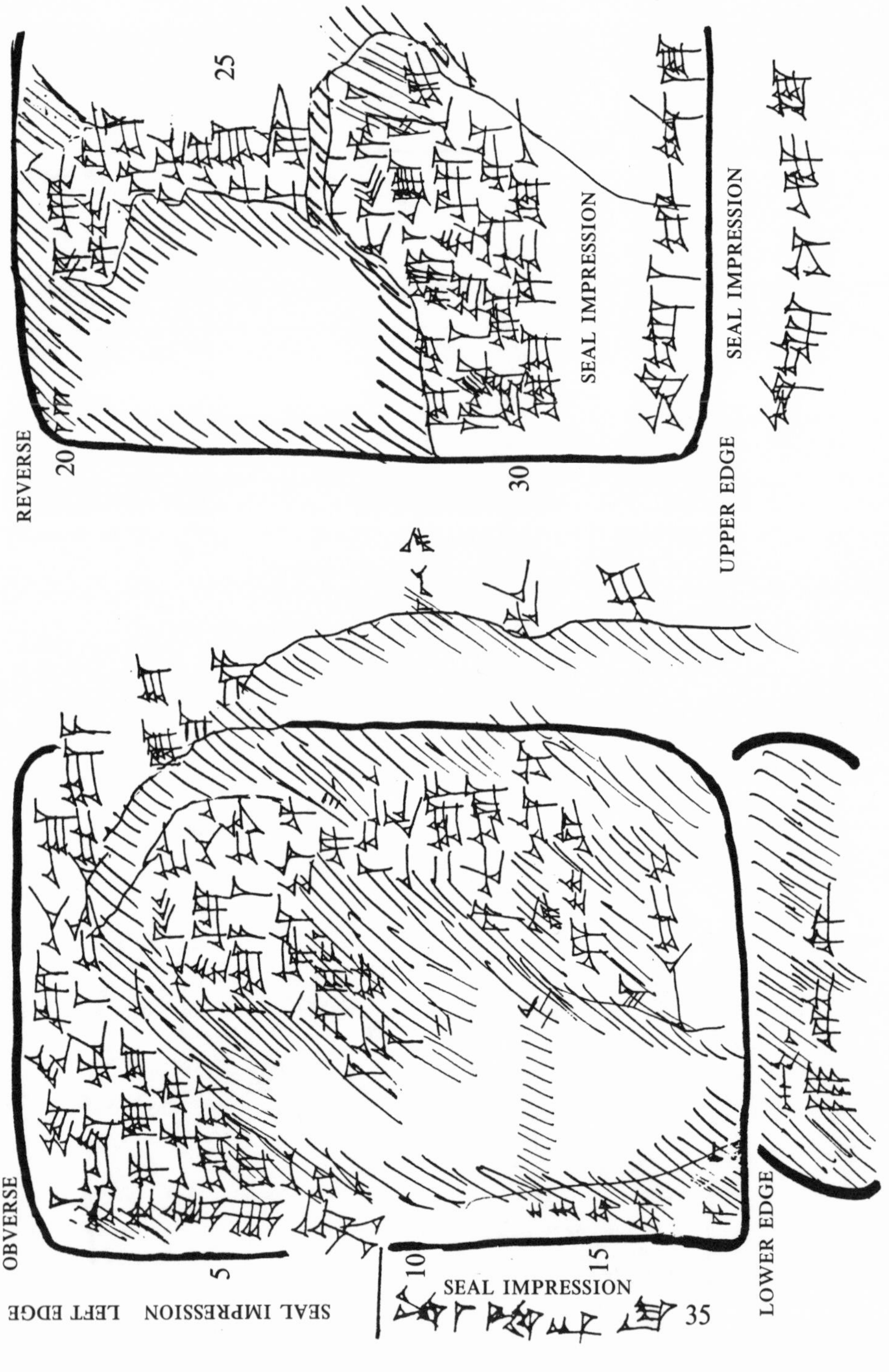
OBVERSE
5
10
15
LOWER EDGE
REVERSE
20
25
30
SEAL IMPRESSION
UPPER EDGE
SEAL IMPRESSION
SEAL IMPRESSION
LEFT EDGE
SEAL IMPRESSION
35

848

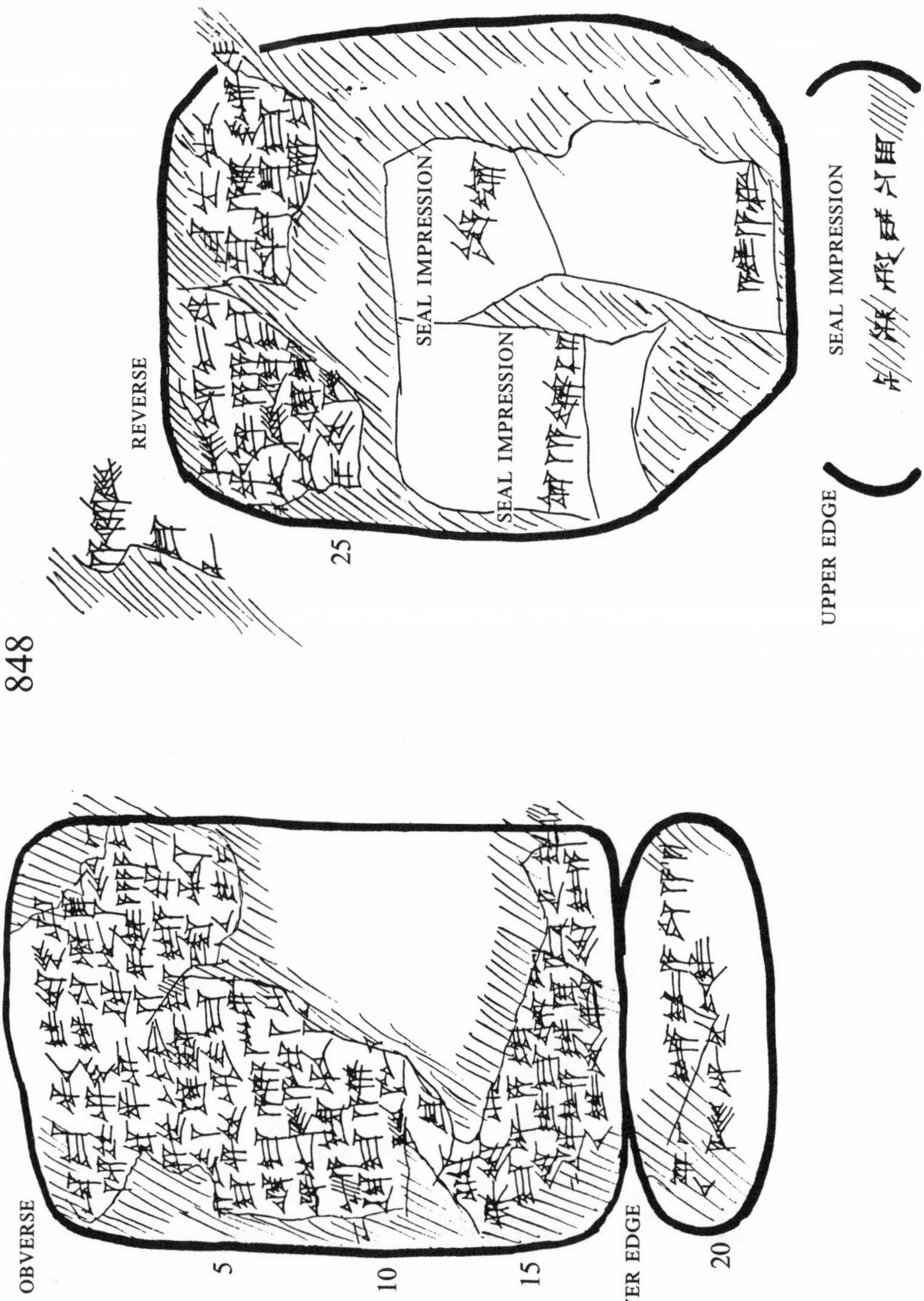
OBVERSE
5
10
15
LOWER EDGE
20
REVERSE
25
SEAL IMPRESSION
SEAL IMPRESSION
UPPER EDGE
SEAL IMPRESSION

849

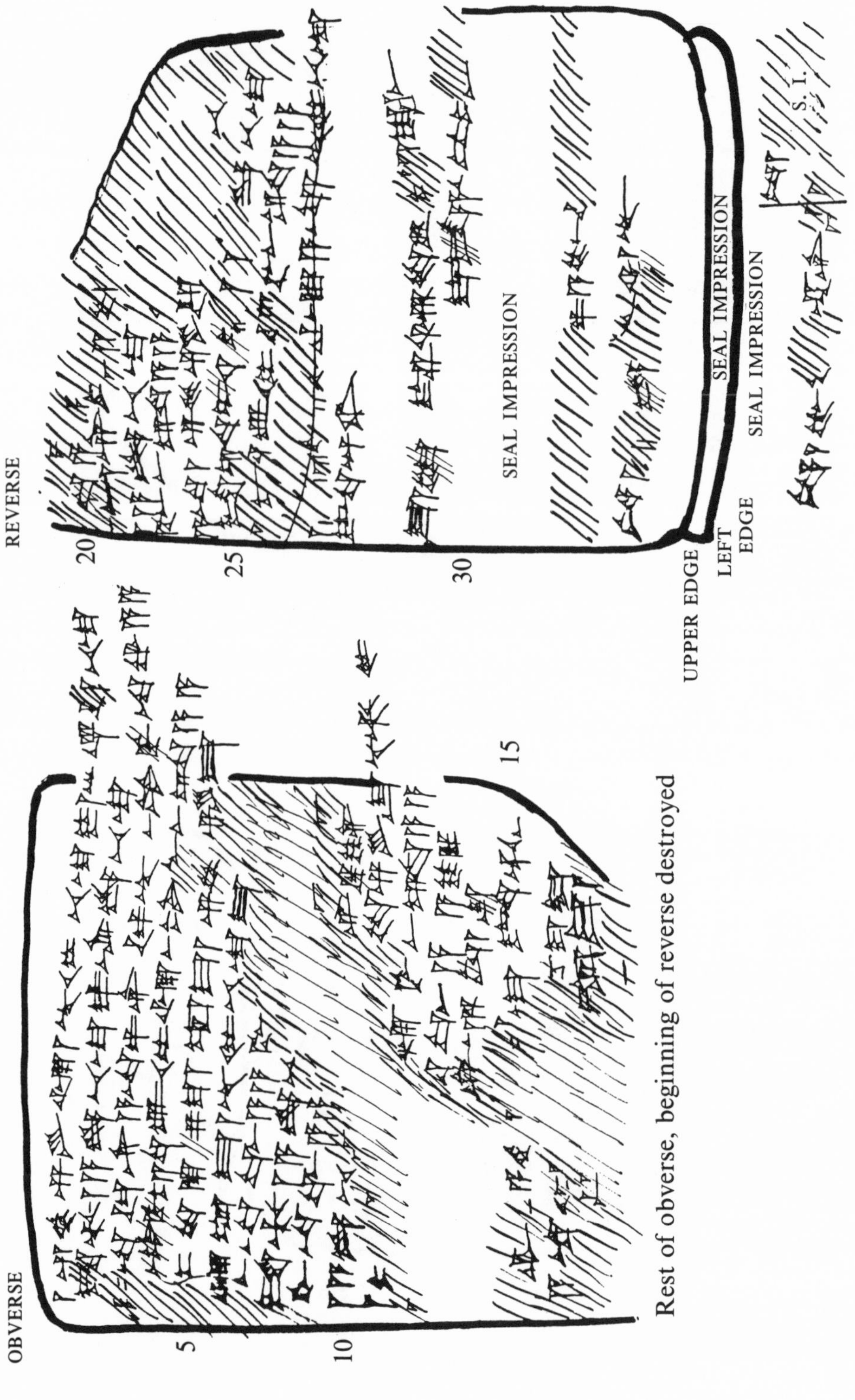
OBVERSE
REVERSE
SEAL IMPRESSION
SEAL IMPRESSION
SEAL IMPRESSION
UPPER EDGE
LEFT EDGE
S. I.
Rest of obverse, beginning of reverse destroyed

850

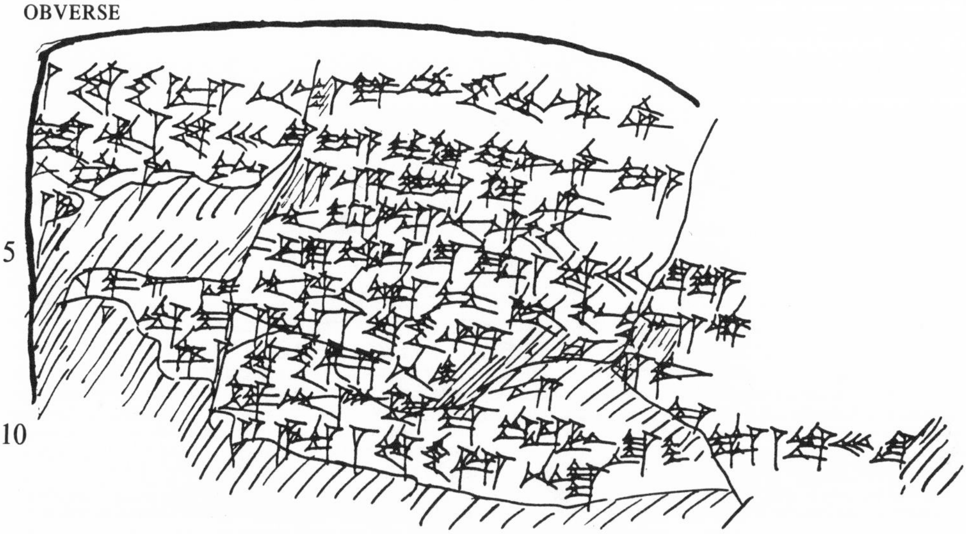

Rest of obverse, beginning of reverse destroyed

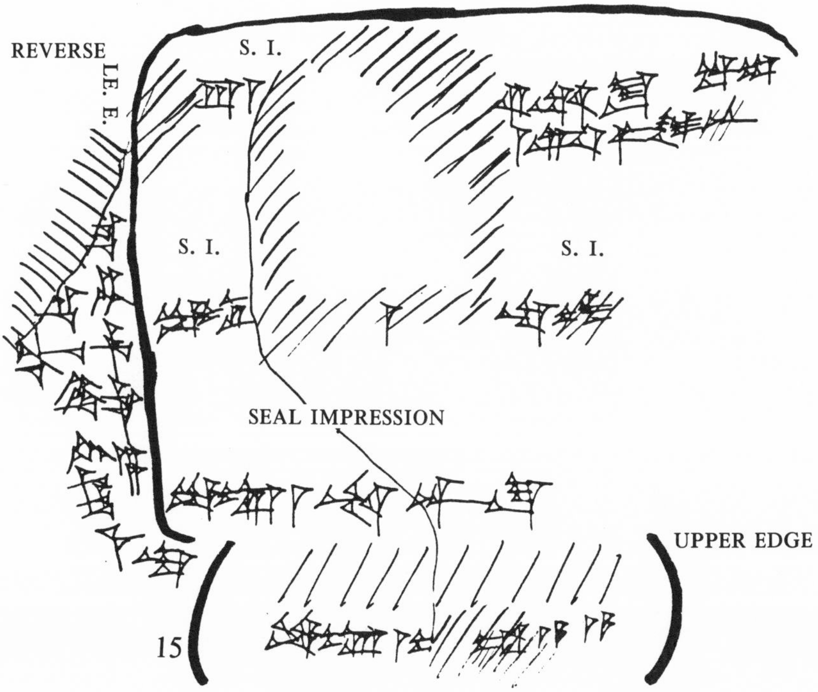

851

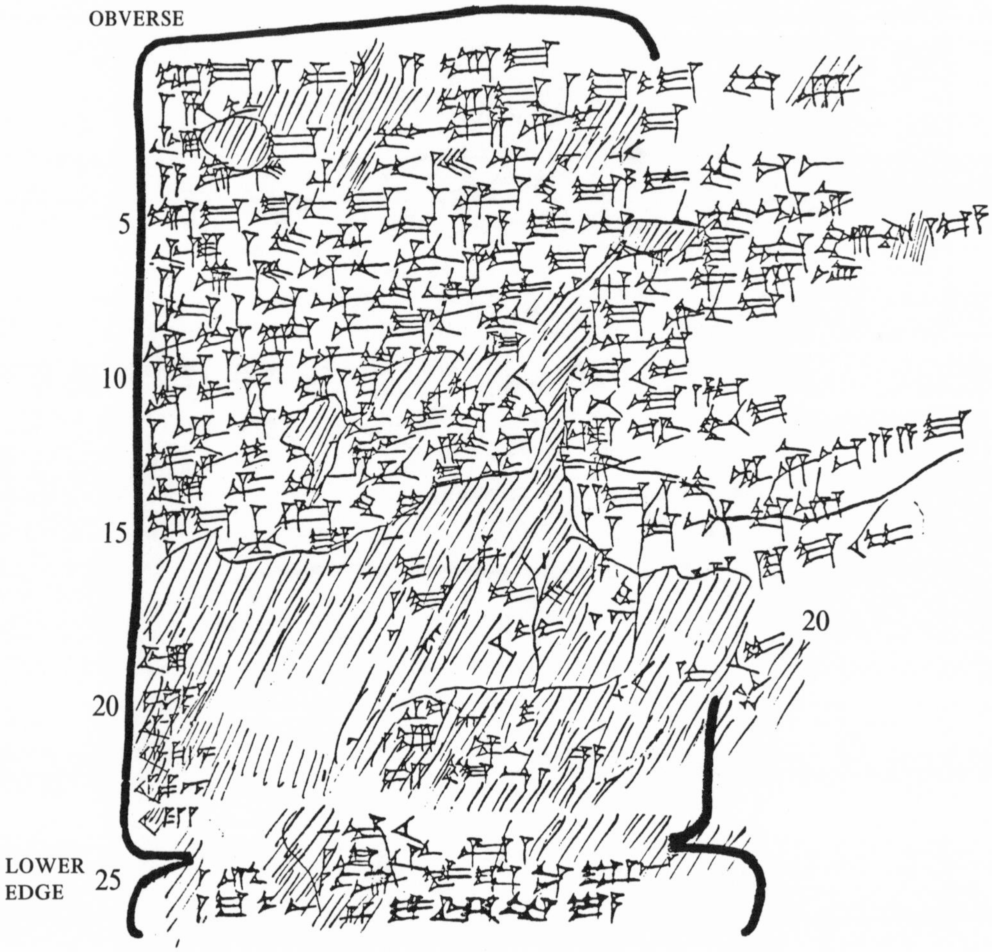

851

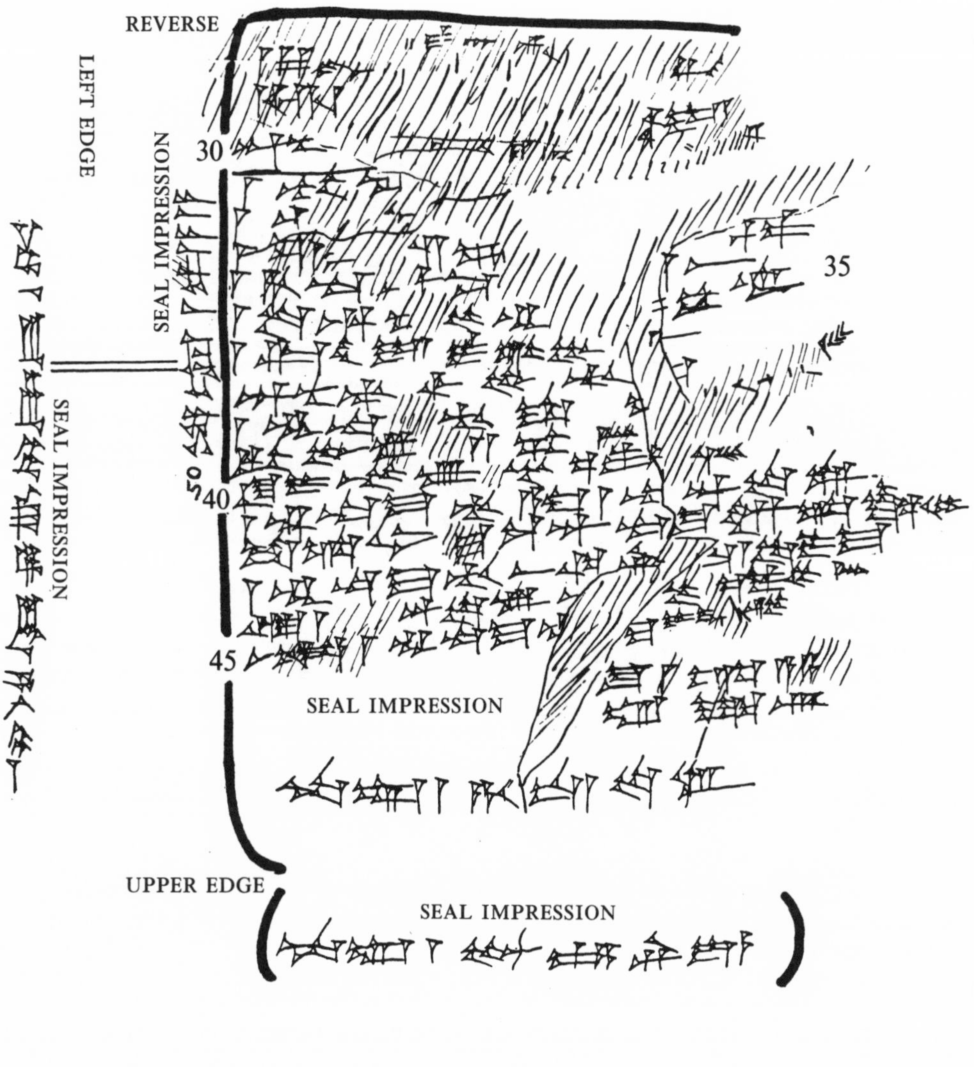
REVERSE
LEFT EDGE
SEAL IMPRESSION
30
35
40
45
50
SEAL IMPRESSION
SEAL IMPRESSION
UPPER EDGE
SEAL IMPRESSION

852

OBVERSE

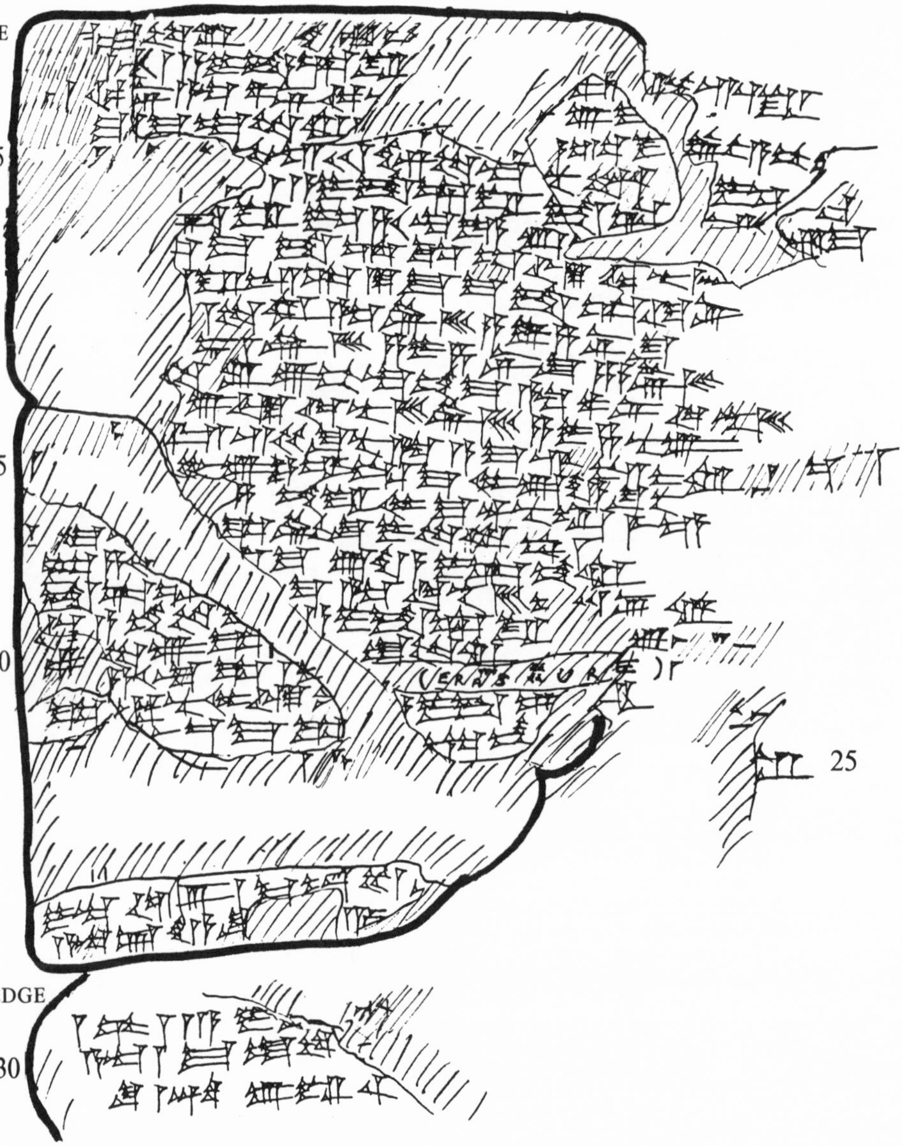

LOWER EDGE

852

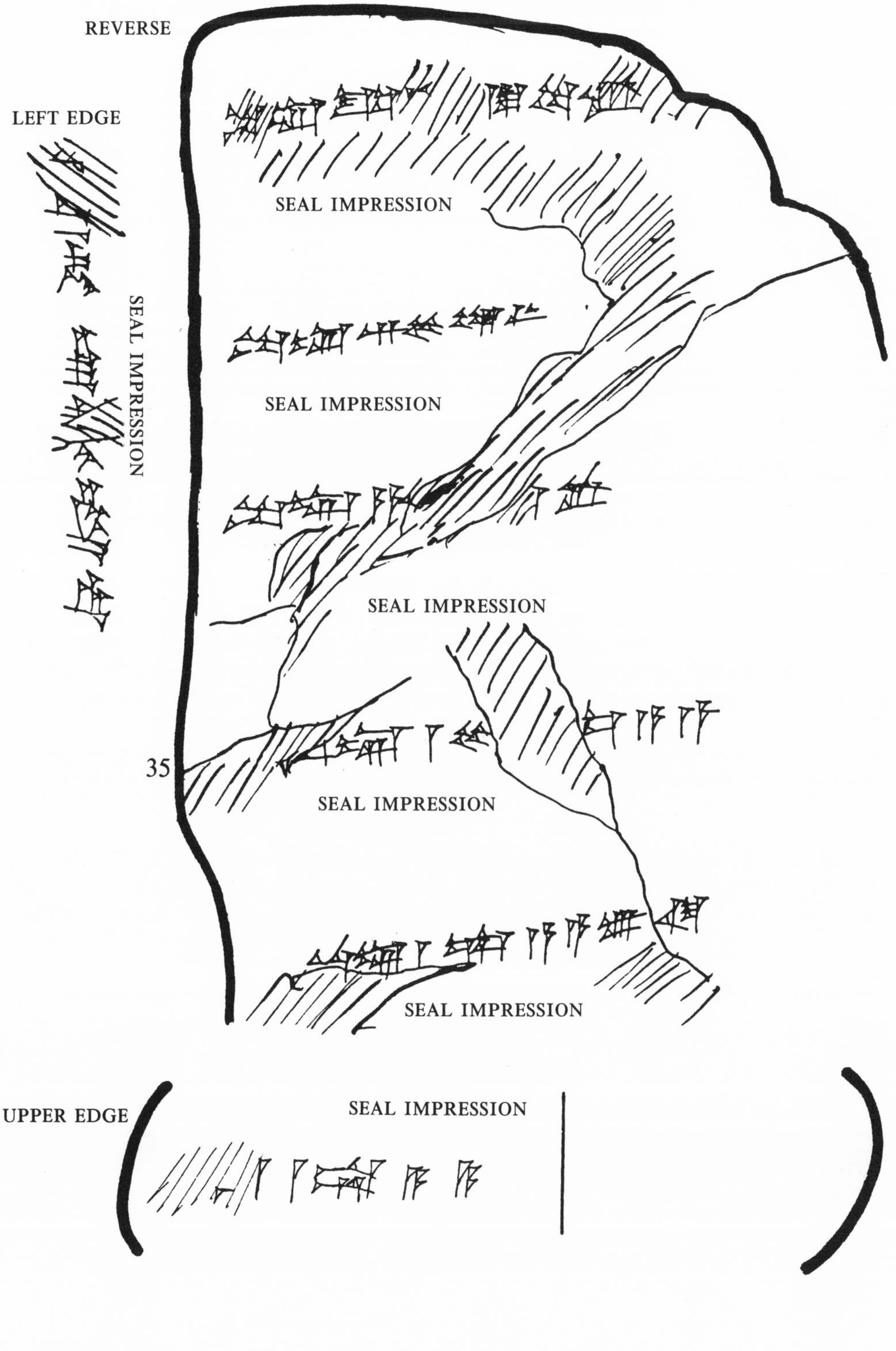
REVERSE
LEFT EDGE
SEAL IMPRESSION
SEAL IMPRESSION
SEAL IMPRESSION
SEAL IMPRESSION
SEAL IMPRESSION
SEAL IMPRESSION
35
UPPER EDGE
SEAL IMPRESSION

853

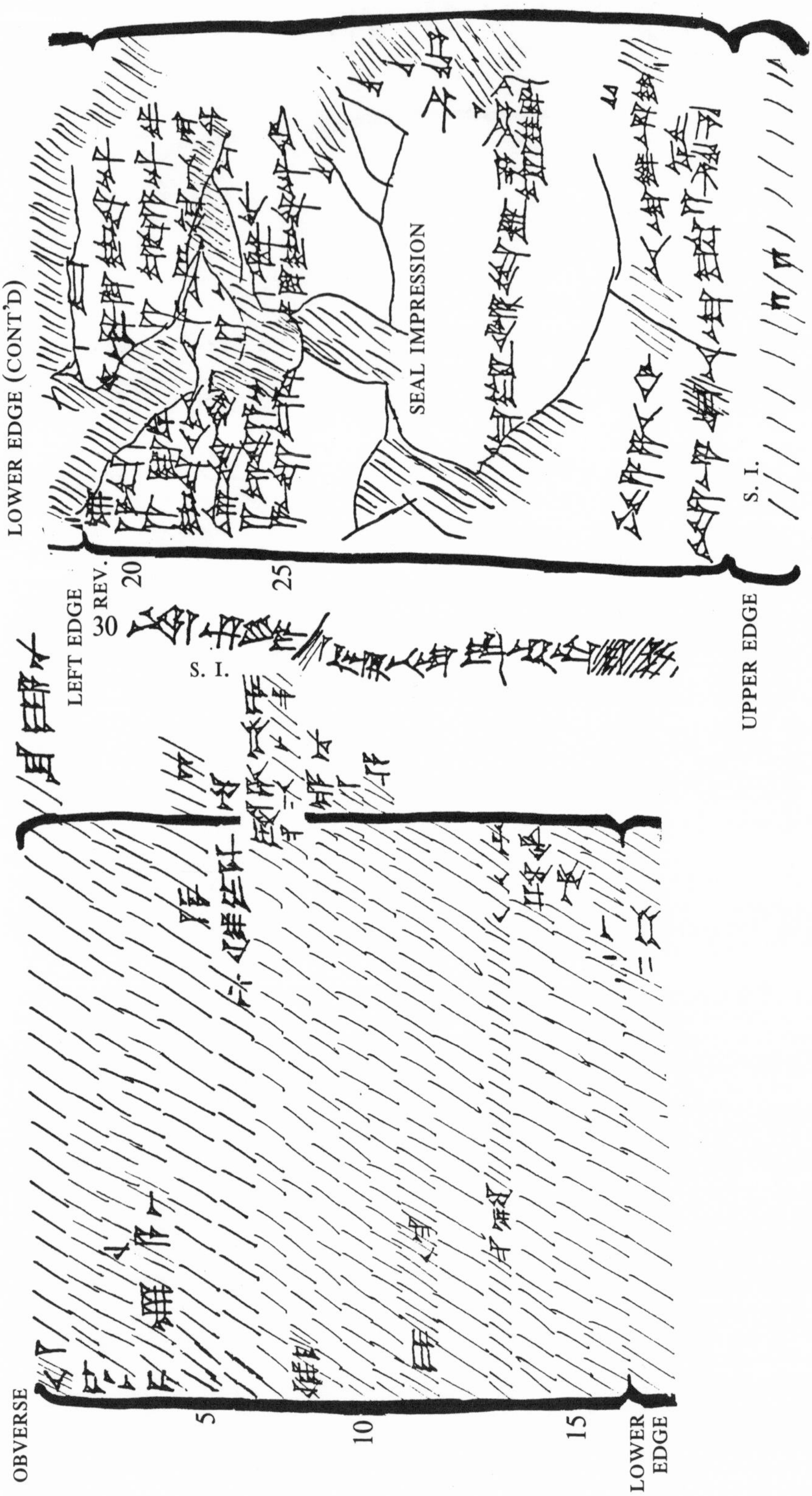
OBVERSE
LOWER EDGE
LEFT EDGE
REV.
LOWER EDGE (CONT'D)
SEAL IMPRESSION
S. I.
S. I.
UPPER EDGE

854

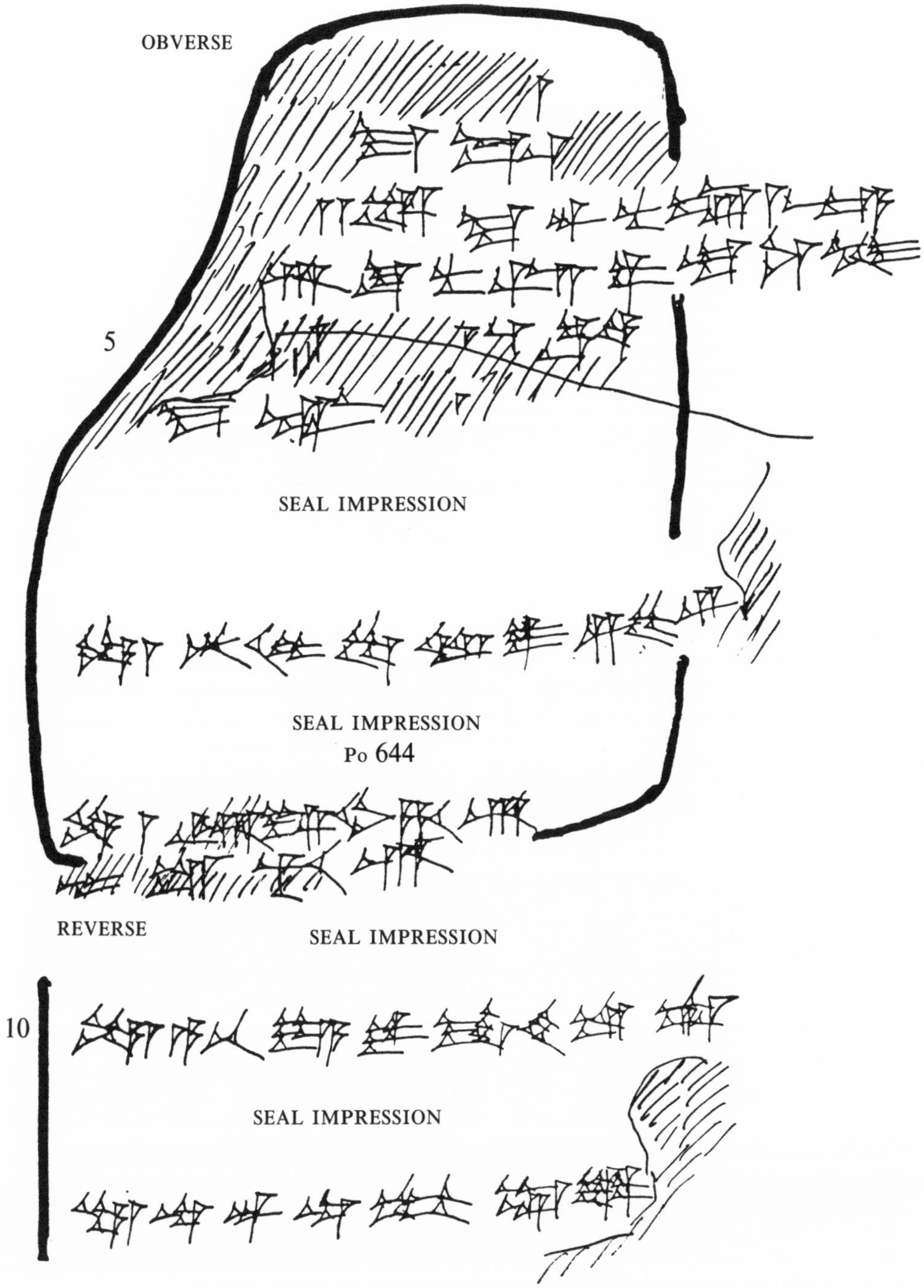
OBVERSE
SEAL IMPRESSION
SEAL IMPRESSION
Po 644
REVERSE
SEAL IMPRESSION
SEAL IMPRESSION

855

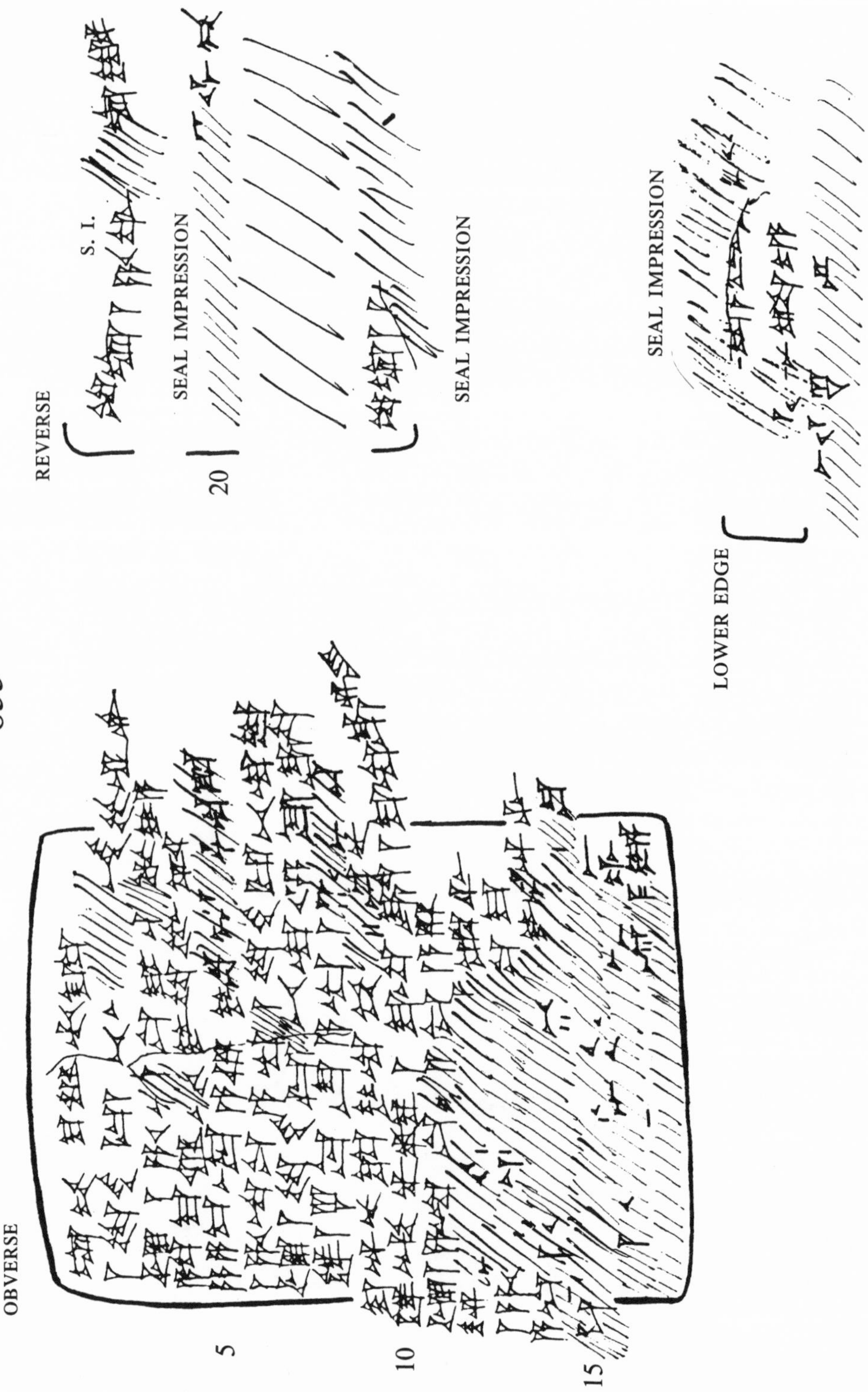
OBVERSE
5
10
15
REVERSE
S. I.
SEAL IMPRESSION
20
SEAL IMPRESSION
LOWER EDGE
SEAL IMPRESSION

856

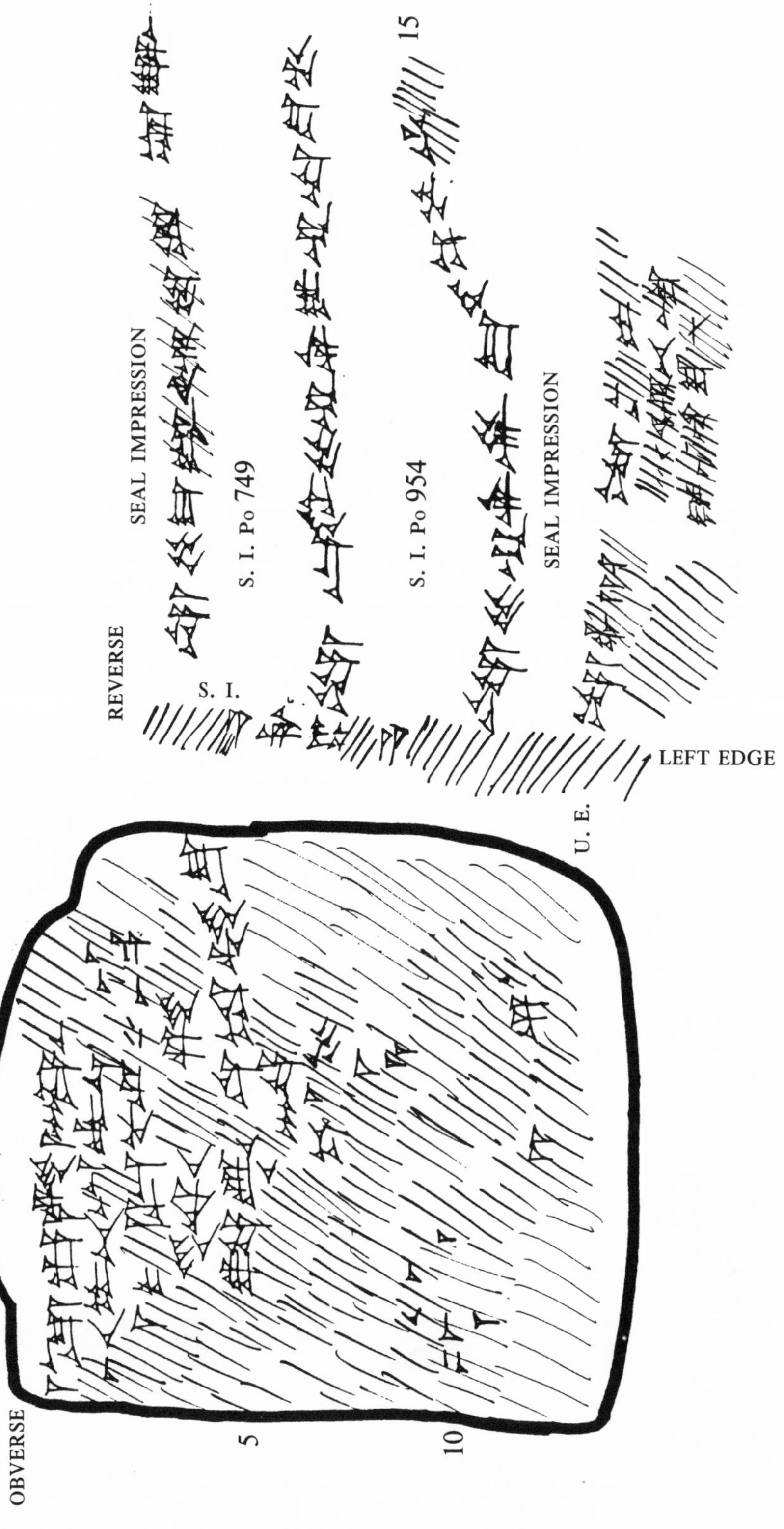
OBVERSE
U. E.
REVERSE
S. I.
SEAL IMPRESSION
S. I. Po 749
S. I. Po 954
SEAL IMPRESSION
LEFT EDGE

857

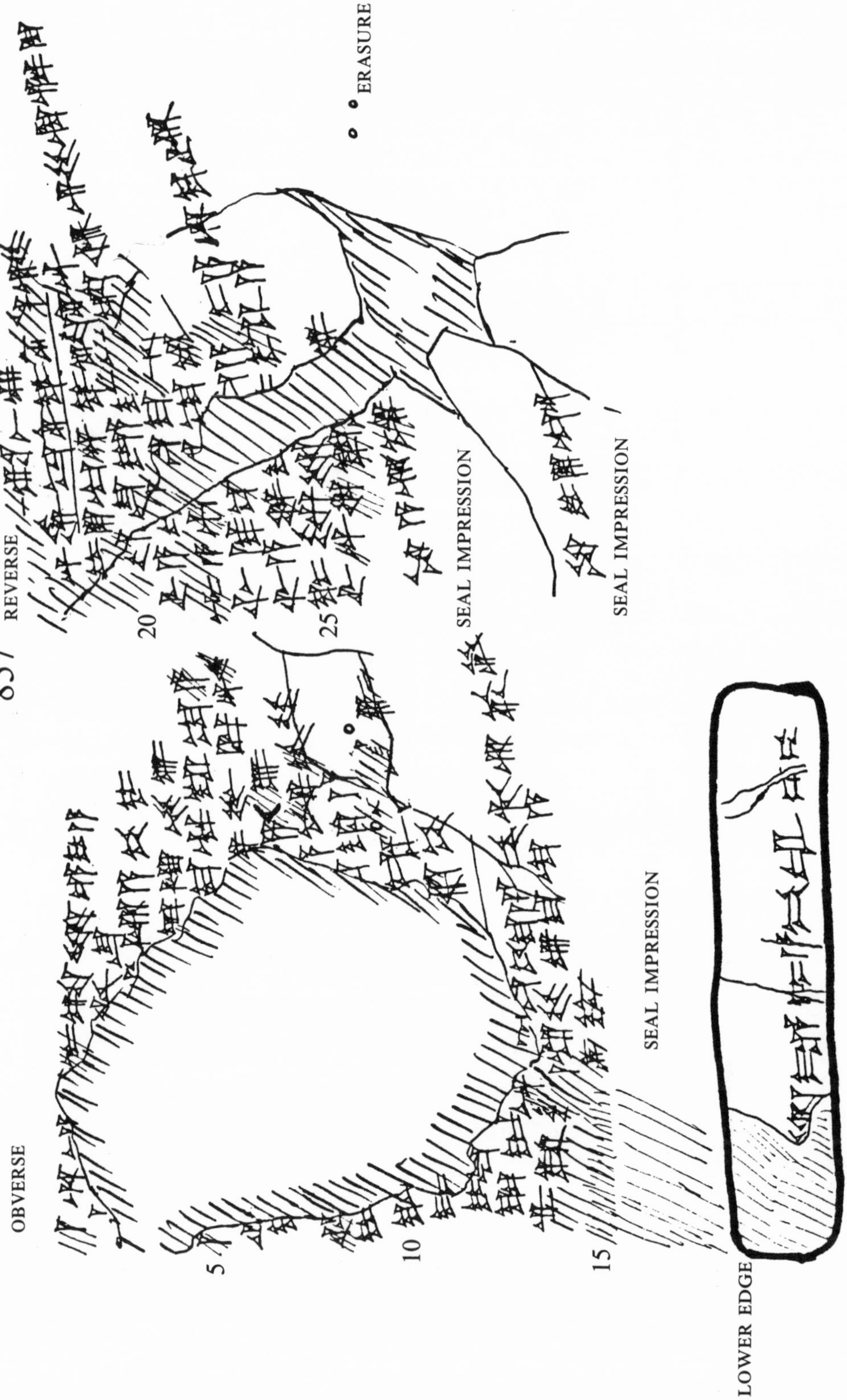
OBVERSE
5
10
15
SEAL IMPRESSION
LOWER EDGE
REVERSE
20
25
SEAL IMPRESSION
SEAL IMPRESSION
ERASURE

858

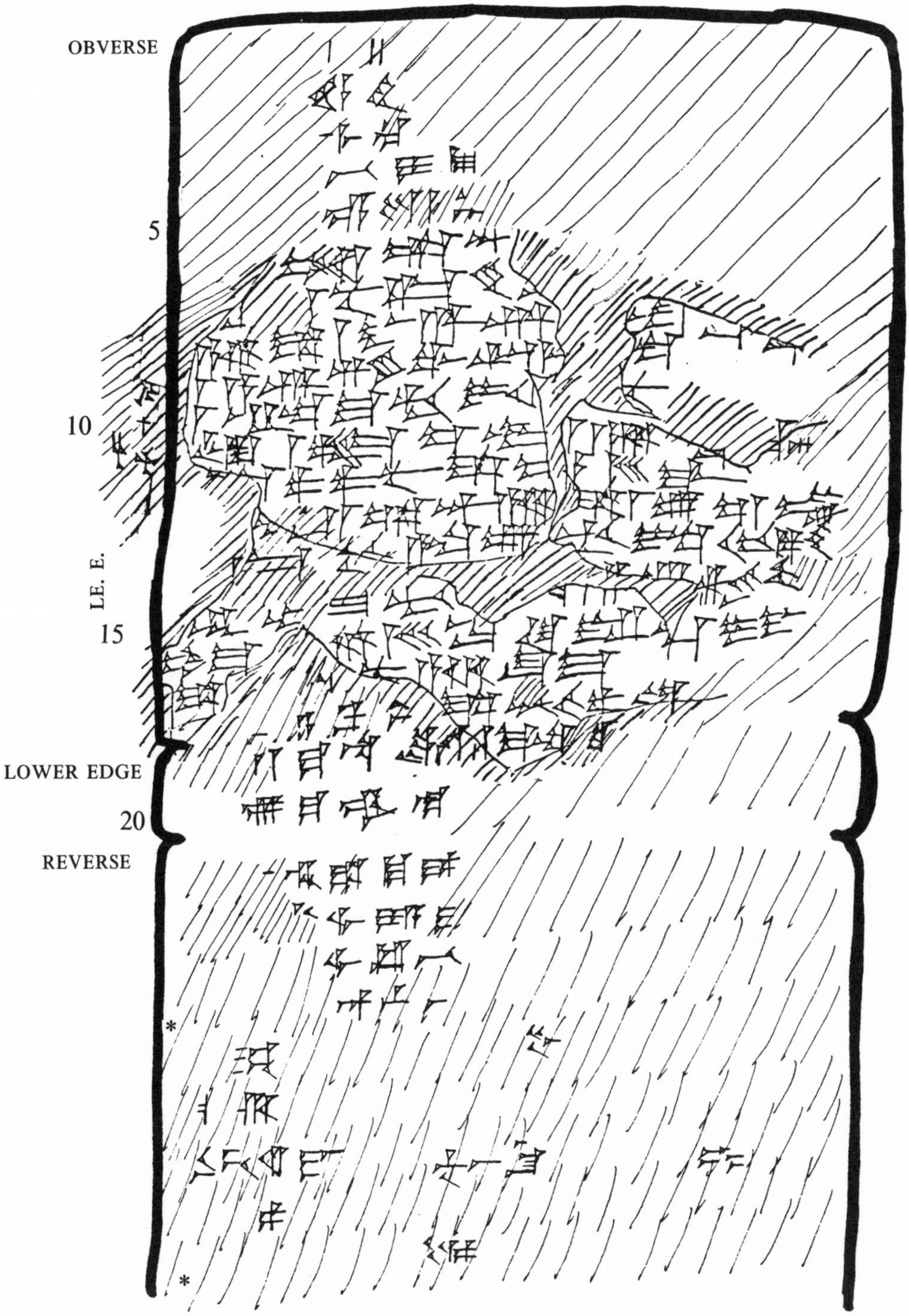

*Additional text; see *THNT*.

859

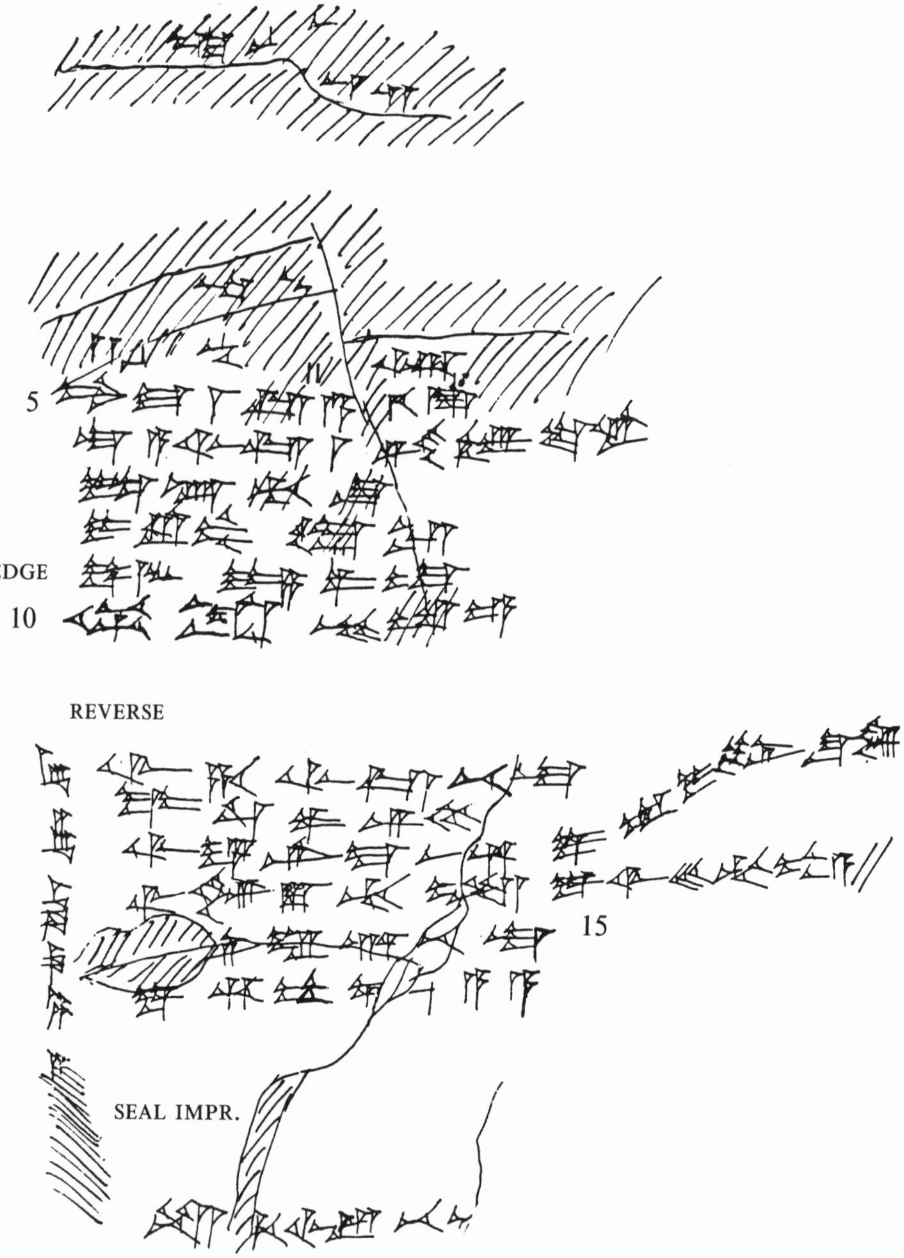
OBVERSE
Beginning of obverse destroyed
LOWER EDGE
REVERSE
SEAL IMPR.
UPPER EDGE
SEAL IMPRESSION

860

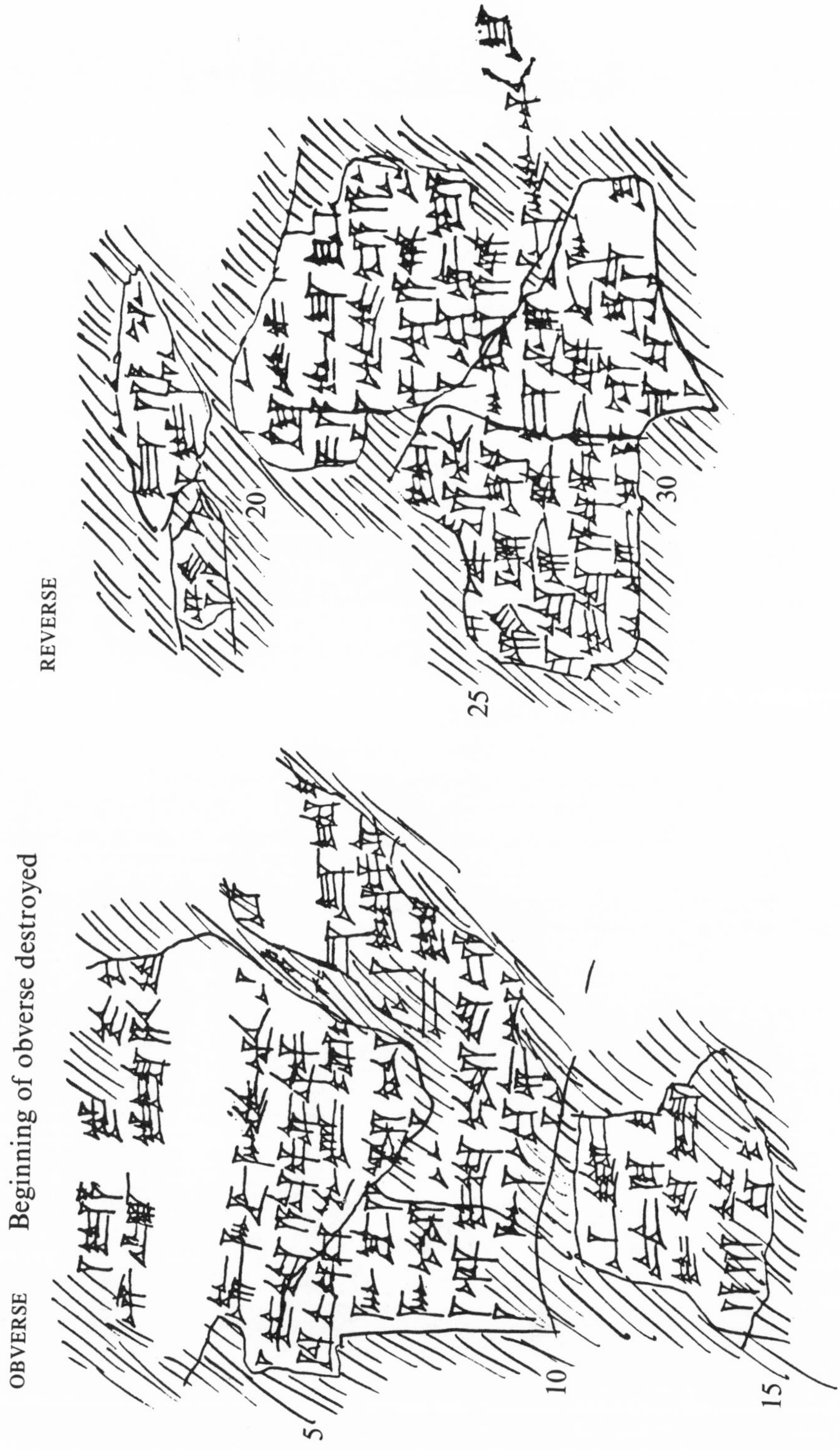

861

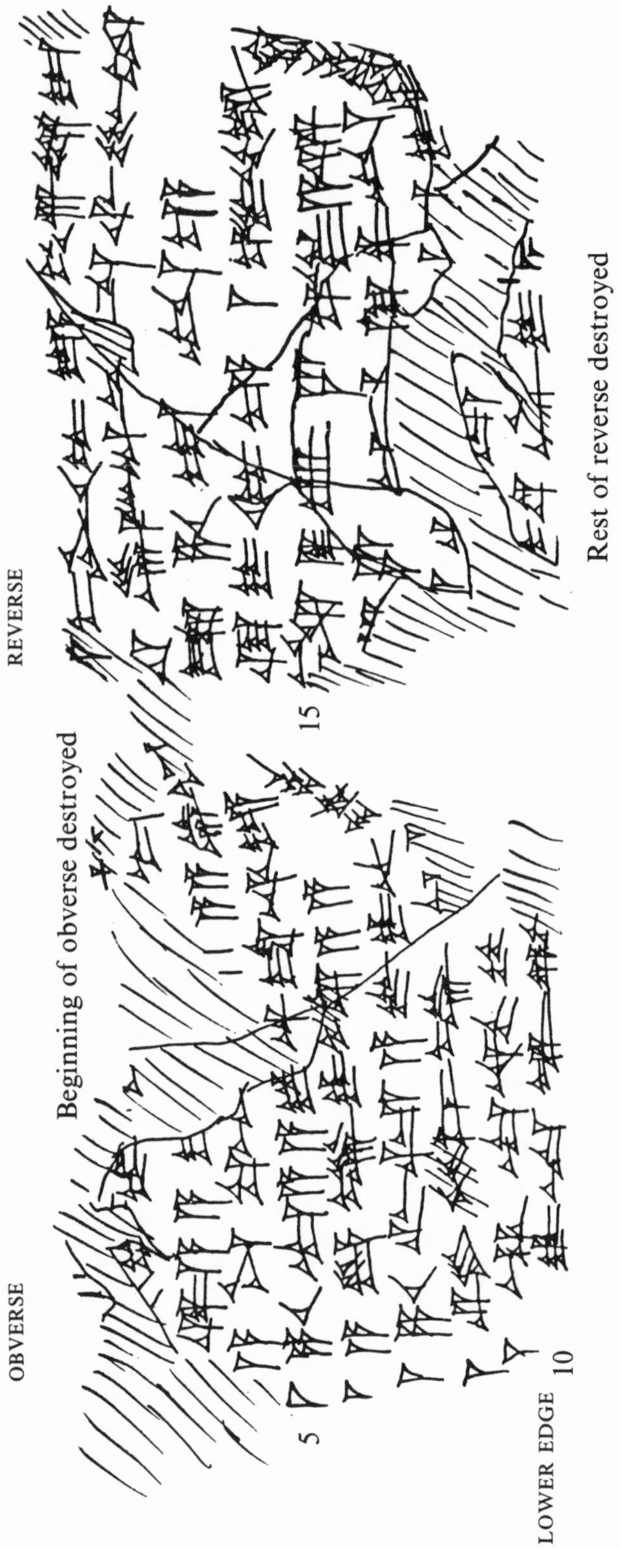
OBVERSE
Beginning of obverse destroyed
5
10
LOWER EDGE
REVERSE
15
Rest of reverse destroyed

862

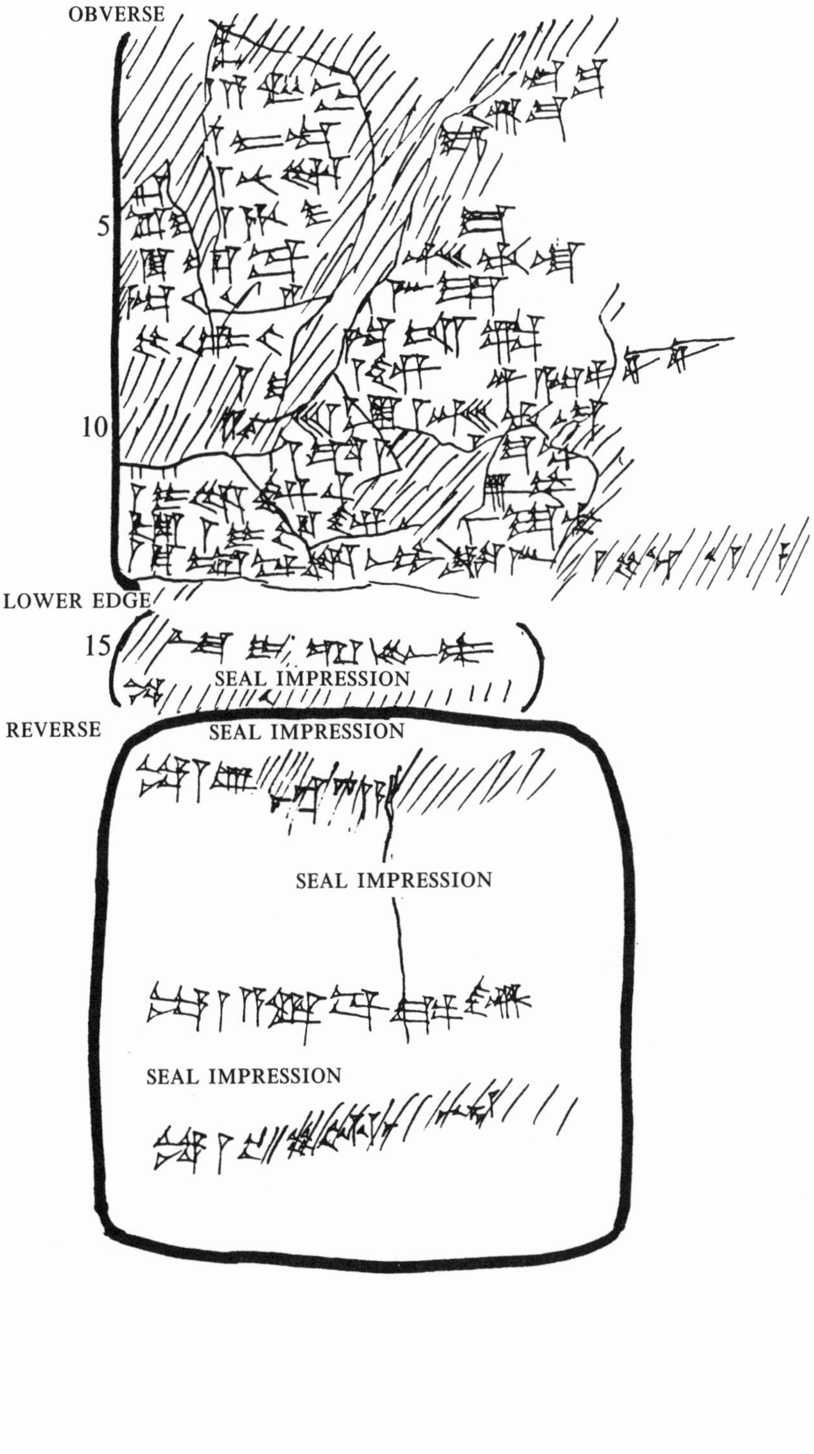
OBVERSE
5
10
LOWER EDGE
15
SEAL IMPRESSION
REVERSE
SEAL IMPRESSION
SEAL IMPRESSION
SEAL IMPRESSION

863

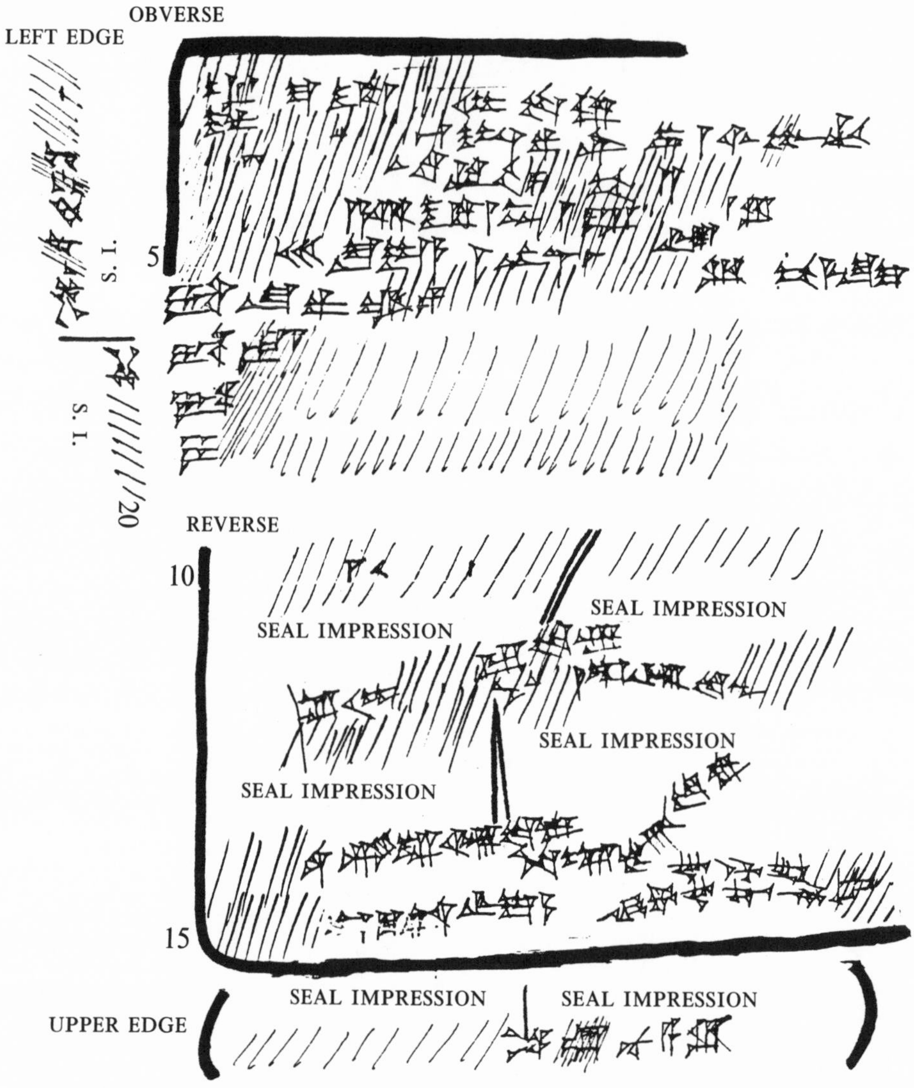
OBVERSE
LEFT EDGE
S. I.
S. I.
REVERSE
SEAL IMPRESSION
SEAL IMPRESSION
SEAL IMPRESSION
SEAL IMPRESSION
UPPER EDGE
SEAL IMPRESSION
SEAL IMPRESSION

864

Beginning of obverse destroyed

OBVERSE

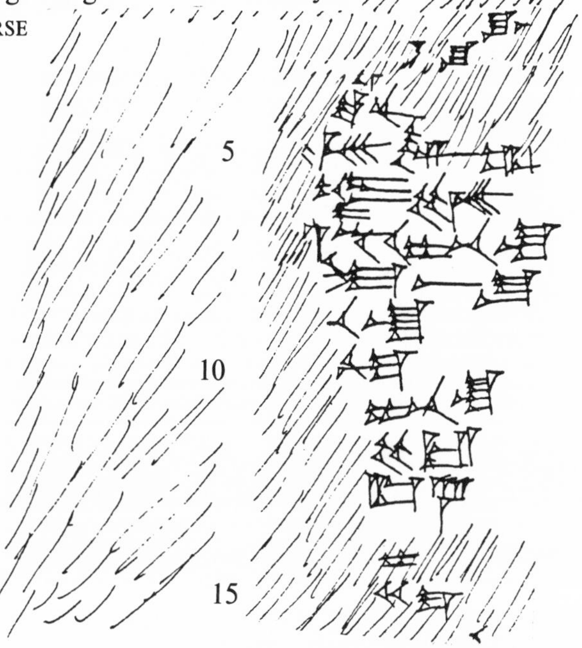

Rest of obverse destroyed

Beginning of reverse destroyed

REVERSE

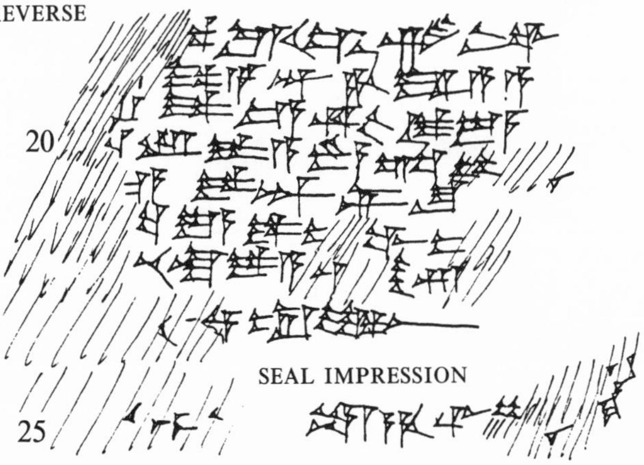

Rest of reverse destroyed

865

OBVERSE

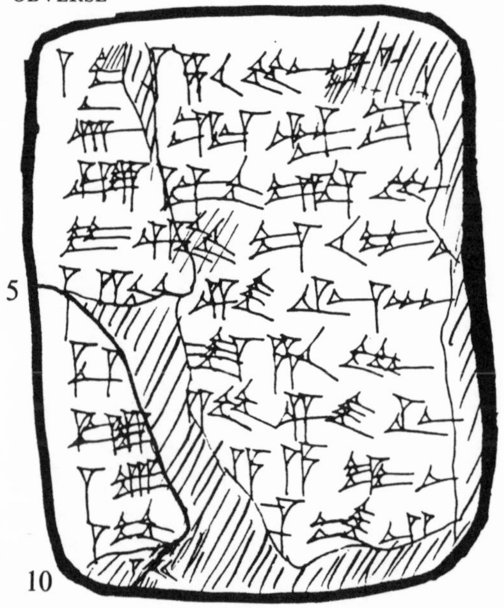

Rest of obverse, beginning of reverse destroyed

REVERSE

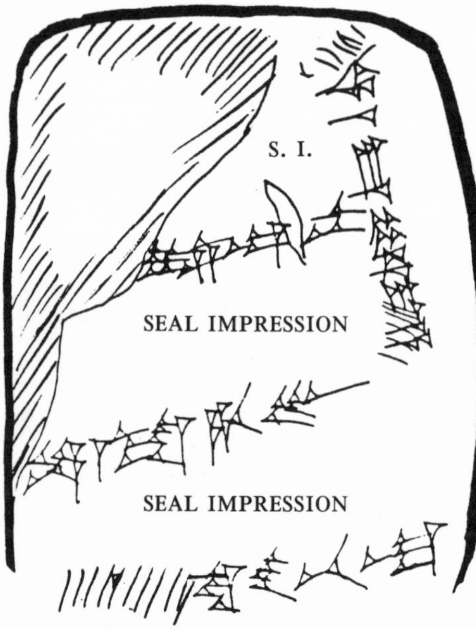

UPPER EDGE

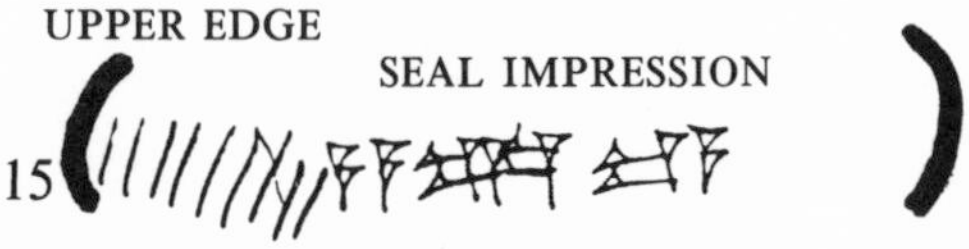

866

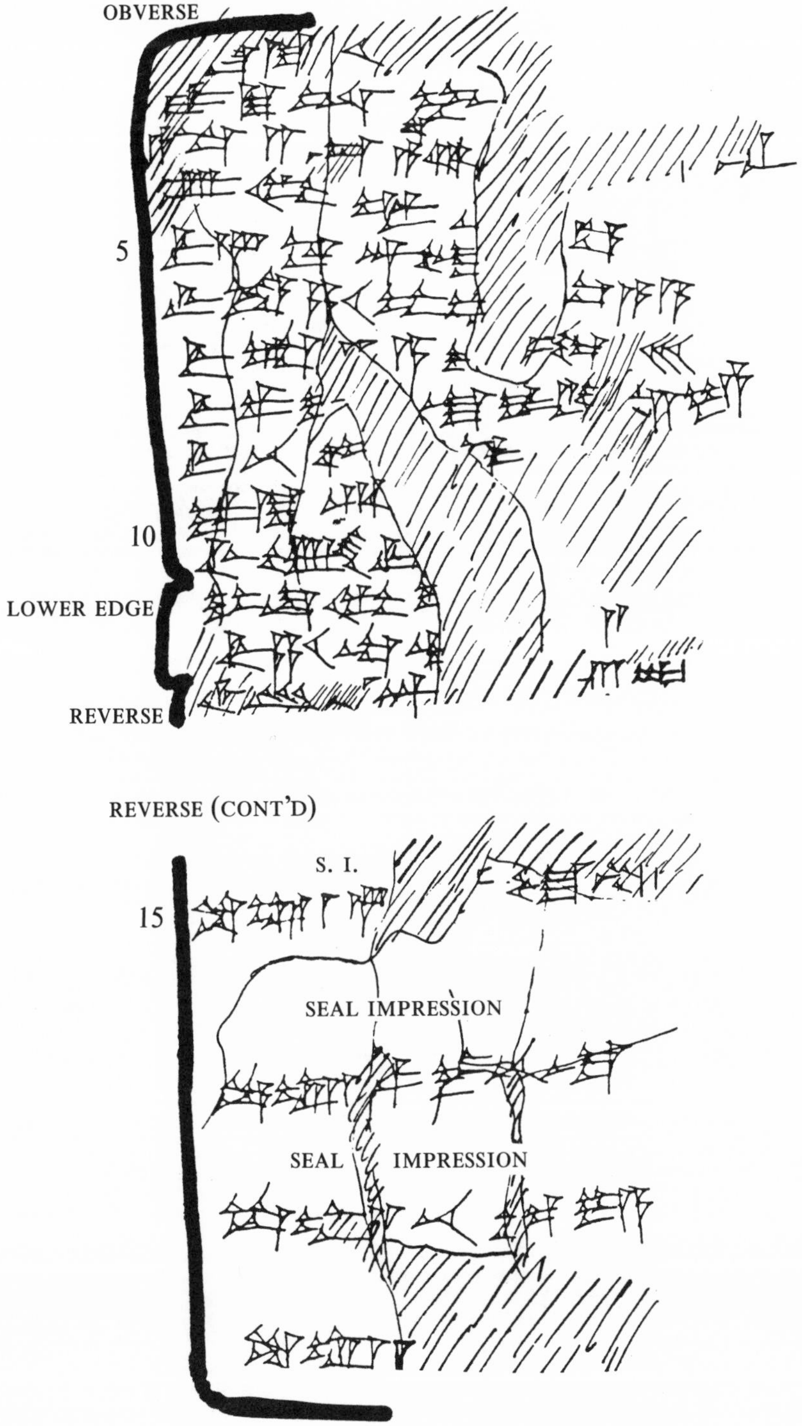
OBVERSE
LOWER EDGE
REVERSE
REVERSE (CONT'D)
S. I.
SEAL IMPRESSION
SEAL
IMPRESSION

867

OBVERSE

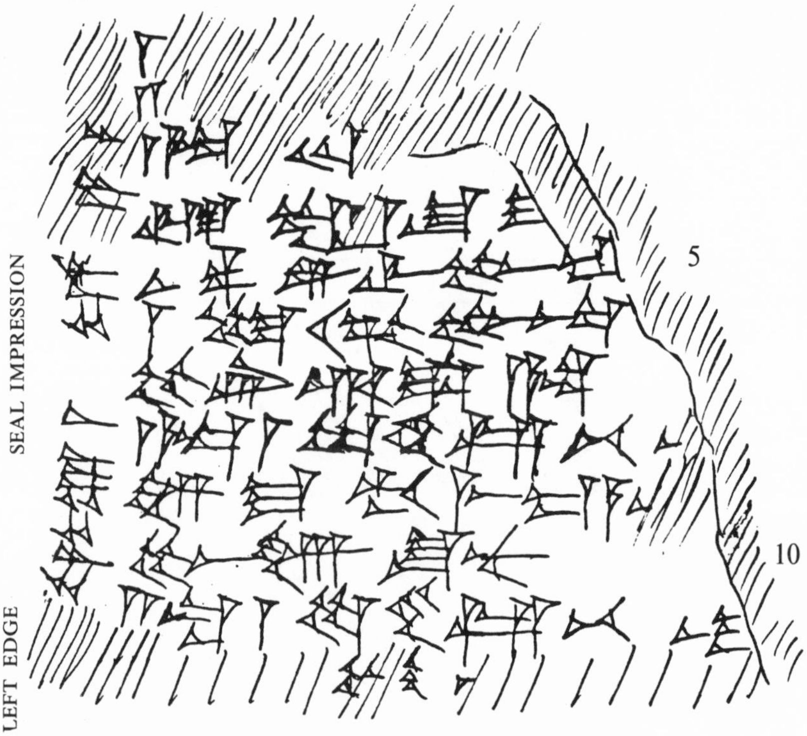

Rest of obverse, beginning of reverse destroyed

REVERSE

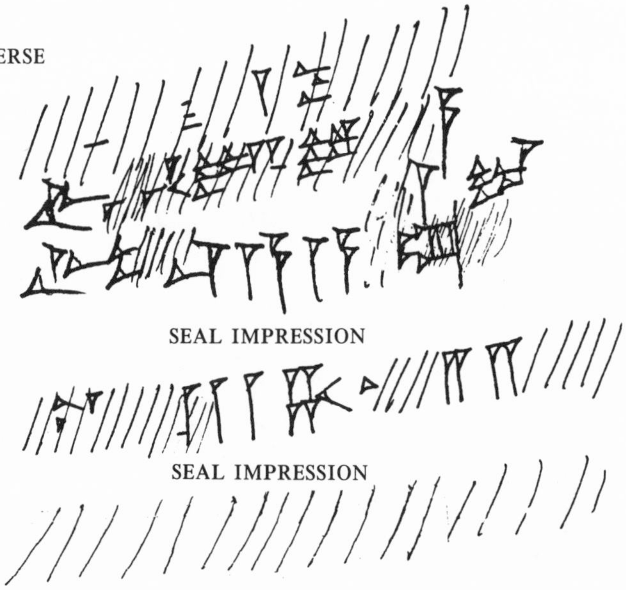

868

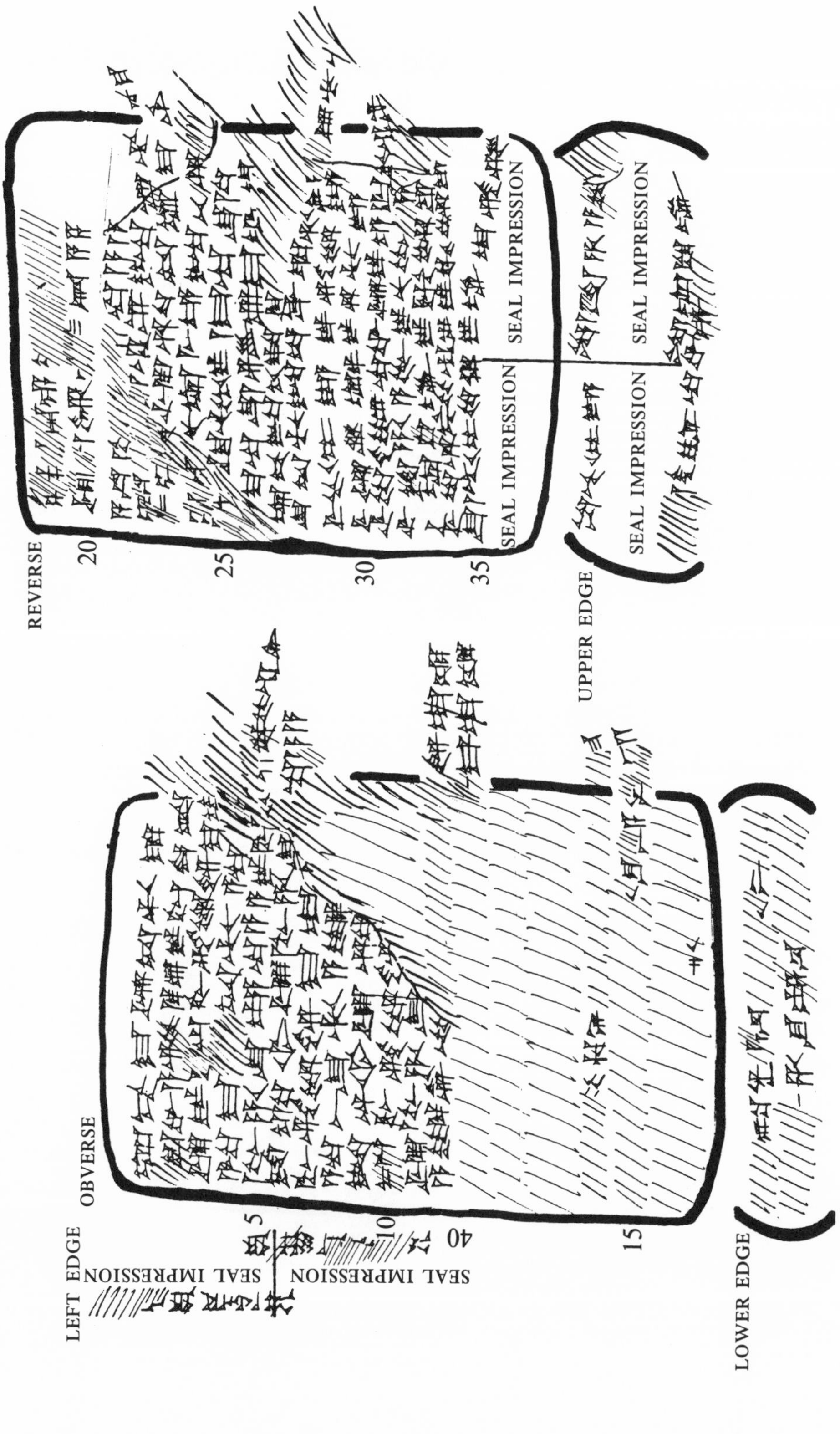
REVERSE
SEAL IMPRESSION
SEAL IMPRESSION
UPPER EDGE
SEAL IMPRESSION
SEAL IMPRESSION
OBVERSE
LEFT EDGE
SEAL IMPRESSION
SEAL IMPRESSION
LOWER EDGE

869 (= 801)*

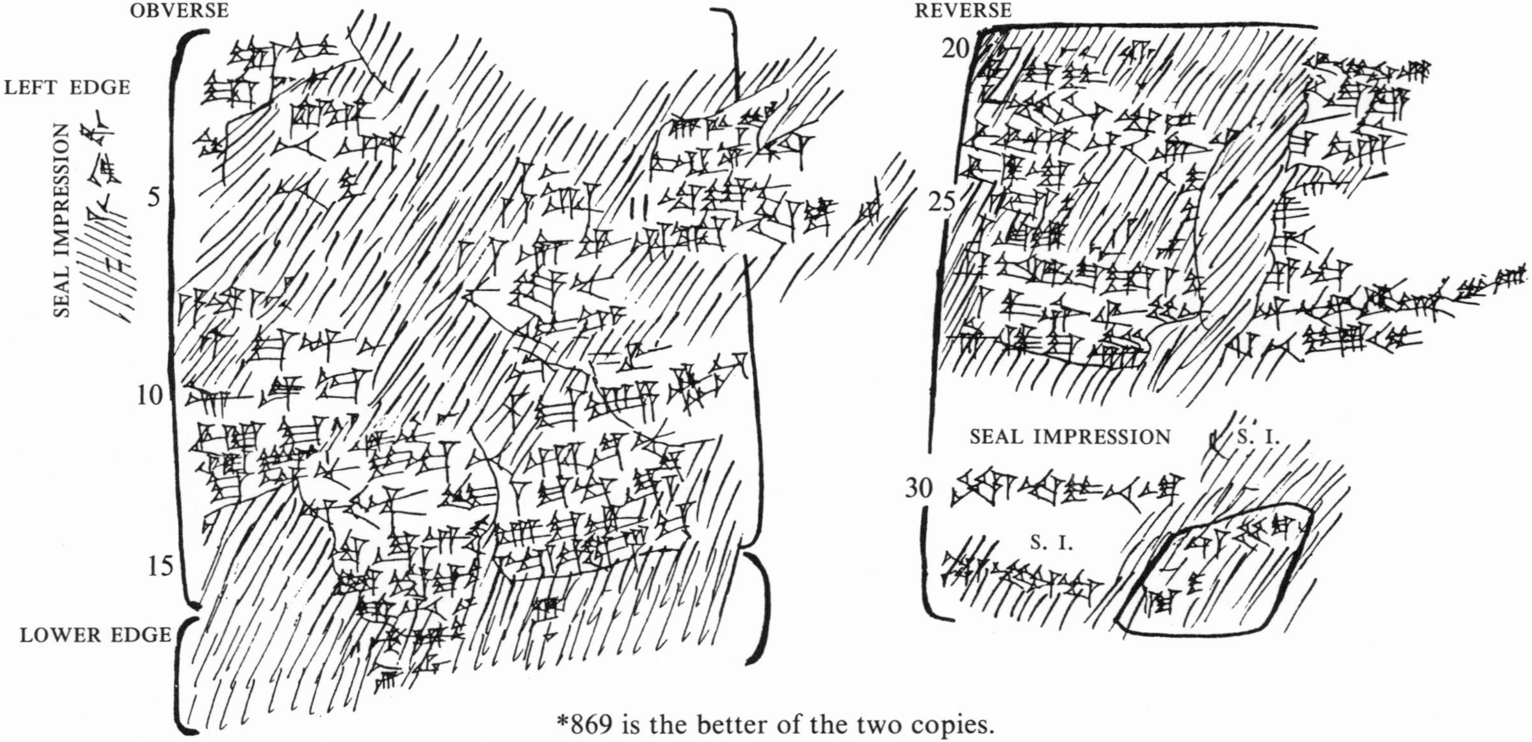

*869 is the better of the two copies.
See comments to this text in *THNT*.

870

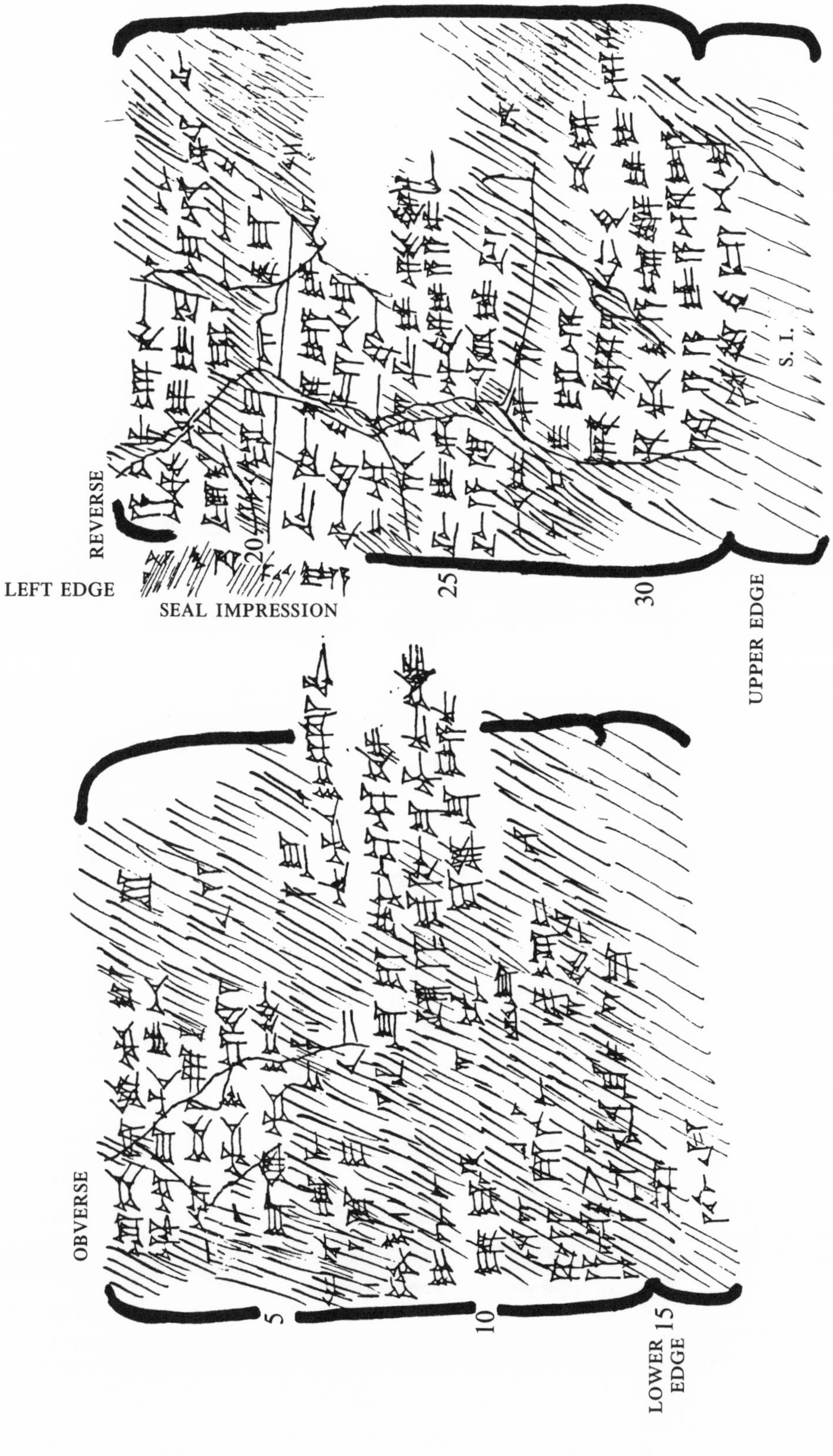
REVERSE
LEFT EDGE
SEAL IMPRESSION
UPPER EDGE
S. I.
20
25
30
OBVERSE
LOWER EDGE
5
10
15

871

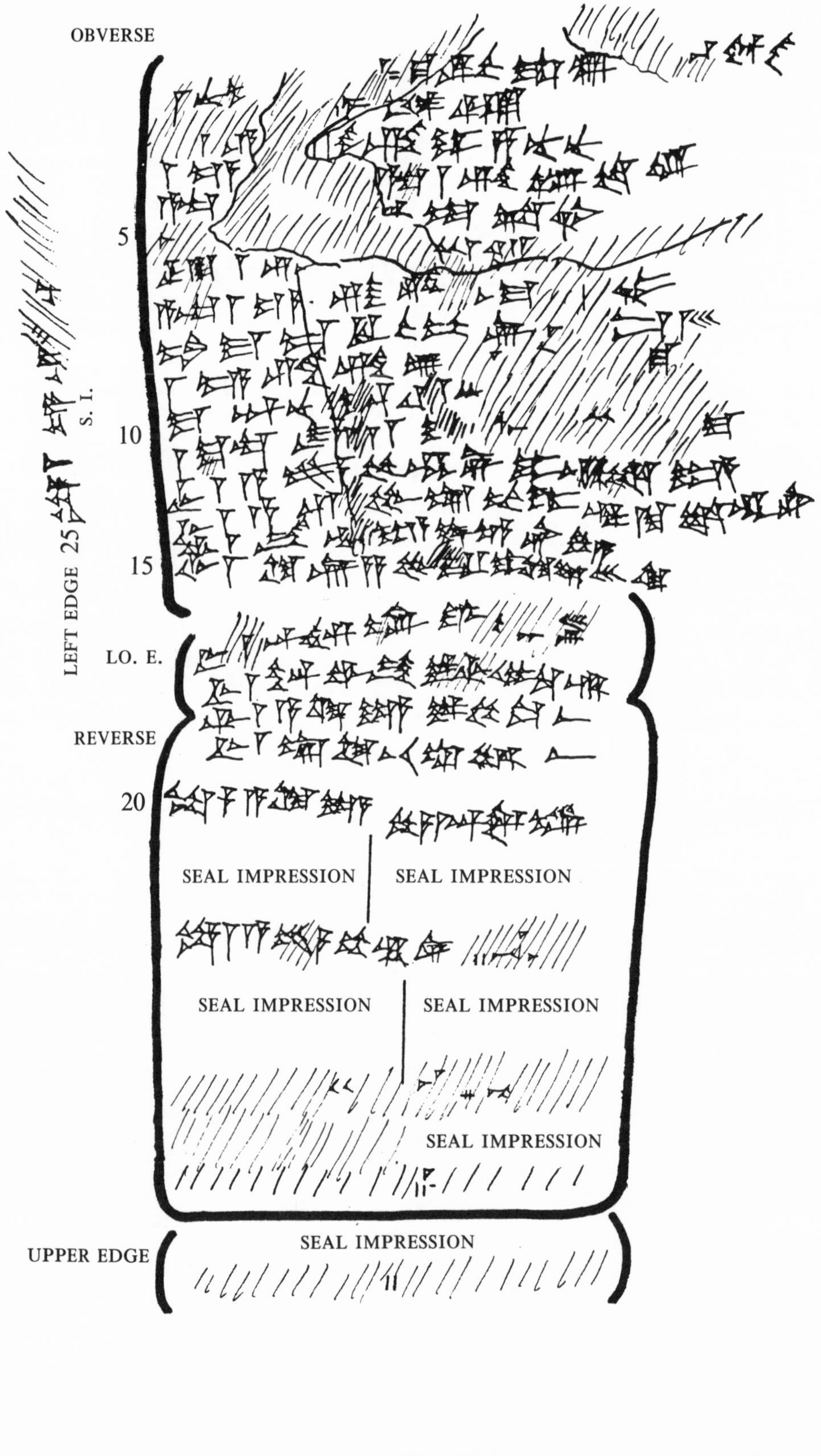
OBVERSE
5
10
15
LO. E.
REVERSE
20
SEAL IMPRESSION
SEAL IMPRESSION
SEAL IMPRESSION
SEAL IMPRESSION
SEAL IMPRESSION
UPPER EDGE
SEAL IMPRESSION
LEFT EDGE 25
S. I.

872

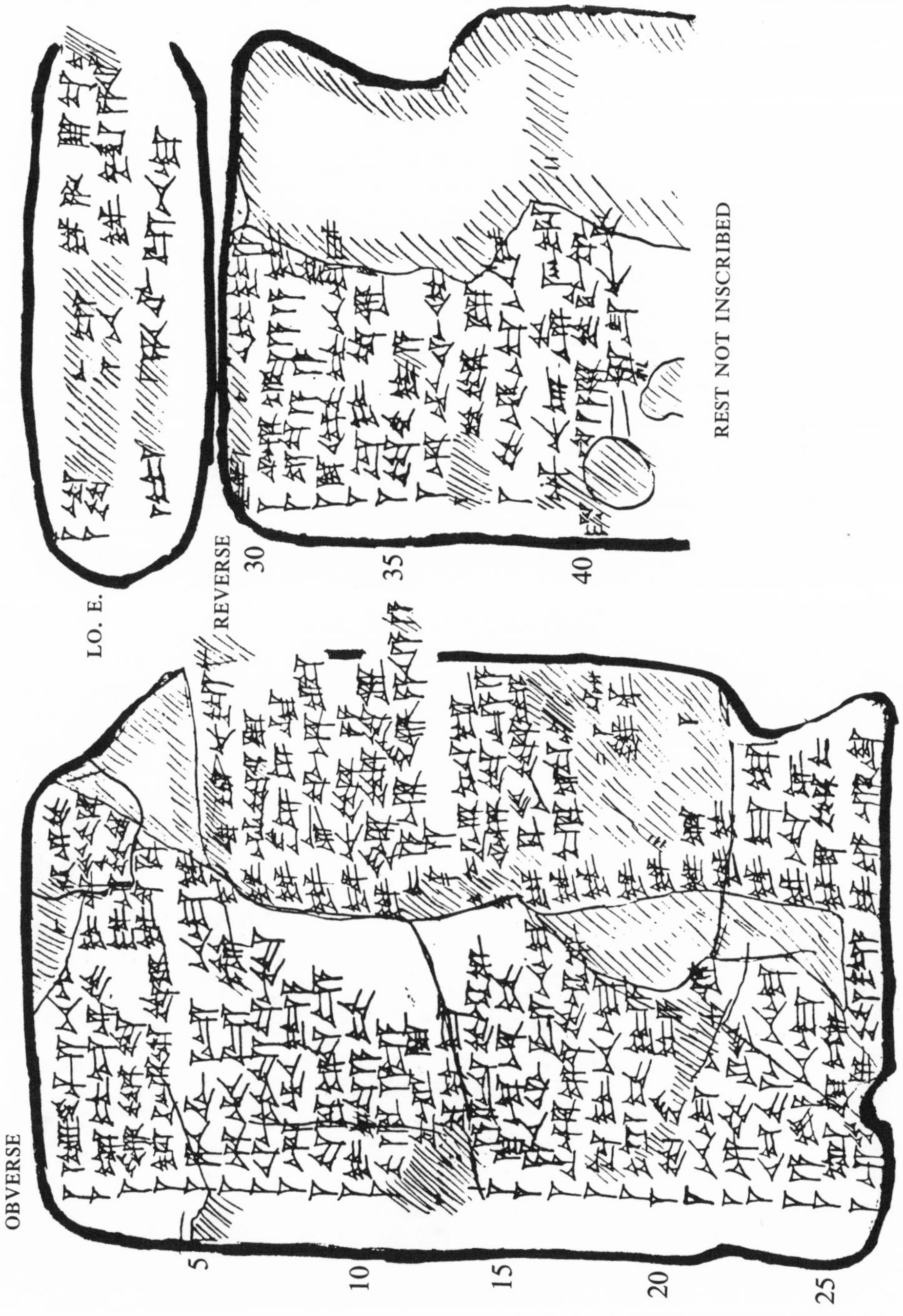

873

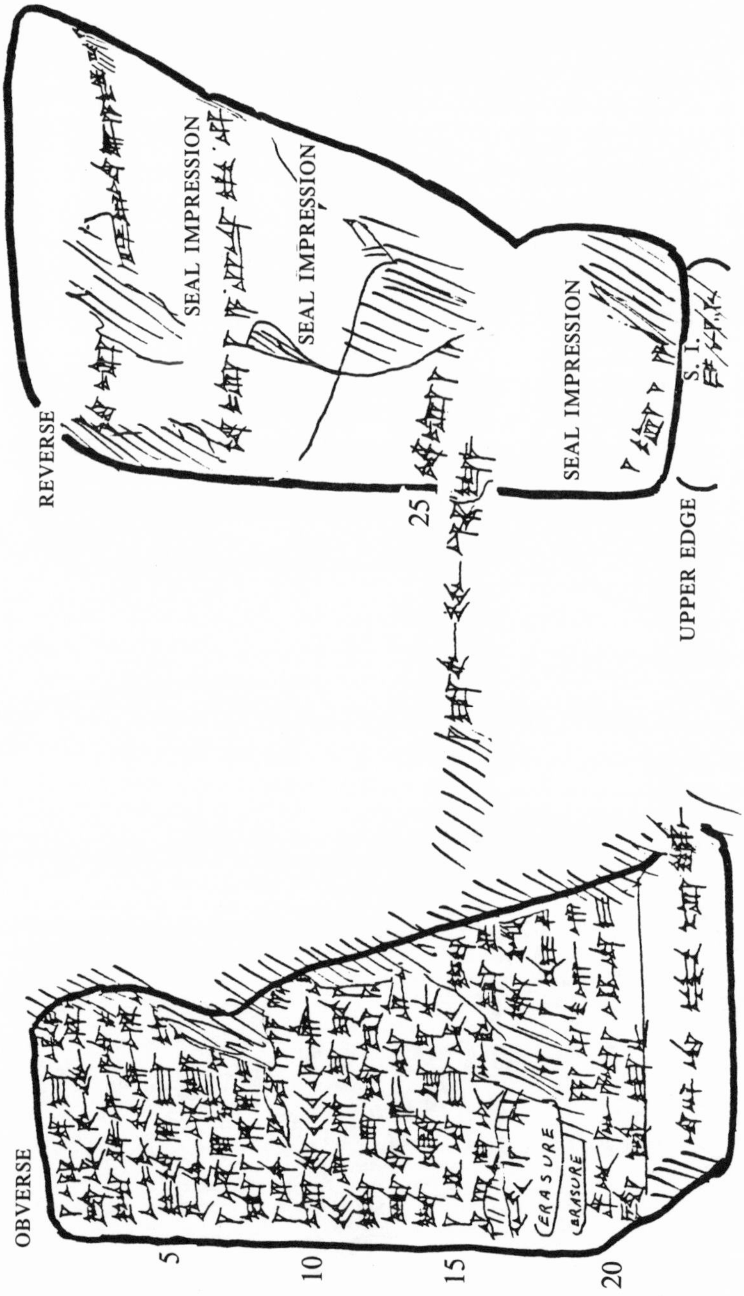
OBVERSE
ERASURE
ERASURE
REVERSE
SEAL IMPRESSION
SEAL IMPRESSION
SEAL IMPRESSION
S. I.
UPPER EDGE

874

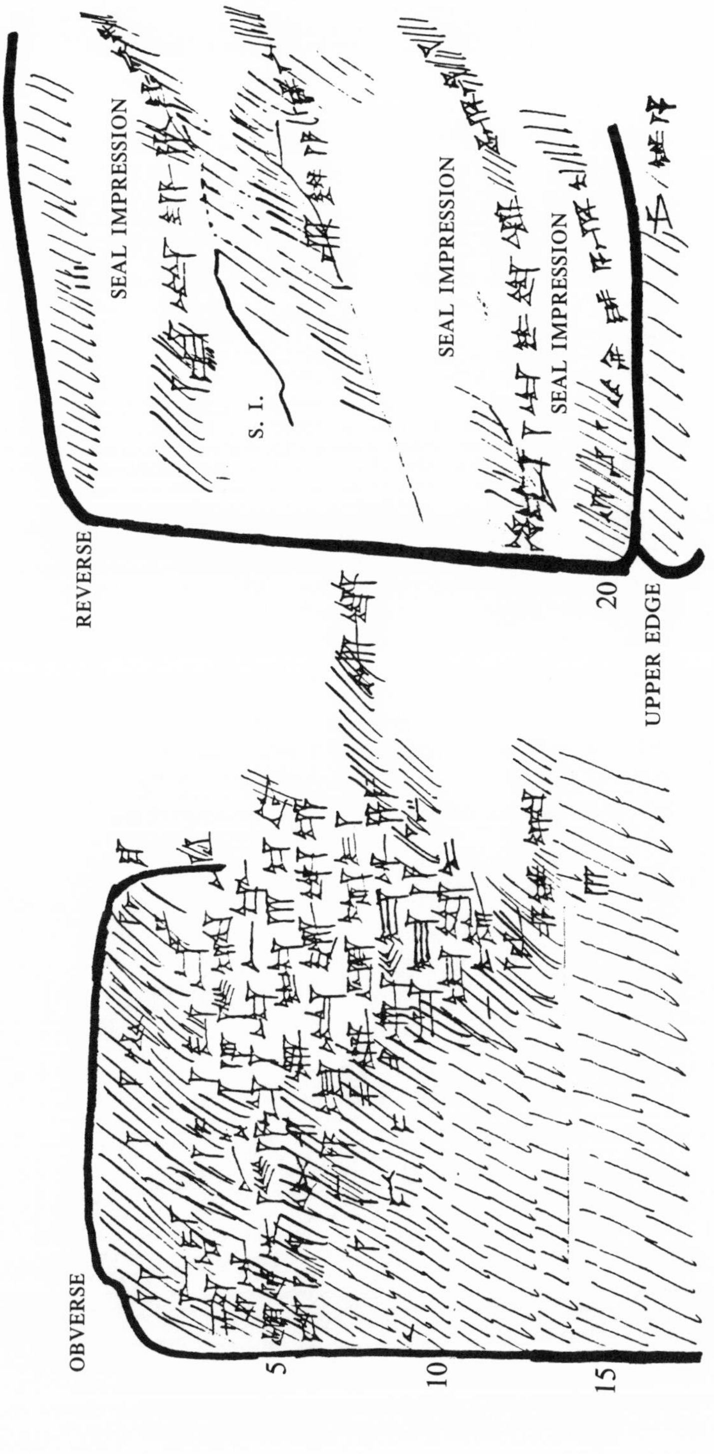
OBVERSE
5
10
15
REVERSE
SEAL IMPRESSION
S. I.
SEAL IMPRESSION
SEAL IMPRESSION
20
UPPER EDGE

875 (= 818)*

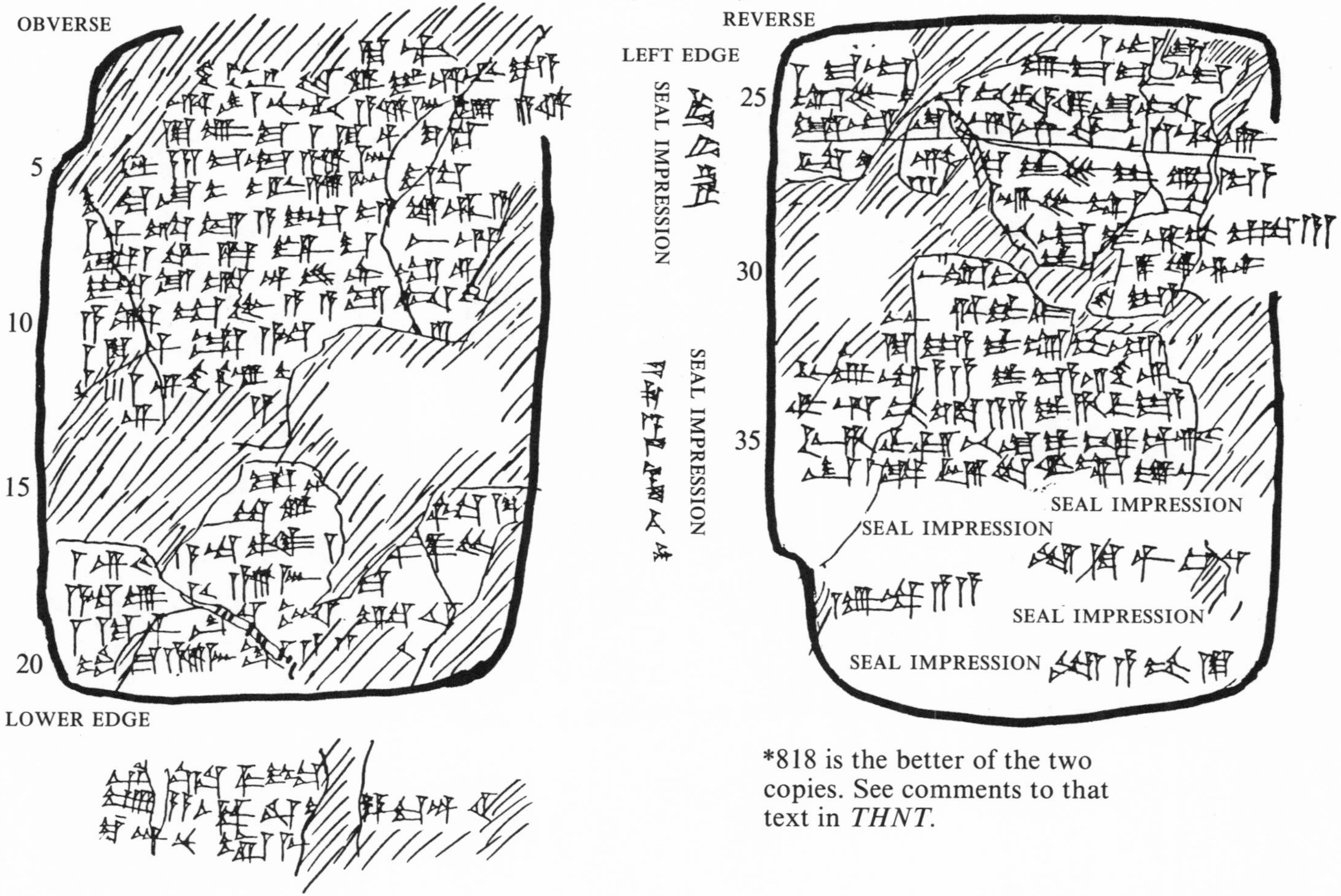

*818 is the better of the two copies. See comments to that text in *THNT*.

876

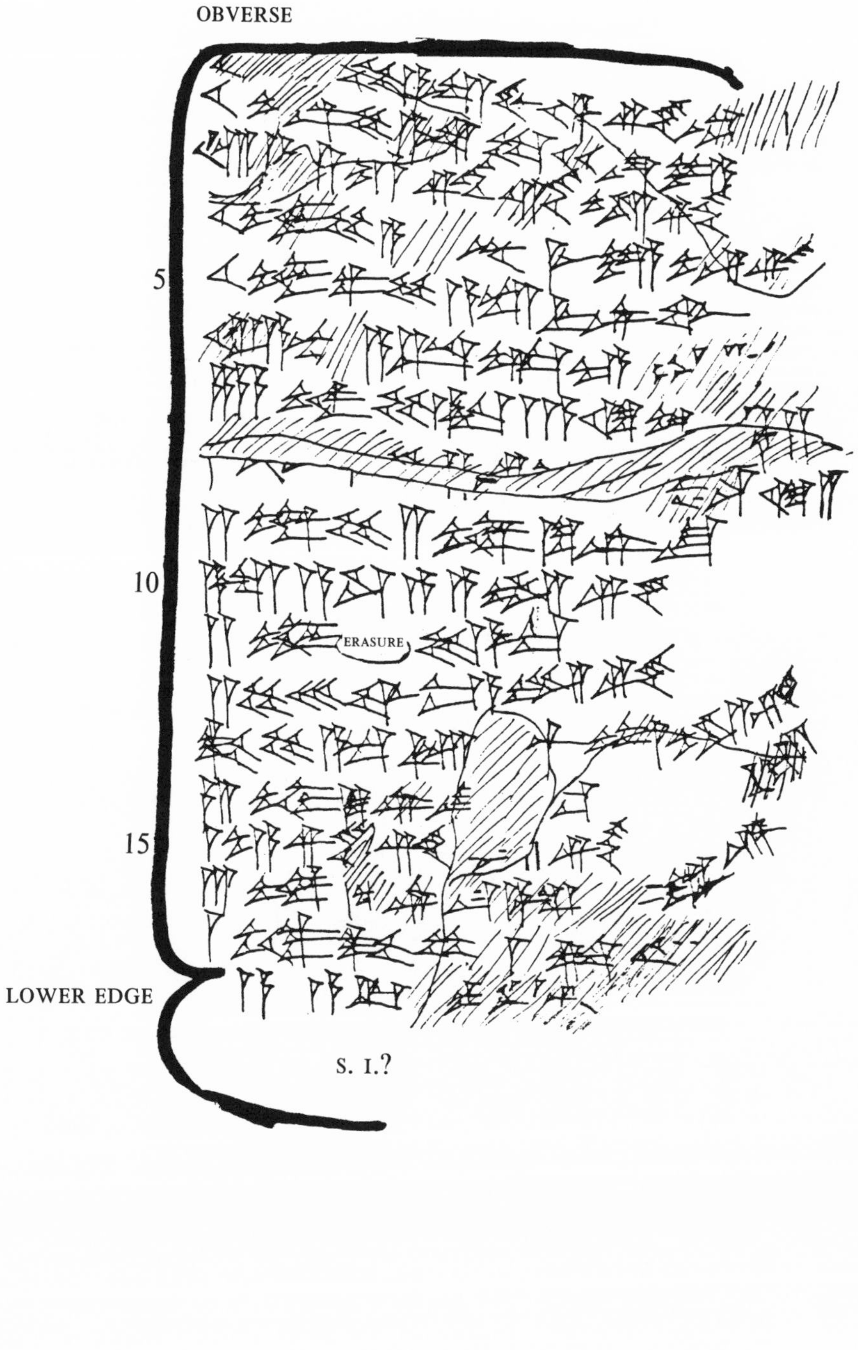

876

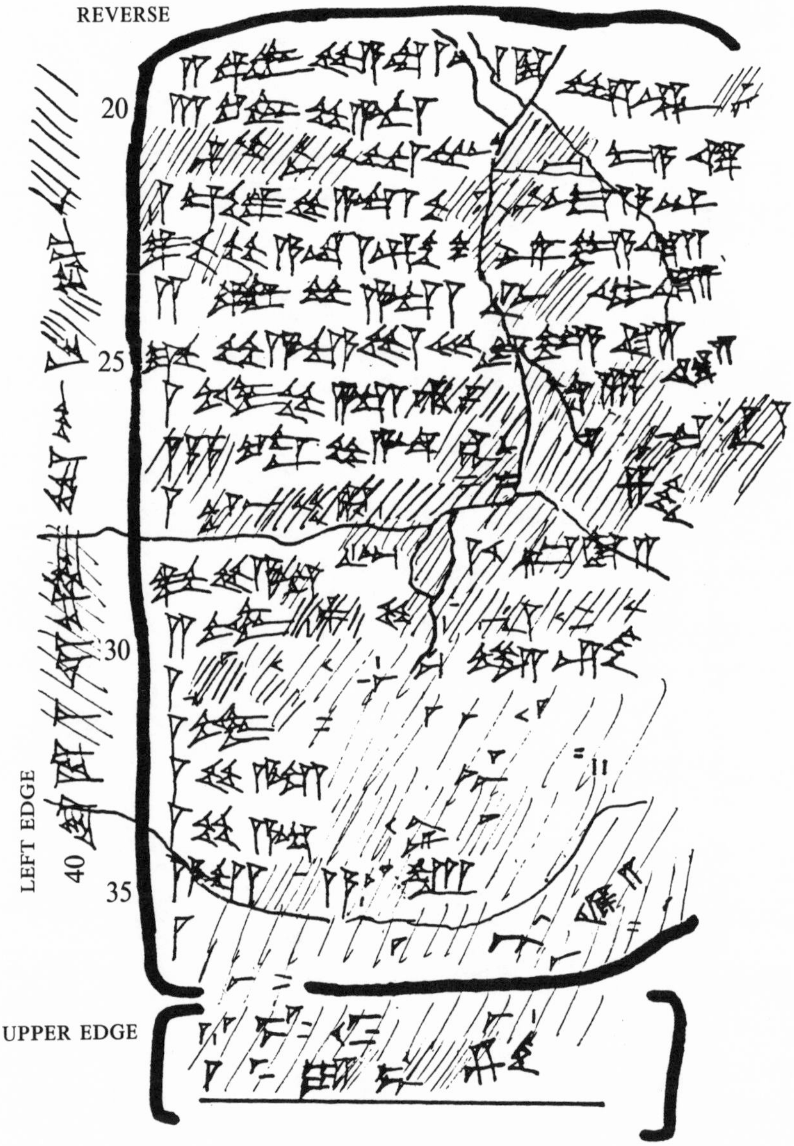

877 (= 712 = 753)*

OBVERSE

Beginning of obverse destroyed

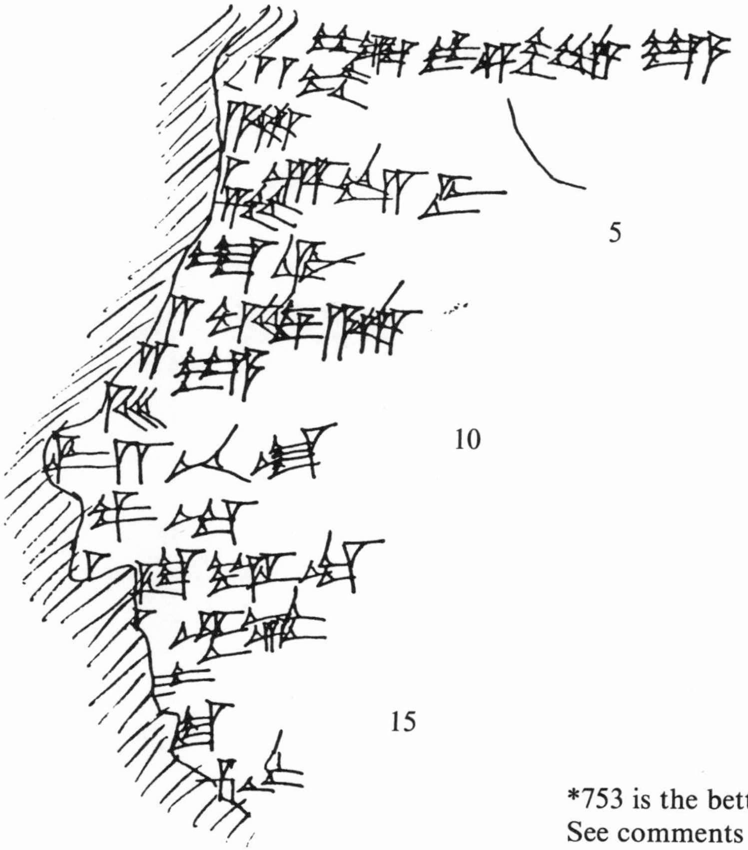

Rest of obverse, beginning of reverse destroyed

REVERSE

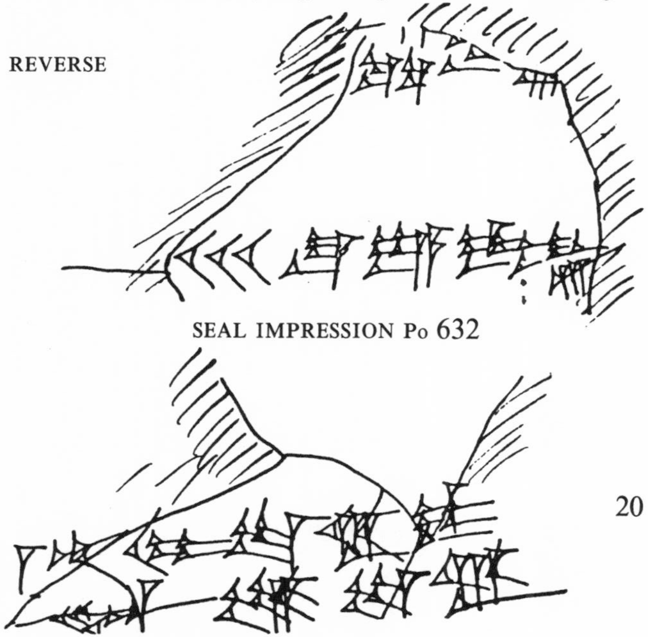

SEAL IMPRESSION Po 632

SEAL IMPRESSION Po 361

Rest of reverse destroyed

*753 is the better of the three copies.
See comments to that text in *THNT*.

878

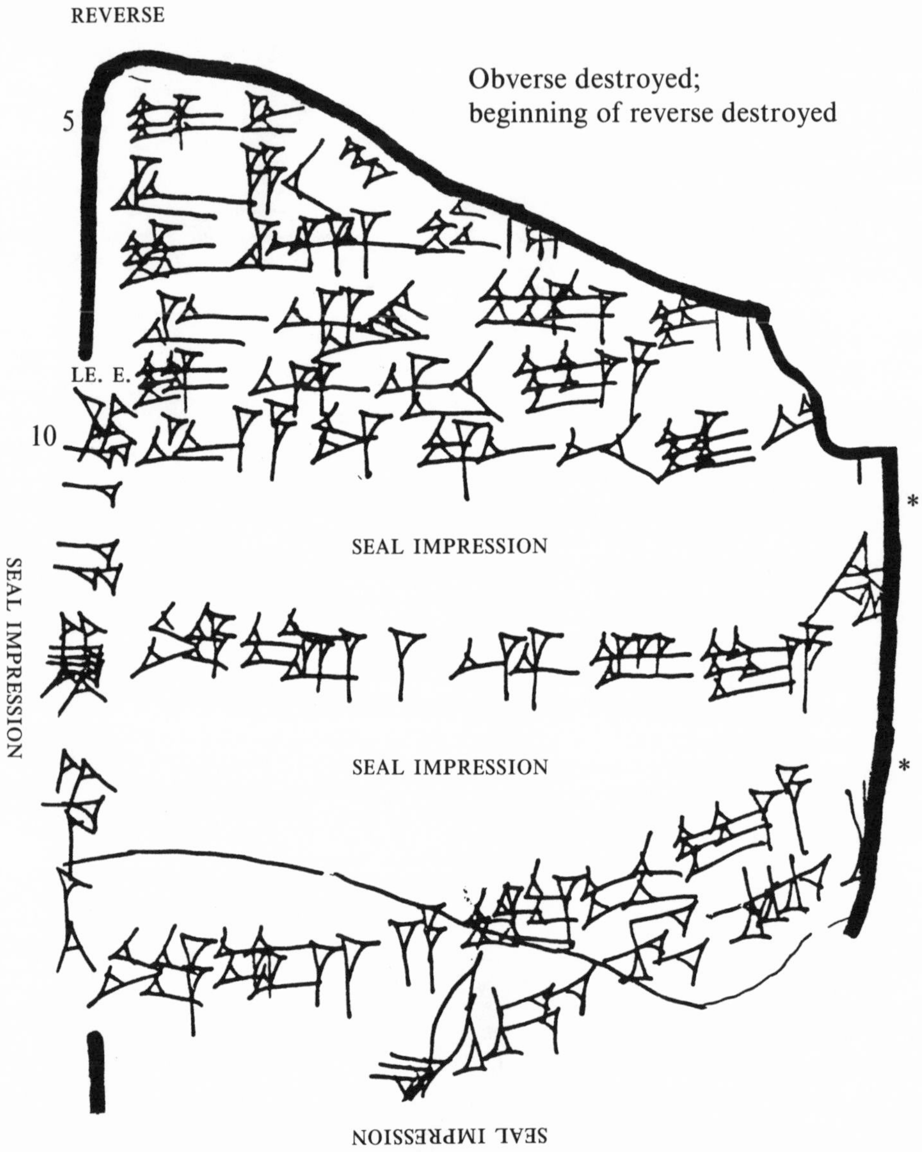

*Additional text; see *THNT*.

879 (= 813)*

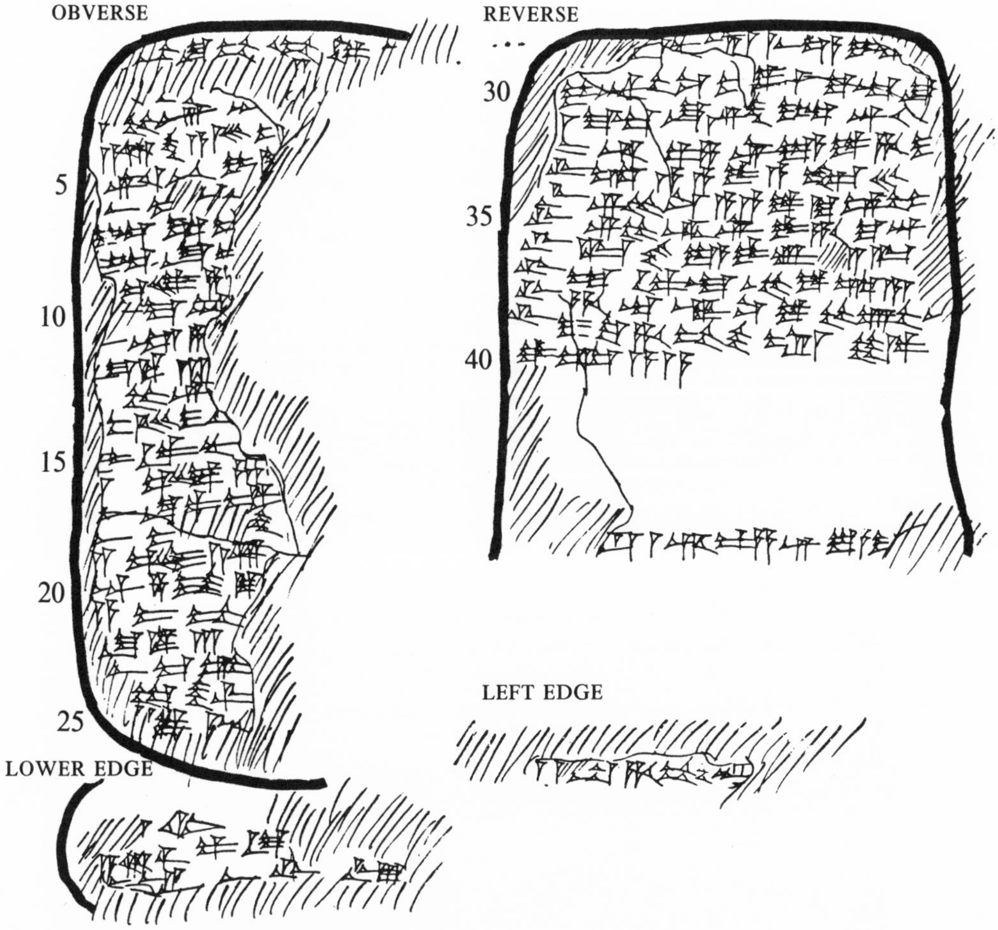

*813 is the better of the two copies.
See comments to that text in *THNT*.

880

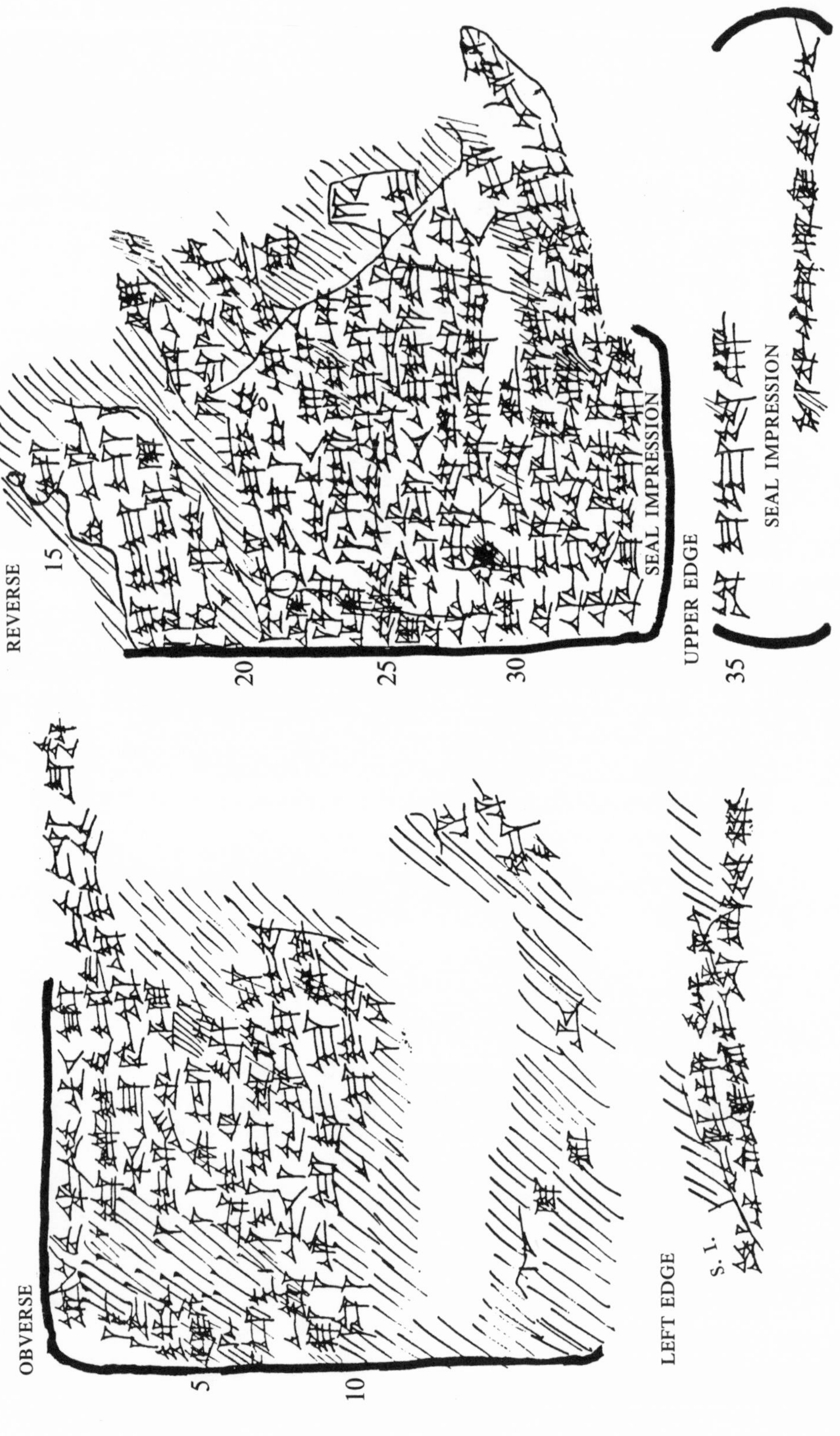
OBVERSE
REVERSE
LEFT EDGE
S. I.
UPPER EDGE
SEAL IMPRESSION
SEAL IMPRESSION

881

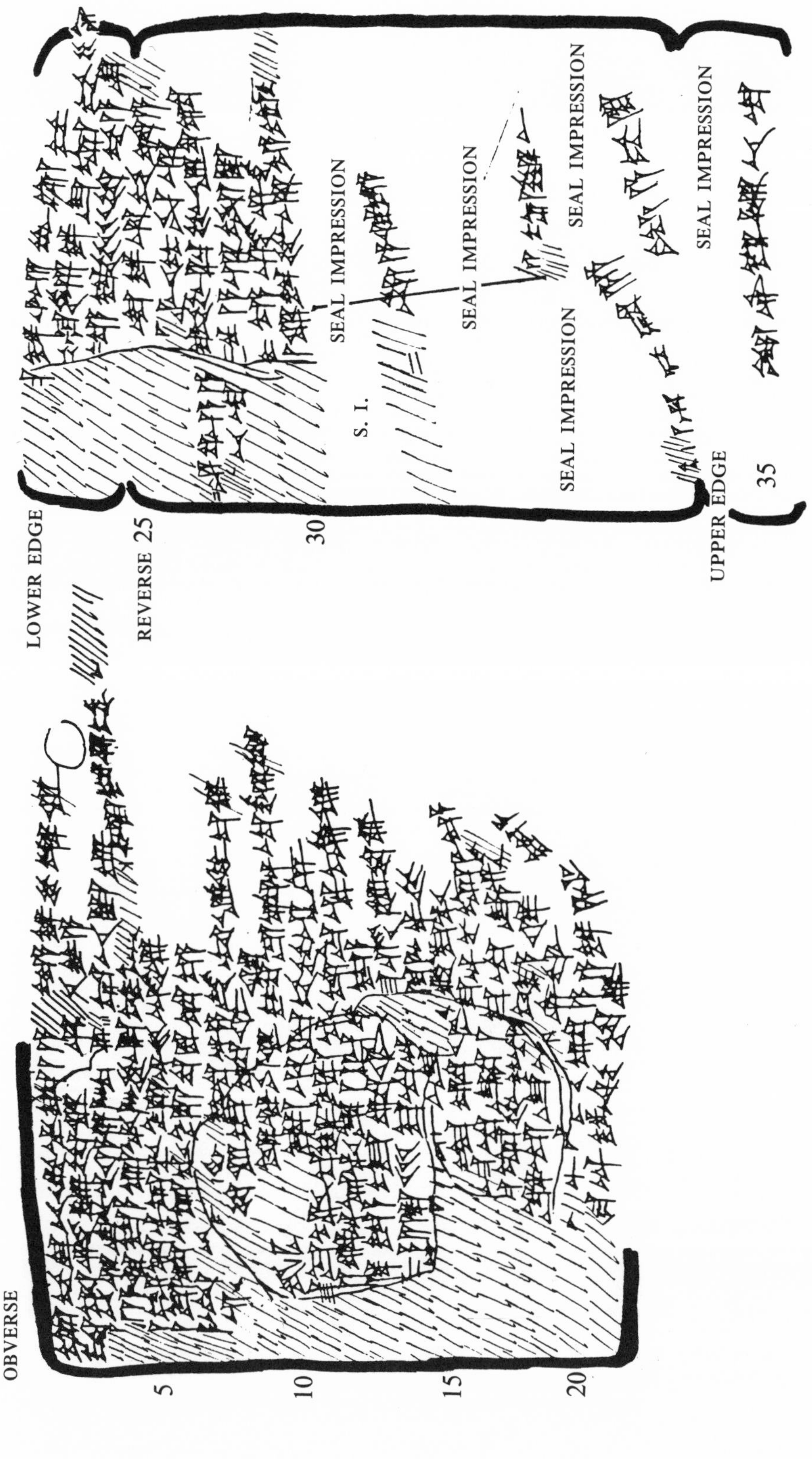
OBVERSE
LOWER EDGE
REVERSE
S. I.
SEAL IMPRESSION
SEAL IMPRESSION
SEAL IMPRESSION
SEAL IMPRESSION
SEAL IMPRESSION
UPPER EDGE